CANADIAN INDUSTRIAL RELATIONS

Jon Peirce

Carleton University

Prentice Hall Canada Inc.

Scarborough, Ontario

For Alex, Lauren, and Elizabeth,
and to Don Wood, with gratitude,
for taking a chance.

Canadian Cataloguing in Publication Data

Peirce, Jon
    Canadian industrial relations

Includes index.
ISBN 0-13-082602-2

1. Industrial relations — Canada.   I. Title.

HD8106.5P44   2000   331'.0971
C00-930047-4

Publisher: Pat Ferrier
Acquisitions Editor: Mike Ryan
Senior Marketing Manager: Ann Byford
Copy Editor: Dawn Hunter
Production Editor: Sarah Dann
Production Coordinator: Deborah Starks
Photo/Permissions Research: Elaine Freedman
Art Director: Mary Opper
Cover Design: Julia Hall
Cover Image: Photonica/H. Kuwajima
Page Layout: Arlene Edgar

© 2000 Prentice-Hall Canada Inc.,
Scarborough, Ontario
Pearson Education

2 3 4 5   QC   04 03 02 01

Printed and bound in the United States of America.

Visit the Prentice Hall Canada Web site! Send us
your comments, browse our catalogues, and more.
www.phcanada.com Or reach us through e-mail at
phcinfo_pubcanada@prenhall.com

Prentice-Hall, Inc., Upper Saddle River, New Jersey
Prentice-Hall International (UK) Limited, London
Prentice-Hall of Australia, Pty. Limited, Sydney
Prentice-Hall Hispanoamericana, S.A., Mexico City
Prentice-Hall of India Private Limited, New Delhi
Prentice-Hall of Japan, Inc., Tokyo
Simon & Schuster Southeast Asia Private Limited,
    Singapore
Editora Prentice-Hall do Brasil, Ltda., Rio de Janeiro

ISBN 0-13-082602-2

Statistics Canada information is used with the permission of the Minister of Industry, as Minister
responsible for Statistics Canada. Information on the
availability of the wide range of data from Statistics
Canada can be obtained from Statistics Canada's
Regional Offices, its World Wide Web Site at
http://www.statcan.ca, and its toll-free access number
1-800-263-1136.

CONTENTS

PREFACE

Like many who teach introductory industrial relations (IR), I've long felt the need for a textbook which is both comprehensive and readable. As most readers will agree, none of the existing introductory texts has managed to be both. To start with, no book can hope to do anything approaching justice to Canadian IR without considering such topics as the public sector, employment legislation, and management—all areas not treated in one or more of the three most commonly-used texts in the field.

There have been a number of things I've done in my attempt to make the book accessible to undergraduates. First, I have not included discussions of highly technical labour economics issues, instead referring interested readers to sources where they can find such discussions. Second, I've used relatively informal language. Third, I've drawn on my extensive work experience for practical examples where possible, to allow the discussion to be carried out at a more concrete, less abstract level. I've also included one or two discussion questions of an experiential nature at the end of each chapter in an attempt to stimulate discussion by attempting to link the text to students' own work experiences. All in all, I believe I've managed to produce a beginning IR text which most students will enjoy reading, and which they therefore will read. While the primary audience is undergraduate university and community college business students, the book can also be used to good advantage in beginning MBA courses, and in courses in related fields such as the sociology of work or labour history. Please see the instructor's manual for some suggestions on how *Canadian Industrial Relations* might be used in a community college setting.

A RAPIDLY CHANGING FIELD

Another important objective has been to reflect emerging trends in the rapidly changing field of IR. While union-management relations and collective bargaining remain at the core, areas once considered peripheral, such as human rights and employment standards legislation, have become increasingly important in recent years due mainly to the entry of large numbers of women, disabled people, and visible minorities into the Canadian labour force. Nor is the labour force all that has been changing. New technology has brought about major changes in the way in which work is done, while trade liberalization and increased foreign competition have led to equally big changes in staffing levels, work scheduling, and remuneration practices in both the private and public sectors. So pervasive have these changes been that today, only a bare majority of employed Canadians work at a full-time job with "standard" hours. Many are self-employed; many more work on a temporary, part-time, or contractual basis, often with little job security, irregular hours, and few benefits. This new "leaner and meaner" economic environment has had important implications for management practice, and even more important implications for unions and the government agencies responsible for workplace regulation.

FEATURES

Among the features of *Canadian Industrial Relations* that have sought to situate IR within the new economic and political environment are the following:

- A detailed discussion, in Chapter 2 (the economy), of the growth in atypical work schedules and Canada's more diverse work force;

- A special section, also in Chapter 2, on the growth in overtime hours and policy measures which could help reduce overtime;

- An expanded employment law chapter (Chapter 7), including a special section on emerging areas of human rights law such as same-sex benefits, violence in the workplace, and non-smokers' rights;

- Special emphasis, in Chapter 6 and 9, on the publicity campaigns unions must engage in to get their message across both to the general public and to their own members;

- A detailed examination, in Chapter 9 (the public sector), of the increasingly restrictive public sector bargaining environment; and

- A discussion in Chapter 12 (strikes) of four recent Canadian strikes, as well as the reasons for the recent resurgence in Canadian strike activity.

CBC ◉ CASE APPENDIX AND VIDEO CASES   The case material at the back of the book has also been prepared with an eye to emerging trends. Health and safety and human rights cases have been included, and labour board and arbitration cases address such topics of current interest as certification procedures for bargaining units composed mainly of part-time workers and employees' use of cellular phones in the workplace. Where appropriate, the cases have been linked to specific chapters of the text. The brief video cases at the end of the book shed additional light on contemporary developments by examining such issues as early retirement, child labour, the Netherlands' innovative approach to work hours, and unionization drives in the private service sector.

WEBLINKS   For those wishing more detailed information on any topic covered in the text, web links have been inserted at strategic points throughout the book. These links are not intended as a substitute for the material contained in the text, but should be a valuable supplement to it. So, too, should the "Suggestions for Further Reading" listed at the end of each chapter.

WHAT THE BOOK COVERS

Chapter 1 (introduction) discusses the importance of the world of work, defines the term "industrial relations," considers some of the most important IR theories, and looks at five different perspectives on the field.

Because the state of the economy is critical to the functioning of the IR system, we consider this next, in Chapter 2. As was indicated earlier, some key issues here are the recent growth of contingent or "atypical" employment, and the recent phenomenon of extensive overtime existing alongside continuing high unemployment.

The next four chapters focus on the roles of management and labour, the two major actors in the IR system. Chapter 3 deals with management, arguably the system's single most important actor. Special emphasis is placed on the evolution of Canadian management practice and on the extent to which management organizations today are making use of innovative or "progressive" approaches to human resource management. The three subsequent chapters deal with labour's role, starting in Chapter 4, which looks at that role from an historical perspective. Chapters 5 and 6 focus more specifically on the role and activities of unions. Chapter 5 examines union membership, growth, and structure and also considers the vexed question of union democracy. Chapter 6 deals with union actions (among them the publicity campaigns mentioned earlier) and impacts, including both economic and non-economic ones.

The following group of chapters is devoted to the IR system's legal aspects. Chapter 7's focus is on employment legislation affecting all workers, but of particular importance to those who don't belong to unions. Special emphasis is placed on new and emerging areas of legislative protection, and on the extent to which legislation is enforced by provincial and federal governments. Chapter 8 deals with private sector labour relations legislation. A major concern here is provincial variations in labour relations legislation. The chapter also discusses the administration of labour relations law, and the extent to which the duty to accommodate disabled workers or members of ethnic and religious minority groups in the workplace is likely to affect the drafting and interpretation of collective agreements. Chapter 9 considers collective bargaining and labour legislation in the public sector. A major focus here is the current state of public sector collective bargaining, which many have argued is in a state of profound crisis.

From here, it's a fairly natural progression to our next group of chapters, which deal with the bargaining process supported by public and private sector labour legislation, with the results of that process, and with the conflict that often arises during collective bargaining. Chapter 10 looks at the negotiation process in some detail. It also examines bargaining structures, which make up an important element of the environment in which bargaining takes place. Chapter 11, on the collective agreement, considers the evolution and philosophy of collective agreements and analyzes a number of sample clauses. The chapter also looks at the types of provisions which today's unions have been most (and least) successful at obtaining.

No IR text would be complete without a discussion of strikes—the most talked-about but perhaps least understood aspect of the IR system. In addition to discussing changing the patterns of strike incidence in Canada and looking at a variety of possible causes for strikes, Chapter 12 features brief descriptions of four recent Canadian strikes. Chapter 13 considers grievances and features an examination of an actual grievance case. A key element of this chapter is its discussion of major criticisms of the conventional grievance process and of alternatives to conventional arbitration, including expedited arbitration, grievance mediation, and preventive mediation.

Chapter 14, the book's conclusion, is an attempt to "pull the pieces together." this chapter looks at the Canadian IR system as a whole in the light of recent developments such as globalization, trade liberalization, and the growth of a contingent work force. This examination focuses on seven key themes and some of the most important findings and policy suggestions related to those themes.

Although the book does not contain a separate chapter on comparative IR, it has sought to incorporate evidence from foreign IR systems where possible, in order to show the Canadian system in international perspective. Similarly, a discussion of key features of Quebec's quite distinctive IR system, such as the extension of collective agreements to non-unionized firms through the decree system, has been incorporated into the text where appropriate.

SUPPLEMENTS

Canadian Industrial Relations is accompanied by a comprehensive supplements package.

INSTRUCTOR'S RESOURCE MANUAL WITH VIDEO GUIDE   (013-082604-9) This comprehensive guide contains a detailed lecture outline of each chapter, suggested answers to discussion questions, and helpful case and video case notes.

TEST ITEM FILE   (013-082605-7) The test item file contains over 1,000 multiple-choice, true/false, and short essay questions. Answers, with page references, are given for all objective questions and suggested answers are provided for essay questions. All questions are rated by level of difficulty (easy, moderate, challenging). The Test Item File is available in both printed and electronic formats.

PH TEST MANAGER   (013-082609-X) Utilizing our new Test Management program, the computerized test bank for *Canadian Industrial Relations* offers a comprehensive suite of tools for testing and assessment. Test Manager allows educators to easily create and distribute tests for their courses, either by printing and distributing through traditional methods or by on-line delivery via a Local Area Network (LAN) server. Once you have opened Test Manager, you'll advance effortlessly through a series of folders allowing you to quickly access all available areas of the program. Test Manager has removed the guesswork from your next move by incorporating Screen Wizards that assist you with such tasks as managing question content, managing a portfolio of tests, testing students, and analyzing test results. It addition, this all-new testing package is backed with full technical support, telephone "request a test" service, comprehensive on-line help files, a guided tour, and complete written documentation. Available as a CD-ROM for Windows 95.

TRANSPARENCY RESOURCE PACKAGE (013-082608-1) Over 100 transparencies in PowerPoint 7.0 have been created for the text, reproducing figures and illustrating important concepts. This package is available in printed and electronic format.

CBC **PRENTICE HALL CANADA/CBC VIDEO LIBRARY** Prentice Hall Canada and the CBC have worked together to bring you five segments from the CBC series *Venture* and *The National*. Designed specifically to complement the text, this case collection is an excellent tool for bringing students in contact with the world outside the classroom.

These programs have extremely high production quality and have been chosen to relate directly to chapter content. Teaching notes are provided in the Instructor's Resource Manual with Video Guide. Please contact your Prentice Hall Canada representative for details.

Acknowledgments

It is a truism that any textbook is a collaborative effort requiring the work of many hands. I hadn't fully realized the extent to which this is true before writing *Canadian Industrial Relations*.

I'd first like to acknowledge the critical contribution of Prentice Hall Acquisitions Editor Mike Ryan, with whom I essentially hatched the plan to write this book while I was teaching at Memorial University and he was the company's Atlantic Canada sales representative. At all times—including some when I wasn't so sure about the venture myself—Mike has been fully supportive of the project and enormously encouraging. Thanks are also due to Prentice Hall's Hardside publisher for Higher Education, Patrick Ferrier, for signing a project by a previously unknown author.

In its initial incarnation, the book was a series of teleconferencing manuals written for use by Continuing Education students at Memorial University. Thanks are due to Memorial's assistant director for Continuing Education, Bob Hyde, for commissioning what in retrospect seems to have been a truly obscene number of manuals. Not only did the manuals represent the rough draft for the textbook; they gave me the confidence to move forward with the larger project. I'd also like to thank the hundreds of Memorial teleconferencing students I taught between 1994 and 1996 for numerous rewarding long-distance classroom experiences and for serving as guinea pigs for the early stage of the project, and my students at Carleton University and the University of Ottawa for serving as guinea pigs for the full text last year and this.

Many people at Prentice Hall have done yeoman service in helping to turn a large, somewhat unwieldy manuscript into a finished product. Special thanks are due to Developmental Editor Amber Wallace, for making the necessary connections to get the book started initially, for making sure the royalty advances went out on time, and for helping me keep things in perspective and not become overwhelmed with the hundred and one little tasks that remain once one has made it through the first draft. Thanks are also due to Production Editor Melanie Meharchand, Copy Editor Dawn Hunter, Photo Researcher Elaine Freedman, Designer Julia Hall, Formatter Arlene Edgar, and Production Coordinator Deborah Starks.

Most of the research for this book was done at the labour library of Human Resources Development Canada in Hull, Quebec. All the staff there have been extremely helpful. Particular thanks are due to librarians Fred Longley and Ed Popoff for initiating me in the intricacies of electronic information systems and generally making it extremely easy to obtain all the materials needed to write the book. I should add that they and their colleagues also deserve considerable credit for creating an environment in which it is a pleasure to work. I would also like to acknowledge the great kindess shown by Mitch Legault of the Work Stoppage Bureau, Workplace Information Directorate of HRDC in providing data used in the strike tables in chapter 12. I'm sure my research days would not have been half so productive anywhere else. Finally, a word of thanks to the mentors who have guided me along the way since I launched my study of Canadian industrial relations some fifteen years ago. At Queen's, Bernie Adell introduced me to labour law, of both the Canadian and international varieties. He has been a valued colleague and friend ever since. Steve Kaliski made labour economics, which I'd been dreading, into *almost* a pleasant experience. And Vinny Mosco and Elia Zureik provided valuable reinforcement and professional confidence-building at a time when not much was going well in my life. Don Wood's contribution was so great that I have dedicated the book to him.

At the Economic Council of Canada, I learned to do serious IR research. It was both a privilege and a pleasure to be part of the Labour Markets and Technological Change group there. Keith Newton, Gord Betcherman, Kathy McMullen, Norm Leckie, and others in that group provided valuable professional guidance and constant intellectual stimulation. We also made great parties together. The connection between work and play which I established at the Council has since become one of the major themes of my professional life.

At the University of Toronto, I benefitted from the guidance and encouragement of Ian Radforth, Hugh Gunz, Frank Reid, and Anil Verma. I am particularly grateful to Anil Verma for useful insights into the strategic choice theory and its application to Canada as well as the relationship between labour relations and employment standards legislation. But my most important influence there was Roy Adams, whose comparative approach has been in large measure responsible for shaping my own approach to the subject. My debt to Roy is apparent in almost every page of this book.

Reviewer Acknowledgments

I would like to thank the following reviewers for their feedback: Dave McPherson, Humber College; Maureen Nummelin, Conestoga College; Joe Rose, McMaster University; Ian Sakinofsky, Ryerson; Marie Sickmeier, University of Manitoba; Basu Sharma, University of New Brunswick. These reviewers' comments, some of which were so helpful as to amount to something close to intellectual midwifery, have done much to strengthen this book. Naturally, I assume sole responsibility for any errors that remain.

J.P.
Ottawa

LIST OF
ACRONYMS AND ABBREVIATIONS

ACCL	All-Canadian Congress of Labour		ICTU	International Confederation of Free Trade Unions
ACLRA	Alberta Construction Labour Relations Association		ILO	International Labour Organization
AFL-CIO	American Federation of Labour- Congress of Industrial Organization		IR	Industrial Relations
			IDI Act	*Industrial Disputes Investigation* Act
BFOQ	Bona fide occupational qualifications		IWA	International Woodworkers of America
CADA	*Collective Agreement Decrees Act*		IWW	International Workers of the World
CAUT	Canadian Association of University Teachers		LLCG	Labour Law Casebook Group
			LRL	Labour relations legislation
CAW	Canadian Auto Workers		MSDS	Material safety data sheets
CCF	Co-Operative Commonwealth Federation		NAFTA	North American Free Trade Agreement
CCL	Canadian Congress of Labour		NAPE	Newfoundland Association of Public Employees
CCU	Confederation of Canadian Unions			
CEP	Communications, Energy and Paperworkers' Union		NDP	New Democratic Party
			NJC	National Joint Council
CEQ	Centrale de l'enseignement du Québec		NLRB	National Labour Relations Board
CFL	Canadian Federation of Labour		NUPGE	National Union of Provincial Government Employees
CIRA	Canadian Industrial Relations Association			
CLC	Canadian Labour Congress		OBU	One Big Union
CLMPC	Canadian Labour Market and Productivity Centre		OECD	Organisation for Economic Co-operation and Development
COLA	Cost of living allowance		OFL	Ontario Federation of Labour
COP	Choice of Procedures		*OLRA*	*Ontario Labour Relations Act*
CPQ	Conseil du patronat du Québec		OPSEU	Ontario Public Service Employees Union
CROA	Canadian Railway Office of Arbitration		PIPSC	Professional Institute of the Public Service of Canada
CSD	Centrale des syndicats démocratiques			
CSN	Confédération des syndicats nationaux (Confederation of National Trade Unions)		PQ	Parti Quebecois
			PSAC	Public Service Alliance of Canada
			PSRA	Public Service Reform Act
CSTEC	Canadian Steel Trade and Employment Congress		*PSSRA*	*Public Service Staff Relations Act*
			PSSRB	Public Service Staff Relations Board
CTCC	Confédération des travailleurs catholique du Canada		QCC	Quebec Construction Commission
			QFL	Quebec Federation of Labour
CTLMC	Canadian Textile Labour-Management Committee		QWL	Quality of Worklife
CUPE	Canadian Union of Public Employees		RBO	Relations by Objectives
CUPW	Canadian Union of Postal Workers		SEIU	Service Employees International Union
CWC	Communications Workers of Canada		SIU	Seafarers' International Union
DFR	Duty of fair representation		TLC	Trades and Labour Congress of Canada
EAP	Employee Assistance Program		TQM	Total Quality Management
ECC	Economic Council of Canada		UAW	United Auto Workers
EI	Employment insurance (formally known as unemployment insurance)		UFCW	United Food and Commercial Workers
			UFW	United Farm Workers
EL	employment legislation		UI	Unemployment insurance (now known as employment insurance [EI]
ETI	Economically Targeted Investment			
FOA	Final Offer Arbitration		USWA	United Steelworkers of America
FTA	Free Trade Agreement		VCC	Venture capital corporations
GATT	General Agreement on Trade and Tariffs		WHMIS	Workplace Hazardous Materials Information System
HEAT	Helping Employees Adjust Together			
HR	Human Resources		WID	Workplace Information Directorate
HRDC	Human Resources Development Canada		WUL	Workers' Unity League
HRM	Human Resources Management			

CHAPTER 1

INTRODUCTION TO
INDUSTRIAL RELATIONS

Today's Canadian work force includes a large number of women and members of ethnic minority groups.

The first part of this chapter considers the significance of work in most Canadians' lives. After a brief discussion of the interdisciplinary nature of our field of study, some definitions for the term "industrial relations"(IR) are offered. A discussion of some of the best-known theories of industrial relations, including the systems framework and the strategic choice theory, follows. Five perspectives for the study of IR are examined, and the chapter concludes with a brief outline of what the rest of the book will cover.

THE SIGNIFICANCE OF WORK

Welcome to the study of industrial relations!

Industrial relations is about the world of work: its joys and sorrows, its satisfactions and frustrations. The importance of work in the lives of most Canadians is immense. Most of us spend about one-quarter of our time working, which is more than we spend doing anything else, except sleeping. Through work, we seek to live our dreams and realize our ambitions. To a large extent, our adult identity is shaped by the work we do and the jobs we hold. We meet many of our friends at work; a good many of us meet our life partners there. A fulfilling job, working among congenial people in pleasant surroundings, can be the source of immense satisfaction. By the same token, unfulfilling work performed in the company of people one finds indifferent or hostile can be the source of such intense frustration that it can affect one's mental health. Landing a job is often an occasion for celebration. Losing one can lead to feelings of inadequacy, guilt, or anger that can last for months or even years. Those people who don't have jobs—for whatever reason—often feel like second-class citizens who aren't contributing to society. Work is addictive to some, so much so that they feel more comfortable at the plant or the office than at home. Even when they are supposed to be on vacation, some people try to maintain constant connection with their work through faxes, long-distance phone calls, or e-mail. Others develop such strong attachment to their work and to their places of work that when they retire (especially if the retirement has been abrupt or involuntary), they find themselves unable to cope with the separation. It isn't uncommon for these retirees to suffer heart attacks or develop severe depression.

Work's economic impact is equally important. The majority of Canadians—except for those lucky few who inherit fortunes or draw winning lottery tickets—derive almost all their income from work-based earnings. Those who lose their jobs generally suffer severely reduced buying power, despite the existence of social support programs like Employment Insurance (EI). When a large number of people in the same community lose their jobs, as when a plant closes or relocates, that community's very existence may be imperilled.

At an even more basic level, work is essential to produce goods and services, like food, housing, telephone service, and electric power, on which we all depend. If people didn't work, or hadn't worked in the past, such goods and services wouldn't be available for our use. When work is interrupted, whether because of a labour dispute or because of a natural disaster like a fire or an ice storm, the disruption of people's daily lives can be severe.

The Changing World of Work

Of late, the world of work has been changing quite dramatically. Until quite recently, most jobs in Canada were full-time and full-year. Most people worked on a regular schedule—typically from 9 to 5, Monday through Friday. Once you found a job, you could generally expect to keep it for a while, assuming that your performance and attendance remained satisfactory. Many people stayed with one employer, or at most two or three, throughout their entire working lives. While changes in occupation weren't unknown, they were the exception rather than the rule.

Over the past 10 to 15 years, the incidence of "atypical" forms of employment has increased dramatically (England, 1987). These include regular part-time work (see Figures 1.1a and 1.1b); casual work; work done on a short-term contractual basis; work performed at home rather than on the employer's premises; and self-employment.

These atypical employment patterns have increased so much that, according to the most recent Statistics Canada data, barely a majority of Canadian workers work under "standard" arrangements. (This point is discussed in far greater detail in Chapter 2). Such dramatically shifting work patterns pose a major challenge for individual workers, for the unions that represent or seek to represent their interests, and for public policy-makers responsible for regulating working conditions. As we'll discuss more fully in Chapter 2, the Canadian work force has been changing no less dramatically. Once predominantly male and almost all White, our work

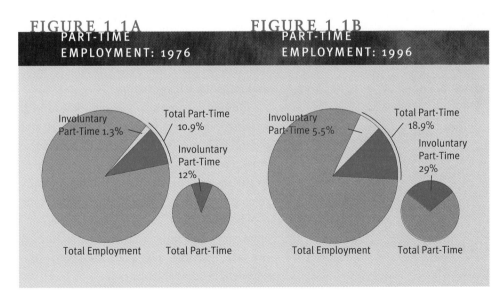

FIGURE 1.1A
PART-TIME EMPLOYMENT: 1976

FIGURE 1.1B
PART-TIME EMPLOYMENT: 1996

Source: CLMPC, 1997

Source: Statistics Canada, Cat. No. 71-201-XPB.

Today, far too many people are working part-time, often in coffee shops like this one, because it is the only work they can find.

An increasing number of women are balancing work and family responsibilities. Between 1978 and 1997, the proportion of women participating in the labour force increased from 45 percent to 57 percent.

force now reflects the diversity of a country with a multicultural population. About 45 percent of all Canadian workers are women and the country's work force includes people from many different ethnic and religious backgrounds.

Our work force also includes people with varying types and degrees of physical and mental disabilities. This new, more diverse work force has also brought new challenges to unions and policy-makers, but especially to employers. For a variety of reasons (some of which are the result of recent legislation), employers are under increasing pressure to provide various physical facilities, like wheelchair-accessible entrances, to meet the needs of workers with physical disabilities; to provide same-sex medical benefits to meet the needs of gay and lesbian couples, or to provide flexible work schedules to meet the needs of single parents or members of religious minorities.

Few young people entering today's work world can realistically expect to stay with one employer, or even one occupation, throughout their entire careers, as many of their parents and grandparents did. This has its advantages and disadvantages. On the one hand, people who frequently change employers or occupations may be less apt to become bored and may achieve more job satisfaction than people who stay in the same place for many years. On the other hand, there is no question that today's increasingly fluid arrangements breed considerable insecurity, as we note in more detail in Chapter 3.[1] As well, generating loyalty and commitment from workers becomes extremely difficult when few of these workers have any assurance that they will still be on the payroll in six months' time. We'll revisit these issues in Chapter 3.

WHAT IS INDUSTRIAL RELATIONS?

Industrial relations is an interdisciplinary subject. It draws on fields as diverse as economics, law, history, business management, political science, psychology, and sociology in analyzing, and proposing solutions for, workplace problems (Dunlop, 1958).

A simple example may help illustrate why many different academic disciplines are necessary to study problems arising out of the world of work. Let's suppose we're trying to explain why union membership rates are higher in Canada than in the United States (This isn't simply a hypothetical exercise. Union-growth analysts have been trying to get at this questions for many years). What "tools" would we need to answer this question?

Union growth is clearly related to broad trends in the economy, like unemployment and inflation. Obviously, anyone looking at the question would need to have some understanding of economics. But this only gets us part of the way. In recent years, union membership rates in Canada and the United States have diverged quite sharply, despite generally similar economic conditions. Clearly, we need more than economics to answer the question fully.

SOURCE LIST OF WORKS RELEVANT TO COMPARATIVE INDUSTRIAL RELATIONS

garnet.berkeley.edu:3333/EDINlist/.labor/.resource/.comp.ind.html

Legislation regarding how unions are certified and who is allowed to join unions can have an important effect on membership rates. If, for example, one government allows unions to become certified through a simple count of signed membership cards while another requires a formal vote, membership rates will likely be higher under the first government, because it is more difficult for a union to become certified where there is a formal election process. Since the United States requires a vote and most Canadian jurisdictions allow certification through signed membership cards, membership rates will likely be higher in Canada, other things being equal (see Figure 1.2). In addition, some governments allow most workers, other than managers, to join unions, while other governments may exclude members of specific groups, like professionals, domestics, and agricultural workers. Other things being equal, the jurisdiction that allows a greater number of occupational groups of workers to belong to unions is likely to have significantly higher union-membership rates (Peirce, 1989). Since American law, as currently interpreted, excludes more potential union members than Canadian law, our country's membership rates again should be higher.

In addition, different political arrangements may be more or less conducive to union growth. Union-growth analysts have generally found that rates go up when a labour or social democratic government is in power and down when a conservative government holds sway (Maki, 1982; Bruce, 1989). Indeed, a labour-oriented party can influence union membership growth even from a balance-of-power or strong opposition position. In Canada, threat of defeat by the CCF party, which was the forerunner to the NDP, was a primary factor inducing Prime Minister Mackenzie King to introduce *PC 1003*, the bill first granting collective bargaining rights to Canadian workers (Morton, 1995). Without such a political party, the possibility of using the political arena to enhance union growth is significantly diminished. The fact that Canada does have such a party (the NDP) while the United States doesn't, arguably contributes to higher membership rates here (Meltz, 1985; Bruce, 1989). So does Canada's multiparty parliamentary system, which has made it much easier for a party like the NDP to get started here than it would be in the United States (Bruce, 1989).

History also plays a role, as well as law and political science. In cities where there is a history of strong, positive labour organizations, unions are likely to have an easier time recruiting new members than in cities lacking such a history, or (perhaps worse still) where unions have made a practice of exploiting their members or becoming involved with organized crime. Since union membership involves a group dynamic, the values attached by a given community to

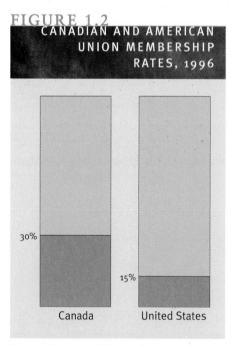

FIGURE 1.2

CANADIAN AND AMERICAN UNION MEMBERSHIP RATES, 1996

30%

15%

Canada   United States

Source: for Canada, WID (1997); for U.S., Bureau of Labor Statistics, U.S. Department of Labor.

union membership may also play a role. Those communities in which union membership is looked on favourably will likely see better success in organizing drives than those where a more individualistic ethic prevails, like high-tech communities. Here, the study of sociology will prove helpful (Kervin, 1988), and psychology is useful in determining what motivates some individuals to join unions, but not others (Kervin, 1988).

Depending on the industrial relations issue we're looking at, many other academic disciplines could come into play. For example, a knowledge of literature would be helpful in analyzing the writings of working people (often an important source of IR knowledge). A knowledge of music and folklore could be very useful in studying work songs, which in turn may offer some important clues to the work process in a given occupation or community (Seeger, 1972). Today, a knowledge of ergonomics could prove extremely useful in understanding contemporary health and safety issues, like the growing incidence of carpal tunnel syndrome among grocery cashiers.[2]

Industrial relations is obviously a subject requiring many different kinds of knowledge. To many (including the author), this is one of the field's enduring fascinations. To others (Laffer, 1974), it is a source of frustration, as is the apparent lack of a single, overarching theory (Heneman, 1969), comparable to, for example, the law of supply and demand in economics. The debate over what the field of industrial relations should include has been raging for some time and seems unlikely to end soon. Suffice to say that, for now, experience suggests the world of work isn't always a neat and tidy place, and that attempts to analyze it as if it were are probably doomed to fail.

Defining Industrial Relations

How should we define "industrial relations"? A possible starting point might be, "the relations between unions and management." That is all right, as far as it goes. Union–management relations *are* at the core of our field. But as we will soon see, and as some of you may have sensed already, the field takes in a good deal more than that.

To begin with, union–management relations in Canada, as in most other industrialized countries, are conducted within a legislative framework devised by government—in this case, both provincial and federal governments, since both have jurisdiction over various aspects of the IR system. Any definition of IR that fails to take governments' role into account is seriously deficient.

It's also inaccurate to confine any definition to the unionized part of the work force. Fewer than 40 percent of all Canadian workers are union members. We can't simply fail to consider the remaining 60+ percent.

In a broader sense, the IR system affects the lives of almost all Canadians, including those who aren't themselves workers, such as children or retired people. If a private-sector firm undergoes a strike, not only are its employees, managers, and their families affected, so are its customers, its suppliers, and not infrequently the entire community in which the firm is located. This is particularly true if that firm happens to be the community's only employer or one of its major ones. In the case of a public sector dispute involving groups like transit workers or sanitation workers, the entire community may feel the effects very quickly, particularly if the service that the striking workers normally provide is one for which there is no readily available substitute. In the case of a big-city transit strike, even people who normally drive to work will be affected because many of those who can't take the subway will also be driving, making traffic heavier and progress slower.

"INDUSTRIAL RELATIONS THEORY: LESSONS FROM A PRIVATE SECTOR MODEL FOR PUBLIC SECTOR TRANSFORMATION"

www.cce.cornell.edu/community/govt/restructuring/labor/reviews/ir.html

A broad definition is needed if we are to take into account all the ways in which the IR system affects people: as workers or managers, as taxpayers, and as consumers. I have not seen a better definition of IR than the one put forward by Thomas Kochan (1980:1): "All aspects of the employment relationship."[3] Almost every other definition—and there are a good many—leaves out one or more important aspects.

To be sure, other disciplines also deal with the world of work. These disciplines include, among others, organizational behaviour (OB), human resource management (HRM), sociology, labour economics, and labour studies. Where industrial relations differs from other disciplines is in what Noah Meltz (1989a) describes as its concern for balancing efficiency and equity, the interests of management and those of workers, as well as its interdisciplinary approach. Thus, while OB and HRM courses tend to take a pro-management approach, and labour studies courses take a pro-labour and often pro-union approach, IR courses seek to make students aware of the needs and interests of both workers and management. While labour economics courses focus on the economic aspects of work, and sociology courses focus on the behavioural and psychic aspects, IR courses treat the different aspects of work as interrelated. In these ways, industrial relations has a valuable, perhaps even unique contribution to make to the study of work-related issues.

THEORIES OF INDUSTRIAL RELATIONS

Dunlop's Systems Theory

As noted previously, few industrial relations experts would maintain that the field possesses a single, strong, explanatory theory. Nonetheless, there have been several attempts at developing such a theory. The most important of these theories is that of John Dunlop (1958). Dunlop (1958:5) defines an industrial relations system as "an analytical subsystem of an industrial society." In his view, the IR system is equally as important as the economic subsystem, but not a part of it. This will be an important point to remember throughout this book, especially when we begin to consider elements of behaviour, like certain types of strikes, that appear to be economically irrational. As we shall soon see, actors in the IR system may and often do have concerns beyond purely economic ones. Economic theory (Dunlop, 1958:5) can't be expected to explain all aspects of these concerns, though it can explain some of them. While there are areas of overlap between the economic and IR subsystems, there are some aspects of the IR system (such as elements of workplace rule making) that fall outside the scope of the economic subsystem.

JOHN DUNLOP'S TESTIMONY REGARDING THE COMMITTEE ON EDUCATION AND THE WORKFORCE TO THE U.S. HOUSE OF REPRESENTATIVES

www.house.gov/eeo/hearings/oi/awp8698/dunlop.htm

At any one time, says Dunlop (1958:7), an IR system comprises certain actors, certain contexts, a body or web of rules governing the actors' workplace behaviour, and a common ideology binding the system together. The actors include managers, workers and their representatives, and government or specialized private agencies (i.e., arbitration panels) appointed by workers and management to handle certain aspects of their relationship. The workers may be unionized or not. It is their job to do the work, following instructions given to them by management, whose job is to provide such instructions (Dunlop, 1958). Government's primary interest is as a peacekeeper and rule maker, though within the public sector government also wears a second hat as employer. The complications resulting from government's dual role here will be discussed in more detail in the public sector chapter (Chapter 9).

The contexts within which the actors operate include market (economic), technical, and power (political) ones. To a considerable extent, these contexts determine the balance of power between the two most important actors (workers and management). Changes in these contexts are likely to produce shifts in that balance of power. Each of the contexts has its greatest impact on a subset of the rules (Anderson and Gunderson, 1982). For example, the market context affects pay and benefit levels (Anderson and Gunderson, 1982), while the power context affects legislation governing union certification and strike procedures.

The web of rules includes substantive rules regarding system outcomes such as pay, benefits, hours of work, and workplace safety, and procedural rules on such matters as collective bargaining, grievance procedures, and transfer or promotion procedures (Dunlop, 1958; Anderson and Gunderson, 1982). For the most part, labour relations legislation (discussed in Chapter 8), or the web of rules established to govern behaviour in unionized workplaces, is of a procedural nature. On the one hand, the assumption here is that as long as the parties are placed on a relatively level playing field through the establishment of appropriate procedures for collective bargaining, the handling of impasses, and the like, they'll negotiate better outcomes than the government could. On the other hand, employment standards legislation (discussed in Chapter 7), or the web of rules applied to all workers but of particular importance in non-unionized establishments), does prescribe certain outcomes. These include minimum wages, maximum hours of work, minimum vacation entitlements, and safety regulations governing the maximum permissible level of discharge of certain substances into the air or water.

It is customary to speak of these two sets of rules as separate entities, and to a large extent they are indeed distinct from one another. At the same time, the two complement each other in some important ways. To begin with, employment standards legislation applies to all workplaces (unionized as well as non-unionized). It is, therefore, illegal for a union and an employer to negotiate any terms and conditions poorer than those provided in employment standards legislation (i.e., a wage below the provincial minimum). Employment standards legislation thus serves as the floor on which collective bargaining can begin. Unions also have an important role to play in enforcing employment legislation in the workplace, in educating workers about their rights under this legislation, and in enhancing minimum legislated standards through the collective bargaining process. Again, these points are discussed in more detail in Chapter 7.

The notion of a common ideology between the actors in the IR system has led to some confusion and a fair amount of debate. By "ideology" Dunlop (1958:16–17) means "a body of common ideas that defines the role and place of each actor and that defines the ideas which each actor holds toward the place and function of the others in the system." Dunlop further suggests (1958:17) that "[t]he ideology or philosophy of a stable system involves a congruence or compatibility among these views and the rest of the system." What has never been clear is just how far the idea of a "common ideology" should be taken. It would probably be fair to say that most North American employers and workers share a common preference for a democratic, capitalist system of government, rather than a totalitarian one like Communism or fascism. This assumption doesn't, however, take us very far towards understanding the extent to which workplace conflict would be restrained or modified as a result of that common ideology. Confusion about this point and various others has led to a number of criticisms of the systems framework over the years.

Criticisms of the Systems Framework

Dunlop's systems framework offers useful insights into the interdisciplinary nature of industrial relations. It also offers a convenient introductory approach to the study of foreign IR systems with which a researcher is unfamiliar. By looking at the actors, the contexts in which they operate, and the web of rules governing the actors' behaviour, one can learn a good deal about such systems.

In many other ways, however, the systems framework has proved disappointing. Dunlop (1958:6) had anticipated that his approach would provide IR with a theoretical core and turn it into "a genuine discipline." While most industrial relationists today would probably agree that IR is a genuine discipline, few would agree that the systems framework has provided a theoretical core that can generate testable research hypotheses. As Anderson and Gunderson (1982:5) note, the most common criticism has been that it is "only a taxonomy which has resulted in descriptive rather than explanatory research."[4]

Another problem is that, by viewing the IR subsystem in at least relative isolation (1958:2), Dunlop tends to minimize the importance of various environmental inputs beyond the three contexts he identifies. But the most serious problem with the systems framework has to do with the role of conflict. Granted, Dunlop doesn't *ignore* the role of conflict; indeed, he suggests that at times, when the actors don't share a common ideology (1958:17), the system will lack stability and may require major changes. He doesn't, however, distinguish between relatively positive or "cathartic" conflict, of the type that can be worked out through collective bargaining and other activities, and destructive or dysfunctional conflict, which could impair or even permanently destroy the actors' relationship. Dunlop also doesn't indicate to what extent conflict is inherent within the employment relationship—or, for that matter, if any kind of conflict at all is inherent. This seems a serious omission, particularly given that his view of the employment relationship is an extremely traditional one in which managers give orders and workers execute them. More generally, Dunlop seems to assume that IR systems possess a greater degree of stability than most actually do. Dunlop's inadequate treatment of conflict has been criticized by earlier writers like Singh (1976) and by more recent ones like Kochan, McKersie, and Cappelli (1984).

Some of the problems just noted were solved when Alton Craig (1967, 1983) put Dunlop's model into more conventional systems form with the use of an input-output framework and a feedback loop (Anderson and Gunderson, 1982:6). Among other things, the input-output framework allows for the use of a broader range of inputs. It also provides a fuller representation of the inputs' role in shaping the IR system's outputs, through various conversion processes, and helps to show the system's connection to and interdependence with other systems instead of representing it in isolation as Dunlop does. Finally, on the important question of conflict, Craig is somewhat more explicit than Dunlop. By identifying the grievance process, strikes, and lockouts as conversion processes, and the latter as system outputs, Craig (1983) implies that some degree of conflict is inherent to the IR system, but that much of it can be worked out through the system's normal operations.

While in many ways an improvement on Dunlop's original framework, Craig's model isn't without its own problems. First, as we'll discuss in more detail in Chapter 3, Craig pays little attention to the role of management. Profit, market share, and the good or service being produced aren't even listed as outputs. The only "organizational" outputs listed are collective agreement provisions. Second, although Craig doesn't explicitly limit his model to unionized workplaces, almost all his conversion processes and system outputs presuppose a collective bargaining process, severely limiting the model's applicability in non-unionized settings. Implicitly at least, the model appears to presuppose a strategy of union acceptance on the part of management. Third, although again Craig isn't explicit on this point, the model appears to assume that most workplace conflict can be contained within, if not worked out through, the IR system. Developments in the past two decades have cast increasing doubt on such an assumption.

The Strategic Choice Model

Concerned that much of the IR literature paid insufficient attention to management's role as a key actor in the system, Thomas Kochan and his associates (Kochan et al., 1984) sought to develop a new theory that would give appropriate emphasis to that role. Kochan et al. were also troubled by Dunlop's notion of shared ideology, which they believe focusses too much on events at the bargaining table and not enough on events at other levels of the organization, where such shared understandings don't necessarily exist (Kochan et al., 1984:20). Still another concern was that industrial relations developments had, in the past, generally been considered in isolation from other developments within unions, governments, and especially within firms. As Kochan et al. see it, to fully understand IR and human resources (HR) strategies, one needs to see how these strategies are linked to firms' larger global strategies and to their strategies at the workplace or shop-floor level.

Beyond that, Kochan and his associates believed conflict had been inadequately handled in much of the IR literature. In their view, one shouldn't necessarily assume that conflict can be worked out within the IR system. The level of conflict is now a question to be measured empirically rather than taken as a given (Verma, 1992). A prime example is a firm's attitude and behaviour towards its unions. In the past, management and unions might have battled vigorously at the bargaining table or in the political arena, but rarely with the idea that the other party shouldn't have the right to exist. By the early 1980s, with anti-union ideology and behaviour becoming more respectable again, especially in the United States, many unionized firms were beginning to give serious thought to removing their unions, while non-unionized firms were hiring consultants or intimidating and harassing suspected union activists in a bid to remain union-free (Anderson, 1989a). Clearly, such attitudes and behaviour would be likely to give rise to a more serious kind of conflict than a bargaining-table dispute over wages.[5] No longer could anyone assume that the IR system would be able to resolve conflict. Collective bargaining is the IR system's main mechanism for resolving conflict. By their actions, the management of the organizations in questions would have indicated their unwillingness, if not outright refusal, to engage in the process. In such circumstances, it would also be extremely difficult to speak of any sort of "shared ideology" between management and unions. How much ideology can management realistically be said to share with unions, when they aren't even willing to sit down at a table and negotiate?

While the systems framework continues to have some applicability within a comparative context, as noted above, overall the strategic choice framework seem to offer a fuller and more accurate explanation of recent North American IR developments. Although the actors have used different strategies in Canada than in the United States, the strategic choice framework is nonetheless applicable here, as well as in the United States. While the framework can apply to unions and governments as well as management, it is of particular importance in explaining management behaviour. Accordingly, a full discussion has been left to Chapter 3.

PERSPECTIVES ON INDUSTRIAL RELATIONS

Another reason to question Dunlop's notion of a shared ideology within the IR system is the existence of a number of different perspectives among industrial relationists (Anderson, Gunderson, and Ponak, 1989; Godard, 1994). Even within unions or management organizations, different individuals may hold different views on key issues. The five perspectives we'll be discussing apply to such things as the individual's primary research focus, the importance individuals attach to unions, the extent to which a person believes conflict is inherent in the IR system, and the individual's location on the political spectrum (right to left). While, as Godard notes (1994:26), not all industrial relationists can be consistently identified with one of the five perspectives, these perspectives nonetheless help to highlight differing opinions within the field on such issues as the role of unions or the appropriate managerial policies to follow to maximize efficiency and productivity. They will be thus be useful throughout the book.

Neoclassical Perspective

Strictly speaking, the right-wing neoclassical perspective is more of a pure economics perspective than an IR perspective. Indeed, the discipline of industrial relations really began in North America as a result of the University of Wisconsin's John R. Commons' recognition that neoclassical economics was inadequate in explaining real-life problems such as poverty and unemployment, and in providing practical solutions to those problems. This recognition permeates such works as his *History of Labor in the United States* (1918), as well as the works of a number of other early twentieth–century writers whom Commons influenced. Throughout the postwar period, few if any leading Canadian industrial relationists adopted the neoclassical perspective, though with the return of competitive labour markets and the ascendancy of the political right in recent years, there have been an increasing number of attempts to apply elements of that perspective to the IR system (Peirce, 1996). Generally, a desire to increase competitiveness has been the rationale behind such attempts. The neoclassical approach has perhaps been more popular in the United States, where, in recent years, it has been adopted by such prominent writers as Troy (1992).

"ECONOMIC THEORY AND HISTORICAL INTERPRETATION: BRIDGING A CENTURY OF DISDAIN BETWEEN ECONOMISTS AND HISTORIANS"
www.delaware.infi.net/~msch/theory5.html

Neoclassicists believe, above all else, in the free and unfettered operation of markets, especially labour markets (Ehrenberg and Smith, 1985). In their view, the labour-management relationship is, in the words of John Godard (1994:27), "a free and equal exchange between two parties with different yet compatible interests." Neoclassicists also believe that managers should have unfettered authority to run their enterprises as they see fit. If workers don't like the way management is running the enterprise, they are always free to quit and find a job more to their liking. Members of this school have little or no use for unions, which they view as organizations that can only increase inefficiency and unemployment by raising wages above the "equilibrium point" (discussed in more detail in Chapter 2) at which labour markets clear and there is full employment. Those adopting the "coercive drive" approach to management, discussed in more detail in Chapter 3, are generally of a neoclassical persuasion and tend to take what Adell (1988a) has described as a "unitary" or "unchained entrepreneurship" perspective on labour law.

Within IR, neoclassicists' primary research focus is on labour markets. Logically enough, since they believe that unions and the government agencies that regulate them shouldn't exist in the first place, they tend to have little or no interest in the practical workings of these organizations. Their research tends to be highly quantitative and statistical, to make heavy use of large databases, and to focus on such issues as unions' impact on wages (Anderson et al., 1989). For the most part, members of this school tend not to concern themselves with questions of conflict, since they believe all such questions can be resolved through the operation of market forces (Godard, 1994:27).

Managerial Perspective

While the neoclassical perspective is closely linked to the discipline of economics, the managerial one is related to organizational behaviour. It arose out of the work of such varied people as F.W. Taylor and Elton Mayo (Gunderson and Ponak, 1995). Many working in personnel and human resource departments take this perspective.

Managerialists' main concern is the motivation of workers, both individually and in small groups. They believe that properly motivated workers will be more productive. Unlike the neoclassicists, they seek to motivate through positive incentives rather than through fear. They also tend to be, at best, ambivalent towards unions. Where unions exist already, they'll often seek to establish a cooperative relationship (Gunderson and Ponak, 1995). For the most part, however, they believe that if intelligent and progressive human resource management policies are followed, unions should be unnecessary, and that while the interests of workers and managers may diverge in the short term, over the longer term they'll converge, again assuming appropriate management techniques are used to link the company's interests to individual workers' needs (Gunderson and Ponak, 1995). Managerialists tend to be particularly interested in employee involvement and other quality of worklife programs, as well as in a variety of incentive-based compensation schemes. Much research conducted from this perspective has focussed on such issues as why some employees are more likely than others to go on strike or take industrial action, and what management techniques and organizational structures will reduce an individual's propensity to engage in industrial conflict (Kervin, 1988:219). While much of this research has been valuable, in general it has paid little attention to the role of unions (Kervin, 1984, 1988; Gunderson and Ponak, 1995). The omission seems somewhat surprising, given that, in Canada at least, only a duly certified union can legally call a strike.

"FIELDS, POWER, AND SOCIAL SKILL: A CRITICAL ANALYSIS OF THE NEW INSTITUTIONALISMS"—A CRITIQUE OF NEW INSTITUTIONAL THEORIES
socrates.berkeley.edu/~iir/culture/page9.html

Institutional Perspective

The institutional perspective has generally been the one adopted by most mainstream industrial relationists. Arising out of the work of people like John R. Commons, this perspective holds that in a competitive market place, individual workers are unable to resist the demands of powerful employers. Unions and collective bargaining are, therefore, needed to balance what would otherwise be a seriously uneven playing field (Barbash, 1984). This perspective entails more government intervention than the two perspectives already discussed, since government is needed to establish and administer labour relations legislation, without which most unions would be unable to function (see Chapter 8). In the view of institutionalists, there's no denying that workplace conflict exists. However, much if not all of it can be dissipated through collective bargaining and other activities of the IR system.

As their name suggests, institutionalists have a strong interest in real-world IR institutions—unions, management organizations, and the government agencies that regulate the IR system. Much of their research tends to be of a practical nature, and many institutionalists have a keen interest in public labour policy issues. While members of this school don't confine themselves to a single research approach, in general (Anderson et al., 1989) institutionalists tend to rely more heavily on interviews and case studies and less heavily on statistical analysis than do neoclassicists. Noted Canadian institutionalists have included H.D. Woods, chairman of a well-known federal task force on labour relations, and the Abbé Gérard Dion, founder of the industrial relations program at Laval University and long-time editor of the Canadian journal *Relations Industrielles*.

ABSTRACTS OF PAST ISSUES OF *INDUSTRIAL RELATIONS: A JOURNAL OF ECONOMY AND SOCIETY* UNIVERSITY OF CALIFORNIA, BERKELEY

socrates.berkeley.edu/~iir/indrel/iir.abstracts/iir.abstracts.html

Reformist Perspective

Members of this school think that collective bargaining and labour relations legislation *could* work, under the right circumstances, but that as things stand, the odds are weighted too heavily in favour of employers, and the rich and powerful in general. While they are supportive of unions in principle (Godard, 1994), they are critical of a system that, all too often, doesn't allow unions to offer workers any real protection, especially in small organizations. Accordingly, reformists seek major economic redistribution, such as changes in the tax system, as well as pay and employment equity and other employment law reforms designed to correct what many of them view as widespread structural and political inequality (Godard, 1994).

One group of reformists, represented most notably by David Beatty (1983, 1987; Adell, 1988a), takes what Adell describes as an "egalitarian individualist" approach to issues of labour law and social justice more generally. In Adell's words, Beatty believes "that the justice of social institutions should be appraised on the basis of their effects on the worst-off members of society" (1988a:116). Beatty would use the *Charter of Rights and Freedoms* to bring about fairer labour relations legislation.

For example, he would use it to remove existing exclusions from this legislation (such as those of management personnel, agricultural workers, and domestics), on the grounds that all workers should have the right to join a union, whether or not they choose to exercise that right (Beatty, 1987; Adell, 1988a). More generally, Beatty views the *Charter* as providing a constitutional guarantee of the right to join a union and to strike (Beatty and Kennett, 1988).[6] But his program for labour law reform doesn't stop with the *Charter*. While this would guarantee fair procedures, workers also need substantive legislative protection of the type provided by human rights and employment standards legislation (Beatty, 1987; Adell, 1988a).

A second group comprises mainly academics in such disciplines as history, sociology, and political science, as well as a few industrial relationists of progressive bent (Haiven, McBride, and Shields, 1990). This group's work focusses quite strongly on issues of power in the workplace and in Canadian society at large. Often they have been critical of the role of the state in maintaining or even fostering existing power imbalances (Haiven et al., 1990). Others have focussed on such issues as discrimination, unsafe working conditions, layoffs and plant closures, and wage inequities (Godard, 1994:31). For example, Canadian legal scholar Harry Glassbeek has long been interested in the issue of corporations' legal liability for workplace injuries and illnesses (Glassbeek and Rowland, 1979).

Radical/Political Economy Perspective

Those holding this perspective, unlike those holding the previous four, believe that widespread inequality is an integral part of capitalist society and can't be overcome under existing economic and political arrangements. In the past, most radicals were of a Marxist or quasi-Marxist bent.[7] They believed that all members of society are divided into two classes: the working class, or proletariat, and the capitalist class, or bourgeoisie. The bourgeoisie, in this view, own the means of production, while members of the working class don't, and are thus forced to sell their labour to those who do. Most workers produce goods or services of far greater value than their wages and the costs of production put together. The difference between the value of the goods or services produced and the total costs of production (including wages) is kept by the capitalists as profits, and is referred to by Marxists as "surplus value."

To the Marxist, trade unions are at best a Band-Aid solution, at worst a distraction from what should be the working class' main mission: to overthrow capitalist society.[8] Classical Marxists thought this would happen through a combination of political means and direct action. Syndicalists (represented in North America mainly by the Industrial Workers of the World) had little use for politics, believing that a giant general strike would eventually bring the capitalist class to its knees. The failure of the

Winnipeg General Strike (described in Chapter 4) meant the end of serious syndical-ism in Canada. Classical Marxism hung on somewhat longer, as Communists con-tinued to play a significant role in the Canadian labour movement through the early fifties (Morton, 1995). Marxist scholarship, however, has played far less of a role in North American than in European industrial relations (Hyman, 1975). One notable exception is the work of Harry Braverman (1974). Taking a Marxist perspective on technological change, Braverman argues that the major effect of such change is to "deskill" workers, thus further increasing managers' and employers' control over the labour process.

Over the past few years, a new political economy school has arisen in North American industrial relations.[9] Members of this school agree with traditional Marxists as to the centrality of power issues and the importance of relating IR to larg-er developments in the economy and society (Godard, 1994; Lipsig-Mumme, 1995). Their prescriptions for change are, however, generally quite different. In place of tra-ditional Marxist calls for the violent overthrow of capitalist society, one hears calls for employee ownership and management of business enterprises (Godard, 1994). In place of calls for unions to serve as foot soldiers in the giant revolution, one hears calls for them to reach out to the communities in which their members live (Lipsig-Mumme, 1995:216) and, at the same time, to operate in a more genuinely interna-tional fashion (Lipsig-Mumme, 1995:218), to better serve the workers of transna-tional enterprises affected by recent North American trade agreements.

Most industrial relationists who take a political economy perspective would agree that there are serious problems with the Canadian IR system as presently con-stituted. Particular difficulties include the inadequate representation of women (Forrest, 1997) and of workers in small firms and peripheral areas of the economy (Lipsig-Mumme, 1995). Few, however, have gone so far as to call for the outright dismantling of the present Canadian IR system. Most appear to believe that, imper-fect though that system may be, workers are still better served with it than they would be without it.

WHAT THE BOOK WILL COVER

This chapter has offered a very basic introduction to industrial relations: what it is, what some leading theories say, and what some different perspectives on the field have to say about such issues as the role of unions and the importance of power and conflict in the workplace.

Since the state of the economy is crucial in determining who'll hold the balance of workplace power, or even who will hold a job, we consider the economy first in Chapter 2. A central issue here is the recent growth of contingent or "atypical" work, and the effect this has had on the actions of management and unions. Another important issue covered in the next chapter is that of work hours and overtime, the latter of which is on the rise.

BUREAU FOR LABOUR STATISTICS
stats.bls.gov:8o/blshome.htm

The next group of chapters is devoted to studying the roles of management and labour, the two major actors in the IR system. We start, in Chapter 3, with management, which most industrial relations experts agree is now the IR system's single most important actor. A key element of this chapter is its discussion of the historical evolution of Canadian management practice. The following two chapters consider the role of labour. Chapter 4 looks at labour's role from an historical perspective. While Chapter 4 considers developments among both unionized and non-unionized workers, Chapters 5 and 6 focus on the role and activities of unions. The former looks at union membership, growth, and structure, while the latter deals with union actions and impacts, including both economic and non-economic ones.

We then move on to the legal aspects of the IR system. Chapter 7 discusses employment legislation affecting all workers, but focusses on that of particular relevance to non-unionized ones. Among the topics we consider here are work standards legislation affecting such things as minimum wages and maximum allowable hours of work, health and safety legislation, human rights legislation, and workers' compensation legislation. We also consider what redress a non-unionized individual has against a dismissal he or she considers to have been arbitrary.

STRATEGIES [SEARCH LABOUR RELATIONS]
strategis.ic.gc.ca

In Chapter 8, we consider private sector labour relations legislation. In addition to enumerating both historical and recent developments in the field, the chapter demonstrates the rationale for such legislation and discusses some of the variations in provincial labour legislation.

Chapter 9 focusses on collective bargaining and labour legislation in the public sector. This sector is of particular interest, both because of the crucial nature of the services it provides and because it has recently been the setting for many of our country's most bitter labour disputes. After examining the historical evolution of public sector collective bargaining and some of the ways in which it differs from bargaining in the private sector, we examine the current state of public sector collective bargaining, which many have argued is in a state of crisis.

The next group of chapters is primarily concerned with the bargaining process and with the conflict that often arises during that process. In Chapter 10, we look at the negotiation process in some detail. We also consider bargaining structures, since they comprise a key element of the environment in which bargaining is conducted. In Chapter 11 on the collective agreement, we discuss the evolution and philosophy of Canadian collective agreements and analyze a number of sample clauses.

Strikes are the aspect of the IR system most familiar to the average reader because of the prominence they receive in the media. After clarifying what a strike is in Chapter 12, we consider the changing patterns of strike incidence in Canada, including changing patterns in different industries and provinces. We then go on to look at a variety of possible causes for strikes. We close the chapter with a look at some of the dispute resolution methods used to prevent strikes, or at least reduce their adverse effect on innocent parties. A highlight of this chapter is its description of four recent major Canadian strikes.

CANADA LABOUR NEWS
www.geocities.com/CapitolHill/5202/Canada.html

Chapter 13 focusses on grievances and the grievance process. Part of the chapter is devoted to an examination of an actual grievance case. In addition, we consider what a grievance is, how a typical grievance process works, and some of the most important criticisms of the grievance process. We close by relating grievances to other forms of industrial conflict, like strikes, and by proposing alternatives to conventional grievance processes.

In the final chapter, Chapter 14, we revisit the Canadian IR system as a whole in light of important recent developments like globalization, liberalized trade, increased work hours, and the growth of a contingent work force. To this end, we examine seven key themes and discuss some of the most important findings related to those themes.

Throughout the book, evidence from foreign IR systems is used where possible to show the Canadian system in a comparative perspective. Similarly, a discussion of key features of Quebec's quite distinctive IR system has been incorporated into the chapters where appropriate.

QUESTIONS FOR DISCUSSION

1) What has *your* experience of work been, to this point? What have you liked best (and least) about it?

2) How has your experience of work compared with your parents', or with that of people of your parents' generation?

3) What are some of the major *strengths* of the systems framework? What are some of its major *weaknesses*?

4) How have Thomas Kochan and his associates sought to address the systems framework's perceived problems through their strategic choice theory?

5) What are the key features of each of the five major perspectives on IR? Which do you find most convincing, and why?

6) How does IR differ from other disciplines that deal with the world of work, such as labour history or organizational behaviour? What has been IR's distinctive contribution to the study of work?

SUGGESTIONS FOR FURTHER READING

Adams, Roy. (1995a). "Canadian industrial relations in comparative perspective." Morley Gunderson and Allen Ponak (Eds.), *Union-Management Relations in Canada* (chap. 17). Don Mills ON: Addison-Wesley. For those interested in learning more about how other countries' IR systems operate, this is a first-rate introduction.

Adams, Scott. Dilbert cartoons (in most newspapers, particularly on Saturdays). The Dilbert strip offers a funny and often extremely penetrating look at the follies and foibles of North American workplaces. It's particularly good on management practice. In addition, Adams has written a number of Dilbert books.

Chaykowski, Richard, and Anil Verma (Eds.). (1992). *Industrial relations in Canadian industry.* Toronto: Dryden. A detailed look at IR practice in 10 Canadian industries, written from a strategic choice perspective.

Godard, John. (1994). *Industrial relations: The economy and society.* Toronto: McGraw-Hill Ryerson. An excellent and very readable textbook written from a political economy perspective. The chapters on management, unions, and the role of the state are particularly good.

Terkel, Studs. (c1975 [1972]). *Working.* New York: Avon. Though possibly a bit dated by now, this series of interviews with more than 100 Americans about their jobs (from business executives to hookers), remains a classic.

ENDNOTES

[1] One can learn a good deal about this insecurity by reading the so-called "GenX" fiction written by and (especially) aimed at people under 35. See, for example, Douglas Coupland's *Shampoo Planet.*

[2] For more information, see the discussion of British Columbia's "Draft Ergonomics Regulation" in Chapter 7.

[3] This same definition has been usefully adopted by Adams (1993).

[4] On this point, see also Wood et al. (1975).

5 For a useful discussion on the distinction between conflict over fundamental issues of principle and what might be described as "instrumental" conflict over issues like wages, see Kervin (1984).

6 As we'll see in Chapter 7, Beatty's belief in the remedial powers of the *Charter* is shared by few other Canadian legal scholars or industrial relationists.

7 For a useful if brief discussion on Marxism and its application to industrial relations issues, see Godard (1994:36–45). I am indebted to Godard's discussion for much of the material in this paragraph.

8 Much of the material in this paragraph has been drawn from Anderson et al. (1989).

9 Readers should note that the term "political economy" is defined somewhat differently here than in Gunderson and Ponak (1995), who use the same term. Those authors don't have the equivalent of this book's reformist or Godard's liberal reformist perspective. Thus, Gunderson and Ponak's political economy perspective includes the work of many people whom Godard and the author would place in the reformist camp.

CHAPTER 2

THE ECONOMY
AND ITS IMPACTS

Conditions in the kitchen shown here look good compared to those in the kitchens Montreal *Star* journalist Sheila Arnopoulos visited during the 1970s, in which large numbers of mainly immigrant workers were putting in long hours.

The state of the economy is critical to the functioning of the industrial relations system, since the economy is largely responsible for determining the relative balance of power between employers and workers. In this chapter, we start by looking at some broad relationships between the economy and the IR system and at the current state of the Canadian economy. Next, we consider how the country's labour force has changed in recent years, with particular emphasis on the growth of contingent and part-time work. We then discuss the concept of a labour market, examining among other things the notion of competitive labour markets, and explaining why such markets seem to have been making a comeback recently. Next, we seek to determine the impact

of globalization and trade liberalization on the Canadian IR system. The rest of the chapter is devoted to unemployment, which remains stubbornly high throughout most of Canada. After defining unemployment and looking at several ways of measuring it, we consider three different types and look at its incidence by age group, industry, and province. Special attention is paid to the recent phenomenon of high unemployment existing side by side with long work hours and a high incidence of overtime.

SOME BASIC DYNAMICS

In the previous chapter, we pointed out that industrial relations is about a good deal more than just money. Nonetheless, at the most basic level, the economy is critical to the functioning of the IR system. When inflation is high, workers may want to join unions to help protect their real wage levels. Since the demand for goods and labour is also generally high in times of high inflation, workers already in unions are more likely to strike in support of wage demands. Knowing that their employers want to get them back to work as soon as possible to avoid losing business, workers also know that their employers are more likely to meet their wage demands. Moreover, even if some unionized workers are laid off because employers believe they can't meet the union's wage demands, when the demand for goods and labour is high (the 'high' end of the business cycle, as it is sometimes called), it is usually relatively easy for them to find new jobs.

ONLINE JOURNAL *WORKING LIFE*
www.lra-ny.com/workinglife/index.html

By the same token, when inflation is low, workers are less apt to seek to join unions to protect their real wages. (They may want to join for other reasons, for example, to protest against what they see as arbitrary management practices, but that is another matter.) Those already in unions are less apt to go on strike over wages. Normally when inflation is low, the general demand for goods and labour is also low (the 'low' end of the business cycle). At such times, it may not be that important for employers to get their workers back on the job, as they may not have a backlog of unfilled orders. Indeed, they sometimes have large unsold inventories and may even welcome a strike as way of reducing their wage bill. Unions are less likely to press wage demands in bad times for two reasons. First, any strike that does occur may last longer, since employers have less incentive to settle than they would in good times. This means that the strike's cost to the workers will be higher than in good times. Second, if workers get laid off because the employer can't meet the union's wage demands without cutting jobs, it may be difficult or in some cases impossible for them to find other jobs when unemployment is already high. Again, as we point out in the chapter on strikes, this doesn't mean that strikes don't take place in bad times. What it does mean is that strikes are less likely to be over wages and more likely to be over other issues.

Granted, the preceding picture has been painted with an extremely broad brush. In the last analysis, each workplace is unique, with its own history, politics, and cast of characters. Still, though such broad economic indicators as the national unemployment and inflation rates don't explain everything about the IR system, they do explain quite a bit, especially at the national level. Table 2.1 offers some sense of these broad relationships from the end of World War II to the present. You can see from the table that periods of high inflation have generally featured increases in union membership and strike activity. Periods of high unemployment and low inflation have usually seen lower union membership rates and strike activity.

Table 2.1

RATE OF CHANGE IN CONSUMER PRICE INDEX, UNEMPLOYMENT RATE, UNION DENSITY RATES, NUMBER OF STRIKES, AND STRIKES AS A PERCENTAGE OF WORKING TIME LOST, CANADA, 1946–1997

Year	CPI Change (%)	Unemp. (%)	Un. Dens.* (%)	Strikes	Strikes as % of Lost Worktime
1946	2.8	3.4	27.9	226	0.54
1947	9.8	2.2	29.1	234	0.27
1948	13.8	2.3	30.3	154	0.10
1949	3.6	2.8	29.5	135	0.11
1950	2.8	3.6	†	160	0.15
1951	10.1	2.4	28.4	258	0.09
1952	3.0	2.9	30.2	219	0.29
1953	-1.2	3.0	33.0	173	0.14
1954	0.6	4.6	33.8	173	0.15
1955	0.0	4.4	33.7	159	0.19
1956	1.8	3.4	33.3	229	0.11
1957	2.9	4.6	32.4	245	0.13
1958	2.3	7.0	34.2	259	0.25
1959	1.7	6.0	33.3	216	0.19
1960	1.1	7.0	32.3	274	0.06
1961	1.1	7.1	31.6	287	0.11
1962	1.1	5.9	30.2	311	0.11
1963	1.6	5.5	29.8	332	0.07
1964	2.1	4.7	29.4	343	0.11

Table 2.1 (continued)

Year	CPI Change (%)	Unemp. (%)	Un. Dens.* (%)	Strikes	Strikes as % of Lost Worktime
1965	2.0	3.9	29.7	501	0.17
1966	4.0	3.4	30.7	617	0.34
1967	3.4	3.8	32.3	522	0.25
1968	4.2	4.5	33.1	582	0.32
1969	4.5	4.4	32.5	595	0.46
1970	3.4	5.7	33.6	542	0.39
1971	2.8	6.2	32.4	569	0.16
1972	4.8	6.2	33.9	578	0.43
1973	7.7	5.5	35.4	724	0.30
1974	10.7	5.3	35.2	1 218	0.46
1975	10.9	6.9	35.6	1 171	0.53
1976	7.5	7.2	36.9	1 040	0.53
1977	7.8	8.1	36.3	806	0.15
1978	9.0	8.4	37.1	1 057	0.32
1979	9.2	7.5	−†	1 049	0.33
1980	10.1	7.5	35.7	1 028	0.37
1981	12.4	7.6	35.4	1 049	0.35
1982	10.9	11.0	35.7	679	0.23
1983	5.8	11.9	36.4	645	0.18
1984	4.3	11.3	37.2	717	0.15
1985	4.0	10.5	36.4	825	0.12
1986	4.1	9.6	36.0	748	0.27
1987	4.4	8.9	35.2	668	0.14
1988	4.0	7.8	34.8	548	0.17
1989	5.0	7.5	34.5	627	0.13
1990	4.8	8.1	34.5	579	0.17
1991	5.6	10.4	34.7	463	0.09
1992	1.5	11.3	35.7	404	0.07
1993	1.8	11.2	35.8	382	0.05
1994	0.2	10.4	35.6	374	0.06
1995	2.2	9.5	34.3	328	0.05
1996	1.6	9.7	33.9	328	0.11
1997	1.6	9.2	34.1	279	0.12

* Union density is defined as the percentage of non-agricultural paid workers belonging to unions. Union density figures are lower than in previous HRDC charts (i.e., the 1993 *Directory of Paid Labour Organizations*) because the number of non-agricultural paid workers used in the calculation for 1996 is higher than that used in previous calculations.

† Data were not collected for these years.

Sources: CPI data, Statistics Canada Cat. No. 62-001-XPB, page i, Table A. Unemployment, Statistics Canada Cat. No. 71-201-XPB. Union membership data 1946–1970, Eaton, 1975. For 1971–1976, Labour Canada, 1992. For 1977, Workplace Information Directorate (WID), Human Resources Development Canada (HRDC), 1996, *Directory of Labour Organizations in Canada.* For 1978–1997, WID, HRDC, 1997, *Directory of Labour Organizations in Canada.* Strike data, 1946–1975, Labour Canada, *Strikes and Lockouts in Canada,* various issues. For 1976–1997, data provided by the Work Stoppage Bureau, WID, HRDC.

TODAY'S ECONOMY

Table 2.1 also reveals that today's economy has quite high unemployment (by historical standards) and low inflation. As we pointed out earlier, high unemployment and low inflation are characteristic of periods at the low end of business cycles and suggest an environment in which employers have a good deal more power than workers and their unions.

But there is growing reason to believe that the changes we are seeing in today's economy aren't simply the result of a cyclical downturn in the economy. Rather, the economic changes appear to be the result of more fundamental changes, like trade liberalization and deindustrialization. Through the early 1970s (Chaykowski and Verma, 1992), relatively high tariffs protected most Canadian businesses from serious foreign competition. Increasingly, this protection is being removed. In the wake of a series of free trade agreements (discussed in more detail later in the chapter), Canadian firms have been forced to compete not just with each other, but with firms in the United States and Mexico, where production costs are generally a good deal lower. They have responded with massive restructuring and downsizing, causing many thousands of workers to lose their jobs, while others have been forced to accept lower pay, fewer benefits, and poorer working conditions.

"HARMONIZATION OF LABOUR POLICIES UNDER TRADE LIBERALIZATION"

www.erudit.org/erudit/ri/v53no1/gunder/gunder.html

As we'll discuss in more detail later, many of the jobs that have been lost during the nineties, particularly manufacturing jobs, aren't expected to come back. While some jobs have been created in the nineties, most of them are in the private-service sector rather than in manufacturing. They typically pay a good deal less than the manufacturing jobs they are "replacing" and they are often part-time. Even if they are full-time, they generally offer employees poorer benefits and less job security than the manufacturing positions did.

Overall, more people have been losing their jobs during the 1990s than at any other time in the last fifty years (Donner, 1994:4). In previous recessions, those laid off were often younger workers with little experience, or older workers with little education and few marketable skills. That is no longer true. The layoffs taking place during the 1990s have spared no one. Younger workers have been hard hit once again, but so have older workers (Foot, 1997). Public sector workers, who were once comparatively well protected in times of economic downturn, are little more immune from layoffs this time around than their private-sector counterparts (see Rose, 1995).

Nor are education or experience any guarantee of job security. People with graduate and professional degrees have been laid off, as have growing numbers of managers (see Payne, 1998).

With even prosperous firms that have posted large profits going in for large-scale layoffs, few people feel their jobs are really secure. Those who do manage to keep their jobs often find themselves working longer and harder than ever before. In recent years, there has been an epidemic of overtime—much of it unpaid. The result is a society in which many people are working far more hours than they want to, while others (the unemployed or partially employed) are working far fewer. For example, many university graduates are working part-time in fast-food establishments and convenience stores because that is the only work they can find.

Another important change has been in the scheduling of work. Until very recently, the majority of working Canadians were full-time employees working on a regular schedule—typically seven to eight hours of work per day, five days a week. The past few years have seen huge growth in a wide range of so-called "atypical" work arrangements, including part-time work, self-employment, home-based work, shift work, work done at irregular hours, and short-term, temporary, and contractual work. Unable to find full-time positions, a growing number of Canadians are piecing together a living out of two or more of these part-time or short-term jobs.

Taken together, these changes have bred considerable economic insecurity and frustration. People in large organizations undergoing restructuring are fearful that they may be the next to go. Working parents forced to put in long overtime hours are resentful that they can't spend more time with their families. And young university graduates who can do no better than flipping hamburgers or pouring coffee are bitter over the waste of their talents and creative energies.

While the economic environment has been changing rapidly, so has the Canadian labour force. Once mainly male and predominantly White, it is now nearly half female and includes growing numbers of ethnic and religious minorities. It is to this changing labour force that we now turn.

THE CHANGING CANADIAN LABOUR FORCE

The **labour force** includes all employed workers and all unemployed ones who are looking for work. Today's Canadian labour force differs in some important ways from the labour force of a generation or two ago. By comparison, it is older, includes more women and members of ethnic minorities, and contains more part-time workers, more self-employed individuals, and more people doing all or part of their work at home. Over the years, the proportion of Canadians working in **primary** industries like agriculture, forestry, and fishing has declined substantially. Throughout most of the postwar period (Craig and Solomon, 1996:51), the proportion working in **secondary** industries like manufacturing has also been declining. In contrast, the proportion working in **tertiary** or **service** industries like utilities, trade, finance, education, and public administration has risen steadily. These changes, some of which have occurred fairly recently, have important implications for Canadian workers and their unions, employers, and governments.

An Older Labour Force

Canada's labour force is aging along with its population. Indeed, it may be aging even more rapidly than the population as a whole, owing to the recent sharp decline in younger workers. In 1978, the labour force contained 3.05 million workers aged 15 to 24; this group comprised 27 percent of the total labour force. By 1997, there were only 2.43 million younger workers in the labour force, comprising less than 16 percent of the total. Over the 19-year period, younger workers' participation rate dropped from 65 to 61 percent.[1] One reason for the drop is that given high youth unemployment rates (almost 17 percent in 1997), trying to find work may not make a great deal of sense. Instead, an increasing number of young people are electing to remain in school—in many cases not because that is what they really want to do, but because they believe it is better for their morale and their future prospects to be in school doing something than unemployed doing nothing (O'Hara, 1993:37).[2]

With youth unemployment still very high, a growing number of young Canadians are reaching their 20s with no work experience at all.

While a more educated labour force could in time make Canada's economy more competitive, an issue of more immediate concern is young people's growing lack of work experience. Between 1989 and 1996, the proportion of people aged 15 to 24 with no work experience doubled from 10 to 20 percent (Statistics Canada, 1997). For those aged 15 to 19, the rate increased from 18 to 34 percent (Statistics Canada, 1997). How to provide these young people with significant work experience continues to be a major challenge for policy-makers.

The aging of the labour force has some important implications for employers, unions, and governments. Motivating older workers can be extremely difficult in organizations with few opportunities for advancement (Reid and Meltz, 1995:34). In such situations, the challenge for HR managers is to make the work itself more interesting, or to find non-monetary ways of honouring older workers for their special skills and knowledge.[3] In the absence of imaginative HR practices, employee burnout can be a serious problem in organizations with a high proportion of older workers—a problem with potentially serious economic consequences for organizations (Minnehan and Paine, 1982) and for individual workers.

Understandably, older workers often place a high premium on job security (Reid and Meltz, 1995:34), since a job loss can be extremely costly. Older workers may have invested many years in an organization and may find it very difficult to obtain a new position. In collective bargaining, they are apt to put relatively greater emphasis on benefits, such as health plans and pensions, and less on up-front wages (Reid and Meltz, 1995). Within unions, they tend to be strong defenders of seniority and are often opposed to new workplace practices that go against traditional, seniority-based approaches. But because older workers generally have less need for up-front wages and a greater preference for additional free time (Gunderson and Riddell, 1993), they may be quite open to reducing overtime hours or even entering into job-sharing arrangements that create or preserve jobs for younger workers (CLMPC, 1997:47–48).

As more and more people born during the postwar "baby boom" enter middle age, **mandatory retirement** has become an issue of increasing concern for workers, employers, and governments alike. All provinces ban workplace discrimination on the grounds of age; however, all but two (Quebec and Manitoba) apply the anti-discrimination provisions only to those aged 64 and under, in effect allowing firms to force workers 65 and over to retire (Reid and Meltz, 1995:35). Proponents say that mandatory retirement at age 65 creates jobs for younger workers and allows older workers to retire with dignity (Gunderson and Riddell, 1993:601). Without mandatory retirement, these people argue, older workers' performance would have to be far more strictly monitored and dismissals of such workers might become more frequent (Gunderson and Riddell, 1993). Another argument in favour of mandatory retirement is that most older workers have pensions that will provide them with adequate post-retirement income. Thus, from an equity perspective, forcing older

Mandatory retirement? It may create jobs, but for many older people, their work is their life.

workers to retire is preferable to keeping large numbers of young people unemployed, given that young people don't have pensions to fall back on.

Opponents argue that forced retirement is simply discriminatory and no more justifiable than discrimination on the basis of sex, race, or religion (Gunderson and Riddell, 1993). They also argue that at a time when increasingly few workers stay with one employer or even a single occupation, and when many parents have interrupted their careers to raise children, it is no longer safe to assume that a worker of 65 will have an adequate pension to fall back on. Others say that with growing pressure on public pension funds (Gunderson and Riddell, 1993), it is counterproductive to increase the pressure on those funds further by forcing people who would rather be working to retire, thus turning them from contributors to the funds into beneficiaries. Other opponents suggest that in an era of widespread hiring freezes, the forced retirement of older workers may not create any additional jobs, but will simply leave "survivors" with heavier workloads.

More Women At Work

Perhaps the most important recent change in the Canadian labour force has been the increase in the number of women working or seeking work. In 1978, just under 45 percent of all women 25 and over[4] were classified as active labour force participants.

By 1997, this figure had risen to 57 percent, and the number of women participating in the labour force had nearly doubled, from 2.98 million to 5.77 million. During this same period, the female share of the labour force grew from 36 percent to 45 percent (see Figure 2.1a). The female participation rate has been virtually unchanged since 1990; however, the overall participation rate (not shown in tables)[5] has dropped from 67.5 to 64.8, which means that the *male* participation rate has gone down substantially.

The growing presence of women in Canadian workplaces has forced employers and employees alike to become more aware of sexual harassment issues. Since many working women have family responsibilities, employers have also had to start paying more attention to work-family issues, like demands for workplace day-care centres, or for more flexible schedules or personal leave time to enable workers to attend to family emergencies.

The increase in the number of working women has had major implications for unions as well. Women now comprise more than 40 percent of all Canadian union members (Murray, 1995:165), and their presence has put issues like paid maternity leave, demands for flexible scheduling, child care, pay equity, sexual harassment, and affirmative action onto bargaining agendas all across the country (Murray, 1995:183–184). Within unions, increased female membership has led to attempts to increase women's participation and to get more women elected to union offices (Murray, 1995:184). Indeed, women's profile within the Canadian labour movement has increased in recent years. The president and secretary-treasurer of the country's largest union, the Canadian Union of Public Employees, are both women, as is a past president of the Canadian Labour Congress.

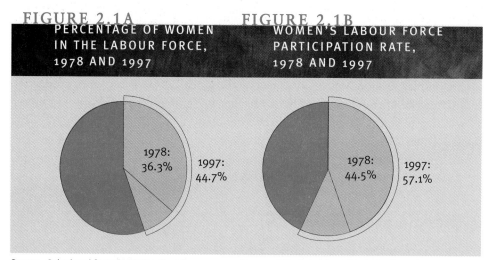

FIGURE 2.1A
PERCENTAGE OF WOMEN IN THE LABOUR FORCE, 1978 AND 1997

1978: 36.3%   1997: 44.7%

FIGURE 2.1B
WOMEN'S LABOUR FORCE PARTICIPATION RATE, 1978 AND 1997

1978: 44.5%   1997: 57.1%

Source: Calculated from Statistics Canada, Cat. No. 71-201-XPB, page 17.

Source: Calculated from Statistics Canada, Cat. No. 71-201-XPB, page 17.

For governments, increased female labour force participation means more demand for a broad range of anti-discrimination legislation, on subjects ranging from sexual harassment to equal pay and employment equity. (Bear in mind that women continue to earn substantially less than men, despite years of pressure from women's groups, unions, and others. In many cases, they also still face discrimination in hiring and promotion opportunities.) As the negative effects on family life of increased overtime become clearer, women both within the labour movement and outside of it may spur demands for changes in employment standards legislation governing overtime.

A More Diverse Work Force

In recent years, ethnic and religious minorities have entered the labour force in growing numbers, due to increased immigration. Employers must ensure that the work environment is free from discrimination against those of different ethnic origins or religions. As a result of the "duty to accommodate," which will be discussed in more detail in the labour relations law chapter (Chapter 7), employers may be obliged to draw up special schedules to allow for time off on religious holidays and for celebrations. They may also need to provide language training for workers for whom English or French is a second language.

Unions, which until comparatively recently were dominated by White males, also need to address the concerns of today's increasingly diverse labour force. As Galt (1994) notes, this may mean using immigrants to organize other immigrants, and being sure that issues of concern to immigrants, such as literacy training and anti-discrimination protection, are on bargaining agendas.

A growing number of workers with physical and mental disabilities have also been entering the labour force in recent years. Again, employers may have a duty to accommodate such employees' special needs by making their premises wheelchair-accessible, providing special equipment, modifying the workers' duties, or altering their schedules so they can keep medical appointments (see Carter, 1997). And as in the case of ethnic minorities, employers must ensure that workers with disabilities aren't harassed by fellow workers or supervisors.

More Part-Time Workers

Since 1976, the proportion of workers employed only part-time has nearly doubled, from just under 11 to just under 19 percent of total employment (see Table 2.2). Of particular importance is the increase in **involuntary** part-time work, or part-time work done by people who would rather be working full-time, but can't find a full-time job. This rate has increased significantly faster than either the part-time rate or the unemployment rate. In 1976, 12 percent of all part-time workers would rather have been working full-time.

By 1993, the proportion of part-time work which was involuntary had tripled to 36 percent, though it has since dropped back to 29 percent in 1996. The rate of involuntary part-time work has been particularly high among workers aged 25 to 44; in 1994, 45 percent of all part-timers from this age group would have preferred full-time work (CLMPC, 1997, Table A2). The rate of involuntary part-time employment has increased to be nearly that of the unemployment rate in some years (see Table 2.3).

In many cases, part-time work arrangements can benefit both employers and workers (CLMPC, 1997:43). This is particularly true in the case of workers with family responsibilities and students attending high school or university. Nonetheless, the growing incidence of part-time work, and especially of involuntary part-time work, raises a number of serious concerns. To begin with, part-timers' wages are generally a good deal lower than those of full-time workers—usually

Table 2.2

	PART-TIME EMPLOYMENT COMPARATIVE PERCENTAGES, AGE 15 AND OVER, CANADA, 1976 TO 1996		
Year	Part-Time as % of Employment	Involuntary P/T as % of P/T	Involuntary P/T as % of Employment
1976	10.9	12.0	1.3
1977	11.6	15.0	1.7
1978	13.3	17.0	2.3
1979	13.8	17.0	2.3
1980	14.4	18.0	2.6
1981	14.9	18.0	2.7
1982	15.9	25.0	4.0
1983	16.8	29.0	4.9
1984	16.8	30.0	5.0
1985	17.0	30.0	5.1
1986	16.9	28.0	4.7
1987	16.6	27.0	4.5
1988	16.8	24.0	4.3
1989	16.6	22.0	3.7
1990	17.0	22.0	3.7
1991	18.1	28.0	5.1
1992	18.5	33.0	6.1
1993	19.1	36.0	6.9
1994	18.8	35.0	6.6
1995	18.6	35.0	6.5
1996	18.9	29.0	5.5

Sources: Part-Time Employment, CLMPC, Table A1 (1976 and 1977); Statistics Canada, Cat. No. 71-201-XPB, p. 5 (1978 through 1996). Involuntary part-time, (1976 through 1994) CLMPC, Table A2; Statistics Canada Cat. No. 71-001-XPB, page B-34 (1995 and 1996). Involuntary part-time as percentage of employment was derived by multiplying part-time as a percentage of employment by involuntary part-time as a percentage of part-time.

from 15 to 35 percent lower, depending on the industry (CLMPC, 1997:Chart 8). Given that part-time workers already work fewer hours than full-timers, the lower wage rates increase the often already serious economic stress on these workers and their families. This is especially true in occupations, like retail trade, that feature a good deal of shift work, and where the availability and predictability of hours is thus a serious concern for workers (CLMPC, 1997:46). Moreover, far fewer part-timers than full-timers enjoy benefits like occupational pensions, paid health and dental plans, and sick leave (CLMPC, 1997:44). In addition, from a national macroeconomic perspective, lower wages and benefits paid to a sizeable number of workers means lower tax revenues and fewer dollars flowing through the economy, which in turn means slower rates of job creation and investment.

Table 2.3

INVOLUNTARY PART-TIME EMPLOYMENT AS A PERCENTAGE OF EMPLOYMENT AND UNEMPLOYMENT, CANADA, 1976 TO 1996

Year	Unemp (%)	Invol. P/T as % of Employment	Invol. P/T as % of Unemployment
1976	7.1	1.3	18
1977	8.1	1.7	21
1978	8.3	2.3	24
1979	7.4	2.3	28
1980	7.5	2.3	31
1981	7.5	2.6	32
1982	11.0	2.7	33
1983	11.8	4.0	37
1984	11.2	4.9	41
1985	10.5	5.0	44
1986	9.5	5.1	45
1987	8.8	4.7	47
1988	7.8	4.5	46
1989	7.5	4.3	44
1990	8.1	3.7	42
1991	10.4	3.7	44
1992	11.3	5.1	49
1993	11.2	6.1	55
1994	10.4	6.9	58
1995	9.5	6.6	68
1996	9.7	6.5	57

Sources: Unemployment, Statistics Canada Cat. No. 71-201-XPB. Involuntary part-time as a percentage of employment was derived by multiplying part-time as a percentage of employment by involuntary part-time as a percentage of part-time as in Table 2.2, from which these data are drawn. Involuntary part-time as a percentage of unemployment is obtained by dividing the data in column 2 of the above table by those in column 1.

Many employers like to use part-time workers because it costs them less. Nonetheless, the growing incidence of part-time work can cause a number of problems for managers. Part-time workers are frequently less committed to their jobs than are full-timers and may be more likely to quit if something better comes along. Low wages, lack of benefits, and frequent lack of job security may lead to lower morale and productivity among part-timers. Scheduling can also become more difficult when there are large numbers of part-timers, particularly in situations where there is also shift work.

For unions, the growing trend to part-time work represents a major challenge. Not surprisingly, a significantly higher proportion of full-timers than part-timers belong to unions (Murray, 1995:168).[6] Part-timers tend to be relatively less attached to their jobs and more apt to quit rather than to stay and try to improve conditions where they are. Many are also concentrated in the private-service sector, where employer opposition to unions has been particularly strong. The fact that part-timers often work in smaller organizations makes them more expensive for unions to organize, and some jurisdictions have also put legislative barriers in the way, such as the requirement that part-timers have separate bargaining units (LLCG, 1984:3–151).[7] While including part-timers in regular bargaining units is probably a more equitable solution, it can also pose problems for unions, since the interests of part-time and full-time workers may diverge significantly (England, 1987:10–13).

Polarization of Work Hours

Related to the trend towards part-time work is a growing polarization of work hours and a decline in the number of people working a "standard" work week of 35 to 40 hours. In 1995, a bare majority (54 percent) of all workers put in "standard" hours, as compared to 65 percent in 1976. The decrease is the result of increases in the proportion of people putting in both short and long hours. Between 1976 and 1995, the proportion of people working fewer than 35 hours per week increased from 16 to 24 percent, while the proportion working 41 or more hours a week grew from 19 percent to 22 percent (Sheridan, Sunter, and Diverty, 1996:C-5). The implications of this broad trend toward polarization of work hours are discussed below, in the section on overtime and unemployment.

More Self-Employed People

The proportion of Canadian workers described as self-employed increased from 13.2 percent in 1978 to 17.8 percent in 1997 (see Figure 2.2). Much of this increase occurred during the last two years. The phenomenon may be a response to tighter EI eligibility rules that took effect in early 1997. It may also in part be a response to the 15 percent decline in public administration employment that occurred between

FIGURE 2.2

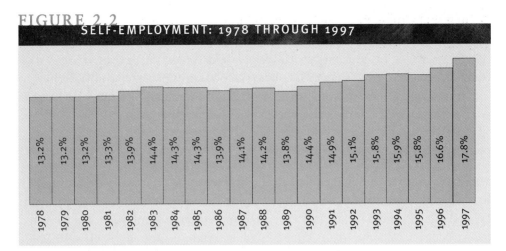

SELF-EMPLOYMENT: 1978 THROUGH 1997

Year	Percent
1978	13.2%
1979	13.2%
1980	13.2%
1981	13.3%
1982	13.9%
1983	14.4%
1984	14.3%
1985	14.3%
1986	13.9%
1987	14.1%
1988	14.2%
1989	13.8%
1990	14.4%
1991	14.9%
1992	15.1%
1993	15.8%
1994	15.9%
1995	15.8%
1996	16.6%
1997	17.8%

Source: Calculated from Statistics Canada, Cat No. 71-201-XPB, page 23.

1993 and 1997 (CANSIM, 1998), as laid-off public servants set up shop as consultants. The most serious implications of self-employment are probably for unions; with fewer people in employee status, they must work harder to maintain their membership levels.

Other Recent Trends

Home-Based Work

Home-based work isn't new in Canada (see England, 1987), but its incidence has been increasing significantly in recent years, thanks to communications and computer technologies that make it easier for work to be done outside central offices. Between 1991 and 1995 (CLMPC, 1997:35), the proportion of paid employees doing all or part of their paid work at home increased from about 6 to about 9 percent. Home-based work was slightly more common among women than among men, and most prevalent in service industries like health care, community services, wholesale trade, and finance/insurance/real estate.

In 1995, nearly half of all home-based workers worked at home because the job required them to do so. Those who chose to work at home most often did so because of better working conditions, other work-related reasons, or savings in time and money (CLMPC, 1997:36).

For individual workers, concerns include isolation and lack of interaction with other people, and the possibility of work intensification or overload. Employers often like having people work at home because building overhead and supervision costs are lower; however, there may be problems in controlling the quality of work done in this way (CLMPC, 1997).[8] For unions, home-based work poses severe challenges both in organizing workers and in monitoring working conditions. The challenges may be equally severe for government agencies, like labour ministries, that are charged with regulating employment standards legislation. How, for example, can anyone monitor health and safety standards (CLMPC, 1997) in a multitude of home-based workplaces, where workers frequently provide their own equipment and furniture?

Flexible Work Schedules

With the recent increase in the number of working women and dual-income families, flexible work schedules can be useful in helping people meet both work responsibilities and family commitments. In 1991, some 16 percent of employed Canadians had the freedom to choose their hours, within certain limits. By 1995 (CLMPC, 1997:32–4), this figure had increased to 24 percent. While there was little difference between men and women, married workers were a good deal more likely to have flexible schedules, as were non-unionized workers (CLMPC, 1997:34). Flextime was much more common in professional, white-collar, and service industries and occupations than in blue-collar or goods-producing ones. Nearly half those in management and administrative occupations had flexible schedules in 1995, compared to only 10 percent in processing and machining occupations. Flextime was most common in the public administration and the finance/insurance/real estate industries.

Flextime is generally popular with workers. While many employers also find it of benefit since it can improve morale and productivity by reducing work-family stress on employees, some dislike it because it complicates scheduling decisions (CLMPC, 1997:31).

Contractual Work

In addition to the growth in part-time work, another important trend is the growth in temporary or contractual work, where a worker is hired for a short term or for a specific job or project. A 1992 study (see Godard, 1994:422) found that 15 percent of all employment was on a temporary or contractual basis. Similarly, Swimmer (1995) notes that short-term and contractual employment increased sharply in the federal government between 1984 and 1992.

There is a great deal of variation in the sorts of contractual arrangements under which people work. Contracts for professionals like computer programmers or researchers may offer high pay and reasonable working conditions. On the other hand, contracts for garment workers assembling goods at home may constitute severe exploitation (see Lipsig-Mumme, 1995:208–209). What is common to almost all temporary and short-term contracts is that they provide little security and few if any benefits like sick leave or a pension plan.[9] These arrangements are popular with employers, since they allow them to avoid the costs of benefits and payroll taxes they would have to pay regular employees (Lipsig-Mumme, 1995:209). Many employers have also found that hiring people only for peak periods allows them to reduce their wage bills considerably. Still another advantage for employers is that temporary or contractual positions tend to be difficult if not impossible to unionize.

Moonlighting

The incidence of moonlighting, or holding more than one job, has increased substantially over the past two decades, from 2 percent in 1976 to 5 percent in 1995 (Sheridan et al., 1996:C-7). However, the pattern of moonlighting appears to have changed somewhat. In the past, most moonlighters were people already employed full-time holding down a second job. Today's moonlighter is more likely to be a younger person, attempting to piece together a living with a series of part-time jobs that among them still may not provide the same number of hours as a single full-time job (Sheridan et al., 1996).

Implications of Recent Trends

Taken together, the labour market trends we have explored suggest that far fewer Canadians today have steady, relatively well-paying jobs with regular work hours and decent benefits than in the past. So many people now work under "atypical" employment arrangements that these arrangements have become all but the norm. A growing number of Canadians work for themselves, and even those working for others are more apt to be employed on a temporary, contractual, or part-time basis. While not all such jobs pay less per hour or day than comparable full-time ones, few provide workers with any real job security or offer much in the way of benefits. When added to the growing number of layoffs resulting from ongoing mergers and restructuring activities, the trend towards atypical employment arrangements has added to Canadians' growing economic insecurity. The trend towards atypical employment arrangements is likewise of concern to unions, since people working under such arrangements are extremely difficult to organize.

"THE ROLE OF LABOUR STUDIES IN INDUSTRIAL RESTRUCTURING: PARTICIPATION, PROTECTION, AND PROMOTION"

www.ilo.org/public/english/130inst/papers/1990/dp19/index.htm

EMPLOYMENT IN DIFFERENT INDUSTRIES

In addition to working different hours, Canadians are also working in different industries than they were 100, 50, or even 20 years ago. In 1997, just over one-quarter (27 percent) of all Canadians worked in goods-producing industries in the primary and secondary sectors. About 5 percent worked in primary industries like agriculture, mining, and fishing, while the rest worked in secondary industries like manufacturing and construction, the former accounting for just over 15 percent of total employment. The service sector provided work for the remaining 73 percent of employed Canadians. About 17 percent worked in trade, 10 percent in health and social services, and 7 percent each in business, educational, and "other" services. Finance/insurance/real estate, accommodation and food services, transportation/storage/communication, and public administration each accounted for about 6 percent of total employment (see Figure 2.3).

Since the beginning of this century, the changes in the distribution of employment by industry have been profound. As we note in the labour history chapter (Chapter 4), Canada was slow to industrialize. In 1911, just before the First World War, just less than 40 percent of all Canadians still worked in primary industries (Ostry and Zaidi, 1979). Of these, the vast majority (34 percent) were in agriculture. Manufacturing and construction employed 17.4 percent of the work force, while another quarter were in the service sector, including government, trade, and finance (Ostry and Zaidi, 1979).

Between 1911 and 1951 (Ostry and Zaidi, 1979), both the secondary and service sectors grew substantially, at the

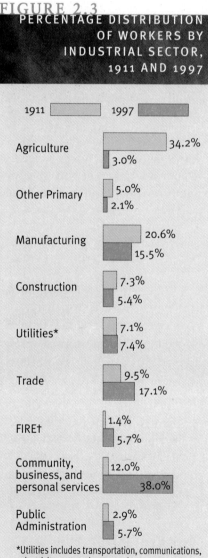

FIGURE 2.3

PERCENTAGE DISTRIBUTION OF WORKERS BY INDUSTRIAL SECTOR, 1911 AND 1997

1911 ☐   1997 ☐

Agriculture 34.2% / 3.0%
Other Primary 5.0% / 2.1%
Manufacturing 20.6% / 15.5%
Construction 7.3% / 5.4%
Utilities* 7.1% / 7.4%
Trade 9.5% / 17.1%
FIRE† 1.4% / 5.7%
Community, business, and personal services 12.0% / 38.0%
Public Administration 2.9% / 5.7%

*Utilities includes transportation, communications, electricity, gas, and waterworks.
†FIRE is Finance, Insurance, and Real Estate

Source: For 1911, Ostry and Zaidi, 1979; for 1997, Statistics Canada Cat. No. 71-005-XPB, Table 3, p. 18, "Labour Force Update," Winter 1998.

expense of the primary sector. By this time, the secondary sector accounted for more than 40 percent of total employment (26 percent in manufacturing), while another 35 percent were working in the service sector. The primary sector had shrunk to just over 21 percent, 16 percent being in agriculture (Ostry and Zaidi, 1979).

Since 1951, there has been a continuing decline in agriculture and other primary industries like mining. Much of this decline can be attributed to mechanization. To give just one example, modern tractors and harvesters enable a farmer to produce far more food today than a generation ago. But in addition to the long-term decline in primary employment, the postwar period has seen a significant decline in secondary industries like manufacturing and construction. Here, too, mechanization has made production more efficient, with the result that factories now require fewer workers to produce the same quantity of goods. Another important cause is deindustrialization (discussed later in the chapter), particularly since the implementation of the Canada-U.S. Free Trade Agreement.

Overall, the Canadian economy's performance has improved somewhat lately. During the past five years (CANSIM, 1998), total employment has increased by about 925 000, while unemployment has dropped by 2 percent (refer back to Table 2.1). Total employment growth has been fairly steady through this period, but the growth hasn't been evenly spread across industries. On the one hand, manufacturing has accounted for about 30 percent of this employment growth, the greater part being in durables rather than non-durables (CANSIM, 1998). In the service sector, more than 400 000 jobs have been added in business and personal services and more than 130 000 in trade. On the other hand, public administration has *lost* more than 110 000 jobs, or about 15 percent of its 1993 total, and jobs have also been lost in utilities and finance/insurance/real estate (CANSIM, 1998). Though job losses in the latter sector haven't been heavy so far (about 15 000, or 2 percent of the 1993 total), the situation will bear close observation over the next few years, given the likelihood of mergers and restructuring in that sector.[10]

The shift in the distribution of employment by industry has significant implications for unions. During the postwar period, employment has declined in manufacturing, mining, and construction—all occupations that tend to be relatively heavily unionized. Recently, employment has also declined in public administration, where unionization rates are extremely high. Most recent increases have been in private service industries like trade and business and personal services, where unionization rates are low and where organizing tends to be difficult. Unions are also concerned that the new private-service sector jobs tend to be poorly paid, are often part-time, and frequently involve home-based work (as in the case of insurance company employees processing claims from home computers). As we noted already, these are all factors that make service sector organizing even more difficult than it would otherwise be.

LABOUR MARKETS: WHAT THEY ARE AND WHAT THEY DO

The significance of labour markets to the IR system should be obvious. Employment levels within any given industry help determine the relative bargaining power of that industry's unions and employers, as well as pay levels within the industry. For countries as a whole, and for provinces within Canada, employment and unemployment levels have long been identified as major factors in explaining union membership growth and decline. At the individual level, the strength of national, occupational, and regional labour markets can play a critical role in determining a college or university student's choice of a major and eventual career choice. This in turn can significantly affect the relative demand for professors in some academic disciplines.

"TRAINING PROGRAMS, ADMINISTERED WAGES, AND LABOR MARKET OUTCOMES: AN INTERNATIONAL COMPARISON," CORNELL UNIVERSITY

socrates.berkeley.edu/~iir/ncw/wpapers/blau/index.html

A **labour market** (Reid and Meltz, 1989) is a mechanism for matching the buyers of labour (employers) with the suppliers of labour (workers). Normally, a labour market isn't a single place, like a farmers' market, although some locations like longshore and construction union hiring halls do serve to bring prospective workers together with potential employers (Reynolds, 1982). What is required in a labour market is that these workers and employers be in sufficiently close communication with one another that relatively standard compensation levels and working conditions can be established for any given type of position (Reynolds, 1982).

It would be a mistake to say that there is a single Canadian or even provincial labour market. There are many different markets, including, most significantly, occupational and regional ones. Except in the most extraordinary circumstances, a carpenter won't be competing for work with a physician or social worker. Nor, for the most part, will British Columbians be competing with Ontarians or Newfoundlanders. (A few exceptions to this generalization are noted below.) Even within the same province, the cost and personal disruption of moving a long distance often makes a province-wide job search impractical, except for very young or unattached workers.

Scope and Operation of Labour Markets

The type of work one does normally determines the scope of the market within which one must compete for work (Reynolds, 1982). Carpenters and other tradespeople usually operate within a local labour market comprising their home towns and the areas immediately surrounding them. Teachers, physicians, and members of other groups licensed by provincial authorities will often be part of a labour market comprising the entire province. For university professors, the market may well be all of Canada, or in some cases even Canada and the United States. In the case of certain highly touted "superstar" business executives, the market may be the entire industrialized world. Athletes, too, particularly professional baseball and hockey players, are increasingly operating within an international labour market. In baseball, for instance, players from the Dominican Republic and other Latin American countries have long been prominent members of major league teams. In recent years, we have seen the arrival of players from other parts of the world, including Japan and Australia, and the more or less permanent assignment of big league scouts to Asian countries.

LABOUR MARKET INFORMATION, NOVA SCOTIA
HUMAN RESOURCES DEVELOPMENT CANADA
www.ns.hrdc-drhc.gc.ca/english/lmi/lmi.htm

Different occupations also tend to communicate job vacancies differently. A construction or longshoring worker may learn of a vacancy at his or her local union hall. Other tradespeople might learn of vacancies through word of mouth or a local newspaper ad. Vacancies in small stores and restaurants are often made known through signs in the windows of these establishments. University teaching jobs are normally advertised through national publications like *University Affairs* or the *Canadian Association of University Teachers (CAUT) Bulletin*. For superstar athletes and business executives, direct personal recruitment appears to be the norm.

What can be said of all labour markets, no matter how broad or narrow their scope, is that they tend to work more efficiently in theory than they do in practice; that is to say, most do a more or less imperfect job of matching employers with prospective workers. We discuss some of the reasons for this imperfect matching in later sections of the chapter.

Competitive Labour Markets

The simplest type of labour market is the competitive one, in which there are so many employers that no single employer can influence the wage rate by varying his or her demand for labour (Lipsey, Purvis, Sparks, and Steiner, 1982:386). All are thus wage-takers rather than wage-setters (Reid and Meltz, 1995). They are also profit-maximizers. This means they will hire as many workers as they need to achieve the greatest possible profits, given the state of the current product market and their level of technology. In such markets, there are also large numbers of workers, all operating on a level playing field and seeking jobs that all pay the same wage. It is normally assumed that workers are either capable of doing the job on hiring or can be trained to do it within an extremely short period. Individual differences in skill or experience are of little importance, so long as a worker is able to perform at a certain minimum standard.

Other things being equal, a wage increase in one firm will make that firm more attractive, and will draw workers away from other firms. However, over the longer term, that same wage increase will reduce the demand for labour in the firm paying it, since it will increase the price of the product. This in turn will lead to a drop in sales, (unless the firm compensates buyers by putting out a superior product), to which the employer may respond by employing cheaper workers or substituting machinery for human labour.

Ideally, such an adjustment process will lead to an **equilibrium wage**, where the supply of and demand for labour are equal and no one willing to work at that rate will be unemployed. In practice, such pure competitive markets aren't common, though there have been signs recently that they are starting to reappear. Where they do exist, they tend to be more common in work of a seasonal, part-time, or temporary nature. A good example is the market for seasonal fruit pickers in Los Angeles, as described in various newspaper articles a number of years ago.

At a given hour (say, 7 A.M.), all those wishing to pick fruit that day position themselves on certain previously announced street corners in certain sections of Los Angeles. Shortly thereafter, trucks come by. They stop, and the drivers announce what the wage for that day is. Anyone willing to work for that wage (say, $5 an hour) gets into a truck and is taken out to the orchards. Anyone not willing to work for the given rate isn't picked up. At the end of each day, workers are paid and then returned to the same street corners where they'd been picked up that morning. The next day, the process is repeated, and so on until the end of harvest season.

The seasonal fruit-pickers' market just described points to some of the limitations of the competitive model as a guide to the way most actual labour markets work, particularly markets for full-time as opposed to seasonal work. Most obviously, employers expecting to retain workers for more than a very short period can't blithely disregard differences in their skill and ability. Such differences generally matter a good deal, even in relatively unskilled jobs requiring little formal education; for any skilled work, they are critical. Related to this, most firms don't have a single, undifferentiated type of work to be performed. Most require a number of different types of work, and many have different requirements even at the entry level. To treat workers as interchangeable, as the competitive model assumes they are, simply doesn't make sense for most employers.

"LABOR AND DEMOCRATIZATION: COMPARING THE FIRST AND THIRD WAVES IN EUROPE AND LATIN AMERICA," UNIVERSITY OF CALIFORNIA, BERKELEY

socrates.berkeley.edu/~iir/iirpub/iirworkpap62.html

The competitive model also fails to take into account the fact that most people work for more than just wages. To begin with, most receive at least a few fringe benefits, like pensions, sick leave, vacation time, and so on. (Some of these are, indeed, required for almost all workers with regular employee status, as we point in more detail in Chapter 7.) Beyond that, most people receive some intrinsic satisfaction from their work. In its purest form, the competitive model we have been discussing can't and doesn't take into account such intrinsic factors.[11] Nonetheless, such factors are of considerable importance in decisions about what field to enter, what firm to work for, and whether or not to stay in a given firm or field. To a degree, but only to a degree, these intrinsic factors *are* taken into account through the notion of compensating wage differentials, to which we now turn.

Compensating Wage Differentials

The notion of compensating wage differentials, like that of competitive labour markets itself, dates back to the classical economists. It was devised to recognize the fact that some jobs are easier, pleasanter, safer, and more secure than others. The main point here is that jobs that are especially difficult or disagreeable must generally pay a higher wage or salary to attract sufficient workers (Reynolds, 1982). For most people, it is pleasanter to work in an office than on a garbage truck. The same applies to jobs requiring a long training period, those offering less security of employment, and those of a seasonal nature featuring long periods of unemployment. Most people need an income all year round, not just for six or eight months of the year. Jobs that provide income for only part of the year need to pay more to compensate workers for the lean months, or to meet relocation expenses to another seasonal job in another location. And jobs in isolated locations need to pay more to compensate workers both for the lack of social life and amenities, and for the higher prices they often must pay for food, fuel, and other necessities.

Two classic illustrations are construction and longshoring work. Here, the work is physically demanding and, not infrequently, dangerous. As well, there is a considerable element of seasonality to the work in both fields. Taken together, these factors justify the relatively high wages paid to construction and longshoring workers.

The element of personal risk likewise explains the comparatively high salaries generally paid to police and firefighters, while the stressful nature of the job explains the high pay given air traffic controllers. For their part, professional athletes can legitimately claim short average careers and the real risk of career-ending injury as factors justifying salaries several times higher than the national average.[12]

Like the competitive labour market theory, compensating wage differentials seem to work better in theory than in practice. There are a number of reasons for this.

1) To some extent, the notion of compensating wage differentials is based on intrinsic job characteristics and personal preferences. These things can be difficult if not impossible to quantify. Many people would probably find making hospital beds a tedious chore at best. But a nurse or orderly might take considerable satisfaction from such work because doing it helped make patients feel more comfortable.

2) The notion of compensating wage differentials assumes that workers are fully informed about all conditions of the job (including its risks) before signing on. This may or may not be a safe assumption. We can reasonably assume awareness of most risks in the case of a candidate for police work or a job in an AIDS clinic. But many situations aren't so clear. Factory workers, for example, may find themselves handling chemicals whose safety hasn't yet been established. Before signing on, they would have had no reason to expect they would be asked to handle such chemicals. Sometimes employers themselves aren't aware of the risks; sometimes they are very much aware of them and in no hurry to communicate that awareness to potential employees. And many job applicants, particularly recent immigrants or others in a poor labour market position, may simply be too afraid to ask what the risks are.

3) There is often an element of discrimination in the application of compensating wage differentials. Such differentials are more apt to be applied to male than to female workers, other things being equal, and to workers of higher socio-economic status and greater labour market power. They are also more likely to be applied to unionized than to non-unionized workers.

Workers in largely male-dominated occupations are often more likely to receive a compensating wage differential because the risks they take tend to be more visible, and the damages they sustain more easily quantifiable, then the risks taken and damages sustained by workers in most largely female-dominated occupations. For example, it is easier both to see and to quantify the economic losses of falls from high construction scaffolds or gunshot wounds sustained in police work than to do so for the nervous breakdowns or repetitive-strain injuries more typical of work in offices or shops.

The traditional high-risk male occupations also tend to be heavily unionized. A union is in a better position to argue that job-related risks should be fully compensated than are most individual workers.[13]

"COMPANY HR POLICIES AND COMPENSATION SYSTEMS: IMPLICATIONS FOR INCOME INEQUALITY," UNIVERSITY OF CALILFORNIA, BERKELEY

socrates.berkeley.edu/~iir/ncw/wpapers/br/index.html

For many immigrant workers and others at the bottom of the socio-economic pyramid, compensating wage differentials seldom if ever apply in practice. While many of these workers work under appalling conditions, often facing such risks as extreme heat and toxic fumes (Arnopoulos, 1974), most typically receive only the minimum wage—if that. Fear of dismissal or deportation often makes them afraid to complain to government agencies about even gross health and safety or minimum wage violations (Arnopoulos, 1974; Sass and Stobbe, 1989).[14]

Economic theory (see Gunderson and Riddell, 1993:428–449; Reid and Meltz, 1995:27–28) suggests that employment standards and health and safety legislation shouldn't be necessary to compensate workers for the undesirable aspects of jobs, since this function should be adequately served by compensating wage differentials. In our view, the fact that such differentials seldom apply in markets comprising mainly immigrants or others with little labour market power underscores the need for protective legislation.

Why Most Labour Markets Are Not Competitive

Actual labour markets, as opposed to the competitive model just described, rarely achieve a state of equilibrium, where the supply of labour matches the demand for labour at the given wage rate. As the situation in Canada today shows, they often feature overtime work for some while others are unemployed, and they often use layoffs rather than wage cuts as adjustment mechanisms (Meltz and Reid, 1989). As well, there are often surpluses of workers in some occupations at the same time as there are shortages in others.

Overtime can exist at the same time as unemployment because, under existing employment standards legislation governing overtime rates, it may be cheaper for an employer to pay existing workers time-and-a-half than to hire new workers at straight time: new workers may be less productive and bringing them on board may entail significant hiring and training costs and additional payroll taxes. While there are ways around both these problems, as we note in the conclusion to this chapter, in the absence of substantial legislative change, many employers prefer to work existing employees longer rather than hire additional ones.

There are a number of reasons why layoffs are often used rather than wage cuts. To begin with, the idea of a fully competitive labour market assumes continual and more or less instantaneous adjustment of wages to demand. In practice, such continual and instantaneous adjustment is impossible. If firms had to adjust their wage rates upwards or downwards each time there were a significant fluctuation in demand for their product or service, there would be administrative chaos. Large numbers of people would be spending their time doing little else but adjust wages. A situation in which no one knew what his or her wage rate was would also be bad for morale, and likely for productivity as well (see Reynolds, 1982). Indeed, as the history of the coal mining industry suggests (Frank, 1976), frequent wage cuts can be a formula for industrial strife.

In unionized establishments, wages are normally "locked in" at a given level for the duration of the contract. Occasionally a contract will contain a "reopener" clause allowing for the renegotiation of wages due to changing circumstances. But in the absence of such a clause, a union is under no obligation to renegotiate wage levels, though it may elect to do so to prevent job losses. Moreover, even at renegotiation time, a union may prefer to take layoffs rather than see its members' wages reduced for several reasons. First, given that layoffs are normally in reverse order of seniority, those affected will be junior members with little clout in the organization. Second, as we point out in more detail in the chapters on unions and strikes (see also the discussion of the asymmetric information perspective in Chapter 12), the acceptance of layoffs may be a necessary part of a union's bargaining strategy, calling the employer's bluff in situations where the union doesn't know whether she is telling the truth about the firm's financial situation. By accepting layoffs rather than a wage cut, the union is imposing costs on the employer (such as lost production and possible lost market share) to balance the costs of foregone wages being imposed on the workers. If, in fact, an employer isn't telling the truth about the firm's financial situation, the union's refusal to accept a wage cut may lead to a better offer.[15]

Minimum wage legislation is another reason why most labour markets don't operate in a fully competitive fashion. Economic theory suggests that such legislation may result in a wage above the equilibrium wage discussed earlier, which in turn may lead to unemployment among those working for the minimum wage (Gunderson and Riddell, 1993:659–660; Reid and Meltz, 1995:30–1). Some have argued that the employment-reducing effects of minimum wage legislation may be particularly severe in the case of teenagers and those working in low-wage sectors like tourism (Gunderson and Riddell, 1993:208–210). However, there is substantial disagreement in the literature about how severe those effects are (Gunderson and Riddell, 1993:211), or whether they even exist (see Reid and Meltz, 1995:31).

There are many other reasons why most actual labour markets do not work the way competitive labour markets are supposed to. Basically, a worker facing a chronic excess supply of labour in his occupation and region has two choices: to change occupations (occupational mobility) or to change locations (geographic mobility). Both strategies are quite problematic in Canada in the late 1990s.

Changing occupations isn't easy, except in some cases for younger workers who have not invested a great deal of time or money in their first occupation and are still searching for a career. If one is changing to a profession or skilled trade, the switch normally requires one or more years of retraining. Since such retraining is generally a full-time business, someone being retrained can normally work only part-time, if at all. Thus, in addition to the direct costs of retraining, which may themselves be considerable, the worker may face a situation where he or she has little or no income for a substantial period of time. These high economic costs and the stress that career changes impose on workers and their families are often enough to deter people from making a career change.

As well, the individual may already have invested years and thousands of dollars in training for the original trade or profession. Particularly at a time of high national unemployment or deficient unemployment, there is little guarantee that he or she will do any better in the new field. Provincial licensing and credentialling policies aiming at restricting entry to certain trades and professions may also pose barriers to would-be career changers. When added to the economic and psychic costs already described, these barriers may make a meaningful career change all but impossible even for the most ambitious and hardy soul.

Canadian workers have traditionally "adjusted" to bad economic times by moving to a part of the country where the economy is stronger. Certain policy makers (see Beauchesne, 1998) continue to believe this is the best solution for continuing high unemployment in such regions as the Maritimes. And for some individuals, particularly those with scarce skills or young people who really have not settled into an occupation or profession, it may indeed be a solution. But it would be a mistake to regard large-scale mobility as any sort of panacea for the country's employment problems. For one thing, Canada's sheer size makes many moves quite costly. Someone moving from, for example, Nova Scotia to Alberta would incur thousands of dollars in direct costs, in addition to any income lost during the transition. Only some of the costs could be claimed as tax deductions, and the worker would be out of pocket at least until tax-refund time the following year. Additional barriers to geographic mobility include family considerations and the difficulty of selling a house (which especially in Atlantic Canada may be the family's only significant financial asset). Linguistic and cultural issues may also be factors, particularly for those contemplating moving into or out of Quebec (Reid and Meltz, 1989).

Beyond that, and perhaps even more important, the mobility solution assumes that there are at least some parts of Canada with low unemployment. Arguably no such area now exists. As Table 2.4 shows, no province has an unemployment rate of less than 6 percent, and only the three Prairie provinces have rates below 8 percent. While those three provinces could perhaps absorb a limited number of new arrivals, none of them has low enough unemployment to absorb a great many. The arrival of large numbers of new workers in any Canadian city would simply mean a displacement of unemployment from the original centres to the new one. In addition, large-scale internal migration might also breed resentment on the part of existing workers who saw their jobs and income levels threatened.

The mobility solution also assumes that Canadians can live equally successfully in any part of the country. Once again, this is at best a dubious assumption. Many people simply don't "transplant well." Consider, for example, the case of an unemployed

Table 2.4

UNEMPLOYMENT RATE (IN PERCENTAGE), CANADA AND PROVINCES, 1977 TO 1997

Year	NF	PEI	NS	NB	QU	ON	MB	SK	AB	BC	CAN
1977	15.7	9.7	10.5	13.2	10.3	7.0	5.9	4.4	4.6	8.5	8.1
1978	16.1	9.7	10.5	12.5	10.9	7.2	6.5	4.9	4.8	8.4	8.4
1979	14.9	11.0	10.2	11.1	9.7	6.5	5.4	4.2	3.9	7.7	7.5
1980	13.2	10.8	9.7	11.1	9.9	6.9	5.5	4.4	3.8	6.8	7.5
1981	13.9	11.2	10.1	11.6	10.4	6.6	5.9	4.6	3.9	6.7	7.6
1982	16.7	12.9	13.1	14.1	13.9	9.7	8.5	6.2	7.7	12.2	11.0
1983	18.8	12.4	13.1	14.8	14.0	10.4	9.5	7.4	10.7	13.9	11.9
1984	20.4	12.9	13.0	14.9	12.9	9.0	8.4	7.9	11.1	14.8	11.3
1985	20.8	13.4	13.6	15.2	11.9	8.1	8.2	8.1	10.1	14.2	10.5
1986	19.2	13.5	13.1	14.3	11.0	7.0	7.7	7.7	9.9	12.5	9.6
1987	18.0	13.1	12.4	13.1	10.3	6.1	7.4	7.4	9.7	12.0	8.9
1988	16.4	12.8	10.2	12.0	9.4	5.0	7.9	7.5	8.1	10.3	7.8
1989	15.7	14.0	9.9	12.4	9.3	5.1	7.6	7.5	7.3	9.1	7.5
1990	17.0	14.9	10.6	12.1	10.2	6.3	7.3	7.0	7.0	8.4	8.1
1991	18.3	17.0	12.0	12.8	12.0	9.6	8.9	7.3	8.3	10.0	10.4
1992	20.2	17.9	13.1	12.8	12.8	10.9	9.7	8.2	9.5	10.5	11.3
1993	20.1	18.1	14.6	12.5	13.2	10.6	9.3	8.0	9.7	9.7	11.2
1994	20.4	17.2	13.3	12.5	12.2	9.6	9.2	7.0	8.6	9.4	10.4
1995	18.3	14.7	12.1	11.5	11.3	8.7	7.5	6.9	7.8	9.0	9.5
1996	19.4	14.5	12.6	11.7	11.8	9.1	7.5	6.6	7.0	8.9	9.7
1997	18.8	14.9	12.2	12.8	11.4	8.5	6.6	6.0	6.0	8.7	9.2

Source: Statistics Canada Cat. No. 71-201-XPB.

man living in Newfoundland. If this worker stays in his home community, he will (usually) still have the support of family and friends. Very possibly he will be able to grow a garden, hunt or fish, and do odd jobs for friends and relatives. While his situation won't be ideal, he'll at least have useful things to do with his time. If, on the other hand, he were to become unemployed in Toronto, having left home to take a job there that ended after a few months, he will have neither his support network nor his garden, and hunting and fishing will be out of the question. Lacking both a support network and useful work, he may well turn to drink or drugs, if not to crime, and become a major social problem. He might be better advised to stay in his home community, unless the move could provide him with specific job skills he couldn't have acquired there.

A Comeback for Competitive Labour Markets?

It has been customary for discussions of competitive labour markets in IR texts (i.e., Meltz and Reid, 1989; Reid and Meltz, 1995:26) to speak of these markets mainly as theoretical constructs, which seldom if ever apply in the real world. Until recently, this may have been the case. From a strict neoclassical perspective, it may also be true that very few markets can ever be *fully* competitive in a society that maintains minimum wage laws, health and safety legislation, and anti-discrimination laws. And it is probably still the case that competitive labour markets are the exception rather than the rule.

Still, is also clear that, over the past decade or so, many labour markets have been moving in a more competitive direction, driven by the same *laissez-faire* ideology that have led to the privatization of many government enterprises, deregulation of regulated ones, and weakening of social programs like unemployment insurance and social assistance (see Reid and Meltz, 1995:26–27). Let us consider, once again, the market for seasonal fruit pickers in Los Angeles. Until recently, such markets were generally found only in seasonal or peripheral industries, and most of the people who worked in them possessed little formal education and few marketable skills. Today, many of the characteristics of this kind of market apply to jobs that people hold on a year-round basis, and many of the people who work in them have a good deal of formal education and many marketable skills.

Like the fruit-pickers' jobs, many part-time jobs in the service sector provide few if any benefits beyond the wage (CLMPC, 1997), and few of these jobs offer much in the way of possibilities for advancement. Many such jobs can be learned in a matter of days if not hours, which means that, in practice, workers can be treated more or less interchangeably. Apart from the exceptional case where the organization has been unionized (as in the case of the B.C. Starbucks coffee shops described by

Murdock, 1997), most private-service sector workers enjoy little job security. Indeed, many can be said to be employed on a "just-in-time" basis (Jenson and Mahon, 1993:7), which means they will be paid only so long as there is work to be done immediately. Such "just-in-time" employment leads not only to considerable economic insecurity, but to severe disruption of family life, since hours are often irregular and extremely variable. The lack of benefits, advancement possibilities, and job and income security are all characteristic of competitive or precarious labour markets, rather than of markets for secure full-time jobs, which have generally existed throughout most of the postwar period (see Lipsig-Mumme, 1995:207).

At the extreme end of the spectrum are industries like the garment industry, which, when they haven't shifted production offshore, have gone back to the use of contractors and homeworkers (Lipsig-Mumme, 1995:208). Exempt from labour legislation and virtually impossible to regulate in any event, such industries may indeed represent a return to the fully competitive labour markets of the nineteenth century (described in more detail in the management and labour history chapters). Now as then, such markets have featured extremely long hours, wretched and often unsafe working conditions, and abysmally low pay.

Driving the apparent return to more competitive labour markets has been a massive wave of economic globalization and trade liberalization. As these developments have had such a severe effect on the economy and on the labour movement, we'll examine them in some detail.

EFFECTS OF GLOBALIZATION AND TRADE LIBERALIZATION

Throughout the world, over the past two decades, there has been a growing emphasis on international trade. Instead of simply producing to meet domestic markets, as many did in the past, businesses must now operate with a continental or even global market in mind. This trend towards globalization has had important consequences for both businesses and workers.

As Anthony Giles (1996:4) notes, world merchandise trade alone increased tenfold between 1950 and 1992. National borders mean far less to business now than they once did, since it is increasingly easy for capital, labour, knowledge, information, and images, as well as goods to flow across those borders (Giles, 1996). The growth in world trade and decline in protective tariffs has clearly meant a greater emphasis on controlling labour costs (Gunderson and Riddell, 1993:215), since domestic producers can no longer rely, as they once did, on those tariffs to shield them from the competition of low-cost foreign producers.

Globalization hasn't been confined to markets. It has also had profound effects on the way in which goods are produced. For example, as Giles points out, quoting Robert Reich, precision hockey equipment is now:

> ...designed in Sweden, financed in Canada, and assembled in Cleveland and Denmark for distribution in North America and Europe, respectively, out of alloys whose molecular structure was researched and patented in Delaware and fabricated in Japan. (1996:5)

With modular production processes of this sort becoming increasingly common, it is now much easier for multinational corporations in particular to shift all or part of their production to countries where labour costs are lower (Giles, 1996). The multinationals' growing clout is one reason for the increasing internationalization of production. According to one estimate Giles quotes (Giles, 1996:6), multinationals now account for about 25 percent of total world production and more than 40 percent of world trade, even though they employ just 3 percent of the world's labour force.

"IS GLOBALIZATION THE CAUSE OF THE CRISIS OF WELFARE STATES?," UNIVERSITY OF CALIFORNIA, BERKELEY
socrates.berkeley.edu/~iir/culture/page9.html

Globalization has also had important political impacts, as the growing dominance of the multinationals, ultimately answerable to no national government at all, weakens the governments' ability to regulate their domestic economies and IR systems. Thus far, it doesn't seem to have had the effect of doing away with distinctive national systems of IR regulation. However, in the longer term, there is a serious danger that governments will pay more heed to the multinationals' demands than to those of their own citizens, for example by weakening environmental regulations, reducing taxation, or cutting domestic social welfare programs to attract or retain transnational investment (Giles, 1996:10). Of particular concern to industrial relationists is the possibility that growing multinational domination of national political agendas will lead to a situation where, even in prosperous Western countries, fundamental workers' rights[16] are subordinated to economic development imperatives, as has long been the case in many Asian countries (Deery and Mitchell, 1993; Verma, Kochan, and Lansbury, 1995).

The Free Trade Agreements

An important element of globalization has been the formation of regional trading blocs in North America, Europe, and Asia (Giles, 1996:5). Major trade agreements have been implemented within each of these blocs.

In North America, a Canada-U.S. agreement (FTA) phasing out both tariff and non-tariff barriers over a 10-year period went into effect in 1989. In 1994, the agreement was extended to Mexico in a new North American Free Trade Agreement (NAFTA). Since then, Chile has been invited to join, and there are plans to create a comprehensive free trade zone throughout the Americas (Craig and Solomon, 1996:49).

The rationale for establishing agreements like FTA and NAFTA goes back to the classical economists and their **theory of comparative advantage,** which you may recall from earlier economics courses. According to this theory (see Reynolds, 1982:90; Reid and Meltz, 1995:47), world output increases and, in the long run, everyone benefits if countries specialize in producing those goods in which they are most efficient. By helping to relocate production to countries where it is more efficient, free trade agreements, in theory, reduce costs and increase the real incomes of citizens in all countries signing those agreements (Reid and Meltz, 1995:47).

Proponents of free trade, such as the MacDonald Royal Commission on the Economic Union, predicted that it would bring a 3 to 5 percent increase in national income over a 10-year period, and that Canada would also benefit from changes in inefficient regulatory regimes, market structures, and work practices that would come into effect as a result of freer trade (Reid and Meltz, 1995:47–48). Opponents (Laxer, 1986; Cohen, 1987) saw major economic dislocation, like layoffs and even plant closings, as well as reduced income even for those workers who kept their jobs. An even more fundamental criticism (see Laxer, 1986) was that the free trade agreement would put Canada's sovereignty at risk by forcing it to harmonize its taxation, social, economic, and labour standards with those of the United States to remain competitive. By the time FTA had been in effect for a few years, others (i.e., Drache and Glassbeek, 1992; Robinson, 1994) were suggesting that it had helped lead to major deindustrialization and loss of manufacturing jobs. These critics also suggested that free trade had weakened the Canadian labour movement severely, both by reducing unions' ability to resist employer demands in the face of widespread layoffs and by increasing employers' ability to resist new union organizing drives.

What has been the trade agreements' overall effect on the Canadian economy? Disentangling the specific effects is extremely difficult, because the trade agreements didn't occur in isolation from other important developments in the Canadian economy, like growing competition from outside North America, widespread technological change, major labour force changes, and the severe recession of the early 1990s (Reid and Meltz, 1995). It is also extremely difficult to say how the United States would have responded had Canada not implemented the FTA, as might have been the case had the Conservatives been defeated in the 1988 federal election. Would the United States have retaliated with a series of non-tariff barriers, whose effect would have been to shut many Canadian businesses out of the U.S. market? Lacking a retrospective crystal ball, one can only speculate.

STATISTICS CANADA "CANADIAN LABOUR FORCE CHARACTERISTICS FROM 1976, UNADJUSTED"

www.statcan.ca:80/cgi-bin/Cansim/cansim.cgi?matrix=3450&cq=&order_id=

What can be said is that, whatever the causes may be, times are much tougher for many Canadians since the first free trade agreement went into effect. Unemployment has generally been higher during the nineties than it was during most of the eighties. As we noted earlier, hundreds of thousands of well-paid, relatively secure manufacturing jobs have been lost (Drache and Glassbeek, 1992; Godard, 1994). While new jobs have been created, most of them have been lower paying and far less secure; many have been temporary or part-time and a fair number have entailed self-employment. As well, the country's social safety net is much weaker than it was 10 years ago. EI benefits are provided to fewer people and run for a shorter period of time, and there have also been major cuts to health care, social assistance, and other social programs. While it is true that such developments might have taken place had the free trade agreements never been signed, at best they hardly suggest that the free trade agreements have benefitted most Canadians.

Meanwhile, whatever the trade agreements' specific impacts may have been, the new economic environment brought about by globalization and trade liberalization has created significant challenges for Canadian businesses. Almost 80 percent of the establishments in the Human Resource Practices Survey conducted by Betcherman, McMullen, Caron, and Leckie (1994:11) report a significant increase in the degree of competition in the five years prior to the survey. Keeping costs down has been a major concern: about 65 percent of the responding firms identify reducing labour costs as a significant element of their business strategies, while an even larger number are concerned with reducing non-labour costs (Betcherman et al., 1994:21). Canadian firms have also been making much more extensive use of computer-based technologies (Betcherman et al., 1994), which certainly *could* reduce their future demand for labour, although this isn't necessarily the case. Similar results were obtained by Reitsma (1993), whose respondents identify automation, reduction of both staff and management, and product specialization as strategies most often used to promote international competitiveness.

UNEMPLOYMENT

What Is Unemployment?

According to Statistics Canada, which conducts a monthly Labour Force survey, an individual is unemployed if he or she doesn't have a job during any given week, but has looked for work at some point during the four weeks preceding the survey. It is important to remember that unemployment is *not* measured by the number of people drawing EI benefits. Some EI recipients are in fact employed, albeit only part-time.[17] Moreover, many unemployed individuals aren't eligible for EI benefits, most notably those who have just entered the labour force and those who have exhausted their benefits.

Different Types of Unemployment

It is useful to distinguish between different types of unemployment, since solving them requires different types of government policy. The three types of unemployment to which we'll refer are frictional, structural, and demand-deficient.

Frictional unemployment affects those who are changing jobs and have a certain period of time between their departure from the first job and arrival at the second. A certain amount of this type of unemployment (probably around 2 percent) is normal in dynamic labour markets. Indeed, its incidence may be higher in a strong economy than in a weak one, since people are more willing to leave jobs they do not really like in good times than in bad. Most economists agree that no special government policies are needed to deal with this type of unemployment, which is usually quite brief, often voluntary, and almost certainly represents a small portion of the total amount of unemployment in Canada today.

Structural unemployment refers to a situation in which there is a mismatch of available jobs and skills, or in which unemployed workers live in different locations from the places where jobs are available. For example, there may be a shortage of skilled computer technicians in Ottawa, while at the same time there is extremely high unemployment among fishers in B.C.

It would seem that the logical solution here would be to retrain the unemployed fishers as computer technicians and then help them move to Ottawa, but as noted earlier, this is often more easily said than done. The unemployed fishers may lack the aptitude, the desire, or the education needed to become computer programmers, and in any case, family considerations and the expenses and trauma involved with moving may make this an impractical idea for many of them.

To the extent that moving *is* a practical and economically rational solution, education and training, along with relocation assistance, are the government policies that best address structural unemployment. But it is important to recognize that in a country as large and geographically and culturally diverse as Canada, structural unemployment will never be easy to overcome.

Demand-deficient unemployment refers to an overall lack of jobs, especially at provincial and national levels. It is this type of unemployment that is most prevalent during depressions like that of the 1930s, or major recessions like those of the early 1980s and early 1990s.

In dealing with this type of unemployment, governments find that education and training by themselves aren't enough, though general training in basic literacy and numeracy can certainly help unemployed workers take advantage of what vacancies there are. Governments have two options available to them here. The first is broad, macroeconomic stimulation to increase demand. This is typically achieved through major changes in monetary, fiscal, and taxation policies or major public works spending, and was the approach taken in the United States and, to a much lesser degree, in Canada during the depression of the 1930s. The second option is reducing work hours to spread the available work around more evenly (Donner, 1994; O'Hara, 1993). Both are discussed in more detail in the chapter's concluding section.

Different Ways of Measuring Unemployment

There has been widespread debate over how accurately the official unemployment rate measures the true level of joblessness in Canada. Some (i.e., O'Hara, 1993) have argued that as high as the official rates are, they severely understate the real unemployment level.

Many economists are prepared to agree that in addition to those officially classified as unemployed, governments should also take into account those known as **discouraged workers.** Such individuals are unemployed, but have stopped looking for work because they believe there are no jobs available for them. Economists do *not* agree about how many people should be classified as discouraged workers. O'Hara (1993:35) suggests that if only those who have given up looking for work during the past six months are counted, the national unemployment rate will increase by about 1 percent.

There is also the issue of whether involuntary part-time workers should be counted as employed or unemployed. Earlier (see Figure 2.2), we pointed out that involuntary part-time work as a proportion of employment rose from 1.3 to 6.5 percent between 1976 and 1995. If each involuntary part-timer had been counted as half-employed, the unemployment rate for the years from 1993 through 1995 would have risen by more than 3 percent, since the involuntary part-time rate was more than 6 percent in each of those years.

Changing National Unemployment Patterns

Overall, Canadian unemployment levels have risen substantially since the end of the Second World War. The 1997 rate of 9.2 percent was more than two-and-a-half times the 1946 rate of 3.4 percent (see Table 2.1). For most of the first quarter-century after the war, the unemployment rate didn't rise above 5 percent, as governments generally practised full employment policies (Morton, 1982:106). Since 1970, it has never fallen *below* 5 percent, and for the past two decades it has been at least 7.5 percent, and often above 10 percent. Although the rate has been dropping slowly over the past five years, it hasn't been below 8 percent since 1990. Were the rate to take into account involuntary part-time workers and discouraged workers, as suggested above, it would have ranged from 13 to 15 percent or even higher during the 1990s. The effects of the recent rise in unemployment have been particularly severe for many Canadians because of the cutbacks in EI benefits and other government-supported social programs that have been occurring throughout the past 15 years or so.

One reason for the rise in unemployment has been governments' abandonment of full employment policies in favour of a concern with deficit and debt levels. Another reason may well be the recent wave of deindustrialization and restructuring discussed earlier in the chapter. Though the manufacturing sector has recovered somewhat during the past five years, it is unlikely to get back anything like the huge number of jobs it lost during the late 1980s and early 1990s (see Godard, 1994:421). Whether the service sector can make up for the loss of so many well-paying manufacturing jobs is at best problematic.

In addition to the number of people unemployed, it is important to consider the **duration** of unemployment, or the length of time people are unemployed. This statistic is of particular significance because those who have been unemployed for a long time often find it very difficult to land another job. In 1980, the average duration for all age groups was about 10 weeks (Gunderson and Riddell, 1993:625). In general, older workers stayed unemployed for longer than younger ones. By 1991 (Gunderson and Riddell, 1993:629), the average duration had increased to more than 18 weeks, and the proportion unemployed for six months or longer had increased from 15 percent to 21 percent. An ominous sign was that even in the good economic years of 1988 and 1989, the average duration of unemployment was significantly higher than it had been before the recession of the early 1980s (Gunderson and Riddell, 1993:628).

Youth Unemployment

While no group has escaped the effects of Canada's rising unemployment rate, the country's young people have been particularly hard hit. The official unemployment rate among workers aged 15 to 24 has been in double digits throughout the past two decades (see Table 2.5). Typically, it has been at least 50 percent higher than the overall rate (Gunderson and Riddell, 1993). Since 1991, it has been more than 15 percent; at the trough of the 1982 to 1983 recession, it was more than 20 percent. Again, it is important to bear in mind that as high as the official youth unemployment rates are, they would be higher yet were it not for the large numbers of young people attending school and university because they really have nothing better to do.

Table 2.5

	UNEMPLOYMENT, AGE 15 TO 24, CANADA, 1978 TO 1997, SELECTED MEASURES		
Year	(2) Unemp., 15–24 (%)	(3) Unemp., All Ages (%)	(2) as % of (3)
1978	14.6	8.4	174
1979	12.8	7.5	171
1980	13.1	7.5	175
1981	13.1	7.6	172
1982	18.6	11.0	169
1983	19.7	11.9	166
1984	17.2	11.3	152
1985	16.3	10.5	155
1986	15.0	9.6	156
1987	13.5	8.9	152
1988	11.9	7.8	153
1989	11.2	7.5	149
1990	12.7	8.1	157
1991	16.2	10.4	156
1992	17.8	11.3	158
1993	17.7	11.2	159
1994	16.5	10.4	160
1995	15.6	9.5	164
1996	16.1	9.7	166
1997	16.7	9.2	182

Source: Statistics Canada, Cat. No. 71-201-XPB, pages 4 & 8.

There are many reasons why continuing high youth unemployment should be of concern. First (Craig and Solomon, 1996:57), it is expensive to provide welfare or EI to unemployed young people, or to keep them in school when they do not really want to be there. (Though tuition fees have risen in recent years, they still cover only a small portion of universities' costs.) Second, unemployed young people are more likely than employed ones to turn to drink, drugs, or crime.[18] The cost of keeping someone in a prison cell or a drug rehabilitation program is far greater than that of providing that person with a full-time job. Third, as noted earlier in the chapter, there is an increasing number of young people with no formal work experience at all. The longer it takes someone to find a job, the more difficult the adjustment to the working world when she does find a job. To put it mildly, a situation in which large numbers of young people reach their twenties without obtaining any work experience can hardly be said to augur well for Canada's future economic growth or international competitiveness.

INTERNET RESOURCES ON YOUTH EMPLOYMENT LINKS PAGE
www.oise.utoronto.ca/~khotta/internet.htm

Unemployment Rates in Different Industries

National unemployment rates can only provide part of the unemployment picture. To gain a fuller understanding of that picture, it is also necessary to consider unemployment levels in different industries and parts of the country.

As Figure 2.4 shows, there is wide divergence in different industries' unemployment rates. For 1996, these rates ranged from a high of more than 13 percent in construction to lows of 3 percent in finance/insurance/real estate and 4.7 percent in public administration. Reflecting the shift to increased service sector employment, unemployment was about 50 percent lower in the service sector than in the goods-producing sector. While the rate was relatively low in agriculture, it was otherwise a good deal higher in primary industries like mining and forestry than in manufacturing. The comparatively high unemployment rates in most goods-producing industries pose a challenge to unions, since they have far more of a presence there than in the private-service industries where unemployment is generally lower.

Unemployment by Province

Provincial unemployment rates vary almost as much as do those of different industries. In 1997, when the national rate was 9.2 percent, provincial rates ranged from lows of 6 percent in Saskatchewan and Alberta to a high of almost 19 percent in Newfoundland. Despite the variation in individual provinces' rates, throughout the past 20 years the provincial *pattern* has been fairly consistent. Newfoundland has normally had at least twice the national rate and the other Atlantic provinces are also well above it. Quebec's rate has usually been slightly above the national one, while British Columbia's has on average been quite near it. Ontario and the remaining

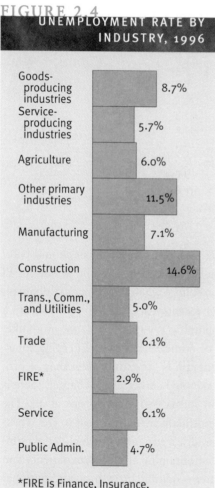

FIGURE 2.4

UNEMPLOYMENT RATE BY INDUSTRY, 1996

Goods-producing industries	8.7%
Service-producing industries	5.7%
Agriculture	6.0%
Other primary industries	11.5%
Manufacturing	7.1%
Construction	14.6%
Trans., Comm., and Utilities	5.0%
Trade	6.1%
FIRE*	2.9%
Service	6.1%
Public Admin.	4.7%

*FIRE is Finance, Insurance, and Real Estate

Source: Statistics Canada, Labour Force Averages, 1996, Cat. No. 71-220-XPB, pg. B-30 & B-32.

Rural parts of Atlantic Canada, like the Newfoundland outport shown above, have unemployment rates far higher than the national average.

western provinces have generally had rates well below the national one (see Table 2.4, on page 50). However, even in these comparatively fortunate provinces, the rate has never been below 5 percent since before the 1982 to 1983 recession. In the five eastern provinces, the rate has almost always been at double-digit levels throughout the past 20 years (see Table 2.6). West of Quebec, unemployment has almost always stayed in single digits, except in British Columbia.[19]

One reason for the disparity in provincial unemployment rates may be a high concentration of layoff-prone resource industries in Atlantic Canada and B.C. (see Heron, 1989:xii). Another reason is the general state of underdevelopment in Atlantic Canada, where wage levels also tend to be a good deal lower than in the

Table 2.6

INCIDENCE OF SINGLE-DIGIT AND DOUBLE-DIGIT UNEMPLOYMENT, CANADA AND PROVINCES, BY EAST-WEST GROUP, 1977 TO 1996		
Group	**Single-Digit (%)**	**Double-Digit (%)**
CANADA	12 (60)	8 (40)
EASTERN PROVINCES	4 (4)	96 (96)
WESTERN PROVINCES	85 (85)	15 (15)

Source: Statistics Canada, Cat. No. 71-201-XPB. Eastern provinces include Newfoundland, Prince Edward Island, Nova Scotia, New Brunswick, and Quebec. Western provinces include Ontario, Manitoba, Saskatchewan, Alberta, and British Columbia. Single-digit unemployment is defined as unemployment of 9.9 percent or less; double-digit, as 10.0 percent or higher.

rest of the country (Craig and Solomon, 1996:56) and where small businesses have historically had a great deal of difficulty obtaining capital (Jackson and Peirce, 1990; ECNL, 1989).

PUTTING THE PIECES TOGETHER

Today's economy is arguably the most difficult one that workers and their unions have had to face since the end of the Second World War. The wave of mergers, restructurings, and layoffs that has taken place over the past 10 to 15 years has left few unaffected. The turmoil has hit public as well as private sector organizations and shows little sign of abating as the decade closes. Many high-paying jobs have been lost in the manufacturing sector, possibly forever. To the extent that these jobs have been replaced, it has been by lower-paying jobs in the private-service sector. This structural shift has posed major challenges for unions, since private-service establishments are generally more difficult to organize than manufacturing firms. At the bargaining table, the tough economic conditions have left most unions fighting to hold on to existing wage and benefit levels, rather than seeking improvements as they generally did in the past.

Throughout most of this period, unemployment has remained stubbornly high. The Atlantic provinces, where the official rate has sometimes approached 20 percent, have been particularly hard hit, as have younger workers. Especially worrisome has been the increase in the average duration of unemployment.

Even those who have continued to be employed have had to adjust to profound changes in the way work is organized and scheduled. Far fewer workers than in the past enjoy any real job security, and there have been large increases in the rates of part-time, temporary, and contractual work, home-based work, and self-employment. These developments have contributed to a general feeling of economic insecurity and frustration among Canadian workers and may be a source of the renewed industrial conflict discussed in Chapter 12.

Two things are particularly disturbing about the most recent spell of high unemployment. The first is how long it has lasted. As the provincial table (Table 2.4) reveals, despite numerous public pronouncements to the effect that the economy is now in recovery, many parts of Canada have clearly still not recovered from the recession of the early 1990s. Some provinces, like Newfoundland and other parts of the Atlantic region, have arguably not recovered from the recession of the early 1980s.

The second is the existence of such continuing high unemployment alongside a rapidly growing rate of overtime work. On average in 1997 (Statistics Canada, 1998:18), nearly one-fifth of all workers—some two million Canadians in all, worked overtime. More than 53 percent of those working overtime weren't paid for their efforts. The highest rate of overtime (30 percent) was in business services, the industry that also had the lowest rate of paid overtime. Those working in finance/insurance/real estate and public administration also put in extensive amounts of unpaid overtime, as did teachers and managers (*Better Times*, 9/97). Over the first four months of 1997, the average overtime worker was putting in nine extra hours per week (*Better Times*, 9/97).

In addition to being a major drain on the national economy, continuing high unemployment rates are emotionally and even physically unhealthy for unemployed workers themselves, and for their family members (see Brenner, 1973; Carrothers, 1979). The solutions governments have attempted to apply during the 1990s clearly have not worked. Given current economic and political constraints, is it possible for governments to make a serious dent in the unemployment rates?

Traditionally, economic theory has prescribed stimulation of the economy, through public works programs or changes in taxation and spending policies, as the best solution for demand-deficient unemployment (see Meltz and Reid, 1989). In the past, governments have used this approach with some success. Right now, however, this option is less attractive, given governments' continuing concern with debt and deficit levels. Many economists like Donner (1994) don't believe that stimulation alone can produce significant and lasting reductions in the unemployment rate.

Given the existence of large amounts of overtime alongside continuing high unemployment, a more appropriate solution might be to spread the available jobs around more evenly by reducing work hours. This solution, the one historically favoured by the labour movement (see Heron, 1989 and Hunnicutt, 1988), seems particularly attractive in view of the growing number of working women and two-earner families in the Canadian labour force. Reducing work hours would provide people with more time to attend to family as well as work responsibilities and might well make them more productive at work (CLMPC, 1997:26). In addition, it could conceivably provide jobs for hundreds of thousands of unemployed Canadians.

One option discussed by Reid and Meltz (1995:46) is the use of EI funds to provide short-term compensation for employees on reduced work weeks. This program has been in effect since early 1982 and appears to have functioned quite effectively during the recession of the early 1980s (see Meltz and Reid, 1989). Under the most commonly used version of this program, employees receive their regular wages for the four days a week they work, and amount equal to the EI benefit for the fifth day on which they don't work. At current EI benefit rates, this would amount to 91 percent of regular wages for a four-day week.[20] The program has long been popular with employees and would appear to be far more equitable than laying off 20 percent of the work force during a recession (Reid and Meltz, 1995:46). However, for reasons which are not at all clear, it has been little publicized during the current downturn and doesn't appear to have been as widely used this time.

In addition to the short-term compensation program already in existence, there are many other possible ways to cut overtime hours. They include an increase in the overtime premium to discourage the use of regularly scheduled overtime; a reduction in the standard hours of work, after which overtime must be paid; and amending employment standards legislation to allow workers to choose to work shorter hours, at a corresponding reduction in pay (Reid, 1997). Another possibility would be to reduce payroll taxes for employers reducing work hours to create or maintain jobs.[21] While none of these options would be completely trouble-free, all seem preferable to the current situation, in which many workers are working far more hours than they would like to be, while many others are working far fewer or even none at all, in both cases often at considerable cost to their physical and mental well-being.

A number of European countries like France and Italy have gone even farther, legislating major reductions in standard work weeks, typically to 35 hours (Hayden, 1998). For the time being, at least, this particular option may not be politically feasible in Canada, since most Canadians appear to prefer voluntary approaches, like reduced hours provisions worked out through collective bargaining (Jackson, 1997; CLMPC, 1997). An approach that may be more feasible is one taken by the province of Quebec, which has for several years been providing financial assistance to firms willing to reduce hours to create or retain jobs (Donner, 1994:42).

It isn't clear which of the above approaches would be most effective at creating additional jobs. At the end of the day, what may be more important than the particular approach taken may be the demonstration that Canadian governments actually possess the political will to mount a sustained attack on the unemployment problem. Thus far, except to some extent in Quebec, there have been few signs that any Canadian government possesses such political will.

QUESTIONS FOR FURTHER DISCUSSION

1) Compare the number of jobs you have held with the number your parents (or children, if you are an older student) have held. Also compare the length of time you have held each job.

2) If you have ever been unemployed for a fairly lengthy period (say, more than three months), what was that experience like? If you have ever been over-worked for a fairly lengthy period, what was *that* experience like? Were there similarities between the two experiences?

3) Explain why, in general, unions fare better at high points of the business cycle and worse at low points.

4) What have been some of the most important changes in the economy over the past 15 to 20 years?

5) Why do many people argue that the changes we are seeing in today's economy are not simply the result of a cyclical downturn?

6) What are some of the major implications of Canada's aging labour force?

7) What are some of the key implications of increased female labour force participation?

8) Why are more people working part-time these days? What are some of the implications of increased part-time work for workers, unions, and employers?

9) What is a competitive labour market, and why are most labour markets not competitive?

10) Why have competitive labour markets been making something of a comeback in recent years?

11) Distinguish between frictional, structural, and demand-deficient unemployment, and discuss some policy solutions appropriate for each.

12) How would *you* measure unemployment in a way that takes into full account the country's or province's loss of productive capacity?

13) In his book *Working Harder Isn't Working,* Bruce O'Hara proposes a legislated four-day week at a little over 90 percent of the worker's previous salary as the solution for continuing high unemployment. Discuss the pros and cons of O'Hara's suggestion.

14) If you agree that shorter hours are needed in Canada, but don't think legislation will work, how do you think shorter hours could best be achieved?

SUGGESTIONS FOR FURTHER READING

Betcherman, Gordon, Kathryn McMullen, Christina Caron, and Norm Leckie. (1994). *The Canadian workplace in transition.* Kingston: Queen's IRC Press. This study offers detailed evidence about how globalization and foreign competition are changing Canadian workplaces.

Better Times (Newsletter of the "32 Hours" organization devoted to achieving shorter work time). This thrice-yearly newsletter provides all kinds of useful information related to shorter working hours. Its discussion of what European countries are doing is probably its greatest strength.

Giles, Anthony. (1996). "Globalization and industrial relations." In *The globalization of the economy and the worker: Selected papers presented at the 32nd annual Canadian industrial relations conference held in Montreal, June, 1995.* Quebec City: CIRA. The best discussion I have seen on globalization and its impact on the IR system.

O'Hara, Bruce. (1993). *Working harder isn't working.* Vancouver: New Star Books. Yes— O'Hara is evangelical at times. But the case he makes for a shorter work week is compelling, and the discussion of how to bring it about offers a wealth of practical suggestions. A must read for anyone seriously interested in the work hours issue.

ENDNOTES

[1] Information on younger workers' participation is drawn from Statistics Canada, Cat. No. 71-201-XPB.

[2] O'Hara (1993:37) estimates that "one fifth of Canada's student population is in school under duress." On page 38, he suggests that if involuntary university students were taken into account, the national unemployment rate would increase by 1 percent.

[3] An approach taken by some organizations is to have older workers mentor younger ones. In this capacity, they have the opportunity to use their hard-earned organizational knowledge.

[4] This discussion of women in the labour force is, of necessity, confined to women 25 and over since data for workers 15 to 24 aren't broken down by sex.

[5] Except as otherwise noted, employment and unemployment data not contained in tables are drawn from Statistics Canada Cat. No. 71-201-XPB.

[6] For a discussion from a slightly different perspective, see Godard (1994:422).

[7] This provision was in force in Ontario's labour relations act until the 1992 NDP government revisions.

[8] This may also be the case when work is done by outside contractors rather than by employees.

[9] In the federal public service, benefits like sick leave aren't provided for contracts of less than six months' duration.

[10] In November 1998, the federal Finance Minister rejected the proposed bank mergers. Shortly after rejection, however, bank officials made it clear that they had no means ruled out further merger bids in the future.

[11] It may be useful to point out that the competitive model was devised by Adam Smith and others in the eighteenth and earyl nineteenth centuries, when only a small portion of the population worked for wages. When Smith's classic *Wealth of Nations* was published, most people were working as farmers, fishers, or artisans, as they also were in Canada. Most wage-earners would have come from among the least-privileged of society; most were likely hard-pressed to provide their families with basic necessities. To them, the notion of intrinsic job satisfaction would have been irrelevant, if not a cruel mockery.

[12] It is left to the reader to decide whether such factors justify paying professional athletes of considerably less than star status salaries which are often 50 to 100 times the national average.

[13] As we'll see in the employment law chapter, workers' compensation boards have traditionally been reluctant to provide compensation for afflictions related to psychological or emotional stress.

[14] Knowing this, some employers deliberately choose to employ work forces made up solely or primarily of immigrants (Sass and Stobbe, 1989:432).

[15] For a more detailed discussion, see Gunderson and Hyatt (1995:313).

[16] Such as the right to bargain collectively or to strike.

[17] EI regulations allow recipients to retain up to 25 percent of their benefits in earnings. Earnings above that threshold are deducted from the recipient's benefits.

[18] The American epidemiologist Harvey Brenner has produced a sizeable body of work relating increases in national unemployment levels to increase in murder and other crimes, liver cirrhosis, and physical and mental hospitalization. For examples, see Brenner (1973) and Carrothers (1979:39). In addition, as Carrothers points out (1979:38), loss of employment, particularly over a long term, can lead to a serious lack of self-esteem both for the unemployed worker and for his or her immediate family and friends.

[19] B.C. has had double-digit unemployment in 9 of the past 20 years (see Table 2.4).

[20] During the 1982 to 1983 recession, the rate was 92 percent since at that time UI benefits were 60 percent of the normal wage.

[21] The option of reducing payroll taxes was the most popular among participants at the "32 Hours" conference held in Toronto, November 22, 1997, and attended by the author.

CHAPTER 3

MANAGEMENT AND
INDUSTRIAL RELATIONS

In today's climate, no group is immune from layoffs.

More than at any other time in the postwar period, management has become the key actor in the industrial relations system. This chapter seeks to explain why this is so, while also outlining some of the new challenges management faces in an era of globalization, trade liberalization, and rapidly changing technology. We begin by outlining some of these challenges, then go on to examine the evolution of management practice from the early industrial period to the present. Special emphasis is placed on those factors that have led the balance of workplace power to shift in management's direction in recent years. Next, we discuss the strategic choice theory, along with some of its implications for the management of industrial relations. The chapter concludes by considering to what extent firms today are living up to the slogan many of them profess: "People are our greatest resource."

MANAGEMENT'S GROWING ROLE IN IR

The growing recognition of management's crucial role in the industrial relations system represents perhaps the greatest single change in the field over the past two decades. Many earlier textbooks (i.e., L. Reynolds, 1982), and indeed even some recent ones (i.e., Craig and Solomon, 1996), do not contain a chapter on management. The assumption here appears to have been that industrial relations is primarily about unions and the government agencies that regulate them; to learn about management, you should take a course in that area.[1] Even when management *was* considered, its role in the IR system tended to be treated as separate from its other activities.

It is impossible to see how anyone can obtain an accurate understanding of the IR system without considering the role played by one of its key actors. As for the separation of management IR activities from other management activities, this may not have been a totally inaccurate reflection of the world of the 1950s and 1960s, when IR functions often appear to have been carried out in isolation from the rest of the firm's activities. Since then, an increasing number of firms have sought to link their IR and HR strategies to their overall objectives. Most recent Canadian IR textbooks' treatment of management (i.e., Anderson, 1989a; Godard, 1994; Thompson, 1995a) has reflected this more sophisticated and integrated understanding of management's IR role.

"TOTAL QUALITY MANAGEMENT IN HIGHER EDUCATION: HOW TO APPROACH HUMAN RESOURCES MANAGEMENT," *TQM MAGAZINE*, VOL. 7, 6, 1995

www.bus.ualberta.ca/yreshef/documents/TQMmgz.doc

At a more practical level, the increasing emphasis on management's role reflects a long-term shift in workplace power away from workers and unions and towards management. This shift has been more pronounced in the United States than in Canada, due mainly to a weaker American labour movement and less strictly enforced labour legislation. Nonetheless, it would be a mistake to conclude that such a shift had not occurred here as well as in the United States. Arguably, the shift *has* taken a different form in Canada; this point will be discussed in more detail later in the chapter.

Continuing high unemployment has probably been the most important factor driving the shift in the balance of workplace power over the past two decades. Other important factors include the privatization of many formerly government-owned enterprises, the deregulation of many previously highly regulated ones, trade liberalization, growing foreign competition, and technological change. Taken together, these forces have led to the emergence of an increasingly market-oriented economy. At the same time, provincial and federal governments, under growing pressure to attack deficit and debt levels, have weakened the social safety net. For example, EI benefits have declined over time as a percentage of the unemployed worker's weekly salary. At the same time, eligibility rules have tightened so that many unemployed part-time workers who would formerly have qualified for EI now do not. These changes in the macroeconomic environment, which were discussed in some detail in Chapter 2, have definitely altered the context within which collective bargaining takes place. As will be noted in this chapter and in Chapter 5, they have significant implications for the strategies of both management and unions.

Obviously, today's economic environment has made life more difficult for workers and their unions. But in many respects it has also complicated managers' lives. To begin with, managers have been no less immune from the effects of downsizing and restructuring than the workers reporting to them. Beginning with the recession of the 1980s, and continuing through to the present, many organizations began flattening their management structures. While this may have improved internal communication and productivity, it also meant that many middle managers lost their jobs (Osterman, 1988), while others found their responsibilities significantly changed. Again, like the workers under them, surviving managers have had to "do more with less"; a recent Statistics Canada survey (*Better Times*, 9/97) found that 31 percent of the country's managers had put in significant unpaid overtime hours during the first four months of 1997. Not surprisingly, in such circumstances, stress-management workshops appear to have become an almost routine feature of corporate life.[2]

There's reason to believe that IR and HR managers may have been particularly hard hit by corporate downsizing and restructuring. Often, the unspoken if not explicit assumption is that "people managers" are more dispensable than others. In times of crisis, they may well be among the first to be let go. Indeed, evidence we'll be discussing later in the chapter suggests that the thinning of IR and HR management personnel has been going on for some time. As well, many find that the nature of their work has changed—often in a way they don't like. In place of the proactive training and development activities that took up much of their time in the past, many are now chiefly occupied in terminating their fellow employees (Berridge, 1995), a situation few find pleasant.

Nor are these the only pressures facing managers in the late 1990s. Globalization, combined with the almost instantaneous availability of information and the free movement of capital from country to country, means that the pace of decision making has stepped up considerably. Changes in technology have meant that competitive advantages, which once could be counted on to last years, may now last only a few months, or even weeks. And growing foreign competition, resulting in large measure from recent trade agreements, has put even more pressure on management to contain labour costs without compromising product quality.

Driving the wave of downsizing and restructuring have been stockholder demands for immediate, short-term profits. According to Kochan and Osterman (1994:113–114), these demands, sometimes reinforced by pressures from finance-oriented managers also of a short-term bent, tend to discourage managers from making long-term investments in human resources. Instead, they are all often encouraged to use the axe to boost their firms' current balance sheets. Whatever its other virtues, such an approach is almost certain to increase labour-management friction, adding further to the stresses on already beleaguered IR and HR managers.

ROLES IN PERSONNEL MANAGEMENT FROM WELFARISM TO MODERNISM: FAST TRACK OR BACK TRACK?
www.dcu.ie/business/research_papers/no.17.htm

Over the past two decades, there appears to have been at least a partial reversion from accommodationist postwar management practice to the more hard-line approach typical of this century's first decades. This same period has seen major reductions in the number of IR and HR management staff, and a diminution in their relative authority and influence within firms. These trends have come on the heels of a much longer (75-year) period generally marked by a progressive liberalization of management practice and a greater emphasis on IR and HR functions within firms. While it is too early to say whether the recent trends represent a fundamental change in direction or a pause within the longer trend, they are certainly disquieting to many industrial relationists and will bear close examination in coming years.

We can better understand recent management trends if we view them in the broader context of the historical evolution of management IR practice in Canada. Accordingly, it is to this evolution that we now turn.

The Evolution of Management IR Practice

Management's major aims are to make a profit and to maintain control of the enterprise. The development of management IR practice reflects management's attempt to achieve these objectives in the face of varying degrees of resistance by workers (and sometimes unions) seeking to maximum their wages and maintain or increase job security—objectives that most managers, most of the time, have seen as largely incompatible with their agendas. As well, particularly since the Second World War, management has had to operate within the constraints of a broad range of provincial and federal government labour relations and employment standards legislation. This legislation, often passed as a direct result of the labour movement's pressure on governments, applies to matters as varied as wages and work hours, the handling of health and safety issues and the accommodation of people with disabilities in the workplace (Carter, 1997).

When worker/union resistance has been relatively effective, management has had to compromise on one or both of its main objectives. In addition, there have always been some organizations that have largely succeeded at reconciling their objectives with those of their employees, and some industries where a cooperative approach is more common than in others. There have also, as we'll see, been periods when worker-management cooperation was easier to achieve and was thus more widely practised than at other times.

JOURNAL OF MANAGEMENT HISTORY
www.mcb.co.uk/cgi-bin/journal1.jmh

Charting the development of management practice is not always an easy task. As Claude George (1968:vii) notes, though there have long been managers, it wasn't until comparatively recently that people began thinking or writing about management in a systematic fashion. And where contemporary developments are concerned (Thompson, 1995a:106), accessibility often becomes an issue. Many firms don't want their management practices made known, for fear of divulging valuable information to competitors. Others want those practices kept secret because they don't want the public made aware of their ethically, or possibly even legally, dubious nature.

Despite these problems, it *is* possible to trace the broad outlines of management IR practice. While there have been variations, most of that practice has taken four basic forms: paternalistic, coercive drive, welfare capitalist, and bureaucratic.

Paternalistic Management

"REPLACING PATERNALISM WITH DATA" BY BRIAN CAULFIELD, NOVEMBER 17, 1997
www.internetworld.com/print/1997/11/17/intranet/19971117-paternal.html

In Canada, prior to the country's first industrial revolution, relatively few people worked for others, at least on a permanent basis; most Canadians were self-employed farmers, fishers, or artisans. Manufacturing establishments were extremely small by today's standards, with an average of only five employees per firm (Godard, 1994). Those who did work for someone else generally worked for a family member, friend, or neighbour; apprentices might well live in the master's house. The mode of control most employers exercised over their employees in this period is best described as paternalistic. In most cases, the owner of a business was also its manager and personally oversaw all work done on its premises.

Legally, workers had virtually no rights; servants who left their masters' employ without permission could be imprisoned (Morton, 1995:133). Still, while working for a relative or neighbour was no guarantee against arbitrary or even abusive treatment, craft traditions, community norms, and peer pressure probably provided some check on at least the more extreme forms of abuse and exploitation that characterized work in the early industrial period in Canada, in Britain, and in the United States. More important, most firms used limited technology and few sought to serve markets beyond their immediate local areas (see Commons, 1909). Indeed, most probably did not seek to compete on the basis of price, relying more on reputation and quality. For these reasons, the profit motive as such did not play the same role in pre-industrial business that it was to play starting in the industrial period (Godard, 1994), and thus it was not necessary for managers to seek to extract the maximum possible "value" from workers—the critical assumption of the "coercive drive" system.

Coercive Drive System

With the growth of factories during the early industrial period, many more people entered into employee status, and many began working for people they had not previously known. The early factory system also saw the growth of a new management class between owners and workers (Yoder, 1962) as the size of factories grew to a point where owners could no longer personally oversee all their workers. The result was the rise of a new supervisory class (foremen or supervisors) between owners and workers, whose sole raison d'être was to extract the maximum possible production from the workers under them (George, 1968). A plentiful supply of labour and an almost total absence of protective government intervention (Yoder, 1962) made it possible for employers and managers to exercise virtually unfettered sway. The one partial exception here was skilled tradespeople, like printers and coopers, who might not always be easy to replace and who, in good times, could often set their own rates (Morton, 1995). However, women and children were often preferred to experienced adult male workers (Yoder, 1962), because their wages were lower and because they were generally considered more tractable.

"POWER, CONTROL, AND BUSINESS SUCCESS,"
THE MOVE FROM TOP-DOWN MANAGERIAL CONTROL
TO WORKER EMPOWERMENT.
www.dealconsulting.com/management/power.html

Fear was what motivated workers in a system where work was irregular and there was no employment security (Yoder, 1962), where most were paid barely enough to keep body and soul together (Morton, 1984), and where the six-day week and ten-hour or even twelve-hour day were the norm. Managerial control was exercised through ever-stricter monitoring of output and enforced through fines and even, on occasion, beatings (Heron, 1989). Not surprisingly, perhaps, such management practices and working conditions led to increased labour-management conflict, as workers sought to beat a system that appeared bent on extracting the last possible ounce of effort from them (George, 1968). With the formation of some of the craft unions described in Chapter 4, and with the Canadian government's growing if grudging recognition of working-class political power, some of this conflict began to be carried out in more organized fashion than had typically been the case in the pre-industrial period.

Scientific Management

The scientific management approach (Taylorism) pioneered by F.W. Taylor is commonly treated in industrial relations courses and texts as part of, or indeed the culmination of, the coercive drive system. Further examination of scientific management, carried out as part of the research for this book, has convinced this author that, when viewed as a whole, the system is both more comprehensive and more complex than it generally has been perceived to be. Viewed from this broader perspective, Taylorism does indeed contain some elements consistent with the coercive drive system. But it also contains other elements much more consistent with the welfare capitalism approach of the early twentieth century, which (in many ways) it undergirded (Anderson et al., 1989:6–7).

"TAYLORISM: F.W. TAYLOR AND SCIENTIFIC MANAGEMENT" BY VINCENZO SANDRONE, UNIVERSITY OF TECHNOLOGY, SIDNEY, AUSTRALIA

www.iserv.net/~mrbill/tqm/taylor.html

Taylor's aim was nothing short of a rationalization of the entire work process. Through detailed time-motion studies, he sought to break individual jobs down into their smallest and simplest components, simplifying each worker's task to allow each worker to achieve the maximum possible output from any given amount of effort. An appropriate quota, based on the results of those time-motion studies, would be set for each job. Those who exceeded it would be rewarded through incentive pay; those who did not meet it would be penalized (George, 1968). Nor was the scientific approach to be confined to job processes; it was also to be applied to such matters as worker selection, job determination, and the creation of a proper working environment. Only if workers and management cooperated in applying this scientific approach to all aspects of work, Taylor believed, could society reap the maximum benefits.

A crucial if highly controversial element of Taylor's program was his rigid separation of managerial work from that performed by ordinary workers. As he saw it, both inefficiency and frustration resulted when labour was asked to take on tasks properly within management's domain, such as "planning, organizing, controlling, methods determination, and the like" (George, 1968:90). Everyone would be happier and things would get done far more efficiently if management took care of all planning and control functions and workers simply executed the orders given to them by management—a situation referred to by Godard (1994:112) as the "think-do" dichotomy.

Like managers under coercive drive, Taylor sought to maximize worker output, and his system provided managers with the means to do so to a far greater degree than had previously been possible. The deskilling of workers associated with his "think-do" dichotomy was also consistent with earlier deskilling brought about, less systematically, during the early industrial period. Beyond that, Taylorism provided a basis for industrial innovations, like the moving automobile assembly line (Godard, 1994; Radforth, 1991), which essentially forced human workers to adapt their pace to that of machines. The criticisms levelled against Taylor and his system on these points (Braverman, 1974; Godard, 1994) seem irrefutable.

In other ways, Taylorism differed significantly from coercive drive management. Appalled at the conflict he saw in late-nineteenth-century factories, Taylor sought to achieve worker-management cooperation—mostly through the substitution of objective quotas for standards arbitrarily determined by foremen. Granted, it was true that such a quota might still, in effect, be unilaterally determined by management, since management would be hiring the experts whose time-motion studies were determining the quotas. This problem could never be fully addressed without a worker representation mechanism legally guaranteeing workers some say in determining their terms and conditions of employment. Still, it can at least be said that Taylor's aim was a harmonious workplace and also one in which workers would be rewarded for superior effort and would share in their firms' gains. In these respects, his system represented a significant advance over conventional nineteenth-century management practice.

THE F.W. TAYLOR PROJECT—ONLINE TAYLOR ARCHIVE
attila.stevens-tech.edu/~rdowns

Particularly notable was scientific management's concern for the total workplace environment—psychological as well as physical. Such concern was especially true among one group of scientific managers initially known as the behavioural school. This school arose out of early efforts to, in George's words, "recognize the centrality of the individual in any cooperative endeavor" (1968:141–142). This school of thought became much more prominent as a result of the now-famous experiments conducted by Elton Mayo and his Harvard colleagues at the Western Electric Company's Hawthorne plant. These experiments had interesting and somewhat surprising results. They revealed that workers' productivity went up not only when lighting was increased, but also when it was reduced. Mayo's conclusion was that if firms wished to increase productivity, they should pay more attention to their workers' needs (Anderson et al., 1989). Accordingly, the behaviourists, now known as the human relations school, started to do just that, focussing much of their attention on such things as individual motivation, group dynamics, and social support for employees (George, 1968; Anderson et al., 1989). Their work eventually led to the development of organizational behaviour as an independent field of study (Anderson et al., 1989).

Welfare Capitalist Management

The link between worker morale and efficiency established by scientific management, broadly applied, provided the rationale for many of the far-reaching changes in management philosophy and practice that occurred between 1900 and 1930. These changes ranged from the provision of employment security and company-paid benefits like pensions, to the establishment of various types of worker-representation systems and company athletic teams and recreational facilities.

A key development was the launching of large numbers of personnel departments in American and Canadian firms. Initially, these departments performed mainly employee welfare functions, as they had in Britain as early as the 1890s (Niven, 1967; George, 1968). Over time, they came to play a larger and more proactive role within organizations. As early as 1903 some writers were suggesting that, in the interest of maintaining labour peace, personnel (or labour) departments should address any worker complaints that could not be resolved between workers and their foremen—in effect serving as informal arbitrators (Carpenter, 1903). Spurred on by the example of innovators like National Cash Register's John Patterson, a number of firms set up departments to do just that. In addition to handling employee welfare issues and resolving disputes, some of the new departments were also used to administer suggestion box systems—another turn-of-the-century innovation (Holman, 1904; Patterson, 1901). During and after the First World War, many firms transferred all or at least a great deal of hiring and firing authority away from line supervisors to the new personnel departments (Slichter, 1929). The move corresponded with a growing shift away from the old temporary employment system to one of relatively permanent job tenure—something that the more enlightened sort of manager had been advocating for some time (Fitch, 1917; Erskine and Cleveland,

1917). If a firm was going to make the substantial investment in workers implied by the provision of job security, it would make sense to use professionally trained people to screen and select those workers.

Personnel departments grew in size and sophistication during the 1920s. A survey conducted in 1930 (Mathewson, 1931–1932) showed that more than 80 percent of all firms were keeping labour turnover records by the end of the decade, and about 40 percent were conducting regular job analyses. In addition, personnel departments were responsible for administering a broad range of employee benefits, including paid vacations, pensions, life and accident insurance plans, stock purchase plans, employee savings plans, low-cost loans, and home-ownership assistance plans. On the development front, personnel departments provided or arranged for on-the-job training for new hires and Americanization courses for new arrivals, helped set up sports teams and other recreational organizations, and arranged night school or correspondence courses for those in need of them (Mathewson, 1931–1932; Slichter, 1929). As if all that were not enough, these departments were also responsible for keeping abreast of the growing body of employment-related legislation.

A number of First World War-era scientific management experiments had found little or no drop in productivity resulting from shorter hours (Nyland, 1989). Supported by those experiments, most major American employers brought in the eight-hour day during the 1920s (Hunnicutt, 1988). Canadian workers also saw their hours shortened, though not to the same extent (Malles, 1976). At the same time, many firms established "works councils" or other worker representation bodies, while others established internal promotion ladders based on merit or converted wage-earning positions to salaried status (Slichter, 1929). Like the benefit plans, the reductions in hours, works councils, and internal promotion ladders were designed to increase workers' loyalty and reduce costly turnover. Another equally important objective was becoming (or remaining) union-free. To a great extent, management sought to operate union-free to help prevent a recurrence of the types of strikes that had occurred in Canada and in the United States at the end of the First World War (Slichter, 1929). To this end, many firms used hard tactics to drive out unions, but then adopted softer paternalistic welfare capitalist practices to keep them out later on (Slichter, 1929:349).

The evidence suggests that welfare capitalist firms in the 1920s were generally successful in achieving their two major objectives. The decade was marked by a large increase in productivity and substantial declines in union membership rates, strikes, and turnover (Slichter, 1929).[3] Some contemporary observers (i.e., Slichter) feared that company benefits had become so pervasive as to sap workers' individual initiative and their drive towards cooperative self-help. Whether or not this was the case, few employers made any bones about the anti-union animus underlying their welfare capitalist practices. This animus, too, troubled thoughtful contemporary observers like Slichter, but by and large those working under welfare capitalist systems in the 1920s appear to have been happy enough to accept an "implicit contract" providing them with job security and relatively good pay and benefits in return for loyalty, commitment, and union-free status. What is not clear is how many, even among male workers, were in fact working under such systems. Observers like Epstein (1932) have suggested that the proportion was small—perhaps 10 to 15 percent. Undoubtedly many workers, especially in peripheral regions like the American South (Hunnicutt, 1988) or Canada's Maritimes, continued to work under authoritarian coercive drive conditions.[4] There is also little evidence to suggest that welfare capitalist provisions were ever applied to any significant number of women. Indeed, the welfare capitalism literature seen by this author makes virtually no mention of female workers. In the North America of the 1920s, as in modern-day Japan (Adams, 1995a), core-worker status appears to have been applied almost exclusively to male workers. All this said, welfare capitalism did have a lasting impact, as evidenced by the degree of conflict that ensued when firms started to abandon it during the 1930s.

With the advent of the Great Depression, many firms, unable to maintain their welfare capitalist practices, reverted to the hard-line coercive drive approach (Osterman, 1988). No better example of the change in thinking can be found than Henry Ford. Ford, known in the 1920s as the pioneer of the eight-hour day and $5 minimum daily wage, and as an employer willing to hire workers with partial disabilities, during the 1930s became notorious for hiring avowed criminals to beat up United Auto Workers seeking to unionize his plant (Gannon, 1972; Lacey, 1986).

In the short term, reversion to coercive drive management led to increased workplace conflict. In the longer term, the result was large-scale unionization (see Osterman, 1988), which in turn led to yet another transformation of management practice, as management organizations were forced to adapt their practices to conform to the new labour relations legislation and the collective agreements made possible by that legislation.

Bureaucratic Management Practice

There is some disagreement in the literature about the extent of change in personnel practice during the early Depression years, prior to the legalization of collective bargaining in the United States. Some (Epstein, 1932) see abandonment of welfare capitalism as total; others (Balderston, 1933; Brown, 1934–1935) indicate that a significant number of welfare capitalist personnel practices remained in place. While personnel budgets as a whole were down and companies' training and recreational activities and suggestion schemes had been cut back, many other elements of "modern" personnel practice seem to have remained in place, including

"Employment procedures, tests, job analysis, [and] time study" (Brown, 1934–1935). Many of those elements would remain in the new jointly administered management regimes that came about as a result of unionization.

By the mid 1930s, collective bargaining had become a major concern of personnel departments (Cowdrick, 1934). In a parallel development, renewed emphasis was placed on supervisor training, since they would have to be the ones to administer the new collective agreements on a day-to-day basis (Cowdrick, 1934). With the legalization of collective bargaining and the signing of large numbers of collective agreements, many firms set up industrial relations departments to carry out collective bargaining and related activities, like grievance-handling. The growth of such departments in turn spurred the growth of large numbers of academic industrial relations departments in the early postwar years.

Under collective bargaining, management practice was based on having workers adhere to two sets of formal, codified rules: those contained in company personnel manuals, administered by management, and those contained in collective agreements, administered jointly by management and unions. Of necessity, personnel practice in unionized firms became quite legalistic, since collective bargaining is a process tightly regulated by legislation. Already quite bureaucratic in large firms—it would have been impossible to run a large, complex organization without clear rules and procedures governing production and personnel policy—non-union personnel policy also became more legalistic during the 1930s and 1940s, as firms were expected to adhere to a growing body of employment standards legislation covering such diverse issues as wages, hours of work, overtime policies, and health and safety procedures. Some unionized practices, like seniority-based promotion, spilled over into the non-unionized sector, as non-unionized firms sometimes found these practices convenient. In other cases, like that of Dofasco Steel, some of those practices, along with high wage levels, might be adopted as part of a broader union-avoidance strategy (Storey, 1983).

"LIFE-TIME EMPLOYMENT, SENIORITY BASED PROMOTION, ENTERPRISE UNIONS," *RELATIONS INDUSTRIELLES*, VOL. 51, 1, 1996

courses.bus.ualberta.ca/orga417/japan.htm

Collective bargaining certainly did not do away with worker-management conflict. The very early postwar period in particular saw a huge wave of strikes in Canada and in the United States (see Chapter 12 for details). However, with workers now able to strike legally and union recognition no longer at issue, these strikes were generally conducted in a more civilized fashion than pre-war strikes had been (see Heron, 1989), and seldom resulted in bloodshed.

Industrial relations departments grew significantly during the postwar period as more firms were unionized and as collective bargaining was conducted over a broader range of issues, making both bargaining and contract administration more complex. A similar pattern of growth occurred in personnel departments, charged with administering an increasingly broad range of benefits, from pensions to insurance plans. Such developments were part of a broader pattern of growth of specialized management staff that was, perhaps, inevitable given many firms increasing size and complexity during this period. By the 1960s, Yoder (1962:47) was suggesting a ratio of one specialized professional and technical IR staff member per 133 employees as a minimum acceptable standard. A later survey discussed by Ash (1967) found a ratio of one IR staffer to every 115 employees. Where the IR function had been decentralized, this ratio was even higher.

While burgeoning benefit plans gave personnel departments plenty to do, there was growing concern that, stripped of their earlier conflict-resolution roles, which had been generally been taken over by IR departments, personnel staff were becoming "managers of records" rather than of people (Owen, 1940–1941; Worthy, 1948). Such concerns continued into the 1960s (Heneman, 1960; Dunnette and Bass, 1963; Sokolik, 1969). By this time, however, others (Fischer, 1968) were predicting a more creative and proactive role for personnel departments. Anticipating to some extent the approach taken in the 1980s by Thomas Kochan and his associates, Fischer suggested that, in the future, the personnel function would assume a more strategic role in the overall management of the enterprise; that it would be responsible for furthering the organization, not just maintaining it; and that top management would become directly involved in the development and deployment of human resources.

A series of economic, social, and political developments beginning around 1970 was to create a quite different IR environment and lead to yet another transformation of management practice. The economic environment had become increasingly difficult as a result of inflation arising out of the Vietnam War and the energy shock of 1973. These new economic pressures meant that management could no longer "buy off" union discontent with large wage and benefit packages, as it often had during the early postwar period (MacDonald, 1967). In any case, a new, more highly educated generation of workers had also come to look for more from their jobs than a paycheque. Riots at General Motors' Lordstown, Ohio, plant in 1970 demonstrated the need for management to attend to workers' intrinsic as well as extrinsic motivation. In the wake of Lordstown and a broad wave of both active and passive rebellion by discontented younger workers (Murray, 1971), many firms began instituting various quality of worklife (QWL) schemes aimed at addressing their workers' intrinsic needs. Some unions signed on. Others resisted, feeling that the QWL programs intruded on their authority to represent workers' interests in the workplace. That debate continues today. In the meantime, complicating matters for suddenly extremely busy IR and HR staff was a new wave of litigation, arising from the broad range of civil rights and employment-related legislation passed during the 1960s and early 1970s. Such legislation, in the view of Arnold Deutsch (1979), amounted to nothing less than a human resources revolution, and meant that human resources would now affect every aspect of the organization, from hiring to marketing to investor attitudes. The legislation would also lead to the increased application of strategic planning and analysis to human resource management (Kochan and Barocci, 1985).

While all this was going on, the American labour movement was running out of steam. Largely as a result of the American Federation of Labour and Congress of Industrial Organizations (AFL-CIO) president George Meany's lack of interest in organizing the unorganized (Goulden, 1972; Winpisinger, 1989), the American labour movement was, by the 1970s, representing an ever-declining share of that country's workers. Politically, it had lost considerable clout as well, chiefly because of the AFL-CIO's willing collaboration with the Central Intelligence Agency (CIA) in overseas cloak-and-dagger work, Meany's support of the Vietnam war and major weapons systems, and his attacks on anti-war protesters, whom he had accused of being Communist-inspired (Goulden, 1972; Robinson, 1990). This reactionary political stance basically severed the AFL-CIO's long-standing ties to Congressional liberals, costing it much-needed political support (Robinson, 1990).

Taken together, these developments would, at least in the United States, lead to a much more management-oriented type of IR. This move to a "new industrial relations" was less widely adopted in Canada than in the United States More broadly, though, in both countries, some of the limitations of the bureaucratic approach to management were becoming apparent. While many firms continue to use the older approach, in whole or in part, many others have spent much of the intervening period searching for alternatives.

THE SEARCH FOR ALTERNATIVES

It would appear that, in recent years, no single type of management practice has predominated as bureaucratic management did during the first quarter century after the First World War. Writing in 1971, Marvin Dunnette confessed to being unsure about the future direction of industrial psychology and personnel practice. Later, Paul Osterman (1988) would arrive at a similar conclusion. Noting the emergence of a broad range of diverse, even contradictory, human resource policies during the previous decade, Osterman said that while the human resource management system of many firms was clearly being transformed, the overall direction of that transformation was difficult to determine. After extensive study and observation, he could do no better than conclude that "something is happening and that the 'something' is extensive" (1988:61–62).

The quest to cut labour costs led many employers to go in for tough concession bargaining, resulting in some cases in two-tier wage systems. Other employers engaged in even more hard-line practices such as layoffs of previously secure employees, shifts of employment outside the firm (often to non-unionized establishments), increased use of temporary and casual workers, the substitution of machinery for human labour, or the relocation of plants to "union-free" areas like the American South (Osterman, 1988; Kochan, McKersie, and Cappelli, 1984). Other employers took an approach focussing on increasing employees' productivity by increasing their loyalty and commitment to the firm. Such employers might adopt employee-involvement or participation schemes, sometimes in connection with new job-security commitments. They also tended to go in for a variety of joint labour-management training programs. Other employers eliminated or reduced traditional distinctions between white-collar and blue-collar work (Kochan et al., 1984). In certain cases, firms simultaneously adopted hard-line practices (concession bargaining or the use of layoffs and the threat of relocation) together with more participative shop-floor practices (Kochan et al., 1984), thus adding to the apparent confusion as to the overall direction of IR and HR practice.

What is clearer is that the relative numbers of IR and HR staff have been declining, and that the focus of their activities has been changing. During the 1960s, as noted previously, an IR staff to total staff ratio of about 1:125 appears to have been the norm. In contrast, a survey conducted by Thompson (1995a) found a ratio of 1:497. Only 22 percent of the firms surveyed had a ratio greater than 1:200; 37 percent had more than 600 employees per IR staff member. As well, both in Britain (Berridge, 1995) and in North America, IR and HR staff are spending an increasing share of their time on activities associated with firms in decline (Kochan and Barocci, 1985), like downsizing employees or arranging for retraining and career or outplacement counselling. It would be interesting to see whether the same pattern holds for IR and HR staff in high-technology firms, since many of these firms are likely still in what Kochan and Barocci describe as a "growth" stage. Unfortunately, this author is not aware of any research on the topic.

The Strategic Choice Theory

The "strategic choice" perspective on IR arose out of concerns of Thomas Kochan and his associates[5] that the then-dominant systems framework gave inadequate attention to the role of management, which in their view had become the dominant actor.

While British IR literature (i.e., Gospel and Littler, 1982) had begun to pay more attention to management, the American literature to date had not done so. It was important, said Kochan et al., to appreciate that management now played a *proactive* role in IR, not the *reactive* role with which it had generally contented itself during the early postwar period. Most recent changes in IR, they argued, were the result of management initiatives. Kochan et al. were also critical of the notion, central to Dunlop's view of the systems framework, that the actors in the IR system shared a common ideology as a result of their experience working together to establish rules. While this may have been true with respect to management IR personnel and union officials working at the collective bargaining level, Kochan et al. suggest it doesn't take into account important decisions affecting IR strategy made at other levels, where there may be no common ideology or shared experience. The systems framework thus overemphasizes the importance of the collective bargaining level and underestimates the importance of other levels. It also tends to underestimate the potential extent of workplace conflict, not all of which can be contained or worked out through collective bargaining.

A key element of the strategic choice theory is that IR and HR policies and strategies are not made in isolation from firms' overall competitive strategies. The human resource strategies a firm follows or the type of stance it takes towards unions are directly related to such "big-picture" decisions as what product line it will enter or remain in, where it will establish new plants, and what type of new technology it will buy. To help readers visualize such linkages, Kochan et al. propose a three-level industrial relations strategy matrix (23) comprising a macro or global level, an employment relationship or collective bargaining level, and a workplace or shop-floor level. The matrix outlines the nature of the IR-related decisions to be made by all three main actors (employers, unions, and government). The authors hypothesize (36) that more effective and lasting changes will occur when there is consistency in strategies across the three levels and a match between the strategies of different actors. Instability is more likely to occur when strategies at different levels are inconsistent.

To see how IR strategies might be integrated with overall firm strategies, let's take a look at some possible employer decisions at all three levels of the strategy matrix. At the macro or global level, a firm that had both unionized and non-unionized plants might decide to invest in new technology for the latter but not the former as a way of putting added pressure on its union and possibly inducing workers to reconsider the value of union membership. Or the firm could also invest heavily in new technology at its unionized sites simply as a way of cutting labour costs, by substituting the new machines for human labour. If the firm were an American one, it could place new plants in a Southern "union-free" zone, both as a way of cutting its labour costs and to put added competitive pressure on existing unionized plants.

While such an option is not possible in this country, a Canadian firm can seek to achieve more or less similar objectives by opening its new plants in remote rural areas where workers may be less likely to unionize. In certain extreme cases (i.e., that of the Michelin Tire Company in Nova Scotia), it may also put pressure on government to change the bargaining structure, to make it next to impossible for a union to succeed in any organizing drive.[6]

Overall, a key assumption behind macro-level management decisions under strategic choice is that union acceptance is no longer a given as it is in the systems framework. As just noted, such decisions may be designed, quite deliberately, to weaken the union's influence or even drive it out altogether (the union-replacement approach). Clearly, the possibility of operating union-free opens up to management a broader range of possible decisions than it would have if it assumed it would have to remain unionized. The same is true for firms not currently unionized. Under strategic choice, they can decide whether to accept unionization, should it occur, or to establish policies and strategies aimed at preventing it (the union-avoidance approach). Firms that have decided to try to remain union-free have the further choice of whether to use a hard-line approach based on fear, or a softer approach based on removing workers' incentive to join unions by providing union-style benefits themselves. Both types of union-avoidance approach have been used in Canada. Service industries like the chartered banks and Eaton's Department Stores have typically resorted to the stick (Lowe, 1980; Morton, 1995). While Eaton's refused to sign a first collective agreement, the banks used such tactics as the transfer of union activists, direct managerial statements to employees expressing disapproval of unions, and the sending of employer memos to employees in branches the union was seeking to organize (Lowe, 1980). In both cases, the basic aim was the same: winning through intimidation. In contrast, the Dofasco Steel Company of Hamilton, Ontario, has remained union-free in an otherwise heavily unionized industry by matching union wage rates, giving employees a profit-sharing plan, and sponsoring large numbers of social and recreational events (Storey, 1983; Thompson, 1995a). Very much in the spirit of the 1920s' welfare capitalism discussed previously, Dofasco has convinced the majority of its employees that, with the firm providing all these benefits, a union isn't needed.

A broad range of factors may underlie a firm's choice of hard or soft union-avoidance tactics. These include the degree of unionization in the industry, worker and community characteristics, managerial values, and many others (Anderson, 1989a). For example, Dofasco management, operating in an industry where unionization is the norm and in a community with a strong labour tradition, undoubtedly know they would face militant opposition were they to use hard tactics to keep their firm union-free. For the banks' management, the situation was quite different. To begin with, the industry had almost no tradition of unionization; thus there was no requirement to meet union wage norms to keep the banks union-free. Coming from an industry with little history of unionization, bank managers perhaps felt freer than would steel plant managers to engage in overtly anti-union behaviour. In addition, bank managers might well have seen the heavily female and part-time work force as easier to intimidate than would steel managers dealing with full-time predominantly male workers, while, for their part, the white-collar bank workers may have felt more ambivalent towards unions than would blue-collar workers. Finally, community characteristics would have played little role in the case of the banks, since the bank branches were scattered all across the various provinces instead of being concentrated in one location, as the steel plant is. The small number of employees in each branch may have been a further impetus to hard-line employer tactics, since workers in larger groups tend to be harder to intimidate than workers in small groups.

"THE TRADITIONAL IR SYSTEM IN NORTH AMERICA" BY YONATAN RESHEF, UNIVERSITY OF ALBERTA
courses.bus.ualberta.ca/orga417/hrmir.htm

At the collective bargaining level, most ordinary management activities are not very different than they would be under the systems framework. Collective bargaining, contract administration, and the establishment and administration of personnel policies continue to be management's major preoccupations at this level. Even here, however, strategic choice opens up some additional options. Particularly in the United States, the threat of relocation to a union-free zone makes it easier for management to wring concessions out of its union (even if it actually has no intention of relocating). More generally, with removal of the union now a serious option, "investment" approaches to collective bargaining (e.g., Fisher and Williams, 1989:187) aimed at building relationships and maintaining long-term industrial peace may assume lower priority (although this will not necessarily be the case).[7] Indeed, management may even seek to provoke a strike it knows the union can't win, with an eye specifically to weakening or even destroying it.

At the workplace or shop-floor level, the strategic choice theory points towards a significant increase in worker-participation schemes, some aimed at individuals, others at small groups. Within the bureaucratic management paradigm, motivational issues were typically handled indirectly, through collective bargaining or in some cases joint union-management committees. Strategic choice suggests a more direct approach to these issues.

With an eye to increasing both motivation and productivity, employers might introduce quality circles or other types of employee-involvement schemes. They might bring in suggestion boxes or introduce some other mechanism for obtaining employee input.

More fundamentally, they could move to self-directed work teams responsible for handling many decisions, including personnel-related ones like hiring, disciplining, and firing normally handled exclusively by management. Work schedules might be changed to allow employers greater production flexibility. With respect to compensation, possible innovations could include profit sharing, gain sharing, employee stock purchases, and pay-for-knowledge, pay-for-performance, and incentive-based bonus plans.

There are a number of ways in which a firm's shop-floor objectives might be related to its objectives at the collective bargaining level. First, increasing employees' job satisfaction through encouraging their participation might allow a firm to get by with smaller pay increases than would otherwise be necessary. Second, if the joint participation programs succeeded and if the union were involved, they could help bring about an improvement in the long-term union-management relationship. Such programs could, unfortunately, also be used to circumvent the collective bargaining process, which is one reason why such programs are often problematic for unions.

Workplace objectives may be even more closely linked to a firm's macro-level ones. This is perhaps most obviously the case when employee participation programs are introduced as part of a union-replacement strategy (another reason why unions must be cautious about endorsing such programs), or in connection with massive layoffs, as in the horrifying but instructive Eastern Airlines case (Woodworth and Meek, 1995). In non-union firms, employee participation schemes may be linked to the firms' desire to remain union-free. Even when such schemes are not part of a broader anti-union strategy, they may well serve to reduce the extent to which the union functions primarily as an advocate for workers by, in effect, making the union co-manager of the enterprise. Some (Halpern, 1984; Verma, 1995) suggest that such a change in the union's role may be best for all concerned. Others (Godard, 1991) are more skeptical, and some (Wells, 1993) are totally opposed to such a change, believing strong unions to be incompatible with employee participation schemes and other elements of what is now known as the progressive human resource management paradigm.

Strategic Choice in Canada

It is possible to argue, as Thompson (1995a) and others have, that the strategic choice theory has not thus far applied to Canada. Certainly no one could deny that Canadian union rates have not gone down, as they have in the United States, or that a great many Canadian employers have been reluctant to use the sort of hard-line union-replacement and union-avoidance approaches taken by many of their American counterparts over the past two decades. The evidence cited by Thompson (1995a), Godard (1995) and others also suggests that publicly, at least, a majority of

Canadian managers continue to maintain a relatively moderate attitude towards unions.[8] In addition, much of the descriptive evidence cited by Kochan et al. in support of the strategic choice theory *is* highly U.S.-specific.

Nonetheless, there are reasons to believe that the strategic choice theory may be applicable to the Canadian situation. We would argue that the different results observed in Canada may have come about not because the theory itself does not apply, but because it has been operating in a different environment, one that has often dictated different choices regarding such issues as a firm's strategy towards unions.

The most important environmental difference is the existence, in the United States, of virtual "union-free" zones, particularly in the South and West. These zones were created as a result of the "right-to-work" provisions of the 1947 *Taft-Hartley* amendments to the *National Labour Relations Act,* which allowed any state that so wished to opt out of union security provisions. As Noah Meltz (1989b) points out, the "right-to-work" provisions have led to extremely low union membership rates in those states where they have been applied. Even more important, from a strategic perspective the existence of "right-to-work" states has, as noted previously, made union-replacement strategies a viable option for U.S. employers. In addition, even employers not immediately seeking to drive their unions out can always use the threat of relocation to extract greater concessions at the bargaining table. Lacking the equivalent of a "right-to-work" zone, Canadian employers have historically found it far more difficult to use union-replacement strategies. It remains to be seen whether the Canada-U.S. and North American Free Trade Agreements will provide Canadian employers with a realistic and feasible equivalent to the American "right-to-work" zone, and thus encourage them to go in for the kind of anti-union strategies that have become common south of the border. The topic is one in need of further research.

As well, most Canadian labour boards provide significantly stricter enforcement of unfair labour practice legislation than does the American National Labor Relations Board (Bruce, 1990). Stricter enforcement means that employers contemplating engaging in such practices as a means of breaking unions or preventing them from forming know they have a far greater chance of being caught than do their American counterparts, and hence are less likely to use those types of union-avoidance or union-replacement practices that might be of questionable legality.

A third important difference is the existence in Canada—in large measure as the result of past efforts of the labour movement and its political allies—of publicly funded medical care and various social programs, including a more generous unemployment insurance program (even after recent cuts).[9] Canada's more generous social safety net has arguably allowed Canadian unions to resist employer demands for concessions more firmly than their American counterparts realistically can, thereby making concession bargaining likelier in the United States than here. For example, striking Canadian workers remain eligible for medical care since our program is publicly funded. Most striking American workers do not, since in the United States medical insurance is typically provided as an employee benefit. As well, the threat of layoff is a more serious one in the United States, since unemployment insurance benefits in most states are less generous and run for a shorter period than do Canadian EI benefits. This, too, should make American unions more likely to grant concessions than Canadian unions, other things being equal.[10]

Overall, it seems illogical to deny the strategic choice theory's applicability to Canada simply because union membership rates have not declined in Canada as they have in the United States, or because concession bargaining has been less widely adopted here. There is no reason to suppose that the theory dictates *any* particular strategy regarding unions; all it does is open up the *possibility* of union-replacement or union-avoidance approaches. In the U.S. environment, marked by a large "union-free" zone and generally lax enforcement of labour legislation, hard-line anti-union approaches are easy and relatively "cheap" for employers. Up until now at least, such strategies have been harder to pursue here, and also relatively "costly" if pursued. The result has been that employers have tended to pursue other strategies, among them mergers, reorganizations, large-scale layoffs, changes in product line, plant closings, and technological changes (Godard, 1995). While such strategies may not lead to a labour board complaint, it would be a mistake to think of them as relatively benign just because most have not entailed a frontal attack on a union. All that these strategies suggest is that given the different Canadian political environment, management here has chosen different ways to cut labour costs than those often used in the United States. The fundamental direction and effect of these changes have remained the same.

Despite the negative impact on workers of many management global-level initiatives, some recent workplace-level ones, like the growth of employee involvement programs, self-directed work teams, job rotation, or multi-skilling, would suggest a move towards a more consensual, or at least a more cooperative, management approach. The next section considers such changes in more detail, with an eye to determining whether they indeed represent a fundamental shift in management practice and policy, as some proponents claim.

"People Are Our Greatest Resource"

All across Canada, firms proudly declare that their people are their greatest resource. There's certainly plenty of talk about "empowerment," and the evidence compiled by Godard (1995), Smith (1993), Betcherman et al. (1994) and others suggests that quite a number of firms *have* adopted management practices that seem to be designed to help workers achieve their individual potential and find greater job satisfaction.

Clearly, Canadian managers today know (or should know) a good deal more than did their predecessors about how to motivate individuals and groups. Most current management practices aimed at improving motivation are not new, after all. John Patterson was using suggestion boxes at his National Cash Register Company by about the turn of the century (Patterson, 1901; Carpenter, 1903). The Scanlon gain-sharing plan was first devised more than half a century ago (Downie, 1989; Godard, 1994). And even socio-technical systems design, possibly the most far-reaching organizational change approach ever used in this country, has been practised for 20 years (Halpern, 1984; Downie, 1989). Over the years, a sizeable body of literature has been written on these and other workplace innovations.[11]

This literature suggests that the *means* are certainly available for any employers and managers wishing to transform their workplaces into what Kochan and Osterman (1994) have described as "mutual gains enterprises," or places where, for the most part, employees and management are working together for their mutual betterment. But has such a transformation actually taken place? If so, to what extent? And if not, why not?

There are, as Godard (1991 and 1994), Kochan and Osterman (1994) and others note, some major obstacles in the way of workplace transformation. One of these is the direct cost to employers of progressive management programs (Godard, 1994, chs. 5 and 6). A more serious and fundamental problem is that these programs seem to be flying in the face of a North American corporate culture more and more exclusively devoted to cutting labour costs. In the introduction to his recent task-force report on work hours and overtime, Arthur Donner points out that both public and private sector organizations in the 1990s "seem more determined to shrink their work forces ... than at any time since the end of World War II" (1994:5). Despite record corporate profits in many industries, headlines announcing further large-scale layoffs are a weekly, if not daily, occurrence. The past five years have seen layoffs in groups previously considered immune, like tenured professors,[12] "permanent" employees of government departments, and employees of large heavily regulated corporations like Bell Telephone Company. In today's climate, relatively few Canadians can say with any certainty that they will still be in their present job at the end of the year.

We noted in the section on welfare capitalism that a primary aim of 1920s' progressive management practices was to build workers' loyalty. Such an aim suggests, almost by definition, that management believes it worthwhile to make a long-term commitment to its workers. While often lacking the anti-union animus of the 1920s' practices, many of today's progressive management practices are likewise based on the notion of cementing workers' loyalty to the organization. We must ask how much sense it makes to try to build workers' loyalty if the organization cannot make any meaningful guarantee of employment security to even its most dedicated and productive

"I am afraid this is not a propitious time for a raise, Adams. Or, as my father would have said, why the devil should I give you a raise? Or, as my grandfather would have said, GET THE HELL OUT OF HERE!"

people. In such circumstances, employee participation programs seem more likely to result in cynicism and decreased morale and productivity than in anything else.[13]

Even those who continue to work are increasingly doing so under conditions unlikely to foster mutual loyalty between them and their employers. As we noted in Chapter 2, Canadian workers are putting in large amounts of overtime—much of it unpaid. As we also noted in Chapter 2, the various "atypical" employment arrangements described by England (1987), including part-time, casual, and contract work, and homeworking, have by now become so common as to be the norm. Once again, the primary rationale is employers' desire to cut labour costs. Particularly common in the private-service sector, such atypical employment arrangements mean not just lower pay but poorer benefits, less job security, and less in the way of legal protection (England, 1987). In some cases (i.e., some Starbucks Coffee stores), the insecurity resulting from these arrangements has driven workers to unionize (Murdock, 1997); however, such cases remain the exception rather than the rule.

If it is problematic to seek to build loyalty among "full-time" workers, it is doubly difficult to do it among people who may not know from one week to the next whether they will continue to have a job, how many hours they will be working, or what their duties will be. What is more, while a single major crisis can be a catalyst for lasting and positive workplace change (Verma, 1995), the atmosphere of constant crisis fostered by the latest wave of restructuring and downsizing makes it extremely difficult for anyone—worker or manager alike—to take a longer view. Within the labour movement, downsizing may have the effect of weakening those favouring union-management cooperation, and strengthening the hand of "hawks," who believe anything other than the labour movement's traditional adversarial stance vis-à-vis management is at best a waste of time, at worst co-optation of the labour movement into the management agenda (CAW, no date). When cooperation schemes can't protect workers' jobs and income, the hawks' appeal to traditional union values is apt to be persuasive.

What is not clear is the extent to which North American managers, and in particular Canadian managers, have been carrying out the latest wave of downsizing and "employment flexibilization" on their own initiative. There is at least some reason to believe that much of this wave has been driven by factors far beyond the control of any individual manager or management group—in particular, by the wave of corporate mergers that has been occurring throughout the decade. These mergers and acquisitions, driven by the ascendancy of shareholder interests over those of other stakeholders and by that of finance within corporate management, appear to have had the effect of relegating human resource issues to the bottom of many management agendas (Kochan and Osterman, 1994:122–123). They have also turned HR and IR managers into mere "agents" of senior management's priorities rather than proactive forces in their own right (Kochan and Osterman, 1994:121). In a climate in which layoff announcements send stock prices up (Kochan and Osterman, 1994:115) and in which, as one American CEO noted, Wall Street analysts attend eagerly to capital spending and downsizing announcements, but go to sleep when told about human resource and training initiatives (Kochan and Osterman, 1994:114), even the most enlightened and far-sighted IR or HR manager often finds it hard to make much headway. Further evidence of IR and HR managers' lowly status within organizations may be their relatively low salaries, compared to managers in sales, marketing, R&D, or finance (Kochan and Osterman, 1994:122–123).

Given the current climate, what is surprising isn't that more workplace innovation hasn't taken place, it's that so much innovation *has* occurred, in the face of some extremely formidable obstacles. For the United States, data cited by Kochan and Osterman (1994:83) suggest moderate diffusion of such innovations as self-directed work teams, job rotation, quality circles, and total quality management (TQM). In about 40 percent of the firms surveyed, 50 percent or more of the employees were attached to self-directed work teams. This same level of penetration was reported by about one-quarter of the firms surveyed for job rotation, quality circles, and TQM. About 55 percent of the firms used work teams somewhere in the organization, while some use was made of job rotation in 43 percent of the firms, TQM in 34 percent, and quality circles in 41 percent.

Comparisons between the United States and Canada as to the degree of innovation are somewhat problematic and should be interpreted with caution. The best available evidence (Godard, 1995) suggests that there has been slightly less diffusion of innovative workplace practices in Canada, except for TQM. Godard (1995:15) finds self-directed work teams used in 36 percent of all firms; for job rotation and TQM, the figures were 34 and 37 percent, respectively. These figures are somewhat, but not greatly, higher than comparable ones reported earlier by such researchers as Smith (1993) and Betcherman et al. (1994).

Godard (1995:12) also finds little change in managerial HR practice between 1981 and 1992, except for a significant increase in employee counselling programs and very modest increases in the use of suggestion boxes and merit pay schemes. Overall, his conclusion is that only a small number of Canadian firms have fundamentally transformed their workplace practices. While various innovations have been adopted, typically they have been adopted in piecemeal rather than comprehensive fashion, which may inherently limit their effectiveness (Godard, 1994:162).

Broadening our perspective somewhat to take in the overall range of Canadian management practice, the current scene suggests considerable diversity, with no single mode being dominant. Despite its limitations, a bureaucratic approach continues to be used in large, unionized industries like the automotive industry. With some important qualifications (see the public sector chapter for details), that same approach continues to be used in much of the public sector, as well. Welfare capitalism continues to hold sway at firms like Dofasco. In other firms, a progressive management paradigm not unlike welfare capitalism, but with greater emphasis on full employee involvement and participation, has been adopted. Adoption of a socio-technical systems approach in unionized settings like the Shell petrochemical plant in Sarnia (e.g., Halpern, 1984) has sometimes resulted in what might best be described as a "consensual" approach to management. Here, the emphasis is on trust, and management's role is not to keep tabs on workers, but rather to help them achieve their objectives. The Shell Sarnia collective agreement is extremely short by Canadian standards. More concerned with outlining broad "framework" principles, like trust and empowerment, than with providing detailed regulation of work processes, the agreement contains no management rights provision and no specific grievance procedure.

But all this is just one side of the story. Many recent developments have moved in quite a different direction from the consensual Shell Sarnia approach. On the one hand, an increasing number of Canadians have, in effect, no boss at all. This group includes not only a growing number of fully self-employed individuals, but also homeworkers and others working off-site under various forms of contractual arrangements (England, 1987; Lipsig-Mumme, 1995). It is impossible to make meaningful generalizations about the management approach underlying such contractual arrangements, since the group to which they apply is so diverse. In some cases (i.e., professionals doing freelance research, writing, or computer consulting), contractual terms may be relatively generous. In others (i.e., women doing sewing work for the garment industry at home), the arrangement may amount to the worst sort of exploitation (Lipsig-Mumme, 1995).

On the other hand, a highly visible aspect of current management practice is the resurgence of the coercive drive approach. To be sure, in speaking of a "resurgence," we must bear in mind that the coercive drive approach probably survived to a far greater extent than many people realize. In much of the private-service sector, particularly in the non-unionized segment of retail trade and in food service, something like this approach has always been the norm. There is nothing new about a situation in which employees of "Mom and Pop" convenience stores or restaurants receive low wages and minimal benefits and are subjected to arbitrary treatment by their employers. What's different about the present situation is that important elements of the coercive drive approach (low pay, minimal benefit, insecure employment, irregular hours) are now used by large chains like McDonald's, which can hardly claim poverty as the excuse for adopting such practices.

What is also different is that such practices now apply to a far broader segment of the work force. Through most of the postwar period, most of the people working in small private-service sector establishments tended to have limited education and few skills. Others, like high-school or university students, might work in that sector part-time or during the summer, but few continued in it after graduation. Today, many a university-educated young person works for Starbucks or McDonald's. An increasing number appear to be doing so not simply to pay the bills until a more suitable position can be found, but believing that this is the best, and perhaps only, job they are likely to hold for the foreseeable future. The fiction of contemporary writers like Douglas Coupland offers a vivid depiction of the plight of these bright but frustrated young "McJobbers."

At no other time in Canadian history have large numbers of highly educated people been made to work under authoritarian coercive drive conditions of employment on a more or less full-time basis. When coercive drive management was the norm, people with university degrees or even high-school diplomas were rare. Those not self-employed would generally have held managerial or professional positions and thus not been subject to such treatment.

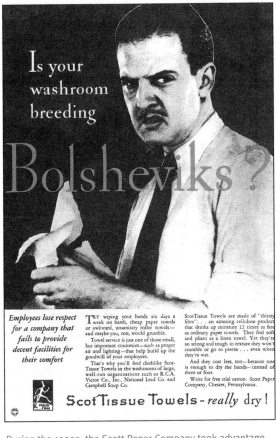

During the 1920s, the Scott Paper Company took advantage of employers' fear of militant employee action to sell its then-new disposable paper towels.

A situation in which large numbers of bright, highly educated people not only are poorly paid and enjoy little or no job security but are made to work under authoritarian conditions seems one ripe for conflict. And there is no doubt that conflict often does occur, though it seldom takes the form of an official strike since relatively few private-service sector establishments are unionized. Often the battle is played out over such seemingly trivial issues as dress codes or regulations regarding personal jewellery.[14] In other cases, a change in hours or scheduling may be the bone of contention. The question here is not whether the conflict will continue, it is what form the conflict will take. To the extent that the new conglomerate unions, like the reconstituted Auto Workers, are successful in organizing the private-service sector (as they have been in the case of at least some Starbucks Coffee stores [Murdock, 1997]), the conflict will likely take on a more collective and public character. Where workers do not unionize, the battles will continue to be played out on an individual or small-group basis over issues like those discussed above.

Elements of the coercive drive approach, like short-term or contractual employment and the imposition of long hours, have also been introduced into sectors (i.e., government) where the primary management approach is different (in this case, bureaucratic). The introduction of such elements of insecurity into previously secure sectors also seems likely to increase workplace tension and conflict. The relatively high public-sector strike intensity observed over the past two years (see Chapter 12 for more details) offers at least modest supporting evidence on this point. On a more positive note, the province of Quebec, where some attempt has been made to draw up "social contracts" providing employment security in return for labour peace, has over the past two years seen very low overall strike intensity. The Quebec experience, also discussed in more detail in Chapter 12, suggests that even in difficult times, more consensual approaches to management may still be possible.

BACK TO SQUARE ONE?

It would be hard to deny that, overall, the balance of workplace power has shifted in management's direction over the past two decades. To be sure, the continued existence of such progressive practices as job rotation and self-directed work teams in a sizeable number of Canadian workplaces suggests that some managers, at least, continue to be concerned about meeting their employees' intrinsic needs for job satisfaction. It is also clear that some managers—it would be impossible to say how many—have come to view the current economic crisis as a good excuse for reverting to authoritarian practices aimed at nothing more than extracting the maximum possible labour from workers for the lowest possible level of compensation. Our examination of both historical and recent evidence suggests that such an "employer militancy" model, as Paul Osterman (1988) describes it, is unlikely to be sustainable over more than the very short term. Here again, the Eastern Airlines case (Woodworth and Meek, 1995) may prove instructive. In that case, a determined employer militancy policy invoked by two successive presidents eventually led to the airline's demise.

In unionized organizations, the employer militancy approach will likely lead to an increased number of grievances, as well as more frequent and longer strikes. Such conflict is far from cost-free, especially if it damages the organization's reputation. In non-unionized establishments, this approach can provoke unionization drives, as indicated by the Starbucks example and by the larger-scale example of depression-era unionization (Osterman, 1988). At the individual level (Osterman, 1988), it can lead to reduced productivity, increased absenteeism, or even theft or sabotage. Overall, as Osterman (1988:89–90) points out, employer militancy seems to be an inherently tenuous approach that may well undermine itself: "Employer strength and union weakness at one point does not imply that the balance of power cannot change in the next period."

INDUSTRIAL RELATIONS/HUMAN RESOURCES MANAGEMENT RESOURCE PAGE: ISSUES, SOURCES, AND PUBLICATIONS
www.mtsu.edu/~rlhannah/IR_HR.HTML

From another perspective, we could argue that recent developments in management practice suggest that many of today's managers and employers have forgotten the lessons that scientific managers were starting to teach as early as 1900. The most important of those lessons is that managers can get more and better work from people through positive, rather than through negative, reinforcement. Again, until this lesson is relearned, increased (and increasingly costly) workplace conflict seems all but inevitable.

QUESTIONS FOR DISCUSSION

1) If you work for someone else, describe your manager's style in terms of the various approaches to management discussed in this chapter. Does the style seem to you to be effective?

2) If you are a manager yourself, what approaches do you use to try to motivate your subordinates?

3) Describe the main stages in the development of management thought, and give some reasons for changes in management approach between one stage and another.

4) How does the strategic choice framework integrate IR strategies with firms' overall strategies?

5) What have been some major innovations in management practice during the past two decades?

6) Why do you think these innovations haven't been more widely adopted?

7) Discuss the evolution of personnel and IR departments, and relate it to the evolution of management practice traced in the chapter.

8) Does the organization *you* work for proclaim "People are our greatest resource?" If so, does it "walk its talk"? Why, or why not?

SUGGESTIONS FOR FURTHER READING

Betcherman, Gordon, et al. (1994) *The Canadian workplace in transition.* (Full bibliographic reference at end of previous chapter). Contains a good deal of useful information on contemporary Canadian management practice.

Godard, John. (1991). "The progressive HRM paradigm: A theoretical and empirical reexamination." In *Relations Industrielles, 46.* Offers a balanced if skeptical appraisal of the progressive HRM paradigm, including barriers to its adoption.

Halpern, Norman. (1984). "Sociotechnical systems design: The Shell Sarnia experience." In J.B. Cunningham and T.H. White (Eds.), *Quality of working life: Contemporary cases.* Ottawa: Supply & Services. This now-classic case remains the best-known Canadian example of a socio-technical systems approach to management using self-directed work teams. For a critique from a labour-left perspective, see the article by Don Wells (1993) listed in the main reference list.

Kochan, Thomas, Robert McKersie, and Peter Cappelli. (1984). "Strategic choice and industrial relations theory." In *Industrial Relations, 23*(1). Perhaps the single most important article on management and IR to have appeared in the past twenty years.

Woodworth, Warner, and Christopher Meek. (1995). *Creating labor-management partnerships.* Reading, MA: Addison-Wesley. Contains a number of very instructive cases, including the eye-opening Eastern Airlines one discussed in the text, and much useful advice on how (and how not) to bring about greater labour-management cooperation in the workplace.

ENDNOTES

[1] The exclusion of management from IR textbooks and courses may, in part, have been a matter of academic turfsmanship, given that IR courses were frequently offered by economics departments and sometimes even combined with labour economics courses. (The Reynolds text cited earlier is designed for just such a split course).

[2] The 1998 Ottawa-Hull "Yellow Pages" lists no fewer than 14 firms specializing in this area.

[3] In Canada, these trends appear to have been somewhat less pronounced. Godard (1994) does not offer evidence on productivity. However, his chart (p. 95) shows a significant

reduction in strike intensity and in union membership rates, but not in the actual number of union members, during the decade. Of course, it may well be that welfare capitalism was less widely adopted in Canada than in the United States. Further research is needed in this area.

4 Hunnicutt notes that New Deal era investigators looking into conditions in Southern textile plants in the early 1930s found widespread use of child labour and work weeks of 50 to 60 hours.

5 Except as otherwise noted, this section is based entirely on the Kochan et al. (1984) article.

6 For a useful if brief discussion of the now-famous Michelin Bill, see Anderson. (1989a:221).

7 The shrinking of IR departments, which tend to contain the group of managers most strongly committed to collective bargaining and union acceptance, may indirectly have had a similar effect.

8 Two important issues arise, however, in connection with the recent survey data cited by such researchers as Thompson and Godard. First, are employers telling the truth? Many might consider it in their interest to profess a moderate attitude while behaving differently. Hence the weakness of questions addressing attitude. At a minimum, such questions would need to be supplemented by behavioural measures of various kinds. Second, are the employers surveyed by Thompson and Godard (and, in particular, responding to the surveys) representative of Canadian employers as a whole? The survey design described by Thompson suggests a strong "bias" in favour of large firms and firms in manufacturing industries, both of which might be expected to be less militantly opposed to unions than smaller firms and firms in service-related industries. We would also expect better-practice firms to be likelier to respond to such surveys than poorer-practice firms, since the latter would be more apt to have "something to hide."

9 For a useful discussion of the link between past strategic behaviour by unions and the labour movement's present ability to defend itself in times of economic crisis, see Lipsig-Mumme (1989).

10 This point is very much worth considering in connection with the 1985 breakaway of the Canadian Auto Workers from its parent American union. The breakaway is frequently ascribed to Canadian workers' greater militancy. We would argue that CAW leaders simply engaged in some quite rational calculation, saw that they could do far better by Canadian members in a separate Canadian environment, and acted accordingly. Whether Canadian workers are possessed of some inherent traits making them "tougher" than their American counterparts seems quite beside the point.

11 For a useful starting-point, consult Cunningham and White (1984) or the references listed at the end of the articles by Downie (1989), Lemelin (1989), or Verma (1995).

12 Sizeable numbers of foreign-language professors at Carleton University were laid off, effective at the end of the 1997–1998 academic year, due to a major reduction in language programs at the university.

13 Once again, the Eastern Airlines case discussed in Woodworth and Meek (1995) is an excellent if chilling illustration. More generally, on the conditions needed to bring about successful employee participation programs, see Woodworth and Meek, especially chapters 6 and 7. For a Canadian perspective, see Downie (1989), Lemelin (1989), and Verma (1995). The most thorough treatment is in the Lemelin article.

14 For example, a female worker at an Ottawa Starbucks was discharged in 1997 for having a pierced tongue, in contravention of company policy. Even as it discharged the young woman, the company admitted she was among their most enthusiastic and productive employees. Along similar lines, see the "Empress Hotel" grievance case in Craig and Solomon (1996:541–543). Dress codes and restrictions on personal jewellery, which might be a matter of relative indifference to professionals otherwise enjoying a fair degree of autonomy at work, take on tremendous importance when (as at Starbucks), workers enjoy little autonomy and a piece of jewellery or headband may be the one way people feel they can make a personal statement.

CHAPTER 4

THE HISTORY OF THE
CANADIAN LABOUR MOVEMENT

Canadian labour has come a long way since the beginning of this century, when many people were still self-employed farmers working their land with horses or mules and simple hand tools.

Like unions in all countries, the Canadian unions we know today are the product of economic, social, and political circumstances, as well as (at least in part) the shapers of their own destinies. In this chapter, we trace Canadian unions through three stages of development—from craft through industrial to public service unionism. Along the way, we also consider the role of government in the development of Canada's labour movement, the nature of political involvement entered into by Canadian unions, and the role played by international unions, or unions headquartered in the United States but with branches in this country.

THE DEVELOPMENT OF CANADIAN UNIONS:
A BRIEF OVERVIEW

Very broadly, today's Canadian labour movement can be described as one that seeks to strike a balance between the pragmatic, economically oriented approach characteristic of American unions and the more politically and socially conscious approach generally taken by European unions. Numerically, too, Canada's union movement, with membership rates of about 35 percent, holds an intermediate position between heavily unionized countries such as Sweden and Denmark, and those with low membership rates such as the United States and Japan (Bamber and Lansbury, 1993; Adams, 1995a).

That movement has come a long way from the small, locally based movement of the early-to-mid nineteenth century. But the evolution has been a difficult and often tortuous one. In addition to overcoming obstacles common to most Western labour movements, such as employer and government opposition (Adams, 1995a), the Canadian movement has had to contend with problems peculiar to this country, such as sparse population, a high degree of outside control over the Canadian economy, general economic underdevelopment (Lipton, 1973), and severe regional imbalances (Heron, 1989). These factors tended to retard the development of an independent Canadian labour movement, as did heavy waves of out-migration of Canadian workers to the United States (Drache, 1984) and the fragmentation of Canadian labour into separate English-Canadian and French-Canadian movements (Drache, 1984; Lipsig-Mumme, 1995).

An even greater obstacle was the tendency of many Canadian workers to affiliate with the U.S.-based international unions (Heron, 1989). There were good reasons why Canadian workers often found the internationals attractive. For one thing, American unions were generally bigger, stronger, and wealthier, with larger strike funds and more experienced organizers (Logan, 1948). For another, an American union card was a valuable possession for a Canadian worker who, due to the seasonal nature of work in much of the country, might well find himself forced to move to Massachusetts or Ohio for at least part of the year (Lipton, 1973; McKay, 1983:137). Still, there were inherent problems with a situation in which Canada's labour movement did not really control its own affairs. After surfacing periodically throughout much of the nineteenth century, these problems would come to a head just after the turn of the century, just before the First World War, and then again during the 1960s and 1970s.

Despite these and other obstacles, the Canadian labour movement has, over time, managed to achieve impressive gains, both for its members and for society at large. Unionized workers have benefitted greatly from the higher wages and benefits, safer workplaces, and generally improved working conditions that have resulted from collective bargaining. Almost all Canadians have benefitted from the minimum wage and other employment standards legislation and from the social programs and universal health-care insurance achieved largely through the labour movement's work in the political arena (Richardson, 1985). Canadian unions continue to fight to maintain these social programs today, even as the wave of globalization, trade liberalization, economic restructuring, and deindustrialization described in Chapter 2 has made it increasingly difficult for them to maintain their members' jobs and incomes.

Heron (1989:xvi) identifies four key periods for the Canadian labour movement when it expanded its membership and goals. These four periods were the 1880s, the end of each world war, and the decade after 1965. Each of the four saw an upsurge of labour revolt during a time of economic transformation; in each, workers were able to "coalesce into a united force capable of articulating and pursuing common goals" (Heron, 1989). In three (all but the 1880s), the role of government was also important. During the First World War, the government used the *Industrial Disputes Investigation Act* to prevent employers from discharging workers for union activity—and thereby hindering the war effort. This encouraged union organization (Morton, 1995), though workers in war industries were still barred from striking. Later, Canada's first general collective bargaining legislation *(PC 1003)* spurred post-Second World War union growth, while the growth of the 1960s and 1970s was mainly the result of public sector legislation such as the *Public Service Staff Relations Act*. It would be a mistake to think of the role of government as having nothing to do with the rise in worker militancy characterizing the three later periods. In all three cases, the passage or extension of the legislation in question was a direct government response to labour militancy, albeit one designed to channel if not blunt that militancy (see Godard, 1994: 260–261).

THE CANADIAN COMMITTEE ON LABOUR HISTORY AND ITS PUBLICATIONS
www.mun.ca/cclh

The Pre-Industrial Period (to 1850)

The earliest recorded strikes in Canada appears to have taken place in the eighteenth century at the royal shipyard in Quebec City (Moogk, 1976:33) and in the fur trade at Lac la Pluie (Lipton, 1973:1). But such disputes were rare in the early pre-industrial period. Most Canadians were self-employed farmers, fishers, or artisans. Those who did work for hire generally did so on a seasonal basis or for a relatively short period of time; few expected to remain employees indefinitely. Employees worked under a paternalistic system (often one of formal apprenticeship). They would normally work side-by-side with their employers and eat with the family (Heron, 1989:2–3).

"ETHNIC AGRICULTURAL LABOUR IN THE OKANAGAN VALLEY: 1880S TO 1960S"

royal.okanagan.bc.ca/cthomson/living_landscapes/articles/wonghome.ht

As we noted in the management chapter, the term "paternalism" does not mean that all employees were well-treated. Employers' treatment of their employees could be arbitrary or even brutal (Heron, 1989:3; Godard, 1994:101–102). At the same time, it's important to remember that work was generally organized in a very different way under pre-industrial craft production than it would have been in any factory. With most transactions being between members of the same community, the quality and dependability of goods mattered as much as, if not more than, their price, and the pace at which work was done was based on the amount of work at hand rather than the clock (Godard, 1994:101–102).

The first significant wave of worker organization appears to have taken place shortly after the War of 1812. By the 1830s, there was significant organization in a number of towns, including Halifax, Quebec City, Montreal, Toronto, Hamilton, and Saint John (Forsey, 1982:9–18). To avoid harsh anti-conspiracy legislation, such as Nova Scotia's 1816 law that provided three-month jail terms for those entering into union contracts (Morton and Copp, 1980; Forsey, 1982; Heron, 1989),[1] unions generally operated as "friendly societies" providing members with a degree of mutual insurance against death, accidents, sickness, or unemployment (Forsey, 1982; Heron, 1989). Most early unions were purely local organizations involving skilled craftspeople such as tailors, shoemakers, carpenters, printers, bricklayers, and masons (Forsey, 1982:30–31). Few were confrontational. Shared craft traditions tended to blur the distinctions between masters and journeymen and apprentices (Heron, 1989:7).

Beginning in the 1830s, with the arrival of large numbers of unskilled Irish, Scottish, and English immigrants, "crowd" behaviour became a factor during times of labour strife (Heron, 1989:5). Such behaviour typically involved direct action against the perpetrator of the alleged wrong, such as the burning of effigies or attacks on owners' or managers' homes. Violence would often ensue, especially if police or troops were called in (Heron, 1989).

"Crowd" behaviour evolved into a more organized form of labour strife with the arrival, in the 1840s, of even larger numbers of Irish immigrants, many of whom found work as canal labourers. These labourers were incensed at the conditions they were expected to endure, including 14-hour days, payment in goods rather than money, grossly inadequate wages, and long waits between paydays (Bleasdale, 1981:124). In response, they took desperate measures. Their tactics ranged from more or less conventional work stoppages to patrolling the canals driving off other potential job hunters and halting navigation on the Welland Canal, or even attacking vessels and their passengers (Bleasdale, 1981:130–136). Although these tactics led to harsh reprisals from both employers and the government, they did often result in higher wages.

Early Labour Organization in Quebec

Effective labour organization was generally slower to develop in Quebec than in the rest of British North America. Like their English-Canadian counterparts, French-Canadian workers did not relish employee status. Most sought to become self-employed and economically independent (Moogk, 1976:15) and would remain employees only until they had saved enough money to achieve that end. Like the Nova Scotia and Canada West legislatures, the royal administration in Quebec had banned workers' associations for fear they would restrain competition in commerce and force up prices (Moogk, 1976:5). Both the courts and public officials persistently rebuffed workers' associations in their quest for economic protection and sought to limit their powers (Moogk, 1976:5).

But the Quebec authorities' suppression of collective activity went well beyond English Canada's criminal conspiracy laws against unions. Public protests over high prices and shortages were treated as sedition (Moogk, 1976). While expressions of craft fellowship were tolerated, they were channelled into the harmless (from the administration's perspective) form of religious confraternities whose activities were limited to devotions and banquets. The confraternities were subordinated to the Roman Catholic church (Moogk, 1976:7). Later, their powers were further limited by a French parliamentary decree that denied them the powers of discipline and compulsion over their members. Without any meaningful economic or political role, the confraternities did not provide Quebec workers with the sort of training in collective organization that English Canada's friendly societies did. The result was that, in the industrial era, Quebec workers lacked such training and were far slower to unionize than workers in the rest of Canada (Moogk, 1976:34–35).

In addition, French-Canadian workers often faced discrimination when they sought work elsewhere in British North America. Often passed over in favour of Irish labourers for canal work, in part because of the Lower Canada Legislative Assembly's desire to "anglicize Quebec by means of immigration" (Drache, 1984:20), they responded by migrating in droves to New England. When they *were* hired in English Canada, they were often given low-end jobs, which again led many to seek their fortune in New England rather than in English Canada (Drache, 1984:21). Quebec workers' tendency to try to improve their lot through emigration proved to be yet another obstacle to union growth in that province.

Labour in the First Industrial Revolution

What is known as Canada's "First Industrial Revolution" began shortly after 1850. Craft shops expanded into sizeable factories, and employers built lumber mills, canneries, and large coal mines. (Heron, 1989:8). Instead of the handful of people employed by traditional craft establishments, these new enterprises often employed hundreds. They also needed to draw on wider markets beyond strictly local areas to stay in business.

With factories selling to expanded markets, profits became all-important. As manufacturers began to sell their goods to people they had never met, they could often compete only on the basis of cost (Commons, 1918). Profits were also necessary to enable employers to pay for all the costly new machinery they had just installed.

To make profits, employers had to control their costs. Since they could generally do little about the costs of raw materials, land, or capital equipment, they focussed their attention on controlling the cost of labour, which they could do something about. To this end, they brought in strict time-scheduling and monitoring of workers' output. Bells and clocks became common in factories, and the new, stricter schedules were enforced through fines and even beatings (Heron, 1989; Trofimenkoff, 1977:213). Work was sped up, mechanized, and simplified as much as possible so that more could be produced in less time with fewer people. With an eye to saving on wages, employers relied less on skilled artisans, flooding the market with cheaper, less skilled workers, including boys and women, (Heron, 1989:8–9) and replacing skilled workers with machines where possible (Morton and Copp, 1980:22; Bercuson and Bright, 1994:78). Many employers were especially partial to female employees because, in addition to commanding lower wages than men, they were seen as docile, clean, quick, and sober (Trofimenkoff, 1977:220).

In reaction to harsher workplace conditions and employers' frequent attempts to deskill their jobs and cut their wages, workers began increasingly to form craft unions, some of which began to affiliate with American internationals (Heron, 1989:10–11). Cigar makers, coopers, molders, machinists, iron-puddlers, and locomotive engineers were among the groups that began to form unions after 1850. By the 1870s, coal miners were also starting to organize (Heron, 1989:10). Inspired by British "New Model" unionism, the new Canadian craft unions sought to formalize their relations with employers and to put themselves on a more secure footing through high dues and strong, centralized leadership (Heron, 1989; Morton and Copp, 1980). A union's bargaining strategy typically consisted of posting its wage demands on the factory or shop doors. If times were good and demand for the product high, the employer might well meet the demands. Otherwise, he would generally refuse the demands, and a strike or lockout might then ensue. Often such a dispute would result in the workers' dismissal; sometimes it would even lead to the union's dissolution. As Morton and Copp (1980:10) note, nineteenth century unions could generally succeed only when there were lasting labour shortages. Still, though strikes remained a very risky business at a time when merely belonging to a union could leave a worker open to criminal conspiracy charges, they became more and more frequent as industrialization progressed, (Heron, 1989:12).

Beyond the Workplace: Making Common Cause

Confederation, increased industrialization, the growth of central-labour organizations in Ontario and Quebec, and growing international awareness of the industrial system's abuses led Canadian workers in the 1870s to mobilize around issues of broad interest to all workers, such as shorter working hours and improved workplace safety (Godard, 1994; Morton, 1995). Nine-hour Leagues in Hamilton and Montreal marked the beginning of broader workers' solidarity in Canada (Heron, 1989:14–15), with their strategy based on a series of strikes to support the demand for shorter hours (Godard, 1994:105). In the short run, the strategy failed, as Toronto printers struck George Brown's *Globe* ahead of schedule in 1872, causing Brown to charge the strikers with conspiracy and preventing the achievement of the nine-hour day for the time being (Morton, 1995:134). But the incident did provide politicians with some evidence of working people's potential political power and may well have been responsible, at least in part, for the Macdonald government's enactment, later in 1872, of a *Trade Union Act* removing peaceful picketing from criminal prosecution (Heron, 1989:17). While this law gave unions little in the way of substantive protection, since employers still had recourse to civil conspiracy actions (Heron, 1989:18) and could still use any number of union-busting techniques (Lipton, 1973:65), what it *did* do was provide unions with some measure of political legitimacy (Godard, 1994:106). In the years to come, the *Trade Union Act* was followed by more substantive legislation, such as the repeal (subject to certain limitations)[2] of the harsh *Masters and Servants Act* prohibitions on strikes (Morton and Copp, 1980; Godard, 1994) and the passage of various provincial Factory Acts, applied mainly to women and children (Morton and Copp, 1980:84). Another, though short-lived, legacy of the period was the Canadian Labour Union, formed in Toronto in 1873 to address larger political issues and, in effect, serve as a kind of national labour federation (Morton, 1995:134).

The Knights of Labor

Expanded industrialization and strong manufacturing sector growth led to a new wave of unionization in the 1880s. The decade saw a revival of the craft unions and the formation of the Provincial Workmen's Association, a Nova Scotia miners' union (Heron, 1989:20). Antagonism between workers and employers became more pronounced during this period, as employers sped up assembly lines and sought to impose even stricter controls on workers in an attempt to extract still more production from them (Kealey and Palmer, 1981:240–241).

At this juncture, with the social costs of industrialization becoming ever more apparent (Kealey and Palmer, 1981:241), the Knights of Labor appeared on the Canadian scene, starting their first Canadian local assembly in Hamilton in 1875 (Craig and Solomon, 1996:115). This organization, which had been founded in Philadelphia in 1869 (Godard, 1994:107), was quite unlike any previous labour organization. As their leaders often said (Kealey and Palmer, 1982), they did not seek to make richer people; they sought to make better people. While conventional craft unions sought to improve the terms and conditions of employment at individual workplaces, the Knights aimed at nothing less than a moral and social transformation of industrial society (Godard, 1994; Kealey and Palmer, 1982).

In pursuit of such transformation, the Knights relied mainly on education and politics. During their brief time in Canada, they opened reading rooms and libraries and supported weekly newspapers, as well as developing producer and consumer cooperatives (Heron, 1989:25–27; Kealey and Palmer, 1981:250). Unlike most other labour organizations of their day (McKay, 1983:125), the Knights admitted women as well as men and unskilled as well as skilled workers, excluding only the Chinese (Kealey and Palmer, 1981; 1982). So broad and so persuasive was their appeal that in Ontario alone they organized at least 21,800 members over their history, according to Kealey and Palmer (1981:245).

Politically, they achieved their greatest gains at the municipal level, including earlier closing hours, union wages for municipal workers, and improved public transit (Kealey and Palmer, 1981:256). At provincial and national levels, while unable to achieve their goal of creating an independent working-class party (Kealey and Palmer, 1981), they did succeed in getting labour's voice heard by the politicians. During the 1890s, both the federal and the Ontario provincial governments implemented many of the Knights' recommendations, including factory acts, bureaus of labour statistics, arbitration measures, extension of the suffrage, and employers' liability acts (Kealey and Palmer, 1981:265). Perhaps most noteworthy of all, the first Monday in September was established as a holiday in 1894 in recognition of the dignity of labour (Morton, 1995:135).

The Knights' role in strikes has generated considerable controversy (Morton, 1995; Godard, 1994; Kealey and Palmer, 1981;1982). Undeniably they were less enthusiastic about strikes than were most conventional craft unions, generally preferring to resolve disputes through conciliation or arbitration instead. At the same time, the record shows that they took part in and even led a good many strikes in Ontario during the 1880s (Kealey and Palmer, 1981:258). It also shows that after a downturn in the economy in the late 1880s, the Knights became more cautious about striking, and that during a London cigar makers' strike, they signed up scab cigar makers and allowed them to use the Knights' label in competition with the cigar makers' union (Heron, 1989:26–27). This action outraged international unionists and caused many to leave the order (Heron, 1989:28). Essentially, it was the beginning of the end for the Knights, though they were to linger on in Canada until the Berlin Convention of 1902. But whether or not the Knights' conception of broad-based industrial unionism was wildly ahead of its time, as Morton (1995:135) suggests, their vision of a genuine alternative culture would inspire former members until well into the twentieth century (Kealey and Palmer, 1981:229–230).

Trades and Labour Congress

The rise and fall of the Knights of Labor were far from the only significant developments on the Canadian labour scene during the 1880s. A more lasting development was the formation, in 1886, of the Trades and Labour Congress of Canada (TLC). This organization, which would remain Canada's major labour confederation until its 1956 merger with the Canadian Congress of Labour, would meet annually to address such labour-related issues as immigration policy, enforcement of factory acts, free education for children, and shorter work hours (Forsey, 1982; Morton and Copp, 1980). Like Samuel Gompers's American Federation of Labor, it did not affiliate itself with any political party, instead lobbying governments on an issue-by-issue basis.

Labour in the Second Industrial Revolution

American Federation of Labor

A second industrial revolution began in Canada during the 1890s. Factories became larger and more capital-intensive (Heron, 1989:30–31; Kealey and Palmer, 1981:235), and supervision grew even stricter under the coercive drive system (discussed in detail in Chapter 3). Not surprisingly, worker-management struggles for workplace control intensified (Heron, 1989; Kealey, 1976). Meanwhile, wages for most workers remained low despite the period's vast accumulation of capital. As late as 1890, Toronto printers were earning $12 for a 54-hour week (Lipton, 1973:79)— and they were among the period's more privileged workers. Less-skilled adult male workers, let alone women and children, generally earned far less (Morton and Copp, 1980; Lipton, 1973; Bullen, 1986; McIntosh, 1987).

Conditions were clearly ripe for a new wave of union organizing. As in the past, Canadian workers found help south of the border. In the middle of his own organizing drive, American Federation of Labor (AFL) president Samuel Gompers realized that if Canada were not organized, all the AFL's efforts might be futile since American employers could procure cheaper Canadian labour (Morton, 1995:136). To prevent this from happening, Gompers enlisted the services of John Flett, a Hamilton carpenter and one-time socialist. Flett's turn-of-the-century campaign proved astoundingly successful. He was responsible for 57 new AFL locals in Canada in 1901 and for most of the 50 new locals added the following year (Morton and Copp, 1980:70). This wave of AFL organizing transformed the Canadian labour movement, firmly setting it on an international path. By 1902, fully 95 percent of all Canadian unionists belonged to international unions. The international direction of the Canadian labour movement was confirmed by Flett's election to the TLC presidency at the organization's 1902 convention, held in Berlin, Ontario (Morton and Copp, 1980).[3]

The Berlin Convention

Up until the Berlin convention, the TLC had been less doctrinally rigid about its unionism than had the AFL. It had included local assemblies of the Knights of Labor alongside traditional craft unions—a practice that the AFL, and Gompers in particular, loathed.[4] Berlin changed all that. After the convention, no national union would be recognized by the TLC when an international union existed, and in no case would more than one central body be chartered in any city or town (Morton and Copp, 1980:74). This prohibition of "dual" unionism led the TLC to expel its remaining Knights assemblies, as well as other national unions organizing the same industries as AFL unions. The 33 expelled unions comprised about one-fifth of the TLC's total membership (Drache, 1984:27).

Historians and industrial relations experts differ on the significance of the Berlin Convention. To some (Morton, 1995:137), the linkage between American and Canadian labour movements established at Berlin was only common sense, since Canadian unionists "wanted to share a North American standard of living." To others (Drache, 1984:26–28), the move effectively split the Canadian labour movement by tying it to an American federation actively seeking to hinder its development as an independent, nationalist, and progressive force. Most likely, the truth lies somewhere in the middle. While Berlin did, to a degree, split the Canadian movement (especially insofar as it maintained TLC control in central Canada, leaving eastern and western unions out in the cold), it did not and could not destroy a persistent nationalist spirit within that movement. That spirit would find expression in a series of nationally oriented union federations, from the National Trades and Labour Congress (later known as the Canadian Federation of Labour) in the first quarter of the twentieth century through the All-Canadian Congress of Labour (ACCL) (1927–1940) to the Canadian Congress of Labour (CCL) (1940–1956). Unlike the TLC, the ACCL and CCL would both seek to organize workers on an industry-wide rather than craft basis, and would place considerable emphasis on political action (Craig and Solomon, 1996:120–123).

Radical Unionism

While the Berlin Convention appeared to set the Canadian labour movement on a moderate as well as international course, there were a good many radical unions operating in Canada during the first two decades of this century. Berlin may even have heightened some unions' radicalism, by confirming that there was no place for them within the mainstream labour movement.

The century's first decade saw a series of increasingly violent strikes, often involving the use of police and volunteer militia to suppress them. Many of these disputes involved street-railway workers. Indeed, it seems that almost every Ontario city of any size had at least one major street-railway strike between 1895 and 1910 (Morton and Copp, 1980:77). These strikes helped develop strong public support for the labour movement (Heron, 1989:34–36), particularly since both workers and railway-riding members of the general public were seeking to have the monopolies placed under public ownership, as most eventually were.

Many other strikes occurred in the coal mines of Nova Scotia (McKay, 1983; Frank, 1983; McIntosh, 1987) and in the mines, logging camps, and railway gangs of British Columbia (McCormack, 1975; Mouat, 1990). On the railway gangs, for instance, a 12-hour day and seven-day week were standard. The work was back-breaking, and accidents, including fatal ones, were far from uncommon. Foremen often drove the men with their fists, and in some cases workers were watched by armed guards (McCormack, 1975:327). Given such conditions, it is hardly surprising that the largely unskilled and immigrant workers should have turned to a radical union like the International Workers of the World (IWW) for help. Like some other unions of its day, the IWW had a **syndicalist** philosophy. This meant that it placed little faith in either collective bargaining or political action, believing instead in a huge general strike that would destroy capitalism (McCormack, 1975:329–330). A belief in direct industrial action made a good deal of sense to the IWW's members, few of whom could vote. Meanwhile, the "Wobblies" were able to provide their members with a good deal of practical help in the here and now. Their organizing was done in at least 10 different languages, and their union halls served as mail drops and dormitories, as employment agencies, infirmaries, and classrooms (McCormack, 1975:328).

IDI Act (1907)

It was a coal strike that led Parliament to pass, in 1907, the *Industrial Disputes Investigation Act*, arguably the most significant piece of labour legislation Canada had yet seen. A nine-month strike of coal miners in the Lethbridge district in 1906 had come close to leaving residents facing a prairie winter without heat (Baker, 1983; Morton and Copp, 1980). The public was appalled by the near miss in Lethbridge, and by the increasing violence of other disputes, such as a strike in a suburban Ottawa lumber yard that left three dead that same year (Morton and Copp, 1980:88). It demanded government action to help stem the increasing labour bloodshed.

The *IDI Act* was based primarily on Prime Minister King's belief that public exposure would moderate the behaviour of unreasonable parties. The Act required all workers and employers in transportation, resources, and utilities industries to submit their disputes to a three-person conciliation board before starting a strike or lockout. Even after the board had issued its report, a further "cooling-off" period was required before any strike or lockout could become legal (Heron, 1989:47). As will be seen in more detail in Chapter 8, *IDI's* basic principles have remained central features of most Canadian labour legislation to this day.

The TLC initially gave the act cautious approval, but quickly changed its mind (Morton and Copp, 1980:89–90). Not only did *IDI* not require collective bargaining; it did nothing to prevent employers from using the "cooling-off" periods to stockpile goods to prepare for strikes, or from imposing yellow-dog contracts barring employees from union membership, recruiting strike-breakers, hiring private police, or firing and blacklisting union activists (Morton and Copp, 1980:89; Heron, 1989:47; MacDowell, 1978:660). In the view of industrial relations author Stuart Jamieson, the act delayed the evolution of mature collective bargaining in Canada (see Morton and Copp, 1980:90).[5]

Even in the short term, *IDI* probably did little to improve labour-management relations. The period just before the First World War continued to be marked by bitter workplace struggles, as managers schooled in the newly fashionable scientific management (discussed in detail in Chapter 3) sought to speed up production lines and extract still more effort from their workers. Socially and politically, as well, the period was one of great ferment and rapid change. In Europe, most mainstream labour movements had by this time adopted some form of socialism (Adams, 1995a:497). While the TLC didn't do this, many workers and union leaders did, moving well beyond the cautious "labourism" that had been Canadian working people's primary political creed for the previous half-century (Heron, 1989:49–51; 1984). None of this was likely to be changed by the requirements for a conciliation board report and cooling-off period before a legal strike could take place.

The First World War and its Aftermath

The First World War saw a rapid increase in union membership, an increase spurred both by rising prices and by wartime labour shortages. Between 1914 and 1919, Canadian union membership more than doubled (Godard, 1994:95) as the wartime organizational surge brought unskilled workers, municipal government employees, and even teachers and other white-collar workers into the labour movement for the first time (Heron, 1989:53–54). These new unionists had grievances that went beyond soaring wartime prices. Unlike the British, French, and American governments, the Canadian government made no attempt to consult with union leaders or socialist politicians during the war, even though the TLC had obediently endorsed the war effort in 1914 (Heron, 1989:53; Morton and Copp, 1980:103). Further frustrated by their inability to elect members to Parliament on a labour ticket (Heron, 1989:56), Canadian unionists turned to radical protest and direct action. The period from 1917 to 1920 saw a wave of strike activity across Canada, inspired at least in part by a worldwide workers' revolt set in motion by the Russian Revolution of 1917 (Heron, 1989:55).

After the largely western-based radicals lost out to the conservative craft unionists at the 1918 TLC convention, they launched a new industrial union known as the "One Big Union" (OBU) with socialist leadership. Their aim was to create a broad-based union free of traditional craft jurisdictional barriers. A key demand was for a six-hour day to reduce unemployment (Heron, 1989:57–58). The launching of the new union was, however, quickly overshadowed by some dramatic events taking place in Winnipeg and a number of other Canadian cities during the spring of 1919.

"CALGARY 1919: THE BIRTH OF THE OBU AND THE GENERAL STRIKE" BY EUGENE W. PLAWIUK

www.geocities.com/CapitolHill/5202/Cal1919.htm

The Winnipeg General Strike

In April 1918, Winnipeg's workers had successfully staged a general strike over city workers' right to strike (Morton and Copp, 1980:115). Just over a year later, on May 15, 1919, they tried the same tactic to show sympathy with the building and metal trades unions, which had been denied collective bargaining rights (Heron, 1989:59). On that day, more than 25 000 workers walked off their jobs, launching a six-week strike (Morton and Copp, 1980:119). Though the Winnipeg strike would spark a wave of 30 sympathy strikes extending eastward to Amherst, Nova Scotia, and westward to Vancouver (Kealey, 1984:203–206), it proved a colossal failure in the end, as all three levels of government combined to crush the strike (Heron, 1989:60–61), continuing a pattern of government repression that had begun during the war with the banning of socialist and radical organizations and the closure of foreign-language newspapers (Morton and Copp, 1980:113). Strike leaders were arrested and threatened with deportation (Morton and Copp, 1980), and the city's police force was dismissed for its pro-strike leanings and replaced by untrained special constables. Most important of all, on "Bloody Saturday" (June 21), the RCMP charged a crowd of strikers, using bullets as well as their horses to suppress the crowd in the most authoritative way possible. Four days later, the strike was over (Morton and Copp, 1980:122).

To all intents and purposes, the collapse of the Winnipeg General Strike marked the end of the radical labour movement in Canada (Morton and Copp, 1980:122–123). Even as many of the Winnipeg strike leaders went off to prison, the OBU was being reduced to insignificance, weakened both by employers who refused to have anything to do with it and by craft unionists who collaborated in undermining its strikes (Heron, 1989:59).

The Postwar Retreat

Ushered in by a severe depression that led to massive layoffs and hopeless strikes against draconian wage cuts (Heron, 1989:60), the 1920s were to prove extraordinarily difficult years for the Canadian labour movement. Continuing government repression, a renewed employer offensive against labour, and deep schisms within the movement itself combined to weaken labour's position dramatically and to bring "fearfulness, fatalism and cynicism" back into the working-class consciousness (Heron, 1989). Throughout most of the decade, union membership fell sharply. So did wage rates, at least during the early part of the decade. (Morton and Copp, 1980:125–126). Ongoing waves of immigration throughout the decade helped ensure that unemployment levels remained relatively high and that unskilled and semi-skilled workers would continue to be easy to replace (Godard, 1994:117).

"LABOUR AGITATION IN THE INTER-WAR PERIOD"
www.acs.ucalgary.ca/SS/HIST/tutor/calgary/labouragitation.html

Having failed at radical industrial action, the labour movement returned to more conventional electoral politics at the start of the decade. Initially this strategy was quite successful, as a fair number of labour members were elected to provincial legislatures during the early postwar years. In Ontario and Alberta, labour parties elected enough members to form coalitions with farmers' parties. These were not, however, political marriages made in heaven. Some modest reforms ensued, but basic disagreements over such issues as work hours, prohibition, free trade, and taxation levels prevented the alliances from lasting very long (Heron, 1989:61–62). By the end of the decade, most mainstream TLC unionists had reverted to the old Sam Gompers method of lobbying individual politicians on single issues of direct concern to unions (Morton, 1995:140).

With wages falling, unemployment rising, and working people generally on the defensive, many early postwar employers found it easy to simply crush unions by intimidating and harassing any workers known or suspected to have had anything to do with them. For those who disliked such heavy-handed tactics, there was the new paternalistic management, or "American Plan" as it was often called.[6] The main idea here was to reduce workers' desire to join unions by providing company-dominated unions, or industrial councils, as channels through which workers could voice their concerns without posing any fundamental challenge to management's authority (Godard, 1994:113–115; Heron, 1989:59–60; Morton and Copp, 1980:130–131; Slichter, 1929). It isn't clear just how widely paternalistic management practices were adopted in Canada. But where they were adopted, they appear to have been fairly successful at keeping unions out (Godard, 1994:117; Slichter, 1929).

Catholic and Communist Unionism

As if the challenges from without were not difficult enough, the 1920s saw the Canadian labour movement split in several different directions. We have already discussed the emergence of a number of different nationalist labour federations unhappy with the TLC's strong ties to the AFL. More serious, perhaps, because it pointed to new schisms within the labour movement, was the emergence of Catholic confessional and Communist union federations. The former had its roots in traditional Quebec nationalism, heightened by the First World War conscription crisis, and in a long-standing tradition of Church involvement in settling labour disputes in the province (Morton and Copp, 1980:131). Since early in the century, Quebec's Catholic hierarchy had been working for a distinctly Catholic unionism that would promote Catholic and francophone values, rather than the secular and socialistic values they saw arising out of the then-dominant international unions (Heron, 1989:60; Boivin, 1982:426–427). Their efforts bore fruit in 1921 with the establishment of the Confédération des travailleurs catholique du Canada (CTCC), which claimed to represent some 26 000 members (Boivin, 1982:427). A key aspect of confessional unionism was the attachment of a priest to each local, ostensibly as an adviser, but more often than not as its de facto president. The CTCC also stressed the common interests of workers and employers, shunning strikes in favour of less confrontational approaches such as conciliation and arbitration.[7] The new Catholic unions clearly represented a serious challenge to the internationals and the TLC (Morton and Copp, 1980:131), since in many cases they were competing for members with the older federations.

The challenge posed by the Communists, who launched their new party in Ontario in 1921, was equally severe. The advent of Communism marked the first time the Canadian labour movement had been used by a political party seeking to achieve its own ends, rather than trying to serve those of the labour movement.

Since the Canadian party took its orders from Moscow, its labour strategies underwent a number of bizarre, even embarrassing, shifts resulting from Soviet policy changes (Morton and Copp, 1980:133–134). Early in the decade, the orders were to "bore from within," taking over the conservative AFL and TLC and transforming them into radical bodies. Unsuccessful in this attempt, the Communists in 1927 turned their attention to the new, more progressive ACCL and sought to bring in a number of like-minded unions in a bid to wrest control of the federation from its founder, Aaron Mosher. All this did was to earn the Communists the enmity of the non-Communist nationalist unions (Heron, 1989:70) and get them expelled from the ACCL (Morton and Copp, 1980:134). In 1930, the Communists formed their own labour federation, the Workers' Unity League (WUL), dedicated to "militant industrial unionism and socialist revolution" (Heron, 1989:70). Finally, in 1935, still under orders from Moscow, the Communists changed their strategy yet again, disbanded the WUL, and rejoined the mainstream labour movement with an eye to forming broad-based anti-fascist alliances.

Clearly, the WUL did much useful work within the Canadian labour movement, particularly by assuming leadership of the great majority of Canadian strikes carried out during the early 1930s (Heron, 1989:70–71). But by fragmenting the already small left-wing opposition to the American-dominated TLC within Canada's labour movement, the Communists also helped delay the emergence of strong, progressive national unionism.

Judicial Fragmentation

The final cause of fragmentation within the Canadian labour movement was neither a union nor a political party, but the British Privy Council, which in the Snider case of 1925 overruled a solid majority of Canadian judges to declare the *IDI Act* unconstitutional because it applied to municipal institutions (Craig and Solomon, 1996:206). Since then, labour law, except in the case of undertakings clearly of a federal nature, has been held to be under provincial jurisdiction. In addition to making life more complicated for all actors in the IR system by in effect establishing 11 IR jurisdictions instead of one,[8] provincial jurisdiction has arguably promoted a decentralized union structure (Murray, 1995) that has made it that much more difficult for the Canadian labour movement to pursue coordinated national economic and political strategies.

Labour During the Depression

The Great Depression of the 1930s offered conclusive evidence of the failure of conventional approaches to economic and political problems. Like many other groups, the Canadian labour movement began to try out a variety of new approaches both in workplaces and in the political arena. It was helped greatly by the American movement, which used a politically sympathetic government to achieve gains it had previously only dreamed of, including the granting of collective bargaining rights.

The Economic Situation

By 1933, one worker in four was unemployed, an increase of more than 300 percent in the national unemployment rate since 1929, and 15 percent of the population was on relief (Morton and Copp, 1980:139–140). For those leaving school, job prospects were poor to non-existent. Many would be condemned to a life of "riding the rods" in search of any work they could get, or an even harder life in the government-sponsored relief camps established in 1932, which provided their inmates with room and board and 20 cents a day in return for six days a week of hard labour (Morton and Copp, 1980; Brown, 1970).

TEXT OF 1933 *WINNIPEG FREE PRESS* EDITORIAL ON ECONOMIC CONDITIONS ON PRAIRIES

www.nelson.com/nelson/school/discovery/cantext/western/1933depr.htm

Few had really secure jobs. Both in the resource industries and in manufacturing, massive layoffs were the order of the day. At Ford Motor Company, employment fell from 7100 to 2174 between 1929 and 1932. Workers often had to bribe their way into even low-paying menial jobs (Manley, 1986:556).

WUL Activity

Under such conditions, most conventional union organizing and strike activity was out of the question, as the major federations hunkered down to protect existing members (Morton and Copp, 1980:142; Manley, 1986:557). The one big exception was the Communists' Worker Unity League, for whom the Depression was tailor-made, since it seemed to confirm the Communists' thesis of the need for broader class struggle (Morton and Copp, 1980:142). In Flin Flon, Manitoba, and Estevan, Saskatchewan, the WUL led bitter and ultimately unsuccessful mining strikes. Though the strikes failed, the courage shown by the workers would inspire many others over the years. The WUL's efforts were more successful in Ontario, where it managed to organize a fair number of furniture, textile, and garment workers despite ferocious redbaiting and frequent repression by provincial police and troops (Morton and Copp, 1980; Heron, 1989).

Government Repression

Government repression was by no means confined to strikers. A common enough feature of 1930s' life generally, it was applied most often and most brutally to the hordes of single, unemployed men who were the Depression's worst victims, and from whom the government seemed to feel it had most to fear (Morton and Copp, 1980:145–146). While the relief camp inmates did not wear uniforms (Morton and Copp, 1980:147), in most other ways they lived and worked under military-style discipline. Inmates were barred from filing group petitions to seek improvement of their wretched conditions, or from making speeches, writing letters to newspapers, or doing anything else "to bring accusations before the tribunal of public opinion" (Brown, 1970:606–607). In 1933, authorities banned May Day parades in Regina and Saskatoon and had the RCMP raid a union hall in Moose Jaw and seize a list of names of "troublemakers" who had refused to work in the relief camps (Brown, 1970:600). Two years later, when unemployed workers made an "On-to-Ottawa" trek to press such radical demands as relief camp workers' right to vote and the removal of the camps from Defence Department control, they were met with RCMP billy clubs in a bloody July 1 riot in Regina (Brown, 1970:610–611; Morton and Copp, 1980; Scott, 1945).

"THE ON-TO-OTTAWA TREK"
www.mala.bc.ca/~nanmsu/ottawa.htm

Though anti-Communist laws were not new to Canada (Scott, 1932), the Conservative government of R.B. Bennett applied them with particular rigour, as did Bennett's provincial allies such as Ontario Premier Howard Ferguson. In 1931, the Communists' Toronto office was raided and eight of its leaders arrested; seven were later imprisoned (Morton and Copp, 1980:145). Other Communist leaders were deported (Morton and Copp, 1980), a phenomenon that had become increasingly common since the First World War (White, 1932).[9] As the decade wore on, similar or even harsher treatment would be meted out to Communists, social democrats, and unionists by the authoritarian governments of Quebec Premier Maurice Duplessis and Ontario Premier Mitch Hepburn, who replaced Ferguson later in the decade (Morton and Copp, 1980:158–160, 163, 191).

Hopeful American Developments

South of the border, meanwhile, things were beginning to look more hopeful, particularly after 1933 when Franklin D. Roosevelt took office as President. Roosevelt's "New Deal" launched large public works projects and, in general, stimulated the U.S. economy greatly, leading to a substantial reduction in unemployment rates by the mid 1930s.

TEXT OF 1935 RADIO ADDRESS BY PM R.B.BENNETT ON THE STATE OF THE ECONOMY
www.rescol.ca/collections/canspeak/english/rbb/sp1.htm

Influenced by business lobbying and by conservatives within his administration, Roosevelt did not give the labour movement the legislated six-hour day and 30-hour week it had been seeking as a means of reducing unemployment (Hunnicutt, 1988). But he saw that he *would* have to give the labour movement a good deal to make up for the loss of the six-hour law. His broad package of reforms eventually included a social security plan generous enough to allow older workers to retire with dignity, and employment standards legislation providing for an eight-hour day and 40-hour week—still far shorter than that worked by most workers in industrialized countries (Hunnicutt, 1988). The centrepiece was the 1935 *National Labor Relations Act,* or "Wagner Act," as it is more commonly known. This bill allowed most American private-sector workers[10] to bargain collectively and to strike without fear of employer intimidation, harassment, or reprisal. Standards for employer unfair labour practice were defined and a National Labor Relations Board established to administer and enforce the act. Free of the fear that hostile employers could fire union organizers and members, American unions signed up hundreds of thousands of new members in the years immediately following passage of the Wagner Act.

ILLINOIS LABOR HISTORY SOCIETY
www.kentlaw.edu/ilhs

Industrial Unionism

A particularly important consequence of the Wagner Act was that it facilitated unionization of unskilled and semi-skilled workers who would otherwise have had difficulty forming unions, since they lacked the scarce skills to withstand employer anti-union initiatives. Many of the country's more foresighted union leaders, such as John L. Lewis of the United Mine Workers, were quick to recognize the huge growth the labour movement might achieve by organizing unskilled and semi-skilled workers in mass-production industries. Unlike traditional craft unionism, the **industrial unionism** envisaged by Lewis and his allies would seek to organize all workers in an industry and would use political action and mass worker mobilization, as well as collective bargaining, in an attempt to achieve its objectives.

Disgusted with what they saw as the AFL craft unions' conservative, elitist, and defeatist strategy, Lewis and other industrial unionists launched a Committee for Industrial Organization within the AFL (Abella, 1975). When its members were expelled from that federation two years later (Morton and Copp, 1980:153), the

Committee became the Congress of Industrial Organization, or CIO (Heron, 1989:73). The CIO's efforts would quickly bear fruit, with the organization of such mass-production industries as autos, steel, rubber, and meatpacking.

Industrial unionism was slower to take hold in Canada, in large measure because Canadian workers still didn't enjoy basic bargaining rights. But CIO organizers nonetheless began working in Ontario, and in February 1937, a proposed 20 percent speed-up of the General Motors Oshawa plant assembly line led to a plant-wide strike that in turn led to a compromise settlement whereby the union won most of its substantive demands without gaining formal recognition (Morton and Copp, 1980; Abella, 1975). With this victory, the Canadian industrial union movement was launched, though it would continue to find the going tough in the absence of legislation protecting basic union organizing rights (Morton and Copp, 1980; Abella, 1975). Over the next few years, CIO unions would be established in Kitchener's rubber plants, Sault Ste. Marie's steel mills, and Montreal dress factories (Morton and Copp, 1980:160–163). In 1939, the TLC would follow the AFL's lead and expel its CIO unions (Heron, 1989:73), which then merged with Aaron Mosher's ACCL to form the Canadian Congress of Labour, or CCL (Morton, 1995:143).

The Founding of the CCF

Desperate for solutions to the Depression, Canadians tried out a broad range of schemes ranging from social credit and religious fundamentalism to varying degrees of socialism (Morton, 1995, 141; Ferguson, 1935). Throughout this period, the Communists were extremely active both in the labour movement and in society at large. Though they won few seats federally or provincially, the ongoing economic crisis caused many Canadians, including some prominent intellectuals and artists, to sympathize if not agree with their approach. Within the labour movement, the WUL's undoubted courage and organizational ability earned respect from radical and non-radical unionists alike.

The most important political development of the period, however, was the founding of the Co-Operative Commonwealth Federation, or CCF, which was launched in Calgary and Regina in 1932–1933 under the leadership of J.S. Woodsworth. The party was made up of socialists, progressive farmers, old-style labourites, and a number of urban intellectuals (Morton, 1995; Underhill, 1932). Its eight-point program included a planned system of social economy, socialization of the banking sector, public ownership of the natural resource sector, socialized medical care, and adequate work or unemployment insurance for the unemployed under federal government auspices (Underhill, 1932).

Though many in the labour movement were initially cool to the new party (Morton, 1995:141), it gained increasing union support over time, earning, for example, the endorsement of Aaron Mosher's CCL. During its first five years, it won only scattered seats, but by the late 1930s it was winning large numbers of seats in B.C. and Saskatchewan. In 1944, it formed the government in the latter province (King, 1944). By this time, it was so strong both federally and in Ontario that it posed a serious threat to both governments. Canada's labour movement finally had an effective political party of its own.

Labour During the War Years

If the Depression's dominant themes had been industrial unionism and political mobilization, that of the war years was legislative enactment of fundamental union bargaining rights. For labour, this period's pivotal event was undoubtedly the enactment, in 1944, of *PC 1003*, the bill granting Canadian workers such basic rights as the right to join a union, bargain collectively, and strike.

The achievement of basic bargaining rights did not come easily. Though wartime labour shortages and government orders-in-council curbing employers' right to fire workers again spurred union organization, Prime Minister King remained convinced of the perfection of the *IDI Act* and unwilling to move beyond it. In a bid to maintain labour peace, the government did, in 1940, put forward an order-in-council urging employers to recognize unions voluntarily. But as L.S. MacDowell notes, this policy was "ignored by employers and never followed by the government itself in the industries under its own control" (1978:662). In the absence of any legislation compelling them to deal with unions, many employers continued to refuse to do so. In a situation of wartime labour shortage, where wages were strictly controlled but prices generally were not (MacDowell, 1978), serious labour strife was virtually guaranteed. A bitter gold mining strike at Kirkland Lake, Ontario, in 1942 and an equally bitter steel strike the following year united the formerly divided labour movement against the government. Both major labour federations demanded that workers be given the same basic bargaining rights American workers had long enjoyed under the Wagner Act (MacDowell, 1978:669). A similar conclusion was reached by the National War Labour Board in 1943, in a report prepared by Mr. Justice C.P. McTague, who had been the conciliator in the Kirkland Lake dispute. Still King did not act (Morton and Copp, 1980:183).

What the McTague report could not do, the growing threat from the left could. In August 1943, the Liberals lost four federal by-elections, two to the CCF (Morton and Copp, 1980). The defeats and the CCF's high poll standings elsewhere appear to have convinced King that if he didn't move the Liberals to the left, he might well lose the next election. Accordingly, he established a system of family allowances and promised full postwar employment and universal medical care (Morton, 1995:143). Most important of all, he finally granted Canadian workers their long-awaited collective bargaining rights.

Collective Bargaining Legislation: *PC 1003*

The legislation providing for those rights, Order-in-Council *PC 1003*, was proclaimed in February 1944, by which time similar legislation had already been put into effect in Ontario and B.C. (Heron, 1989:80). Now, employers could not refuse to bargain with unions that had proved to the new labour relations board that they had the majority support of workers in any given workplace. This meant that strikes for union recognition would no longer be necessary; in fact they would be illegal. Otherwise, the right to strike, within limits, was now protected, but *IDI's* conciliation process (including the "cooling-off" period) would still have to observed before any strike or lockout would be legal (Heron, 1989:80–81). Strikes were *not* legal during the life of a contract. Instead, every collective agreement was assumed to contain a grievance procedure, culminating in binding arbitration, for the handling of disputes over contract interpretation (Craig and Solomon, 1996:207). The new board, to be known as the Canada Labour Relations Board, was charged with overseeing certifications and ruling on unfair labour practices (Heron, 1989:80).

Thanks to favourable wartime conditions, union membership rates had already risen dramatically. Between 1939 and 1945, the number of Canadian union members doubled, while union density increased from 17 to 24 percent of paid non-agricultural workers (Godard, 1994:96). Now, thanks to *PC 1003*, the unions would be able to maintain those gains during the postwar period. Indeed, membership rates continued to rise during the late 1940s, aided both by the legislation and by a booming postwar economy that proved conducive to union growth.

Maintaining Union Security: The "Rand Formula"

Another piece of legislation that may have contributed to postwar union growth by enhancing unions' security was the so-called **"Rand Formula,"** introduced in 1945. The formula, devised by Justice Ivan Rand to help settle a Ford Motor Company dispute he was arbitrating, did not require employees to join unions that had been certified for their bargaining units, but did require them to pay union dues, since all bargaining-unit employees, whether union members or not, benefitted from the union's efforts on their behalf. Free of the threat of compulsory union membership, which they bitterly opposed, most employers adopted the dues "checkoff" whereby employees' union dues were deducted at the source. This gave unions a solid financial basis of support and helped ensure their survival (Heron, 1989:85).

With the war over, the federal government could no longer maintain its jurisdiction over labour legislation. But in 1948, it enacted a slightly modified version of the wartime order, the *Industrial Relations and Disputes Investigation Act of 1948* (Morton and Copp, 1980:198). The new law was intended to serve as a model for the provinces and to provide some degree of uniformity for labour law across the country (Carter, 1995:62). To a degree, it did. Within two years, every province had adopted some version of the federal legislation. Many provincial acts, however, were significantly more restrictive than the federal one; this was particularly the case for the Atlantic provinces and Alberta.[11] The one area of uniformity was the compulsory conciliation provision, a holdover from the old *IDI Act*, which was adopted in every province except Saskatchewan.

Postwar Strikes

The Ford strike just mentioned was but one of a huge wave sweeping across Canada during the early postwar years. Workers needed substantial wage increases to keep pace with postwar inflation. And thanks to the new labour legislation, even the unskilled could now strike to support wage demands without risking dismissal or harassment from their employers. In 1946 alone, a year that saw the highest level of Canadian strike activity since 1919, strikes shut down the entire B.C. logging industry, the Ontario rubber industry, the entire steel industry, the Southam newspaper chain, and central Canadian ports (Heron, 1989:84). Though often long and sometimes bitter, these strikes were of a different character than the ones that had swept Canada after the First World War. With union recognition as such no longer at issue, the primary aim now was not mass mobilization, but the winning of specific contract demands. While picket lines continued to be tense places, bloodshed and loss of life were far rarer than in pre-war strikes. Thanks again to the new legislation, the strike had become less of a political weapon and more of an economic one (see Heron, 1989:85 and Morton, 1995:145).

Women: The Forgotten 50 Percent

While *PC 1003* and the Rand Formula were certainly of great benefit to male workers, especially blue-collar workers in industries important to the war effort, it is doubtful whether this legislation was of much immediate benefit to female workers. The legislation didn't apply to public sector workers (except in Saskatchewan); by and large these workers continued to be legally barred from joining unions. In the private-service sector, where many other women worked, any significant degree of unionization would simply not be in the cards for the foreseeable future.[12]

Since most heavy industries had been unionized, the new labour legislation might have benefitted the sizeable contingent of women who had left their homes to take wartime defence plant jobs—except for one minor detail. With the end of the war, women were leaving those plants in droves. To help ensure that the exodus continued, governments closed workplace day-care centres and cancelled wartime tax concessions

As this photo suggests, logging could be an extremely dangerous business.

An illustration from Dante's *Inferno*? Actually, it's a rather typical scene from a 19th century factory.

Brutal suppression of strike activity, as in the case of the Winnipeg General Strike, was more the rule than the exception before Canadian workers received official bargaining rights.

Quebec workers take to the streets in a demonstration against the authoritarian regime of Premier Maurice Duplessis.

Even before World War II was over, advertisers were campaigning hard to ensure that "Rosie the Rivetter" would turn back into "Henrietta the Homemaker" as soon as possible after the end of hostilities.

Long hours and low wages were the rule for Canada's immigrant workers.

United Food and Commercial Workers urge a boycott of Gainer's meats during their now-famous 1986 strike in Edmonton.

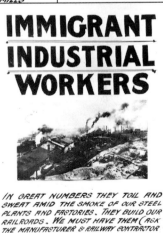

Immigrant workers were often forced to toil under appalling conditions.

(Roberts and Bullen, 1985:387). Not surprisingly, the female proportion of the labour force dropped from 31 to 23 percent between 1945 and 1946 (Bland, 1983:681), while marriage and birth rates soared. After the war, the country's advertisers did their part to complete the metamorphosis of "Rosie the Rivetter" into "Henrietta the Homemaker" by painting bright pictures of an appliance-filled future in which women were portrayed primarily as consumers (Bland, 1983:707). At home with her washer and dryer and high-gloss paste wax, a woman would have little reason to concern herself with such things as unions and labour legislation.

Labour During the 1950s

After the radicalism of the 1930s and rapid expansion of the 1940s, the 1950s were a decade of consolidation and stabilization, if not stagnation. Except in the provinces (Quebec, Alberta, and Newfoundland) where governments maintained repressive anti-union policies, unions were generally accepted, but had to operate within fairly narrow bounds. In return for this acceptance, they were expected to concentrate on wages and benefits and not concern themselves with more fundamental questions of control or management of the enterprise (Heron, 1989:86–87). In addition, they also lost the mid-term strike and other traditional tools of direct action (Heron, 1989:91–92). With the mid-term strike barred in favour of the grievance procedure, many believed union leaders were increasingly being made to function as the managers of discontent. Whether or not this was the case, it was definitely true that they now had to function in an increasingly bureaucratic and legalistic workplace environment, one in which administrative and negotiating skills were more important than the ability to mobilize workers or move a crowd (Heron, 1989:86–89).

At the bargaining table, unions racked up impressive gains for their members. Wages increased dramatically, and the eight-hour day and five-day week became the norm. Paid vacations, pensions, and medical plans were all brought in (Roberts and Bullen, 1985:393–394). For the first time, ordinary workers were able to buy cars, appliances, TV sets, and other items of which they had previously only dreamed (Heron, 1989:99). At the same time, more and more union members tended to view their unions instrumentally, as essentially their business agents. Attendance at union meetings dwindled, except at negotiation time (Heron, 1989). Later, this growing lack of membership commitment would come to trouble both unionists and academic industrial relationists. For now, the movement's relative placidity appeared to suit the times quite well. Overall, it was an era of economic and political conservatism. Few people, within the labour movement or outside of it, cared to rock the boat.

Union membership rates edged up to 34 percent in 1958, then started a slow drop towards the trough of 28 percent they would reach six years later. There were a number of possible explanations: public perception that union leaders had become "fat cats" and that unions had lost touch with "the little guy"; negative fallout from disclosures of union corruption and violence in the United States;[13] the apparent saturation of unions' traditional power bases in manufacturing, mining, construction, and transportation; and an unsympathetic Conservative government headed by John Diefenbaker.

With the Cold War, Communists had gradually been pushed to the sidelines during the late 1940s. By 1950, CCFers and others had rid the CCL of any remaining Communist influence (Morton, 1995:145). The TLC had been slower to get in on the Cold War hysteria, but in 1949 it suspended its largest Communist organization, the Canadian Seamen's Union (Heron, 1989:90); five years later it also got rid of the west coast fishermen's union (Heron, 1989). In hindsight, the TLC may have come to regret expelling the Seamen's Union, which was replaced with the gangster-ridden Seafarers' International Union (SIU), leading to one of the sorriest chapters in Canadian labour history (Heron, 1989). Using intimidation, beatings, and sweetheart deals with companies to defeat other unions, SIU leader Hal Banks would leave a black mark on the Canadian labour movement for years to come. Only after six years and 75 proven instances of violence would the Canadian Labour Congress (successor to the TLC) expel the SIU (Morton and Copp, 1980:233–236).

The Communist purges definitely ended that party's influence within the Canadian labour movement. Surprisingly, they didn't seem to benefit the social democratic CCF, now the only remaining labour-oriented party on the left. Far from growing as a result of its old rival's demise, it fared poorly in most federal and provincial elections through the 1950s (Morton and Copp, 1980:227). Only after the party modernized itself, diluting its socialist agenda and broadening its appeal to middle-class voters after the fashion of the British Labour Party (Heron, 1989:110), would it do better at the polls. This new, more centrist party, known after 1961 as the New Democratic Party (NDP), would play a critical role in the expansion of collective bargaining to the public service and liberalization of federal labour legislation by virtue of the balance-of-power position it held in several Liberal minority governments (Heron, 1989:110–112). Provincially, its impact would be even greater, as NDP governments elected in three Western provinces between 1969 and 1972 would introduce a broad range of progressive labour legislation on issues ranging from occupational health and safety to technological change (Heron, 1989:112).

"THE CONTRIBUTION OF EMPLOYEE PARTICIPATION AND VOICE TO THE SUCCESSFUL IMPLEMENTATION OF NEW TECHNOLOGY, WORK ORGANIZATION AND TRAINING": INSIGHTS FROM FOUR PAPER MILLS

socrates.berkeley.edu/~iir/ncw/wpapers/voos/index.html

Federation Mergers

The decade's major event, in terms of labour politics, was the merger of the two great federations, the TLC and CCL, which took place in 1956, just a year after the American AFL and CIO had merged under the presidency of George Meany. The two long-standing rivals formed a new organization, under the presidency of Montrealer Claude Jodoin, known as the Canadian Labour Congress. The merger appeared to make a good deal of sense, since it would end the union raiding that had become common during the postwar period and would also allow for the pooling of scarce organizational resources (Morton and Copp, 1980:216–220).

Amid the labour movement's growing bureaucratization, there were a few reminders of its stormier past. In 1957, Quebec Premier Maurice Duplessis crushed an illegal strike at Murdochville, Quebec, that resulted when the Gaspé Copper Company refused to recognize a duly certified Steelworkers' local. Provincial police stood by as strike-breakers stoned picketers and hoodlums ransacked the union office. Eventually, two-thirds of the strikers lost their jobs and the union was sued for nearly $3 million (Morton and Copp, 1980:228). In 1959, Newfoundland Premier Joey Smallwood, himself a former socialist and union organizer, decertified the International Woodworkers of America (IWA) during a bitter, but legal, loggers' strike in Badger. A few days later, after vigilantes had smashed the IWA headquarters in Grand Falls, employers signed agreements with a new local union created by Smallwood himself (Morton and Copp, 1980:230–231).

Automation

Fears that technological change, or automation as it was then known, would displace and deskill large numbers of workers resurfaced at the end of the 1950s. The switch from steam to diesel locomotives threatened the jobs of thousands of railroad firemen. The switch to computerized typesetting was an even greater threat to printers' jobs. In numerous other occupations, from mining and logging to banking and postal work, rapidly emerging new technologies transformed the way work was done, in the process putting thousands of workers' jobs and skills at risk.

In a few cases, such as longshoring in Montreal, comprehensive modernization agreements were worked out. Like a similar agreement on the Pacific Coast, the Montreal agreement allowed employers to proceed with mechanization and automation of longshoring work in return for job protection for those working full time on the docks (Picard, 1967). Others were not so lucky. Many Toronto printers lost "their jobs, their savings, and ... their craft" (Morton and Copp, 1980:240) in a lengthy, bitter, and ultimately hopeless strike against computerized typesetting at the city's daily newspapers. During the early 1970s, both the federal government and the three

Western provinces with NDP governments wrote modest protection against the effects of technological change into their labour acts. But the legislation proved largely ineffectual, mainly because labour boards were extremely reluctant to intervene, even in cases where the legislation had clearly been violated (Peirce, 1987).[14]

The Canadian Labour Movement's New Face

The 1960s was a decade of renewed radicalism and questioning of conventional wisdom and received authority in most areas of Canadian life, from economics and politics to music and personal morality. The labour movement was no exception. By the end of the decade, it wore a very different face, mainly as a result of something previously considered unthinkable—full-scale unionization of the public sector, including federal and provincial public servants.

Unlike private sector unionization, which had evolved gradually, public sector unionization came very quickly to Canada once the forces leading to it had been set in motion. Through the 1950s and into the 1960s, the notion of parliamentary sovereignty had been used to deny public sector workers collective bargaining rights. As the sovereignty argument eroded and public sector workers became more militant, there were growing demands that they be allowed to join unions.

By the end of 1964, full collective bargaining rights, including the right to strike, had been granted to most of Quebec's public sector workers (Hébert, 1995:202). Meanwhile, federal public servants, frustrated with years of lagging pay, the transformation of their workplaces into large impersonal bureaucracies (Heron, 1989:106), and an unsympathetic Conservative federal government, were demanding similar rights. Elected in 1963, Lester Pearson's Liberal government initially promised federal public servants collective bargaining rights with binding arbitration (Swimmer, 1995:369). A nation-wide postal strike in 1965 and the Liberals' tenuous minority position, in which the pro-labour NDP held the balance of power, pushed them to go further than that. The result was a piece of comprehensive collective bargaining legislation, the *Public Service Staff Relations Act (PSSRA)*, which broke new ground in a number of different ways. Most notably, the bill gave the union the right to choose between binding arbitration and the conventional conciliation-strike route of resolving disputes (Swimmer, 1995). A Public Service Staff Relations Board was set up to administer the act and determine appropriate bargaining units (Swimmer, 1995:370). To safeguard the public health and welfare during public service strikes, the bill also established a procedure for designating employees whose services were deemed essential (Swimmer, 1995:377).

PSSRA had a number of significant impacts on the labour movement all across the country. To begin with, a number of provinces (including Newfoundland and

New Brunswick) soon followed the federal government's lead, passing their own "mini-PSSRA" bills legalizing full public sector collective bargaining, including the right to strike. Other provinces (including Ontario and Alberta) granted public servants bargaining rights, but substituted binding arbitration for the right to strike. By the early 1970s, some form of collective bargaining covered every provincial government worker in Canada (Fryer, 1995:343–346). By decade's end, collective bargaining rights had likewise been extended to all the country's teachers and health care workers. *PSSRA* and its provincial counterparts also facilitated unionization of professionals and other private sector white-collar workers. Once they saw their public sector colleagues benefitting from unionization, they came to realize that they could, as well. By the 1970s, an increasing number of private sector professionals had taken out union membership (Thompson, 1982).

Even more important, *PSSRA* and the various provincial laws brought large numbers of women into the Canadian labour movement for the first time, since women made up a large proportion of the public sector work force. Among other things, this development would have a significant impact on the public sector unions' bargaining agendas. Unions with large female memberships soon began to demand improved maternity leave provisions, provisions allowing for more flexible working hours, and other benefits reflecting the reality of women's dual roles as workers and homemakers. The relatively greater concentration of professionals in public sector unions led to a greater emphasis on intrinsic working conditions than one would find in most blue-collar unions, and bargaining table demands for in-service training and joint labour-management committees (Ponak: 1982, 351–353).

Private Sector Militancy

The 1960s also saw increased militancy in Canada's private sector unions. In 1966, strikes had reached their highest level in 20 years (Godard, 1994:96), spurred by rising inflation. The middle of the decade saw the previously mentioned postal strike, the country's first national railway strike, a strike along the St. Lawrence Seaway, and disputes at Heinz Foods, Canada Packers, International Nickel, and in B.C.'s logging industry (Morton and Copp, 1980:248–251). Across the country there was a wave of wildcat strikes (in 1966 these amounted to one-third the total number of strikes) and increasing rank-and-file rejection of contracts negotiated by union leaders (Heron, 1989:104; Morton, 1995:109). Alarmed at the growing turbulence in the country's industrial relations system, Prime Minister Pearson struck a Royal Commission under the direction of Dean H.D. (Buzz) Woods of McGill University to see what could be done (Morton and Copp, 1980:253–254). The Woods Task Force report, released in early 1969, recommended relatively minor changes such as the formation of employer associations to balance unions and the creation of a public interest disputes commission to deal with strikes in essential industries. Overall, its message was that the Canadian IR system was, if not perfect, probably among the least of possible evils and that industrial conflict was an inevitable price to be paid for living in a democratic society (Morton and Copp, 1980:262–264).[15]

Changes in Quebec

Nowhere did the Canadian labour movement change more quickly during the 1960s than in the province of Quebec. The changes were greatest of all within the former confessional union movement, which by this time had gone through a number of different metamorphoses to emerge as the leading exponent of radicalism in the province.

Forced to become more militant to compete with other federations that were actively organizing in the province, the CTCC had, during the Second World War, dropped its "Catholic-only" clause and opposition to strikes and started operating more like a conventional trade union (Boivin, 1982:427). Later, under the leadership of Jean Marchand, it played a leading role in the Asbestos strike of 1949 and the opposition to the Duplessis regime during the 1950s. In 1960, it severed its remaining ties with the Catholic church and renamed itself the Confédération des syndicats nationaux (CSN). Buoyed by Duplessis's replacement by Liberal premier Jean Lesage, the CSN grew rapidly in both size and influence during the 1960s. A key player during the "Quiet Revolution," the federation benefitted particularly from the unionization of public sector workers mentioned previously (Boivin, 1982:429–430).

In 1965, Marchand left the CSN for Ottawa, where he would eventually join Pierre Trudeau's cabinet. After his departure, the federation took an increasingly radical and separatist course under Marcel Pépin, losing much of its mainstream public support as the result of a major hospital strike in 1966 and a Montreal Transit strike during Expo 1967 (Boivin, 1982). By 1968, the CSN had expanded its efforts to the quest for a "Second Front" outside collective bargaining, which sought alliances between the labour movement and other progressive organizations such as tenants' groups and credit unions in local "political action committees" (Heron, 1989:117). With other provincial labour organizations, such as the Quebec Federation of Labour (QFL) and teachers' union (CEQ) also taking an increasingly radical stance (Heron, 1989), the CSN in 1971 published two radical manifestos that made the case for an independent and socialist Quebec (Boivin, 1982:430).

Brought together, at least for the time being, by their radicalism, the three major federations in 1972 established a "Common Front" for public sector negotiations with the provincial government involving some 250 000 workers (Boivin, 1982). The failure of those negotiations led to a massive public sector strike, the largest in

Canadian history, which would eventually lead to the jailing of the leaders of all three federations for defying back-to-work orders (Heron, 1989:118). Though the strike spread to the private sector, becoming a general strike in some parts of the province, it ended about a week later (Heron, 1989). The "Common Front" days were to be the high-water mark for both labour radicalism and labour unity in the province. Within two years of the great strike, dislike of the CSN's radicalism had prompted three large groups to break away from the federation (see below for more details). Moreover, the QFL and CSN were back at loggerheads over the organization of construction workers on the James Bay construction site (Boivin, 1982:431), though they remained united in their dislike of the Liberal government. The election of a separatist and pro-labour Parti Quebecois (PQ) government in 1976 arguably helped reduce Quebec labour radicalism, although there would be resurgences, especially in the PQ's second term, when it froze the right to strike and rolled back public sector salaries by almost 20 percent (Heron, 1989:128).

A New Breed of Worker

The young people entering the work force for the first time during the 1960s posed problems both for employers and for the unions seeking to represent their interests. More highly educated than their parents had been, these young people had been raised in a culture of permissiveness and brought up to believe there should be a good deal more to a job than a paycheque. With their disdain for dress codes and traditional social mores generally, they found it hard to adjust to life in mainstream organizations with conventional top-down management practices.[16]

Often they gave their union leaders nearly as hard a time as their employers. Many were impatient with unions' often bureaucratic ways of doing things and with seniority-based systems that left them at the bottom of the ladder. Also, their bargaining agenda often conflicted with that of older, more established workers. Many of the older workers had bought into the postwar compromise whereby unions negotiated for wages and benefits and intrinsic concerns were, in effect, left outside the factory gate or office door. For young people raised with such high expectations of work and life, and who had seldom known real, grinding poverty, the old compromise simply wasn't good enough. It wasn't enough that a job be secure and pay a decent wage, it had to be interesting and socially worthwhile as well.

Younger workers' unhappiness with established ways of doing things was probably a factor in the high rate of wildcats and contract rejections during the 1960s. Later (as we noted in Chapter 3), it would prove a stimulus to the broad range of quality of worklife initiatives introduced during that decade—often in the face of union leaders' indifference or outright hostility.

Those Left Behind

Again, many didn't share in the general prosperity of the 1960s and early 1970s. In big cities like Montreal, immigrant workers, mainly women, continued to toil 50 to 60 hours a week or even longer, exposing themselves to heat, cold, toxic chemicals, and grossly inadequate sanitation in abattoirs, factories, hotels, and restaurants. If they were lucky, they would receive the minimum wage. Many did not. Fearing deportation or dismissal, most of those who didn't were afraid to complain. Even the few who did had no guarantee of success, given the lack of inspectors and of political will to enforce minimum wage and health and safety legislation (Arnopoulos, 1974). For Ontario's farm workers, conditions were little better. At a time when the average industrial wage was $3.17 an hour and the Ontario minimum wage $1.60, the *top* 54 percent of farm workers were averaging $1.71 an hour; fully 94 percent of all fruit and vegetable workers were getting less than the provincial minimum (Ward, 1974:302). Despite such pathetically low wages and primitive working conditions, the provincial government did not extend the minimum wage or other basic employment standards to farm workers (Ward, 1974).

A NEW ERA OF RESTRAINT

Despite a number of differences with the federal government, the Canadian labour movement was, in 1974, in the strongest position it had been in since the end of the Second World War. The wave of public sector legislation that followed *PSSRA* had brought hundreds of thousands of new members into the Canadian labour movement for the first time. Union membership rates had risen from 29 percent of the country's labour force in 1964, to 35 percent in 1974 (Godard, 1994:96–97). Across the country, labour relations acts had been liberalized. A 1971 revision to the *Canada Labour Code* had removed the *Code's* long-standing exclusion of professionals and brought in the country's first technological change provisions. During the early 1970s, similar liberalizations had occurred in several provincial labour acts, including those of New Brunswick, Manitoba, and Saskatchewan.

Politically, as well, the labour movement was in a strong position in 1974, thanks to the growing popularity of its ally, the New Democratic Party. Federally, the NDP held the balance of a power in a minority Liberal government; provincially, it formed the government in three of four Western provinces (Manitoba, Saskatchewan, and British Columbia) and was also a significant player in Ontario.

STATISTICS CANADA "CANADIAN LABOUR FORCE FROM 1926–1975"

www.statcan.ca:80/cgi-bin/Cansim/cansim.cgi?matrix=600&cq=&order_id=

Starting in 1974, all this changed. With the 1973–1974 energy crisis and subsequent wave of inflation and unemployment, the country's economic and political climate turned notably more conservative. The 1974 federal election was an omen of hard times to come. In that election, the NDP lost half its seats (including that of its leader, David Lewis) and its balance-of-power position as Pierre Trudeau's Liberals swept to a strong majority. The next year, B.C.'s NDP government was defeated, and in 1977, the party lost power in Manitoba.

Though he'd ridiculed wage-price controls during his 1974 election campaign, Trudeau introduced a comprehensive three-year program on Thanksgiving Day, 1975 (Reid, 1982). The labour movement was outraged. In protest, it withdrew labour representatives from most tripartite government bodies, such as the Economic Council of Canada, and staged a one-day general strike against the controls and the government's Anti-Inflation Board in 1976. To some (i.e., Panitch and Swartz, 1988), the controls mark the beginning of the end of free collective bargaining in Canada. Even those (i.e., Reid, 1982:501) who felt the controls had been on balance effective and believed the labour movement's fear about them had been largely unfounded admitted that the program "had imposed severe strains on both the social fabric and the industrial-relations system."

When "normal" collective bargaining resumed in 1978, it was in an environment increasingly hostile to workers and their unions, particularly the public sector unions. A wave of public sector strikes, particularly a series of lengthy disputes involving Canada Post (Swimmer, 1995:385–386) and the Montreal Transit system, had soured many Canadians on the whole idea of free collective bargaining in the public sector. By the late 1970s, there were numerous calls for the federal government to abolish its workers' right to strike. Despite strong public pressure, it did not do that. But it did severely restrict its workers' right to strike in two other ways: by increasing the proportion of workers designated as "essential" and thus compelled to work during a strike (Swimmer, 1995; Panitch and Swartz, 1988), and through an increased use of back-to-work legislation (Panitch and Swartz, 1988:31), a device also used by provincial governments.

A second energy crisis, starting in 1979, launched the country into a new inflationary spiral as serious as the 1973–1974 one had been. Federal and provincial governments responded, once again, with wage control legislation—legislation this time aimed exclusively at the public sector. Federal wage restraint legislation limited increases to 6 percent in the first year and 5 percent in the second (Swimmer, 1995). Some provinces' legislation was even more restrictive. This was especially true in Quebec, where the PQ government in 1982 imposed a 20 percent reduction on public sector workers' salaries (Hébert, 1995:222–223), and in B.C., where wage restraint legislation was accompanied by legislation effectively giving the provincial cabinet the authority to terminate any public sector worker unilaterally, under the guise of restraint (Panitch and Swartz, 1988:41).

The 1980s Recession and Its Aftermath

Beginning in 1981, Canada plunged into its most serious recession since the Second World War. In 1983, some 1.3 million Canadians (or more than 12 percent of the country's work force) were officially unemployed (Heron, 1989:125; Morton, 1995:151). In some parts of the country, such as Newfoundland, the official unemployment rate was more than 20 percent.[17] Food banks, which had not been seen since the Great Depression, began to appear in major Canadian cities as unemployment increased and more and more people exhausted their unemployment benefits (Heron, 1989:125–127).

Though the economy started to recover in the mid 1980s in central Canada, many of the high-paying jobs lost in manufacturing and resources never came back. Thereafter, high unemployment would be a more or less permanent feature of the Canadian labour market (Heron, 1989:125; Morton, 1995:151–152). The new jobs that replaced those well-paying jobs were mainly in the low-paying, hard-to-organize private-service sector. Knowing they had few other options if they wanted to replace the thousands of members lost in manufacturing and resources during the recession, the unions made a valiant effort to organize the service industries, focussing their attention on the chartered banks and on retail giants like Eaton's. But Eaton's refused to sign a first collective agreement (Morton, 1995:152), and the bid to unionize the banks proved largely unsuccessful due to determined employer resistance marked by the frequent intimidation, harassment, and transfer of union activists (Lowe, 1980).

A Harder Management Line

In such a difficult economic environment, workers and unions were reluctant to press demands too hard, while management felt it could safely take a much tougher stance in dealing with unions. By the early 1980s, management was starting to bring its own list of demands to the bargaining table. These demands often included outright wage freezes or even rollbacks, reductions in paid holiday time, and cuts in employer-paid benefit plans (Heron, 1989:136–137). By the mid 1980s, some employers were demanding that unions accept **two-tier wage schemes**, whereby new hires were paid far less than experienced workers. To back up their demands for concessions, employers often forced a strike or locked out their workers. Increasingly, they used the threat of closing down or relocating the plant to achieve concessions (Heron, 1989). Given the tough economic environment and increasingly unsympathetic political climate, such threats seemed all too real to most workers. The new employer militancy approach (discussed in some detail in Chapter 3) was most used often in historically anti-union Alberta. There, construction employers virtually destroyed the building trades unions in 1984 by means of a lockout that enabled them to break an expired collective agreement legally (Heron, 1989:136), while Peter Pocklington tried and failed to break the United Food and Commercial Workers (UFCW) union at his Gainer's meatpacking plant in Edmonton during a bitter strike that attracted nation-wide attention (Godard, 1994:380–381).

The Mulroney Years

Life became even more difficult for the Canadian labour movement following the 1984 landslide election of a Conservative federal government under Brian Mulroney. Sharing much of U.S. President Ronald Reagan's political ideology, if not his person-al dislike of unions, Mulroney pushed an agenda featuring large-scale privatization of public enterprises, deregulation of regulated ones, free trade with the United States, and relaxation of foreign investment controls. The effect of this agenda was to great-ly increase foreign competition for Canadian businesses, thereby putting even more pressure on employers to cut labour costs. This in turn led to even more plant clo-sures, a proliferation of mergers and acquisitions, large-scale layoffs, the substitution of technology for human labour, and harder work and longer hours for those who remained—all in the name of "rationalization" (Heron, 1989:134).

Schisms and Breakaways

As if it didn't face difficult enough challenges in its battles with employers and gov-ernments, the Canadian labour movement during this period was becoming increas-ingly divided against itself. The period was marked by major schisms within labour federations, a growing number of breakaways of Canadian branches from U.S.-based international unions, and a number of serious incidents of **union raiding,** or attempts by one union to sign up members of another (Godard, 1994:244).

THE CANADIAN FEDERATION OF LABOUR Traditionally more conservative than most other unions, the building trade unions had long been unhappy with the Canadian Labour Congress (CLC). Major irritants included the CLC's support for the NDP and its refusal to move to a block voting pattern, similar to that of the AFL-CIO, that would give union leaders more power (Heron, 1989:151; Morton, 1995:151). But nothing upset these labour traditionalists more than the CLC's granting of partial autonomy to its Quebec arm, the Quebec Federation of Labour, which allowed con-struction unions that had broken away from the internationals to remain affiliated. CLC leaders, reluctant to aggravate an already difficult situation in Quebec, did not act despite the building trades' protests that the dual unions violated the CLC's con-stitution, whereupon 12 of the construction unions, representing about 350 000 work-ers, withheld their congress dues in 1980 (Heron, 1989; Morton, 1995). A year later, the CLC suspended the building trades unions; in 1982, most of them formed their own federation, a new Canadian Federation of Labour based on internationalism and the apolitical, bread-and-butter approach of Samuel Gompers (see McCambly, 1990).

The building trades' secession from the CLC mirrored a similar schism that had taken place a few years earlier within the Quebec labour movement. Alarmed at what they saw as the CSN's growing radicalism at the time of the Common Front strike in 1972, about 30 000 private sector workers, mainly in textiles, woodworking, and construction, had left the CSN to form their own federation. Like the CFL, this new organization, known as the Centrale des syndicats démocratiques (CSD), was established on apolitical business unionist principles (Boivin, 1982:431,436). Subsequently, other splits inspired by the CSN's radicalism saw groups of 30 000 civil servants and 5000 aluminum workers leaving to form their own independent labour organizations (Boivin, 1982).

The CFL operated quite successfully for 15 years. But in 1997, crippled by the loss of 40 percent of its members after the International Brotherhood of Electrical Workers returned to the CLC, it ceased to operate as a central labour body, leaving its long-time rival as English Canada's only umbrella labour organization (McKinley, 1997). The Federation's venture capital fund, which we discuss in more detail in Chapter 6, was not expected to be affected.

BREAKAWAYS FROM U.S. INTERNATIONALS   The secession of the Canadian branches of U.S. international unions from their parent organizations was not new in the 1980s; however, the trend towards Canadianization of the labour movement gained a higher public profile as the result of several widely publicized breakaways, including most notably that of the Canadian Auto Workers (CAW) from the United Auto Workers (UAW) in 1985.

By the late 1960s and early 1970s, the Canadian branches of U.S.-based international unions had begun breaking away from their parent unions and forming independent unions. The reasons ranged from dislike of U.S. control over the Canadian labour movement and resentment at the poor servicing of Canadian branches, to more specific disagreements over bargaining strategy and political issues such as Canadian unionists' support for the NDP or the Americans' support for the Vietnam War (Heron, 1989:149).

The growing number of secessions from the internationals led the CLC to establish a number of autonomy guidelines for the Canadian branches of U.S. internationals in 1970 and 1974 (discussed in more detail in Chapter 5). By 1980, the CLC reported that the guidelines were providing more freedom for the Canadian branches of internationals (Heron, 1989:150–151). Still, the wave of secessions continued apace. The communications workers left their American parent in 1972, the paper workers in 1974, and energy and chemical workers in 1980 (Heron, 1989:152).

The Canadian Auto Workers' 1985 secession from the United Auto Workers was based to a large extent on bargaining strategy. The Canadian division had refused to go along with the international's concession bargaining approach in the previous round of negotiations and eventually reached a settlement differing significantly from the American one. The bitter dispute that resulted eventually became a major factor in the CAW's departure from the UAW (Craig and Solomon, 1996:186–18; Godard, 1994: 248–249).

UNION MERGERS AND RAIDING   To make up for the membership lost through economic restructuring and deindustrialization, many of the big industrial unions, such as the steelworkers and autoworkers, were forced to look farther afield, to workers in totally unrelated industries. Often they turned to the unorganized. Occasionally, however, they turned to workers already represented by a union, as in the now-celebrated dispute between the CAW and the United Food and Commercial Workers (UFCW) over the right to represent fisheries workers in Atlantic Canada.

In 1987, the 23 000-member Newfoundland branch of the UFCW announced its decision to affiliate with the CAW. The ensuing battle between the two unions, eventually won by the CAW, went before the courts as well as the labour boards and proved a major embarrassment to the labour movement (Craig and Solomon, 1996:170; Heron, 1989:152). The brouhaha did lead to a major change in the way the CLC handles jurisdictional disputes. Until 1988, it had employed a permanent umpire to rule on such disputes. After the CAW-UFCW episode, it brought in tough new anti-raiding rules and gave its executive committee the responsibility of settling jurisdictional disputes itself. But while both these changes probably made sense, they didn't put a stop to raiding. In 1992, the CLC's executive committee imposed heavy sanctions on the International Woodworkers of America's Canadian division for raiding the Canadian Paperworkers Union (Craig and Solomon, 1996:170–171).

Canadian Labour in the Brave New Global Order

As was discussed in some detail in Chapter 2, the past decade has seen fundamental change in the economic and political environment. These changes have led to equally major changes in the way work is organized and scheduled, in unions' strategies, and in national governments' willingness and ability to regulate economic and IR-related issues.

Free Trade and Its Implications

The single most important development here has arguably been the formation of a North American trading bloc (Lipsig-Mumme, 1995), following the implementation of Canada-U.S. and North American free trade agreements in 1989 and 1994,

FIGURE 4.1

A SCHEMATIC OUTLINE OF EVENTS IN THE HISTORY OF TRADE UNION MOVEMENTS IN THE UNITED STATES AND CANADA

The United States

1869 *Knights of Labor*
— uplift unionism
— membership not restricted
— craft and mixed locals

1886–1955 *American Federation of Labor (AFL)*
— a loose federation of craft-oriented unions
— excluded Knights of Labor because of dual unionism
— little activity in politics
— each affiliate was autonomous
— preferred little government intervention

1038–1955 *Congress of Industrial Organizations (CIO)*
— unions expelled from AFL
— wanted to unionize unskilled labourers
— wanted industrial unions
— more active in politics than AFL
— organized mass production workers

1955 *AFL-CIO*
— merger of AFL and CIO affiliated unions
— no-raiding pacts between unions affiliated with each federation
— craft and industrial unions
— conservative philosophy
— supports Democratic party
— code of ethical practices
— little control over affiliates

Canada

1875–1910 *Knights of Labor*
— active in Que., Ont., and N.S.
— uplift unionism
— membership not restricted
— craft and mixed locals
— problems with R.C. Church in Que.

1908–1927 *Trades and Labour Congress (TLC)*
— included Knights of Labor, N.S. Provincial Workman's Assoc. and other Canadian unions
— nationalistic in orientation
— dominated by regional interests
— wanted more Canadian control

1919–1956 *One Big Union (OBU)*
— mainly in western Canada
— dissatisfaction with TLC
— opposed to craft unions
— felt TLC structure not suited to western Canada
— influenced by radical IWW
— played an active role in Winnipeg General Strike of 1919
— became part of CLC in 1956

1927–1940 *All-Canadian Congress of Labour (ACCL)*
— remnants of CFL or 1908, OBU, and CBRE
— wanted industrial unions
— critical of American control
— critical of conservative philosophy of TLC

1940–1956 *Canadian Congress of Labour (CCL)*
— Canadian branches of CIO unions
— remnants of ACCL
— wanted to unionize unskilled labourers
— wanted industrial unions
— active in politics
— organized mass production workers
— wanted less control from U.S.
— wanted more government action than TLC

1956 *Canadian Labour Congress (CLC)*
— merger of TLC and CCL affiliated unions
— no-raiding pacts between unions affiliated with each federation
— craft and industrial unions
— less conservative philosophy than AFL-CIO
— has supported NDP, but link now being revisited
— code of ethics
— little control over affiliates
— standards of self-government to apply mostly to Canadian districts of international unions

FIGURE 4.1
(continued)

1982–1997 *Canadian Federation of Labour (CFL)*
- formed by construction unions
- has some non-construction unions
- wanted more voting power in CLC
- non-partisan political stance
- closer ties with government than CLC
- no raids between CFL and CLC

1991 *Federal Public Service Strike*
- sign of increasing public sector militancy
- result of government imposition of wage freeze
- PSSRB found Treasury Board guilty of bargaining in bad faith with PSAC

1996 *General Motors Strike*
- pattern bargaining in auto industry survived, after a tough fight
- one of many recent strikes in which work intensification and overtime were major issues

1997–1998 *Ontario Teachers' Strikes*
- two of many political strikes against Ontario government, 1996–1998
- a protest against Bill 160, centralizing power over public education in Toronto
- ended abruptly as teachers' unions returned to work
- further wave of teachers' strikes in 1998 over loss of preparation time

Union Developments in Quebec

1900 *Major strike in Quebec City, arbitrated by Archbishop of Quebec*
- confessional unions formed across the province
- meetings dominated largely by clergy
- influenced by Papal encyclicals

1921–1960 *Canadian and Catholic Confederation of Labour (CCCL)*
- founding convention in Hull, Quebec, in 1921
- brought workers together into a confederation
- wanted to keep workers Catholic and French-speaking
- dominated largely by clergy until 1940s
- adhered largely to teachings of Papal encyclicals

1947 *Asbestos strike*
- a turning point in Quebec's economic and social history
- broke ties between government and church
- lay leaders began to play major role in unions after mid-1940s

1960 *Confederation of National Trade Unions (change of name to CNTU)*
- dropped Catholic from name
- has about ten sectors
- became radical during the 1970s, but more pragmatic during the 1990s
- smaller than Quebec Federation of Labour (provincial arm of CLC)
- part of "Common Front" in 1972 and 1982
- QFL and CNTU cooperate and raid

1991 *Social Contracts*
- response to recession of early 1990s
- signed by both CNTU and QFL unions
- mainly in metal and pulp and paper industries
- guarantee long-term labour peace in return for employment stability, joint union-management administration of the agreement

Source: Adapted from Craig and Solomon, 1996.

respectively. In a related move (Reid and Meltz, 1995:47), Canada in 1994 signed on to a broad range of worldwide tariff reductions resulting from a new round of negotiations under the General Agreement on Trade and Tariffs (GATT).

With the formation of broader regional trading blocs, not just in North America but in Europe and Asia as well, it is no longer possible for Canadian employers, workers, or unions even to pretend Canada can insulate itself from larger world economic developments. More immediately, the recent wave of globalization and trade liberalization has had the effect of intensifying the wave of restructuring begun during the late 1980s. By early 1998, restructuring had moved beyond the manufacturing sector. In banking, for example, two proposed mergers (of the Royal Bank and Bank of Montreal and of the Toronto Dominion Bank and Canadian Imperial Bank of Commerce) would have seen control of half the country's domestic banking assets and 70 percent of its total banking assets in the hands of just two banks. As noted in Chapter 3, the Finance Minister rejected these proposed mergers in November 1998. However, the banks may well attempt other mergers in the future.

Already there have been signs that the free trade agreements have had an effect on collective bargaining settlements. In early 1998, for example, workers at Maple Leaf Foods Company in Brampton, Ontario, narrowly approved a deal that saw average wages reduced by more than 40 percent. The deal, which seemed to refute the conventional industrial relations wisdom that Canadian workers would never go in for concession bargaining, was attributed almost entirely to the free trade agreements. Quite simply, without a drastic reduction in labour costs, it appeared that Canadian meat producers could no longer compete with lower-cost producers in the United States and Mexico.

In this new economic order, the wave of plant closings described earlier in the chapter has continued and perhaps even increased. So, too, have the waves of layoffs discussed in Chapter 3. Workers' job security has been a major casualty, as many firms have adopted a "lean production" mode whereby they retain only a small core of permanent workers, using short-term, temporary, or contractual workers to meet peak-period demands. Those few who remain more or less steadily employed must often work longer and harder than in the past, since there are now so many fewer regular employees. The result is a situation where many workers are putting in long overtime hours while unemployment rates remain high (O'Hara, 1993). As we noted in Chapter 2, "atypical" work arrangements, with workers provided little if any job security and few benefits, have by now become so common as to be all but the Canadian norm. The growth of atypical work arrangements poses major organizing challenges for unions, since part-time and temporary workers are normally a good deal more difficult to organize than full-timers.

The Public Sector Squeeze

The decade has been particularly hard on public sector workers. In 1991, the federal government's imposition of a wage freeze caused the Public Service Alliance of Canada to launch its first-ever full-scale national public service strike (Swimmer, 1995). At provincial levels as well, most public sector workers have had to endure wage freezes if not outright rollbacks, and suspension of normal collective bargaining procedures (Fryer, 1995). The growing incidence of the latter has raised concerns about the possible permanent dismantling of public sector collective bargaining (Swimmer and Thompson, 1995:1). Downsizing and program cuts have meant that, as in the private sector, there have been fewer people to do the work needing to be done. Beyond that, large-scale health-care and education restructuring initiatives in Alberta and Ontario have led or are leading to massive layoffs. While different provinces have taken different approaches to the question of public sector restructuring, few public sector workers have escaped unscathed.

Labour's Response

The labour movement has responded in various ways to the unusually severe economic and political pressures just described. In English Canada, especially in the public sector, it has begun to turn more militant again, after a number of years of relative quiescence. In 1996 (see Chapter 12 for more details), the proportion of working-time lost due to strikes was more than twice that of the previous year. In 1997, that proportion increased again (HRDC, 1998). Triggering the increased strike intensity was a pronounced increase in public sector strike activity, much of it in Ontario and much of it a direct protest against provincial government policies (HRDC, 1998). In a number of cases, such as the 1997 Ontario teachers' strike, the aim was as much to win public support as to achieve better collective agreement provisions. In the private sector, the proportion of time lost due to official strikes did not increase nearly as dramatically. However, there were a growing number of informal and unofficial job actions that seemed to point to the likelihood of more formal conflict in the future. In early April 1998, for example, Vancouver taxi drivers blocked off access to the city's airport for several hours in a dispute over proposed increases in licensing fees. Later that month, angry Newfoundland fishers blockaded the main Revenue Canada office in St. John's to protest the planned elimination of the federal government's TAGS compensation program for unemployed fishery workers in the Atlantic fish industry(Peirce, 1998a).

Union Consolidation

At a more strategic level, the past decade has also seen the consolidation of Canada's previously highly fragmented union movement, mainly through a variety of mergers (Heron, 1989; Murray, 1995). The most notable of these involved the Communications

Workers of Canada, Energy and Chemical Workers Union, and Canadian Paperworkers Union, which in 1992 joined forces as the Communications, Energy and Paperworkers Union of Canada, or CEP. The Canadian Auto Workers and Steelworkers have also been heavily involved in merger activity during the decade (Murray, 1995:178; Craig and Solomon, 1996:190–193). These larger unions are likely to be in a better position to carry out intensive organizing and otherwise provide a broad range of services to their members than the smaller ones they replaced.

Closely related to the merger trend, in fact a direct result of it, has been the evolution of a number of industrial unions, including the Auto Workers and Steelworkers, into general or conglomerate unions claiming to represent all workers, not just those in a particular industry. While the trend has led to some jurisdictional disputes such as the CAW-UFCW one discussed earlier, it also offers hope for many currently unorganized private-service sector workers, since the big conglomerate unions have the money and the staff to carry out organizing drives and have increasingly shown interest in signing up private-service sector workers in a bid to bolster their flagging membership ranks. For example, the Steelworkers, who had already been organizing groups as diverse as zoo and security guards, hotel and restaurant workers, and Montessori teachers, increased their private-service sector organizing following their 1993 merger with the Canadian section of the Retail, Wholesale and Department Store union (Murray, 1995:178). The CAW has recently organized at least two British Columbia branches of the Starbucks coffee chain (Murdock, 1997). Most dramatically of all, the Teamsters Union recently declared "North America-wide war" on McDonald's after the chain closed a branch in Saint-Hubert, Quebec, that had just won official union certification (King, 1998). The move received the strong support from officials at both the Quebec Federation of Labour and the Canadian Labour Congress (King, 1998).

Revisiting the NDP Link

Earlier, we indicated that the English-Canadian labour movement has generally relied on the New Democratic Party to help it achieve its political objectives, such as labour law reform or improved health and safety legislation. Union support was critical to the election of NDP provincial governments in Ontario, Saskatchewan, and British Columbia early in the 1990s. As in the past (Heron, 1989), these governments often proved disappointing to their labour supporters once in office (Lipsig-Mumme, 1995:207). This was especially true in Ontario, where, in 1993, the NDP government imposed a "social contract" suspending free public sector collective bargaining and forcing workers to take unpaid days off (Murray, 1995:189). Loss of labour support, especially from the public sector unions, was clearly a factor in the NDP's disastrous 1993 federal election showing and in its defeat in the 1995 Ontario election. Though the party rebounded somewhat in the 1997 federal election, doing particularly well in the Atlantic region, its failure to win a single Ontario seat suggested that the tensions resulting from the "social contract" had not yet been resolved. Similar tensions may be emerging in Quebec regarding the labour movement's link to the Parti Quebecois, as a result of provincial government cutbacks to health care and education.[18] At the time of writing, the labour movement's strategy regarding the NDP remains unclear, particularly in Ontario. What can be said is that the party will have to win far more votes nationally than it did in the two previous federal elections if it is to remain a strong voice on behalf of labour and ordinary working people.

Labour Strategy in Quebec

In Quebec, the labour movement has responded very differently to the economic crisis than it has in the rest of Canada. During the 1970s, the Quebec labour movement was by far the most radical in the country. Now, supported by a succession of provincial governments that have taken a far more active role in socio-economic planning than even most NDP governments in English Canada, its strategy has become one of tripartite cooperation with employers and government in the interest of creating and maintaining jobs (Lipsig-Mumme, 1995; Boivin and Déom, 1995). Increasingly, both the Quebec Federation of Labour (QFL) and Confederation of National Trade Unions (CSN) have signed on to long-term peace agreements, agreements that, unlike the botched Ontario experiment, can legitimately be called social contracts, since the unions have been full partners in negotiating and implementing them (Boivin and Déom, 1995:461). The most widely publicized examples are in the steel industry (Verma and Warrian, 1992:128–129); others have been negotiated in the pulp and paper and garment industries (Boivin and Déom, 1995:461). In return for a long-term guarantee of labour peace (generally for five years or more), the union receives employment security for its members and is given joint administration of the agreement. In addition, employees are provided with full information about the firm's financial situation. To help compensate the union for giving up its right to strike for five years or longer, most agreements allow for arbitration of monetary clauses after three years (Boivin and Déom, 1995).

While it is not clear just how widely the Quebec social contracts have been adopted, they do appear to have had a positive effect on labour-management relations in the province. After long being among the country's most strike-prone jurisdictions (Anderson and Gunderson, 1982:227; Gunderson, Ponak, and Hyatt, 1995:380), by 1997, Quebec was among the country's *least* strike-prone provinces, accounting for only about 6 percent of all working-time lost due to strikes, even though it is home to about one-quarter of the country's union members (HRDC, 1998).

MOVING INTO THE TWENTY-FIRST CENTURY

As the decade and century draw to a close, Canada's labour movement finds itself in an increasingly embattled position. The problems are perhaps most obvious in the public sector, where many union members enjoy few substantive bargaining rights. Winning back those rights, in the face of continuing federal and provincial government cutbacks, will be a major challenge for the labour movement.

Throughout most of the past 25 years, it has generally been assumed that the nationalization of the Canadian labour movement was a healthy development (Lipsig-Mumme, 1989). In the new, global economy marked by strong regional trading blocks, this may no longer be such a safe assumption (Lipsig-Mumme, 1995). Perhaps genuinely international unions (not the U.S.-dominated organizations that up to now have been referred to as such) are the logical answer to globalization and the growing power exerted by multinational corporations. In deciding how best to adapt to the new global economic order, Canada's unionists will have to weigh the possible merits of such broad-based bargaining against the likely loss of autonomy it will entail (see Lipsig-Mumme, 1995:218).

These are not the only challenges the labour movement will face. The link between labour and the NDP (or PQ in Quebec) will bear continuing examination. Unions will need to continue to refine their organizing and mass-mobilization techniques to reach the growing number of part-time private-service sector workers and homeworkers. And they will need to broaden their efforts to build coalitions with church and women's groups, social justice organizations, and environmental groups to achieve such objectives as a shorter work week (*Better Times*, 1997) and family-friendly work schedules.

Canada's relatively steady union membership rates are in contrast to the situation in the United States, where rates have been dropping steadily for the past 30 years (Murray, 1995:164). The labour movement's ability to maintain those rates, in the face of an increasingly difficult economic and political environment, suggests that it possesses considerable resiliency. It will need all that resiliency and more if it is to meet the challenges it is likely to face at the beginning of the twenty-first century.

QUESTIONS FOR DISCUSSION

1) What did you know about unions and Canadian labour history at the start of this course? What was your impression of unions and what they do?

2) What were some of the barriers to unions found in most industrialized countries?

3) What were some barriers unique to Canada?

4) How did the Quebec labour movement develop differently from the English-Canadian one?

5) Why was the Canadian labour movement closely tied to the American one for many years? What factors contributed to the loosening or severing of many of those ties?

6) What was the significance of the Berlin Convention of 1902 to the development of the Canadian labour movement?

7) Explain why the First World War marked a watershed in the history of the Canadian labour movement.

8) Why did the Canadian labour movement become more militant during the two world wars?

9) How did the industrial unionism introduced during the 1930s and 1940s differ from traditional craft unionism?

10) Did the industrial unionism concept succeed in bringing unionization to all Canadian workers who wished to join? Why, or why not?

11) Do you think Mackenzie King helped or hindered the development of the Canadian labour movement?

12) How has the Canadian labour movement benefitted from its affiliation with political parties such as the NDP? Why are many in the labour movement now reviewing the linkages between it and the NDP (and the Parti Quebecois in Quebec)?

13) In your view, what are the biggest challenges facing the Canadian labour movement today? How can it best meet those challenges?

SUGGESTIONS FOR FURTHER READING

Heron, Craig. (1996). *The Canadian labour movement: A short history.* Toronto: Lorimer. First published in 1989, this has become a classic thanks to its readable style and the vivid picture it portrays of the lives of Canadian working people. The introductory section provides an extremely useful discussion of the barriers to the formation of an independent Canadian labour movement.

MacDowell, Laurel Sefton, and Ian Radforth (Eds.). (1991). *Canadian working class history.* Toronto: Canadian Scholars' Press. An extremely useful collection of articles covering many different aspects of Canadian labour history, from pre-Confederation days right through to modern times. Contains a number of articles on the role of women and immigrants—information that is often hard to obtain elsewhere.

Morton, Desmond. (1990). *Working people: An illustrated history of the Canadian labour movement.* Toronto: Summerhill. Another very readable history of the Canadian labour movement that has gone through several editions. Excellent illustrations. Those with a real taste for history may wish to compare Morton's institutionalist perspective with Heron's political economy one. Both books are well worth reading.

ENDNOTES

1 As noted by Heron (1989:13), similar legislation was passed by the Canada West legislature in 1847.

2 As noted by Morton and Copp (1980:34), the revised act excluded workers in positions involving public safety, such as gas and water and railway strikes. These workers still had no legal right to strike.

3 Since the First World War, Berlin has been known as Kitchener.

4 In fairness, Gompers's dislike of dual unions was not without cause. In 1885, according to Morton and Copp (1980:58), his own Cigar Markers Union had been undercut in a strike by the Knights, who had imposed their own rival union label.

5 This contention seems logical enough, given that Canada was the last major western industrialized country to grant its workers collective bargaining rights.

6 As Morton (1995:138) notes, the nickname is somewhat ironic, given that the plan was invented by none other than Canada's own Mackenzie King, during his stint as labour consultant to the Rockefellers.

7 As Boivin (1982:437) notes, between 1915 and 1936, the Catholic unions accounted for only nine, or less than 2 percent, of the strikes officially called in Quebec.

8 That is, 11 *private sector* jurisdictions. When the various public sector jurisdictions are taken into account, the number becomes several times that.

9 In 1931 alone, according to White, there were more than 7000 deportations. Between 1903–1928, deportations had averaged slightly more than 1000 per year.

10 Domestics and farm workers were excluded, as was management.

11 On early postwar Atlantic labour law, see Forsey (1985). On Alberta's law, see Finkel (1986).

12 I am indebted to Forrest (1997) for many of the ideas contained in this paragraph.

13 See Morton and Copp (1989:233–234). In 1959, these disclosures would lead to the passage of the *Landrum-Griffin Act,* which imposed substantial restrictions on unions' internal operations with an eye to preventing further union racketeering.

14 Through 1985 (Peirce, 1987:69), the Canada Board had accepted only 1 of 25 technological change applications brought before it under the federal legislation.

15 On a similar note, see Crispo (1982).

16 For much of this discussion, I'm indebted to Heron (1989:103–104).

17 Real unemployment rates were likely much higher, as readers will recall from the discussion of alternative measures of unemployment in Chapter 2.

18 A CBC Radio News report on August 25, 1998 indicated that a number of teachers had heckled Premier Lucien Bouchard during a political speech the night before.

CHAPTER 5

UNION MEMBERSHIP
AND STRUCTURE

Volunteer union officials, like the steward shown here talking to a member about her grievance, put in hundreds of thousands of unpaid hours each year and are really what keep the organizations going in many cases.

Unions are the organizations most directly responsible for representing the interests of Canada's working people. We begin this chapter with a brief look at what unions are and at the functions they serve. Next we look at changing patterns of union membership, both for Canada as a whole and within different industries and provinces. Among the issues considered here is the divergence between Canadian and American union membership rates. The chapter then considers the structure of the Canadian labour movement, looking at activities carried out at the local, provincial, and national level, and at the role played by international unions based outside Canada—a distinctive feature of the Canadian labour movement. We conclude with a discussion of union democracy, or the extent to which unions are responsive to their members' wishes.

UNIONS: A QUICK OVERVIEW

Unions have been defined as workers' associations formed to enhance their power in dealings with employers (Craig and Solomon, 1996:9), particularly in negotiating the terms and conditions under which work is performed and in handling workers' grievances. But while collective bargaining and grievance-handling are their core functions, unions do many other things as well. In Canada, as in most other countries, many unions are heavily involved in political action aimed at passing legislation that will advance the interests of working people. Beyond that, union political activities may include joining coalitions with other organizations such as anti-poverty groups, and serving on joint union-employer industry panels aimed at the advancing the interests of a particular industry, such as the Canadian Steel Trade and Employment Conference (Verma and Warrian, 1992). In recent years, unions have also become increasingly involved in publicity campaigns of various kinds. Some of the campaigns are rather specifically focussed on mobilizing support for specific bargaining items. Other are designed to call public attention to problems of a more general nature, such as ongoing cutbacks in the federal and provincial governments. We will be looking at the various types of union activity in more detail in the union action section of the next chapter.

Before we get to that, it's important to look at the changing patterns of union membership in Canada, and at the structure of the country's labour movement, to get a better sense of how unions operate and why they operate as they do. As we'll soon see, while overall union membership rates have remained quite stable, there has been considerable change in the composition of the labour movement. In particular, the movement includes many more women and many more professional and white-collar workers than it did just a generation ago. As well, the movement's structure has changed significantly, with new labour federations springing up both at the national level and in Quebec, and many traditional industrial unions expanding their organizing efforts in an attempt to attract workers from the private-service sector. It is to these questions of union membership and structure that we now turn.

UNION MEMBERSHIP

National Membership Trends

Except for brief periods of decline during the early 1920s, 1930s, and 1960s, Canadian union membership has grown steadily throughout most of the twentieth century. In 1911 (Eaton, 1975, not shown in table), there were about 130 000 union members in Canada. By 1945, that number had grown to just over 700 000. As of 1997 (see Table 5.1), there were just over four million Canadian union members. Through the 1990s, union membership has not declined, but it also hasn't increased.

Table 5.1

	UNION MEMBERSHIP AND UNION DENSITY, CANADA AND THE UNITED STATES, 1945–1997			
Year	Union Membership Canada (thousands)	Union Membership U.S. (thousands)	Union Density Canada (%)	Union Density U.S. (%)
1945	711	12 254	24.2	30.4
1946	832	12 936	27.9	31.1
1947	912	14 067	29.1	32.1
1948	978	14 272	30.3	31.8
1949	1 006	13 936	29.5	31.9
1950	—	14 294	—	31.6
1951	1 029	15 139	28.4	31.7
1952	1 146	15 632	30.2	32.0
1953	1 220	16 310	33.0	32.5
1954	1 268	15 809	33.8	32.3
1955	1 268	16 217	33.7	31.8
1956	1 352	16 446	33.3	31.4
1957	1 386	16 498	32.4	31.2
1958	1 454	15 571	34.2	30.3
1959	1 459	15 438	33.3	29.0
1960	1 459	15 516	32.3	28.6
1961	1 447	15 401	31.6	28.5
1962	1 423	16 894	30.2	30.4
1963	1 449	17 133	29.8	30.2
1964	1 493	17 597	29.4	30.2
1965	1 589	18 269	29.7	30.1
1966	1 736	18 922	30.7	29.6
1967	1 921	19 668	32.3	29.9
1968	2 010	20 017	33.1	29.5
1969	2 075	20 186	32.5	28.7
1970	2 173	20 990	33.6	29.6
1971	2 231	20 711	32.4	29.1
1972	2 388	21 206	33.9	28.8
1973	2 591	21 881	35.4	28.5
1974	2 732	22 165	35.2	28.3
1975	2 884	22 207	35.6	28.9
1976	3 042	22 153	36.9	27.9
1977	3 149	21 632	36.3	26.2
1978	3 278	21 757	37.1	25.1
1979	—	22 025	—	24.5
1980	3 397	20 968	35.7	23.2
1981	3 487	20 647	35.4	22.6
1982	3 617	19 571	35.7	21.9
1983	3 563	18 634	36.4	20.7
1984	3 651	17 340	37.2	18.3

Table 5.1 (continued)

Year	Union Membership Canada (thousands)	Union Membership U.S. (thousands)	Union Density Canada (%)	Union Density U.S. (%)
1985	3 666	16 996	36.4	18.3
1986	3 730	16 975	36.0	17.4
1987	3 782	16 913	35.2	16.5
1988	3 841	17 002	34.8	16.1
1989	3 944	16 960	34.5	15.7
1990	4 031	16 740	36.2	15.2
1991	4 068	16 568	34.7	15.3
1992	4 089	16 390	35.7	15.1
1993	4 071	16 598	35.8	15.8
1994	4 078	16 748	35.6	15.5
1995	4 003	16 360	34.3	14.9
1996	4 033	16 269	33.9	14.5
1997	4 074	N/A	34.1	N/A

Notes: Union density is defined as the percentage of non-agricultural paid workers belonging to unions. No figure is reported for 1950 because the reference date of Labour Canada's survey was changed from Dec. 31 to Jan. 1 in that year. No survey was conducted in 1979. Data for Canada are not strictly comparable before and after 1978 because the number of paid non-agricultural workers was adjusted upwards after that year. Data for the United States are not strictly comparable before and after 1983 because of the different sources used by Kumar for U.S. union membership figures. Union membership data were not available for 1997.

Sources: For Canada, 1946–1970, Eaton, 1975. For 1971–1976, Labour Canada, 1993, *Directory of Labour Organizations in Canada*, p. xvi, Table 1. For 1977–1997, HRDC, 1996 and 1997, *Directory of Labour Organizations in Canada*. For the U.S., 1945–1992, Kumar, 1993. For 1993–1996, Bureau of Labor Statistics, U.S. Dept. of Labor. The Dept. of Labor statistics are not entirely consistent with those used by Kumar; however, the differences are not great.

This stagnation of union membership growth is in sharp contrast to the roughly 400 000 member increase posted between 1980 and 1987 and nearly 1 million member increase posted between 1970 and 1977.

Union density, or the percentage of organizable workers belonging to unions,[1] has also generally increased throughout most of the century, again excepting brief periods of decline during the early 1920s and 1960s. It should be noted, however, that union density has not increased over the past two decades and that it has been declining slowly but fairly steadily since 1984.

HUMAN RESOURCES DEVELOPMENT CANADA PAGE LINKS TO MANY FEDERAL AND PROVINCIAL UNIONS, LOCALS, AND LABOUR COUNCILS

www.eoa-hrdc.com/3540/html/unions.htm

In 1921, the first year for which we have density data, Canadian union density stood at 16 percent (Eaton, 1975). This figure dropped to 12 percent through most of the 1920s, but rose steadily during the 1930s and soared during the Second World War, reaching a level of just more than 24 percent by 1945 (see Table 5.1). From 1945 through 1958, union density rose steadily to just more than 34 percent. The next six years saw a decline, to just more than 29 percent in 1964, but then membership rates started rising again, peaking at 37.5 percent in 1977. Between 1977 and 1984, union density hovered between 35 and 37 percent; since 1984, it has been slowly declining to its current level of 34 percent.

Why have union membership and density rates risen and fallen as they have? As we pointed out in the previous chapter, labour shortages during both world wars increased workers' power relative to that of employers and made it easier for them to join unions. In addition, the extension of the *IDI Act* to all war industries encouraged union organization, especially during the First World War (Morton, 1995:139). The declines in membership and density levels during the 1920s were due largely to a determined employer anti-union offensive, facilitated by a postwar depression and by the government's dropping of wartime *IDI* restrictions against intimidation and harassment of union activists. The two major periods of growth during the post-Second World War period, those from 1945 to 1958, and 1965 through 1977, can be closely linked to legislative changes making it easier for workers to join unions. As we noted in the labour history chapter, *PC 1003*, passed in 1944, extended unionization rights to most blue-collar workers. The decade or so following passage of this legislation saw the organization of large numbers of semi-skilled workers in heavy industries such as autos, steel, rubber, and meatpacking. Similarly, large numbers of public servants and other public sector workers such as teachers and nurses entered the labour movement during the decade or so after the passage of major public sector legislation across Canada.

 "KEY EVENTS IN THE HISTORY OF THE ILGWU
www.ilr.cornell.edu/library/Bookshelf/HotTopics/UNITE/
UNITE_Merger/KeyEvents_ILGWU.html

The lack of any major new legislative initiatives comparable to *PC 1003* or the more recent *Public Service Staff Relations Act* may be one reason why union growth has slowed over the past two decades. As for the recent stagnation in growth and decline in density, the major reason is probably the loss of hundreds of thousands of manufacturing jobs, most in heavily unionized sectors (Morton, 1995:153; Godard, 1994:421). Yet despite severe losses in traditional manufacturing strongholds, the Canadian labour movement as a whole has fared better than those of many other industrialized countries, such as Britain, Japan, Australia, and the United States (Bamber and Whitehouse, 1993:310), all of which have experienced significant declines in union density since 1980.

Changing Union Membership Components

Growing Unionization of Women

While overall Canadian union density rates have remained fairly steady, this apparent stability masks many changes in the composition of the Canadian labour movement. Forty years ago, the typical Canadian union member was white, male, and employed full-time at a blue-collar job. Today, nearly half the country's union members are women (see Figure 5.1), and people from many different religious and ethnic minorities have joined the labour movement. As we will see later on, sizeable numbers of part-timers have become union members, and white-collar workers are now nearly as likely to be members as blue-collar workers.

BIBLIOGRAPHY OF WOMEN'S LABOR HISTORY, FROM ILLINOIS LABOR HISTORY SOCIETY
www.kentlaw.edu/ilhs/bibliogw.html

Perhaps the single greatest change has been the growing number of women in the labour movement. As late as 1967, fewer than 20 percent of the country's union members were women. The male union density rate (41 percent) was well over twice the female density rate of 16 percent.

Virtually all of the 100 percent increase in overall Canadian union membership since 1967 has come from women (Akyeampong, 1997). As a result, women now make up almost 46 percent of the country's union members, and their density rate of just under 30 percent is nearly that of men at 32 percent (see Tables 5.2 and 5.3). The two major reasons for this large increase in female union membership are women's

FIGURE 5.1

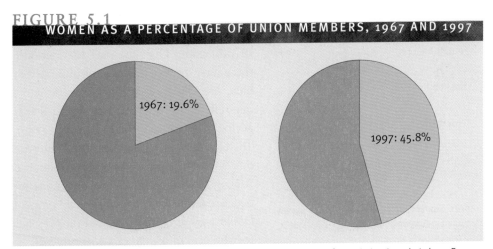

WOMEN AS A PERCENTAGE OF UNION MEMBERS, 1967 AND 1997

1967: 19.6%

1997: 45.8%

Source: For 1967, CALURA (1967); for 1997 (January to September average), Statistics Canada Labour Force Survey, Cat. No. 71-001-XPB, as quoted in Akyeampong (1997).

growing participation in the labour force (discussed in detail in Chapter 2) and the extension of unionization to the public sector, where large numbers of women work. By 1991 (Swimmer and Thompson, 1995:4), some 60 percent of all public sector union members were women; in the private sector, the figure was only 22 percent.

It is somewhat harder to pinpoint the reasons for the corresponding decline in male union density. However, one reason may well have been the recent wave of deindustrialization (also discussed in Chapter 2), which has resulted in the loss of hundreds of thousands of manufacturing jobs, many in traditionally heavily unionized sectors.[2]

Union Membership by Province

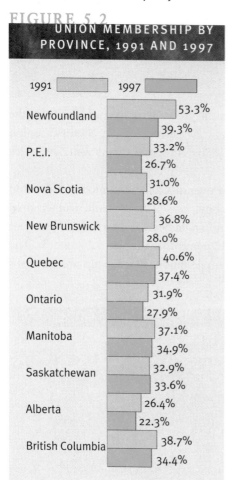

FIGURE 5.2

UNION MEMBERSHIP BY PROVINCE, 1991 AND 1997

1991 [   ]   1997 [   ]

	1991	1997
Newfoundland		53.3%
	39.3%	
P.E.I.		33.2%
	26.7%	
Nova Scotia		31.0%
	28.6%	
New Brunswick		36.8%
	28.0%	
Quebec		40.6%
	37.4%	
Ontario		31.9%
	27.9%	
Manitoba		37.1%
	34.9%	
Saskatchewan		32.9%
	33.6%	
Alberta		26.4%
	22.3%	
British Columbia		38.7%
	34.4%	

Sources: Sources: for 1997: Labour Force Survey as quoted in Akyeampong (1997), p. 48, Table 2; for 1991, CALURA, 1993:25.

For some time, there has been a good deal of variation in provincial union membership rates. In 1997, provincial union density rates ranged from a low of just over 22 percent in Alberta to a high of more than 39 percent in Newfoundland (see Figure 5.2). In 1991, the range was even greater: from 26 percent in Alberta to 53 percent in Newfoundland.[3] By and large, provincial rankings stayed pretty much the same. Quebec, British Columbia, and Manitoba ranked above the national average both times, while Ontario, Nova Scotia, and Prince Edward Island were well below it.

What accounts for differing provincial union membership rates? The subject is one of increasing interest within the Canadian IR profession. Over the past two decades, there have been a number of studies that have shed light on various aspects of the question (see, for example, Maki, 1982; Meltz, 1989b; Ng, 1992; Martinello, 1996). To date, however, the definitive study on this important issue has yet to appear. Among the determinants most often identified are *industrial structure*, the type of *labour legislation* in place, and the presence (or absence) of *pro-labour governments*.

Certain industries, such as forestry and transportation, have traditionally been heavily unionized. Certain others, such as agriculture and finance, have traditionally had few unions. It follows that provinces with large numbers of heavily unionized industries should, other things being equal, have higher union membership rates than provinces with few such industries. The existence of strong forestry, pulp and paper, and (until recently) fishing sectors in Newfoundland and British Columbia is likely one reason for these provinces' relatively high density rates. Conversely, Prince Edward Island's focus on agriculture and lack of a strong industrial base may be one reason why that province has generally had union density rates well below the national average.

CONSTRUCTION LABOUR RELATIONS ALBERTA
www.clra.org

An equally if not more important factor is the type of labour legislation a province has in place. Clearly, certain types of provisions can help union growth, while other types are more likely to retard it.[4] For example (Peirce, 1989), some provinces have relatively liberal exclusion policies governing who can and cannot join unions, barring only management and confidential labour relations personnel. Others have more restrictive policies that serve to prevent people such as professionals, domestics, and farm workers from joining unions in addition to the groups already mentioned. Not surprisingly, membership rates are generally higher in the provinces with liberal exclusion policies than in those with restrictive ones.

Another relevant factor is the presence of a pro-labour (NDP or Parti Quebecois) government that can help the labour movement advance its cause in the political arena. As Maki (1982) has suggested, such governments can help increase union membership both directly, by passing legislation designed to make it easier for unions to attract new members, and indirectly, by improving labour's public profile (as when unionists are appointed to cabinet positions), thus making union membership seem a more attractive proposition. Maki's study has directly linked the presence of NDP governments to higher union membership rates. Similar comparative studies (see Freeman, 1989; Bean, 1994) have linked support for labour or social democratic parties to increased union membership rates in various countries that are members of the Organisation for Economic Co-operation and Development (OECD).

More recent evidence lends support to Maki's study. Except for Newfoundland, all of the provinces whose union membership rates are above the national average have at some point had NDP or PQ governments. In contrast, only one of the provinces (Ontario) with below-average density rates has ever had an NDP or PQ government, and in that case the government served just one term, which may not have been long enough to have made a lasting difference.[5]

Unionization Rates by Industry

Union membership rates vary even more by industry than they do by province. For 1997, density rates ranged from just more than 2 percent in agriculture to 66 percent in public administration (see Table 5.2).[6] Other heavily unionized industries included utilities and transportation/communication/storage, both "quasi-public" in that they are marked by a high degree of public ownership and regulation (see Murray, 1995). Manufacturing and construction had density rates near the national average, while trade and finance/insurance/real estate were both well below it.

Over the years there have been major shifts in the composition of Canadian union membership by industry. While the public sector has been making up an increasingly large share of the labour movement, the proportion contributed by traditionally heavily unionized private-sector industries such as manufacturing and construction has been steadily declining. In 1966 (Murray, 1995:167), manufacturing accounted for 39 percent of the country's union members. By 1977 (Chaison, 1982:151), its share had dropped to 28 percent; by 1997 (see Table 5.2), that figure was less than 20 percent. As Murray (1995:167) notes, this shift has been the result both of declining density rates and of an absolute decline in the numbers of union

Table 5.2

UNION MEMBERSHIP AND DENSITY BY WORK STATUS AND INDUSTRY, 1997		
Work Status	**Membership (thousands)**	**Density (%)**
Full-time	3 096	33.2
Part-time	451	21.7
Industry		
Goods-producing industries	957	31.8
Agriculture	3	2.2
Other primary	68	28.5
Manufacturing	679	33.2
Construction	123	26.6
Utilities	84	62.1
Service-producing industries	2 590	30.8
Trans., comm. and storage	338	44.1
Trade	229	11.9
FIRE*	62	9.4
CBPS[†]	1 436	33.8
Public Administration	525	65.5

* FIRE = Finance, Insurance and Real Estate
[†] CBPS = Community, Business and Personal Services

Sources: Labour Force Survey (1997), as quoted in Akyeampong (1997), p. 48, Table 2.

members employed in the manufacturing sector. Between 1966 and 1997, the manufacturing density rate dropped from 44 percent (Murray, 1995) to 33 percent (Table 5.2). This decline can hardly be considered surprising, given that, between 1977 and 1997 alone, the number of union members employed in manufacturing dropped by nearly one-quarter, from 869 000 (Chaison, 1982:151) to 679 000 (Table 5.2). Similarly, in construction, the industry's share of the country's union members dropped from 10 percent in 1977 (Chaison, 1982:151) to 8 percent through the 1980s (Rose, 1992; WID, 1997) and 3.5 percent in 1997 (Table 5.2). The decline in this industry's density rate was even greater than the corresponding decline in manufacturing. In 1977 (Rose, 1982:400), about two-thirds of all construction workers were union members. By 1997 (Table 5.2), the rate had dropped to 27 percent, or just over one-quarter.

In contrast, membership rates have been rising for such private-service industries as trade and finance/insurance/real estate. For example, in 1977 (Chaison, 1982:151), fewer than 8000 union members were employed in finance, insurance, and real estate. This figure represented only about 0.2 percent of the country's total union membership. By 1997, there were about 62 000 union members from this sector, or just under 2 percent of the national total (Table 5.2). Similarly, in trade, the number of union members rose from 132 000 to 229 000 between 1977 and 1997, while the industry's share of total Canadian union membership increased from 4 percent to 6.5 percent. While such increases are certainly encouraging to the labour movement, it remains to be seen whether the private-service sector, which in much of the Western industrialized world has typically had lower membership rates than either the public sector or private goods-producing sector (see Clegg, 1976), can make up for the heavy membership losses that have already occurred in such traditional strongholds as manufacturing and construction, and that could well occur in the public sector as cash-strapped governments follow the lead of Ontario and Alberta and downsize and restructure public services such as health care and education.

Other Union Membership Components

PUBLIC VERSUS PRIVATE SECTOR STATUS   As has been the case for some time (see Rose, 1995), the public sector continues to be far more heavily unionized than the private sector. In 1997 (Akyeampong, 1997), more than 72 percent of Canadian public sector workers were unionized, as opposed to just under 22 percent of the country's private sector workers. The extremely high unionization rates in such sectors as public administration (66 percent), education, and health care explains why nearly half the country's union members come from the public sector, even though only slightly more than one-quarter of all Canadians are employed there (Swimmer and Thompson, 1995:4).

FULL VERSUS PART-TIME STATUS   As has also been the case for some time (see England, 1987), part-time workers are significantly less likely to be union members than full-timers. In 1997 (Akyeampong, 1997), the density rate for full-timers was just over 33 percent, compared to a rate of just under 22 percent for part-timers. The lower unionization rate for part-timers may reflect, among other things, the greater difficulty and expense of organizing these workers, many of whom work in the traditionally non-union private-service sector.

AGE AND EDUCATIONAL ATTAINMENT   Generally, union membership rates do not appear to be very strongly affected by individuals' age or educational attainment,[7] except that very young workers (those aged 15 to 24) are far less likely than others to be union members. For workers aged 15 to 24, the 1997 density rate was just under 11 percent. For other age groups, the range was from 32 to 44 percent, the latter being the rate for workers aged 45 to 54. The likeliest explanations for the extremely low density rate among young workers are the high proportion of young workers who work part-time (see Chapter 2 for more details) and the frequency with which young people tend to change jobs. As is noted in more detail in the section on job tenure, those who don't keep their jobs for very long are extremely unlikely to become union members.

Educational attainment appears to be of little more importance than age in determining a worker's union membership status. The likeliest to join unions were people with university degrees (37 percent), possibly reflecting a high concentration of educated individuals in the heavily unionized public sector, which more than balanced out the large number of excluded managers and administrators with university degrees. Next likeliest to join were those with a postsecondary certificate or diploma (34 percent) and those with Grade 8 or less (33 percent). Those least likely to join were individuals with some postsecondary education, whose 1997 density rate was just under 23 percent.

FIRM SIZE   Those working in large establishments are far more likely to be union members than those working in small ones. While only 12 percent of those in firms with fewer than 20 employees were union members, the ratio rose to 31 percent in firms of 20 to 99 employees, 47 percent in firms of 100 to 500 employees, and 58 percent in firms of more than 500 employees. Given these figures, the fact that most recent job growth has been in small or medium-sized businesses does not augur well for the Canadian labour movement.

JOB TENURE   As with firm size, union density rates rise with increased job tenure. Only 13 percent of all workers with a year or less on the job belong to a union, and the density rate is still low (20 percent) for those with one to five years' service. After five years, the likelihood of union membership is greatly increased. For those with five to nine years' tenure, the density rate is 36 percent, and for those with more than 14 years, it rises to 58 percent. Although this last group of experienced workers makes up only 20 percent of the country's employed labour force, it accounts for nearly two-fifths of all Canadian union members.

Canadian Versus American Union Membership Rates

Many of the same factors that explain differing union membership rates in different Canadian provinces may also help explain differing Canadian and American union membership rates. While a number of studies of both Canadian and American union membership growth have found economic factors to be of great significance (Ashenfelter and Pencavel, 1969; Bain and Elsheikh, 1976; Eastman, 1983), economic factors arguably do little to explain the growing divergence in Canadian and American union membership rates over the past 35 years, a period when Canada and the United States have had roughly similar economic experiences and when their economies have become increasingly integrated.

"U.S. LABOR WARS: BOTTOM TO TOP" BY KIM MOODY
www.wilpaterson.edu/~newpol/issue20/moody20.htm

In 1965, as Table 5.1 shows, American union density was just slightly higher than that of Canada, both being around 30 percent. By 1980, the Canadian rate had risen to almost 36 percent, or more than half again greater than the U.S. rate of just over 23 percent. Since 1986, the Canadian rate has invariably been more than twice that of the United States.

Industrial relations scholars have put forward a variety of explanations for the growing divergence in the two countries' membership rates. One is differing public labour policy. In Canada, such policy has generally been more supportive of unions than it has in the United States.

First, union security is more carefully guarded in Canada than in the United States. Every Canadian jurisdiction has in place some version of the Rand Formula (discussed in detail in the labour history chapter) providing for dues checkoff deductions at the source. In contrast, many U.S. states (the so-called "right-to-work" states) have no union security protection in place. The existence of this sizeable "right-to-work" zone may be the single most important difference in the Canadian and American labour policy environments. As Noah Meltz (1989b) points out, union density rates in the "right-to-work" states are generally extremely low, sometimes even in single digits. Overall, the difference in density rates between the right-to-work states and those with union security provisions in place is far greater than that between any two Canadian provinces (Meltz, 1989b).

Second, the process by which a union becomes certified is generally quite different in Canada and the United States. In most Canadian jurisdictions, certification has traditionally been through a count of signed membership cards.[8] As a result of the 1947 *Taft-Hartley Act*, which was designed specifically to curb unions' powers, any American union wishing to gain certification since then has had to go through a formal election. This is a process that many have argued gives employers the opportunity to intimidate and harass union activists and influence employees' opinion (Weiler, 1980 and 1983a; Mills, 1989). Such arguments are supported by studies showing increasingly low union success rates in elections held since 1950 (Weiler, 1983a).

Third, collective bargaining rights for public sector workers are generally a good deal stronger in Canada. In the United States, these rights were provided at the federal level through a 1961 executive order by President John F. Kennedy (Mills, 1989:536–537). They have generally not included the right to strike. At the state level, nearly two-fifths of all states, as of 1985, did not permit their employees to engage in collective bargaining as such, while only 11 states permitted employees to strike at all, and then usually under very limited circumstances (Mills, 1989:530). As we will see in more detail in the public sector chapter, most Canadian public sector workers *do* enjoy the right to strike and, in general, possess more collective bargaining rights than their U.S. counterparts (Mills, 1989:412). These greater rights appear to have made union membership a more attractive proposition for Canadian than for American public sector workers.

Finally, labour relations legislation appears to be more strictly enforced in Canada than in the United States. A study by Peter Bruce (1990) of the handling of employer unfair-labour-practice cases in the United States[9] and in Ontario finds that cases in Ontario were dealt with more quickly, were more likely to result in a conviction, and were far less likely to be appealed to the courts. Bruce's conclusion is that, in Ontario, employers contemplating engaging in unfair labour practice would likely be deterred, knowing that they would have a high probability of being convicted, whereas in the United States, they would be much more likely to proceed, given the low probability of a timely conviction there. Given that employer opposition has been shown to be a significant factor in explaining union growth and decline (see Kochan, McKersie, and Cappelli, 1984; Freeman, 1989), Canada's generally stricter enforcement of labour legislation is probably at least in part responsible for this country's higher union membership rates.

The political environment is also significantly different in the two countries. For the past 60-odd years, Canada has had a social democratic party (known first as the CCF and now as the NDP) dedicated to advancing unions' interests in the political arena. While not strong by European standards, the NDP has often held power provincially in Canada and on a number of occasions has held the balance of power federally. In all of these situations, it has been in a position either to pass union-friendly labour legislation directly (as it has done in B.C., Saskatchewan, Manitoba, and Ontario when it formed the government there) or to demand that its coalition partner pass such legislation as the price of continued NDP support (as it appears to have done in the case of *PSSRA*). Lacking such a party, the American labour movement has often had considerable difficulty advancing its legislative agenda, as its failure to win passage of President Jimmy Carter's labour law reform bill during the late 1970s illustrates. Overall, the evidence suggests that the NDP has helped increase or at least maintain union membership rates in Canada, while conversely, the lack of a labour or social democratic party may help explain the recent decline in union density in the United States (see Bruce, 1989; Meltz, 1989b).

Yet another difference is the extent of union organizing efforts in the two countries. As Ian Robinson (1990) notes, Canadian unions have generally made far more effort to organize unskilled workers than have their American counterparts. The difference between Canadian and American organizing efforts was particularly great during the last years of George Meany's presidency of the AFL-CIO. Like many conservative craft unionists before him, Meany cared little about the fate of unskilled workers and generally gave organizing a low priority. Indeed, he was quoted in a national news magazine as saying that the size of the American labour movement made no difference to him (Goulden, 1972; I. Robinson, 1990). Canadian unionists never shared this lackadaisical attitude towards organizing; not surprisingly, this country's unions greatly out-organized those of the United States, to the degree that in some years, despite the two countries' difference in size, Canadian unions actually signed up more new members than American unions did (Rose and Chaison, 1990)![10]

Despite the apparently strong evidence of growing divergence of Canadian and American union density rates, some (including most notably Troy [1992]),[11] have argued that this divergence is no more than a short- to medium-term trend and that in the longer run, economic factors such as globalization and trade liberalization will lead to a new convergence of those rates at a level much lower than the current Canadian one. Moreover, even those who have thus far emphasized the divergent nature of the Canadian and American labour movements (e.g. Robinson, 1994) have admitted that major economic changes such as those brought about as a result of the North American Free Trade Agreement (NAFTA) could lead to a convergence of labour legislation, which in turn could lead to major reductions in Canadian union membership rates. At the same time, provincial jurisdiction over labour legislation means that such a process of convergence is less likely to come about than it would otherwise be, or will at least take longer than it might otherwise, given that changes must be made to not one but many sets of labour legislation.

UNION STRUCTURE

Canadian labour organizations conduct their business at local, provincial, national, and in some cases international levels. In general, the Canadian labour movement operates in a quite decentralized fashion, at least by international standards (see Rogow, 1989a:158–161 and Chaykowski, 1995:231). The Canadian Labour Congress, Canada's largest and most important central labour body, has little power over the unions affiliated with it, other than the power to expel, suspend, or reprimand them for offences such as raiding other unions. By international standards, as well, Canadian unions carry out a great deal of their bargaining at the local union-local plant level, a situation in sharp contrast to that prevailing in many European countries such as Germany and Sweden, where bargaining has normally been conducted at industry or even national levels (Fuerstenberg, 1993; Hammarstrom, 1993).[12] Canada's decentralized bargaining structure has sometimes been identified as a possible cause of its relatively high strike incidence (see Chapter 12 for more detail on this point).

Canada's union structure is also generally considered quite **fragmented**. This means that by international standards, Canada has a large number of small unions. While Table 5.3 shows that some Canadian unions are quite large, representing upwards of 100 000 workers, many of these big unions are in the public sector.

Table 5.3

TEN UNIONS WITH LARGEST MEMBERSHIP, 1997	
Union (federation)	Membership (thousands)
Canadian Union of Public Employees (CLC)	451.5
National Union of Public and General Employees (CLC)	309.0
National Automobile, Aerospace, Transportation and General Workers Union of Canada (CLC)	205.0
United Steelworkers of America (AFL-CIO/CLC)	200.0
United Food and Commercial Workers International Union (AFL-CIO/CLC)	197.0
Public Service Alliance of Canada (CLC)	167.8
Communications, Energy and Paperworkers Union of Canada (CLC)	167.5
Fédération des affaires sociales inc. (CSN)	97.0
International Brotherhood of Teamsters (AFL-CIO/CLC)	95.0
Service Employees International Union (AFL-CIO/CLC)	80.0

Source: Workplace Information Directorate, Human Resources Development Canada, *Directory of Labour Organizations in Canada*, 1997, p. xix.

In the private sector, there is still a good deal of fragmentation, despite recent mergers such as that of the Communications, Energy, and Paperworkers unions and a fair amount of diversification and expansion on the part of traditional industrial unions like the Autoworkers and Steelworkers (see Murray, 1995:177–178). One result of such fragmentation can be **dual unionism,** or competition between two or more unions to represent workers in the same sector. Such competition can lead to friction or even, sometimes, violence, as the case of competition within Quebec's construction industry, discussed later in this section, will illustrate. As recent observers like Lipsig-Mumme (1995:218) suggest, it could also hinder the Canadian labour movement's attempts to form effective international sectoral alliances. Finally, and perhaps of greatest relevance to the average Canadian union member, smaller unions simply cannot offer the same range of services that larger ones can. While size isn't everything, it can make a good deal of difference when it comes to issues such as organizing, research, publicity, and legislative lobbying. By and large, bigger unions have the funds to pay for more of these kinds of services, which (as we point out in the next chapter) are becoming increasingly important elements of unions' day-to-day activity.[13]

Union Locals

A union local (sometimes referred to as a local union) organizes workers within a given geographic area (most commonly a city). In some cases, it will represent all workers in its area; in other cases, it represents only workers at a particular work site. Public sector locals may represent all workers throughout a municipal region or even an entire province (Godard, 1994:226).

In some cases, a union local will remain unaffiliated with any labour federation. In this case, the union is known as an **independent** local and the local is the union. More often, however, a union will affiliate with a provincial and federal federation (most often the Canadian Labour Congress, described in detail below). In this case, the local is the union's basic building block (see Figure 5.3)

Locals in different types of unions tend to operate somewhat differently from each other. For example, in **craft** unions (those representing workers from a single occupation, such as carpenters or bricklayers) and professional-employee unions, bargaining is often conducted at the local level (Chaison and Rose, 1989). In addition, in craft unions in particular, the membership may be widely dispersed over a large geographical area, making it difficult for part-time volunteers to provide effective service (Godard, 1994). In such cases, the local will sometimes employ an individual known as a business agent to serve as chief spokesperson at negotiations, handle grievances, deal with members' problems, and liaise with other unions. In addition, business agents can often serve as trustees for the locals' health, welfare, and pension

FIGURE 5.3

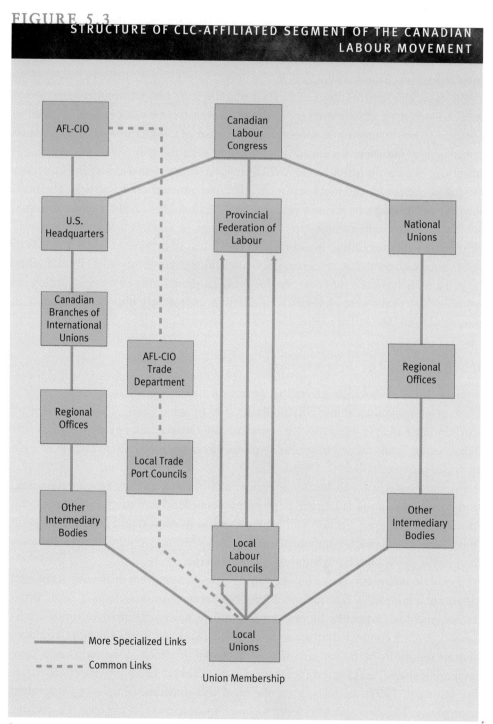

STRUCTURE OF CLC-AFFILIATED SEGMENT OF THE CANADIAN LABOUR MOVEMENT

Source: Craig and Solomon, 1996.

funds (Godard, 1994). Industrial and public service unions, where bargaining is often conducted at the industry, provincial, or even national level (as in the case of federal public servants) do not normally employ business agents, though these unions do often use provincial and national representatives to provide some of the same services a business agent might otherwise perform. In these cases, the local officers with whom members have most contact are **shop stewards.** Generally unpaid, shop stewards work for the union on a part-time basis. Their major responsibility is usually investigating grievances and representing members at grievance hearings; however, they may also be involved in such activities as recruiting new members or encouraging participation at meetings (Godard, 1994).

Whichever type of union a worker belongs to, the local is the level of the union with which he or she is generally most familiar. It is at the local's meetings, normally held monthly, where officers are elected, policies established, the broad outlines of bargaining strategy set,[14] and strike votes taken. Though attendance at monthly meetings is generally extremely low, for reasons to be discussed shortly, meetings involving the election of officers or discussion of possible strike action will normally see a far better turnout.

As is the case with many other organizations, much of the local's work is done by a variety of committees. Typically a union will use both standing, or permanent, committees to deal with ongoing issues such as bargaining, grievances, pensions, and finances, and ad hoc committees created for a particular purpose, such as job action committees to plan strike strategy, or strike committees to coordinate strike activities. Many of these committees entail a heavy time commitment on the part of participating members. Grievance committees, for example, often meet weekly, and individual committee members may spend additional time discussing the details of grievors' cases with them individually. Job action committees may meet weekly or even more often during the lead-up to a possible strike, and of course being part of a bargaining committee may entail several hours of work a day, or perhaps even some all-night sessions during negotiations. While many union leaders are concerned, and rightly so, about the low attendance figures for most monthly meetings, these figures must be balanced against the hundreds of volunteer hours put in each month by the members of a typical union's many committees.

In addition to their provincial and federal affiliations (discussed in detail in the next section), most locals are affiliated with one of Canada's 120-odd district labour councils. These councils, funded by a per capita tax on the locals (Craig and Solomon, 1996:156), are designed to advance the labour movement's interests at the local and municipal levels. In practice, this could mean anything from running an information booth at a Labour Day fair to providing a union perspective to the media on contemporary economic and political developments or lending support to

Municipal and district labour councils such as this one help raise the profile of unions and the labour movement in communities all across Canada.

a striking union in the area (Craig and Solomon, 1996). In larger centres, in particular, district labour councils can be a potent force. For example, the Toronto and District Labour Council was heavily involved in organizing protest actions against the Ontario provincial government in 1997 and 1998.

National and Provincial Labour Federations

Some unions, most typically those representing professionals such as nurses (Boivin and Déom, 1995) or university professors, choose to remain completely independent of affiliations with other unions.[15] Most unions, however, see distinct advantages in joining forces with other unions at national and provincial levels. Unions working together through a labour federation, or association of unions, often find they can accomplish many things that they could not have achieved on their own.

By far the most important labour federation in Canada is the Canadian Labour Congress (CLC), which represents about 60 percent of the country's union members. The organization's policies are established and constitution amended at its biennial conventions, attended by thousands of delegates from affiliates. It is also at these conventions that the CLC elects its officers and decides whether to admit, suspend, or expel individual unions (Godard, 1994:245). In between conventions, an executive council made up of the CLC's president, vice presidents, and secretary-treasurer is responsible for policy decisions (Godard, 1994).

The CLC does not normally engage in collective bargaining with employers. Its major functions are: (1) representing the Canadian labour movement politically, (2) providing services, such as research and organizing assistance, to its affiliated unions, (3) managing relations between its affiliated unions, (4) enforcing its ethical code, and (5) representing the Canadian labour movement internationally.

Political Representation

As we point out in the union action section of the next chapter, unions need to become involved politically to influence the passage of the legislation affecting workers and their unions. Over time, the Canadian labour movement has found that it makes sense to coordinate much of its political activity in Ottawa, the seat of Parliament.[16]

The CLC's political representation takes a variety of forms. Among the most important of these is liaison with the labour movement's political partner, the NDP. In addition, the CLC uses various other means in seeking to influence government legislation and policy. These include lobbying of Cabinet members and government officials, the issuing of press releases in response to economic developments, and the preparation of briefs or research studies on issues it considers of major importance. During the 1980s, the CLC presented briefs to parliamentary commissions investigating subjects such as unemployment and concentration in media ownership (Craig and Solomon, 1996:164). On issues it considers critical, the CLC will play a more active role in public debate; for example, in the case of the Canada-U.S. Free Trade Agreement, it issued numerous public statements and campaigned against the deal during the 1988 federal election campaign (Craig and Solomon, 1996). When it feels its advice is not being heeded, it will go even further, organizing demonstrations and publicity campaigns in the hope of spurring the government into action. This was the case in 1993, when the CLC organized a massive Parliament Hill demonstration to protest what it saw as the job-killing effects of the free trade agreements (Craig and Solomon, 1996:165).

Assistance to Affiliated Unions

The CLC provides a broad range of services for its members, many of which (particularly smaller unions) lack the money or expertise to carry out for themselves. Such services can include labour education (discussed in more detail in the union action section of the next chapter), research for collective bargaining, and organizing assistance (Godard, 1994:244–245).

Maintaining Relations Between Affiliates

Next to its political work, the CLC's most important activity is maintaining (or trying to maintain) harmonious relations between its affiliated unions. Of particular concern here are jurisdictional disputes, or battles over which union will represent a given group of workers. Such disputes have become increasingly common in recent years as the big industrial unions, seeking to make up for the membership lost through deindustrialization and economic restructuring, have been forced to look farther afield for new members. In most cases, these unions have focussed on organizing the unorganized, but on occasion they have attempted to sign up workers already belonging to another union—an action known as union raiding. Raiding is a serious concern to the CLC, since it not only saps the morale of many of those involved and wastes valuable money and human resources that should be directed elsewhere (Godard, 1994:244), but can also cause the entire labour movement major public embarrassment.

The most serious incident of this kind involved the Canadian Auto Workers (CAW) and United Food and Commercial Workers (UFCW). In 1987, the CAW began to sign up Atlantic fishery workers already represented by the UFCW. After a battle that ended up being heard by both labour boards and courts, the CAW won the right to represent the 23 000 fishery workers (Craig and Solomon, 1996:170). The dispute led the CLC to change the way it handles jurisdictional disputes. Until 1988, it had used a standing umpire. Finding that this approach had not helped solve the CAW-UFCW dispute, the CLC decided to handle future disputes of this kind internally, through its own executive committee. It also adopted tough new anti-raiding rules (Craig and Solomon, 1996:170–171). While these changes probably made sense, they have not been enough to prevent other instances of raiding, such as the International Woodworkers of America's raid of the Canadian Paperworkers' Union, for which, in 1992, the IWA was cut off from all CLC services and its officers barred from participation on CLC or provincial labour federation boards and committees (Craig and Solomon, 1996).

Though regrettable, union raiding is probably inevitable in the current environment of constant economic restructuring, one in which unions must compete increasingly fiercely for members. One change that *could* help would be to grant the CLC additional disciplinary powers, such as the ability to levy fines. To date, however, there have been few signs that any affiliates would be willing to grant the Congress such expanded powers.

Maintaining the Code of Ethics

To help ensure that its affiliates behave honourably, the CLC has written into its constitution a code of ethics. This code prohibits corrupt leadership practices and specifically guarantees union members the right to have honest and democratic elections, to run for union office, and to get fair treatment from their union's officials. The CLC's executive is charged with enforcing this code, although here, as in the case of union raiding, its powers are quite limited (Godard, 1994:244). In 1956, the CLC did expel the Teamsters union for gross corruption, following a U.S. Congressional investigation that found widespread corruption among the union's leaders (Craig and Solomon, 1996:171).

"TEAMSTERS/DNC MONEY LAUNDERING SCANDAL" FROM THE U.S. REPUBLICAN PARTY NATIONAL COMMITTEE RESEARCH DIVISION

www.rnc.org/research/scandal/teamdnc.htm

International Representation

Canada is active in a number of international labour organizations, including most notably the International Labour Organization (ILO) and International Confederation of Free Trade Unions (ICFTU). The ILO is a United Nations agency that investigates workers' rights and working conditions all around the world and sets international standards, or conventions, that apply to all member countries. These conventions have been established for issues such as freedom of association, the right to strike, hours of work, and the abolition of forced labour (LaBerge, 1976). Its powers are mainly limited to those of persuasion since, like the CLC, it lacks any real power to enforce its rulings (Godard, 1994; Craig and Solomon, 1996). The ICFTU is heavily involved in training unionists and in establishing and maintaining workers' rights in developing countries, where such rights are often far from a given (Craig and Solomon, 1996; Fashoyin, 1991). As the body representing the majority of Canada's unionists, the CLC represents the Canadian labour movement in these organizations, often playing a key leadership role. For example, former CLC president Shirley Carr was vice president of the ICFTU, while she and another former CLC president, Joe Morris, have both served as head of the ILO workers' group (Craig and Solomon, 1996:172).

CANADIAN INTERATIONAL LABOUR NETWORK

labour.ciln.mcmaster.ca

Provincial Labour Federations

Provincial labour federations play an extremely important role in Canada, since most labour legislation is under provincial jurisdiction; hence the importance of maintaining a strong political presence at the provincial as well as federal level. The CLC has 12 provincial and territorial labour federations affiliated with it. Like the national federation, the provincial ones generally carry out activities that most unions lack the resources to carry out for themselves, such as political and legislative lobbying, research, and labour education. Their range of activities is often extremely broad. For instance, in one recent year (OFL, 1994), the Ontario Federation of Labour (OFL) submitted briefs on subjects ranging from workers' compensation and unemployment insurance to the possible incorporation of physicians and sustainable economic development. The Federation also carried out a substantial research program on health-related issues, successfully lobbied the provincial government to stop the introduction of user fees for drugs for seniors, organized an international symposium on the arts and labour, and held seminars on homeworking and teleworking, in addition to making plans for a joint conference with the Ontario Environment Network and helping to develop a dispute resolution process to deal with forest land-use claims.[17]

Quebec's Special Situation: Multiple Federations

Every province and territory except Quebec has a single provincial labour federation affiliated with the CLC. Like the other provinces, Quebec has its CLC affiliate, the Quebec Federation of Labour. There are, however, two important ways in which Quebec's union structure is different from that in other provinces. First, unlike any other province, Quebec has several different labour federations, as well as a sizeable number of independent unions not affiliated with any federation. The most important of the federations is the Confédération des syndicats nationaux (CSN), the former Catholic confessional federation that, as we pointed out in the labour history chapter, has undergone many metamorphoses since its formation just after the First World War. With about 250 000 members, or just over 6 percent of Canada's total union membership, the CSN is now heavily involved in promoting joint labour-management ventures (see Lipsig-Mumme, 1995:214)—a major change from its hard-line militancy of the 1960s and early 1970s. Other Quebec-wide federations include the education federation, the Centrale de l'enseignement du Québec (CEQ), and the Centrale des syndicats démocratiques (CSD), a small group of mainly private sector unions that left the CSN during the 1970s in protest over that federation's radicalism. The CEQ, formerly a confessional federation like the CSN with membership restricted to elementary and secondary schoolteachers, has evolved into a broad-based secular industrial union representing all workers in education, including caretakers and maintenance staff as well as teachers (Boivin and Déom, 1995:467). Like the CSN, it has a history of militancy and continues to practise a strongly politically conscious brand of social unionism. In contrast, the CSD, most of whose members work in the clothing, chemical, and metal industries, operates according to business union principles and has taken a militantly apolitical stance (Boivin and Déom, 1995). The independent unions, which represent about one-quarter of the province's union members, have been most active in the public and parapublic sector, the two most important independent organizations being those representing civil servants. The large number of workers represented by the independents has been a significant concern to the federations; however, since 1987, this concern may have eased a bit as the proportion of workers represented by the independents has stayed roughly the same (Boivin and Déom, 1995:468).

Unlike any other Canadian province, then, but like many European countries, Quebec has a situation where a number of different labour federations are actively competing for new members, both with each other and with the independent unions. As in the case of many European countries, such as Germany and the Netherlands (Bean, 1994:27), Catholic opposition to the secular and (so the church hierarchy maintained) radical orientation of the dominant mainstream secular federation was a big reason for the establishment of a separate Catholic federation. Even after the secularization of the major confessional federations (the CSN and CEQ), politics has played a role in the further fragmentation of the Quebec labour movement, most notably in the departure of the conservative CSD unions from the CSN. The existence of multiple labour federations in Quebec has always been a source of friction and on occasion has resulted in violence, as in the case of the QFL's and CSN's pitched battles over the organization of James Bay construction workers during the 1970s (Boivin, 1982:431). At the same time, it cannot be denied that when the federations have pulled together, as they did during the 1972 Common Front strike, the result has been a provincial labour movement of unusual cohesiveness and strength. Thus the jury must remain out on the question of whether Quebec's multiple federations have strengthened or weakened the province's labour movement overall.

The second distinctive feature of Quebec's union structure is the unusual degree of freedom granted the CLC's Quebec affiliate, the QFL. Unlike other provincial CLC affiliates, the QFL has always been in the position of having to compete for members, which almost by definition makes its situation a special one. When the debate over Quebec independence began to heat up, it was able to make the case that it would need special powers and more money than other provincial labour federations if it was to continue to attract new members. The CLC responded in 1974 by granting the QFL what amounted to partial autonomy, yielding its usual jurisdiction over labour education and local labour councils, and allowing the provincial federation to recoup funds for national services that provided Quebec members no tangible benefit, such as unilingual English newspapers (Boivin, 1982:433). Twenty years later, the CLC went even further, granting its Quebec affiliate what some have referred to "sovereignty-association" status within the national federation. A 1994 agreement worked out at the Congress' convention in Toronto gave the QFL powers that would normally be granted only to a national labour organization, such as the right to designate its own representatives to activities held by international

CUPE president Judy Darcy—one of far too few female union officials in Canada today. From Craig and Solomon, 1996.

labour groups like the ILO and ICFTU. In addition, the QFL president was automatically made a voting member of the Congress's executive, and the QFL was given the right to observe its own protocols on matters such as internal jurisdictional disputes and labour education, as well as control over the money that the CLC would normally have allocated for these activities (Boivin and Déom, 1995:465).

Quebec's "special status" within the CLC has often been a source of friction and resentment, especially for conservative international unions like those representing the building trades. As we noted earlier, this special status was a major reason why the building trade unions left the CLC in 1982 to form the now-defunct Canadian Federation of Labour (CFL). Undoubtedly there are others within the CLC who resent the QFL's special status. But given Quebec's always-delicate political situation and the realities of operating in an environment where the QFL must compete for members with strongly and avowedly nationalist federations, "sovereignty-association" status may represent the only feasible way for the CLC to keep its Quebec affiliate from leaving altogether.

National and International Unions

Canada is among the few industrialized countries to have a sizeable number of union members represented by unions headquartered outside the country. Generally known as "international" unions, these organizations are in reality American unions with Canadian branches. Their role in the Canadian labour movement has been a source of controversy throughout this century. It continues to generate controversy even at a time when some observers (i.e., Lipsig-Mumme, 1995) have begun to argue for closer links between unions in Canada, the United States, and Mexico in response to the continental integration resulting from the Canada-U.S. and North American Free Trade Agreements.

In the labour history chapter, we pointed out that there were good reasons for Canadian unionists in the late nineteenth and early twentieth centuries to choose to be represented by American unions. Bigger, more experienced, and stronger American unions could provide money and logistical and organizing support that simply wasn't available in this country. Moreover, at a time when many jobs were still seasonal, an American union card served almost as a meal ticket for many Canadian workers forced to seek employment in the United States (see Lipton, 1973 and McKay, 1983).

But if there were good reasons for the "internationalization" of the Canadian labour movement in the late nineteenth and early twentieth centuries, there have been equally good reasons for its more recent Canadianization, which has taken place mainly over the past 30 years. Numerically, as Table 5.1 shows, the American labour movement is far weaker than it was during the early postwar period. Union density in the United States is now less than half what it was in 1947; indeed, the actual number of union members in that country has dropped by more than one-third since 1976 despite a sizeable increase in its labour force. As a number of observers have pointed out, the decline in the size of the American labour movement has been mirrored by a decline in its political clout (see Lipsig-Mumme, 1989; Robinson, 1990 and 1994; Peirce, 1995).

Far from being stronger than the Canadian labour movement, as it was through the early years of this century, the American labour movement is now considerably weaker than its northern counterpart. This growing weakness has led many Canadian unionists to question the value of continued affiliation. After all, if American unions lacked the money and human resources to conduct organizing campaigns at home (see Chaison and Rose, 1991:28–29), how much help could they realistically be to their Canadian affiliates? In these circumstances, many Canadian unionists have suggested that Canadian members are paying more in international dues than they're getting back in benefits, making continued international affiliation a losing proposition.

Nor are these the only forces that have led to the nationalization of the Canadian labour movement. Arguably the single most important development here has been the growth of public sector unionism in Canada. Excluded from unionization in most jurisdictions, public sector workers were an insignificant part of the Canadian labour movement through the early postwar period.[18] Once public servants and other public sector workers were granted the right to bargain collectively, they joined the labour movement in huge numbers (Rose, 1995). It was estimated that by the beginning of the 1980s, nearly half the country's union members worked in the public sector (Ponak, 1982:345; Rose, 1995:22). By the early 1990s, that figure was roughly 55 percent (Rose, 1995:22).

Almost by definition, public sector unions are national unions. It is difficult to imagine how a union based in another country could provide effective representation to Canadian public servants, schoolteachers, or health-care workers. Indeed, any serious attempt by an American union to organize Canadian public sector workers, particularly federal or provincial public servants, would likely raise major concerns around issues of national sovereignty. Moreover, Canadian public sector workers would generally have little if anything to gain from affiliation with an American union, given the far less liberal public sector bargaining legislation in the United States (see Craig and Solomon, 1996:183).

In the private sector, issues leading many Canadian unions to break away from their American internationals have included disputes over strike funding and bargaining strategy and political disagreements. As we noted earlier, some international head offices strongly disapproved of their Canadian branches' support for the social democratic NDP; for their part, many Canadian unionists were strongly opposed to their internationals' support for the Vietnam War. More generally, the 1960s and 1970s were a time of growing nationalism and questioning of authority across Canada, a time when many Canadians were becoming increasingly displeased with the degree of American ownership of and control over this country's economy. In such a volatile political climate, (see Ponak, 1982:349), the labour movement could not expect to escape unscathed. To many Canadian unionists, a situation in which their unions were controlled outside the country had become unacceptable as such, beyond specific disagreements over bargaining strategies or political affiliation.

Taken together, the developments just described have transformed the Canadian labour movement from a primarily U.S.-based one to a primarily national one. In 1920 (Chaison, 1982:152), Canadian national unions represented just over 5 percent of the country's union members. As recently as 1962 (see Table 5.4), more than 70 percent of all Canadian union members still belonged to internationals. By 1980, half the country's union members were in Canadian-based national unions; as of 1997, that figure stood at more than 65 percent (Table 5.4). As Table 5.3 indicates, the country's three largest unions, and six of its ten largest, are now Canadian-based.

The best-known secession of a Canadian union from its American international parent was undoubtedly that of the Canadian Auto Workers from the United Auto Workers, in 1985. Here, the major issue was the Canadian branch's refusal to accept the international's concession bargaining strategy. But the CAW's breakaway from the UAW was just one of a sizeable number taking place through the 1970s and 1980s and into the 1990s. Unions such as the Communication Workers and Paperworkers

Table 5.4

| | **Number of Unions** | | | **Number of Members (thousands)** | | |
	National	International	Other	National	International	Other
Year	N (%)	N (%)	N (%)	N (%)	N (%)	N (%)
1962	51 (11.5)	108 (24.3)	285 (64.2)	335 (23.5)	1 025 (72.0)	63 (4.4)
1978	88 (16.6)	121 (22.8)	321 (60.6)	1 553 (47.4)	1 638 (50.0)	87 (2.6)
1990	234 (23.0)	61 (6.0)	721 (71.0)	2 563 (63.6)	1 283 (31.8)	184 (4.6)
1997	233 (23.0)	51 (5.0)	727 (71.9)	2 663 (65.4)	1 217 (29.9)	195 (4.8)

NATIONAL VERSUS INTERNATIONAL COMPOSITION OF UNIONS AND UNION MEMBERS, SELECTED YEARS, 1962–1997

Source: Workplace Information Directorate, HRDC, *Directory of Labour Organizations in Canada*, 1997, p. xii.

broke completely away from their American "parents," while others, such as the National Association of Broadcast Employees and Technicians and Brotherhood of Railway, Airline, and Steamship Clerks, drafted their own constitutions and elected their own officers while maintaining a loose affiliation with their parent unions (Craig and Solomon, 1996:187).

CANADIAN AUTO WORKERS
www.caw.ca

Even Canadian unions remaining within their internationals have often been able to achieve a significantly higher degree of autonomy and self-sufficiency than they previously enjoyed (Godard, 1994:250). In large measure, this appears to have been the result of the CLC's autonomy guidelines, passed in 1970 and again in 1974. These guidelines include: the election of Canadian officers by Canadians; the right of Canadian officers and members to determine union policies dealing with national affairs; the authority for Canadian officers to speak for their union in Canada; separate affiliation for Canadian sections in international labour bodies; and assurance from the internationals that Canadian members could take full part in their country's social, economic, cultural, and political life (Heron, 1989; Craig and Solomon, 1996).

CANADIAN LABOUR CONGRESS
www.clc-ctc.ca/links/index.html

Whether the guidelines have succeeded in reducing the number of secessions is an interesting question, but one that is very difficult to answer, given the available evidence (see Chaison and Rose, 1989). What can be said is that the pace of secession has slowed considerably, if not halted altogether, in recent years. In 1997, the proportion of union members belonging to international unions (Table 5.4) was virtually unchanged from what it had been in 1994 (Murray, 1995:177). As was noted earlier in the chapter, if anything the trend now may be back in the direction of some kind of internationalism, given the increasing global and continental economic integration described in detail in Chapter 2.

UNION DEMOCRACY

Union democracy is of interest to the labour movement for many reasons, not least because actual or even perceived lapses in democracy can hurt the movement's public image, causing it to lose much-needed support. Cynics sometimes say that the very notion of union democracy is an oxymoron. Others (i.e., Craig and Solomon, 1996:173) suggest that, given the serious constraints under which unions often operate, their achievements in the area of democracy are admirable. The issue has been of increasing interest both to unionists and to the general public since the 1950s, when widespread corruption was revealed in such American unions as the Teamsters and the Longshoremen's. These revelations were followed by a number of congressional investigations of labour racketeering, and eventually by the passage, in 1959, of the *Landrum-Griffin Act,* which imposed strict controls on the internal operations of American unions, including the possibility of an appeal to the Secretary of Labor for a judicial recount in cases where there was reason to believe that a union election had been rigged (Craig and Solomon, 1996:181–182).

Union democracy is not an easy concept to define. Anderson (1979) has suggested that it means, essentially, the ability to influence decisions that are important to members and to participate effectively in its affairs. A more comprehensive definition by Edelstein and Warner (quoted in Chaison, 1982:166) has described democracy as:

> ... a decision-making system in which the membership actively participates, directly or indirectly through its representatives, in the making and implementation of policy and in the selection of officials, for all levels, on the basis of political equality and majority rule. Furthermore, the system operates on the basis of the accountability of officials, the legitimacy of opposition, and due process for the protection of the rights of individuals and minorities.

It doesn't take a Ph.D. in political science to appreciate that doing all these things amounts to a tall order for any union. Indeed, a close reading of the definition reveals significant tension between a number of the objectives, such as operating through majority rule while still respecting the rights of individuals and minorities. If this is what is expected of unions, no wonder their actual achievements in the area of democratic operation often fall short of expectations. Indeed, one reason for some perceived lapses in union democracy—not to say that actual lapses do not occur—is the tremendously high expectations people have for it. In part, this is the result of the way unions position themselves among the few democratic institutions in society willing and able to stand up to big business and other powerful and monied interests. And in part it's because, at the national or societal level, as the union-impacts section of the next chapter will explain in more detail, trade unionism *is* clearly and closely related to democracy. With respect to unions' internal operations, however, things may turn out to be a bit different. Usually, union constitutions will provide that everyone be treated equally. In practice, though, some members and, particularly, officials, may turn out to be more equal than others. In the sub-sections that follow, we'll try to provide some explanations for this apparent paradox, closing the discussion with a comparison of evidence of union democracy in Canada and the United States.

Components of Union Democracy

A review of the Edelstein-Warner definition just quoted reveals a number of key components, including membership participation, selection of officials, legitimacy of opposition, and due process. In addition, we might add freedom from outright corruption and fraud, since this is the aspect of union democracy (or the lack thereof) that has the potential to arouse the greatest public concern. Since this last point is so important, let's begin with it.

Freedom from Corruption

At a bare minimum, unions should operate within the law. They should hold regular meetings, and treasurers should provide regular reports of how members' dues are spent. Officials should not resort to violence, intimidation, or other bully-boy tactics either in their dealings with their own members or in dealings with others (such as members of other unions or prospective members they are trying to organize). They should avoid having anything to do with organized crime, and they should not make "sweetheart" deals with employers behind their members' backs. Nor should they refuse to carry a member's grievance forward simply because the grievor or his or her father may happen to have run for office against a member of the current executive.

Any union (or any other organization) that cannot abide by these rather minimal standards is not only acting undemocratically; it is violating the most basic precepts of morality and common decency. The Landrum-Griffin legislation was passed precisely to avoid further instances of such essentially criminal union behaviour, which the record shows was quite common in the United States during the 1940s and early 1950s. This type of unionism has fortunately been rare in Canada, with the notable exception of American import Hal Banks and his Seafarers' International Union, who regularly resorted to beatings and intimidation (Morton, 1995:147). Perhaps because this type of behaviour has been rare in Canada, there seems to have been little pressure for a "Landrum-Griffin North" (Craig and Solomon, 1996).

Membership Participation

No two observers agree on exactly what proportion of union members attend meetings regularly; all agree that that proportion is very low. Two older sources quoted by Strauss (1991:213) estimate 2 to 6 percent and 5 to 7 percent, respectively, while a more recent estimate cited by Chaison (1982:166) is in the 10 to 15 percent range. Why is attendance at most meetings so low? And what do these low attendance figures really mean?

It is common to attribute such poor attendance to apathy, or to union leaders' tight control over meeting agendas, which leads members to believe they will have little chance to provide meaningful input even if they do attend (see Chaison, 1982). Certainly many members do feel, if not apathetic, at best instrumental towards their union; it's there if they need it, and they will turn out for strike votes and elections, but they have no wish to become involved in the organization's day-to-day operations. As for the issue of leaders' control over agendas, there is no doubt that this happens on occasion. However, we have no way of knowing how frequently it happens. Anecdotal evidence suggests that apathy (or instrumentalism) is a more significant factor here than any attempt by leaders to control the agenda. Indeed, many leaders would dearly love to have better attendance; it would make them look better and also give them a better "read" on what their members are thinking.[19] The problem is, how to get better attendance without resorting to tactics that members might regard as undemocratic.

A brief comparison of today's situation to that prevailing in many unions in the nineteenth century may be instructive. It appears that few of these unions had attendance problems; the Nova Scotia carpenters' union described by McKay (1991:169) boasted average turnouts of more than 150—an extraordinary record by today's standards. In this case, peer pressure and a strong craft tradition apparently helped ensure good attendance. Moreover, like most unions of its time, the Carpenters was a fairly small, homogeneous group of men, most of whom worked together during the day and would have welcomed the opportunity to socialize with their work mates in the evening. Being men, few would have had to worry about who would look after the children during their absence.

Many of today's unions are large, heterogeneous organizations representing people doing many different jobs. The person one sits next to at a union meeting may be someone one doesn't know. This fact alone is enough to explain why modern North

American unions, especially big industrial and public service unions, would find it difficult to play the same role as that played by the Nova Scotia carpenters' union. Especially in the public sector unions, many members are women, which means they *do* have to worry about who will look after the children.[20] Beyond that, for women and men alike, there is the problem of overcommitment. The nineteenth-century unionist likely participated in just two organizations: his union and his church. Today's unionist, especially if he or she has children, often belongs to or participates in a staggering number of organizations, ranging from Home and School associations and children's sports teams to civic improvement groups, musical and cultural organizations, and church groups. As if all that were not enough, even people of modest means now have access to an array of home entertainment technology which their grandparents could only have dreamed of. Given what the union meeting must compete against in modern workers' crowded schedules, is it really any wonder that it often loses out?

Moreover, attendance figures in and of themselves may not mean all that much. As Anderson suggests (1979:488), what's most important may not be the number of bodies in the chairs, but whether those who have come feel free to participate actively and without fear of being suppressed if their ideas don't happen to agree with those of the leadership. Given members' crowded schedules and the child-care problem, there may be no realistic way for today's unions to ensure high attendance at ordinary meetings, although this author has heard of at least one imaginative idea, used by a nurses' association in Newfoundland, that tied the granting of scarce travel funds to satisfactory attendance. If attendance is high when important business such as strike votes or contract terms is being discussed, and if members who do attend feel free to participate fully in the discussions, this may be the best anyone can hope for. The evidence suggests that turnout generally *is* high when important issues are stake (Godard, 1994:241) and that, contrary to popular belief, leaders do their best to get as much membership input as they can, particularly on those important issues.[21] Whether members always feel free to participate in the way they would wish is another question, one to be taken up in the next section.

Selection of Officers and Legitimacy of Opposition

In a democratic union, at a minimum there should be regular election of officers. Those opposing the "official" or incumbent slate should have the opportunity to express their views to members through official union publications and in other ways. Finally, there should be at least a certain degree of turnover in union presidents and other officials, to ensure that the organizations receive the benefit of fresh thinking and prevent ruling cliques from becoming unduly entrenched. While we would not expect incumbent union presidents to be defeated often, given the inherent advantages incumbents possess in unions as in most other political organizations, a situation in which they were *never* defeated would not augur well for union democracy.

More research is needed on the question of what opportunities are provided to opposition slates to express their views through union publications and other channels. As for the matter of turnover, the evidence is mixed. A study conducted by Gary Chaison and Joseph Rose (1977) showed that Canadian union presidents were defeated for re-election less than 15 percent of the time. However, between 1963 and 1972 nearly 80 percent of both national and international unions experienced at least one presidential turnover (Chaison and Rose, 1977; Chaison, 1982). Far more common than defeat at the polls were retirements attributed to age, health, union rules against successive terms in office (which some would argue are themselves a healthy sign of union democracy), or changes to other positions (Chaison, 1982:165). The fact that nearly four-fifths of the unions surveyed changed presidents in a decade suggests that a healthy degree of renewal may well be taking place, although we would need to know what influence the outgoing president had in the choice of his or her successor before making such an assertion with any degree of certainty. Here again, further research is needed.

Due Process

Unions possess a considerable degree of power over their members, including the power to discipline them. Penalties can include loss of union membership, which in turn can lead to loss of one's employment and livelihood in situations where only union members can be employed, or where hiring is conducted through the union, as in the building trades (Craig and Solomon, 1996:180–181). Organizations that have such great power over their members have the responsibility to use it wisely and fairly, especially in situations where someone's livelihood may be at stake. Ideally, those disagreeing with their union's disciplinary action should have the right to a prompt and fair hearing before a neutral third party or parties. In practice, it would appear that this ideal is seldom realized. The Canadian Auto Workers appears to be among the few Canadian unions that have established an impartial panel made up entirely of people from outside the organization to hear members' complaints about internal union actions (Craig and Solomon, 1996:181; Murray, 1995:182). What appear to be more common are internal procedures for handling such complaints, procedures that start at the local level and if not resolved there may end up before the union's executive board or even at its annual or biennial convention. Such a procedure is apt to be extremely time-consuming, to put it mildly (Craig and Solomon, 1996:181). What is not clear is the extent to which unions may have developed speedier, more informal internal dispute resolution processes comparable to the expedited arbitration systems found in a number of industries and jurisdictions. (These are discussed in some detail in the grievance chapter). Given the bad press unions could receive from disgruntled individuals who had suffered lengthy delays in getting their cases heard, some sort of "expedited review" system would appear to be in their enlightened self-interest.

Limitations on Union Democracy

There are a variety of reasons why unions generally find it impossible to fully achieve the lofty democratic ideal suggested in the Edelstein and Warner definition discussed earlier. One argument often advanced (see Godard, 1994 and Murray, 1995) is the "iron law of oligarchy," one originally formulated by the political theorist Robert Michels. This theory argues that as political leaders stay in power, they become increasingly less responsive to their constituents and more concerning with simply staying in power. Godard (1994:238) points out that the "iron law of oligarchy" may be of particular relevance to union leaders, who unlike business leaders may have little or nothing to fall back in if they lose their jobs, except perhaps a shop-floor job, and for whom staying in office would thus appear to be of great importance.

Certainly there are some Canadian union leaders who may well be more concerned with getting re-elected than with formulating the wisest possible long-term policies for their organizations. At the same time, there is at least modest evidence to suggest that the "iron law" may not be working very strongly in Canada. As noted earlier, most Canadian union presidents appear to serve for fairly limited periods; as we will point out below, the same is generally true at the national level, at least for CLC presidents—in stark contrast to the situation prevailing in the United States within the AFL-CIO. Moreover, it is also worth noting that any union or federation wishing to prevent the "iron law" from taking effect has a number of options at its disposal, including term limits for leaders or stipulations that new people be regularly rotated onto their executives.

Other limitations to union democracy may be rather more intractable, since they have to do with the inherent nature of a union as a collective majoritarian political organization in which, at least occasionally, the wishes of the minority must be sacrificed to those of the majority. For example, an individual may feel hard done by because the union has refused to carry a grievance on overtime pay forward. But the union is perfectly within its rights to do so, providing it has considered the case on its merits and its decision is not the result of discriminatory treatment. After all, a union cannot possibly carry all or even most grievances through to arbitration. The union official handling the case may have decided that the case was not winnable, or may simply have felt that scarce union funds might be better used to try to save a member's job in a dismissal grievance than to try to recoup $50 in overtime pay. Subject to the broad limitations of duty of fair representation provisions, union officials must be given latitude in matters of this sort if their organizations are to represent the bargaining unit as a whole effectively.

Strikes are an even better example of situations where the wishes of the individual must often be subordinated to the needs of the union as a whole. At such times, strict discipline is generally necessary. In particular, it is absolutely essential that a striking union be able to call its members out on picket duty and that those members obey the picket captain's orders. Failure to maintain an adequate picket-line presence could lead to the collapse of the strike; failure to follow a picket captain's orders could in certain situations lead to arrest, injury, or possibly even loss of life. Similarly, if enough members crossed a picket line and continued working, the strike could also collapse. This explains the fines and other forms of discipline that unions sometimes impose on members who cross picket lines, as well as the ostracism with which such workers are often greeted by co-workers once the strike is over.

Collective bargaining is yet another core union process that is arguably impossible for any union to conduct in a fully democratic fashion. A union may go to great lengths to solicit members' input on the initial bargaining package; almost all Canadian unions submit their tentative agreements to the membership for an up-and-down ratification vote. But bargaining itself is, as we'll see in the negotiation chapter, a delicate process often very heavily dependent on the personal chemistry of the chief union and management negotiators. If a union had to go back to the membership every time a demand was dropped or it changed its position in any way, the flow of negotiations would be seriously interrupted, and it is unlikely a settlement could ever be reached.

One other point must be made concerning limitations on union democracy arising from the nature of unions as political organizations. Most of us probably think of democracies as also being *meritocracies*, in which the best person for any given job is assigned that job regardless of whom he knows, how long he has been with the organization, or what sort of socio-economic background she comes from. Unions do not seem to function entirely as meritocracies. Seniority within the organization does appear to matter, as does knowing officials or other important members. To a degree, at least, individuals have to "work their way up" the union ladder. Someone generally also has to become known by key senior members and officials before being entrusted with a leadership position, no matter what skills and abilities he or she has. To a degree, this sort of "internal seniority system" keeps unions from acquiring fresh ideas and new perspectives. The question here is, to what degree do unions' "internal seniority systems" prevent genuinely talented people from working their way into leadership positions as quickly as they should?

Here, at least modest light has been shed by a study of Canadian union presidents by Solomon, Andiappan, and Shand (1986). These researchers sought to relate the time it took individuals to rise to the presidency of Canadian national unions to such personal characteristics as the individual's age and educational background, as well as to such organizational characteristics as the union's size. Solomon and his associates found that, on average, it appeared to take a fairly long time (about eight years after assuming elected or appointed office within the union) for someone to be elected president. Though university graduates still took a fairly long time (just under seven years) to reach the presidency, this was significantly less time than the ten-plus years it took non-university graduates to do so. Presidents of larger unions and those deriving most or all of their income from their union salaries also took longer to "reach the top," indicating that seniority and trust factors may be more important in leadership situations where there is more at stake.

Taken together, these findings suggest that while seniority definitely matters, so do a person's qualifications. It would be interesting to compare the characteristics of union officials with the characteristics of officials of political parties or civic organizations with an eye to determining the relative mix of seniority and education or other qualifications in each case. Very possibly unions are not unique among voluntary organizations in placing importance on personal connections and seniority within the organization.

Safeguards for Democracy

Although there are a number of limitations to how democratic a union can be, there are also a number of safeguards that, taken together, help to ensure active membership participation, the legitimacy of opposition, and the upholding of due process.

First, as noted earlier, many leaders not only permit but encourage active participation on the part of their membership. As Godard (1994:240) notes, it is often in their enlightened self-interest to do so, since committed members are likelier to support strikes and a union with a reputation for encouraging member participation may have an easier time recruiting new members.

Second, members who are unhappy with their leadership have a number of options available to them. Most obviously, they may vote an incumbent slate out at the next election. In this regard, if an executive has been in office for a long time, even a close election (say, of 55:45 proportions) can serve as a kind of "warning shot across the bows" and make the executive more responsive to the membership after the election.[22] Disgruntled rank-and-filers can also reject tentative contracts, engage in wildcat strikes (Godard, 1994:241), or (in extreme instances) move to have the union decertified. All of these actions can have serious consequences both for the leadership and for the union as a whole; thus the threat of any of them is something a wise union official will not take lightly.

Third, there are a number of legislative safeguards for union democracy, in addition to those contained in union constitutions and those of labour federations such as the CLC. Most jurisdictions have in place a duty of fair representation provision that has the practical effect of requiring unions to consider each member's grievance seriously. While such provisions don't mean that a union must carry every grievance through to arbitration (a practical impossibility, as we'll see when we get to the grievance chapter), it does mean that any possible bias in a union's handling of grievances (i.e., refusal to carry forward grievances filed by "dissident" members) is likely to be scrutinized rather thoroughly by the labour board. In most cases, the effect of these duty-of-fair-representation provisions is to induce union officials to bend over backwards not only to be fair, but to be *perceived* as fair. A number of jurisdictions also have in place provisions that require unions to conduct secret strike votes before calling any strike. It appears that most Canadian unions already require such votes as a matter of course.

Union Democracy in Canada and the United States

Overall, Canadian unions appear to be significantly more democratic than their American counterparts. To begin with, there has been far less outright corruption here than in the United States. Thugs of the Hal Banks variety have been mercifully rare here—and far too common south of the border. For example, a succession of presidents of the Teamsters Union, which was expelled from both the American AFL-CIO and CLC for corruption (Craig and Solomon, 1996:86–87), were convicted of serious criminal offences, and for years it was routine for Teamster officials to use gangsters to protect themselves (Craig and Solomon, 1996). Corruption was also rampant in some of the building trade unions and in the longshoring unions, at least one of which was also expelled from the AFL-CIO.

CORPORATIONS AND LABOUR UNIONS RETURNS ACT
www.canada.justice/gc.ca/FTP/EN/Laws/Chap/C/C-43.txt

One reason why labour leaders of Hal Banks type have been rare in Canada may be most Canadian jurisdictions' duty-of-fair-representation provisions—something that does not exist in American legislation. The possibility of an aggrieved member taking the union before the labour board very likely acts as a brake on seriously undemocratic union conduct. In contrast, under a system where a member's only recourse is a cumbersome internal review procedure, followed by the courts, leaders might be more willing to engage in undemocratic behaviour, knowing there is little likelihood they will be called to account.

Most important of all is an issue that has rarely been treated in the union democracy literature, though it is noted by Edelstein and Warner: union democracy at the national level. Here there are profound differences in the ways in which the Canadian and American labour movements have operated, at least since the creation of the CLC in 1956. CLC presidents function as just that—presidents. That is to say, they are elected, serve for a relatively short period of time, and then move on to other things. In contrast, the "presidency" of the major American federations (first the AFL, now the AFL-CIO) has in practice functioned more as a monarchy. At least two long-serving AFL presidents (Samuel Gompers and William Green) died in office. The first president of the merged federation, George Meany, died shortly after his last convention, at which he was so ill that he had to be wheeled on and off the convention floor (A. Robinson, 1981). Only in 1995, when Meany's successor, Lane Kirkland, was replaced by John Sweeney, did one witness a change in the federation's presidency resulting from some cause other than the incumbent's death or disability. And even Kirkland served for 15 years and was well into his seventies when he retired.

With no serious possibility of an electoral challenge, AFL and AFL-CIO presidents have often conducted themselves in quite high-handed fashion. For example, under Gompers, the strong minority of AFL members favouring socialism and comprehensive industrial democracy was always ruthlessly suppressed (Galenson and Smith, 1978).[23] Despite such strong rumblings from the rank-and-file, Gompers appears never even to have considered the possibility of forming a labour party in the United States (Galenson and Smith, 1978). Later, under Meany, the AFL-CIO placed a low priority on organizing, despite many executive council members' obvious desire to expand the federation's efforts in this area (Goulden, 1972; Reuther, 1976; Winpisinger, 1989). As well, during the Vietnam era, Meany almost single-handedly put the federation firmly behind the government's policies (Goulden, 1972; Dulles and Dubofsky, 1984). When unionists dared oppose the Johnson administration's Vietnam policies, Meany not only cut them off at AFL-CIO conventions; he publicly attacked them as traitors and Communist sympathizers (Goulden, 1972).

Not only was the conduct of Gompers and Meany extremely undemocratic; there is reason to believe that it did not serve the country's union members and other working people at all well. For example, had the American labour movement established its own political party, as almost all other Western labour movements have, it might have been in a better position to combat the extreme anti-unionism of the Reagan administration. Meany's support of the Vietnam War and other reactionary foreign policies effectively severed the labour movement's ties to Congressional liberals (Peirce, 1995) as well as alienating young people from the labour movement (I. Robinson, 1990). And had Meany devoted more money and resources to organizing, American union membership might well not have declined as sharply as it did even during the relatively prosperous 1960s and 1970s (see Table 5.1), which again would have left it in a better position to withstand the neoconservative assault of the 1980s. It is hard to imagine any CLC president persisting in such misguided and undemocratic actions as those engaged in by Gompers and Meany, given the very real likelihood of defeat at the next election.[24]

More research is clearly needed on specific aspects of Canadian versus American union democracy at the national level. It would, for example, be useful to know what happens to "unofficial" resolutions at AFL-CIO and CLC conventions, and more generally how policy is made in both federations. For now, even the brief discussion we have provided should suffice to show that the Canadian labour movement has generally functioned a good deal more democratically at the national federation level than has the American one, and that this more democratic functioning appears to have benefitted the Canadian labour movement.

QUESTIONS FOR DISCUSSION

1) If you are a union member, how do you feel about how your union is serving you? If you are not a union member, how would you feel about joining one?

2) At which points did Canadian union membership increase significantly? At which points did it decrease? What were the reasons?

3) How have union membership rates by industry been changing in recent years?

4) In which provinces is union membership highest? In which is it lowest? Why, do you think?

5) Thirty-five years ago, Canadian union membership rates were roughly the same as those in the United States. Now Canadian rates are more than twice those of the United States. Why has this situation changed? Do you think Canadian rates will continue to be significantly higher than American rates in the future?

6) What are some of the main effects of Canada's fragmented union structure? Are there signs that this situation is starting to change?

7) Discuss the role played by union locals and municipal and district labour councils.

8) Do you think low attendance at most monthly union meetings is a serious problem? If so, then how might union officials correct the problem?

9) Discuss the role played by provincial and national labour federations, particularly the CLC.

10) How does union structure in Quebec differ from that in all other Canadian provinces?

11) Why have many Canadian unions been merging in recent years? Do you think the trend is healthy for the country's labour movement?

12) How would you define union democracy? Do you think the standards set by Edelstein and Warner in the definition discussed in the text are too high?

13) Are Canadian unions more or less democratic than American unions, in your view?

14) Are there inherent limitations to union democracy? If so, how can unions be more democratic within those limitations?

15) In your view, does the Canadian labour movement pay sufficient attention to the needs and aspirations of female unionists? If not, what could it do to make itself more "woman-friendly"?

SUGGESTIONS FOR FURTHER READING

Chaison, Gary. (1996). *Union mergers in hard times: The view from five countries.* Ithaca and London: Cornell Univ. ILR Press. A thought-provoking study of recent union mergers in the United States, Britain, Australia, and New Zealand, as well as Canada. Chaison's prediction is that in years to come Canadian union fragmentation will be greatly reduced and that large conglomerate unions such as the CEP and CAW will become "centers of mergers of activity and will come to rely on absorptions for continued growth."

Goulden, Joseph. (1972). *Meany.* New York: Atheneum. A well-written and thoroughly researched biography that goes a long way towards linking the decline of the American labour movement to Meany's inattention to organizing and misguided political strategies.

Strauss, George. (1991). "Union democracy." In G. Strauss et al. (Eds.). *The state of the unions.* Madison: IRRA Press. A useful discussion of a difficult concept.

ENDNOTES

1 In Canada, union density is normally defined as the percentage of paid non-agricultural workers belonging to unions. A rationale for excluding agricultural workers from the union density "denominator" is that such workers have often been excluded from unionization and in any case seldom join. However, as Murray (1995:162) points out, this rationale is not entirely consistent since members of other groups excluded from unionization rights, such as managers and confidential IR personnel, *are* counted as part of that denominator.

2 Aggregate union membership rates used in this book are generally higher than the disaggregated rates drawn from Akyeampong's Labour Force survey data. In note 1 of his article, Akyeampong explains the difference as follows: "CALURA density rates in the construction industry in particular have traditionally been higher than those captured by household

surveys like the Labour Force Survey, mainly because CALURA union membership includes both the unemployed and retired, and the household surveys do not." For this reason, provincial union density rates cited in Figure 5.2 appear to have fallen more sharply than they actually have, since the 1991 provincial union density data were drawn from CALU-RA, whereas the 1997 data were drawn from the Labour Force Survey. The overall situation regarding union membership data is far from satisfactory, but no better solution than using HRDC data for aggregate rates and Statistics Canada data for disaggregated rates seemed to be available at the time of writing.

[3] See note 2.

[4] For a more detailed look at legislative provisions and their effect on union growth, see Ng (1992) and Martinello (1996).

[5] The four NDP or PQ governments in provinces with above average density levels served for at least 10 years.

[6] The data contained in Table 5.2 do not provide anything approaching a complete breakdown by industry group; however, these were the only 1997 data available at the time of writing.

[7] Except as otherwise noted, all the information contained in the next three paragraphs has been drawn from Akyeampong (1997).

[8] This has begun to change in recent years, as a number of provinces have moved from the card count to the vote. Newfoundland made such a change in 1994, and Ontario did so in June 1998.

[9] In the United States, private sector labour legislation is under federal jurisdiction.

[10] In fairness, Meany's successors, Lane Kirkland and more recently John Sweeney, have given considerable attention to organizing (on Kirkland, see Winpisinger, 1989). However, by the 1980s, years of benign or not-so-benign neglect had left the American labour movement in such a weakened condition that many unions lacked the money and the people to mount effective organizing campaigns and instead made a conscious decision to devote their resources to protecting the interests of existing members (Chaison and Rose, 1991). For a more detailed discussion, see Lipsig-Mumme (1989).

[11] At least to a certain extent, Troy's arguments appear to have been accepted by Coates (1992).

[12] In Sweden, bargaining was conducted at the national level from the 1950s through the mid 1980s. After several years of shifting back and forth, bargaining was moved to the industry level for 1993 (Hammarstrom, 1993).

[13] For an interesting and useful discussion covering a number of the issues addressed in this section, see Chaison (1997).

[14] Specific tactics are more often planned by the local's negotiating committee. However, the negotiating committee must make sure it is in sync with the general membership's wishes, or it will have an extremely difficult time arriving at an agreement that the membership is willing to ratify.

[15] In the case of university professors, it should be noted that the profession's national organization, the Canadian Association of University Teachers, provides at least some of the same services that a labour federation would.

[16] Similar political functions are carried out by provincial labour federations in provincial capitals.

[17] Environmental issues, most of which involve multiple stakeholders, offer an excellent example of how the labour movement can put its specialized expertise (in this case, knowledge of negotiating strategy) to use in other public forums. In recent years, a special type of bargaining, known as multilateral negotiation, has evolved to address such environment-related issues as native land claims and cleanup of toxic waste sites.

[18] Rose (1995:21) cites one study that estimates that there were about 40 000 Canadian public sector union members in 1946. As Table 5.1 shows, this figure would have comprised less than 5 percent of all Canadian members at the time.

[19] Godard (1994:240) has noted that some local leaders have gone to the extent of offering door prizes or arranging social events after meetings in their bids to increase attendance. Elsewhere, this author has heard of unions that served wine and cheese at the meetings to try to get more members to turn out.

[20] Inadequate child care is often cited in the literature as a factor explaining women's low attendance at union meetings and the low proportion of union officers who are women.

[21] At least one union to which this author has belonged sent out monthly mailings soliciting members' opinions on a variety of issues. While it may be that the union would have achieved a higher response rate with e-mail than it did with its print questionnaires, the basic principle was a good one. Here again, with "hard copy" mailings as with meetings, there is all too frequently the problem of overload.

[22] On the other hand, a close election may make an incumbent executive unduly conservative and fearful of pursuing new initiatives, particularly those involving cooperation with management. Such an executive may find it necessary to put up a show of toughness in a bid to shore up sagging support.

[23] It is instructive to remember that a 1902 AFL convention saw a full 46 percent of the delegates voting in favour of a motion advocating socialism and cooperative industrial democracy, and that a decade later, a socialist candidate opposed Gompers for the federation presidency and won a full one-third of the vote. (Galenson and Smith, 1978:51).

[24] See Lipsig-Mumme (1989) for a much more detailed discussion of these points from a strategic choice perspective.

CHAPTER 6

UNION ACTIONS
AND IMPACTS

Union member votes on the employer's final offer as a steward looks on.

Building on the discussion of the previous chapter, this chapter examines the kinds of actions unions take in support of their objectives and the economic and social impacts they have, both at the workplace and in Canadian society as a whole. We begin with a brief overview of union actions, and the way in which these actions have changed in recent years. We then take a more detailed look at a broad range of union activities, from traditional ones such as collective bargaining and political action, to modern ones such as the creation of union-sponsored venture capital corporations and joint participation with management in a variety of employee involvement schemes. Next, we examine unions' wage impacts, both on employers and on other, non-unionized

workers. After a brief look at the ways in which unions achieve their wage goals, the chapter goes on to consider unions' productivity impacts and effects on the management of organizations, before concluding with a discussion of their broader effects on Canadian society as a whole.

UNION ACTIONS

The question of the methods or actions that unions use to achieve their objectives has been of interest to industrial relations experts for more than 100 years. In a classic 1897 work entitled *Industrial Democracy,* Sidney and Beatrice Webb suggest that unions rely primarily on three methods: mutual insurance, collective bargaining, and legal enactment.[1]

As was pointed out in the labour history chapter, the mutual insurance function of unions was extremely important in the days before unemployment insurance, publicly funded health care, and sick and disability leave. Union benefit funds could help tide unemployed workers over periods of cyclical depression and support the families of workers killed or injured at work, or incapacitated due to illness. By representing themselves as "mutual benefit societies" or "friendly societies," unions were also able to get around harsh nineteenth-century legislation banning them as criminal conspiracies in restraint of trade (Forsey, 1982; Heron, 1989; Craig and Solomon, 1996). Much of the unions' traditional mutual insurance function has been taken over by government. However, some elements of it survive, such as the Supplementary Unemployment Benefits contained in auto workers' collective agreements, which top up government EI payments to a level near the worker's normal wage (Craig and Solomon, 1996:78). With continuing cutbacks to government social programs, unions may well start returning to some of their older mutual insurance activities more frequently.

SHEET MUSIC FOR "SOLIDARITY FOREVER"
www.kentlaw.edu/ilhs/solidarity.html

Unions' collective bargaining activities are still generally carried on more or less as the Webbs envisaged, though the range of issues brought to the table is now often considerably greater. As for legal enactment, unions have been among the strongest supporters of higher minimum wages, health and safety legislation, anti-discrimination laws, and a broad range of social programs of benefit to all working people—not just union members. Again, this emphasis on working on behalf of all working people is in line with the Webbs' original emphasis.

Even today, the Webbs' three methods are at the core of what most unions spend a good deal of their time doing. But the range of union activity has expanded a good deal over the past century, and to some degree its character has also changed. In the area of collective bargaining, for example, while most bargaining continues to be adversarial, a growing number of unions have entered into more cooperative arrangements with management. In some cases, unions have taken on what amounts to something approaching joint governance of the workplace—a role that would have been totally foreign to the unionist of 50 years ago and that continues to arouse considerable controversy within the Canadian labour movement even now (CAW, no date; CPU, 1990; USWA, 1991).[2] In the political arena, unions have also expanded their role, moving beyond support for specific pieces of labour-related legislation to more or less permanent alliances with parties such as the NDP, and less formal arrangements with women's, environmental, anti-poverty, and church groups and other progressive organizations and the creation of "humanity" or "justice" funds to support specific causes (Godard, 1994:218). They have also become adept at using publicity campaigns to help achieve their objectives and at using their members' savings and pension funds to promote local and regional development and job creation through a broad range of labour-sponsored venture capital corporations and pension pools (Jackson and Peirce, 1990:40–44; Boivin and Déom, 1995:459–460; Jackson and Lamontagne, 1995; Jackson, 1997 and 1998). Finally, Canadian unions have long been and continue to be involved in a broad range of educational ventures (CWC, 1990; CUPE, no date; Fisher and Peirce, 1995; White, 1995).

Thus, while their general objectives remain the same as those of unions in the past, today's unions tend to operate within a far broader context. They also have available to them strategies and technologies which the unionists of, for example, the 1940s could only dream about. The discussion that follows takes into account both that broader context and some of those strategies and technologies.

Collective Bargaining

Overall, the Canadian industrial relations system can fairly be described as voluntarist. This means that in unionized workplaces, most outcomes are left to be negotiated between the union and management rather than being established through legislation, as is the case in some European countries such as France (Goetschy, 1993). As a result, collective bargaining is, almost by definition, a core activity for virtually all Canadian unions.

The bargaining process itself will be considered in some detail in the chapter on negotiation, and thus need not be discussed here. But it may be worth taking a brief look at some of the ways in which that process has changed in recent years.

First, collective bargaining now addresses a far broader range of issues than it generally did early in the century, when agreements might be just one or two pages long and were usually limited to such core issues as wages, hours of work, holiday and overtime pay, and union security provisions (see Giles and Jain, 1989). During the early postwar period, as was noted in Chapter 4, unions began to negotiate a broad range of fringe benefits such as paid vacations, sick leave, pensions, and medical and hospitalization insurance (Heron, 1989; Giles and Starkman, 1995). More recently, demands from an increasingly diverse work force containing growing numbers of women have caused unions to negotiate maternity and paternity leave provisions, flexible schedules, workplace day-care centres, and in some cases anti-discrimination and anti-harassment provisions that go beyond the requirements of human rights legislation. At the same time, the introduction of labour-saving technology into workplaces has caused unions to seek (albeit often unsuccessfully) to negotiate protection against job or income loss resulting from such technology. The introduction of new chemicals and other potentially hazardous substances has led to the negotiation of clauses regarding their use, as well as the employer's responsibility to provide appropriate safety equipment and training in the handling of such substances (see Giles and Starkman, 1995:367). Finally, growing concern for members' well-being both on and off the job has led many unions to negotiate employee assistance programs to help employees with drug, alcohol, financial, or other personal problems. The addition of this broad range of issues to such core issues as wages and hours of work has tended to make bargaining a longer and more complex process than it was in the past.

CANADIAN ASSOCIATION OF LABOUR MEDIA
www.calm.ca

Second, while most collective bargaining continues to be adversarial, or **distributive,** a growing proportion of it is now of an **integrative,** or problem-solving nature (Downie, 1982 and 1989; Craig and Solomon, 1996). Integrative bargaining's most obvious use is in cases involving clear "win-win" issues, such as health and safety (Chaykowski, 1995:237); however, this type of bargaining has sometimes been more widely applied, even in cases involving monetary issues (Downie, 1982:323). A recent, essentially integrative approach developed by Robert Fisher and William Ury and known as **principled bargaining** (see Chaykowski, 1995:247) emphasizes the separation of issues from personalities, a focus on the parties' underlying interests, and the invention of options that give rise to mutual gain rather than win-lose situations. There is evidence to suggest that principled bargaining has been adopted by major companies like Petro-Canada, Bell Canada, and Algoma Steel, and prominent unions such as the Communications, Energy and Paperworkers, Steelworkers, and United Mine Workers (Chaykowski, 1995:247–248).

Clearly, any move towards principled bargaining entails a significant shift in attitude. Whereas in conventional bargaining, mistrust of the other side and a focus on short-term tactics designed to give one's own side the advantage are the norm, principled bargaining requires a good measure of trust and a willingness to take the long view in dealings with the other side. To union leaders trained to distrust management, as many have traditionally been, it may be extremely difficult to make the necessary attitudinal change.[3]

Joint Union-Management Ventures at the Workplace

The same types of challenges posed by a shift from distributive to principled bargaining apply, to an even greater degree, to unions' participation in joint ventures with management designed to increase worker morale and productivity. Such ventures can range from single-issue labour-management committees to broad gain-sharing plans such as the Scanlon Plan (see Downie, 1982:330–332). They can also include quality circles, self-directed work teams, and employee stock ownership plans (Verma, 1995).

"EMPLOYEE OWNERSHIP AND THE HIGH-EFFICIENCY WORKPLACE" BY DAVID JACKSON, COLUMBIA UNIVERSITY

socrates.berkeley.edu/~iir/ncw/wpapers/jacobson/index.html

In a few cases, unions and management have negotiated joint governance arrangements whereby the union becomes, in effect, a full partner in management of the organization (Verma, 1995:299–300). Such arrangements would seem to entail a radical transformation of the union's role, from that of workers' advocate to that of administrator and perhaps even manager of discontent. They also open up far greater possibilities for direct communication between management and employees—possibilities that run the risk of reducing the union's influence in the workplace. (See Lemelin, 1989:452–455).

Joint governance arrangements clearly offer many important, perhaps even unique opportunities for unions, but they also pose many challenges. If, for example, in its role as co-manager, a union has agreed with management on the need to cut costs, but rank-and-file members are pushing hard for immediate, up-front wage increases, what will union negotiators do at the bargaining table, and how will the demand for wage increases affect the union's continued participation in the joint governance scheme? Moreover, participation in such schemes often requires union members and officials to learn new skills. Traditionally, motivational and political skills were most important for union leaders. But if a union is co-managing an organization, its officials and those of its members involved in joint governance committees will also need to learn business-related skills such as finance, economics, and accounting (see Verma, 1995:299).

Union participation in joint cooperation and employee involvement schemes has often proven quite controversial, both within individual unions, in the Canadian labour movement as a whole, and among IR academics. Some regard increased employee involvement as inevitable given globalization and increased competitiveness. Such writers argue that unions have no choice other than to participate in employee involvement programs. If unions don't participate, they suggest, management will introduce the programs anyway, and the interests of neither individual workers nor the union will have been well-served.[4] Others (i.e., Godard, 1991) are more skeptical, while still others (i.e., Wells, 1993) oppose any union participation in such ventures, basically on the grounds that for a union to assume any significant co-management role amounts to a conflict of interest with its core role as the workers' advocate. Within the labour movement, some unions (i.e., CAW, no date) have adopted policies of outright opposition to joint cooperation schemes, while some of the schemes' strongest supporters, such as the CEP and Steelworkers, have insisted on being given a major role as a condition of participation (Verma, 1995:297).[5] Arguably the current economic environment, which has seen many large-scale layoffs even in highly profitable organizations, has made such joint ventures a dicier business from the unions' perspective. With large-scale layoffs occurring despite unions' best efforts to increase productivity, even former supporters may wonder what's in the schemes for them. At a minimum, such continuing layoffs could serve to strengthen the hand of union "hawks" opposing cooperation, thus making it more difficult for unions to enter into any new programs, as well as weakening the internal political position of leaders disposed towards cooperation.

Joint Participation Outside the Workplace

Canadian unions are also involved in a variety of joint ventures with management outside the workplace. Among other things, unions and management groups have formed a number of sectoral councils to address such issues as training, economic restructuring, trade policy, and labour-management cooperation on an industry-wide basis. One of the first such councils was the Canadian Textile Labour-Management Committee (CTLMC), formed in 1967 in the wake of a bitter strike at the Dominion Textile plant in Quebec (Thomason, Zwerling, and Chandra, 1992:264). Comprising nine management representatives and nine from the textile unions, the committee has not formally involved itself in collective bargaining as such but has sought to improve the bargaining process by ensuring that the parties are provided with accurate information about the real state of the industry (Thomason et al., 1992:266). In addition, the CTLMC has involved itself with issues ranging from domestic and foreign trade policies to productivity, occupational health and safety, and education and training. The committee appears to have been at least partly responsible for a major improvement in labour-management relations and a significant reduction in strike incidence in the textile industry (Thomason et al., 1992:264–266).

"WHO RECEIVES FORMAL FIRM-SPONSORED TRAINING IN THE U.S.?" BY CRAIG OLSON, UNIVERSITY OF WISCONSIN, MADISON

socrates.berkeley.edu/~iir/ncw/wpapers/olson/html

Another important sectoral initiative is the Canadian Steel Trade and Employment Congress (CSTEC), formed jointly by the major steel companies and the United Steelworkers of America (USWA) in 1985 (Verma and Warrian, 1992:124). Since its formation, CSTEC has been heavily involved in trade issues, a special concern being the targeting of unfair foreign competition. The Congress's other major concern has been providing employment assistance for displaced steelworkers, of whom there have been a great many due to ongoing restructuring in the industry. Such assistance is provided under CSTEC's HEAT (Helping Employees Adjust Together) program, which (under an agreement with the federal government has since 1987) has been provided with the same amount of per capita funding to assist displaced workers as would otherwise have been given to the Industrial Adjustment Service (Verma and Warrian, 1992). HEAT's services have included provision of job market information, training in starting a business, relocation assistance, and personal financial planning and retraining (Verma and Warrian, 1992:125).

Canadian unions have also been involved in a number of tripartite, or labour-management-government initiatives. Tripartism has never been as strong in Canada as in many European countries, such as the Netherlands and Sweden (Adams, 1995:506), and generally has had its ups and downs here. While a fair number of tripartite consultative bodies were established during the 1960s and 1970s, in 1976 the labour movement withdrew its representatives from most of them, including the Economic Council of Canada, in protest over the federal government's imposition of wage-price controls (Craig and Solomon, 1996:138). More recently, however, unions have joined with management and the federal government in launching the Canadian Labour Market and Productivity Centre (CLMPC) (Adams, 1995; Murray, 1995). Much of the CLMPC's work has been on relatively uncontentious issues such as training and labour market information (Adams, 1995); however, over the past few years it has broadened its focus, doing important research on issues as varied as work hours (CLMPC, 1997), the impacts of labour-sponsored venture capital corporations (Jackson and Lamontagne, 1995), and women in the workplace (Craig and Solomon, 1996:54).

Political Action

Almost all unions engage in some kind of political action. To a large extent, unions' ability to achieve their objectives depends on the types of legislation and government policies in place. They cannot hope to influence legislation or government policy without in some way becoming involved in the political process, whether through lobbying government on specific issues or through more formal connection with a political party.

This said, the form of political activity taken varies greatly within the Canadian labour government. Unions and labour federations differ particularly with respect to affiliation with a political party. The Canadian Federation of Labour, for example, was always strongly opposed to any such affiliation (McCambly, 1990). In Quebec, a similar position is taken by the Centrale des syndicates démocratiques (CSD), which feels so strongly on this point that it has written into its constitution an article stating that any adoption of a particular ideological position would require a referendum of the organization's entire membership (Boivin and Déom, 1995).

In the Canadian context, however, labour organizations such as the CFL and CSD have been probably the exception rather than the rule. Most Canadian unions are explicitly committed to **social unionism,** a type of unionism that believes that the role of unions is to further workers' well-being as a whole, outside the workplace as well as within it (Godard, 1994:217). Almost by definition, a commitment to social unionism entails a formal, or at least informal, affiliation with a political party, since acting on behalf of the working class as a whole necessitates winning passage of a broad range of legislation that will benefit workers and lower-income Canadians. This is something that is extremely difficult to do through ad hoc lobbying on specific issues. While affiliation with a political party is no guarantee of success, it does arguably improve unions' chances, by providing them with an experienced partner to assist them in their political ventures on a steady basis.

In English Canada, the labour movement has most often chosen the NDP or its forerunner party, the CCF, as its political partner. In general, the links between the labour movement and the NDP have become closer over the past two decades. Unions are allowed a given number of delegate slots at NDP conventions (Godard, 1994:218), and many choose to affiliate directly to the party, a decision that allows them to play in active role in formulating its policy (Murray, 1995:189). In Quebec, most labour activists support the Parti Québécois, or the federal Bloc Québécois party (Boivin and Déom, 1995:458–459). The support, however, is typically of a more individual and ad hoc nature than the formal affiliation of unions with the English NDP. Only one Quebec central labour organization, the Quebec Federation of Labour, or provincial wing of the CLC, has formally endorsed the PQ (Boivin and Déom, 1995).

CANADIAN ASSOCIATION OF LABOUR MEDIA
www.calm.ca

There is no doubt that the NDP-CCF and PQ have often been of great benefit to the labour movement. As we pointed out in the labour history chapter, the threat of a CCF victory was arguably the major factor responsible for passage of Canada's first collective bargaining legislation, *PC 1003*. Later on, the NDP's balance-of-power position in a minority Liberal government was crucial in winning passage of the *Public Service Staff Relations Act*. More recently, NDP and PQ provincial governments have been responsible for a variety of pro-labour laws ranging from the removal of restrictive exclusions from unionization rights and the liberalization of certification procedures[6] to anti-strike-breaker bills, first-contract arbitration, and technological change provisions.

But there have also been many strains between the labour movement and the NDP or PQ, particularly when these parties have formed a provincial government and have been forced to make unpopular spending cuts directly affecting some of their union supporters. In 1982, the PQ government unilaterally imposed a 20 percent public sector salary reduction for the first three months of 1983, then unilaterally extended the existing agreements until the end of 1985 (Hébert, 1995:222). This action infuriated the public schoolteachers and other public sector workers, who had been among the PQ's strongest supporters, and caused much of the province's labour movement to withdraw support from the party in the 1985 election, which the PQ lost. Similarly, in 1993, Ontario's NDP government infuriated public sector unions by imposing a "Social Contract" providing for a three-year public sector wage freeze and unpaid days off. Public sector and many private sector unions withdrew their support from the NDP, which went down to disastrous defeat in the 1995 Ontario election, following an even worse performance in the 1993 federal election, for which the "Social Contract" legislation was largely blamed (Morton, 1995). More recently, relations between the PQ and Quebec's labour movement have again been severely strained by the government's large-scale cutbacks in health care and other social areas. But while the current strains between the Ontario and Quebec labour movements and their political partners are real and may not go away quickly, over the longer term it seems most likely that these labour movements will reaffirm their support for the NDP and PQ. They will do so not because they necessarily agree with all the decisions that

NDP and PQ governments make, but because in the larger scheme of things, having a regular political partner is better for the labour movement than not having one,[7] and if the unions sever their ties to the NDP and PQ, they are unlikely to find other political parties willing or able to meet their needs.

Not all politics is carried out in parliaments and legislative assemblies. As the economic environment becomes more globalized, many Canadian unions are finding themselves increasingly concerned with international development issues and with related problems of workers' rights, child labour and the like, as well as with issues such as child poverty, hunger, and regional underdevelopment at home. To help address these issues, a number of unions have established social justice or humanity funds. The Canadian Auto Workers' Social Justice Fund requires participating employers to donate one cent for each straight-time hour worked by each bargaining unit worker to a designated charity, food bank, or international relief effort (Godard, 1994:218). The Steelworkers' Humanity Fund, established on a similar checkoff basis, addresses itself to international labour issues, including support for core labour rights such as workers' freedom of association and reduction of child labour. With increased global trade, the Humanity Fund has become particularly interested in developing codes of conduct that would support basic human and labour rights for Canadian firms doing business overseas, and with linking trade and foreign aid to support for those basic rights by Third World governments. As globalization increases, such funds could well become a much more prominent aspect of Canadian union activity, since they are potentially very useful vehicles for linking Canadian and overseas labour organizations.

Publicity Campaigns and Member Communication

Like almost all other modern organizations, today's unions are finding that they have to spend an increasing amount of their time and energy communicating, both with their members and with the public at large. To keep members abreast of what they are doing, unions send out regular newsletters and other publications such as special pre-strike bulletins, develop telephone trees, post notices on union bulletin boards, and occasionally use other mediums such as the Internet. To tell their story to the general public, they use the full range of modern media, from traditional newspaper and magazine ads, to radio, TV, and (once again) the Internet.

Union publicity efforts serve a variety of purposes. In some cases, such as the CEP's recent ad on work hours in the *Ontario New Democrat*, the purpose is to inform both the union's own people and sympathetic members of the general public (in this case New Democrats) about what the union is doing on a particular issue. In other instances, like that of the Carleton University ad protesting cutbacks to

Carleton University's CUPE locals, representing support staff, advertise their voicemail account where students can register their protest.

support services, the aim is to build coalitions with other stakeholders—in this case the university's students. In still other cases, like those of the Ontario Secondary School Teachers' Federation against education cutbacks or the CUPE ad against Ontario's two-tier health care, the aim is to protest government policy. While many union ads tend to be negative, at least insofar as they are critical of existing economic and political conditions and seek to change them, unions also run a variety of positive ads. A number of the union ads appearing in the *Ontario New Democrat* do not address specific issues but are designed merely to emphasize the unions' general support for the NDP.

The strongest and most controversial type of union publicity campaign is the **boycott,** or negative publicity campaign

The Ontario Secondary School Teachers' Federation urges citizens to join their campaign to protest education cutbacks in the province.

designed to induce the public not to purchase the goods or services of the company in question. Boycotts are frequently though not always launched in the context of a strike or lockout or union recognition dispute. Perhaps the best-known example is the grape-and-lettuce boycott undertaken by the late Cesar Chavez and his fledgling United Farm Workers (UFW) union in the United States during the late 1960s. The boycott was widely credited with helping the UFW win bargaining rights for thousands of farm workers, mainly Mexican-American immigrants, who up to that point had been working under wretched conditions for extremely low wages.

Two major boycott campaigns were launched in Ontario early in 1998. The first was the "We're not bringing home the bacon" campaign undertaken by the United Food and Commercial Workers

Let us never return to the days when the wealthy enjoyed the best of care and the poor entered through the back door.

Treatment for the POOR Only
No patients received for clinics after 9:30 A.M. and 2:30 P.M. Doors will be locked at these hours

Yes to Canada's Health Care system, with quality services for all.

Canadian Union of Public Employees

CUPE ad offers *Canadian Forum* readers a stark reminder of what two-tier health care could be like.

SUPPORT FARMWORKERS

BOYCOTT GRAPES & LETTUCE

United Farmworkers' grape and lettuce boycott was one of the most successful boycotts ever undertaken and was widely credited with helping the union win bargaining rights for California farm workers.

Union against Maple Leaf Foods, with whom the UFCW had been locked in a series of bitter strikes since August 1997. The second and more controversial campaign was one launched by the Ontario English Catholic Teachers' Association against firms found to have donated money exclusively to the governing Conservative party, to which the teachers are opposed because of the education cutbacks leading to the fall 1997 strike described in detail in the strike chapter (Lakey, 1998). The teachers' union boycott was particularly controversial because it was a **secondary** boycott (a boycott of an ally of one's adversary rather than the adversary itself)[8] and because, in the eyes of some, it amounted to punishing people for their political beliefs.

UNIONS IN BUSINESS

The severe recession of the early 1980s caused many labour organizations to start working proactively to create jobs and promote local and community development. It was at this time that labour-sponsored venture capital corporations (VCCs) began to appear.

Among the first, and by far the largest of the labour-sponsored VCCs, was the Quebec Solidarity Fund, launched in 1984 with support from the Quebec government (Jackson and Peirce, 1990:42; Boivin and Déom, 1995:460). Like other labour-sponsored VCCs, the Solidarity Fund offers investors a variety of tax credits, including an RRSP deduction as well as a provincial equity tax credit (Boivin and Déom, 1995:460). By 1993, the Fund had accumulated almost $800 million in assets and attracted just under 200 000 investors, nearly half of whom were QFL members, and was accounting for about half of all risk capital invested in Quebec (Boivin and Déom, 1995). It is generally recognized that the Fund has been responsible for creating or saving many thousands of jobs in the province.

Since its inception, the Fund has invested in a broad range of small and medium-sized enterprises in such sectors as communications, EDP software and service, and forest products, and has created specialized sectoral funds in biotechnology, environmental industries, and aerospace (Jackson and Peirce, 1990; Boivin and Déom, 1995). Among its more recent ventures, the Fund helped finance Entourage, a new employee-owned firm launched by former Bell Canada technicians in the Ottawa region who are CEP members (Jackson, 1998).

Though it is the country's largest and probably its best-known labour-sponsored VCC, the Solidarity Fund is far from being the only such organization in Canada. Other such VCCs include Working Ventures*, founded by the Canadian Federation

---

* Working Ventures, administered by an independent company, was not expected to be affected by the CFL's 1997 decision (*Globe & Mail*, 8/22/97) to cease operating as a central labour body.

of Labour (Jackson and Peirce, 1990:43; Murray, 1995:188), First Ontario Fund, the Manitoba Federation of Labour's Crocus Investment Fund, and B.C.'s Working Opportunities Fund (Jackson, 1998:4). The last three of these funds have been particularly interested in supporting employee-owned firms (Jackson, 1998). In addition, the Solidarity and Crocus Funds and B.C.'s Working Opportunity Fund have, since the 1980s, directly supported a broad range of community economic development projects. For example, the Working Opportunity Fund invests in community loan funds serving small business (Jackson, 1998:10).

Unions and labour federations have also been heavily involved in social housing. Nationally, the CLC played a key role in establishing the Cooperative Housing Foundation; at the local level, many local labour councils sponsored cooperative housing projects during the 1970s and 1980s. In Cape Breton, the non-profit Cape Breton Labourers Development Corporation funds the construction of affordable homes for International Labourers Union members. In B.C. during the 1980s, the labour movement supported a progressive board of directors at Vancouver City Savings Credit Union, which resulted in a number of innovative affordable housing projects (Jackson, 1998:11).

Through their members' pension funds, unions control many hundreds of millions of dollars. An idea that has lately been gaining increasing currency both in the United States and, to a lesser degree, in Canada is that of using these funds to promote such socially desirable objectives as community development, affordable housing, and small-business growth (Jackson, 1997). The vehicle normally used for this purpose is an Economically Targeted Investment (ETI), a pooling mechanism that allows pension funds to channel a certain portion of their assets into such worthwhile ventures (Jackson, 1997).

Vancouver's Greystone Properties is a good example of a Canadian ETI. This organization, sponsored by 28 pension plans jointly trusteed by construction unions and construction companies, now has assets of some $250 million and has become a major investor in affordable housing in Vancouver. The fund is used to finance construction projects that provide jobs for union members affiliated with the participating pension plans, and also to provide mortgages for low- and middle-income people in a city whose housing costs are among the country's highest. In addition to achieving these worthy social objectives, Greystone has provided above-average returns to its sponsors (Jackson, 1997). In the eyes of at least one observer (Jackson, 1997:2), Greystone represents a model that could be replicated across Canada, especially with construction union pension funds.

In some cases, unions and their members have also bought significant or even controlling interests in the firms for which members work. Most often, this strategy has been used in single-industry resource towns where the corporate owners want to pull out even though the enterprise remains viable (Jackson, 1998:3). While many unions are critical of employee buyouts, arguing that it isn't the union's or workers' job to save management from the consequences of its own mismanagement, the Steelworkers have been a notable exception (Jackson, 1998:5). Since the early 1990s, this union has encouraged viable buyouts, both directly and through venture capital funds. By now, it has had enough experience to be able to provide support for those locals contemplating a buyout (Jackson, 1998). Its most notable success has been in the case of Algoma Steel in Sault Ste. Marie, Ontario. Here, a firm on the brink of collapse (Verma and Warrian, 1992:121–124) was rescued and turned around, thanks to an employee buyout that saw the firm's 6000 workers acquire a 60 percent interest in the company (Steed, 1994; Jackson, 1998:3). Other buyouts of note have occurred in the pulp and paper industry, at Spruce Falls in Ontario and Tembec in Quebec. In these cases, unionized workers represented by the CEP bought major interests in their mills and managed to keep most of their jobs (Jackson, 1998:3–4).

The preceding discussion has touched on only a few of the ways in which unions have begun to function, in effect, as business organizations, mobilizing their members' capital and in some cases using it to leverage other funds to create and save jobs, build affordable housing, and promote community development. Given government's growing reluctance to fund direct job creation schemes, this aspect of union action seems likely to expand in the coming years and will bear close observation by students of industrial relations.

Education

The labour movement has a long and proud record of involvement in education. As we noted in the labour history chapter, nineteenth- and early twentieth-century union halls often served as libraries, forums for public lectures and seminars, and venues for a broad range of educational and cultural activity. The tradition of union education has continued to the present day. Although there is not space in a general industrial relations textbook to do more than skim the surface on the subject of unions' educational ventures, even a cursory look will suffice to give some idea of the extent of their involvement.

"LABOUR EDUCATION FOR 2001," ADULT EDUCATION RESEARCH CONFERENCE, BRUCE SPENCER

www.athabasca.ca/html/staff/academice/brucesp/laboured.htm

While many union-sponsored courses focus on technical issues of immediate concern such as organizing, bargaining strategy and shop steward training, others have addressed broader issues such as women in the labour movement and unions and the environment (CUPE, no date; Fisher and Peirce, 1995). Over the years, the CLC has run weekend institutes and week-long summer programs covering a broad range of subjects (R. White, 1995). In Newfoundland, the Newfoundland Association of Public Employees (NAPE) has been a major player in this area, as has the Canadian Union of Public Employees (CUPE). NAPE's offerings have included training in public speaking and leadership, which has gone a long way towards building up members' confidence when placed in situations requiring them to speak in public (Fisher and Peirce, 1995). CUPE's courses, many offered in French as well as English, have included ones in political action, pay equity, technological change, and assertiveness training. The union has placed special emphasis on health and safety training; among its offerings, in addition to general health and safety courses, are specialized courses aimed at health-care workers, municipal sewage-treatment-plant workers, social-service workers, and those who must deal with asbestos in the workplace (CUPE, n.d.).

A number of unions have begun to offer courses on contemporary political and economic issues of special relevance to their members. CUPE's offerings have included "Contracting Out and Privatization—Ways of Winning," a subject of obvious interest to the union's members given the wave of privatization that has taken place over the past 15 years (CUPE, n.d.). The Communications Workers of Canada (CWC) and its successor union, the Communications, Energy, and Paperworkers Union (CEP) have also offered courses and developed educational materials on various "hot topics." During the early 1990s, the CWC conducted ongoing education on the subject of free trade (CWC, 1992). More recently, the CEP has developed a series of articles, videos, and other materials on work hours for insertion into its leadership development and steward training courses (J. White, 1997b).

Unions' Expanded Scope of Action

Unions continue to spend a great deal of their time negotiating collective agreements, handling members' grievances, and seeking to achieve passage of pro-labour legislation. But in addition to these traditional core activities, today's unions have entered into a broad range of partnerships with management, both within workplaces and beyond the workplace. Politically, their sphere of interest has widened, to encompass coalitions with anti-poverty and other social justice groups at home and with foreign unions and Canadian NGOs promoting economic development and human and labour rights overseas. And particularly over the past 15 years, many unions have entered the world of business, learning how to use available funds such as pension monies to promote job creation, community development, affordable housing, and other social objectives. In the field of labour education, a number of unions have expanded the labour "curriculum" beyond traditional core subjects such as collective bargaining and grievance handling, to encompass highly technical courses in specific areas of occupational health and safety, and employment law and personal development courses in areas such as stress management and retirement planning (CUPE, n.d.).

Supporting all these efforts has been an increasingly sophisticated publicity apparatus. Like most other organizations in today's media-driven society, unions have become increasingly aware of the need to communicate their message both to members and to the general public. To this end, they have not hesitated to use the full gamut of media approaches, from traditional newspaper and magazine ads to direct mail campaigns and the establishment of Web sites on the Internet.

"USING THE DUNLOP REPORT TO FULL ADVANTAGE: A STRATEGY FOR ACHIEVING MUTUAL GAINS" BY THOMAS A. KOCHAN, MIT, 1995
www.ilr.cornell.edu/library/e_archive/Dunlop/Kochan.html

This new, expanded scope of union action has not been uncontroversial, either within the labour movement or outside of it. As noted earlier, some unionists feel a union has no business affiliating with a political party. A fair number might argue against a checkoff-based fund such as the Steelworkers' Humanity Fund, on the grounds that it should be up to the individual union member to decide which charities and non-profit organizations he or she will support. At least one major Quebec labour federation, the Centrale des syndicats démocratiques, has been skeptical about the merits of the Solidarity Fund (Boivin and Déom, 1995:460), and more national unions than not seem to be opposed to employee buyouts, even in cases where the rank-and-file strongly support the buyout (Jackson, 1998:5). Economically targeted investment vehicles for employee pension plans have been no less controversial (Jackson, 1997).

While the debates over these issues seem unlikely to end any time soon, the fact remains that most Canadian labour organizations have expanded their scope of action in one or more of the areas just mentioned. To give just one example, the Canadian Federation of Labour, which was always adamantly opposed to any kind of political affiliation, became a major player in the area of labour-supported business ventures. The areas into which a union or labour federation chooses to expand will depend on a variety of factors, including the organization's traditions and history, its membership composition, its members' interests, and the economic pressures facing the industry in which it operates. Some may wish (or need) to expand into more "new" areas than others. But in today's environment of more or less perpetual economic crisis, few if any unions can afford the luxury of simply burying their heads in the sand and concentrating solely on "minding the shop." While Canadian union membership rates have not declined anywhere near as sharply as those in the United States have, the pressures on Canadian union membership are nonetheless real (Murray, 1995:170–171; Lipsig-Mumme, 1995). In the coming decades, the ability to mount effective publicity campaigns and to use members' accumulated funds to create or save jobs may become increasingly critical to a union's survival. Our prediction, therefore, is that the scope of union action will continue to expand.

UNION IMPACTS

Not surprisingly, given the broad range of activities in which we have just seen that they engage, unions have an equally broad range of impacts on their members' wages and working conditions, on the productivity and overall performance of the firms in which their members work, and on the Canadian economy and Canadian society as a whole. Many of these impacts, especially the wage impacts, have been studied extensively. A 1986 U.S. review article (Lewis, 1986) considers more than 200 studies on wage impacts alone. Gunderson and Riddell (1993) review 11 Canadian studies on the same subject.

To a large extent, the union impacts likely to be of greatest interest to any given industrial relationist will depend on that person's overall perspective on IR (discussed in detail in Chapter 1). Pure economists and others of a neoclassical persuasion are apt to be most interested in unions' wage impacts. Students of organizational behaviour and other managerialists are likely to focus on the way unions affect management and overall firm productivity. Institutionalists may be most interested in positive productivity effects resulting from unionized workers' having a greater say in how firms are managed. For their part, reformists and people taking a political economy perspective are apt to emphasize unions' macro-level effects on Canadian society as a whole. Our view is that one must take *all* the above effects into account to have a good understanding of how unions operate in Canada today.[9]

Wage Impacts

Direct Union Wage Impact

While unions are certainly about more than just money, it's unlikely that most people would remain members for very long if their unions could not negotiate a higher wage than they would otherwise receive. In simplest terms, a **direct union wage impact** is the premium a worker receives for union membership. It can be expressed as the *difference* between the wage a unionized worker and an otherwise equally qualified non-unionized worker would receive for doing the same job, as the following equation shows: DUWI = W(uw) – W(nuw), where W(uw) is the average wage for unionized workers doing any given job, and W(nuw) is the average wage for non-unionized workers doing that same job.

To be sure, the question of how large any direct union wage impact is will typically be much more complex than the previous discussion would suggest. The whole assumption behind the calculation of direct union wage impacts is that other things, such as workers' experience and skill levels, are equal. Often they are far from equal. Because unionized firms generally offer higher pay and sometimes better working conditions as well, they tend to attract (and are able to hire) more highly qualified people than non-unionized firms. It may, therefore, be difficult to say to what extent a "union" wage impact is a simple premium for union membership, and to what extent it is a premium for greater skill or experience (Gunderson and Riddell, 1993:390–391).

Over the years, advances in statistical techniques have made it possible for researchers to "control" for differences in labour quality and job characteristics (Gunderson and Riddell, 1993; Gunderson and Hyatt, 1995:323; see also l. Reynolds, 1982:133–135). While there are still significant methodological problems[10] in determining the precise direct union wage impact for any country as a whole, the 11 Canadian studies reviewed by Gunderson and Riddell (1993:394–396) found that impact to be in the 10 to 25 percent range, a finding generally in line with earlier U.S. studies (L. Reynolds, 1982:485–486; Lewis, 1986). Some more recent U.S. studies discussed by Gunderson et al. (Gunderson and Hyatt, 1995:325) have yielded slightly higher estimates, typically in the 20 to 30 percent range. Since union wage impacts tend to be somewhat higher during recessions because collective agreement provisions "lock wages in" for the duration of the contract (Gunderson and Hyatt, 1995), it is possible that these higher recent impacts can be attributed mainly to the recent recession.

What's clearer is that direct union wage impacts are not the same for every worker, or in every industry. In general, these impacts tend to be greater for blue-collar than for white-collar and for less skilled than for more-skilled workers (Gunderson and Hyatt, 1995:325; Gunderson and Riddell, 1993:397; Reynolds, 1982:496–497). The impacts may be especially high in industries such as construction (Guderson and Riddell, 1993:397; Reynolds, 1982:485–486). In the United States, the evidence suggests that the impacts are greater for Black workers and women than for White male workers (Reynolds, 1982:486); in Canada, there is some evidence of greater impacts for women, though this evidence is far from conclusive (Gunderson and Riddell, 1993:398). Studies from both countries suggest that direct union wage impacts are generally greater in the private than in the public sector (Gunderson and Riddell, 1993; Gunderson and Hyatt, 1995:326).

Impact on Fringe Benefits

Most workers do not receive all their pay as up-front wages. Usually a portion of the total compensation package is paid in fringe or non-wage benefits for such things as pensions, vacations, medical and dental insurance, holidays, and sick leave (Gunderson and Riddell, 1993:406). Unionized establishments generally pay a greater portion of the total compensation package in fringe benefits than do non-unionized ones; thus their impact on fringe benefits is typically greater than their impact on up-front wages (Gunderson and Riddell, 1993:406–407). There are a number of reasons for this. For one thing, the average unionized worker is likely to be older and in a higher tax bracket than the average non-unionized worker, and hence to favour deferred forms of compensation, such as pensions, which are non-taxable. These benefits may be particularly attractive because, due to economies of scale, they can be purchased relatively inexpensively, especially in larger establishments (Gunderson and Riddell, 1993:407). Again, since unionized workers are older and in most cases would have had the chance to save up money over the years, they tend to prefer to take more of their total compensation in the form of increased leisure (i.e., longer vacations and holidays) than as up-front pay (Gunderson and Riddell, 1993:230). Their greater average age also helps explain their relatively greater interest in medical insurance and pension plans.

Unionized firms also tend to favour pensions and other forms of deferred payment because they help "lock workers in," thereby reducing costly turnover. In addition, pensions and other work benefits serve as work incentives, since older workers who stand to lose a lucrative pension if they are let go will likely work harder than they otherwise would to prevent that from happening (Gunderson and Riddell, 1993:408).

Indirect Union Wage Impacts

Indirect union wage impacts are the effects unions have on the wages of non-unionized workers. As various commentators point out (Gunderson, 1989; Gunderson and Hyatt, 1995:325–326), unions can affect the wages of non-unionized workers through a broad range of market, institutional, and legislative mechanisms. Economic theory would suggest that over the longer term, unions should reduce wages in the non-unionized sector, as employees from the unionized sector who are laid off when the unionized wage rises above the equilibrium level "spill over" into the non-unionized sector, thereby reducing wages there as well (Gunderson and Riddell, 1993:325–328). In practice, it is quite difficult to determine the overall impact of unions on non-unionized workers' wages in Canada. In general, the consensus is that this effect has been modest—probably less than 3 to 4 percent (Gunderson and Hyatt, 1995:327; Gunderson and Riddell, 1993:401). But it would be misleading to think of the indirect union wage effect as being uniform across the economy. Some non-unionized workers have lower wages due to unionization, while others, including most notably White males, may see their wages rise (see Gunderson and Hyatt, 1995:327).

What we are really talking about here are two quite different kinds of indirect union wage impact, impacts that pull wages in different directions and apply to different types of workers. The depressing or so-called "crowding" effect predicted by economic theory (Gunderson and Riddell, 1993:385–386) will typically apply to lower-skilled workers with little labour market power. (The case of the Los Angeles fruit pickers discussed in Chapter 2 is an excellent example here). The so-called "threat" effect applies in situations where non-unionized employers increase their employees' pay, often to levels at or near those paid to unionized workers, in order to forestall a unionization drive or prevent employees with scarce skills from quitting and going to work in a unionized firm (Gunderson and Riddell, 1993:387–389). *This* type of indirect wage impact, also sometimes known as the "as-if-unionized" impact, most often applies in situations involving highly skilled workers such as professionals or skilled technical staff. The reasoning here is that if the firm pays workers the same or nearly the same wages as they would receive if unionized, they will have less incentive to join the union, particularly if, along with higher wages, the workers receive union-style benefits and some kind of in-house grievance system. In effect, this type of indirect union wage impact is a soft union-avoidance tactic since the primary aim is to reduce workers' demand for union services.

Unions and Wage Dispersion

In addition to increasing their members' wages relative to those of non-unionized workers, unions may affect national income distribution in various ways. Because unions tend to reduce wage differentials related to skill, age, experience, and seniority, there is less wage dispersion among unionized than among non-unionized workers (Gunderson and Riddell, 1993:402). To put it another way, there appears to be significantly less difference between the best-paid and worst-paid unionized workers than between the best-paid and worst-paid non-unionized workers. At the same time, unionization tends to increase overall dispersion by creating a wage differential between unionized and non-unionized workers (Gunderson and Hyatt, 1995:325). A number of studies from both Canada and the United States have shown that the former effect is stronger, which means that overall, unions tend to reduce wage dispersion throughout the economy as a whole (Gunderson and Hyatt, 1995; Gunderson and Riddell, 1993:402). Other things being equal, we would expect similar results from unions' efforts in the political arena, since they generally tend to support redistributive economic and social policies such as progressive taxation policies, high levels of unemployment insurance and welfare benefits, and pay and employment equity programs.[11]

How Unions Achieve Their Wage Goals

In the section on union actions, we noted that unions use a variety of approaches to achieve their objectives, approaches that can range from collective bargaining to work for a labour-oriented political party or publicity campaigns. Here, we focus in slightly more detail on the methods unions use to achieve their wage objectives.

BARGAINING LAW AND ARBITRATION - AN OVERVIEW OF U.S. COLLECTIVE BARGAINING

fatty.law.cornell.edu/topics/collective_bargaining.html

In Canada, collective bargaining is the major method used by most unions to achieve their wage objectives. This is not, however, the only method Canadian unions use. Some seek to keep wages up by restricting entry to the trade or profession (as by increasing entrance requirements for professional training or denying accreditation to those licensed in other jurisdictions). Others seek to fix non-union wages (as by supporting higher minimum wage or equal pay legislation) to reduce the relative cost of union as opposed to non-union labour, thereby maintaining or increasing the demand for union labour. Still others seek to change the environment within which bargaining is conducted (by supporting changes in labour legislation that make union certification easier or supporting changes to a more centralized structure that will make it easier for the union to call an effective strike).[12]

Union Impact on Productivity

There is considerable disagreement within the industrial relations profession as to whether, on balance, unions serve to increase or decrease firms' productivity. The arguments on both sides have been usefully summed up by Freeman and Medoff (1979 and 1984).

"THOUSANDS RALLY IN SEOUL TO PROTEST UNEMPLOYMENT AND ILLEGAL FIRINGS" BY STEVE ZELTER, LABOURNET

www.igc.org/igc/ln/hg/korea.html

Neoclassicists and others primarily interested in unions' economic impacts (the "monopoly" perspective described by Freeman and Medoff) argue that unions reduce productivity by raising wages above competitive levels, by reducing output through the strikes they call, and by forcing management to agree to restrictive work rules that result in the substitution of capital for labour, and hence increased unemployment (Freeman and Medoff, 1979:75; Gunderson and Hyatt, 1995:328). Institutionalists and others primarily interested in workplace equity or equity within society as a whole argue that far from reducing productivity, unions often have positive effects on it. These include reduced quit rates and improved morale and worker-management cooperation resulting from union grievance processes and other mechanisms that give workers a sense that they have some say in what goes on in the workplace. Unions can also induce management to use more efficient production methods and even, perhaps, more effective personnel policies. In addition, they can increase productivity by collecting information about the preferences of all workers, information that can help the firm select better personnel policies and a more appropriate mix of wages and fringe benefits (Freeman and Medoff, 1979:75). For their part, managerialists as well as some institutionalists argue that unions can have either positive or negative productivity effects, since what is most important is whether a union helps or hurts relations between workers and management. From this perspective, what may be of greatest interest are management's policy towards unions and the union's willingness to enter into a cooperative relationship with management (Godard, 1994:374–375). For example, if a union opposes an employee involvement initiative, the program's chances of success will clearly be reduced (Verma, 1995:297–298).

Which position is closest to the truth? The one thing almost everyone *can* agree on is that the question is an extremely difficult one to answer. As the previous discussion has suggested, some union effects are clearly positive, while others are clearly negative, and still others can be either positive or negative depending on the particular situation. Complicating matters still further is the fact that in many situations, particularly where what is being "produced" is a service rather than a tangible good, it may be extremely difficult if not impossible to measure productivity. In such cases, asking whether unions increase or decrease productivity may not be at all useful. Here (assuming we were trying to determine the effects of unionization in a recently unionized establishment), it might be far more useful to start by asking workers whether they found they were getting along better or worse with their supervisor than they were before the union came in, or whether they felt more or less confident than before about their ability to do their job. Even where productivity can be measured, the union's impact on the labour-management relationship may still be much the most important factor. Where this is positive, it can lead not just to improved bargaining and communications (Gunderson and Hyatt, 1995:329), but to a broad range of problem-solving behaviour in all areas of workplace life, which in turn can result in reduced accident and illness rates, lower grievance and strike rates, and even reduced down time and spoilage. Conversely, where the union's impact on the labour-management relationship is negative, the results can include greatly increased sickness, accident, and industrial conflict rates and increased down time and spoilage. At the end of the day, both positive and negative impacts of this kind may turn out to be more important than the generally modest union wage impacts discussed earlier in the section.

Union Impacts on Management of the Organization

People from all different perspectives on IR agree that union impacts on the management of organizations are substantial. Where they disagree is on whether such impacts are beneficial. From a comparative perspective, these impacts appear to be greater in North America, with its detailed collective agreements regulating many different aspects of workplace behaviour, than in Europe, where agreements are apt to be more general (see Giles and Starkman, 1995:340) and unions do not generally have a significant effect on firms' day-to-day operations, a fact that may help explain North American managers' greater opposition to unions (Adams, 1995a:502).

In North America, unionization constitutes a significant limitation on management's freedom to run the enterprise as it sees fit. Here, management authority is specifically limited by any collective agreement provision; to counter such limitations, almost all management organizations insist that collective agreements contain management rights clauses, which generally have the effect of referring to management any matter not specifically addressed in the agreement. In Canada, unionization invariably brings with it a grievance process, since all jurisdictions' labour legislation requires collective agreements to include a process for the handling of disputes arising over the interpretation of the agreement (Carter, 1995:63).

Unions' most important impacts on the management of firms come through the aforementioned grievance processes, work rules laid out in collective agreements, and joint participation with management on various committees. For the average worker, and perhaps for management as well, it is the grievance process that is of greatest importance. Most significantly, the grievance process offers an avenue of redress for any worker who feels she or he has been unjustly dismissed. The chances of reinstatement following a dismissal grievance are more than 50 percent (McPhillips and England, 1995:81), whereas the non-unionized worker has no chance of reinstatement, except in the few jurisdictions offering the equivalent of a dismissal grievance process to certain non-unionized workers. The wish to avoid a costly and possibly embarrassing dismissal grievance process undoubtedly deters many managers from engaging in arbitrary dismissals. If managers are unduly timid, fear of a dismissal grievance may even keep them from firing people who should be let go. In lesser matters, as well, the grievance process serves as a brake on what might otherwise be capricious or arbitrary management behaviour. Indeed, the threat of possible grievances typically causes management to operate in a very different way in a unionized establishment than it would in a non-unionized one. Now it must operate in accordance with two sets of rules: company policy and the collective agreement. As we noted in the management chapter, this makes the whole process of managing more formal and more legalistic. To the extent that the collective agreement brings a degree of certainty to what might otherwise be a confused, chaotic management process, the firm will likely benefit. To the extent that its work rules stifle creativity and innovation and cause people to become more concerned about legalistic observance of the contract than about doing their jobs better, the firm is likely to suffer. No theory can tell us whether the positive or negative effects are more likely to prevail; the only way to tell is to go to individual workplaces and do detailed case studies. Here again, the nature of the individual labour-management relationship may be pivotal. Where there is a positive relationship, both sides may be willing to exercise some discretion in interpreting the collective agreement. Where the relationship is bad, both sides are more apt to "go by the book" in almost every instance, a process that can prove extremely counterproductive or even paralyzing if carried to extremes.

The work rules contained in collective agreements address a broad range of issues. Unless limited by legislation (as in the case of many public servants) or by management rights provisions stating that layoffs and promotions are totally within management's discretion, collective agreement provisions are apt to use seniority as a criterion (if not *the* criterion) for promotion, and reverse seniority as the criterion for layoffs. Unions generally like seniority-based promotion and layoff provisions because they prevent management from promoting or laying people off in an arbitrary fashion (Godard, 1994:319–320). Without seniority provisions, employers facing an economic downturn might lay off more senior workers, because they would normally be earning higher wages, or might simply lay off any workers management didn't like. While the use of seniority to govern promotions is more controversial, relatively few collective agreements use seniority as the sole basis for promotion; much more common are provisions that state that seniority will be one criterion along with skills and ability (Giles and Starkman, 1995:362).

Other union work rules may apply more specifically to the work process. In some cases, workload itself may be limited. This was the case with the longshoring agreements of the 1960s, where a minimum gang size and maximum allowable load size might well be stipulated (see Picard, 1967). More recently, it has often been the case with agreements in education. Public schoolteachers' agreements have sometimes limited class size; university professors' agreements have sometimes stipulated a normal or maximum number of courses a professor will be expected to teach.

Another important group of work rules has to do with procedures governing work force reduction. In addition to provisions requiring that layoffs be in reverse order of seniority, unions may negotiate total or partial restrictions on management's ability to contract out work to outside firms. They may also negotiate restrictions on management's ability to implement technological change, such as requirements that the union be given a period of advance notice or that affected workers be provided with retraining opportunities. Finally, contracts may provide for a layoff notice period greater than that required by employment standards legislation or for training, job search assistance, or other benefits for employees facing layoff.

In addition to the impacts resulting from grievance procedures and the work rules contained in collective agreements, unions also affect the management of organizations through their joint participation, with management, in a number of committees or other forms of joint governance mechanism. The most important of these committees are the joint health and safety committees required in all jurisdictions. Here, unions often play a key role, both by educating and informing workers on the issues and by helping to ensure that the committee is not just a token. Unions also play an important role in the pay equity process through their involvement in job-evaluation procedures (Gunderson and Hyatt, 1995:330). Beyond that, collective agreements often provide for a variety of labour-management committees. Many agreements provide for a general labour-management committee; less common, but far from unheard-of, are more specific committees designed to address such issues as technological change (ECC, 1987; Peirce, 1987). While the scope and powers of these committees vary greatly, they do involve a good many workers, at least to some degree, in the day-to-day management of the organization—a development that most industrial relationists and many managers probably regard as healthy.

Union Impacts on Society as a Whole

The previous discussion suggests that within the workplace, unions can have both positive and negative effects. For society as a whole, the situation is rather more clear-cut. Here, particularly in the social and political spheres, the impacts appear to have been almost entirely positive. It is largely thanks to unions, through their participation in politics, that Canadians have publicly funded medical care, unemployment insurance, public pensions, and other worthwhile social programs. Note here that the labour movement could not have achieved these results without a political partner (today the NDP, formerly the CCF), nor could the NDP or CCF have achieved them without the labour movement's active support. Earlier, we noted that the CCF and NDP have not only passed legislation providing for pro-labour legislation and social programs when they have been in government, they have also forced governments from other parties to pass such legislation when they have held the balance of power in minority governments, or when there has been a serious threat that those governments would lose to the CCF or NDP in the next election. It's important to note as well that the CCF, in particular, did not really get off the ground until it started attracting strong support from unionists during the Second World War (Heron, 1989). More recently, the NDP was strengthened by the increased support it started receiving from the CLC and affiliated unions beginning with the 1979 federal election (Morton, 1995; Murray, 1995). In the four federal elections held starting in 1979, the party posted some of the best results it had ever achieved. The critical role played by the labour movement within the NDP is also shown, in a negative way, by the party's appalling showing in the

1993 federal election, in which organized labour withdrew much of its support, particularly in Ontario. Without strong, steady support from the labour movement, the NDP has little chance of remaining viable as a national political party.

The labour movement has made other important contributions to Canadian society. Over the years, it has done a great deal to raise the profile of health and safety issues, educating members, managers, and the general public alike. While Canadian workplaces are still far from safe, as the employment law chapter will show in more detail, they are safer than they would be without the work of unions, which have played a particularly important role in the joint health and safety committees required in all Canadian jurisdictions. Unions have also worked to bring in affirmative action, pay equity, anti-discrimination legislation, and other human-rights measures benefitting all Canadians. Overall, we can only agree with Desmond Morton (1995:154), that "[m]uch that has made Canada a humane and civilized society has come from the social vision of its labour movement."

One other point about unions' broader impacts should be made: their effect on the members who participate in their day-to-day operation and governance. More than 50 years after they had left the Knights of Labor (Kealey and Palmer, 1981), former members recalled their time in the Order as one that transformed their lives, giving them new vision and new hope. More recently (Murray, 1995:183), union activists have spoken highly of the impact that participation in the union has had on their personal development and understanding of society.[13] In some cases, union participation has marked the beginning of a worthwhile political career. In many more, union activists have taken the skills and self-confidence that they have learned through their participation and applied them to the problems faced by civic organizations such as school boards, zoning boards, or hospital boards. It would be an exercise in futility to attempt to measure the value of these activists' previous union participation through any sort of conventional cost-benefit calculus, but almost certainly that participation has helped make a difference to their communities.

ARE UNIONS STILL NEEDED?

One need not read newspapers more than occasionally to be aware of the frequency with which a certain type of article or letter about unions appears. Though these pieces vary somewhat in tone, their basic point is nearly always the same. Unions were very much needed, the authors concede, in the late nineteenth and early twentieth centuries, when most workers were wretchedly paid and forced to work under appalling conditions. Today, however, almost all workers are well paid, management has become totally enlightened, and working conditions everywhere are first-rate. Given these facts, which the authors regard as obvious to anyone with even a slight knowledge of the world of work, unions today are essentially redundant. All they do, according to the writers, is create friction by filing grievances and calling strikes, without providing any positive benefits to the people they claim to be representing.

"THE FUTURE OF WORK: TODAY'S YOUTH NEEDS UNIONS— AND UNIONS NEED THEM"
www.policyalternatives.ca/edumon/article15.html

While such articles seldom draw on any specific factual evidence in support of their thesis, they appear to represent a belief that a fair number of Canadians share. It is a rare week when we do not hear someone in a grocery store, pub, or laundromat making essentially the same point. Though these articles cannot really be taken seriously on their own account, they may nonetheless be an appropriate way to conclude our discussion, first, because they reveal just how misinformed much of the Canadian public is about unions and what they do,[14] and second, because in their misguided way they do raise some important issues concerning unions' overall impacts.

Those who have read the previous chapters with any care will immediately recognize the erroneous factual basis for the sort of article we've just been talking about. Chapter 2, on the economy, showed that many workers' earnings and overall economic situations are declining. Chapter 3, on management, showed that in many cases management practice is becoming less, rather than more, enlightened than in the recent past. In addition, the health and safety section of Chapter 7, on employment law, will reveal some of the many health and safety problems continuing to face Canadian workers. All of this is hardly evidence supporting the thesis that unions have outlived their usefulness.

More significant than such blatant factual errors is the articles' implication that Canadian society would somehow be better off without unions. It seems appropriate, in the circumstances, to ask what Canadian society would be like without unions, and what kinds of societies do not have free trade unions, in the sense in which we would understand them.

Since the second question is somewhat simpler, let's begin with it. Virtually every country we would consider democratic has free trade unions which advance their members' interests and, usually, those of the country's working people as a whole. On the other hand, fascist and other authoritarian regimes and military dictatorships generally do not allow unions at all, or at the very least constrain their activities severely. Before and during the Second World War, for example, all three Axis powers banned or dissolved their country's unions (Kuwahara, 1993:223; Pellegrini, 1993:131; Fuerstenberg, 1993:178). More recently, union rights have been sharply curtailed in a number of Asian countries with authoritarian regimes, such as Singapore and Malaysia (Bean, 1994). In Communist countries, such as the former

Soviet Union, unions have most typically been absorbed into the larger state apparatus and given no independent role of their own in the IR system (Héthy, 1991). Quite
simply, it would appear that free trade unions go hand-in-hand with democracy. To
this end, the International Labour Organization (ILO) has established a number of
freedom of association conventions guaranteeing workers the right to join unions,
bargain collectively, and strike (Clarke, 1993:267), as have the national governments
of many European countries.[15]

As for what Canadian society would be like without unions, the most immediate
and obvious differences would be noticed at the workplace. To start with, many fewer
Canadians would enjoy any real protection against dismissal or other arbitrary action
by their employers. And many fewer would have any part in setting the terms and
conditions of their employment. This would become a privilege enjoyed only by a
select group of professionals, entertainers, and middle- to upper-level managers.
Health and safety laws would be less strictly enforced, even if the laws themselves did
not change; the same would likely be true for human rights laws. Moreover, the
already strong trend towards less secure work and more part-time, temporary, and
contractual work would very likely accelerate without the brake now placed on it by
union collective agreement provisions.

In addition to losing unions' workplace representation, working people would also
lose political representation, since the one national party pledged to advance their
interests, the NDP, would almost certainly cease to exist without a labour movement
to support it. Publicly funded health care might not disappear immediately, but support for it would certainly diminish, as would support for EI, social assistance, and
other social programs, and public arts funding. Supporters of health care and public
arts funding would definitely find their job much harder if they were forced to operate without the labour movement's financial support and the NDP's political support.

In a more general way, the question is perhaps best answered by two more. If
there were no Canadian labour movement, what other group in contemporary
Canadian society would be big enough and strong enough to provide a significant
check to the economic and political clout of big business and the political right
(Crispo, 1982)? And what other group would be in a position to advance the economic and political interests of the broad spectrum of ordinary working Canadians?
Such questions are, admittedly, far from new or original. Expanded only slightly, they
form much of the basis of the institutionalist perspective on industrial relations
described earlier. They are nonetheless perhaps worth asking, given that the advocates
of a union-free society have thus far had little to say in response to either one.

Fortunately, such questions are likely to remain purely hypothetical. As we pointed out earlier, the practical need for unions appears if anything to be increasing,
rather than decreasing. From a broader perspective, a society without free unions
would almost certainly be one in which few Canadians would care to live.

QUESTIONS
FOR DISCUSSION

1) If you are in a union, what kinds of activity does it engage in? What kinds have you, personally, been involved with? If you aren't in a union yourself, ask a friend or relative who is and find out what sort of things their union has been doing.

2) How has the range of union activities been expanding in recent years? Do you think this expansion has been healthy, overall?

3) Should unions affiliate with political parties? If not, how should they pursue their political objectives?

4) Should unions engage in business ventures such as labour-sponsored venture capital corporations? Why, or why not? What about employee buyouts of failing businesses?

5) Why do public sector unions place such heavy reliance on publicity campaigns?

6) What are unions' major impacts on wages?

7) What are some problems in evaluating union wage impacts?

8) What are unions' major impacts on productivity and management of the organization? Why are these impacts often extremely difficult to measure?

9) What are some of the major impacts unions have on society as a whole? How do they achieve these impacts?

10) Do you agree with those who argue that unions have outlived their usefulness in Canada? Why, or why not?

SUGGESTIONS
FOR FURTHER READING

Freeman, Richard, and James Medoff. (1984). *What do unions do?* New York: Basic Books. Classic study of unions' impacts that implicitly argues that most economists have looked at union impacts from far too narrow a perspective. The comparison between the "monopoly" and "collective voice" perspectives on unions is particularly useful.

Jackson, E.T., and François Lamontagne. (1995). *"Adding value: The economic and social impacts of labour-sponsored venture capital corporations on their investee firms."* Ottawa: CLMPC. Useful study of this important new mechanism.

ENDNOTES

1 For a useful if brief discussion of the Webbs, see Craig and Solomon, (1996:76–80).

2 For a useful overview of the key issues here, see Verma (1995).

3 And for managers trained to distrust unions, as well; however, this is not the focus of the present chapter.

4 Anil Verma tends to fall into this camp, although less so in his 1995 Gunderson and Ponak chapter than in many of his earlier works, such as the 1987 and 1989 articles cited in the reference list. With some reservations, Lemelin (1989) also takes this position.

5 It is generally accepted throughout the industrial relations literature that the union must be involved as a full partner in any joint cooperation schemes if the schemes are to succeed. For a classic and still very useful statement, see Kochan (1979, quoted in Downie, 1982). Another useful list can be found in Lemelin (1989).

6 In British Columbia, the Social Credit government in 1984 instituted the requirement of a certification vote (Craig and Solomon, 1993:145). That requirement was removed by an NDP government in 1992 (Craig and Solomon, 1993:215).

7 Comparative analysis lends some support to this point. Internationally, the major example of a labour movement that operates without the regular support of a labour or social democratic political ally is the American one. At 15 percent density, it is among the world's weakest labour movements. Density has also been dropping significantly in Japan (Bamber and Whitehouse, 1993:310), a country whose labour movement is dominated by largely apolitical enterprise unions.

8 In connection with this point, however, it must be noted that when your adversary is the government itself, *only* a secondary boycott is possible; no one can realistically boycott a government (other than, perhaps, by leaving the province or country in question).

9 For an interesting and much more detailed discussion of the issues raised in this paragraph, see Godard (1994:210–221). An equally interesting discussion from a quite different perspective may be found in Reynolds (1982:492–498).

10 These problems raise technical statistical issues that in this author's view are far too complex to be discussed in an introductory industrial relations textbook. Students with an extensive background in labour economics and statistics who wish to pursue these issues further will find useful discussions in Gunderson and Riddell (1993:388–397) and Gunderson and Hyatt (1995:322–324).

11 For a useful discussion around some of these points, see Godard (1994:217–219).

12 For most of the material in this paragraph, I am indebted to Gunderson and Hyatt (1995:318–322) and to Gunderson's discussion in the previous (1989) edition of the book, pp. 353–356. Some use has also been made of Murray (1995:184–190).

13 This author has observed this same attitude in his industrial relations students, many of whom have been local union activists.

14 For further evidence on this point, see LaBerge (1976) and Hannigan (1986).

15 Thus far, the Supreme Court of Canada has not seen fit to establish freedom of association as a basic constitutional right under the Charter of Rights and Freedoms. See the labour relations law chapter for further discussion of this issue.

CHAPTER 7

EMPLOYMENT LEGISLATION

"Promises, promises." PSAC members demonstrate in Ottawa in September 1998 to protest federal government's decision to appeal the Human Rights Tribunal's pay equity award of billions of dollars in back pay to federal public servants.

Employment legislation applies to most workers, but is of special interest to those who don't belong to unions, since they aren't covered by labour relations legislation. In this chapter, after a brief discussion of employment legislation's (EL) general significance and the groups of workers to whom it applies, we start by considering work standards legislation

governing such matters as minimum wages and overtime regulations. Next, we look at dismissals and the non-unionized worker. From there, we go on to consider human rights legislation, one of the areas of employment legislation that has been changing rapidly of late. We continue with a discussion of health and safety legislation. This discussion emphasizes the joint labour-management safety committees that are a distinctive feature of the Canadian legislative framework. We conclude with a consideration of workers' compensation legislation and a broad look at overall trends in Canadian EL.

EMPLOYMENT LEGISLATION: AN OVERVIEW
Why EL Is Needed

There are a number of reasons why legislation covering the broad spectrum of workers,[1] not just those belonging to a union, is needed. First, as we noted earlier, only about one-third of all Canadian workers belong to a union. Many workers who do not belong to a union don't even have the legal right to join one (Beatty, 1983). Considerations of fundamental equity suggest that some kind of legislation is needed to protect certain basic rights for all workers. For example, it seems unduly harsh to suggest that a worker should be required to join a union to be assured of a safe workplace.

SWEATSHOP WATCH
www.sweatshopwatch.org/swatch/index.html

In addition, a number of important workplace issues, particularly human rights issues such as sexual harassment and religious discrimination, may be inherently difficult to regulate through collective bargaining alone. As we point out in Chapter 10, much collective bargaining is based on the notion of a settlement zone, or the range of overlap between union and management positions. Inherent in the notion of the settlement zone is the possibility of some kind of compromise, which in turn strongly implies that the issue in question can be quantified. Thus, while we can apply the notion of a settlement zone to monetary issues, it is virtually impossible to apply it to issues such as health and safety or sexual harassment. Where, realistically, is the basis for compromise on issues of this type? Will the collective agreement provide for a workplace free from harassment on Mondays, Wednesdays, and Fridays, but grant no protection on Tuesdays and Thursdays? Will it offer health and safety protection to those working in the plant but not to its office workers? At a minimum, collective bargaining over such issues needs to be supplemented by a process that applies to all workers.

Nor is the lack of a settlement zone the only difficulty likely to arise. By definition, collective bargaining is a majoritarian political process.[2] A union made up mainly of men might well decide that wages and benefits were more important than a sexual harassment provision, and vote to have their negotiators pursue the former at the expense of the latter. Then, too, what's gained at the bargaining table can also be lost there, particularly in a difficult economic climate like the present one. Once again, a largely male-dominated union, forced to choose between loss of wages and benefits or dropping of a sexual harassment provision, could well opt for the latter. While the minority female membership might not think much of the male members' concept of solidarity, under current labour legislation they would have little recourse, other than perhaps splitting off and forming their own union at the next available opportunity.

With human rights legislation in place, the likelihood of problems such as these is greatly reduced. Moreover, since human rights issues are generally handled by a specialized body, such as a human rights commission, they may well be addressed more effectively by such a commission than if they are left solely to union officials, who often do not have the time or resources to become experts in such a specialized area. This is not to say that unions don't still have a role to play in addressing human rights issues covered by specific legislation. They do, and as we shall soon see, that role is and continues to be an important one. But it is also a more limited and, arguably, more manageable one than they would have in the absence of such legislation.

 ## CANADIAN HUMAN RIGHTS ACT
insight.mcmaster.ca/org/efc/pages/law/canada/canada.H-6.head.html

Jurisdiction and Administration of EL

Like most labour relations legislation, most employment legislation falls under provincial jurisdiction. Here again, the major exception is workers employed in undertakings of a clearly federal nature, such as the railroads, airlines, telephone companies, and chartered banks. These workers fall under federal jurisdiction and are covered by the relevant sections of the *Canada Labour Code* and the *Canadian Human Rights Act* (see McPhillips and England, 1995:74). As for administration, work standards (employment standards) legislation is typically handled by a branch of the labour ministry, as is health and safety legislation. Human rights issues are generally handled by separate commissions, as is workers' compensation.

Coverage Under EL

Employment legislation applies to most, but by no means all, Canadian workers. Some jurisdictions exclude certain groups completely from coverage under their employment standards acts, while others do not apply particular provisions to certain groups.

Overall, exclusions are not as broad as for labour relations legislation, nor do they appear to be quite as broad as they were in the early 1980s, when England (1987) found large numbers of workers falling outside the protection of many jurisdictions' employment standards laws. Still, the remaining exclusions raise significant equity concerns, particularly given that some of those excluded are among the country's least fortunate workers and some are also excluded from unionization rights under labour relations legislation. In Nova Scotia, the Governor-in-Council may exempt the members of certain professions from coverage under the province's labour standards code. He or she may also exempt specified employees or classes of employees from the province's pregnancy leave and parental leave provisions. In Prince Edward Island, farm labourers, salespeople, and home care workers are exempt from the application of most sections of the employment standards act. Home care workers are also exempt in Quebec, as are senior managers, while in Saskatchewan, employment standards legislation does not apply to management or to those employed primarily in farming, ranching, or market gardening. (The above list of exclusions should be considered suggestive rather than definitive.) As McPhillips and England note (1995:75), there is always the possibility that Section 15 of the *Charter* could be used to find such exclusions unconstitutional. However, the fact that these exclusions have remained in place for so long (16 years) after the *Charter* took effect is anything but comforting.

The Significance of EL

EL, as well as labour relations legislation, is important to IR and HR practitioners because (as noted above) it applies to such a large portion of the work force and takes in such a broad range of issues. As you'll see throughout this chapter, EL applies to virtually every aspect of the employment relationship, from the preparation of job application forms and conducting of job interviews to the handling of layoffs and outright dismissals.

Employment legislation is so important and so pervasive in its application that the IR or HR practitioner who isn't familiar with at least its broad outlines cannot be considered fully qualified. There have been far too many cases where lack of familiarity with this legislation has led otherwise sensitive and knowledgeable practitioners to do things such as continue to use application forms calling for photos,[3] or ask job applicants whether or not they are married. At best, such actions don't do a firm's reputation any good; at worst, they can be a serious embarrassment or even a legal liability.

EL's practical importance, then, should be obvious. Managers need to know it to be sure they and their organizations are operating legally. Workers need to know it to be sure they are obtaining everything they are entitled to. Beyond that, employment legislation bears an interesting relationship to labour relations legislation. While the two operate in quite different ways, there are also important ways in which they complement each other.

CANADIAN BILL OF RIGHTS

canada.justice.gc.ca/FTP/EN/Laws/chap/C/C-12.3.txt

In particular, EL (sometimes referred to as minimum standards legislation) serves to establish a kind of floor below which unions cannot go in collective bargaining. A union cannot legally enter into an agreement paying a wage below the provincial minimum, nor can it legally bargain an agreement requiring workers to work a seven-day week or take only one week of vacation. On the other hand, unions are perfectly free to negotiate terms and conditions of employment more favourable to their members than those prescribed by the relevant employment legislation, and in most cases, they do just that.

In addition, unions may serve as useful "enforcement agents" for the legislation, which government often fails to enforce sufficiently, due to a lack of personnel or other resources. A union may play this role directly, through the grievance process, or indirectly, by educating its members about their rights under EL. The health and safety system, discussed in more detail below, offers an excellent illustration of this point. Instances of workers exercising their legal right to refuse to work in situations they consider unsafe are rare in non-unionized workplaces (McPhillips and England, 1995:91), a fact that suggests that unions' role in enforcement may be critical.

Recently, EL and labour relations legislation have come to intersect in another important way. Grievance arbitrators have increasingly been expected to apply human rights legislation, such as bans on discrimination against people with disabilities, in the course of resolving collective agreement disputes (Carter, 1997:185). The duty to accommodate such workers, or those of religions requiring special work schedules, has been more and more broadly imposed on employers and unions, even to the point where modifications to the collective agreement have been required in order to bring agreement provisions in line with human rights legislation (Carter, 1997:196–198). As Carter points out (1997:202–204), this new obligation to interpret collective agreements in the light of human rights legislation has significantly changed the role of arbitrators. Over time, it could come to change collective bargaining itself, as employers and unions alike take the duty to accommodate into account in fashioning collective agreement provisions.

WORK STANDARDS LEGISLATION

Work standards legislation[4] covers what might broadly be referred to as terms and conditions of employment, with the notable exception of health and safety issues.

Among the provisions found in most Canadian work standards laws are those governing minimum wages, maximum permissible hours of work, overtime pay, minimum annual vacation entitlements, paid holidays, termination notice periods, and maternity leave. Provisions found in some, but not all, Canadian legislation include those governing paternity or family leave, adoption leave, clothing or special apparel payments, child employment laws, minimum-age levels for employment, bereavement and sick leave, and maximum permissible board and lodging charges (McPhillips and England, 1995:76). Overall, there is a good deal of variation within Canadian jurisdictions.

Some Specific Provisions

Minimum Wages

As of early 1998 (see Table 7.1), the general minimum wage ranged from $5.00 per hour in Alberta to $7.20 per hour in the Yukon. Three provinces had separate rates for workers under 16 or under 18, all roughly 10 percent below the adult minimum.[5]

MINIMUM WAGE DEBATES

www.nationalpost.com [Site Search "minimum wage"]

Hours of Work and Overtime Pay

Here there is a great deal of variation among the different jurisdictions. About half the jurisdictions have no maximum number of hours an employer can have employees work without first obtaining a labour ministry permit (see Table 7.1; also see Gunderson and Reid, 1998). In those provinces that do have daily maximums, the range is from 8 (Ontario) to 16 (Newfoundland). The point at which overtime must be paid varies from 40 to 48 hours in a week. Normally, overtime must be paid at 1.5 times the employee's regular wage rate; however, three provinces, all in the Atlantic region, have set overtime at 1.5 times the provincial minimum wage. In three provinces (Ontario, Manitoba, and Saskatchewan), employees have the right to refuse to put in any overtime after working a given number of hours within any day or week (Gunderson and Reid, 1998).

Vacation Entitlement

Every province except Saskatchewan requires a minimum of two weeks of paid vacation per year, with 4 percent of earnings. In Saskatchewan, the minimum is three weeks with 3/52 of earnings. Many, but not all, jurisdictions require three weeks'

Table 7.1 SPECIAL FEATURE: SELECTED EMPLOYMENT STANDARDS PROVISION IN CANADA

Subjects	Jurisdictions					
	Federal	Alberta	British Columbia	Manitoba	New Brunswick	Newfoundland
Hours of work and Overtime pay	Maximum: 48 in a week. Overtime at 1 1/2 times the regular rate after 8 in a day and 40 in a week.	Maximum: 12 in a day. Overtime at 1 1/2 times the regular rate after 8 in a day and 44 in a week.	No maximum. Overtime at 1 1/2 times the regular rate after 8 in a day and 40 in a week, and at 2 times the regular rate after 11 in a day and 48 in a week.	No maximum. Overtime at 1 1/2 times the regular rate after 8 in a day and 40 in a week. Employees can refuse to work any overtime after these hours.	No maximum. Overtime at 1 1/2 times the minimum wage after 44 hours in a week.	Maximum: 16 in a day. Overtime at 1 1/2 times the minimum wage after 40 in a week.
Minimum wages	Same as general adult minimum wage rate in each provincial or territorial jurisdiction.	Generally: $5.00 per hour (01/04/92). Under 18 attending school: $4.50 per hour (01/04/92).	Generally: $7.15 per hour (01/04/98).	Generally: $5.40 per hour (01/01/96).	Generally: $5.50 per hour (01/07/96).	Generally: $5.25 per hour (01/04/97)
Annual vacations with pay (Length of employment is with the same employer.)	Two weeks with 4% of earnings; Three weeks after 6 years with 6% of earnings.	Two weeks with 4% of earnings; Three weeks after 5 years with 6% of earnings.	Two weeks with 4% of earnings; Three weeks after 5 years with 6% of earnings.	Two weeks with regular pay; Three weeks after 4 years with regular pay.	Two weeks with 4% earnings.	Two weeks with 4% of earnings. Three weeks after 15 years with 6% of earnings.
General holidays with pay	New Year's Day Good Friday Victoria Day Canada Day Labour Day Thanksgiving Day Remembrance Day Christmas Day Boxing Day	New Year's Day* Alberta Family Day* Good Friday* Victoria Day* Canada Day* Labour Day* Thanksgiving Day* Remembrance Day* Christmas Day*	New Year's Day Good Friday Victoria Day Canada Day Labour Day Thanksgiving Day Remembrance Day Christmas Day British Columbia Day	New Year's Day Good Friday Victoria Day Canada Day Labour Day Thanksgiving Day Remembrance Day* Christmas Day	New Year's Day Good Friday Canada Day New Brunswick Day Labour Day Christmas Day	New Year's Day Good Friday Memorial Day Labour Day Christmas Day

* means no requirement that employees be paid if they are not normally scheduled or required to work on that day

Table 7.1
(continued)

	Northwest Territories	Nova Scotia	Ontario	Prince Edward Island	Quebec	Saskatchewan	Yukon Territory
	Maximum: 10 in a day and 60 in a week. Overtime at 1 1/2 times the regular rate after 8 in a day and 40 in a week.	No maximum. Overtime at 1 1/2 times the minimum wage after 48 in a week.	Maximum: 8 in a day and 48 in a week. Overtime at 1 1/2 times the regular rate after 44 in a week.	No maximum. Overtime at 1 1/2 times the regular rate after 48 in a week.	No maximum. Overtime at 1 1/2 times the regular rate after 43 in a week (to be reduced to 40 by October 1, 2000).	Maximum: 44 in a week unless the employee agrees otherwise. Overtime at 1 1/2 times the regular rate after 8 in a day and 40 in a week.	No maximum. Overtime at 1 1/2 times the regular rate after 8 in a day and 40 in a week.
	Generally: $6.50 per hour; and $7.00 per hour in areas distant from the highway system. (01/04/91). Under 16: $6.00 per hour; and $6.50 per hour in areas distant from the highway system. (01/04/91).	Generally: $5.50 per hour (01/02/97)	Generally: $6.85 per hour (01/01/95). Students under 18 working no more than 28 hours in a week or during a school holiday: $6.40 per hour (01/01/95).	Generally: $5.40 per hour (01/09/97).	Generally: $6.80 per hour (01/10/97)	Generally: $5.60 per hour (01/12/96).	$7.06 per hour (01/04/98). $7.20 per hour (01/10/98).
	Two weeks with 4% of earnings; Three weeks after 5 years with 6% of earnings.	Two weeks with 4% of earnings.	Two weeks with 4% of earnings.	Two weeks with 4% of earnings.	Two weeks with 4% of gross wages; Three weeks after 5 years with 6% of gross wages.	Three weeks with 3/52 of earnings; Four weeks after 10 years with 4/52 of earnings.	Two weeks with 4% of earnings.
	New Year's Day Good Friday Victoria Day Canada Day First Monday in August Labour Day Thanksgiving Day Remembrance Day Christmas Day	New Year's Day Good Friday Canada Day Labour Day Remembrance Day* Christmas Day	New Year's Day Good Friday Victoria Day Canada Day Labour Day Thanksgiving Day Christmas Day Boxing Day	New Year's Day Good Friday Canada Day Labour Day Christmas Day	January 1st Good Friday (or Easter Monday*) Dollar Day* (i.e. Victoria Day) National Holiday July 1st Labour Day* Thanksgiving Day* December 25*	New Year's Day Good Friday Victoria Day Canada Day Labour Day Thanksgiving Day Remembrance Day Christmas Day Saskatchewan Day	New Year's Day Good Friday Victoria Day Canada Day Discovery Day Labour Day Thanksgiving Day Remembrance Day Christmas Day

Source: HRDC, *Workplace Gazette*, Summer 1998.

paid vacation for more senior workers; the threshold for the longer vacation kicks in after anywhere from four to 15 years' service with the same employer. In Saskatchewan, employers must give employees four weeks' paid vacation after ten years of service (see Table 7.1).

Paid Holidays

The various jurisdictions provide employees with anywhere from five to nine holidays per year. Usually employees must be paid for these days; however, in a few cases, there is no requirement that employees be paid if they are not normally required to work on that day (see Table 7.1).

Notice of Individual Termination

In general, the notice that an employer must provide to a worker being terminated is quite short[6] (not shown in table). In the federal jurisdiction, the notice period is two weeks for all employees. In seven provinces, it can be as short as one week for recent hires. Typically, an employee must have worked at least three months to be eligible for any required notice at all. Except for the federal jurisdiction, most jurisdictions have a "sliding scale" for notice periods, which generally increase to eight weeks for employees with 10 or more years' service. In the Yukon, individual termination provisions do not apply to unionized workers; in New Brunswick, they do not apply to workers covered by a collective agreement. About half of all jurisdictions require an employee who wishes to quit to give notice.

Group Termination Provisions

Every Canadian jurisdiction except Prince Edward Island has special group termination provisions that take effect when a large number of workers are terminated in a short period of time, most often as a result of a plant closure or major downsizing (not shown in table). The special provisions are designed to take into account the hardship that may be faced not just by the affected workers individually, but by the entire community, particularly when the business being closed or downsized is the community's only or major employer. Given the large number of plant closures that have occurred in recent years, these group termination provisions are of increasing importance to workers and their unions, and have also attracted growing interest from the academic industrial relations community (Gunderson, 1986).

Notice periods for group terminations are frequently a good deal longer than those for individual terminations, and in many cases the length increases on a sliding scale based on the number of workers affected. Depending on the jurisdiction and the number of employees involved, the notice period may be as short as the individual termination period or as long as 18 weeks; however, most notice periods fall in the 8- to 16-week range. Normally, in addition to notifying affected employees, the employer must notify the Minister of Labour (or the equivalent) and the union if the establishment is unionized. In five provinces, notices must contain specific information such as the number of employees being terminated, the names of the employees, the effective date of the terminations, and the reason for the terminations. The federal jurisdiction, British Columbia, Manitoba, Ontario, and Quebec all require or may require the employer to set up a joint planning committee to address the issue of re-employment for the workers being terminated. The federal jurisdiction provides for severance pay in addition to the required notice period. Here, employers must give the employees being terminated notice about the amount of severance pay, vacation benefits, wages, and any other pay and benefits to which they are entitled.

Pregnancy and Parental Leave

Provisions include the right to paid or unpaid leave during pregnancy and after the birth or adoption of a child (not shown in table). They also generally stipulate that the worker be reinstated into her old position following her return to work. Ontario, whose provisions are fairly typical, allows up to 17 weeks' pregnancy leave and 18 weeks' parental leave. British Columbia allows up to 32 weeks' combined leave, but will grant five more weeks for the parent of a child whose physical, psychological, or emotional condition requires additional care.

How Effective Is Work Standards Legislation?

In today's economy (discussed in Chapter 2), work standards legislation is of increasing importance, particularly to younger workers, part-timers, and those in low-end jobs in the private-service sector, for whom unionization is generally not a realistic prospect. Given the importance of this legislation, the question that should be asked is how effectively it addresses the needs of Canadian workers. Does it provide coverage for the least fortunate workers? Are its provisions adequate to meet workers' basic needs? And are enforcement mechanisms sufficient to ensure that workers can obtain their rights under the legislation?

Complete answers to these questions would require a detailed examination of every Canadian jurisdiction's work standards legislation and of the mechanisms through which that legislation is enforced. Such an examination must await other hands. However, on the evidence now available, the answers to the preceding questions are far from reassuring.

Coverage for All

Basic equity considerations suggest that work standards legislation should apply to all workers, or at a minimum all workers whose exclusion from certain provisions (i.e., overtime pay) is not compensated for by above-average pay and status, as in the case of most managers. Nonetheless, a number of groups of workers other than managers continue to be excluded from all or part of various jurisdictions' work standards acts. Members of some of these groups, such as domestic workers, farm workers, and home care workers, are among the country's least fortunate workers. Some are also excluded from labour relations legislation, a situation that leaves them with no protection at all. With the growth of "atypical" employment situations described in Chapter 2, it is becoming increasingly important for governments to provide protection for part-timers, homeworkers, and others in such "atypical" employment relations. Thus far, however, most Canadian governments appear to have done little along these lines.

WORKPLACE EQUITY

info.load-otea.hrdc-drhc.gc.ca/~weeweb/homeen.shtml

Granted, the special conditions under which some of these groups work make it difficult to apply the same work standards laws that would be applied in a more conventional industrial setting. The nature of home care work, for example, makes it very difficult to apply conventional hours of work and overtime regulations; the same could be said of vacation pay with respect to farm workers. But such difficulties should not lead to the blanket exclusion of entire groups from protection under work standards legislation. While exclusion of certain groups from the operation of specific provisions may well be necessary, such exclusions should be accompanied by separate codes outlining appropriate standards for the occupation in question.

Adequacy of Protection

Considerations of basic equity suggest that the minimum wage should be enough to enable a worker to provide basic necessities for himself or herself, a partner, and an average-sized family of two children. Similarly, hours of work and vacation provisions should ensure workers adequate rest and time to themselves or with families, while overtime pay provisions should offer adequate compensation for the loss of time and rest and for the extra stress that overtime work entails.

Even a cursory examination of the minimum standards required under various work standards laws suggests that existing legislation (even if enforced) is a long way from providing most workers with the basic necessities of life or sufficient free time. At the beginning of 1983 (LLCG, 1984:4–29), minimum wages ranged from $3.50 to $4.25 per hour. Shortly before that, a study by the National Council of Welfare

(LLCG, 1984:4–37) had found the net minimum wage income falling well below the income one could expect from social assistance for units of three people and more in every province except Quebec. Between 1975 and 1987, real minimum wage income fell by more than 30 percent in Alberta, B.C., and Quebec and by more than 20 percent in the remaining provinces (Gunderson, Myszynski, and Keck, 1990). While the Gunderson et al. study finds some erosion of real income for most Canadians, this erosion appears to have been most serious for those at minimum wage jobs, most of whose incomes were already well below the poverty level.

Over the past decade, the situation has not improved, except in B.C. and Ontario, where NDP governments legislated major increases during the early 1990s. Elsewhere, the situation has worsened. As Table 7.1 shows, most provinces' minimums are in the $5 to $6 range, which is substantially less, when adjusted for inflation, than the $3.50–$4.25 range of the early 1980s. Most Canadian minimums are also well below the $5.15 U.S. minimum when exchange rates are taken into account (Bureau of Labor Statistics, 1997). Yet the U.S. minimum itself has fallen sharply as a percentage of the average industrial wage, dropping from 54 percent of the average in 1950 to 37 percent in 1996 (BLS, 1997).

Regarding hours of work, paid vacations, and holidays, the situation is no better. The two weeks' vacation required under most jurisdictions' work standards legislation is a fraction of the amount available to most European workers (Owen, 1989; *Better Times,* 1997 and 1998). Restrictions on long hours (see Table 7.1; also Gunderson and Reid, 1998) are minimal. As we pointed out earlier, only three jurisdictions give workers the right to refuse overtime. About half of all jurisdictions have no maximum number of hours a worker can be allowed to work in a day or week, and even those jurisdictions that have maximums generally set them at a very high level (12 hours a day in Alberta, 16 in Newfoundland). Overtime pay provisions are also inadequate. In some cases workers cannot receive overtime until they have worked 44 hours in a week, and in three Atlantic provinces, overtime is based on the provincial minimum rather than on the worker's actual wage, a situation that could lead to a worker's receiving less for overtime than for regular hours. Even in jurisdictions where the 50 percent overtime premium is "fairly" based on the worker's regular wage, the premium is generally acknowledged to be insufficient to prevent many employers from making heavy use of regularly scheduled overtime rather than hiring additional workers to meet increased demand.

Adequacy of Enforcement

Enforcement of minimum standards legislation has been a problem ever since such legislation was first introduced, as minimum wages for children and female workers (see McCallum, 1986). Then and now, inadequate funding for inspectors, lack of political will, and a desire on the part of those administering the legislation to accommodate rather than prosecute all but its most intransigent violators appear to have been the norm.

Roy Adams' 1987 study of the Employment Standards branch of the Ontario Ministry of Labour finds no effective procedure available to help unorganized employees resolve disputes with their employer over the application of the Employment Standards Act.[7] Routine inspections of workplaces are rare, dropping significantly between 1980 and 1986, and even rarer are cases where an employer is prosecuted for victimizing employees seeking to exercise their legal rights under the act. Adams also finds a high level of non-compliance with provincial minimum wage provisions and notes that most awards under the act occurred after the employee had left employment (LLCG, 1991:982). His conclusion is that the Employment Standards branch is operating primarily as a collection agency, and not even a very good collection agency at that, since its procedures had corrected minimum wage violations in fewer than 2 percent of the cases he studied (LLCG, 1991:992).

In Ontario at least, work hours legislation also appears to have been enforced quite laxly. A 1987 Ontario Task Force report on hours of work and overtime found that in 1985, more than 140 000 workers in the province had worked weeks of more than 60 hours on a regular basis (LLCG, 1991:995). Even making liberal allowance for exempted personnel, such as managers and those working in occupations that did not require Labour Ministry overtime permits for excessively long hours, about 32 500 workers were illegally working such long work weeks in 1985. The Task Force also estimated that for every overtime hour worked with a permit, 24 had been worked without one (LLCG, 1991:995–996). Since then, as we noted in Chapter 2, the overtime situation has almost certainly worsened.

Overall, work standards enforcement mechanisms in Ontario have been so weak that they appear to have given employers little real incentive to comply with the law (LLCG, 1991:996). Such lax enforcement is in sharp contrast to the generally strict and effective enforcement of unfair employer labour practice provisions under most Canadian jurisdictions' labour relations legislation (discussed in the next chapter), and it raises serious questions about governments' commitment to maintaining effective work standards legislation. The implications of the current situation are troubling, to say the least.

THE INDIVIDUAL EMPLOYMENT CONTRACT

Non-unionized workers are under **individual** employment contracts (whether or not the contract has ever been written down). An individual contract of employment, which is essentially "a contract for the payment of compensation for service" (LLCG, 1984:2–1), confers obligations on both employee and employer. The employee must report for work regularly, perform his or her duties honestly and faithfully, obey lawful and safe orders, and avoid gross misconduct such as drunkenness or insubordination (McPhillips and England, 1995:76–77). For professional and managerial employees, avoiding any conflict of interest (as would be created if an employee solicited his or her employer's customers) may be an important element of the express or implied contract (McPhillips and England, 1995:77).[8] Employers, in addition to abiding by any relevant statutes such as employment standards or human rights laws, must pay employees regularly and cannot change their duties, status, or level of pay significantly without the employees' consent. Most important of all, they can only dismiss employees for just cause or with sufficient notice (McPhillips and England, 1995). A firm's economic difficulties do not constitute just cause. Any dismissal for just cause must be well founded in the conduct of the employee (Christie, 1980:362). As for the question of what constitutes "sufficient notice" for any given employee, this is an important, but sometimes difficult, issue that will be discussed in more detail shortly.

Dismissals and the Unorganized Worker

Perhaps the single most important difference between collective bargaining legislation and the legislation governing non-unionized workers is in the area of protection against dismissal. A unionized worker who has been dismissed may seek redress (up to and including reinstatement with full pay for any time lost between the termination and the arbitration award) under the grievance procedure of his or her collective agreement. Though other types of grievance often do not get carried forward to arbitration, in most cases dismissal grievances will be if the worker insists, if only so that the union can avoid a possible duty of fair representation complaint for failing to do so. Ordinarily in dismissal cases, the onus of proof is on the employer to demonstrate that the employee should be discharged; the standard of proof required by most arbitrators is high. Given these facts, a discharged worker stands more than an even chance of being reinstated (Christie, 1980:81). The substantial protection that union membership thus provides against arbitrary dismissal has frequently been cited in union-membership-joining and union-growth studies as a major reason why workers wish to join unions.

Dismissals may be of two types: express (outright) or "constructive." A "constructive" dismissal occurs when the employer unilaterally makes a major alteration in an employee's pay, status, or workplace responsibilities, such that the employee believes she or he is no longer being asked to do the same job on the terms initially agreed upon, and feels invited, if not compelled, to resign. If, for example, a middle-level manager found herself assigned to sweep floors, she would logically interpret the reassignment as a demotion and consider it a constructive dismissal. In a case involving the Burns Foods Company,[9] a foreman named Baker was suddenly advised that his position had become redundant and offered alternative work at lower pay as a beef boner or security guard. When he refused, he was dismissed. The court ruled that Baker's removal from the position he had held for nearly 30 years constituted a constructive dismissal, since at no time did the company argue his work was unsatisfactory. But the notion of constructive dismissal does not apply to minor, or sometimes even fairly significant changes, such as lateral transfers, providing they do not involve lower pay or a demotion. In a case involving Lloyd's Bank,[10] a manager sued for constructive dismissal after being transferred from the bank's Vancouver branch to an equivalent position, at higher pay, at the bank's smallest branch in New York. The court ruled this a lateral move rather than a demotion in denying the plaintiff's constructive dismissal suit.

Whether a dismissal is express or constructive, the non-unionized employee has two options available: an action under work standards legislation (discussed in the previous section) or redress at common law, through the courts. Either way, reinstatement is normally not available (Christie, 1980), except in the three jurisdictions (mentioned below) that offer some kind of equivalent to the grievance procedure for non-unionized employees. Elsewhere, the best the aggrieved non-unionized employee can hope for is reasonable notice, or money in lieu thereof. Under work standards legislation (see above), the notice period is extremely short, even for employees with many years' service. For more recent hires, it is all but non-existent. Unjust dismissal actions at common law can lead to substantially larger awards (sometimes from six to 24 months of salary[11] in the case of professional or managerial employees or those with very long service). However, when a worker goes to court, the outcome is never certain, the process is normally quite long and stressful, and lawyers' fees can eat up a large portion of the award. The courts may not, therefore, be a realistic option for most workers other than professionals, managers, top-level athletes and entertainers, or those with extremely long periods of service. Still, awards have been increasing in recent years. Awards of 12 to 24 months' salary are no longer uncommon (McPhillips and England, 1995:81). Given the large amounts of money that may be at stake and the potential of damaging a firm's reputation and hurting the morale of other employees, it behooves employers to exercise extreme care in the way in which they discharge employees. Dismissal is an extremely stressful experience in the best of circumstances. Employers and managers must take care not to aggravate an already emotionally loaded situation by such ill-advised and heartless actions as termination in the presence of fellow workers, personal abuse, or false accusations of serious misconduct such as theft. It is precisely this kind of behaviour that can trigger a substantial increase in an unjust dismissal award, whether or not separate punitive damages are awarded.[12]

In determining the size of awards, judges still rely quite heavily on a 1960 case involving an advertising director named Bardal and *The Globe & Mail*.[13] While there was never any allegation of improper conduct or unsatisfactory performance, Bardal was summarily dismissed after refusing to resign with six months' notice and one month's salary. The factors used by the court in arriving at an award of a year's salary included the nature of the employment, the employee's length of service, his age, and the availability of similar employment, as well as his experience, training, and qualifications. In addition to the "Bardal" factors, courts take into account whether the employee has made any attempt to mitigate (lessen) the damages by seeking other, substantially similar work. Employees have the duty to mitigate; however, in these cases the onus is on the employer to prove that the employee has not made an attempt to find suitable work.

Dismissal Adjudication for Non-Unionized Employees

Three jurisdictions (Nova Scotia, Quebec, and the federal jurisdiction) provide some kind of arbitration or adjudication in dismissal cases for non-managerial, non-bargaining-unit employees with more than a certain length of service. The qualifying period for application of the laws (10 years in Nova Scotia, five in Quebec) sharply reduces the number of cases brought under the adjudication procedures.

The adjudication process most studied is that carried out under the *Canada Labour Code,* which provides for adjudication of dismissal grievances of non-managerial, non-bargaining-unit employees with more than a year's service. Under this procedure, the adjudicator can either reinstate or award damages in lieu of reinstatement (McPhillips and England, 1989:50–51). However, a recent study (Eden, 1993) suggests that experience under this section of the *Code* has been more or less similar to experience in the unionized sector. Of 279 dismissal cases decided under this section of the *Canada Code* between 1978 and 1989, 61 percent were sustained, a figure roughly comparable to that for dismissal grievances. In general, it appears that the same concepts of progressive discipline being applied by arbitrators in the unionized sector are being adhered to by adjudicators under the *Code* (Eden, 1993).[14]

It is not entirely clear why more jurisdictions have not followed the lead of the federal jurisdiction, Nova Scotia, and Quebec by providing some kind of adjudication procedure for non-unionized workers' dismissal grievances. Some writers have suggested that opposition from unions may be one reason, given that the availability of a dismissal grievance procedure for non-unionized workers might reduce workers' incentives to join unions. On the other hand, workers in various European countries (such as Germany) have a variety of options for handling grievances (including dismissal grievances), some of which also do not involve the union (Fuerstenberg, 1993:181); there is little evidence that these countries' union membership rates have declined as a result.

Given the fundamental importance to workers of having some kind of protection against arbitrary dismissal and the very real likelihood of stable if not declining Canadian union membership rates for the future, the issue warrants further investigation.

HUMAN RIGHTS LEGISLATION

The basic purpose of human rights legislation is to prevent discrimination. Such legislation, in force in every Canadian jurisdiction, prohibits workplace discrimination on a broad range of grounds. For example, the federal human rights act bars discrimination on the basis of race, national or ethnic origin, colour, religion, age,[15] sex, sexual orientation, marital status, family status, disability, and conviction for which a pardon has been issued (CCH, 1998b).[16] Most provinces' grounds are fairly similar, but there are some minor variations. Despite public pressure, Alberta has not yet included sexual orientation as a prohibited ground; interestingly enough, it *does* include source of income, a prohibition presumably meant to prevent discrimination against social assistance recipients. Certain other provinces, such as Newfoundland, also include political opinion as a prohibited ground.

Every province exempts bona fide occupational qualifications (to be discussed in more detail below). In addition, a number of jurisdictions, including most of the Atlantic provinces, exclude occupations of a religious or philanthropic nature. For example, a Catholic school may require that its staff be Catholic or adhere to traditional Catholic values (i.e., staff cannot live together outside marriage).

Human rights legislation is normally enforced on the basis of individual complaints to the appropriate commission or council (McPhillips and England, 1995:82), although in a few cases proactive investigations may be conducted.

THE 50TH ANNIVERSARY OF THE UNITED NATIONS' ADOPTION OF THE UNIVERSAL DECLARATION OF HUMAN RIGHTS
206.191.130/eng/50th.cfm

Bona Fide Occupational Qualifications

A bona fide occupational qualification (BFOQ) allows employers to discriminate for legitimate business reasons. Most Canadian legislation specifically allows discrimination on this basis (McPhillips and England, 1989:55). Obvious examples include physical strength requirements for police and firefighters, vision requirements for pilots and air traffic controllers, and appearance requirements for clothing models. A less obvious example would be a clause in an employment contract barring a spouse or close relative of the current employee from employment at the same firm, on the basis that nepotism, or even the perception of nepotism, is bad for morale and thus constitutes a legitimate business reason for the prohibition.

There have been two broad and somewhat interrelated trends in the use of BFOQs. The first has been towards an increasingly narrow construction, on the part of courts and adjudication tribunals, of what constitutes a legitimate business reason for discrimination. A generation ago, airline flight attendants were always female. As well, they normally had to be within a certain, quite narrow, size range and were generally grounded on reaching a certain age. Airlines justified these requirements on the basis that their customers wanted a certain type of image in flight attendants. The flight attendants successfully countered with the argument that they had serious work to do (including providing emergency first aid as well as serving coffee and drinks) and that the gender, age, and size requirements had nothing to do with that work and should thus be eliminated. Now, there are often older flight attendants on airplanes, as well as an increasing number of men working in this position. There is little evidence that the quality of service has suffered as a result.

Tests of an employee's ability to meet bona fide occupational requirement must directly address that requirement, not its second cousin. While courts and tribunals continue to allow police forces and fire departments to require strength as a condition of employment, they are generally no longer allowed to impose minimum height and weight requirements. Such tests, it was found, had the effect of systematically discriminating against most women and even many male members of certain minority groups. They also might not be a totally reliable predictor of a person's strength, since a small person who works out every day may well be stronger than a giant couch potato. Granted, even with specific strength tests in place, a woman or member of certain ethnic minority groups is still at a disadvantage. Other things being equal, a bigger person will have an easier time carrying 150 pounds of dead weight down a ladder than a smaller person. But no one can argue that this is not a legitimate test of the kind of work a firefighter will be called upon to do, and at least a woman or ethnic minority group member now has the opportunity to lift weights five hours a day to prepare for the ordeal.

The second trend has been the application of the duty to accommodate those who cannot comply with legitimate business requirements because of their sex, religion, or some other factor that constitutes a prohibited ground of discrimination. This duty applies up to the point where an employer would suffer "undue hardship" by making the required accommodation (see Carter, 1997). As we note elsewhere in this chapter and in the next one, the duty to accommodate has, in recent years, been construed increasingly broadly. In the now well-known case of Bhinder v. CNR,[17] the Supreme Court of Canada ruled that the railroad's hard-hat rule discriminated against a Sikh electrician who was required by his religion to wear a turban, even though the requirement had not been made for discriminatory reasons. At that time, the Court also ruled that though the rule was discriminatory, it could be considered a BFOQ since its aim was to protect workers' safety. However, in the later Central Alberta Dairy Pool case,[18] the Court changed its direction, indicating that Bhinder would have incurred only a minimal added safety risk by working without a hard hat and that the employer could have accommodated him by placing him in a different job (LLCG, 1991:1007–1019). Since then, employers have been expected to modify jobs, buildings, and work schedules to accommodate people with disabilities and those of different ethnic and religious backgrounds who cannot work regular hours (see Carter, 1997). What remains unclear from the cases reported to date is exactly what would constitute "undue hardship" under the duty to accommodate.

Application of Human Rights Legislation

Human rights legislation applies to all stages of the employment relationship: from initial application and interviewing to the job itself to eventual retirement or termination. It's crucial for human resource, personnel, and IR staff to know this legislation, since they must use it on a daily basis. As we noted at the beginning of the chapter, failure to act in accordance with this legislation can cause a firm embarrassment or even lead to legal action.

Hiring Process

In some jurisdictions, including the federal jurisdiction, there are specific provisions that prohibit, on job application forms or at job interviews, the inclusion of questions related to any of the forbidden grounds of discrimination. In jurisdictions whose human rights legislation does not contain the provisions, such questions should still not be asked by employers. However, someone who feels that information related to a prohibited ground of discrimination was the reason he or she was not hired must prove that the information was the basis for the decision in jurisdictions without express job application provisions (McPhillips and England, 1995:83). The ban, it should be noted, applies not only to questions intended to elicit information directly (i.e., asking a person's date of birth), but also to those intended to elicit it indirectly (i.e., asking when a person graduated from university, from which it would usually be easy to infer an age range).

Job applicants who do not wish prospective employers to know information related to a prohibited ground of discrimination should not include it on their resumes. If such information is necessary for legitimate business reasons (i.e., date of birth for company benefit plans), it can be obtained once the person is on payroll (see McPhillips and England, 1989).

On the Job

At the most obvious level, human rights legislation bars such grossly unequal treatment as paying men and women different rates for the same work, or establishing separate locker room facilities for people of different races. With regard to pay, a number of jurisdictions have moved beyond equal pay for equal work to adopt the more sophisticated concept of equal pay for work of equal value (see the discussion of pay equity below).

Employers have the duty to do everything in their power to prevent harassment on any of the prohibited grounds and, where it occurs, to find the offenders and deal with them appropriately, to minimize the likelihood of any recurrence. Under the federal act, hate messages on the basis of any prohibited ground of discrimination are specifically barred. In a 1988 case involving the Canada Employment and Immigration Commission,[19] a black employee who received racist notes through interoffice mail was awarded $4000[20] when the human rights tribunal found that the employer had done nothing to try to bring the perpetrators to justice. Among other things, the head of security had not informed police, sought legal advice, or asked other black employees if they had been the target of similar hate mail (LLCG, 1991:1054–1058).

A special focus in recent years has been sexual harassment. A number of jurisdictions include special human rights provisions on this form of harassment, and many organizations have established sexual harassment policies, perhaps driven by the fear that if they do not establish and enforce such policies, they may be held liable not just for harassment of subordinates by supervisors, but also that of co-worker by co-worker (McPhillips and England, 1995). A growing trend has been to the recognition that a "poisoned climate," created through such actions as posting magazine pin-ups on office walls or telling crude, sexually oriented jokes, may make women feel unwelcome and should thus be considered a form of harassment, even if the actions are not directed against a particular individual (McPhillips and England, 1995). In a not unrelated development, many organizations have become increasingly aware of the threat of workplace violence, especially to women and in situations where employees must work late at night. Nova Scotia's draft report on workplace violence (discussed below), which would include violence under the provincial health and safety act, is an early and worthwhile attempt to address this extreme form of harassment in a systematic fashion.

Ending the Employment Relationship

Termination of an employee on the basis of any prohibited ground of discrimination is illegal in all jurisdictions. Human rights commissions' remedies (discussed below) include the right to reinstatement in such cases. A major exception is mandatory retirement, legal in all jurisdictions except Quebec and Manitoba, which have barred it as a form of age discrimination. For example, Ontario's Human Rights Act has placed a cap of age 64 on its age discrimination provision (Reid and Meltz, 1995:35). It is not clear whether many of the assumptions under which mandatory retirement policies were initially established still apply today; thus we should expect to see these policies challenged in the near future.[21]

Remedies for Human Rights Violations

Human rights commissions generally have a broad range of available remedies. If an employer has not hired someone for discriminatory reasons, or has terminated someone for such reasons, the employer may be made to hire or reinstate that individual with back pay. In addition, the worker may be given compensation for any expenses resulting from the discriminatory practice, such as legal costs (LLCG, 1991:1019). As noted earlier, where discrimination has led the victim to suffer a loss of self-respect or hurt feelings, the commission may order compensation. The commission may also order the employer to change the discriminatory practices in question.

Under the Ontario act (Swinton and Swan, 1983, in LLCG, 1984:4–137–138), if the initial investigation of a complaint by an officer does not result in a settlement, conciliation is used. Where this is unsuccessful, the commission may convene a board of inquiry. Board findings may be appealed to the courts on issues of facts or law. With the consent of the Attorney General, offenders may also be prosecuted in the courts; however, this method is rarely used, as the commission normally prefers to seek an accommodation (Swinton and Swan, 1983, in LLCG, 1984).

Human Rights Legislation for Unionized Workers

Unionized workers have additional protections available to them, beyond those already discussed. For example, human rights codes apply specifically to unions, which can be subjected to human rights complaints if they discriminate against any of their members (McPhillips and England, 1995:87). As well, the duty of fair representation provisions found in most jurisdictions' labour acts bar bad faith, arbitrary, or discriminatory behaviour, on penalty of a complaint to the labour board. Finally, collective agreements often contain non-discrimination provisions, as well as provisions specifically pertaining to such areas as sexual harassment. Such provisions can be enforced through the grievance procedure, which may well be a more efficient and effective process than those provided under human rights legislation (McPhillips and England, 1995; also see Carter, 1997; LLCG, 1991:1007).

WORKERS' RIGHTS ARE HUMAN RIGHTS:
UNITED STEELWORKERS' CONFERENCE
www.uswa.ca/ENGREL/humrght.htm#Agenda

Pay and Employment Equity

Pay Equity

Despite the improved workplace conditions brought about by human rights legislation, women and members of ethnic minority groups continue, in many cases, to be at a severe disadvantage on the job. The average female worker in Canada receives only about 70 percent of the average male's pay (McPhillips and England, 1995:83). It appears that a significant portion of the gap still results from outright discrimination (McPhillips and England, 1995). Another significant portion is due to job segregation, which results in women being clustered in typically lower-paying traditionally "female" occupations such as child care and secretarial work (McPhillips and England, 1995) and finding it difficult to enter traditionally "male" occupations that pay more.

Pay equity legislation, providing that workers be given equal pay for work of equal value, is now in place in most jurisdictions. In three jurisdictions (Quebec, Ontario, and the federal jurisdiction), it applies to both public and private sectors (LLCG, 1991:1028); elsewhere it applies only to the former. Such legislation resulted from the growing recognition that traditional "equal pay for equal work" provisions could be easily evaded and in any case were not doing enough to close the male-female wage gap. Under the federal pay equity legislation, the criterion to be used in assessing the value of work performed by employees in the same establishment is the "composite of the skill, effort, and responsibility required in the performance of the work and the conditions under which the work is performed" (LLCG, 1991). Furthermore, separate establishments maintained primarily to allow for the continuation of male-female differentials are treated as the same for purposes of the legislation, and employers are also barred from reducing anyone's salary to eliminate pay discrimination (LLCG, 1991).

Pay equity recently received national attention when the Canadian Human Rights Tribunal ordered the federal government to pay back-salaries, with interest, to a group of 200 000 current and past employees in female-dominated occupations[22] who had been receiving less than males in comparable occupations (Aubry, 1998; May, 1998). For example, the work of librarians, a female-dominated occupation, was regarded as comparable to that of historians, a male-dominated occupation. In late August (PSAC, 1998), the government announced it would appeal the Tribunal's decision, sparking a wave of outrage among federal public servants across the country. (The public service unions' response to the government's action is discussed in more detail in the public sector chapter).

Employment Equity

The purpose of pay equity is to correct pay imbalances for women already working (Robb, 1987). Employment equity seeks to break down patterns of occupational segregation that have, in the past, made it difficult for women or, sometimes, members of various other groups such as ethnic minorities or people with disabilities, to enter certain occupations. In 1986 (LLCG, 1991:1047), the federal government enacted the *Employment Equity Act*, designed to apply both to federally regulated employers and to all employers receiving federal government contracts of more than $200 000 (LLCG, 1991; also McPhillips and England, 1995:86). The four groups to whom this act specifically applies are women, aboriginal people, people with disabilities, and visible minorities. The act does not impose specific hiring quotas (McPhillips and England, 1995), but does require affected employers to implement employment equity (i.e., fair representation of the four designated groups within the work force) by identifying and eliminating employment barriers against members of those groups (LLCG, 1991:1047–1048; CCH, 1998b). Beyond simply removing discriminatory barriers, employers are expected to initiate positive hiring policies and practices to help ensure that members of the designated groups are fairly represented in their work forces.[23] They are also required to monitor and report on employment equity progress on an ongoing basis and to consult with employees and, where the organization is unionized, the union regarding the implementation of their employment equity programs (CCH, 1998b). There are limits to how far employers are expected to go in implementing employment equity. Specifically, the legislation provides that they will not be expected to assume undue hardship,[24] hire or promote unqualified people, or create new positions to ensure equitable representation of designated group members (CCH, 1998b).

HEALTH AND SAFETY LEGISLATION

As Giles and Jain (1989:341) have aptly pointed out, "Work kills, maims, and sickens at a horrifying rate." For many, the seriousness of the situation with regard to occupational health and safety in Canadian workplaces was brought home by the 1992 Westray Mine disaster, in which 26 miners were killed in a coal mine explosion in Pictou County, Nova Scotia (Richard, 1997:I, vii). Judge Peter Richard, commissioner of the provincial board of inquiry looking into the causes of the tragedy, found "a complex mosaic of actions, omissions, mistakes, incompetence, apathy, cynicism, stupidity, and neglect," with a few "well-intentioned but misguided blunders" added to the mix (Richard, 1997:I, viii). Richard's report concluded that mine management disregarded critical safety factors and "appeared to regard safety-conscious workers as…wimps" (Richard, 1997:I, ix). While the report was severely critical of mine management on many counts, it came down especially hard on it for failing to take proper measures to control coal dust, a primary cause of the explosion (Richard, 1997:I, 347). Despite several previous "near-misses," management had done little or nothing to remove coal dust from the mine, or to collect and test coal dust samples to monitor their combustibility, thus ignoring its own policies as well as violating the requirements of the provincial *Coal Mines Regulations Act* (Richard, 1997). The report was also severely critical of the provincial government, in particular its Labour Department, for making no effort to enforce its demands that management correct the numerous safety violations that government inspectors had found at the mine, some as recently as 10 days before the explosion (Richard, 1997:I,347–348).

To what extent is the Westray pattern of willful employer neglect of employees' safety and government's inability or unwillingness to enforce its own safety regulations typical of Canadian workplaces as a whole? The issue of occupational health and safety is a complex one, as Judge Richard himself admits in his report. Many occupational accidents do not have any single or simple cause. There are also many conscientious employers who recognize that safety is in their own as well as their workers' best interests, and do what they can to make their workplaces safer. Finally, some workers are the authors of their own misfortune.[25] Sometimes an injury or

As the Westray Mine disaster demonstrated, unsafe working conditions remain a fact of life in far too many Canadian mining operations.

death is the result of simple carelessness or ignorance on the part of employees, and sometimes it is the result of "macho" practices (driving without a seat belt, operating welding equipment without goggles, going out on a boat without life preservers) that may have been perpetuated for any number of reasons.

THE CANADIAN CENTRE FOR OCCUPATIONAL HEALTH AND SAFETY ACT

canada.justice.gc.ca/FTP/EN/Laws/chap/C/C-13.txt

Whatever the reasons, Canada's record in occupational health and safety is and has long been appalling. Between 1976 and 1981, Canada ranked worst in work injury incidence in a group of eight countries studied by the ILO, with an average rate of about 11 injuries per 100 workers (Digby and Riddell, 1986, in LLCG, 1991:1071). During that same period, Canada was second only to West Germany in a group of nine ILO countries in workplace fatalities, with a yearly average of about 10 per 100 000 workers (Digby and Riddell, 1986, in LLCG, 1991:1072). In 1983, job-related injuries or illness killed 761 Canadians and nearly one million people, or roughly one worker in nine, were injured on the job. While Canada's record has improved somewhat in recent years, with a drop in the number of accidents reported from just over 620 000 in 1989 to just over 455 000 in 1992 (McPhillips and England, 1995:87), far more clearly needs to be done.

The Canadian approach to health and safety is twofold: prevention where possible, compensation where prevention doesn't succeed (McPhillips and England, 1989:58). The two main preventive methods used are the "external system," whereby specified health and safety standards are established legislatively, and the "internal system," which provides for joint labour-management safety committees (required in all Canadian jurisdictions)[26] as a means of promoting safer workplace practices. The legislation is often contained in a specific health and safety statute applicable to all employers. It is sometimes supplemented by various statutes applicable to certain industries only, and administered by different government departments (McPhillips and England, 1989).

The External System

There are two main components to the external system. The first is detailed laws, often geared to the circumstances of particular industries, compelling employers to operate in a safe manner. The second is a general "performance duty" imposed on both employers and workers, obliging them to promote health and safety at work (McPhillips and England, 1989).

Safety legislation is often extremely detailed, specifying how many parts per million of a given substance may legally be discharged into the air or water, or at what temperatures and under what conditions certain foods must be stored in restaurants. It also covers such issues as required sanitary facilities, the qualifications needed by workers to work in a given industry, and the manufacture and use of equipment. In some cases, it imposes specific obligations on workers, as by requiring that restaurant workers wash their hands after visiting the washroom or that construction workers wear hard hats on job sites. Legislation may also require training or successful completion of a test before workers are allowed to perform potentially hazardous work, such as operating certain types of heavy equipment or working on high construction scaffolds. In other cases, it requires periodic inspection of equipment, such as elevators.

LABOUR STANDARDS

info.load-otea.hrdc-drhc.gc.ca/~lsweb/homeen.shtml

Under the "performance duty," employers are obliged to ensure the health and safety of all workers on the site, whether they employ them or not. Employers are also obligated to notify the government of any serious accidents or illnesses that occur, as well as of any hazardous substances in use on the work site (McPhillips and England, 1989:58–59). Workers, for their part, are obliged to take reasonable care to protect their own health and safety and that of their co-workers while on the job. In certain occupations, particularly those involving frequent contact with the public, "taking reasonable care" entails obtaining a periodic medical examination to ensure one does not have a contagious disease that could easily be spread at the workplace. In some jurisdictions, the performance duty also confers an obligation on the suppliers of tools and equipment to ensure that the tools and equipment are in good condition and comply with the statutory safety standards (McPhillips and England, 1989:59).

Though external legislation has undoubtedly helped make Canadian workplaces safer than they would otherwise be, the system is far from perfect. Ultimately, any system of external legislation can only be as good as its enforcement mechanism. To suggest that health and safety legislation has typically been haphazardly enforced in Canada may be putting the matter charitably. In general, governments have preferred to accommodate employers rather than prosecute them for safety violations. Another problem is that inspectorates have been inadequately staffed, and inspectors have often been reluctant to issue stop-work orders on large or politically sensitive projects, particularly those backed by the provincial government (like Westray Mines), preferring to leave the hard decisions to their superiors (McPhillips and England, 1995:92).

The situation in Ontario offers some examples of just how inadequately safety legislation has been enforced. There, where the labour ministry has jurisdiction over about 150 000 workplaces, inspections dropped from 38 000 to 29 000 between 1983–1984 and 1988–1989. In other words, only one workplace in five was inspected at all in the latter year (LLCG, 1991:1104), a seriously inadequate percentage, especially in non-unionized workplaces that do not have a union grievance procedure to rely on. During this period, the Health and Safety Branch issued more than 250 000 orders demanding that employers correct various safety violations. Of these orders, only 693 resulted in prosecutions and 450 in convictions. As well, "stop orders" compelling employers to correct violations before resuming work were rare, amounting to only 2 percent of all orders at the beginning of the study period and 4.5 percent at the end (LLCG, 1991). Where a conviction was obtained, the penalty was arguably far from severe enough to serve as a deterrent. During the study period, the average fine increased only from $3194 to $4515. The low incidence of prosecutions led the Ontario Public Service Employees Union (OPSEU), the union representing provincial health and safety inspectors, to complain that the inspectors had been prevented by their superiors from initiating prosecutions for violations (LLCG, 1991). Many, though not all, of OPSEU's allegations were confirmed by an independent task force struck by the Deputy Minister to investigate the union's complaints. It is perhaps revealing that the rate of prosecutions and convictions did increase after the task force investigation (LLCG, 1991), although the rates of both remained extremely low (well below 1 percent of orders).

In recent years, provincial governments appear to have been taking a somewhat tougher line on chronic safety violators. Both in Ontario and elsewhere, the level of fines has increased. By the early 1990s, Ontario had begun to issue fines in excess of $100 000 in extreme cases, and criminal prosecutions, though rare, had occurred (McPhillips and England, 1995:93). But the Westray disaster shows just how much further Canadian jurisdictions have to go in enforcing health and safety standards.

Inadequate enforcement is not the only problem. Another is the failure of legal standards to address the hazards that contribute to the majority of occupational injuries (LLCG, 1991:1101), a problem that becomes more serious all the time as new substances and equipment are introduced into Canadian workplaces. Still another problem is that the safety standards may be set too low to provide adequate protection against certain hazardous substances. As Edward Tucker (1986, in LLCG, 1991:1099–1100) points out, regulatory practice in Ontario has generally entailed bringing worst-practice firms in line with the industry average, thus serving to sanction existing exposure levels rather than improving them when new evidence suggests a tougher standard would be warranted. The main thrust of Ontario's regulatory concern is suggested, in Tucker's view, by the fact that the Labour Ministry has rarely selected standards that would lead to significant compliance costs for industry (Tucker, 1986, in LLCG, 1991).

The Internal System

While external safety legislation is important, no legislation can cover every possible workplace situation. An important feature of Canada's health and safety system is, therefore, its "internal responsibility system," whereby management and labour both assume responsibility for workplace safety. A key assumption here is that prevention is more likely to occur when workers are actively participating in the process; the worker who operates a particular machine is often the one who best knows that machine's potential hazards and how to get around them (Swinton, 1983, in LLCG, 1991:1126). While the internal system is normally intended to work in tandem with the external one, Nova Scotia's health and safety act contains a unique provision stating that the internal system (encompassing all workplace parties) is the foundation upon which the act is based (CCH, 1998c:551-1 to 551-2). The internal system's three major components, as outlined in Ontario's 1978 *Occupational Health and Safety Act*,[27] are joint health and safety committees, the right to refuse unsafe work, and the right to be informed about workplace hazards (CCH, 1998c:1125–1126).

Joint Committees

Joint labour-management health and safety committees are required in all jurisdictions in workplaces of more than a certain size—20 employees being the usual minimum (McPhillips and England, 1995:89). In workplaces below the minimum-size threshold for a committee, a workplace health and safety representative is generally required.

Committees are normally expected to have equal numbers of worker and management representatives. In many jurisdictions, their maximum size is 12 (CCH, 1998c:1805). On average, they meet once a month, though they are sometimes not required to do so more than quarterly. Their powers and functions are established through provincial legislation; in general, those powers are merely advisory, in that an employer cannot normally be forced to comply with a committee's recommendations unless mandated to do so by a government official (CCH, 1998c:1801). What the committee can do is call in a government inspector, who may issue a stop-work order or other directive if the work practice appears sufficiently dangerous. In most jurisdictions, employers are required to pay committee members for time spent preparing for and attending meetings and doing committee business (see CCH, 1998c:1922). In Ontario, an employer is obliged to respond within 21 days to any written committee recommendation (CCH, 1998c).

Committees are usually given a fair degree of latitude. In most jurisdictions, they have the power to handle employees' health and safety complaints, to establish health and safety training and education programs, to take part in health and safety-related inquiries and investigations, to access government and employers reports relating to employees' health and safety at their work site, and to request any information necessary from an employer to identify existing or potential workplace safety hazards (CCH, 1998c). There is some variation in committees' functions in different jurisdictions. Under the *Canada Code*, they are obliged to maintain records pertaining to the disposition of employees' health and safety complaints and to cooperate with any occupational health service established at the workplace. Other specific duties include accompanying government safety inspectors on "walkaround" inspections of work sites, investigating serious accidents, and helping to resolve work refusal cases (discussed in more detail below). In Quebec, committees have the additional responsibilities of designating a physician in charge of health services and working with the provincial Occupational Health and Safety Commission to develop recommendations for safe work practices (CCH, 1998c:1811).

How effective are the joint committees? A number of commentators (i.e., Bryce and Manga, 1985; McPhillips and England, 1989, 1995) have indicated that the presence of a joint committee seems to lead to a significant reduction in workplace injuries. Others, including Robert Sass (1993), a pioneer in introducing joint committees during the 1970s, have concluded that the committees are ineffectual. An obvious problem here is that many workplaces simply do not have committees. As McPhillips and England argue (1995:89), a minimum threshold of 20 employees may be too small, especially at a time when many jobs are in small and medium-sized businesses. A single representative may not be as effective as a committee in representing workers' health and safety interests—particularly a representative handpicked by management. Second, it is generally recognized that committees need the active cooperation of top management if they're to operate effectively. While enlightened managers may be prepared to recognize that a strong health and safety committee is in their best interest, as well as their workers', not all managers are enlightened. Those opposed to committees may flout the law by simply refusing to establish one (McPhillips and England, 1989), by holding meetings infrequently, or by not granting the committee any budget or any real power. While more research is needed on the conditions under which joint committees can function most effectively, the evidence to date suggests that the committees can work, but only when management gives them a fairly free hand. The minimum establishment size required in most jurisdictions raises the question of whether some alternative mechanism is needed to ensure adequate protection of workers' safety in small businesses. Perhaps where there are a number of similar businesses (i.e., restaurants) within a given city or town, there could be a committee for all the restaurants in that area, including at least one representative from each area restaurant.

Right to Refuse Unsafe Work

A key component of any internal safety system is allowing workers the right to refuse any work they honestly consider unsafe, pending an investigation by a neutral third party (normally a provincial health and safety inspector). This right is granted to workers in all Canadian jurisdictions. Most jurisdictions require "reasonable" grounds or the "likelihood" of risk; in Alberta and Newfoundland, the right is more narrowly applied to situations of imminent or immediate danger (McPhillips and England, 1995:91). In most jurisdictions, anyone refusing unsafe work must formally report the situation to management (CCH, 1998c:601). Under the *Canada Code*, the worker must also notify the health and safety committee, or representative where no committee exists. If management intervention fails to resolve the situation, the next step is for either the worker or employer[28] to notify a government safety inspector (CCH, 1998c). If the safety inspector upholds the worker's decision, she or he can continue to stay off work until the situation is corrected to the inspector's satisfaction; otherwise the employee must return to work. The one major exception, under both the *Canada Code* and provincial legislation, is that no one can refuse to work where the refusal would put someone else's life, health, or safety directly in danger (CCH, 1998c:1315).

 CANADIAN CENTRE FOR OCCUPATIONAL HEALTH AND SAFETY
www.ccohs.ca

Though workers in most jurisdictions run the risk of loss of pay if no alternative work is available to them after a refusal, the worker is normally protected from discharge or other disciplinary action for exercising a legal right to refuse work under the health and safety act (CCH, 1998c:1316), providing the worker has duly notified the employer and, where appropriate, a government inspector. However, several studies (i.e., LLCG, 1984:4–359; McPhillips and England, 1989:62) find that, at least in Ontario, the vast majority of refusals to work occurred in unionized settings. Failure to exercise the legal right to refuse work in non-unionized settings could result from a (possibly justified) fear of employer reprisal, simple ignorance of the law, or both. Whatever the reasons, the evidence suggests that unions have an important role to play in ensuring the adequate enforcement of safety legislation. It also suggests the need for stronger mechanisms to protect non-unionized workers, such as the equivalent of a dismissal grievance procedure in cases where a refusal to work triggered the dismissal.

Before leaving this subject, we should point out that in some cases, workers have not only the right but the duty to refuse unsafe work. If, for example, a worker were ordered to dump toxic waste into a stream, she or he would legally be required to refuse, on the basis that workers are obliged not to break any law. (To be sure, it would normally be the employer, rather than the employee, who would be prosecuted for this illegal action [CCH, 1998c:2316]). Similarly, Alberta's health and safety act requires workers not to operate any tool, appliance, or equipment if they have reason to believe that the equipment will cause an imminent danger to them or anyone else on the work site (CCH, 1998c:2317).

Notification of Hazardous Materials (WHMIS)

The third and far from least important component of the internal system is the right to know (Swinton, 1983), specifically, the right to be informed about the actual or potential danger posed by various hazardous substances that may be used in the workplace. Each jurisdiction has its own Workplace Hazardous Materials Information System (WHMIS) provisions. Under the federal *Hazardous Products Control Act*, suppliers are required to classify the products they sell according to the amount of risk entailed in handling those products. They are also required to provide appropriate labels that will enable workers to tell at a glance what kind of substance they are working with (CCH, 1998c:60, 560). These labels must include the product's brand or generic name, that of the supplier, appropriate hazard symbols indicating the type of hazard potentially posed by the product, information on how to handle the product safely, and any appropriate first-aid measures (CCH, 1998c). Material safety data sheets (MSDS) must provide detailed descriptions of the product's chemical composition, any hazardous ingredients it contains, its fire or explosion hazard, its toxicological properties, and appropriate preventive and first-aid measures (CCH, 1998c:60, 820).

For their part, employers must ensure that controlled substances are labelled, to obtain and distribute material safety data sheets, and to educate workers about any hazardous substance used or produced at the workplace (CCH, 1998c:100). They are also required to provide workers and supervisors with a copy of the regulations (McPhillips and England, 1995:92). Under Ontario's law and that of most other jurisdictions, trade secrets can be exempted from WHMIS regulations. In Ontario (CCH, 1998c:14:700), employers may apply to the Hazardous Materials Information Review Commission for an exemption for information contained on a label or MSDS that they believe to be confidential business information. However, even if the exemption is granted, the confidential information must be released to a doctor in a medical emergency (CCH, 1998c).

Workers' Compensation

Workers' compensation legislation is the major mechanism used to compensate the victims of workplace accidents or work-induced illness.[29] Normally, workers' compensation is under the control of a provincial board whose primary responsibilities are to collect levies from employers and pay benefits to disabled workers. The basic principle of the system is that it is "no-fault." This means that a worker need not prove employer negligence to be eligible for benefits, but is also precluded from seeking further remedies through the courts. To be eligible for benefits, the worker must have suffered an accident or disease that arose out of and during the course of employment, disabled him or her beyond the day of the accident, and was not the result of his or her own willful misconduct, except in cases of death or serious disablement (CCH, 1998c:15.403).

Funds used to pay compensation benefits are drawn from a levy on employers, based on the nature of the industry and the size of the employer's wage bill (McPhillips and England, 1995:94). In high-risk industries, employers pay higher rates than in low-risk ones. In the past (see McPhillips and England, 1989), the tax was based on the number of claims filed by the industry as a whole. Such a system may actually have served as a disincentive to safe practice, since conscientious employers who did their best to maintain safe workplaces were forced to pay the same amount of tax as laggard or negligent ones. To correct this problem, most jurisdictions now use a system of "experience rating" whereby employers whose claims are above the industry average must pay higher premiums (CCH, 1998c:15,103), while those with good safety records pay less.

Workers may qualify for either temporary or permanent disability benefits. The main basis for compensation is the level of disability sustained by the victim; benefit levels generally range from 75 to 90 percent of the victim's regular salary. Every jurisdiction has imposed a cap on the maximum earnings covered by workers' compensation; in 1997, these ranged from $35 900 in Prince Edward Island to $56 100 in Ontario, with most falling within the $40 000 to $50 000 range (CCH, 1998c:15, 502).

A problem in the past was that employers were under no obligation to rehire disabled workers, either in their old position or a different one, in situations where a worker recovered from an injury or illness. Prior to experience rating, they would have had little incentive to do so. In some jurisdictions, however, this situation has begun to change. In Ontario, the Workers' Compensation Act was amended in 1989 to require reinstatement of workers medically able to perform their previous duties. In cases where the worker can not perform his or her previous duties, but can do some job within the organization, the employer is expected to offer the worker the first available opportunity of suitable employment. A duty to accommodate (for example, by redesigning the workplace) applies here as in the case of other workers with disabilities (McPhillips and England, 1995:95). In Newfoundland, which up until the 1990s had the country's highest workers' compensation levies, the provincial compensation board has recently taken a number of measures to improve the situation. These have included a reduction of benefit levels, including elimination of the "employer top-up" whereby employers would make up the difference between employees' benefit levels and their regular wages, in an attempt to provide disabled workers with more incentive to get back into the workplace (English, 1995, 1996). Other changes have included the introduction of individual employer experience rating and of a rehabilitation program whereby a disabled worker is assigned to a single workers' compensation caseworker throughout his or her disability (English, 1995, 1996). The idea here is that workers are more apt to be rehabilitated if they form a close working relationship with a single caseworker.

In redesigning compensation systems to encourage rehabilitation, workers' compensation boards must walk a fine line. The problem is to provide those who want and are able to return to work with appropriate incentives to do so without denying those who cannot their legitimate benefits, or pressuring them to return to work before they are really ready.

A RAPIDLY CHANGING FIELD

Unlike labour relations legislation (discussed in the next chapter), which has seen few major changes over the past 25 years, employment legislation has been changing constantly throughout most of that period. Human rights legislation, pay equity and employment equity, and joint health and safety committees are but a few of the more important innovations. Generally, the legislative changes have, from the workers' perspective, been positive, in that they have provided workers with additional protections against discrimination and poor working conditions. However, this has not always been the case. The Ontario government, for example, in line with its general policy of deregulation and of shifting power in the direction of business and employers, has passed **Bill 136**, weakening pay equity and the Employment Standards Act. It has also been seriously considering other changes to the Employment Standards Act that would allow employers to make people work more hours before they would become eligible for overtime pay (*Better Times*, various issues). Along similar lines, recent changes to workers' compensation legislation have reduced benefit levels, limited appeals to the compensation board's decisions,[30] and limited compensation for mental stress, except in cases where the stress was a reaction to a "sudden and unexpected traumatic event" (*Canada Labour Views*, 1997).

Even as this chapter was being written, new areas of legislative concern were emerging. Recent efforts in various jurisdictions have sought to provide protection for gays and lesbians under human rights legislation, same-sex benefits for the partners of gays and lesbians, ergonomic workplace designs, improved indoor air quality, rights for non-smokers, and protection against workplace violence. There has also been growing recognition of the problems faced by certain groups, such as the obese, on the grounds of their appearance. The scope of this book precludes a detailed treatment of these emerging areas of human rights legislation, but we will try to give a sense of some of the most important recent developments, allowing more space for issues seldom discussed in the existing literature, and which may thus be new to readers.

Inclusion of Sexual Orientation in Human Rights Acts

As noted earlier, sexual orientation is now a prohibited ground of discrimination in all Canadian jurisdictions except Alberta.[31] The growing awareness of this issue by governments mirrors a similar growth in awareness within much of the labour movement (Hunt, 1997).

Same-Sex Benefits

Closely related to protection of gays and lesbians from workplace discrimination is the issue of providing benefits to same-sex partners comparable to those for which heterosexual partners are eligible. Already, some employers had been doing so voluntarily, among them the regional municipality of Greater Toronto (*Toronto Sun*, 1998), while in Saskatchewan, the Human Rights Commission ruled in April 1998 that same-sex couples have the same right to employment benefits as heterosexual ones (Pacholik, 1998). The movement picked up considerable steam following an April 1998 Ontario Court of Appeal ruling that a section of the federal Income Tax Act was unconstitutional because it restricted survivor benefits from registered pension plans to spouses of the opposite sex (Ditchburn, 1998). In late June, the federal government said it would not appeal the ruling, a decision that paved the way for other jurisdictions to extend same-sex pensions and other benefits. Shortly after the federal government's announcement, the British Columbia government announced it would extend pension benefits to public employees with same-sex partners, becoming the first province to do so voluntarily (Ditchburn, 1998).[32]

Ergonomics

There has been growing recognition that ergonomics, or appropriate, "people-friendly" workplace designs, can help reduce injuries and thus benefit both workers and employers. Given Canada's deplorable workplace injury record, the subject has assumed considerable importance; in 1996 *Relations Industrielles*, the national industrial relations journal, devoted an entire issue to it. A hopeful sign is British Columbia's issuance of a draft ergonomics regulation and code of practice (CCH,

1998c, paragraph 95.307) under its Workers' Compensation Act, which regulates occupational health and safety in the province. The purpose of the regulation is to attempt to reduce workplace injury and occupational disease by controlling ergonomic factors such as the physical demands of work, workplace design, environmental conditions, clothing, equipment and tools, and work organization (CCH, 1998c). Employers would be required to identify existing ergonomic factors that might expose workers to the risk of adverse health and safety effects, to assess those risks, and to take steps to eliminate or at least minimize those risks. Afterwards, they would be required to monitor and evaluate, at least annually, the effectiveness of any measures taken to comply with the regulation. In addition, they would be required to educate workers on the adverse health effects resulting from ergonomic factors (CCH, 1998c).

Indoor Air Quality

Closely related to ergonomics, if not part of it, is the question of indoor air quality. With growing numbers of people working in buildings without adequate ventilation, respiratory illness and other medical problems related to poor air quality are on the increase across the country.

While this author is not aware of specific legislation on this subject, Nova Scotia's Occupational Health and Safety Council has prepared a discussion paper on indoor air quality (CCH, 1998c, paragraph 95.311). Noting that poor indoor air can affect workers' health, safety, and performance, the Council identifies contaminants generated inside buildings, the generation of heat from computer systems, overall building deterioration, secondhand smoke, overcrowding of office space, and faulty design of heating and ventilating systems as its major causes. Of these, faulty ventilation would appear to be the most serious culprit: it was responsible for more than half the cases of indoor air pollution reported in the province between 1971 and 1989 (CCH, 1998c). The paper proposes specific strategies for dealing with these problems, including walkabout inspections, better temperature and humidity control, educating workers on safe practices, and the establishment of workplace smoking policies (CCH, 1998c).

Rights of Non-Smokers

As just noted, smoking policies are an integral part of any serious attempt to improve indoor air quality. Often, however, employers have found it difficult to implement strict smoking policies because of the strong reaction from employees who smoke, though in some jurisdictions legislation may make it easier for them do so than in the past.

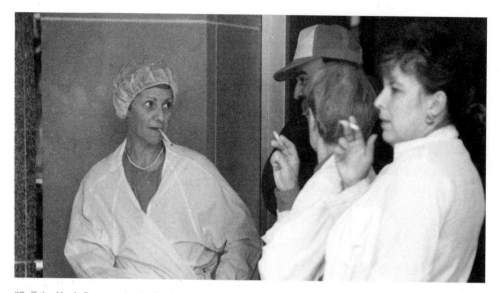

"Puff the Magic Dragon—Not!" Smoke in the workplace is becoming an increasingly divisive and difficult issue for workers and managers alike.

A pioneering effort in this field was Ontario's Smoking in the Workplace Act (1989), which prohibits smoking in an enclosed space, although it also allows the employer to permit smoking in a designated zone (McPhillips and England, 1995:88).

Few other workplace issues arouse such strong emotions or raise such complex problems as workplace smoking. To the serious smoker, who is usually addicted to "the weed," the right to keep on puffing is a basic human right that should not be denied or abridged under any circumstances. To the non-smoker, secondhand smoke is an enemy which risks clogging his chest or polluting her lungs; for those who already have asthma or some other respiratory condition, it can pose serious risks indeed.[33] To these people, the right to a smoke-free environment is both a human right and an important, perhaps even critical health and safety issue. To employers, caught in the middle, smoking can be the source of serious morale problems and division between workers. It can also have important economic implications. Heavy smokers forced to leave their offices to smoke outside or in a designated area may lose as much as 5 to 10 percent of their working time to the habit. As a proven cause of fires, smoking can lead to higher insurance costs if employers permit it; as an equally proven cause of many different kinds of illness, smoking can lead to higher disability leave incidence, more sick days, reduced productivity on other days, and increased medical insurance premiums.[34]

There have been a number of recent cases involving secondhand smoke. Most concern a refusal to work because of the smoke. In general, the case law and arbitral jurisprudence in this area have followed trends in the larger "right to refuse unsafe work" category. For the most part, this right has been upheld, except where refusal would create a dangerous situation (as in prisons and hospitals), and the policies of employers seeking to curb workplace smoking have also been upheld.[35] But in a 1994 case involving a correctional officer at an Ontario detention centre,[36] the guard exercised his right to refuse work at the detention centre. The health and safety officer investigating the case found that, because some of the inmates were smokers, poor air quality was an integral part of the work environment; moreover, any refusal to work could endanger the life, health, or safety of inmates or co-workers. The guard's refusal was, therefore, suspended.

Workplace Violence

With more and more businesses remaining open all night and a general increase in violence throughout society, workplace violence has become of increasing concern to many employees, especially women. On occasion, fear of such violence has formed the basis of a refusal to work, as in the Sharon Moore case of 1995.[37] Moore, a bar waiter, had refused to serve a patron she had seen acting abusively towards other customers and who had been involved in altercations with other female wait staff.[38] The manager denied that the patron was dangerous. Six days later, the patron returned and asked Moore for a drink, whereupon she refused to serve him and left work, claiming illness. After the manager warned her she would be terminated if she refused to serve the patron again. Moore again refused and was dismissed. Her complaint was upheld on the grounds that she had legitimate reasons to believe a dangerous situation existed and that the employer should have treated the case as a health and safety issue and called in an investigator. Since he had not done so, the validity of her refusal could not be tested and the refusal had, therefore, to be treated as legitimate. Of particular concern to the Board was the lack of a worker-selected health and safety representative; had such a representative been in place, it argued, the situation would probably not have escalated as it did.

Recognition of the growing risks to employees posed by workplace violence, especially in certain industries such as correctional services, health care, and retail food and beverage services, has led the Nova Scotia Occupational Health and Safety Advisory Council to prepare a report on the subject. The primary aim was to recommend the content of legislation designed to help protect workers from on-the-job violence (CCH, 1998c, paragraph 95.329). The paper proposed that violence should be identified as an occupational hazard under provincial health and safety legislation, and that provisions against it should be applied to all workplaces covered by the health and safety act. Under the proposed regulation, employers would be required to identify potentially hazardous workplace situations and to offer training and educational programs that would help employees reduce the risks of violence.

In addition, they would be required to report any such incidents to the workplace health and safety committee for corrective action under the provincial health and safety act. Finally, they would be required to provide victims of violence with prompt first aid and emotional support and to establish procedures for reporting, investigating, and documenting any incidents of violence occurring in their workplace.

OBESITY

Obese people find themselves discriminated against in many subtle and some not-so-subtle ways. Their condition often makes it more difficult for them to get hired,[39] and on occasion they may be fired solely on the basis of their weight.[40] To be sure, there are some occupations in which weight could constitute a bona fide occupational qualification. After a severely overweight major league baseball umpire dropped dead from a heart attack in the middle of a game a few years ago, the major leagues tried to make other obese umpires lose weight to help prevent a recurrence of the tragic incident. Given the highly stressful conditions under which the umpires work, few appear to have regarded the weight-loss demands as unreasonable. But many (perhaps most) obesity cases do not involve any sort of bona fide occupational consideration.

In his 1997 study of the issue, Harris Zwerling notes that one American state (Michigan) prohibits discrimination specifically on the basis of weight. No Canadian jurisdiction does so, and only British Columbia has found obesity as such to be a covered disability under human rights legislation banning discrimination against people with disabilities. Ideally, he suggests, Canadian jurisdictions should add obesity to the list of protected classifications under their human rights codes (Zwerling, 1997:646). Since this isn't likely to happen in the near future, other jurisdictions should, in Zwerling's view, follow B.C.'s lead and treat obesity as a covered disability, without requiring claimants to prove that their obesity has an underlying involuntary medical cause (Zwerling, 1997:620).

The issue of obesity raises the larger and even more difficult question of the extent to which it is legitimate for employers to require employees to maintain a certain image or type of appearance on the job. When, to what extent, and under what circumstances is appearance a bona fide occupational qualification? Few would dispute that it is for clothing models or ballerinas. As well, few would likely dispute the legitimacy of uniform requirements for police and members of the armed forces, or even civilian dress codes for bus drivers, salespeople, and wait staff in fancy hotels and restaurants. The problem comes when employers move beyond specific dress codes (stipulating, for instance, a uniform or a jacket and tie) and require a "neat appearance" or that hair not be "untidy." Here we enter the realm of subjectivity. Even in the same establishment, two different supervisors may not agree on what constitutes neatness or acceptable hair length. Consider, for example, the Empress Hotel case (Craig and Solomon, 1996:541–543), in which a waiter was suspended for wearing a pony-tail, in the absence of a policy against them, and in a context where males were permitted to wear earrings. In this case, the only formal requirement was that hair be neat. While the case does not say specifically that the dismissal would be over-turned, the list of criteria suggested by the arbitrator at the end indicates that rein-statement would be a virtual certainty, given the ambiguity of the policy and the lack of consistency with which it was enforced. Given the growing prevalence of tattoos, earrings, and other forms of personal jewellery among young people, dress codes and restrictions on personal jewellery could well prove a major source of friction between employers and employees, especially in coffee shops, restaurants, and other private-service sector establishments.

As we have just seen, Canadian employment legislation is in a state of almost constant flux. Almost every year, new human rights concerns seem to emerge, along with new approaches to old problems in more established areas such as health and safety and workers' compensation. The collective creativity shown by Canadian leg-islatures in coming up with solutions to both old and new problems is really quite extraordinary.

There remain, however, two serious concerns. First, despite the Charter, many individuals and groups of workers continue to be excluded from even basic protec-tion, particularly under work standards legislation. Second, enforcement mechanisms have not only failed to keep pace with the onrush of new legislation; they have proved inadequate to enforce existing legislation, such as work standards provisions govern-ing minimum wages and overtime hours. Here, the most damning evidence is the extreme rarity with which the right to refuse unsafe work appears to be exercised in non-unionized establishments. If some of the same creativity already applied to draft-ing legislation could now be used to design adequate enforcement mechanisms, Canadian workers would be much better served.

QUESTIONS FOR DISCUSSION

1) What are some practical consequences of knowing (or not knowing) employ-ment legislation? Have you ever experienced any of these consequences, whether positive or negative?

2) Why is EL needed? What is its significance?

3) What are some major areas covered by work standards legislation?

4) What are three major problems with this legislation?

5) What protection does a non-unionized worker have against arbitrary dismissal in most jurisdictions? In practice, do most non-unionized workers have a meaningful remedy? Why, or why not?

6) Where do non-unionized workers have additional protection through adjudication of dismissal grievances? How does this system work?

7) What are the main grounds of discrimination prohibited under human rights legislation?

8) To which aspects of the employment relationship does HRL apply?

9) What is the purpose of bona fide occupational qualifications (BFOQs), and how can employers test for them? What are some recent trends with regard to BFOQs?

10) Distinguish pay equity from employment equity. Why do many people argue that both are needed?

11) Why is health and safety legislation of particular importance?

12) Distinguish the external system from the internal system.

13) What role do joint committees play within the internal system?

14) How does workers' compensation operate within most Canadian jurisdictions? What are some problems with it?

15) What are some emerging areas within EL?

16) How does EL "intersect" labour relations legislation?

17) What are some important differences between EL and labour relations legislation?

SUGGESTIONS
FOR FURTHER READING

Adams, Roy. (1987). "Employment standards in Ontario: An industrial relations systems analysis." *Relations Industrielles, 42.* A very important study illustrating the Ontario government's inability or unwillingness to enforce its employment standards legislation. More such studies are needed for other jurisdictions and other types of employment legislation, such as health and safety laws.

Bryce, George, and Pran Manga. (1985). "The effectiveness of health and safety committees." *Relations Industrielles, 40*(2). A useful early study of joint health and safety committees. Bryce and Manga are cautiously positive about the committees' impacts of the committees.

Eden, Genevieve. (1993). "Industrial discipline in the Canadian federal jurisdiction. *Relations Industrielles, 48*(1). A study of adjudication of dismissal grievances in the federal jurisdiction that suggests that experience under this system is roughly comparable to that under grievance arbitration in unionized establishments.

Richard, K. Peter (Commissioner). (1997) *The Westray Story: A Predictable Path to Disaster.* No place of publication given: Province of Nova Scotia. Not for the faint of heart! A chilling indictment of Westray management's callous disregard for workers' safety, and the Nova Scotia government's appalling lack of political will in enforcing its own legislation.

Zwerling, Harris. (1997). **"Obesity as a covered disability under employment discrimination law: An analysis of Canadian approaches."** *Relations Industrielles, 52*(3). Interesting article on an emerging, but as yet seldom-studied, area of employment law. Makes a reasonably strong case for treating obesity as a prohibited area of discrimination under human rights legislation.

ENDNOTES

[1] It is not strictly accurate to say all workers are covered by EL. Certain groups are excluded in some jurisdictions. However, fewer workers and groups are excluded from EL coverage than from labour relations legislation coverage.

[2] For an interesting and very thoughtful critique of this aspect of collective bargaining, see Beatty (1983).

[3] In a 1996 survey of one of his introductory IR classes, the author found that 40 percent of the students had at one time or another been asked to include a photo on a job application form.

[4] The term "work standards" legislation has been used here to avoid possible confusion between "employment standards legislation" and "employment legislation," the term used to describe all the different types of legislation discussed in this chapter. It should be noted, however, that the term "employment standards" legislation is often used for this purpose. For example, the federal Human Resources Department uses it to describe the legislation outlined in Table 7.1.

[5] Except as otherwise noted, the source for all information about the first four types of provisions described here is HRDC's *Workplace Gazette,* summer 1998:93–94.

[6] Except as otherwise noted, the source for the information about termination and pregnancy and parental leave provisions is CCH (1998a).

[7] Adams' article, which first appeared in *Relations Industrielles,* 42, is quoted at length in LLCG (1991:980–992).

[8] For very senior people, especially those in a financial portfolio, contracts may even stipulate that employees cannot solicit the employer's customers for a given period after they have left the employer's service.

[9] Baker v. Burns Foods Ltd. (1977), 74 D.L.R. (3rd) 762 (Man. C.A., Matas J.A.) at 763-4, quoted in LLCG (1991:2-88 through 2-90).

[10] Reber v. Lloyds Bank International Canada (1984), 52 B.C. L.R. 90 (B.C.S.C., Mackoff J.) at 92–96, rev'd (1985), 7 C.E.E.L. 98 (B.C.C.A., Esson J.A.), quoted in LLCG (1991:2-90 through 2-92).

[11] As noted by McPhillips and England (1989:50), "salary" normally includes any fringe benefits the employee would have received had she or he remained on payroll.

[12] Normally they are not. The more usual method would appear to be for judges simply to "tack on" some extra months to existing awards. However, punitive damages may be awarded in extreme cases of abusiveness or severe negligence, as in the Vancouver Hockey

Club case discussed in LLCG (1991:2-147), where an injured hockey player was denied proper medical treatment and forced to play injured until, in his weakened condition, he was seriously hurt.

[13] Bardal v. *The Globe & Mail Ltd.* (1960), 24 D.L.R. (2nd) 140 (Ont. H.C., McRuer C.J.H.C.) at 141-7, quoted in LLCG (1991:2-129 through 2-131).

[14] It should be noted that these findings do not please Eden, a critic of the whole notion of progressive discipline. For her detailed critique of this system of industrial justice, see (1992). Progressive discipline: An oxymoron. *Relations Industrielles, 47*(3).

[15] Except for those below the minimum working age or over 65.

[16] Except as otherwise noted, all information on human rights legislative provisions has been drawn from this source.

[17] (1986) 9 CEEL 135.

[18] Alberta Human Rights Commission v. Central Alberta Dairy Pool (1990), 90 C.L.L.C. para. 17.025 (S.C.C.).

[19] Hinds v. Canada Employment and Immigration Commission (1988), 10 CHRR 015683 (Can. Hum. Rights Tribunal).

[20] This amount may seem very small. However, under the federal act, the maximum amount an individual can receive in punitive damages was (and still is) $5000.

[21] See Beatty (1983) for a useful critique of traditional mandatory retirement policies and an elegant partial solution, which would impose mandatory retirement not at a given age, but after a given number of years of service.

[22] Because some men work in these occupations (i.e., as librarians), about 5000 to 10 000 of the employees receiving back payment cheques will be men, according to Aubry (1998).

[23] Here, "fair representation" is based on a comparison reflecting the minority group's representation in either the Canadian work force as a whole or the segment of the Canadian work force from which they employer would logically hire new employees (i.e., the local labour pool).

[24] Implicitly, this language once again suggests the notion of the duty to accommodate.

[25] In this connection, I cannot help thinking of the gas station employee I once saw sitting on the top of one of the station's gas pumps, smoking.

[26] In Alberta and Prince Edward Island, such committees are set up at the discretion of the minister (McPhillips and England, 1995).

[27] Ontario's act was not the first providing for committees. In 1972 (Swinton, 1983), Saskatchewan's comprehensive *Occupational Health Act* provided for them. Earlier, a number of unions had obtained such committees through the collective bargaining process, and Canadian Labour Congress policy had stated that joint committees should be a cornerstone of occupational health and safety programs.

[28] Both must do so under the *Canada Code.*

[29] As various commentators note, it remains difficult to prove a relationship in the latter case. See, for example, CCH (1998c, 15, 406).

[30] The workers' compensation board was renamed the Workplace Safety and Insurance Board, effective January 1, 1998·

[31] In April, 1998, the Supreme Court of Canada ruled Alberta's omission of sexual orientation from its human rights code unconstitutional (Hutchinson, 1998). Initially, Premier Ralph Klein indicated he would not challenge the decision on Charter "override" grounds; however, following a storm of protest from the right, he began to waver on the issue. It is not clear, at this writing, what the government intends to do.

[32] In addition to Ontario, Nova Scotia had already been forced to do so as a result of a court ruling (Ditchburn, 1998).

[33] At Memorial University, where smoking was banned in all campus buildings, students used to congregate in droves just outside classroom buildings for a smoke between classes. The clouds of smoke drifting up from the sidewalks below caused several of us in the Business School minor respiratory problems; however, one colleague, who was asthmatic, was forced to keep an inhaler in her office because the billowing smoke not infrequently induced attacks.

[34] As some readers are probably aware, a good many insurance companies offer substantially reduced rates to non-smokers.

[35] Ben's Bakery v. Bakery, Confectionery and Tobacco Workers' International Union, Local 466, arbitration decision, Halifax, N.S., Oct. 20, 1993, in CCH (1998(c), par. 95-312.

[36] O'Neill v. Ministry of Labour and Quinte Detention Centre, Ontario Office of Adjudication, Dec. 23, 1994, Decision Number OHS 94-48, in CCH (1998(c), par. 95-317.

[37] Sharon Moore v. Barmaid's Arms, Ont. Labour Relations Board, 3284-94-OH, Mar. 23, 1995, in CCH (1998(c), par. 95-328.

[38] As a former bartender, I can attest that Moore had not only the right but, under any province's liquor laws, the obligation to refuse to serve a patron she believed dangerous. In addition to constituting an unjust dismissal, the manager's actions in forcing Moore to serve such a patron would have constituted a violation of the liquor laws.

[39] See Saskatchewan's Davison case, discussed in Zwerling (1997:631, note 60).

[40] See Quebec's Rioux case and Ontario's Vogue Shoes case, discussed in Zwerling (1997:642-3 and 627-32), where two women were discharged solely on this basis. In connection with obesity cases, it would be interesting to see if (as one suspects) this basis for discrimination is used far more often against women than against men. If so, such discrimination itself might itself be a possible basis for Charter action.

CHAPTER 8

LABOUR RELATIONS LEGISLATION

Union and management representatives meeting with a conciliator from the labour ministry. Compulsory conciliation has been a prominent feature of Canadian labour legislation since the early years of this century.

Labour relations legislation (LRL) is of pivotal importance in any industrial relations system. It addresses such issues as how a union can become certified, when a strike or lockout may legally occur, and what constitutes an unfair employer or unfair union labour practice. In this chapter, we start by considering the rationale for LRL. Next, we take a brief look at the development of LRL in Canada, including the role played in recent years by the Charter of Rights and Freedoms. From there, we go on to examine some of the major features of Canadian LRL and to compare it to labour relations legislation in the United States. We then discuss some of LRL's main functions, illustrating our discussion with specific provisions from various Canadian laws. This discussion is followed by an examination of some key variations in different provincial

acts, and by a brief look at Quebec's special system of legislation. We conclude
the chapter with a discussion of how LRL is administered. Note that, in this
chapter, we generally confine ourselves to private sector labour relations legisla-
tion. Public sector legislation is considered in the next chapter.

THE RATIONALE FOR LRL

Legal scholars, philosophers, historians, and industrial relations experts have all written quite extensively on the rationale for labour relations legislation (LRL). Probably
the simplest and most compelling explanation for having such legislation is to prevent
the suffering, chaos, and injustice that would almost certainly occur in its absence.
This is not a theoretical or hypothetical statement. For more than 100 years, significant industrial activity was carried out in Canada without any legislation to protect
workers' right to bargain collectively or to strike. Some of the results of this lengthy
"experiment" were discussed in Chapter 4 (labour history). They included frequent
loss of life, serious injury, and extensive property damage resulting from strikes; an
almost total lack of protection for workers against even the most arbitrary actions on
the part of their employers; grossly inadequate protection of workers' health and
safety; and a very low standard of living for most ordinary Canadians.

In a world in which most people must work and relatively few work at jobs they
would voluntarily undertake, conflict between employers and workers is all but
inevitable. The question is not whether there will be conflict; it is rather what form it
will take.[1] In the absence of legislation regulating industrial conflict or providing
workers with the right to join unions, many strikes take on the character of pitched
class warfare.[2] Through the last century and most of the first half of this one (as the
labour history chapter shows), this kind of strike was far too common. It remains
common, even in the postwar period, in countries where governments do not legitimate industrial conflict or accept workers' right to organize and bargain collectively.[3]

CANADA LABOUR CODE
canada.justice.gc.ca/FTP/EN/Laws/L/L-2.txt

Under labour relations legislation, the possibility of violence leading to serious
injury or loss of life is still there (as the recent tragic Giant Gold Mine strike demonstrates), but it is greatly reduced. Disputes are easier to settle, since most are over
specific terms and conditions of employment rather than more intractable issues
such as the union's right to exist.[4] In most cases, employers and unions are able to
maintain reasonably effective long-term working relationships despite the occasional strike. Thus regulated and with severe limits put on unfair practice by either side,
a strike becomes less like class warfare and more like, say, a hockey game: rough,

occasionally dangerous, but not usually anarchic. Most conflict will eventually be resolved through collective bargaining, strikes, and other activities of the IR system (Barbash, 1984). Indeed, there are those (i.e., Dubin, 1959) who would argue that conflict comes to play an essentially constructive role, once it has been regulated and limited by labour relations legislation.

Another important rationale for LRL and the collective bargaining it supports is the opportunity the latter provides for a degree of worker input into management decisions, indeed for some measure of worker self-government. As Paul Weiler (1980:29–32) notes, under collective bargaining, "[m]anagement must spell out its workplace rules; employees must be given a vehicle for collectively voicing their objections when their rights seem to be under siege." To Weiler, such an exercise in self-government is of value in and of itself, above and beyond the superior economic results it is likely to produce when compared to what most individual workers could likely obtain through individual negotiations with their employers. Essentially similar arguments have been advanced by other institutionalists, such as Alan Flanders (1970, in LLCG, 1991:153–164).

To be sure, not everyone would agree with Weiler's positive assessment of collective bargaining. Over the years, it has often been criticized from both the right and the left. Neoclassicists like Milton Friedman (1962, in LLCG, 1991:30–32) see unions as an intrusion on individuals' freedom to choose. Others, such as Posner (1977, in LLCG, 1991:49–50), while admitting that unions' effects may be fairly complex, see them as leading to losses for consumers who buy from unionized industries, some stockholders and suppliers in those industries, and workers who lose their jobs due to union wage impacts. Managerialists (discussed in Freeman and Medoff, 1979, in LLCG, 1991:168–182) primarily resent the loss of control unions mean to employers and managers. On the left, reformists such as David Beatty (1983) criticize collective bargaining for leading to a tyranny of the majority and taking little, if any, account of the needs of the "worst-off" classes in industrial society, such as domestics and farm workers. Further left, radicals such as Leo Panitch and Donald Swartz (1988, in LLCG, 1991:59–60) suggest that "free collective bargaining" is pretty much an oxymoron, given the coercive way in which the state has used its power in recent years, and its pronounced bias towards capital and business interests throughout the postwar period. Similarly, Richard Hyman (1983, in LLCG, 1991, 34–35) argues that "industrial democracy" is likewise a contradiction in terms, since work organization in modern societies is carried out under an inherently undemocratic authority structure.

LABOUR ADJUSTMENT BENEFITS ACT
canada.justice.gc.ca/FTP/EN/Laws/L/L-1.txt

Despite these and other criticisms such as the belief that unions gave away too much by giving away the right to strike during the life of the agreement (see Adell, 1988a), most Canadians, inside the labour movement and out, would probably agree that labour relations legislation and collective bargaining have helped produce a society where workers are economically better off and have more workplace rights than did those of their grandparents' generation. Imperfect though the Canadian system of LRL doubtless is, most believe that both workers and Canadian society as a whole are better served with it than they would be without it.

THE EVOLUTION OF CANADIAN LRL

As we noted in the labour history chapter, Canada was slow to develop collective bargaining and to pass collective bargaining legislation. Indeed, Canada was among the last industrialized countries to grant private sector workers the right to join a union, doing so only in 1944, several decades later than countries such as Sweden and Denmark, and about a decade later than the United States.[5] In the case of Canadian public sector workers, most of whom did not receive full bargaining rights until the late 1960s or early 1970s, the lag was generally even greater. Among the major reasons for the slow evolution of unionism and collective bargaining in Canada were the country's comparatively late industrialization; its linguistically, regionally, and religiously fragmented labour movement; determined employer opposition; and a particularly unsympathetic federal government.[6]

Through much of the nineteenth century, unions were regarded as conspiracies in restraint of trade in Canada and in many European countries (Adams, 1995:496). This notion ended with the *Trades Union Act* of 1872, which declared that the purposes of unions were not to be considered unlawful simply because they might be in restraint of trade (Carter, 1989:30). However, the protection applied only to those unions that took the trouble to register with the government, which few if any apparently did, thereby rendering it all but meaningless in practice (Morton, 1990:27). Overall, the act offered unions few positive benefits. Employers could still harass, dismiss, and blacklist union activists without fear of government reprisal.

Conciliation Legislation

The rest of the century saw little major change to Canadian labour legislation, although an 1877 amendment to the *Masters' and Servants' Act* meant that employees could no longer be sent to jail for striking or leaving their employers' service (Morton, 1990:34).[7] A much more significant development was the introduction of conciliation legislation around the turn of the century. In 1900, the government created a

Department of Labour with a conciliation service (Heron, 1989:46). At the same time, it passed the *Dominion Conciliation Act*, allowing the labour minister to appoint a conciliation board either at one of the parties' request or on his own initiative (Carter, 1989:30). The idea behind the conciliation process, which remained voluntary, was that once people became aware of the issues of labour disputes from reading the conciliation board's published report, public pressure would compel the two sides to settle those disputes (Carter, 1989). Similar principles were written into the *Railway Labour Disputes Act* of 1903 (Carter, 1989). In 1907, with the passage of the *Industrial Disputes Investigation Act,* conciliation became compulsory. Now, no union in a transportation, resource, or utilities industry could strike nor could an employer lock workers out until the conciliation board's report had been published and a further "cooling-off" period had elapsed (Heron, 1989:47). Compulsory conciliation has remained a cornerstone of most Canadian LRL to this day, although three-person board reports are now rare and the process has evolved into something much more closely resembling mediation in most cases (Carter, 1989).

The *IDI Act* seemed to favour the labour movement and initially won the Trades and Labour Congress' cautious support (Morton, 1990:89). Its greatest benefit to unions may have been in legitimizing very weak unions, which would otherwise have had little hope of getting their point across to the general public (Morton, 1990). More often, though, the time delays simply gave employers the opportunity to stockpile production, fire and blacklist union activists, or hire strike-breakers and private police (Morton, 1990; Heron, 1989). The act did little to promote union growth. Since it did not provide such basic rights as the right to join a union or go on strike, it didn't put an end to the kind of bitter, violent recognition disputes that had led to its enactment in the first place. If anything, these strikes became more frequent through the 1930s and 1940s, an added source of frustration being that, by this time, American private sector workers enjoyed the right to bargain collectively and to strike, thanks to the New Deal *Wagner Act* passed in 1935. A key feature of the *Wagner Act* was its specific prohibition of such unfair employer labour practices as intimidation or harassment of union members or the formation of a management-dominated company union. Another important feature was the establishment of a separate agency, the National Labor Relations Board, to administer and enforce the act (Carter, 1989:32). The NLRB mechanism was particularly welcomed by unionists since, in the past, labour matters had customarily dealt with by the courts, which in general were not well disposed towards unions (Carter, 1989).

Between 1937 and 1943, a number of Canadian jurisdictions did adopt certain features of the *Wagner Act,* the most comprehensive of these being Ontario's Labour Court, which came into effect in 1943. This act was in many ways similar to *Wagner* but didn't fully meet with the labour movement's approval because administration was left to the courts rather than being turned over to a separate administrative agency, as in the United States (Carter, 1989:32–33).

PC 1003: Basic Bargaining Rights for Canadian Workers

During the war, the lack of basic bargaining rights became an issue uniting the long-divided Canadian labour movement, which had grown considerably stronger due to wartime labour shortages (Carter, 1989; Heron, 1989:78). By 1943, one Canadian union member in three was on strike—a rate that exceeded that of 1919, the year of the Winnipeg General Strike (Heron, 1989:78). Alarmed at the situation, Prime Minister Mackenzie King commissioned a report from the National War Labour Board. The report, written by Justice Charles McTague, told the government in no uncertain terms that only full union bargaining rights comparable to those granted American workers would put an end to the wave of strikes and violence (Morton, 1990:182–183). Not until the next year, however, faced with the very real possibility of a CCF victory in the next election (Heron, 1989:78–80; Morton, 1995:143) did King grant Canadian workers these rights. He did so through a wartime order-in-council, *PC 1003*, which contained most of the Wagner protections and mechanisms, including a separate board to administer the act as well as the right to bargain collectively and to strike. Now, employers could not refuse to bargain with a legally certified union that had demonstrated to the labour board it could command majority support in any given workplace (Heron, 1989:80). The Canadian act's major difference from the Wagner model was its incorporation of IDI's compulsory conciliation, an incorporation apparently made at King's insistence (Morton, 1989:168). When labour legislation returned to provincial jurisdiction with the end of the war, the federal government passed a permanent statute, the *Industrial Relations and Disputes Investigation Act* (1948), which incorporated most of the wartime order's major features. Within the next two years, most provinces had passed their own labour acts guaranteeing basic union rights (Heron, 1989:86), though some provincial acts, especially in Alberta and the Atlantic region (Finkel, 1986; Forsey, 1985), were far more restrictive than the federal one.

ALBERTA LABOUR
www.gov.ab.ca/lab/index1.html

Unlike most previous Canadian labour bills, *PC 1003* and its offspring did help promote union growth, since employers were now specifically forbidden from interfering with unions in any way. The 1945 *Rand Formula* guaranteeing union security may also have contributed, since unions now had a firm financial basis to help ensure their survival (Heron, 1989:85). Nonetheless, as we noted in the labour history chapter, many Canadian workers, including most of the country's female workers, still could not join a union. This situation did not change until after 1967, when the federal government passed the *Public Service Staff Relations Act (PSSRA)*. Among other things, *PSSRA* legalized collective bargaining for federal public servants and gave them the right to choose between binding arbitration and the traditional conciliation-strike route. Within a few years, provincial public sector workers across Canada were covered by some kind of collective bargaining act. Some, like *PSSRA*, included the right to strike; others, like the administrative model adopted in Ontario[8] and Alberta, substituted binding arbitration. During the late 1960s and early 1970s, collective bargaining rights were also extended to other public sector workers, such as teachers and nurses. Again, some jurisdictions gave these groups the right to strike, while others forced them to submit their disputes to arbitration. (This issue is covered in more detail in the public sector chapter).

ALBERTA LABOUR STATUTES AND REGULATIONS
www.gov.ab.ca/lab/regs.html

The Impact of the Charter

Since the passage of public sector bargaining legislation, Canadian LRL has seen few important changes and no fundamental ones. This is not what most would have predicted following the enactment of the *Canadian Charter of Rights and Freedoms* in 1982. Many observers believed that the Charter would significantly affect the fundamental balance between legislatures and courts (see Carter, 1989:40–41). Some, notably David Beatty (1987; also Beatty and Kennett, 1988) thought the effect would be positive, as the courts used the Charter to strike down unjust labour laws. Others feared that unions would be the losers and that they would fare less well before the courts than before labour boards, whose activities courts might now severely circumscribe, reversing a long-term trend towards granting more power to labour boards and less to the courts (Arthurs, 1988; see also Carter, 1982). Neither the enthusiasts' hopes nor the skeptics' fears have been realized. The Charter's overall effect on Canadian LRL might best be described as underwhelming. If its freedom of association clause has not been used to provide workers with positive protection for the right to join a union, to strike, or to picket (England, 1988; Fudge, 1988), neither has the document been used to reduce labour boards' jurisdiction or to reduce unions' ability to use members' dues for political as well as collective bargaining objectives.[9] In general, courts have been reluctant to use the Charter to reshape the IR system (Carter, 1995:70; Swinton, 1995). What is perhaps most surprising is that the Charter has not been used to provide even minimal "defensive" protection for freedom of association, as by striking down exclusion laws (discussed in more detail later in the chapter) that bar domestics, farm workers, and professionals from union membership in several Canadian jurisdictions.

"ROLE OF THE CANADA LABOUR RELATIONS BOARD"
home.istar.ca/~clrbccrt/ingclrb.htm?57,30

The Duty to Accommodate

Though Canadian LRL's content has not changed much of late, its interpretation is changing dramatically. This is primarily the result of the passage of various types of employment legislation (discussed in detail in the previous chapter), in particular, human rights legislation. Thus far, the new human rights legislation has had its greatest effect on the grievance procedure, where arbitrators have been obliged to interpret collective agreements in the light of anti-discrimination provisions contained in human rights acts. Ever since the landmark O'Malley v. Simpson-Sears case (1986), intent to discriminate need not be proved for a finding of illegal discrimination to be reached. Now, a concept of "constructive" or "systemic" discrimination applies, under which workplace rules and collective agreement provisions can be found discriminatory, regardless of their intent, if they have a disproportionate effect on an individual employee (Carter, 1997:188). Since the advent of "constructive" discrimination, both unions and employers have been required to accommodate such adversely affected employees up the point of "undue hardship." The requirement has been construed to extend far beyond the protection of women and minority group members from sexual, religious, and racial harassment, to the provision of special treatment such as the drawing up of different work schedules for members of religious groups whose beliefs forbid work on certain days, or the redesign of jobs to allow individuals with disabilities perform them more easily (Carter, 1997:190–197). As Carter has shown (1997:197–198), the duty to accommodate may even extend to rewriting collective agreement provisions or agreeing to waive their application. This kind of requirement would seem to fly in the face of core collective bargaining principles, such as equal application of all collective agreement provisions and the barring of special treatment for individual workers without the union's express consent and approval (Carter, 1997:186). As the arbitral jurisprudence in this area grows and workers become more aware of their rights under human rights legislation, the duty to accommodate will likely pose increasing challenges for employers, unions, and arbitrators alike.

MAJOR FEATURES OF CANADIAN LRL

Legislative Fragmentation

To those familiar with other industrial relations systems, the most notable feature of the Canadian system of labour relations legislation is its extreme fragmentation. Unlike the situation prevailing in the United States, where private sector labour law is under federal jurisdiction, most Canadian private sector workers fall under provincial jurisdiction, thanks to a British Privy Council decision in the 1926 Snider case (discussed in the labour history chapter), which placed labour relations in the provinces' constitutional domain. As a result, each province has had to write its own private sector labour relations act.

The one exception to the general pattern of provincial jurisdiction is workers in enterprises of a clearly federal or interprovincial nature, such as the railroads, airlines, chartered banks, and telecommunications companies. These workers, who together make up about 10 percent of the country's union members, are governed by the *Canada Labour Code*. Federal public servants fall under the *Public Service Staff Relations Act;* provincial public servants and most other public sector workers, such as teachers and nurses, fall under a broad array of provincial public sector laws (see Swimmer and Thompson, 1995:7–8).[10]

In all, there are about three dozen different pieces of labour relations legislation in effect in Canada. Such extreme legislative fragmentation poses a number of difficulties, not least of which is the simple confusion of keeping all these laws straight (Carter, 1989:28). For the practitioner, mastering all the different acts can pose a formidable challenge, although there are, as we'll see, broad patterns of similarity among many of the acts that make this task a bit less formidable than it might at first seem. As Carter (1995:55–56) notes, labour boards and courts sometimes find it difficult to decide whether a given enterprise should fall under provincial or federal jurisdiction. As well, provincial jurisdiction has definitely contributed to the emergence of a highly decentralized bargaining structure (see Anderson, 1982; Rogow, 1989a), for example by making it more difficult for an industry to conduct negotiations at the national level (Carter, 1995). Given that Canada's decentralized bargaining structure has often been implicated as a cause of its relatively high incidence of strikes, the implications of provincial jurisdiction may be more profound than many realize. Moreover, in an economy that is becoming increasingly globalized, the lack of a single clear national standard in labour relations legislation could prove a barrier to international trade and global competitiveness.

On the positive side, the existence of many different sets of labour legislation may well contribute to innovation and change, as in the case of the many new dispute resolution procedures introduced in British Columbia while Paul Weiler (1980) was head of that province's labour board.[11] Whether the advantages of a system that allows for comparatively low-risk legislative innovation and experimentation outweigh the disadvantages posed by Canada's decentralized bargaining structure and lack of a single national standard for labour relations legislation is a question each reader must answer individually.

Emphasis on Processes

A key assumption behind Canadian LRL is that it should operate primarily through free collective bargaining between employers and unions (Godard, 1994:278). It follows then, that LRL should not normally prescribe outcomes (i.e., a given wage level or set of working conditions), but should rather confine itself to laying out processes that will allow free and fair collective bargaining to take place. The idea here is that the parties, who know each other and must work with each other and with the collective agreement on a daily basis, are in a better position to fashion an agreement that meets their particular needs than a group of legislators or a labour board would be.

Two types of provisions would seem to represent an exception to this emphasis on processes rather than outcomes. The first of these are first-contract arbitration provisions allowing for the imposition of an initial collective agreement in cases where the labour board believes an employer has not bargained in good faith with an eye to concluding an agreement. The second are provisions, now found in almost every labour act except Ontario's,[12] that allow labour boards to certify a union with less than majority support in situations where the board believes that the employer's unfair labour practices have prevented the employees' true wishes from becoming known. At first glance, both types of provision may seem like heavy-handed government intervention in the collective bargaining process. Closer inspection, however, reveals that, far from serving to stifle free collective bargaining, these provisions are designed to further it, by serving as a deterrent to grossly unfair labour practice.[13] In this respect, it may not be too far-fetched to compare them to the penalty kicks occasionally imposed in soccer matches. Such drastic measures are not put into effect every day; nor was it anyone's intention that they should be. Generally, labour boards will impose a first agreement or certify with less than majority support only as a last resort. Indeed, at least one observer (Godard, 1994:290–292) suggests that even these remedies may be inadequate, and that given what amount to rather minimal disincentives to unfair employer labour practice, it is surprising more unfair practices are not committed.

Closely related to Canadian LRL's emphasis on processes is its voluntarism, or belief in the ability of employers and unions to resolve disputes on their own, without compulsory government intervention (Godard, 1994:278). A belief in voluntarism clearly underlies the development of several innovative new dispute resolution methods, such as grievance mediation. Here, the consent of both parties is normally required before the process can go forward (Joyce, 1996). The major exception to Canada's generally voluntarist approach to dispute resolution is the retention of compulsory conciliation provisions in most jurisdictions' labour acts. One study (Gunderson, Myszynski, and Keck, 1989) did find the provisions to be associated with a somewhat lower level of strike incidence. It is, however, debatable whether this justifies such widespread government intervention into the bargaining process, particularly in private sector disputes without a substantial public interest component.[14]

One other point should be made. The parties are not absolutely free to write any provisions they wish into collective agreements, because they are bound to abide by any relevant legislation, such as employment standards and human rights laws. Normally it is illegal for an agreement to contain any terms less favourable to employees than those found in the jurisdiction's employment standards act. For example, the parties cannot agree to a wage less than the provincial minimum or a shorter vacation period than that provided under the employment standards act. They also cannot agree to provisions that discriminate against any group, such as separate pay scales for women and men.

No Mid-Term Strikes

Another key tenet of Canadian labour relations legislation is the "peace obligation" imposed on both unions and employers during the life of the agreement. While the agreement is in force, a union cannot strike and an employer cannot lock out its employees. Every jurisdiction's labour act stipulates that disputes over contract interpretation must be settled through a grievance process culminating, if need be, in binding arbitration. While the parties are free to devise their own process, they are not free to do away with it (Carter, 1995:64).

Broad Worker Protection

Overall, Canadian LRL provides workers and their unions with a reasonably broad range of protection in a number of areas. As noted earlier, first-contract arbitration provisions and provisions allowing labour boards to certify with less than majority support give workers and unions at least some protection against employers' unfair labour practices. Union security and dues checkoff provisions, required in a number of jurisdictions, have helped unions establish a firm financial footing. And striking workers enjoy a number of safeguards, ranging from Quebec's and British Columbia's absolute prohibition of replacement workers to most provinces' guarantee that they can get their jobs back once the strike is over (Carter, 1995:65).[15] On the other side of the ledger, the duty of fair representation provisions found in most Canadian jurisdictions afford workers a measure of protection against arbitrary treatment at the hands of union leaders, which may make hesitant workers feel more comfortable about joining unions.

Canadian Versus American Legislation

Canadian LRL originally evolved out of the American *Wagner Act* (1935). In many ways, it still strongly resembles its American ancestor. In other ways, it has taken some quite different directions.

The existence of provincial jurisdiction may well have helped Canadian legislation to change more and more often than has been the case in the United States, where the legislation is under federal jurisdiction and any change can affect many millions of workers. Both countries' laws tend to emphasize processes rather than outcomes and to be relatively voluntarist in their overall orientation. However, the American legislation has remained truer to its voluntarist heritage. First, almost all Canadian jurisdictions have compulsory conciliation provisions. Second, Canada's compulsory grievance arbitration, which is not part of the *Wagner* model,[16] represents a significant degree of government intervention into the IR system. Third, the United States has no equivalent of Canada's first-contract arbitration or anti-scab laws. Indeed, U.S. law allows for the permanent replacement of striking workers (Carter, 1995), except in cases where a dispute has arisen over illegal activities, such as the employer's attempt to get rid of the union. In these cases, permanent replacements are illegal and strikers have a right to get their jobs back (Sims, 1996:Chapter 9).

In other areas as well, Canadian law offers workers and unions significantly greater protection than U.S. law. For instance, union security is generally stronger in Canada, which has no equivalent to the "right-to-work" provisions of the 1947 Taft-Hartley amendments to *Wagner*. Even more important, union certification is significantly easier in Canada than in the United States, thanks to the count of signed members still used by a majority of Canadian jurisdictions, in contrast to the American requirement of a formal vote and election campaign. In addition, laws against unfair employer labour practice appear to be more strictly enforced here (Bruce, 1990).

MAJOR FUNCTIONS OF CANADIAN LRL

Certification and Decertification

Overseeing the certification process is arguably the single most important function of Canadian labour relations legislation. Before *PC 1003*, a Canadian union could win bargaining rights only through voluntary recognition or a strike (Craig and Solomon, 1996:213). As was noted earlier, strikes over recognition tended to be long and bitter and often resulted in bloodshed; thus the establishment of a procedure through which unions could obtain legal recognition of bargaining rights was crucial to bringing about some measure of labour peace.

The certification process begins with an application from a union to the labour board to represent the workers in a proposed bargaining unit. The application, a copy of which is normally delivered to the employer (see *OLRA*, sec. 7[2]), must include a written description of the proposed bargaining unit and an estimate of the number of individuals in the unit. It generally must also include a list of the names of the individual workers in the proposed bargaining unit and their status as union members; however, this information is not given to the employer (see *OLRA*, sec. 7[13]).

At this point, the labour board has two jobs to do: (a) determine the appropriate bargaining unit, and (b) ascertain the union's level of support. To assist it in determining the appropriate bargaining unit, the board will allow employers or, in some cases, individual workers who object to the union's proposed unit to submit a proposal for a unit they prefer (*OLRA*, sec. 7 [14]).[17] In making its determination, the labour board will take into account both the union's and employer's wishes (*OLRA*, sec. 8); in Ontario, it may conduct a special poll of employees to determine their wishes in the matter (*OLRA*, sec. 9[1]). The board may also consider such factors as the community of interests of the workers involved, traditional or customary bargaining units in the industry in question, and the way in which the proposed bargaining unit would fit into the employer's administrative set-up (Godard, 1994:281–282; Craig and Solomon, 1996:213–214), with the workers' community of interest normally being of greatest importance (Craig and Solomon, 1996:214).

To become certified, unions in all Canadian jurisdictions must reach two threshold points: (a) a level of support that will entitle them to apply for certification (whether this is determined through a card count or a formal election), and (b) a level that will entitle them to become officially certified as the representative for the bargaining unit in question. Typically, the level of support required to apply for certification is lower than that at which certification will be granted. In Alberta and Ontario, where a vote is always required, it will be triggered if the union can produce evidence that 40 percent of the proposed bargaining unit have joined the union. To reduce the chances of employer interference, most Canadian labour acts requiring a vote also require that the vote be held very soon (within 5 to 10 working days) after the certification application has been filed. In B.C., whose arrangements are fairly typical of provinces that do not normally require a vote, 45 percent support is needed to apply for certification. With signed membership cards from 55 percent or more of the proposed bargaining unit members, the union will automatically be certified. If support is between 45 and 55 percent, a vote must be held.

Where a vote is required, simple majority support is always enough to certify the union. However, various jurisdictions differ as to whether the union must receive votes from a majority of the bargaining unit or simply a majority of those voting. Most jurisdictions, including Ontario and the federal jurisdiction, allow certification based on a majority of those voting; a few jurisdictions, including Quebec and Manitoba (see Craig and Solomon, 1996:218) require support from a majority of bargaining unit members—a situation that in effect allows abstentions to count as negative votes. Newfoundland has come up with a compromise whereby the union must receive support from a majority of those voting in situations where at least 70 percent of the proposed bargaining unit have voted.

Traditionally, labour boards made their decisions about the appropriate bargaining unit before deciding whether a union would or would not be certified as that unit's representative. Lately, however, there has been a growing trend towards the prehearing or "quickie" vote—again with an eye to minimizing employer interference in the certification process (see Craig and Solomon, 1996:217–219).[18] Such a vote will normally be granted if either party requests it, and in Ontario, it has become standard (see *OLRA*, sec. 8[4]). In cases where the proposed bargaining unit is in dispute, the board may direct that one or more ballots be segregated and that the ballot box be sealed until after it has decided on an appropriate bargaining unit. If a hearing is necessary, the board will conduct it after the certification vote is held, but before the ballots are counted. In some jurisdictions, including Ontario (*OLRA*, sec. 9[2]), the board may certify the union pending final determination of the bargaining unit, providing it is satisfied that any dispute over the bargaining unit cannot affect the union's right to certification.

Decertification is a process whereby union members who are unhappy with the way in which their union has represented them can get rid of that union in favour of a different one, or no union at all. Any bargaining unit employee may apply to the board for decertification; however, the application will normally be entertained only near the collective agreement's expiry date,[19] or in cases where the union has not managed to negotiate a collective agreement within a reasonable length of time after certification (one year in Ontario). From this point, the process is quite similar to the certification process. Again, a copy of the application must be delivered to the employer and the union. If a sufficient percentage of the bargaining unit applies for decertification (40 percent in Ontario) the board will direct that a decertification vote be taken and will set about determining the appropriate bargaining unit for the purpose of that vote. Normally the percentage requirements for decertification are identical to those for certification. In Ontario and many other jurisdictions, if a majority of those voting favour decertification, the union will be decertified (see *OLRA*, sec. 63[14]).

As Craig and Solomon note (1996:223), decertification provisions are an essential element of public labour policy. Among other things, such provisions help enhance union democracy by providing workers with a way of getting rid of unions which have been ineffective, or that have treated them unfairly or arbitrarily. At the same time, high levels of decertification activity are hardly a sign of a healthy IR system. Most typically, they are associated with a rise in employer anti-union tactics and unfair labour practice activity (see Godard, 1994:139 and Barbash, 1988), though as Godard notes, decertification may also be linked to increased union raiding (discussed in detail in Chapter 5).

Remedying Unfair Labour Practice

An inadequately enforced labour act would not amount to much. Accordingly, a major purpose of Canadian LRL is to set standards for unfair labour practice and provide remedies for it. Unfair labour practice provisions apply both to employers and unions. In some cases, they also apply to individuals.

Employers are barred from participating in or interfering with a trade union, from discriminating against union members, or from seeking to induce employees not to join a union. In some jurisdictions, including Ontario (see below), the hiring of professional strike-breakers is specifically defined as an unfair labour practice. When a union has been certified, an employer cannot refuse to bargain with it or engage in mere "surface" bargaining not aimed at concluding a collective agreement (see *OLRA*, sec. 17). Once bargaining begins, an employer cannot alter wage rates or other terms and conditions of employment until the conciliation process has run its course (see *OLRA*, sec. 86[1]). During organizing drives, employers are barred from issuing any threats or promises to workers or attempting to influence the unionization process by hiring additional workers, who, in most cases, would likely vote against unionization (Godard, 1994:286–287). They are also barred from closing down and relocating all or part of their operations in an attempt to avoid or get rid of a union (Godard, 1994:287).

For their part, unions are barred from interfering with the formation and operation of employers' organizations (*OLRA*, sec. 71), as well as from interfering with other unions that have won the right to represent given groups of workers. In most provinces, including Ontario (*OLRA*, sec. 74), they are bound by a duty of fair representation provision, which forbids them from acting in an arbitrary or discriminatory manner, or in bad faith in representing bargaining unit members. Unions cannot use intimidation or coercion to seek to compel people to join (*OLRA*, sec. 76), and are specifically barred from trying to persuade employees to join at the workplace during regular working hours (sec. 77).[20] They are also forbidden from suspending or otherwise disciplining members for refusing to engage in unlawful strikes (*OLRA*, sec. 85).

As will be noted in more detail in the "Administration" section, labour boards are primarily responsible for administering and enforcing labour relations acts. They have a broad range of remedies available, including the power to issue cease and desist orders, the power to order unfairly discharged employees reinstated with or without compensation (*OLRA*, sec. 96[4]), and the ability, where appropriate, to alter a bargaining unit determined in a certificate or defined in a collective agreement (*OLRA*, sec. 99[7]). In extreme cases, they may certify a union with less than majority support in almost all jurisdictions except Ontario,[21] or impose a first collective agreement through arbitration in those jurisdictions that make first-agreement arbitration available. Many labour acts (i.e., *OLRA*, sec. 104) also stipulate that violators can be prosecuted through the criminal courts. However, it would appear that criminal prosecution is seldom used, as most labour boards prefer to take a more accommodative approach (Carter, 1995:68; Godard, 1994).

Maintaining Union Security

Without protection for their right to carry out legitimate activities in the workplace and a regular source of income, few unions would last for very long. Protection is provided in all jurisdictions through provisions stating that no employer or employers' organization shall participate in or interfere with the formation, selection, or administration of a trade union or with the union's activities (see *OLRA*, sec. 70), and similar provisions barring employers or other unions from interfering with a duly certified union's bargaining rights (see *OLRA*, sec. 73[1]). Income protection is assured in most jurisdictions through some version of the *Rand Formula* (discussed earlier in the chapter). In Ontario, section 47(1) of the *Labour Relations Act* provides for the regular deduction of union dues from all bargaining unit members, whether or not they are union members. Non-members will have their deductions reduced to take account of pension, insurance, and other benefit plans available only to members (sec. 47[2b]), and those with a religious objection to joining a union or paying union dues may have their dues money paid to a recognized charity (sec. 52[1]).

Regulating Industrial Conflict

Strikes

Canada generally regulates strikes more strictly than do most other countries. As we note in more detail in the strike chapter (Chapter 12), most jurisdictions require the appointment of a conciliator before a strike can become legal. American private sector labour law does not require conciliation prior to strikes, nor has that of most other countries, with the notable exception of New Zealand (Bean, 1994:116–7). Generally a strike will be legal only after the conciliator has reported his or her lack of success to the minister and a certain length of time (normally 7 to 14 days) has elapsed. While this is now becoming less common, some jurisdictions maintain a second stage of conciliation, culminating in a public report. Several jurisdictions, including British Columbia and Ontario (*OLRA*, sec. 79[4] and 79 [7]), require a secret strike vote. Two jurisdictions (Saskatchewan and Ontario) give the employer a say in whether or not a strike will continue. In the former, the employer may ask the labour board to conduct a vote on the employer's last offer; in the latter, the employer may make a similar request of the minister (*OLRA*, sec. 42[1]). Saskatchewan's law also allows the union, or the lesser of 100 workers or 25 percent of the bargaining unit members, to apply for such a vote (Craig and Solomon, 1996:227).

Although this is not the Canadian norm, two jurisdictions (Alberta and B.C.) have special provisions for handling emergency disputes in the private sector, in cases where the government believes the public health or welfare is being seriously endangered. The Alberta legislation provides for the establishment of a public emergency tribunal to mediate the dispute and, where necessary, hand down a binding arbitration award (Craig and Solomon, 1996:235). The B.C. legislation allows the government to block a planned strike or lockout and substitute mediation, designation of essential employees, and appointment of a public interest inquiry board (Craig and Solomon, 1996).

There are also restrictions on employers' conduct during a labour dispute. Just as unions cannot strike, employers cannot legally lock out until the conciliation process has been exhausted and the appropriate time delays have passed. Quebec and British Columbia ban the use of replacement workers, within certain limits, while Ontario (*OLRA*, sec. 78[1]) bans professional strike-breakers, as does Manitoba. Most Canadian jurisdictions provide for the reinstatement of workers following a legal strike. Manitoba specifically bans the use of permanent replacement workers (Carter, 1995:65).

Grievances

As we pointed out earlier, a distinctive feature of Canadian labour legislation is that strikes during the life of the collective agreement are illegal. Instead, every Canadian jurisdiction's labour act requires that collective agreements establish a grievance process, culminating in final and binding arbitration, to settle disputes over the interpretation or application of the agreement (e.g., *OLRA*, sec. 48[1]). Most provinces also have a provision in their labour acts stating that if a collective agreement does not make specific reference to a grievance procedure, it shall be deemed to contain such a provision (e.g., *OLRA*, sec. 48[2]).

VARIATIONS IN PROVINCIAL LEGISLATION

Over the years, different provinces' labour relations acts have begun to vary a good deal in a number of ways. While the basic core of the acts is usually quite similar, there are now a number of differences in such important areas as eligibility for coverage under the legislation, certification procedures, duty of fair representation provisions, first-contract arbitration, technological change, replacement worker provisions, and the availability of alternative dispute resolution procedures such as grievance mediation and expedited arbitration.

To the beginning student, labour relations acts seem to present a great welter of minute, confusing detail, often written in highly technical language. It is definitely not our intention to drown readers in a sea of mind-boggling detail. At the same time, we *would* like to offer some guidance on the question of which types of provisions and which acts seem to offer the greatest (or least) protection to workers and their unions. To this end, we consider a number of provisions with an eye to determining their relative impact on unions and employers. The provisions we will be examining include those governing exclusions from coverage under labour relations legislation, certification procedures, first-contract arbitration, expedited arbitration, technological change, duty of fair representation, the use of replacement workers in strikes, and management's right to communicate and right to manage. The results of this examination are summarized in Table 8.1. In the discussion below, "liberal" provisions are those generally favourable to workers and their unions, while "restrictive" provisions are those favourable to employers (or unfavourable to workers and unions).[22]

As Table 8.1 reveals, the most liberal labour act overall is that of British Columbia, where seven of the nine laws considered here are liberal and only two are restrictive. Clustered behind B.C. are Manitoba (five liberal and two moderately liberal), Saskatchewan and Quebec (five liberal and one moderately liberal), and the federal jurisdiction (five liberal laws). The remaining jurisdictions all have more restrictive than liberal laws, the most restrictive being Alberta and Nova Scotia, with only one moderately liberal and six restrictive provisions each. It may be of interest that all the liberal jurisdictions except the federal jurisdictions have had an NDP or PQ government for at least two full terms. Of the remaining provinces, only Ontario has ever had such a government, and then for just one term.[23]

Exclusions

In many European countries, the right to join a union has been written into freedom of association provisions in national constitutions. This is not the case in Canada, where the Supreme Court has ruled that the *Charter of Rights and Freedoms'* guarantee of freedom of association does not apply to workers' rights such as collective bargaining, striking, or picketing (Adell, 1988b; Arthurs, 1988; Cavalluzzo, 1988; England, 1988). Far from providing positive protection for workers' right to join a union, Canadian LRL continues to exclude the members of a number of occupational groups from coverage.

Table 8.1.

VARIATIONS IN PROVINCIAL LABOUR LAWS

Jurisdiction	Laws								
	1	2	3	4	5	6	7	8	9
Federal	L	L	L	L	NA	L	ML	NA	NA
Alberta	R	R	ML	R	NA	R	R	R	NA
B.C.	L	L	L	L	L	L	L	R	R
Manitoba	L	L	ML	L	L	L	ML	R	NA
New Brunswick	ML	L	NA	R	NA	L	R	R	NA
Newfoundland	L	R	NA	L	NA	R	R	NA	NA
Nova Scotia	R	R	ML	R	NA	R	R	R	NA
Ontario	R	R	L	L	L	R	ML	R	NA
P.E.I.	R	L	NA	L	NA	R	R	R	NA
Quebec	ML	L	L	L	NA	R	L	NA	L
Saskatchewan	L	L	ML	L	L	L	R	NA	NA

Notes: NA = not applicable, because in the author's judgment the law in question cannot meaningfully be classified as either liberal or restrictive.
L = Liberal; ML = Moderately Liberal; R = Restrictive.
Law 1: Exclusions
Law 2: Certification procedure
Law 3: Union's duty of fair representation
Law 4: First-contract arbitration
Law 5: Expedited arbitration
Law 6: Technological change
Law 7: Replacement workers
Law 8: Employer's freedom to communicate
Law 9: Employer's right to manage

Sources: CCH (1998d); Craig and Solomon (1996).

Aside from their philosophical significance, exclusion provisions are of considerable practical relevance to the labour movement, since they can play an important role in union membership growth. Other things being equal, provinces with more liberal exclusion policies should have higher union membership rates than those with restrictive policies simply because they will have a larger pool of potential members to draw from. The evidence suggests that this has indeed been the case. In 1997 (see Table 5.4), the three provinces with the highest union membership rates, Newfoundland, Quebec, and British Columbia, all had liberal or moderately liberal exclusion policies. The three provinces with the lowest rates, Alberta, Prince Edward Island, and Ontario, all had restrictive policies. Significantly, Alberta, whose exclusion policies are the country's most restrictive, had by far the lowest membership rates.[24]

"No place in the sun." Though they're among the country's poorest workers, agricultural workers are exclud-ed from unionization rights in several Canadian provinces, including Ontario. To make matters worse, sever-al provinces also exclude them from coverage under employment standards law.

While some writers (i.e., Beatty, 1983) disagree, most Canadian industrial rela-tions experts would justify the exclusion of management and confidential labour rela-tions personnel, found in almost all Canadian jurisdictions, on the grounds that their inclusion in unions could create a conflict of interest. The real questions here may be who is a manager and what proportion of an employee's time is spent on confiden-tial labour relations matters.[25] In the case of professionals, however, most would likely agree that the rationale for their continued exclusion is at best unclear (LLCG, 1984:3–25), given that many now work not as independent practitioners but as salaried employees. Nonetheless, four provinces continue to exclude members of the legal, medical, dental, and architectural professions, and three exclude professional engineers[26] Even less defensible is the exclusion of agricultural workers and domes-tic workers, each of whom are also excluded in three provinces. Industrial relations experts have been calling for the abolition of these exclusions ever since the 1968 Woods Task Force Report (LLCG, 1984:3–27), with some going so far as to describe the agricultural exclusion, in particular, as blatantly political.[27] Thus far, their pleas appear to have fallen on deaf ears. What is surprising is that the Charter has not had more effect here. Ironically, exclusion laws have changed far less in the past 15 years than they did in the 15 years before the Charter took effect.

The federal jurisdiction and four provinces (B.C., Saskatchewan, Manitoba, and Newfoundland) can be said to have "liberal" exclusion policies, since their legislation excludes only management and confidential labour relations personnel (see Table 8.1). Two provinces (New Brunswick and Quebec) can be characterized as having "moderately liberal" policies, since their acts exclude small numbers of workers other than managers or confidential personnel. (New Brunswick excludes domestic workers, while Quebec excludes farm workers in units of less than three.) The remaining provinces' exclusion policies can be described as "restrictive," since they exclude large numbers of workers beyond the basic management-confidential exclusion. Alberta, P.E.I., and Nova Scotia continue to exclude members of all five professions listed above; in addition, Alberta excludes domestics and most agricultural workers. Ontario excludes domestics, most agricultural workers, professionals (except for engineers), and those engaged in fishing and hunting.

Certification Procedures

As we indicated earlier, Canadian jurisdictions' certification procedures vary significantly. Of greatest importance here is whether a jurisdiction requires a vote for all certifications, or will allow certification based on a count of signed membership cards. Some analysts argue that the card count allowed in many Canadian jurisdictions is one of the reasons why Canada has higher union membership rates than the United States (see Bruce, 1990; Ng, 1992). Where a vote is required, such analysts argue, there is more opportunity for employers to influence the process, as by suspending, transferring, or harassing union activists or by warning employees of the dangers of unionization (Weiler, 1983).

The federal jurisdiction and six provinces (New Brunswick, P.E.I., Quebec, Manitoba, Saskatchewan, and British Columbia) have liberal certification procedures, since they allow certification through a card count providing certain conditions are met. The four remaining provinces have restrictive certification procedures, since they require a vote for certification in all cases.

In recent years, the tendency has been for more jurisdictions to require a vote. Until 1984, when B.C. began to require a vote (Craig and Solomon, 1996:215), certification through card count was the norm throughout Canada. After 1984, other provinces began to follow suit. For example, Alberta moved to the vote in 1988 (Craig and Solomon, 1996), while Newfoundland did so in 1994. Another recent tendency has been towards greater "politicization" of the certification process. For example, B.C.'s NDP government dropped the previous Social Credit government's requirement of a vote in its 1992 revisions to the province's labour code (Craig and Solomon, 1996). But, when a Conservative government replaced the NDP in Ontario in 1995, one of its first acts was to amend the labour relations act so as to require a vote (CCH, 1998d).

Duty of Fair Representation

At first glance, one would think duty of fair representation (DFR) provisions might be detrimental to unions, since they impose certain definite obligations on them. We would argue that DFR provisions likely benefit unions, since they can help reassure potential members that they have some protection against arbitrary or discriminatory treatment by union officials and thereby induce more people to join. Most DFR provisions forbid the union from showing bad faith or acting in an arbitrary or discriminatory fashion towards any bargaining unit member, whether or not that individual happens to be a union member.[28] The Quebec provision also forbids the union from displaying "serious negligence" towards any bargaining unit member.

Four jurisdictions (Ontario, Quebec, B.C., and the federal jurisdictions) could be characterized as having "liberal" DFR provisions, since their provisions apply to the negotiation process as well as to contract administration. Four other jurisdictions (Saskatchewan, Manitoba, Nova Scotia, and Alberta) could be said to have "moderately liberal" provisions, since their DFR clauses apply only to unions' handling of grievances.

First-Contract Arbitration

First-contract arbitration provisions may be of considerable help to unions, since (at least in principle) they can deter employers in a first-contract situation from refusing to bargain seriously to prevent the union from achieving a collective agreement. A 1987 study by Jean Sexton finds that the provisions had a positive effect in helping Quebec unions achieve an initial collective agreement.

Eight jurisdictions (the federal one and the provinces of British Columbia, Manitoba, Newfoundland, Ontario, Prince Edward Island, Quebec, and Saskatchewan) have some kind of first-contract arbitration provision in effect. While there is quite a bit of similarity to most of these provisions, there is some variation regarding the length of contract that will be imposed. Most jurisdictions will impose an agreement for only one year, but in two (Ontario and Saskatchewan), the agreement must be for at least two years, a period of time that commentators such as Weiler (1980) suggest may be necessary if the union is to achieve a lasting bargaining relationship with the employer. There is also some variation in the conditions under which the board or an arbitrator acting under the board's direction will impose a first agreement. Most jurisdictions allow considerable ministerial discretion on this point. The Ontario legislation stands out in that it directs the board to appoint an arbitrator in any case where it has found that the employer has refused to recognize the union's bargaining authority, has adopted any "uncompromising" bargaining position, or has in the board's judgment not made a reasonable effort to conclude a collective agreement.

We would classify the eight jurisdictions having first-contract arbitration provisions in place as "liberal," and the three remaining jurisdictions as "restrictive" in that they offer no special protection to unions in the delicate first-contract situation. Further research is needed to determine whether the procedure has worked better in jurisdictions where the initial contract is imposed for two years rather than one, and whether Ontario's mandatory procedure has achieved significantly different results from the discretionary procedure in place in most other jurisdictions.

Expedited Arbitration

The purpose of expedited arbitration (to be discussed in more detail in the grievance chapter) is to achieve a speedier and more informal resolution of grievances. It can benefit unions in a number of ways. First, it can significantly reduce the cost of arbitration (Rose, 1986). Second, by speeding up the dispute resolution process, it can help make union members feel better about the kind of service the organization is providing them. Third (and not unrelated to the two previous points), by offering an inexpensive alternative to conventional arbitration, it allows for the resolution of a greater number of workplace problems. Again, this should have the effect of increasing members' satisfaction with their unions, since a common criticism of conventional arbitration is that it allows for the final resolution of only a tiny proportion of the total number of grievances filed.

Four provinces (B.C., Manitoba, Ontario, and Saskatchewan) have some kind of expedited arbitration procedure in effect. In all four cases, expedited arbitration can be combined with some form of grievance mediation, thereby further reducing the costs of arbitration and increasing the number of cases resolved (Rose, 1996; see also Weiler, 1980). We would classify the four provinces having expedited arbitration provisions as "liberal." Interestingly, this is one case where a gain for the union is not necessarily a loss for the employer. Employers as well as unions can benefit from lower arbitration costs, quicker resolution of problems, and the resolution of a greater number of workplace difficulties. Indeed, one reason for the growing popularity of expedited arbitration may well be that it offers a "win-win" situation for all concerned.

Technological Change

Technological change is of serious concern to unions, both because it is sometimes used specifically to weaken unions (Godard, 1994:137) and because it can have the effect of destabilizing workplace relations and undermining collective agreement protections (Godard, 1994; Peirce, 1987). Five jurisdictions (B.C., Manitoba, New Brunswick,

Saskatchewan, and the federal jurisdiction) have in place some kind of technological change provision requiring employers to give notice before making a technological change that will affect workers' jobs or incomes.

In practice, legislated technological change provisions have not afforded workers and their unions a great deal of protection, in large measure because labour boards have been reluctant to enforce the legislation even in cases where an employer is in clear violation (see Economic Council of Canada, 1987; Peirce, 1987). Still, the provisions may encourage otherwise reluctant employers to bargain over the issue, and, therefore, are probably better than no provision at all. Therefore, we would classify the five jurisdictions with some kind of technological change provision in place as "liberal," and the remaining provinces as "restrictive," in that they offer workers no legislative protection against the adverse effects of this change.

Use of Replacement Workers

One of the most hotly debated issues in industrial relations is whether employers should be allowed to replace striking workers. Those taking a neoclassical or managerial perspective generally argue in favour of this right, on the grounds that management should be free to run enterprises as it sees fit, and that to take away the right would be to tilt the balance of power too much in the union's favour (see Godard, 1994:295). Others point out that the practical effect of allowing replacement workers is to undermine the union's legal right to strike, particularly in the case of low-skilled jobs, where workers can easily be replaced (Godard, 1994:295–296; Beatty, 1983). In addition, the use of replacement workers can lead (and has, in fact, often led) to picket-line violence, or even loss of life.[29] In this regard, the Giant Gold Mine case, where nine workers were killed in an explosion in a replacement worker situation, is but one of many painful illustrations from recent Canadian labour history.

Quebec, which pioneered anti-scab legislation in 1977 (Boivin, 1982), prohibits the use of replacement workers hired after negotiations begin, but before the end of a strike, or who are supplied by another employer or by a contractor. The legislation also bans multi-establishment employers from using a worker at a struck or locked-out establishment elsewhere, or from bringing employees from other establishments into the struck or locked-out one. British Columbia's legislation is similar, but also bars' employers from bringing in someone from outside to substitute for a non-bargaining unit employee temporarily performing the work of a striking bargaining-unit employee. In addition, the B.C. law states that no non-bargaining unit employee can be required to do the work of a striker at the same location. Ontario had similar legislation on the books during the early 1990s, but it was repealed when the present Conservative government came to power in 1995.

The two jurisdictions that prohibit the use of replacement workers should be classified as "liberal" on this issue. Ontario, which bans the use of professional strikebreakers, and Manitoba, which does that and also prohibits replacement workers from being hired permanently after the strike, can be classified as "moderately liberal." The federal jurisdiction should also be classified as moderately liberal, since recently enacted changes to the *Canada Labour Code*, discussed in Note 15, provide protection against the use of replacement workers in cases where the purpose of bringing in those workers was to undermine the union, rather than to pursue legitimate bargaining objectives. The remaining jurisdictions should be classified as "restrictive" as they offer striking workers no protection against replacement workers.

Employer's Freedom to Communicate

Seven jurisdictions (Alberta, B.C., Manitoba, New Brunswick, Nova Scotia, Ontario, and P.E.I.) have in place provisions specifically granting employers the right to communicate with their employees, within certain limits. These provisions appear to be on the increase; in 1984, the Labour Law textbook (3–67) indicated that they were in place only in B.C., Manitoba, and Ontario.

Alberta's provision is typical; it states that an employer can express his or her views "so long as (s)he does not use coercion, intimidation, threats, promises, or undue influence." Manitoba's and Ontario's provisions specifically exclude interference with unions from permissible employer communications. The P.E.I. provision differs in that it specifically allows employers to express their views on "collective bargaining, or terms and conditions of employment," so long as they do not use coercion, intimidation, threats, or undue influence. In B.C., the provision allows employers to communicate to an employee "a statement of fact or opinion reasonably held with respect to the employer's business."

Although these provisions have not, thus far, occasioned a great deal of discussion in the IR literature, they are far from uncontroversial. Defenders argue that providing employers the right to communicate with employees is little more than a fair balance of the rights given to unions to make their case. They also point out that unions have more than sufficient protection from other legislative provisions (found in all Canadian acts) barring employers from having a hand in the formation or operation of a union or from interfering with its operations. Critics, for their part, argue that, whatever other legislative provisions might say, *these* provisions open the door to employers wishing to influence the unionization process—a process in which employers should have no say whatever. Of particular concern to the critics are employer free speech provisions in the three jurisdictions that also require a vote for certification (Alberta, Nova Scotia, and Ontario), and the P.E.I. provision, which specifically permits direct communication on collective bargaining issues and might, therefore, be seen as encouraging employers to make an "end run" around unions by communicating with employees directly on these issues.

Our view is that although these provisions will not necessarily lead to increased employer interference with unions, they have the potential to do so.[31] For this reason, we would classify all jurisdictions having such provisions in place as "restrictive." Further research is needed to determine whether these provisions have had an adverse effect on new union certifications or have contributed to an increase in unfair employer labour practice.

Employer's Right to Manage

Seven jurisdictions (Alberta, B.C., Manitoba, New Brunswick, Newfoundland, P.E.I., and Quebec) have written "right to manage" provisions into their labour acts. The Alberta, Manitoba, and Newfoundland provisions relate exclusively to discipline and discharge. In contrast, B.C.'s provision relates both to discipline and discharge and to making "a change in the operation of the employer's business reasonably necessary for the proper operation of that business." The Quebec provision has a rather different emphasis. It gives employers the right to suspend, transfer, or dismiss employees for a "good and sufficient reason," the proof of which must be provided by the employer. Exercising one's legal rights under the labour code (such as the right to join or help organize a union) does not constitute such a "good and sufficient reason" for dismissal, since employers are specifically barred from penalizing employees for this reason.

The rationale for most of the "right to manage" provisions seems unclear. Generally, employers write management rights clauses into collective agreements; in addition, the residual management rights doctrine that most arbitrators apply grants employers the right to discipline and discharge as they see fit, subject to the limitations of the collective agreement, even in the absence of a specific management rights provision. Provisions applying only to discipline and discharge would, therefore, appear to be redundant, though in borderline cases an arbitrator might conceivably use the legislation to arrive at a pro-management decision. The B.C. provision is more troubling, since it could potentially have the effect of undermining that province's technological change provision. Here again is a situation where more research is needed on the effects the provisions have had. We would classify Quebec's provision as "liberal," since its main emphasis appears to be on protecting employees' rights. The B.C. provision, on the other hand, should be classified as "restrictive," given its potential for undermining existing union rights. For the time being, we would not classify the remaining "right to manage" provisions as either liberal or restrictive, given that it isn't clear they would have much practical effect either way.

Other Provisions

Six jurisdictions (the federal jurisdiction and all provinces from Ontario westward) allow individuals with religious objections to joining a union or paying union dues to apply to the labour board for exemption in situations where they would otherwise be expected to join the union or pay dues. Normally, the amount of money that would have been paid in dues is then remitted to a charity agreed upon by the worker and the union (see Craig and Solomon, 1996:241–242). Some argue that such provisions weaken unions by depriving them of potential members and revenue. Our view is that such provisions are unlikely to do much harm since only a very small number of workers will likely wish to avail themselves of them. In any case, it could also be argued that both individual unions and the Canadian labour movement as a whole will, in the long run, be better off for not forcing workers' consciences in such matters. We have, therefore, not included these provisions in our "liberal/restrictive" classification scheme.

With regard to unfair labour practices, several jurisdictions have written specific "reverse onus" provisions into their legislation. These provisions, which apply particularly when an employee is dismissed or otherwise disciplined during a certification drive, state that during critical periods like certification drives, the employer will be assumed to have disciplined the employee for reasons relating to union activity unless and until the employer proves otherwise. There would be a strong argument for classifying jurisdictions with such reverse onus provisions in place as "liberal," except that there is some reason to believe labour boards may operate in the same way even when specific reverse onus language is not in place.[30] Once again, research is needed to determine whether unfair labour practice cases are handled substantially differently in provinces with and without reverse onus provisions in their labour acts.

LRL in Quebec

Special mention should be made of Quebec's labour relations legislation, since in some ways that province's collective bargaining procedures and administrative mechanisms differ quite markedly from the rest of Canada's. Here, we focus mainly on private sector legislation; features applying to the public sector will be discussed in the next chapter.

While Quebec is probably best known to the English Canadian IR community for pioneering anti-strike-breaking legislation and the strike-right for public servants, the most distinctive feature of its legislative regime is arguably its decree system, whereby collective agreements are extended to the non-unionized sectors of an industry. In effect since 1934 (Boivin and Déom, 1995:476), the decree system was established to encourage collective bargaining and to eliminate competition over wages and working conditions among firms in the same industry (Boivin and Déom, 1995). Decrees

Signs like the warning to potential strike breakers shown in the above picture aren't needed in provinces, such as Quebec, which have banned the use of replacement workers during strikes.

are found mainly in low-wage industries comprising large numbers of small and medium-sized firms, such as men's and women's clothing, security guards, garages, bread distribution, hairdressing, and waste removal (Boivin and Déom, 1995:477).

Under the *Collective Agreement Decrees Act* (*CADA*), unionized firms, which are normally the biggest ones in any given industry, negotiate an agreement in the normal fashion. Then, those employers and unions wishing to have their agreement extended decide on the contents of the agreement that would eventually bind all employers and employees in the industry (Boivin and Déom, 1995). Such agreements are normally narrower in scope than standard agreements, since permissible provisions for an extension are limited to wages, hours of work, working days, vacations with pay, and classification of operations and of employers and employees (Boivin and Déom, 1995). Certain provisions are specifically barred from extended agreements; these include any having to do with the activities, administration, or funding of a union or employer's association or with the minimum prices to be charged to the public for certain services (*CADA*, section 9.1[1]). Once the parties have decided on their agreement, they send it to the Labour Minister, who publishes it in a major French and English newspaper and in the province's official gazette. Those with objections normally have 45 days to file them, though a shorter time frame may be imposed if the Minister believes that the urgency of the situation requires swifter action (*CADA*, section 5). If the Minister believes that the provisions of the proposed agreement "have acquired a preponderant significance and importance for the establishment of conditions of employment" and do not pose a serious inconvenience for enterprises competing with out-of-province businesses (*CADA*, section 6[2a]), he or she may then extend the agreement to the entire industry, with or without any modifications she or he may deem appropriate (*CADA*, section 6.2). Decrees are normally for a period not exceeding 18 months (*CADA*, section 37); however, the Minister may at any time extend the term of a decree for a period up to a further 18 months (*CADA*, sections 8, 37). If the Minister rejects an application for extension, she or he must inform the applicant in writing and provide reasons for the decision (*CADA*, section 6.3). Administration and enforcement of decrees is through joint committees made up of equal numbers of representatives from employers and unions that have signed the agreement, and financed by payroll taxes levied both on employers and employees (*CADA*, sections 16–24).

FAIR WAGES AND HOURS OF LABOUR ACT
canada.justice.gc.ca/FTP/EN/Laws/L/L-4.txt

Special, highly centralized arrangements govern labour relations in the construction industry, itself a decree sector. Administration of the Quebec construction labour relations act[32] is carried out by the Quebec Construction Commission (QCC), which is also charged with verifying the credentials of prospective construction workers (Act, section 4, especially 4[3]). In general (see below for an important exception), only those workers holding a QCC competency card are legally entitled to work in construction in the province (*CADA*, sections 36 and 39). Union certification as such does not exist in Quebec's construction industry (Boivin and Déom, 1995:479). Instead, all workers must belong to one of the five labour organizations legally entitled to represent construction workers: the QFL-Construction, the Quebec Council of Construction Trades, the CSN-Construction, the CSD-Construction, and the North Shore Association (Boivin and Déom, 1995; Act, section 28). Bargaining is carried out between these unions and one of five sector-based employers' associations over matters specific to the sector. Issues common to all sectors are negotiated between the unions and a general construction employers' association to which all construction employers must belong (Act, sections 40–41, 61.1). Though the sector-based associations are the sole bargaining agents for issues other than the common ones, they may (if they wish) delegate their bargaining authority to the general association (Act, section 41).

In a 1993 amendment to the construction act that infuriated unions and led to a series of wildcat strikes (Boivin and Déom, 1995:480), the government, in effect, deregulated the residential construction industry by stating that the act did not apply to most work done on single-family dwellings (see Act, section 19[10]). The unions' opposition was understandable, given that the amendment had the effect of no longer requiring those engaged in residential construction work to be union members, which in turn would almost certainly lead to a decline in unionization in Quebec's construction industry as a whole. The move appears to have been a response to contractors' complaints about high labour costs in residential construction (Boivin and Déom, 1995:480). It is not clear what the overall effect of the 1993 amendment has been, or whether competitive pressures will lead the government to opt for further deregulation elsewhere in the industry.

Perhaps because of the decree system, employers' associations, which in English Canada are limited mainly to the construction industry, play a much more prominent role in Quebec than they do elsewhere. The province has about 90 such organizations representing some 25 000 employers, mainly in the decree sectors or in construction. Many of them are directly engaged in negotiating with unions. In 1969, most of those associations joined forces to create a confederation of employer associations known as the Conseil du patronat du Québec (CPQ). The CPQ does not engage in collective bargaining as such, instead focussing its energies on legislative lobbying, public relations, and research (Boivin and Déom, 1995:468). The existence of such a federation has arguably enabled the Quebec business community to speak with one voice to a far greater extent than would be possible in any other province.

Another unique feature of Quebec LRL is its Essential Services Council, established in 1982. The Council's main function is to ensure that sufficient employees are designated as essential to protect the public health, safety, and welfare during labour disputes affecting public services (Boivin and Déom, 1995:471). Since its activities apply mainly to the public sector, they will be discussed in more detail in the next chapter.

Finally, Quebec has differed significantly from other provinces in the way it administers LRL. In 1969, it replaced its labour relations board with a three-tier system including certification agents, labour commissioners, and general commissioners to deal with certification and unfair labour practice issues. A Labour Court was also established to handle appeals from commissioners' and general commissioners' decisions and to deal with criminal prosecutions brought under the Labour Code (Boivin, 1989:424–425). The idea was that such a specialized tribunal, staffed with IR and human resource specialists, would reduce recourse to the courts on labour-related matters. It proved unable to achieve this objective and was also widely criticized for its lengthy delays in rendering decisions (Boivin, 1989:425). As a result, the government in 1987 passed legislation replacing the court with a labour relations board that would function in basically the same way as other provinces' boards (Boivin, 1989). However, for reasons not clear to the author, the legislation had still not officially been proclaimed at the time of writing.

HOW LRL IS ADMINISTERED

Labour Boards

As Donald Carter (1995) notes, Canadian labour relations legislation is administered through three different institutions: labour relations boards, arbitrators (working either singly or in panels), and the courts. Of the three, labour relations boards are by far the most important. Found in every province except Quebec, which for the past three decades has used a labour court instead (see above), these boards are administrative tribunals that derive their authority from the collective bargaining law they administer (Carter, 1995:65). Their major functions are overseeing union certification and decertification and policing unfair labour practice; however, in recent years their jurisdiction has expanded to include the power to issue directives concerning illegal strikes and lockouts and to determine whether the parties are bargaining in good faith (Carter, 1995:66). As well, a number of boards, including Ontario's (*OLRA*, section 43[4]), can arbitrate first-contract disputes.

Labour relations boards normally report to the government through the labour ministry, but are regarded as having some autonomy from that ministry (Carter, 1995:65). In general, they are tripartite. Most comprise independent chairpersons and representatives from both management and the labour movement (Carter, 1995). Ontario (*OLRA*, section 110[2]) also provides for one or more vice-chairs. In larger jurisdictions, labour board appointments are full-time; in smaller ones, they are more apt to be part-time. In all cases, labour boards employ a staff of civil servants to perform research and various other functions (*OLRA*, section 110[2]). Normally, a panel of three, headed by a chair (or vice-chair) and containing at least one member from the union and management sides is considered a quorum. However, when necessary, the chair or a vice-chair may sit alone in a number of jurisdictions (see *OLRA*, section 110[12–14]).

THE FULL RANGE OF CLRB WORK

home.istar.ca/~clrbccrt/$pub_e.htm#infocirc?68,27

Labour relations boards have quite extensive powers. In Ontario, these include the power to subpoena witnesses and compel them to give evidence under oath; to require any party to produce documents; to accept such evidence as the board deems proper, whether or not that evidence would be admissible in the courts; to require employers and unions to post board notices; to enter workplaces to inspect work processes and interrogate workers and managers; to conduct representation, strike, and ratification votes; and to bar unsuccessful applicants for certification for a period up to one year (*OLRA*, section 111[2]). They also have a broad range of remedies available to them, including (as noted above) the power to issue cease and desist orders, to certify a union with less than majority support (except in Ontario) where an unfair labour practice has prevented employees' true wishes in the matter from being made known, and to order unfairly discharged employees reinstated with or without compensation. While most labour acts provide substantial fines for violation,[33] labour boards rarely resort to criminal prosecution, even for serious and willful violations of the labour act, generally believing that prosecution will do little good and will likely only serve to embitter the parties even further (Godard, 1994:291). Instead, the approach they generally take is the non-punitive "make-whole" one from civil law (Godard, 1994:289), which requires the guilty party to right past wrongs and to restore the victim to the position he or she would have been in had the offence in question not been committed. This means that instead of fining or jailing an employer for unfairly discharging an employee during a union organizing drive, the board would normally order the employee reinstated with back pay (Godard, 1994:289–290). In some cases, unions have been awarded damages to compensate them for the extra expenses resulting from the employer's breach of the labour act (Carter, 1995:69). Where a board has found that the closing of an establishment was motivated at least in part by anti-union animus, it has ordered employers to make cash settlements with displaced employees and/or offer them equivalent jobs in the employer's other establishments (Godard, 1994:290).

Typically, labour board proceedings are more informal and less legalistic than proceedings before a court, though some have suggested that the gap between the two has narrowed of late (Arthurs, 1988:30). There is no requirement that parties to a labour board proceeding be represented by a lawyer (Carter, 1995:65), although an increasing number are (see Arthurs, 1988:30). In general, labour boards are more concerned with finding practical and workable solutions that will win broad acceptance in the industrial relations community than with laying down long-term legal precedents. To this end, they usually take an accommodative approach in addressing workplace problems. Often a labour relations officer is assigned to a dispute, in the first instance, to help the parties resolve the problem on their own. If an accommodation is reached, the board will not hear the matter (Arthurs, 1988:68). As well, the board will sometimes refuse to act if the conduct in question has ended by the time of the hearing; in Ontario, it has had a policy of not issuing an order to remedy illegal strike or lockout action if the strike or lockout has ended before the hearing, except in cases where there has been a clear pattern of such misconduct (Arthurs, 1988).

For the labour movement and many academic industrial relationists, labour boards have a number of advantages over the courts. In general, problems are resolved more quickly and expeditiously by boards. Since unions often have fewer resources than employers, this greater speed of resolution may be critical. In addition, labour boards, which normally include both union and management representatives, have tended to be more even-handed than the courts, which overall have tended to favour employers far more often than labour (Arthurs, 1988:20; England, 1988:169). Some have also noted that because labour boards are made up of IR practitioners and have expert staff available to them, they tend to be more knowledgeable about IR and more sensitive to its implications than do most judges, who may or may not have special training and expertise in the field. At the same time, there have been concerns that in their quest to be accommodating, labour boards have failed to take sufficient steps to prevent employers from committing unfair labour practices (Godard, 1994:289–292), and that existing penalties do not serve as much of a deterrent against such practices (Godard, 1994:290–291).

Arbitrators

While labour boards are the most important of the institutions that administer LRL, they are by no means the only ones. It is arbitrators who are chiefly responsible for interpreting and administering collective agreements. At one time (Carter, 1995:69), three-person panels comprising a union nominee, a management nominee, and a neutral chair were the norm for grievance arbitration. Now, however, single arbitrators are increasingly being used, as many on both sides of the union-management divide have come to the conclusion that their decisions are just as good and arrived at more quickly and at less expense than those reached by three-person panels (Carter, 1995; see also Rose, 1986).

CLRB "REPORT ON PLANS AND PRIORITIES 1998–1999"
home.istar.ca/~clrbccrt/rpp_eng.htm

Initially, the expectation was that collective agreement arbitration would be essentially a private arrangement between the parties. Over the years, however, it has become more of a mixed or hybrid public-private system (Carter, 1997). There have been two reasons for this evolution. First, as Carter notes (1997), arbitrators have for some years been expected to apply external legislation, such as employment standards and human rights provisions. For example, in Ontario, section 48(12[j]) of the *Labour Relations Act* specifically requires arbitrators and arbitration panels to "interpret and apply human rights and other employment-related statutes, despite any conflict between these statutes and the terms of the collective agreement." The trend towards interpreting collective agreements in the light of external legislation has accelerated in recent years with the growth of the "duty to accommodate" arising out of human rights legislation (Carter, 1997). Second, in many jurisdictions (including Ontario), government has become increasingly involved in the arbitration process through expedited arbitration or mediation-arbitration systems utilizing a single arbitrator or mediator-arbitrator chosen by the Labour Minister (e.g. *OLRA*, sections 49 and 50, respectively). Such systems were set up largely to remedy some of the deficiencies long apparent with the conventional arbitration process, such as its costliness and lengthy time delays (Thornicroft and Eden, 1995:267). As we will note in more detail in Chapter 12, the evidence to date (i.e., Rose, 1986) suggests that expedited arbitration systems have indeed managed to achieve significant time and money savings without (apparently) resulting in any decline in the quality of awards.

Courts

The third institution through which LRL is administered is the court system. Prior to LRL, all labour-related legal matters were dealt with in the courts. As noted above, the outcomes were seldom favourable to workers, given that judges, in the words of Harry Arthurs (1988:19), proved "singularly inventive" in finding remedies to help protect employers against workers and labour unions, including a broad range of injunctions, severe limitations on picketing and union organizing, and convictions on both civil and criminal conspiracy charges. Even during the early postwar period (Carter, 1995:66), courts continued to exercise substantial power in regulating strikes, picketing, and bargaining-table behaviour. As the role of labour boards has expanded, that of the courts has diminished. While in principle the courts continue to play an important role, given their power to review arbitral and labour board decisions, enforce provincial labour acts, and interpret the Canadian Constitution (Carter, 1995:69), in practice their only remaining function of any importance is issuing injunctions limiting or, in some cases, barring picketing altogether (see Godard, 1994:297).[34] As was noted earlier in the chapter, fears that the Charter of Rights and Freedoms would be used to return control over most labour-related matters to the courts have thus far proved largely unfounded, as the courts have generally been reluctant to use the document to reshape the IR system (Carter, 1995:70). However, there is always the possibility that the courts could start to assume a more activist role, justifying it on Charter-related grounds.

THE IMPORTANCE OF LABOUR RELATIONS LEGISLATION

Labour relations legislation is critical in any IR system because it establishes rules for the conduct of industrial conflict and provides workers with some input into management decisions that affect their working conditions. In general, Canadian legislation is fairly voluntarist in that it regulates mainly processes, leaving most outcomes to be determined by the parties through collective bargaining. A notable exception is the compulsory conciliation procedure found in most Canadian labour acts.

Canada was among the last industrialized countries to grant its workers bargaining rights. It granted most private sector workers these rights in 1944 through wartime Order-in-Council *PC 1003*. However, public sector workers were generally denied the right to unionize until the 1960s and the passage of the *Public Service Staff Relations Act*. Within a decade after *PSSRA's* passage, almost all Canadian public sector workers had been granted bargaining rights, although many did not receive the right to strike. Since *PSSRA*, there has been little fundamental change in Canadian labour relations legislation. The Charter of Rights and Freedoms, which came into effect in 1982, has had very limited impact on labour-related matters, due to judges' general reluctance to use the document to reshape the IR system. Perhaps the most significant recent development has been a growing tendency to apply external legislation, particularly human rights legislation, to the interpretation of collective agreements. The duty to accommodate minority group members, people with disabilities, and others inadvertently discriminated against by workplace arrangements or collective agreement provisions has been held to apply up to the point of undue hardship. In some cases, arbitrators have held that this duty entails providing special work schedules for people whose religion forbids them to work on certain days; in others; it has led to the rewriting of collective agreement provisions or the waiving of their application (Carter, 1997).

CLRB REGIONAL OFFICES

home.istar.ca/~clrbccrt/reg_elst.htm?46,19

In Canada, most labour relations legislation is under provincial jurisdiction, the exception being enterprises of a clearly interprovincial nature, such as the railroads, airlines, and telecommunications companies, which fall under federal jurisdiction. Most Canadian labour acts are fairly similar to the American *Wagner Act* and to each other; however, in recent years significant patterns of interprovincial variation have arisen. Some key areas of variation include exclusions from coverage under labour relations legislation, certification procedures, first-contract arbitration, the right to use replacement workers during a strike, and management free speech provisions.

Labour relations legislation is administered by labour relations boards, arbitrators, and the courts. Of the three, labour relations boards are by far the most important. Their major functions are overseeing certifications and decertifications and policing unfair labour practice; however, in recent years their jurisdiction has expanded to include the handling of many strike-related matters. In addition, some boards have the authority to arbitrate a first contract. Although labour boards have a broad range of powers, they generally use an accommodative approach in resolving problems, rarely resorting to criminal prosecution. With the growth in importance of labour boards, the courts' role in labour-related matters has diminished considerably, and is now generally confined to issuing injunctions ordering unions to restrict or end picketing activities during strikes.

HIBERNIA AND LABOUR RELATIONS

www.wob.nf.ca/News/1998/Feb98/special_projects.htm

While most Canadian labour legislation has not changed in any fundamental way since the granting of public sector bargaining rights, the ongoing wave of globalization and free trade agreements may increase pressure on policy-makers to relax worker protections to promote economic development (Carter, 1995; Peirce, 1996). In particular, there may be pressure to harmonize Canadian to American labour relations standards, although this may not be easy to do given that, as we noted early in the chapter, Canada itself has not one but many different sets of standards, owing to the fact of provincial jurisdiction. In this connection, the growing trend towards a certification vote instead of a card count in Canadian labour acts may be a sign of things to come and will bear observation in the years ahead. It will also be interesting to see whether other provinces follow Ontario's lead and remove the labour board's authority to certify without majority support as a remedy for grossly unfair employer labour practice. If Ontario proves a trend-setter in this matter, we could be seeing the end of what has been a critical difference between the Canadian and American IR systems: this country's significantly stricter enforcement of labour legislation.

QUESTIONS FOR DISCUSSION

1) Get a copy of your province's labour relations act. Read it. Pay special attention to its preface or introductory paragraphs explaining its purpose. Does its purpose seem to be more closely related to maintaining industrial peace and promoting collective bargaining or to promoting economic growth?

2) What's the rationale for labour relations legislation (LRL)?

3) Describe the main stages in the evolution of Canadian LRL.

4) What are some major features of Canadian LRL? Compare and contrast it to American LRL.

5) What are some important provincial variations? Which ones may be of particular importance to union membership growth or decline?

6) Would your province's labour act best be described as liberal or restrictive? Why?

7) What are some distinctive features of Quebec LRL? Do any aspects of the Quebec system seem worth adopting elsewhere?

8) How is LRL administered in Canada?

9) How much effect has the *Charter* had on Canadian LRL?

10) What has been the impact of the duty to accommodate on the interpretation of Canadian LRL? What don't we yet know about that impact?

11) What are some issues which in your view Canadian LRL in general (or your province's act in particular) should be addressing but isn't?

SUGGESTIONS
FOR FURTHER READING

Adell, Bernard. (1998). Law and industrial relations: The state of the art in common law Canada. In G. Hébert et al. (Eds.) *The state of the art in industrial relations.* Kingston and Toronto: Queen's Univ. IRC and the Univ. of Toronto Centre for Industrial Relations. Contains a very useful discussion of perspectives on labour law.

Beatty, David. (1987). *Putting the 'Charter' to work: Designing a constitutional labour code.* Montreal: McGill-Queen's Univ. Press. Few labour lawyers or academic industrial relationists share Beatty's faith in the *Charter,* but he makes a compelling case nonetheless.

Bruce, Peter. (1990). "The processing of unfair labour practice cases in Canada and the U.S." *Relations Industrielles, 45.* Extremely interesting comparative study that points to stricter Canadian enforcement of labour legislation as a major cause of this country's higher union membership rates.

Carter, Donald. (1997). "The duty to accommodate: Its growing impact on the grievance arbitration process." *Relations Industrielles, 52*(1). An important article that shows just how far human rights legislation has affected arbitrators' interpretation of collective agreements.

Labour Law Casebook Group. (1991). *Labour law: Cases, materials and commentary* (5th ed.). Kingston: Queen's IRC Press. 1991. A rich source of both factual material and sophisticated interpretations of major trends in Canadian labour law. Indispensable for anyone with a serious interest in the subject.

Labour Law Under the Charter: Proceedings of a Conference ...Kingston: Queen's Law Journal and Industrial Relations Centre, 1988. Very useful set of essays explaining (or in some cases speculating about) the *Charter's* impact on labour law and the IR system. Of particular note are the introduction by Adell and the essays by Arthurs, England, Cavalluzzo, Kuttner, Fudge, and Beatty and Kennett.

Weiler, Paul. (1980). *Reconcilable differences: New directions in Canadian labour law.* Toronto: Carswell. A lucid, often witty, and always thought-provoking discussion by a man who, as chair of the B.C. labour relations board during its glory days, was "present at the creation" of many major innovations in Canadian labour law.

ENDNOTES

1 See Hebdon (1992) for an excellent discussion of this topic. For an equally interesting discussion with a slightly different emphasis, see Godard (1994:75–83).

2 On this point, see the industrial confict perspective discussed by Kervin (1984).

3 In the Philippines, for example, as noted by Jimenez (1993:233), a major cause of increased strike activity during the 1960s was management's unwillingness to recognize unions or bargain with them.

4 See Kervin (1984) on this point.

5 In Sweden (Hammarstrom, 1993), basic bargaining rights were achieved in 1906. In Denmark and in Australia, recognition came even earlier, in 1899 and 1904, respectively (Scheuer, 1992; Davis and Lansbury, 1993). In the United States, recognition came in 1935 (Carter, 1995).

6 For a more detailed discussion of the reasons for the slower evolution of unionism in North America than in Europe, see Adams (1995a:496–501).

7 As Morton notes, railway workers and others in positions where public safety was involved where excluded from the amended act's protection. The exclusion thus set in motion the beginnings of the pattern of differential regulation of private and public sector workers still in effect in most of Canada today.

8 Since 1994, Ontario's public servants have had the right to strike.

9 On this point, see the Lavigne case, involving an Ontario community college instructor who did not like the fact that his union was using his dues for political causes with which he disagreed. The Supreme Court ruled in favour of the union, declaring that the union's freedom to spend dues for the collective good of the membership constituted a reasonable limitation on the Charter's freedom of association provision. For a more detailed discussion, see Swinton (1995:66–8).

10 Every Canadian jurisdiction has at least one act applying to some part or other of the public sector. Though Saskatchewan's public servants are under the province's general labour act, special acts are applied to public schoolteachers, police, and firefighters. The proliferation of public sector laws has been most extreme in Ontario, where separate acts apply to civil servants, police, firefighters, teachers, and hospital workers (Swimmer and Thompson, 1995:7–8).

11 Under the "laboratory of democracy" argument from political science implicitly advanced by Carter (1995:56), provinces or states are more likely to introduce legislative innovations than national governments because the risk in introducing the innovations at this lower level is far less. The "laboratory of democracy" argument also suggests that successful experiments will spread to other jurisdictions, as has indeed been the case in Canada. Some of Weiler's innovations, such as the use of grievance mediation in connection with expedited arbitration, have since spread to several other provinces.

12 Ontario's Conservative government recently (June, 1998) deprived the labour relations board of the ability to impose certification with less than majority support as a penalty for grossly unfair employer labour practices (G. Adams, 1998).

13 While the provisions just described are directly mainly at employers, a number of jurisdictions, including Nova Scotia and Alberta, have adopted comparable provisions aimed at unions giving the labour board the power to dismiss a certification application in cases where the union's unfair practice resulted in employees' true wishes not becoming known.

14 For a useful and more detailed discussion of this point, see Godard (1994:349–50).

15 In the federal jurisdiction, striking workers' rights have recently been strengthened by changes in the *Canada Labour Code* that bar the use of replacement workers where that use is determined to be engaged in for the purpose of undermining the union rather than in pursuit of legitimate management bargaining objectives. In addition, striking employees in the federal jurisdiction are now entitled to maintain employer-administered or third-party insurance programs without interruption by the employer, providing that the employees or their unions pay the full premium costs of such benefit plans for the duration of the strike or lockout. These changes are based directly on recommendations of the Sims Commission. For a useful discussion, see Sims (1996:Chapter 9).

16 Significantly, Saskatchewan, the one province that adopted a more or less 'pure' Wagner model, did not initially require grievance arbitration, changing its law to do so only in 1994.

17 The *OLRA's* provision refers only to employers.

18 This trend toward a "quickie" vote appears to have accompanied the broader Canadian trend away from simple card counts and toward certification votes. In jurisdictions using a simple card count, employer interference would be less of an issue and the need for a quick vote less compelling.

19 In Ontario, the application must be made during the last two months of agreements of three years or less. For longer agreements, the application must be made during the last two months of the agreement's third and subsequent years (*OLRA*, section 63[2]).

20 This provision also applies to employers who might be trying to persuade employees not to join. One suspects, however, that it is aimed primarily at unions. Note that employer free speech provisions such as *OLRA*, sec. 70, would appear to conflict with this provision— unless one assumes that employers contact employees only at their homes after working hours.

21 In June, 1998, the Ontario government removed this power from the Ontario Labour Relations Board (G. Adams, 1998). The policy change is widely believed to have resulted from the Board's certification of a union at a Wal-Mart department store in the face of a 151 to 43 vote against certification (*Canada Labour Views*, 1997:3–4).

22 Except as otherwise indicated, factual information about existing legislative provisions has been drawn from CCH (1998d).

23 Had Table 8.1 been prepared while Ontario's NDP government was still in power, that province would have had five liberal laws and one moderately liberal one. One of the Conservative government's first acts on taking over from the NDP in 1995 was to amend the labour relations act by restoring professional exclusions removed by the NDP and changing the certification procedure from a card count to a vote.

24 See Peirce (1989) for a more detailed discussion of the points raised in this paragraph.

25 For an interesting discussion of these issues, see LLCG (1984:3–16 to 3–25).

26 Thompson (1982:385) suggested that the professional exclusions then in force in five jurisdictions were "clearly exceptional," and that those provinces would likely "join the

national pattern" in time. Given that over the past 15 years, there has been no lasting change—Ontario dropped its professional exclusions in 1992 only to re-insert them in 1995—his forecast would seem to have been optimistic, to put it mildly.

[27] See Beatty (1983) for an interesting and quite philosophical discussion of this exclusion, and of the philosophy behind Canadian exclusion policies more generally.

[28] The Ontario Labour Relations Board has specifically ruled that the union's obligations to represent workers fairly extends to those who are not union members. See Craig and Solomon (1996:450).

[29] Quebec's anti-scab bill, discussed in the text above, was brought in following a picket-line incident that led to loss of life.

[30] In this connection, the linguistic vagueness of many of the provisions is quite troubling. For example, what constitutes "undue" influence over employees? How can a labour board distinguish between reasonable and "undue" influence? And what constitutes a "fact or opinion reasonably held" under the B.C. legislation?

[31] Several labour lawyers with whom the author has talked regarding this matter indicate that this is in fact the case. As well, the discussion in Godard (1994:296) strongly implies that this is the case, since the discussion does not mention any specific legislative provisions. For a more detailed discussion, see LLCG (1984:3–62 through 3–64).

[32] The full title of the statute, "An Act Respecting Labour Relations, Vocational Training and Manpower Management in the Construction Industry," is far too cumbersome to be used in the text.

[33] In Ontario (*OLRA*, section 104[1–2]), these can go up to $2000 per day for an individual and $25,000 per day for a corporation or union.

[34] As Godard notes (1994:297), in British Columbia, even this function has been assumed by the Labour Relations Board. It is not clear to this writer why more provinces haven't followed B.C.'s enlightened lead. Having all labour-related matters including picketing administered by a single tribunal would seem to be both more consistent and more efficient.

CHAPTER 9

LABOUR RELATIONS AND COLLECTIVE BARGAINING IN THE PUBLIC SECTOR

"Blackboard Jungle."
Thousands of teachers could
well lose their jobs in ongoing
educational restructuring
across Ontario.

The public sector is of critical importance in the Canadian IR system because of the often essential nature of the work it performs and because public sector strikes can have severe consequences for the general public. It is also important because nearly half the country's union members work there, and because, like public sectors throughout most of the industrialized world, it has recently been under severe stress because of government fiscal crises. After noting these points and indicating who should be considered a public sector employee, we begin with a discussion of the evolution of public sector collective bargaining, an evolution quite different from that of collective bargaining in the private sector. From there, we go on to consider some special

features of public sector bargaining, including employee and employer differences, legislative differences, the narrower scope of bargaining generally permitted there, and special dispute resolution methods such as conventional and final-offer arbitration and the controlled strike. We conclude the chapter with a look at the current state of public sector labour legislation and collective bargaining.

THE IMPORTANCE OF THE PUBLIC SECTOR

The public sector is important to IR students for a variety of reasons. First and perhaps foremost is the often essential nature of the work it performs. Public sector workers teach our children, care for our sick, and look after the needs of social assistance recipients, in addition to performing a host of other jobs ranging from garbage collection and snow removal to issuing driver's and marriage licenses. In many cases, there is no readily available substitute for the services provided through the public sector (Gunderson and Reid, 1995:158). If a shoe factory goes on strike, it is normally easy enough to obtain another brand of shoe. But if public schoolteachers go on strike (as happened in 1997 and 1998 in Ontario), parents can't simply turn around and find another school. If public transit workers go on strike (as happened in 1991 in Toronto), people *can* try to get to work or to medical appointments some other way, but the result is a serious inconvenience for many, real hardship for some, and frayed nerves, snarled traffic, and fouled air all around. Thus the effects of public sector strikes tend to be more severe than those of private sector ones (Gunderson and Reid, 1995), and also more readily apparent.

The public sector is also important because it makes up a sizeable share of the country's work force and a very large share indeed of its union membership. In recent years, public sector unions and leaders have played an increasingly important role in the Canadian labour movement (Rose, 1995:47). Given the high proportion of women in many public sector fields, women are particularly prominent in the public sector labour movement, representing a clear majority of total public sector union members and of the membership in two key sub-sectors: health care and education (Swimmer and Thompson, 1995:5). With their high proportion of female members, the public sector unions have become leaders in the fight for paid maternity leave and employment and pay equity (Swimmer and Thompson, 1995).

Finally, the public sector is important to IR students because of the state of crisis it is in, not just in Canada but throughout most of the industrialized world (Beaumont, 1995). Faced with growing and seemingly intractable deficits, and increasingly unable or unwilling to balance the books by increasing taxes, governments everywhere have sought to reduce the one cost seemingly within their control: that of public sector workers' compensation. For the most part, cost reductions have not been obtained through collective bargaining (Swimmer and Thompson, 1995). Across the country, governments have resorted to legislation freezing public sector pay or even reducing it, sometimes by as much as 8.5 percent (Fryer, 1995).[1] Aside from legislation freezing salaries and/or suspending collective bargaining, Canadian government strategies for reducing public sector labour costs have included privatization, contracting out, downsizing, reorganization of work, and a greater use of "atypical" work arrangements such as part-time or temporary work, fixed-term contracts, homework, and even volunteers (Rose, 1995:35). Over the past five years, major restructuring of the health-care and education systems imposed unilaterally by provincial governments in Alberta and Ontario has led, and is still leading, to hospital and school closures and widespread layoffs (Haiven, 1995:268; Thomason, 1995:303).[2] Not surprisingly, such hard-line government tactics have led to increased union militancy and higher rates of public sector strikes (again, a worldwide phenomenon).[3] Through the first half of the 1990s (Workplace Information Directorate, 1998), public sector strikes accounted for roughly 15 to 25 percent of all person-days lost.[4] In 1996, this figure increased to 42 percent; by 1997, it had reached 55 percent. During the fall of 1998, more than 130 000 secondary school teachers across Ontario, upset at the loss of preparation time and the government's imposition of a heavier teaching load took strike action (Mahoney, 1998; Galt, 1998; Green, 1998). In Ottawa, public servants angered by the federal government's plan to appeal the Human Rights Tribunal's pay equity award held a massive demonstration on Parliament Hill on September 21, 1998 (PSAC, 1998).

WAGES LIABILITY ACT

canada.justice.gc.ca/FTP/EN/Laws/Chap/W/W-1.txt

Through most of the 1990s, free public sector collective bargaining has been more the exception than the rule. The suspension of bargaining rights in the federal public service has become so routine that at least one observer (Swimmer, 1995:405) has suggested that the government might well remove the right to collective bargaining permanently. Similar sentiments have been expressed by observers of the provincial scene. With regard to Quebec, Gérard Hébert (1995:227–228) notes that many have asked whether public sector collective bargaining in the province has become passé; for his part, he believes it died in 1982 (Hébert,1995:230). Only slightly less pessimistically, John Fryer (1995:365) believes provincial public service collective bargaining will survive, but only in a significantly altered form. The question of the survival of public sector collective bargaining is one to which we shall return at the end of the chapter.

Who Is a Public Sector Worker?

For the purposes of this discussion, the public sector includes the federal and provincial civil services, municipalities, health care, education, and government enterprises such as the CBC and Ontario Hydro. Between 1977 and 1996, the percentage of working Canadians employed in the public sector remained relatively steady at between 21 and 24 percent; however, this apparent stability masks important changes occurring in many parts of the public sector. Since the mid-1980s, certain parts of that sector, notably health care, education, and municipal work, have grown more rapidly than others (Rose, 1995:31). Between 1984 and 1994, provincial government employment grew only modestly, while federal government employment was largely stagnant (Rose, 1995). Because of severe budgetary restraints affecting virtually all levels of government across Canada, the prospects for continued growth are extremely doubtful. Indeed, as we noted in Chapter 2 (the economy), employment in public administration *declined* by about 15 percent between 1993 and 1997. As for health care and education, which have been the main public sector growth areas, governments may find it more difficult to cut employment in these sectors than in their own departments. Given Canada's aging population, the demand for health care, in particular, should continue to increase. However, ongoing restructuring efforts in provinces such as Alberta, Ontario, and B.C. (Haiven, 1995; Thomason, 1995) could lead to lasting employment reductions in these sectors. Indeed, as Table 9.1 shows, by 1996, employment in education had begun to decline from the peak reached in 1994. While health-care employment continued to increase, it was doing so at a far slower rate than it had for most of the recent past. The modest increase in health care was not enough to make up for the declines in public administration and education employment; thus the actual number of Canadians working in the public sector was lower in 1996 than in 1994, and the proportion was down by more than 1 percent (see Table 9.1).

Because union density rates are far higher in the public than in the private sector, public sector workers make up a much larger share of the country's union members than of its work force. While many private sector unions saw their membership rolls drop during the 1980s and early 1990s, major public sector unions such as CUPE continued to grow (Rose, 1995:25), as did teachers' unions, nurses' unions, and police and firefighters' unions (op. cit.). Rose (1995:24) estimates that in 1992, public sector unionists accounted for almost 55 percent of the country's union membership, a significant increase from its 43 percent share in 1984 (Rose, 1995:23). Since 1992, as we noted already, there have been some declines in public sector employment, especially in public administration, due mainly to downsizing, privatization, and contracting-out. These declines have led to drops in membership in a number of public sector unions, particularly in the federal public service. As Rose (1995:25)

Table 9.1

			Health/			Pub. as
Year	**Pub. Adm.**	**Education**	**Welfare**	**Total Pub.**	**Total**	**% of total**
1977	723.8	716.9	796.2	2 236.9	9 978.2	23.4
1981	793.3	732.1	931.2	2 456.6	11 398.0	21.6
1986	829.1	798.9	1 113.0	2 741.0	12 094.5	22.6
1991	872.9	888.5	1 314.1	2 975.5	12 916.1	23.0
1994	877.4	959.0	1 388.2	3 224.6	13 291.7	24.3
1996	820.1	929.0	1 425.7	3 174.8	13 676.2	23.2
1997	791.0	962.0	1 425.0	3 178.0	13 941.0	22.8

EMPLOYMENT (IN THOUSANDS), CANADIAN PUBLIC SECTOR AND VARIOUS SUB-SECTORS SELECTED YEARS 1977–1997

Pub. Adm. = Public Administration

Total Pub. = Total public sector employment (sum of public administration, education, and health and welfare). Government enterprise employees are not included.

Data used are unadjusted annual averages for the various years.

Note: The ratio of public to total employment is significantly lower here than in Swimmer and Thompson (1995:4, Table 1) because we have included self-employment in total employment figures, whereas Swimmer and Thompson have not. Their total employment figure includes only those in employee status in the public and private sectors.

Source: Statistics Canada, Cat. No. 71-201-XPB (Historical Labour Force Statistics)

notes, PSAC has been in a decline for more than a decade. Still, high density rates allowed the public sector, according to our estimates, to account for just over 49 percent of the country's union membership in 1996.[5] While this rate may well decline further over the next few years given the likelihood of continuing cutbacks in public sector employment, public sector unionists are almost certain to remain a critical element of the country's labour movement for the future.

THE DEVELOPMENT OF PUBLIC SECTOR UNIONISM

Why Public Sector Unionism Developed Slowly

Two important facts about the growth of Canadian public sector unionism should be noted at the outset. First, it came a good deal later than private sector unionism. Most Canadian public sector workers did not acquire the right to join unions until after the passage of the *Public Service Staff Relations Act (PSSRA)* in 1967—23 years after private sector workers acquired that right through *PC 1003* (discussed in the labour history and labour law chapters). Such a time lag between the granting of private and public sector union rights is quite normal in Western industrialized countries. In the United States, the lag between the *Wagner Act* and President Kennedy's executive order granting federal public servants limited bargaining rights was 26 years (Mills, 1989:536–537). Likewise, there was a lag of several decades between private and public sector bargaining rights in such European countries as France (Lorwin, 1954) and Sweden (Johnston, 1962).[6] The reason for such a lag is that the problem of providing essential public services under an IR regime that permits public sector workers to strike is one that few governments seem ready to confront until they have had substantial experience with private sector disputes.

The second important fact about Canadian public sector unionism is that, in contrast to private sector unionism, which developed rather slowly, it "emerged full-blown in a very compressed time span" (Ponak, 1982:343). In 1960, aside from some outside municipal workers, public schoolteachers (Ponak, 1982:344), and those in the province of Saskatchewan, very few public sector workers had joined unions. By the mid to late 1970s, the vast majority had (Ponak, 1982:350). The extremely rapid evolution of public sector collective bargaining meant that certain growing pains were inevitable. In particular, finding appropriate bargaining structures and dispute resolution procedures proved (and continues to prove) extremely difficult (Ponak, 1982).

The Early Years: Public Employee Associations

The late emergence of Canadian public sector collective bargaining should not be taken to mean that public sector employees never engaged in any form of collective action. There was some form of public sector employee organization as early as the late nineteenth century (Rose, 1995:31), and by the end of the First World War, associations of public employees had become fairly prominent (Ponak, 1982:345; Fryer, 1995:347). Although these associations were to prove critical to the eventual emergence of full-blown public sector unionism, they initially operated very differently from trade unions. Among other things, they sought to avoid confrontation with employers, had no compulsory membership requirements, did not affiliate with labour federations, and included management personnel up to the most senior levels (Ponak, 1982:345). While the associations undertook various social activities, they also played a consultative role by presenting to government employees' concerns about wages and working conditions (Fryer, 1995:347).

Throughout the pre-war period and well into the postwar period, such consultation marked the limit of permissible collective action for the vast majority of Canadian public sector employees. Before the Second World War, with even most private sector workers effectively barred from joining unions due to employer opposition and the lack of protective legislation, any significant degree of public employee organization was simply not a serious possibility.[7] After the war, labour relations legislation in every jurisdiction except Saskatchewan continued to exclude public sector workers, other than some municipal workers (see Graham, 1995) and a few public schoolteachers. Public employers were generally opposed to unionism on the grounds that collective bargaining would inevitably lead to strikes and thus to disruption of essential services and possibly even threats to public safety (Ponak, 1982:347). Another, even more fundamental basis for opposition to public employee unionization was the sovereignty notion (see Fryer, 1995). What this notion means is that government bodies such as legislatures are vested with certain powers, especially over fiscal matters, that cannot be shared or taken away. Collective bargaining would, so sovereignty proponents argued, be unconstitutional in that it would diminish those powers by forcing revisions in government budgets (Ponak and Thompson, 1989:376–377). The clearest statement of the doctrine was made in 1964 by Quebec Premier Jean Lesage: "The Queen does not negotiate with her subjects!" (Ironically, just a year after issuing this lofty pronouncement, Lesage found himself essentially doing just that, as his province became the second, after Saskatchewan, to grant public sector workers full collective bargaining rights, including the right to strike.)

In addition, many public sector workers, particularly white-collar and professional ones, didn't like what they saw traditional unionism as representing. Many were skeptical about the possibilities of collective action and most disliked the adversarial tone characteristic of union-management relations in industrial settings. Professionals generally believed collective action, especially strikes, to be unprofessional; historically most had worked under a collegial system whereby their views were incorporated into management decisions (Thompson, 1982) and could rely on professional associations to protect their economic self-interest. Others believed that the nature of their public service obligations, including particularly the need to maintain continuous service, ruled out collective bargaining (Ponak, 1982:346). It should also be noted that, prior to the Second World War, most government departments and other public sector organizations were generally quite small. For the most part, those working in such organizations would have known their co-workers and immediate superiors and subordinates quite well. In such small, intimate organizations, it may have been easier to work out problems informally than it would be later on, when government departments and other public sector organizations grew into large, impersonal bureaucracies (see Heron, 1989).

Association-Consultation: The NJC Experience

Through the early 1960s, the most common form of public employee action was association-consultation, whereby members of employee associations would consult, either formally or informally, with public sector management to express employees' concerns regarding pay, working conditions, and other aspects of the employment relationship. Perhaps the best-known consultative body was the National Joint Council (NJC), established in 1944 to address the needs of federal public servants. Comprising representatives from about a dozen civil service staff associations (the Staff Side) and senior government officials (the Official Side), the NJC would meet when necessary to consider such issues as recruitment, training, hours of work, promotion, discipline, tenure, pay, health, welfare, and seniority (Ponak, 1982:348). When the two sides managed to reach agreement on an issue, a recommendation would be made to Cabinet. Since the Council included senior government officials, the idea was that its recommendations would be quickly accepted by the government. All too often, this did not happen. For one thing, the scope of discussable issues was narrower than the Staff Side had expected. Most notably, wages were outside the NJC's jurisdiction, which forced the associations to submit salary briefs directly to the government (Ponak, 1982). Another serious problem was the lack of any mechanism to resolve disputes between the two sides. If the Official Side said "No," the matter was determined unilaterally by government, and that was that (Ponak, 1982). As well, the NJC's decisions were merely advisory. While its recommendations would usually be accepted by government in the end, often there were preliminary rejections, lengthy delays, and amendments to the recommendations, all of which had the effect of breeding considerable frustration on the part of civil servants (Ponak, 1982:349).

By the 1950s, the NJC's lack of any real power caused an increasing number of staff associations to question its value. Throughout the 1950s and into the 1960s, the lack of wage increases, the rapid growth of government departments into large, impersonal bureaucracies, and a general climate of social change and questioning of authority helped move most public servants away from association-consultation and towards conventional trade unionism (Heron, 1989; Ponak, 1982:349). The latter began to look more and more attractive after New York City schoolteachers won a hefty wage increase in the aftermath of a widely publicized strike in 1961 (Ponak, 1982:349). Recognizing that consultation was simply not meeting their members' needs, the associations began deleting no-strike clauses, excluding management personnel, hiring full-time staff, and affiliating with major labour federations such as the CLC (Ponak, 1982). The "last straw" was when John Diefenbaker's minority Conservative government rejected an NJC-recommended wage increase as inflationary (Swimmer, 1995:368–369). After his government fell (over a different issue), public service bargaining rights became a major issue in the ensuing election campaign, and the Liberals, under Lester Pearson, promised that, if elected, they would grant those rights with binding arbitration (Swimmer, 1995:369).

Transition to Collective Bargaining

Elected in 1963, Pearson and his Liberals had struck a commission to develop a model for public service bargaining when they were overtaken by a series of events, of which the most important was an illegal nation-wide postal strike in 1965 (Swimmer, 1995). The strike, to which most Canadians were reasonably sympathetic (Swimmer, 1995), apparently made government officials realize that, for many public employees, arbitration would no longer suffice. Also propelling the Liberal government towards granting fuller public service bargaining rights was its tenuous minority position, with the balance of power held by the pro-labour NDP. When, after the success of the postal strike, many of the old associations began demanding the right to strike, the government (as a matter of political expediency) came up with the then-novel choice of procedures mechanism (Swimmer, 1995), which it later enshrined in the *Public Service Staff Relations Act (PSSRA).*

PSSRA and Its Impacts

Passed in 1967, *PSSRA* gave federal servants the right to join unions. The unions were given the right to choose between binding interest arbitration and the conventional conciliation-strike route at the start of each bargaining round. To protect the public safety, union members designated as essential (*PSSRA*, section 78[1]) are not allowed to strike. To compensate for this limitation on the right to strike, the employer is not allowed to lock workers out (*PSSRA*:371). The legislation also created the Public Service Staff Relations Board (PSSRB) to administer the act. One of the Board's major functions was to determine appropriate public service bargaining units. The PSSRB determined those bargaining units along occupational rather than departmental lines, which meant a complicated system of 76 bargaining units (*PSSRA*, section 78[1]).[8]

After *PSSRA*, public sector unionization grew very quickly. There were three reasons for this. First, the existing associations proved an ideal membership base for the public service unions. For the most part, association members joined one of the public service unions en masse, eliminating the need for extensive membership campaigns (Ponak, 1982:350). Second, public employers generally accepted unionization. The lack of employer opposition meant that certification could proceed quite rapidly once the unions had signed up the old association members. Finally, *PSSRA* was to set in motion a wave of legislation providing first provincial public servants (Fryer, 1995:343) and then other public sector workers, such as teachers and nurses, with collective bargaining rights. By the early 1970s, every province had granted its public servants the right to join unions (Fryer, 1995). Some provinces adopted a variation of *PSSRA*, providing the right to strike; others (including Alberta and Ontario[9]) adopted an administrative model with binding arbitration as the dispute resolution procedure (Fryer, 1995:345–346).

The unionization of public sector employees had a dramatic effect on both the size and character of the Canadian labour movement. Between 1965, when Quebec liberalized its labour act to grant public servants the right to unionize, and 1978, the end of the great wave of public sector legislation, Canadian union membership more than doubled from 1.59 million to 3.28 million. The country's union density rate also increased sharply, from 29.7 percent to 39.0 percent (Chaison, 1982:149). No less dramatic was the change in the labour movement's character. In 1960, most union members were male and blue-collar (Ponak and Thompson, 1995:423). By the 1970s, many were women and many of the male members were white-collar workers or professionals. The Canadian Union of Public Employees (CUPE) had become the country's largest union (Morton, 1995:149). Its heavily female membership and those of other public sector unions would push demands for maternity leave, flexible work hours, and anti-discrimination provisions, while professionals and white-collar workers pushed professional development issues, such as support for in-service education and travel to conferences (see Ponak, 1982:351). Initially, the new union members were often less militant than their private sector counterparts. Particularly in white-collar and professional units, they tended to favour cooperative mechanisms such as joint committees, to prefer arbitration to strikes, and to be somewhat reluctant to file grievances (Ponak, 1982:351–352).

CANADIAN UNION OF PUBLIC EMPLOYEES
www.cupe.ca

From the 1960s through 1975, public sector unions negotiated significant improvements in wages and working conditions. Special attention was paid to the correction of long-standing salary anomalies in lower-paid, largely female-dominated job classifications (Fryer, 1995:349). Throughout most of this period, public sector collective bargaining operated quite well with only moderate government interference in the form of back-to-work legislation, much of that being in Quebec (Ponak and Thompson, 1995:440).[10]

PROVINCIAL AND TERRITORIAL GOVERNMENT EMPLOYMENT, WAGES, AND SALARIES
www.statcan.ca:80/cgi-in/Cansim/cansim.cgi?matrix=2866&cq=&order_id=

End of the Golden Age

This "Golden Age" of public sector collective bargaining, as it has since become known, ended abruptly on Thanksgiving Day 1975, with the federal government's imposition of a three-year program of wage and price controls. (These were discussed extensively in the labour history chapter.) While the controls applied to all workers, they appear to have demonstrated to government the political advantages of restraining public sector compensation (Ponak and Thompson, 1995:444).

At this time, as well, a number of governments began to take a harder line in their approach to labour issues generally and public sector labour issues in particular.[11] At least in part, they may have been responding to growing public outrage at the frequent, lengthy strikes in the Montreal Transit system and the post office, a feeling that the highly publicized "public be damned" attitude of certain postal union leaders did little to diminish (Swimmer, 1995:385–386). In 1978, as inside postal workers were negotiating their first agreement after the end of controls, the federal government passed legislation to extend their contract until after the upcoming federal election (Swimmer, 1995), confident that the postal workers would not find much sympathy from a public that had been deprived of mail service for six weeks in 1975. The late 1970s also saw sharp reductions in federal government employment levels, which up till then had been increasing steadily since the beginning of the decade (Swimmer, 1995:377, Table 3). On another front, the government moved to restrict public servants' bargaining rights substantially in a series of amendments to *PSSRA* introduced in 1978. While the amendments, including restriction of the right to strike, extension of managerial exclusions, introduction of the lockout right, and the tying of arbitration awards to private sector compensation norms, were eventually withdrawn in the face of strong public opposition (Thompson and Ponak, 1995:427), they pointed the direction for future federal public service labour policy. In Quebec, the government took the first steps towards the comprehensive essential services legislation it passed in 1982 (Hébert, 1995:214).

Perhaps not surprisingly, public sector unions responded to these developments with a show of increased militancy. For example, they were among the leaders in the labour movement's nationwide protest against the Trudeau government's wage and price controls. Beginning in 1976, the public sector share of total person-days lost to strikes began to increase (Gunderson and Reid, 1995:138–139). Starting around 1980, the percentage of disputes settled through arbitration began to decline, suggesting, among other things, a preference for strike action as opposed to arbitration on the part of public sector workers (Ponak and Thompson, 1995:437).[12] The public sector also began to feature high grievance rates (Ponak and Thompson, 1995:429). Overall, public sector union members had begun behaving more like their private sector counterparts, due to an increasingly difficult economic environment, as well as the growing restrictions placed on their activities by governments across Canada.

The 1980s: Wage Controls and Restraint

In 1982, the federal government responded to a second wave of inflation by imposing another round of controls. This time the controls were applied exclusively to wages and only in the public sector. By 1983, every province had followed Ottawa's lead and limited public sector compensation in some way or another (Ponak and Thompson, 1989); six provinces had adopted formal control programs of their own (Fryer, 1995:350). The harshest measures were taken in Quebec, where public sector workers saw their pay rolled back by about 20 percent (Hébert, 1995:222), and in British Columbia, where a right-wing government not only imposed a public sector wage freeze, but also made drastic (25 percent) cuts in government employment levels (Morton, 1989:177; Thompson and Ponak, 1992:308). In Alberta, where public servants and many other public sector workers did not have the right to strike, arbitrators were ordered to take the government's ability to pay into account in fashioning public employee arbitration awards (see Haiven, 1995:246).

EFFECTIVE WAGE INCREASES FOR NEW SETTLEMENTS
www.statcan.ca:80/cgi-in/Cansim/cansim.cgi?matrix=4058&cq=&order_id=

The wave of retrenchment was not limited to compensation issues. In 1982, in the wake of a disagreement over designation levels in an air traffic controllers' dispute, the Supreme Court of Canada ruled that the government had the sole right to determine the level of service to be provided (Swimmer, 1995:381). The decision in effect removed most of the PSSRB's adjudicative role and led to a sharp increase in federal public service designation levels after 1982 (Swimmer, 1995:379–381). In 1983, the Alberta government passed legislation outlawing hospital strikes in the province (Haiven, 1995:254). Meanwhile, in Quebec, a government weary of the public sector strikes that it had often been forced to end through legislation, passed essential services legislation designed to protect the public's health and safety during labour disputes.[13] In 1982, it established an Essential Services Council to manage and maintain essential services during public sector disputes (Boivin and Déom, 1995:471). The Council's major task is to evaluate whether the essential services set out in a list or an agreement between the parties are essential to ensure the public health and safety during the strike, and to verify that those services are being provided (Boivin and Déom, 1995:482). Under the essential services legislation, the parties must come up with an agreement on the definition of essential services before any strike can become legal. If the parties cannot agree, the union's list of proposed services is submitted to the Council for approval (Boivin and Déom, 1995). The Council's remedies include the power to issue back-to-work orders, to require the parties to go back to the bargaining table, or to accelerate an arbitration procedure (Boivin and Déom, 1995).

Having already unilaterally extended existing public sector agreements until December 1985 (Hébert, 1995:222), the Quebec government placed further restrictions on public sector unions with its 1985 *Act respecting the process of negotiation of the collective agreements in the public and parapublic sectors*. The Act provided for province-wide bargaining on most issues, though some local issues could be negotiated at that level. Management committees were made up of an equal number of representatives from the various management associations and government departments concerned. The Treasury Board chairman provided the terms of reference to all management committees, and no agreement could be signed that went against those terms of reference, or without explicit Treasury Board approval (Hébert, 1995:223–224). In effect, this gave the Treasury Board complete control over the entire collective bargaining process (Boivin, 1989:429). The Act also established a separate, autonomous Compensation Bureau, to study and publish wage comparisons between the public and private sectors (Hébert, 1995:225). On the union side, the right to strike was made subject to a whole gamut of dispute resolution procedures and time restrictions, including mediation, a notice to the Minister about the mediation report, an essential service designation process, and a seven-day notice concerning the strike date (Hébert, 1995:24). In addition, the right to strike was removed completely for all matters negotiated at the local level (Boivin, 1989:429). While the Act was bitterly opposed by the province's unions (Boivin, 1989:430), their opposition was unavailing, although they did have the satisfaction of seeing the government that had introduced it defeated in the December 1985 provincial election.

The attack on public sector unions went farthest in British Columbia where, in 1987, a sweeping revision of labour relations legislation sought to shift the balance of power away from workers and unions and towards employers (Shields, 1990). Though the B.C. government's attack on labour was not confined to the public sector, its effects were felt most sharply there. Among other things, Bill 19, passed by the Social Credit government of William Vander Zalm, replaced the province's tripartite labour relations board with an Industrial Relations Council headed by a commissioner selected by the government (Shields, 1990:52). This "labour czar" was given sweeping powers to impose mediation, binding conventional or final-offer arbitration, or a public interest inquiry board on the bargaining process (Shields, 1990:58). With regard to essential services, the Labour Minister was given the power to declare a category of workers essential whenever a dispute posed a threat to the province's economy or to residents' health, safety, and welfare. In the public sector, collective bargaining was subjected to the "ability to pay" clause, which made the government's ability to pay the primary consideration in all public sector settlements. In effect, this marked the abolition of free public sector collective bargaining over wages and its replacement with a state of permanent[14] wage controls, with compensation levels to be determined unilaterally by Cabinet (Shields, 1990).

STATISTICS CANADA "FEDERAL PUBLIC SECTOR EMPLOYMENT, WAGES, AND SALARIES"

www.statcan.ca:80/cgi-in/Cansim/cansim.cgi?matrix=2718&cq=&order_id=

Bill 19 was never accepted by the province's labour movement, which responded by boycotting the Industrial Relations Commission established under the legislation (Shields, 1990:62–63). In addition, it was sharply criticized by prominent third-party neutrals such as mediator Jim Dorsey (Shields, 1990:65), then-Liberal leader Gordon Gibson (Shields, 1990:63), and even by some members of the business community who felt that the bill gave the government too much power in industrial relations matters. The bill was also unpopular with the general public, who according to various public opinion surveys would have preferred a less confrontational approach to industrial relations (Shields, 1990:63–64). While the immediate cause of the Vander Zalm government's collapse was the Premier's unsavoury financial dealings (Shields, 1990:71), the labour bill may also have played a role (Shields, 1990).

The 1990s: Retrenchment and Restructuring

The 1990s have been by far the most difficult period for public sector workers since they began bargaining collectively. Like the 1980s, the present decade has been marked by public sector wage freezes and rollbacks and the suspension of collective bargaining (Fryer, 1995:350). The result has been that pay increases for most public sector workers have lagged well behind the inflation rate (Fryer, 1995:351; Swimmer, 1995:383). However, governments in this decade have gone even further than did those of the 1980s. For one thing, sharp reductions in federal transfer payments have put severe pressure on the provinces, causing many of them to reduce programs and services and lay off public sector workers (see Fryer, 1995:351). For another, a number of provinces, including most notably Alberta and Ontario, have engaged in wholesale restructuring and downsizing of their public services—a process that has already cost many public sector jobs and will almost certainly cost many more. Such developments as privatization, contracting-out, and the use of short-term and temporary contracts have all served to put public sector workers' jobs increasingly at risk (Rose, 1995:35). Not surprisingly, public sector unions have emphasized job security issues on the comparatively rare occasions when they have been able to engage in collective bargaining (Rose, 1995:45). Also not surprisingly, given the growing lack of job security and what Rose describes as governments' "uncanny ability to provoke public sector unions" (Rose, 1995:47), those unions have begun to take an increasingly militant line, urging their members to vote against governing parties in elections (see Aubry and Bryden, 1998), waging aggressive publicity campaigns against the government policies that are costing members their jobs, and accounting for an increasingly large share of the country's strike incidence.

The Federal Government and the 1991 Public Service Strike

Once again, the federal government set the tone for public sector bargaining across the country. On February 26, 1991, Finance Minister Michael Wilson told federal civil servants that any wage increases could only be achieved at a proportional cost in jobs (Fryer, 1995:351; Swimmer, 1995:398).[15] Moreover, annual wage increases greater than 3 percent would not be considered for the next three years (Swimmer, 1995:398). This hard-line stance, taken at a time when the government was proposing many changes to public servants' working conditions through the "PS 2000" initiative, turned employees against "PS 2000," which promised greater employee empowerment through a streamlining of classification and staffing procedures (see Swimmer, 1995:396–398, 400). How, cynical employees started asking themselves, could the government seriously be preaching empowerment at a time when it was removing its own employees' right to bargain over money? Even more important, the government's action would lead to a full-scale public service strike, the first in the country's history, in September of 1991. Though in one sense the public servants could be said to have lost the strike, since the government legislated them back to work and unilaterally extended their old agreement with a wage freeze for the first year and a 3 percent increase for the second (Swimmer, 1995:399–400), in another sense they and their union, the Public Service Alliance of Canada (PSAC), may have come out ahead. Prior to the strike, many members of the general public appear to have shared government officials' prevailing view of public servants as underworked, overpaid "fat cats."[16] Thanks to an astute public relations campaign and a conciliation board report that recommended a 6 percent increase for PSAC's administrative group in the first year and a smaller amount in the second, the union was able to correct that misperception and demonstrate to the public that the vast majority of public servants were hard-working men and women attempting to get by on modest salaries (Swimmer, 1995). The union was also helped in its PR campaign by a PSSRB finding that the government had not bargained in good faith, which demonstrated to the public that the government had in effect provoked the strike it was now trying to outlaw (Swimmer, 1995:400). In the long run, PSAC's militancy may have helped the union's internal solidarity as well, though its decision to punish non-designated members who worked during the strike did little for morale in the short term (Swimmer, 1995).

While the union's tough stance may have won it both respect and improved pension and work-force adjustment benefits (Swimmer, 1995), it didn't change the government's wage control policy. Indeed, in November of 1992, just slightly over a year after the massive public service strike, the government took an even harder line in unilaterally extending the wage freeze for a further two years. This meant that federal public servants had a wage increase of only 3 percent over a four-year period (Swimmer, 1995:401), a rate far below inflation even in the recessionary 1990s. At a time of major government restructuring and downsizing, including the elimination of prominent government agencies such as the Economic Council, Science Council, and Law Reform Commission, the new wage freeze destroyed what little credibility the government had left with the public service unions. Abandoning its traditional stance of political neutrality, PSAC vowed to work for the Conservatives' defeat in the 1993 federal election (Swimmer, 1995:400).

When the Conservatives lost to Jean Chrétien's Liberals in that election, public servants and their unions were cautiously optimistic. Liberal governments had generally been, if not sympathetic, less unsympathetic to public servants than Conservative ones. Moreover, the Liberals had in their "Red Book" of campaign promises pledged to restore free collective bargaining in the federal public service. Once the Liberals took office though, their prescription for the public service was more of the same medicine provided by Mulroney and his Conservatives. Wages were unilaterally frozen for a further two years, until 1997; worse still, the government axed 45 000 civil service jobs, or nearly one-quarter of all federal public employment (Swimmer, 1995:405; Craig and Solomon, 1996:362). Those who remained have had to work harder to do both their own work and that of their now-departed colleagues. In addition, thanks to changes resulting from the 1992 *Public Service Reform Act (PSRA)*, it became much easier for the government to replace full-time, permanent employees with short-term, temporary, or casual ones who would receive no benefits and not be eligible for union membership (Swimmer, 1995:397–398). In the face of these and other developments, not least of which is the government's tough line on pay equity, federal public servants find themselves beleaguered on almost every front as the millennium approaches.

The Provincial Scene

While this is cold comfort, federal public servants have not been alone in facing wage freezes, major downsizing and restructuring initiatives, and more difficult working conditions for those who have managed to keep their jobs. All across Canada, similar initiatives have been taken by governments of every conceivable political stripe. In many cases, governments have gone beyond previous wage control programs in unilaterally changing the way in which public services are delivered, and thus in which public sector employees must do their jobs. So extensive has the scope of unilateral government action become that across Canada, free public sector collective bargaining is now the exception rather than the rule.

"Not-so-Green Gables." PEI's public sector workers lost a full month's salary in 1994 due to a government-imposed rollback.

In the generally depressed Atlantic region, federal cuts to transfer payments have hit particularly hard, leaving already hard-pressed provincial governments with little or no room to maneuver. In Newfoundland, the provincial government imposed a one-year wage freeze in 1991, later extending the freeze for a further three years. In 1994, the government's actions in slashing pension fund payments to teachers, closing schools, and reducing teachers' job security provoked a three-week province-wide teachers' strike. Pension contributions to other public employees were reduced that same year, and those employees were required to take 1.5 days off without pay in each of the two succeeding years (Fryer, 1995:353–354). Elsewhere in the region, governments took even harsher measures. In Nova Scotia, after a two-year wage freeze beginning in 1991, the government unilaterally imposed five unpaid days off on all public sector workers in mid-contract, following this action in 1994 with a further 3 percent cut to the pay of all public sector workers earning more than $25 000 per year (Fryer, 1995:354). In Prince Edward Island, the government imposed an 8.5 percent rollback on all public sector compensation in 1994, even though public sector workers had voluntarily agreed to a 6 percent reduction for four months just two years earlier (Fryer, 1995:355).

In Quebec, governments have gotten into the habit of unilaterally extending public sector collective agreements. Successive extensions in 1991, 1992, and 1993 meant that no collective bargaining was conducted over a six-year period, and public sector workers received only a 3 percent wage increase throughout those six years (Hébert, 1995:226–227). In addition, the 1993 extension was accompanied by legislation ordering all public employers to reduce their wage bill by 1 percent in each of the next two years. As in the case of the Ontario "social contract" discussed below, the reduction was to be achieved by means of unpaid holidays, unless the unions were prepared to agree on other ways of achieving the savings (Boivin and Déom, 1995:476). Another piece of legislation passed at about the same time ordered all government departments and public agencies to reduce their supervisory staff by 20 percent between 1993 and 1996, and their overall work force by 12 percent between 1993 and 1998. Outraged unions sought to mobilize their members and the general public against the wage freeze legislation and the work force reductions, but to no avail (Boivin and Déom, 1995).

More recently, with PQ Premier Lucien Bouchard becoming a belated convert to the balanced budget brigade, the province has embarked on widespread cutbacks in health care and education that have infuriated erstwhile public sector union supporters, just as the Levesque government's cutbacks did during the 1980s. Hospital closings, a particularly sore point, were a major issue in the November 1998 provincial election campaign, and may well have cost the PQ some votes.

ONTARIO EDUCATION ALLIANCE
worldchat.com/public/tab/oea/oeawho.htm

In Ontario, an NDP government under Bob Rae, faced with ballooning budget deficits, sought to recoup more than $2 billion in savings from its 900 000 public employees without resorting to layoffs (Craig and Solomon, 1996:362). Rather than unilaterally imposing legislation, the government initially sought to achieve this objective through a "social contract" to which it hoped the public sector unions would agree (Fryer, 1995:357). When the unions did not agree, the government passed its "Social Contract Act" in 1993. The act, bitterly opposed by the province's labour movement and also by three of the party's own backbenchers, provided for a three-year wage freeze and up to 12 days of unpaid leave per year in the event the wage freezes did not achieve sufficient savings. Those earning less than $30 000 per year were exempted, pay equity adjustments were left unaffected, and employers and unions reaching agreement before the deadline for implementation had their payroll reduction targets reduced by 20 percent (Fryer, 1995:358). For the most part, varying numbers of unpaid "Rae Days" proved necessary throughout the public sector (Craig and Solomon, 1996:363). Throughout the life of the social contract, the term would be used contemptuously to refer to what many public sector workers regarded as their betrayal by the party that had come to office with their support and pledged to defend their interests. Probably the legislation's main effect was to seriously weaken, if not destroy, the relationship between the province's labour movement and the NDP. The party failed to win a single Ontario seat in the 1993 federal election and was soundly defeated by Mike Harris' Conservatives in the 1995 provincial election. Though the NDP fared somewhat better in the 1997 federal election, it still failed to win a single Ontario seat, suggesting that the four-year-old wounds had not yet healed.

Draconian though it may have seemed in 1993, the Rae government's approach now appears almost benign when compared to that of the Conservative government that succeeded it. Abandoning a 50-year tradition of pragmatic, consensus-oriented conservatism in Ontario, the Harris government took office committed to implementing its strongly ideological "Common Sense Revolution" featuring large tax cuts, massive cuts in government spending, and major restructuring in health care and education. In 1996 and early 1997, public service cutbacks led to a series of province-wide one-day general strikes (*Collective Bargaining Review,* 1996–1997). Later in 1997, the province ushered in a new era of educational restructuring when it passed Bill 160. The bill severely restricts and will eventually eliminate local school boards, effectively concentrating control over the province's educational system in Toronto. The government's education agenda also includes shorter vacations, longer school days, and more classes with less preparation time for teachers (see Galt, 1998). In protest over these changes, the province's teachers staged an illegal three-week strike during the fall of 1997 (see Chapter 12 for a detailed discussion) and further strikes during the fall of 1998 (Green, 1998). At issue was the loss of preparation time, which teachers see as necessary both to ensure they are adequately prepared for their classes and to recharge themselves for seven periods of teaching per day (Galt, 1998).

In health care, the government's changes have been no less dramatic. Major restructuring initiated by the provincial government is leading to the closure of many hospitals, the merger of others, a reduction in the services offered patients, and the deinstitutionalization of many long-term patients (Marshall, 1998). Many services formerly provided in hospitals will now be provided through home care of various kinds, and the government appears interested in contracting out much of the home care service now provided by public sector workers (Marshall, 1998). The implications are extremely serious both for employment and for unionization in the health care sector (Marshall, 1998; Haiven, 1995:264–267), especially since most of the contractors will likely be non-union, pay at or near the provincial minimum wage, and make heavy use of part-time and casual labour (Haiven, 1995:266).

The Prairie provinces have responded in various ways to the recent economic crisis. In Manitoba, the government froze public sector wages for a year in 1991. Though normal negotiations took place in 1992, resulting in a three-year contract

(Fryer, 1995:356), the government did not allow that agreement to stay in place for long. In February 1993, the Finance Minister asked the public sector unions to accept a "voluntary" reduction in pay and benefits. When the unions did not agree, the government legislated 10-day unpaid layoffs for each of the next two years.

In Alberta, an ideologically driven far-right government under Premier Ralph Klein has, in effect, sought to balance the provincial budget on the backs of public sector workers, cutting public expenditures by 20 percent to balance the budget over a three-year period ending in 1997. Cuts ranged from 8.3 percent in social services to 12.4 percent in education and 17.6 percent in health care (Fryer, 1995:360; Thomason, 1995:303). In education, the budget cuts resulted in the complete elimination of adult education funding, a 50 percent reduction in kindergarten funding, and a 5 percent cut in teachers' salaries (Thomason, 1995:303–304). These moves were accompanied by a major consolidation of public school boards and elimination of those boards' taxing authority (Thomason, 1995:280, 303).[17] In health care, still deeper cuts were made without consultation with the unions involved and with little consultation even with management (Haiven, 1995:268). Not surprisingly, health care professionals have been on a collision course with the government ever since. As this chapter was being completed (September 1998), a full-blown crisis was developing in obstetrics, with the province's obstetricians refusing to accept new patients.[18] Meanwhile, the government has been equally hard on its own employees, initially forcing them to

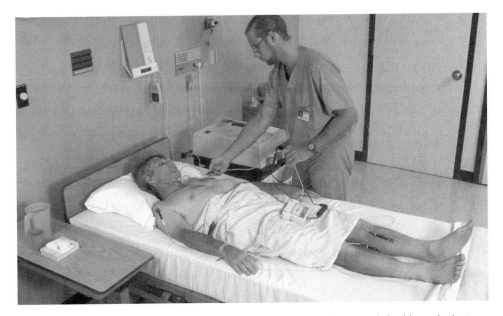

Health care workers like this nurse are coming under increasing stress due to cuts in health care budgets across Canada.

accept a 5 percent pay reduction comprising unpaid days off and a freeze on increments (Fryer, 1995:360), and later taking away four statutory holidays as well.

Public sector collective bargaining has fared better in Saskatchewan, where an NDP government took over in 1991. After a series of rotating strikes by government employees, their union agreed to accept a five-year agreement providing for modest wage increases and a cost-of-living adjustment in its late stages. The agreement expired in September 1996 (Fryer, 1995:359–360). Even here, however, with a government committed to maintaining free public sector collective bargaining, public sector workers have not been immune from restructuring, such as that resulting from the widespread closure of rural hospitals (Ponak and Thompson, 1995:418), or from frequent back-to-work orders when they have gone on strike.[19]

In British Columbia, also an NDP province since 1991, a genuine social contract was arrived at through collective bargaining in the health care sector (Fryer, 1995; Haiven, 1995; Marshall, 1998). In 1992, the government signed an agreement that gave its employees, whose pay had been frozen for a decade under the previous government's Compensation Stabilization Program, wage increases of 6 and 2 percent for the first two years and full cost of living for the final eight months (Fryer, 1995:361). The "social accord" in health care, which was negotiated in 1993, broke new ground in Canadian public sector bargaining. Designed to help B.C.'s health care system shift to a community-based "wellness" model, the agreement provided for a reduction of 4800 acute-care jobs, to be achieved through attrition, early retirement, and a reduced work week rather than layoffs (Haiven, 1995:268). Additional features included a modest (1.5 percent) wage hike, an early retirement fund, job security provisions, a labour adjustment program to help workers being transferred to community-care facilities, a guarantee of no expansion in contracting-out, and the involvement of workers in decision-making, including decision-making regarding new community health programs (Haiven, 1995:268–269; Marshall, 1998). Building on this achievement, the B.C. government subsequently negotiated a new agreement with its own employees that did not provide for a general wage increase, but did give the union considerable authority in improving work systems and redesigning the delivery of service (Fryer, 1995:363–364).

DISTINCTIONS BETWEEN PUBLIC AND PRIVATE SECTOR BARGAINING AND LABOUR RELATIONS

By now, it should be clear that public sector bargaining differs from bargaining in the private sector in a number of important ways. In this section, we consider in more detail some of the many important differences between collective bargaining in the two sectors. The distinctions we focus on include employer differences, employee and union differences, and legislative and policy differences, including those in dispute resolution mechanisms. Not only are these distinctive features of public sector bargaining of inter-est in and of themselves; they are worth examining to determine whether they are likely to help or hinder the transformation of public sector IR from its current state of crisis (see Chaykowski and Verma, 1992), a point we discuss in the conclusion to this chapter.

Employer Differences

Government's Dual Role

The single most important employer difference between public and private sector bar-gaining is the dual role government plays, as the employer of public sector workers and as legislator. This dual role gives it a degree of power that private sector employ-ers can only dream of possessing. Particularly in times of economic crisis, governments often find it irresistibly tempting to pass legislation to achieve objectives they haven't been able to achieve at the bargaining table (Haiven, 1995:243–244; Ponak and Thompson, 1995; Swimmer and Thompson, 1995:6). As we noted earlier in the chap-ter, government's desire to reduce inflation or the deficit has often led it to introduce public sector wage controls, freezes, or rollbacks. Government's desire to protect Canadians from the effects of public sector work stoppages has also caused it to make frequent use of back-to-work legislation, particularly since 1975. From 1950 through 1993, the federal and various provincial governments resorted to such legislation on 62 occasions, 50 of them between 1975 and 1993 (Ponak and Thompson, 1995:440). Even when government has not intervened, the threat of such intervention has often been enough to induce unions to accept a settlement proposed by the government, as in the case of the 1991 Toronto Transit strike (Craig and Solomon, 1996:412–413).

The vast power government possesses in its dual role as employer and legislator can be a source of considerable frustration to public sector workers and unions, who often spend months in painstaking negotiations, only to see their hard-earned results overturned by a single stroke of the legislative pen. Government's power may also be a source of frustration to public sector managers, who sometimes find themselves forced to administer a government-imposed solution they don't like and had no hand in fashioning. In this connection, it is worth noting that a 1989 study by David Zussman and Jak Jabes found a significantly higher degree of frustration and lower degree of job satisfaction among public than among private sector managers.

Diffusion of Management Authority

Another key difference between private and public sector collective bargaining is the far greater diffusion of management authority in the latter. In most private sector orga-nizations, management responsibility is well defined and clearly established (Ponak and Thompson, 1995:424). Unions can usually come to the table knowing whom they are bargaining with and (for the most part) where those negotiators stand.

In the public sector, on the other hand, there is typically a "bewildering fragmentation of authority among numerous management officials" (Ponak and Thompson, 1995). In some cases, this fragmentation is inherent. Government departments, for example, normally have both an administrative and a political role. While federal and provincial public servants typically spend most of their time on their administrative functions (i.e., program delivery or policy analysis), reporting to the deputy minister as public servants, they ultimately report to the minister, who may assign them to political chores having little to do with their administrative work or even in direct contradiction to it. Given that few ministers are likely to want to give up the power to use public servants more or less as they see fit, this situation seems unlikely to change any time soon. Even where public sector workers do not potentially have political responsibilities, there is still typically a division of management authority between elected officials and the line management who administer public sector organizations on a daily basis (Swimmer and Thompson, 1995:5). Often this division of authority is not a happy one, as elected officials' political agendas or lack of labour relations and administrative experience may lead them into more or less serious conflict with line management (Swimmer and Thompson, 1995).

To a degree, the diffusion of public sector management authority is deliberate, reflecting policy-makers' assumptions about the value of checks and balances, political versus non-political decision making, and local versus centralized control (Swimmer and Thompson, 1995). Responsibility for education decisions, for instance, has typically been divided between locally elected school boards and the provincial education ministry (Swimmer and Thompson, 1995).[20] In the civil service, while global resource allocation remains a cabinet function, the desire to appear impartial with regard to public service hiring and promotion has led most Canadian governments to vest responsibility for recruitment, transfer, and promotion in ostensibly politically neutral civil service commissions (Swimmer and Thompson, 1995).

Such fragmentation is exacerbated by the fact that many public bodies are funded from several different sources, each of which is likely to want to influence how the money is spent. In urban transit, for instance, local transit commissions are generally financed through a combination of user fees, municipal subsidies, and provincial grants. Provincial governments, various municipal governments, citizen groups, and the transit commissions' management all seek to play some role in the collective bargaining process (Swimmer and Thompson, 1995). These groups' objectives may well differ. Citizen groups may be primarily interested in improving or at least maintaining the level of service, while provincial and municipal governments may be more concerned with keeping costs down. The existence of so many different claimants inevitably makes decision making and the collective bargaining process much more complex (Swimmer and Thompson, 1995) Not infrequently, the internal or intraorganizational bargaining that must take place before the union's proposals can be seriously addressed is as complex, if not more so, as the bargaining between the management and union sides (Swimmer and Thompson, 1995:425; also see Walton and McKersie, 1965). Such intraorganizational bargaining may be particularly difficult where the government is directly involved in negotiations. In health care, where governments have increasingly been more and more directly involved in recent years, frustrated employers and municipal governments may even side with unions against the province (Haiven, 1995:243).

To bypass the difficult and time-consuming multilateral bargaining that normally ensues in such situations, public sector unions may seek (sometimes successfully) to do an "end run" around the management bargaining team to deal directly with a public official they believe will be more sympathetic to their cause, such as a mayor or provincial premier (Ponak, 1982:354–355). While such intervention can bring an end to the particular dispute in question, it may also impose excessive long-term costs on taxpayers in addition to being a source of frustration for public sector managers, who not unjustifiably resent the loss of authority and lack of trust implied by such actions. Even in cases where elected officials do not intervene in such a direct way, political competition between officials of different parties or representing different levels of government can aggravate the problem of management fragmentation still further (Ponak and Thompson, 1995:425), again making bargaining more complex and increasing the frustration of public sector workers and the unions representing them.

Where negotiations have not been centralized at the federal or provincial level, a common phenomenon over the years has been phantom bargaining (Ponak, 1982:354), whereby formal negotiating authority is ostensibly vested in a management group, such as a health care employers' association, but the key player, in this case the provincial government, that controls the purse strings, is not represented at the table. The absence of parties with any real authority from the bargaining table in such situations has sometimes led unions to refer to the government as the "phantom at the bargaining table" and to complain that without direct government representation, collective bargaining amounts to little more than going through the motions (Ponak, 1982).

In attempting to get around these various difficulties, Canadian governments have tried a number of different approaches. Quebec has customarily taken a highly centralized approach to public sector bargaining (Hébert, 1995; Haiven, 1995:240), although in recent years large-scale disputes resulting from that centralization have induced the government to bring in a degree of decentralization through a two-tier (provincial and local) bargaining system (Hébert, 1995; Boivin and Déom, 1995). In health care in that province, and also in New Brunswick, the government actually sits at the bargaining table as the management representative (Haiven, 1995:244). In contrast, Alberta and Ontario have historically played a much more passive role, providing little guidance beyond issuing overall budgetary guidelines for the entire sector (Haiven, 1995). For its part, Saskatchewan has taken a middle-of-the-road position, allowing the employers' association to represent management, but also having a government observer sit at the bargaining table (Haiven, 1995).

Perhaps the most significant recent changes have taken place in British Columbia, where the government has provided for negotiations in seven different public sub-sectors (Ponak and Thompson, 1995:445). Under the 1993 *Public Sector Employers' Act,* each sub-sector other than the provincial civil service has its own employers' association responsible for coordinating human resource activity within the sub-sector, including collective bargaining (Fryer, 1995:362). The government is directly represented in these employer associations and has representatives in each sub-sector's governing body and the power to approve bylaws (Fryer, 1995:362–363).

The new B.C. public sector bargaining arrangements appear promising. Thus far, they have generally resulted in constructive negotiations, including those leading to the social contract in health care discussed earlier in the chapter. It remains to be seen, however, whether other provinces will adopt such arrangements, or whether in B.C. itself they will survive a change in government (Fryer, 1995:364). Overall, it appears that Canadian governments and public sector employers are as far from consensus as ever about the most appropriate arrangements for public sector bargaining. After several decades of varied experience, most are still "groping for the right organizational form for labour relations" (Ponak and Thompson, 1995:425).

Economics Versus Politics

It is only a slight oversimplification to suggest that the currency of private sector bargaining is money, while that of public sector bargaining is political power. While private sector employers and unions are far from unconcerned about politics, at the bargaining table their major battles tend to be over monetary issues such as wages, benefits, hours of work, and levels of employment. In contrast, though public sector employers and unions are certainly concerned about money, particularly at a time of continuing government budget cutbacks and work force reductions, public sector bargaining itself remains primarily an exercise in political rather than economic power (Swimmer and Thompson, 1995:2). In private sector strikes, the union's aim is normally to induce employers to make a better offer out of fear of losing business and perhaps permanent market share. In public sector strikes, as in the case of the

1997 Ontario teachers' strike discussed in Chapter 12, the aim is more often to turn public opinion against the government, with an eye to pressuring the government into changing those policies that the union feels are hurting its members.

Notably, the costs of disagreement tend to be quite different in the private and public sectors. While private sector strikes almost invariably impose costs, in terms of lost profit and longer-term market share, strikes may actually benefit public sector employers economically, since their revenues remain the same, but their expenses are reduced by the amount of the striking employees' forgone wages and benefits (Ponak and Thompson, 1995:425–426). Here the costs are mainly political ones, particularly in the case of disputes that seriously inconvenience the public for a lengthy period of time, such as postal or transit strikes or strikes of municipal garbage collectors. Irate at the loss of the service in question, angry residents will deluge ministers' or municipal officials' offices with letters, phone calls, faxes, and e-mail messages demanding the restoration of the service at any cost and threatening to vote the government out of power at the first possible opportunity. Politicians' fear of not being re-elected may help explain why, in good times, striking public sector workers have sometimes received extremely, perhaps even overly generous settlements—and why in bad times they have often been legislated back to work.

MINISTER OF PUBLIC WORKS AND GOVERNMENT SERVICES REGARDING BILL C-24

w3.pwgsc.gc.ca/comm/min/text/spch3-e.html

A point that has perhaps not been made often enough (see Gérin-Lajoie, 1993) concerns the lack of an economic "bottom line" in public sector bargaining and the effect such a lack may have on union-management relations and the bargaining process. In the private sector, if a firm is losing profits and market share, management and the union may not agree on the cause of the problem, but at least they'll be able to agree there *is* a problem. The recognition of this common problem and of a common interest in keeping the enterprise afloat may just be enough to get the parties to start thinking about innovative possible solutions. In the public sector, where there normally is no economic bottom line, and where revenues typically have no direct link to either the quantity or quality of the good or service produced (Ponak and Thompson, 1995:426), it's often much harder for the parties to agree on what their problems are, or even necessarily that there is a problem. With no decline in profit or market share to serve as a "wake-up call," public sector managers in times of crisis may see their employees coming into work and apparently doing their jobs as usual, without recognizing that serious morale problems resulting from government restructuring or downsizing have seriously affected the quality of service these employees are providing to the public. Even those aware of a problem may not be able to convince their superiors of its seriousness, in the absence of concrete quantitative indicators such as a drop in sales revenues. Lacking any sort of basic agreement as to what the major problems are, a union and a management organization will generally find it exceedingly difficult to work out solutions, a difficulty likely to be aggravated by the generally quite severely restricted scope of public sector bargaining (described below).

Employee and Union Differences

Employee Differences

By and large, and increasingly so in today's tough economy, public sector workers have the same concerns as private sector ones (Ponak and Thompson, 1995:427). Job security, the maintenance of real income levels, work hours, and workload (see Chapter 12 for details) are of prime importance in both sectors.

This said, there *are* a number of significant differences between public and private sector employees, and also between the ways in which public and private sector unions tend to operate. Public sector union members are much more likely than their private sector counterparts to be female, professional, and white-collar. In 1991, 60 percent of all public sector union members were female, compared to 22 percent in the private sector (Swimmer and Thompson, 1995:5). In some sectors, such as health care and social services, more than 80 percent of the union members are women (Swimmer and Thompson, 1995). In addition, the public sector contains more than its share of unionized white-collar workers, and virtually all the country's unionized professionals (Ponak and Thompson, 1995:428).

These differences may have mattered more in the early years of public sector bargaining than they do now, in part because, unlike many blue-collar male union members in the private sector, most women and white-collar and professional men in the public sector had little experience with traditional unionism and initially tended to dislike some of its more adversarial features, such as strikes, picketing, and the filing of grievances. Indeed, during the first decade or so of widespread public sector bargaining, public sector workers tended to be less strike-prone, less apt to file grievances, and more interested in joint employee-management committees and other consultative mechanisms than their private sector counterparts. Because so many were women, they were also extremely interested in such issues as pay and employment equity, maternity leave, and workplace day-care centres; because so many were professionals, they tended to put a premium on professional development issues such as in-service education and funding for travel to conferences. And because times were generally quite good and their unions didn't find it hard to win better wage and benefit packages, those unions could afford to devote a good part of their energy to negotiations over intrinsic issues.[21]

Beginning in the mid 1970s, public and private sector unionism began to converge as public sector unionists generally grew more militant. There were a number of reasons for this. First, having had some experience with unions, public sector workers may have learned to be less afraid of unionism's more adversarial and confrontational aspects. Second, particularly after the imposition of wage-price controls in 1975, many public sector workers undoubtedly *felt* more confrontational. Times were tougher, and governments were no longer anywhere as ready as they had been to accede to generous wage and benefit packages. Worse still, a number of them were beginning to restrict public sector union rights. Taken together, these developments arguably helped the country's public sector workers realize they were no longer (if they ever had been) specially privileged beings, but rather were subject to the same economic pressures as their private sector counterparts.

Today, as noted previously, economic issues are just as important for public sector workers as for those in the private sector. Political issues, however, are generally far more important because, in its dual role as employer and legislator, government has restricted public sector union activities even more severely in this decade than it did in the 1980s. For the most part unable to work out problems at the bargaining table, public sector workers and their unions have increasingly been forced to turn to political action and a broad range of publicity campaigns in an attempt to win public support for their cause.

Pay and employment equity issues, in particular, remain a central concern for the heavily female memberships of public sector unions. Here, the federal government's apparent abandonment of its traditional leadership role (Weiner, 1995), as signalled by its recent (August 1998) decision to appeal the Human Rights Tribunal's pay equity award to current and past federal public servants, appears to have tapped a reservoir of deep resentment, if not rage, on the part of those affected. PSAC, the union representing most federal public servants, responded by declaring September 14, 1998, a day of mourning and urging its members to wear black, in addition to calling a mass Parliament Hill demonstration for September 21 (PSAC, 1998). The union also urged its members to vote against the government in a September 14 federal by-election in Sherbrooke, Quebec, a move that may well have meant the difference in the Bloc Quebecois candidate's narrow win over the Liberal (Aubry and Bryden, 1998). Though one can only speculate as to the union's future strategies and the government's response, it seems entirely possible at this writing (September 1998) that Parliament Hill demonstrations and the wearing of black will be only the first moves in a long, drawn-out battle over pay equity.

Earlier, we noted that intrinsic concerns over the nature of work are of considerable importance to public sector workers, many of whom are professionals with a strong sense of commitment to their profession and to serving the public. Such concerns still exist, though again, because of the general suspension of public sector bargaining in recent years, unions have seldom been able to address these concerns at the bargaining table. Often these concerns are the source of great frustration to dedicated professionals. For example, nurses resent the fact that health care restructuring and other government cutbacks mean they can't give patients the quality of care they believe they deserve. Similarly, Ontario public schoolteachers resent the loss of preparation time resulting from provincial government policy, which means they will not be as well prepared for classes and will also not have time to recharge and regroup during a long day. University professors (as the author can attest from personal experience) resent the fact that large classes and severe reductions in teaching assistant hours[22] mean they can no longer assign essays, or at least must assign fewer and shorter ones and grade them less carefully.

Put simply, most public sector workers today are anything but "happy campers." Given governments' almost universal preoccupation with reducing the deficit and cutting taxes, the situation seems likely to get worse before it gets better.

Union Differences

THE IMPORTANCE OF PUBLICITY   While public sector unions are obviously concerned with specific issues of particular relevance to their members (class size for teachers, shift schedules for nurses), overall their bargaining agendas tend to be fairly similar to those of private sector unions—when they can bargain at all. What's different is the way in which they attempt to achieve their objectives. Given that members of the general public are important stakeholders in all public sector activity, both as consumers of public services and as taxpayers, public sector unionism is inherently political, with many of its efforts directed towards winning and maintaining public support both for public sector unions' specific rights and for the government spending that undergirds the services public sector workers provide. In recent years, the relative importance of political action and publicity campaigns has increased, due to the decline in public sector bargaining activity.

As Swimmer and Thompson (1995:2) note, the media are far more important in public sector than in private sector bargaining, as both sides seek to win the hearts and minds of everyday citizens. This is particularly true during labour disputes. The media played a prominent role both in the 1991 federal public service strike (Swimmer, 1995:400) and in more recent disputes such as those involving Ontario's teachers and postal workers (to be discussed in detail in Chapter 12). But public sector unions' publicity efforts are not confined to times when there is a work stop-page. Most are regularly involved in campaigns aimed both at the general public and their own membership (Lawson, 1998; Marshall, 1998). For example, in 1996 PSAC responded to the federal government's privatization and contracting-out of national parks with an article in the union's magazine, *Alliance* (Mitchell, 1996), following it up later in the year with a direct mail campaign featuring articles that showed the public, in a humorous way, some of the possible effects of the govern-ment privatization campaign. For its part, the Canadian Union of Postal Workers has used such varied means as bus ads, stamps, billboards, and leaflets to attack the government for increasing its members' workload and to let the public know what kind of effect the increased workload will likely have on postal service (Lawson, 1998), while CUPE has run a series of hard-hitting magazine ads (see Chapter 6) dramatizing its attack on Ontario's health care restructuring plan by suggesting that the plan is likely to lead to a two-tier health care system comparable to that of Victorian England. While some observers, such as Warrian (1996), argue that polit-ical protest and other such pressure tactics will generally be futile, so long as pub-lic sector unions are generally prevented from bringing their concerns to the bargaining table, it is difficult to see what alternative they have.

UNION FRAGMENTATION   Union representation can be quite fragmented in the public sector, particularly in health care and education. In large, industrial settings like auto plants and steel mills, a single union typically represents all employees or at least the great majority of them (Haiven, 1995:241). For the most part, the industri-al union model also holds in government departments, although in the federal gov-ernment, the large number of occupational groupings under *PSSRA* has led to fragmentation of a different sort (see Swimmer, 1995). This is not the case in health care. In hospital settings (Haiven, 1995), there are normally at least three unions rep-resenting health care workers: a nurses' union, a general service union for mainte-nance and support staff, and a "paramedical" unit for skilled technical staff like dietitians, X-ray technologists, and physiotherapists. To make matters even more complicated, several different unions may be competing for the right to represent the same group of workers (Haiven, 1995:241–242)—a phenomenon likely to become even more common in the near future because of hospital closures and mergers (Marshall, 1998). CUPE represents many hospital maintenance and support staff, but it is far from being the only union in the field. The Service Employees International Union (SEIU), International Union of Operating Engineers, and various government employee unions also represent many of these same workers (Marshall, 1998; see also Haiven, 1995:241–242). The result of this kind of "balkanization" is that bargaining becomes more difficult, since there is a rarely a single union that can come to the bargaining table representing all employees in a provincial sub-sector (Haiven, 1995:241–242). In education, while the degree of union fragmentation is less pronounced, the industrial union model has also seldom taken hold, except to a limited degree in Quebec, where the Centrale de l'enseignement du Québec has begun to serve as an industrial union representing all education workers from care-takers to classroom teachers (Boivin and Déom, 1995:467). In the public schools, teachers are normally represented by a provincial teachers' federation; support staff are normally represented by a union such as CUPE. Similarly, at the university level, professors are generally represented by a certified staff association, while support staff are again represented by a union such as CUPE. In some cases, separate unions may represent office support staff and maintenance staff. While the separation of professionals from support and maintenance staff may make sense in terms of build-ing industrial relations "communities of interest," from another perspective it may make it harder for those working in education to come up with imaginative and equi-table ways to deal with spending reductions in that sector. So long as university pro-fessors and support staff are represented by different unions and bargain at different times, they are likely to see themselves as, at least to a certain extent, pitted against each other. As the author can again attest from personal experience, this is a situa-tion that can lead to a good deal of bitterness.

 PUBLIC SERVICES INTERNATIONAL
www.world-psi.org

Legislative and Policy Differences

There are a good many legislative and policy differences between the private and pub-lic sector. The two most important ones are the far greater degree of fragmentation and variation in dispute resolution methods found in the public sector, and the sig-nificantly greater extent to which governments restrict public sector unions' rights with respect to such matters as bargaining-unit determination and the scope of bar-gainable issues.

Legislative Fragmentation

For the private sector, each province has a single labour act more or less closely modelled after the American Wagner Act (Ponak and Thompson, 1989). While there are some relatively minor differences in dispute resolution procedures, almost all jurisdictions require some type of conciliation before a strike or lockout can become legal.[23]

In contrast, jurisdictions vary greatly with respect to the coverage of particular groups under public sector legislation. At one extreme is Ontario, with separate laws for almost every public sector group, including civil servants, teachers, hospital workers, police, and firefighters. At the opposite extreme are the federal jurisdiction and New Brunswick, each of which has a single private sector act and a single public sector one. In between are provinces such as Saskatchewan and British Columbia, which apply their general labour acts to a number of different public sector groups, but have special acts for teachers (in both provinces), for police and firefighters (in Saskatchewan), and for provincial civil servants (in B.C.). Quebec (see Hébert, 1995:201 and Boivin and Déom, 1995:473–474) has a hybrid system whereby all groups fall under the jurisdiction of the general labour act, but many groups also have specific legislation governing such things as bargaining structure, the scope of collective agreements, and in particular the maintenance of essential services (see Table 9.2).

Table 9.2

PUBLIC SECTOR COLLECTIVE BARGAINING LEGISLATION				
Jurisdiction	**Municipal**	**Police**	**Firefighters**	**Hospitals**
FEDERAL	*Can. Code*	*None (RCMP)**	*PSSRA*	*PSSRA*
B.C.	General lab. act; Pub. Sec. Employers' Act	General lab. act; Pub. Sec. Employers' Act	General lab. act; Pub. Sec. Employers' Act	General ab. act; Pub. Sec. Employer's Act
ALBERTA	General lab. act	Police Act	General lab. act	General lab. act
SASK.	General lab. act	Police Act	Fire Dept. Act	General lab. act
MANITOBA	General lab. act	Gen. lab. act; Police Act; City of Wpg. Act	Gen. lab. act; Fire Dept. Arb. Act.	General lab. act
ONTARIO	General lab. act	Police Act; Ont. Prov. Police Act	Fire Dept. Act	General lab. act; Hosp. Disputes Arb. Act
QUEBEC	General lab. act (lab. code)	Lab. Code, Div. II;‡ Police Act; Prov. Police (Sûrété) Act	Lab. Code, Div. II	Lab. Code, Pub. Serv. Act
N.B.	General lab. act	Gen. lab. act; Police Act	General lab. act	Pub. Serv. Act

Table 9.2 (continued)

Jurisdiction	Municipal	Police	Firefighters	Hospitals
N.S.	General lab. act	General lab. act	General lab. act	General lab.act
P.E.I.	General lab. act	General lab. act Police Act	General lab. act	General lab. act
NFLD.	General lab.	Gen. lab. act Royal Nfld. Constabulary Act	General lab. act; St. John's Fire Dept. Act	Pub. Serv. Act

Jurisdiction	Teachers	Civ. Service	Govt. Enterprise
FEDERAL	*PSSRA*	*PSSRA*	*Can. Code*
B.C.	Gen. lab. act; Ed. Act; Pub. Sector Employers' Act	Pub. Serv. Act	Gen. lab. act; Pub. Sector Employers' Act
ALBERTA	Gen. lab. act	Pub. Serv. Act	Gen. lab. act
SASK.	Education Act	Gen. lab. act	Gen. lab. act
MANITOBA	Education Act	Gen. lab. act; Civ. Serv. Act	Gen. lab. act
ONTARIO	Education Act	Civ. Serv. Act	Civ. Serv. Act; Gen. lab. act
QUEBEC	Gen. lab act; Pub. Serv. Act	Gen. lab. act; Pub. Serv. Act; Civ. Serv. Act	Gen. lab. act; Pub. Serv. Act; Civ. Serv. Act
N.B.	Pub. Serv. Act	Pub. Serv. Act	Pub. Serv. Act
N.S.	Education Act	Civ. Serv. Act	Gen. lab. act
P.E.I.	Education Act	Civ. Serv. Act	Geb. lab. act
NFLD.	Education Act	Pub. Serv. Act	Pub. Serv. Act

* The RCMP are excluded from unionization rights under both the *Canada Labour Code* and *PSSRA*.

The *Public Sector Employers' Act,* providing for public sector employer associations, applies to all public sector collective bargaining in the province except for the provincial civil service.

‡ Unlike those covered by the main part of Quebec's *Code du Travail,* police and firefighters are forbidden to strike and must submit disputes to binding arbitration.

Note: Public service acts are general acts applying to several different branches of the public sector. Civil service acts, where applicable, apply only to the provincial civil service or (occasionally) to employees of certain government enterprises.

Source: Adapted from Thompson and Swimmer (1995:7–8) and updated by the author.

The variation in dispute resolution procedures is equally great. Most provinces do not permit police and firefighters to strike, but all grant that right to municipal employees and most grant it to employees of government enterprises. In between, there is little consensus. Seven jurisdictions permit civil servants to strike; four (Alberta, Manitoba, Nova Scotia, and P.E.I.) do not. Eight jurisdictions permit teachers to strike, while three (Manitoba, Saskatchewan, and P.E.I.) do not. Likewise, eight jurisdictions allow hospital workers to strike while three (Alberta, Ontario, and P.E.I.) do not.

Most jurisdictions appear to offer little in the way of consistent policy rationale for their choice of public sector dispute resolution methods. P.E.I., which has long had one of the most restrictive labour acts in Canada (Forsey, 1985; Peirce, 1989), does not allow any public sector workers except municipal employees to strike. At the opposite extreme are the federal jurisdiction, where all workers who have the right to bargain collectively have, at least in principle, the right to choose strike action (see Table 9.3), and B.C., where all public sector workers have the right to strike, subject in most cases to essential service designations. In between, New Brunswick and Quebec allow all groups except police and firefighters to strike—an exclusion that would probably make sense to most Canadians given the essential nature of the work performed by these groups.

Elsewhere, however, the right to strike seems to have been applied more or less randomly. Alberta, for example, allows teachers to strike, but not civil servants or hospital workers (see Table 9.3). Manitoba is just the opposite; there hospital workers can strike, but teachers and civil servants cannot. Ontario allows both teachers and civil servants to strike, but not hospital workers; in Nova Scotia, teachers and hospital workers as well as police can strike, but not civil servants.

ALBERTA FEDERATION OF LABOUR
www.afl.org

Why is there so little consistency in Canadian jurisdictions' public sector legislation? It may be some comfort to realize that Canadian jurisdictions are not alone in this regard. In Germany, for example, career public servants, or *Beamte*, are barred from striking, unlike most other public sector groups (Beaumont, 1995:413; Jacobi, Keller, and Muller-Jentsch, 1992:259). Police and the armed forces are barred from striking in France, Italy, and Britain (Jacobi et al., 1995), while in Japan many municipal workers are allowed to strike, but virtually all other public sector workers are not (Matsuda, 1993:23). Canada is also not alone, among federal systems, in having different bargaining and strike rights for public sector workers in different jurisdictions. For example, in the United States, where public sector law is generally under state jurisdiction, about one-quarter of all states allow their employees to strike

(Mills, 1989). Most states allow their employees to bargain collectively, but some do not (Mills, 1989). But though the differential application of public sector strike rights to different groups and in different jurisdictions is not unique to Canada, Canadian jurisdictions have carried this trend farther than any other known to the author.

Table 9.3

	DISPUTE RESOLUTION PROCEDURES IN VARIOUS PUBLIC SECTOR JURISDICTIONS					
Juris.	Municipal	Police	Firefighters	Hospitals	Teachers	Civ. Service
FED.	Strike (Yukon/NWT)	NA	COP*	COP*	COP*	COP*
B.C.	Strike*	Strike*	Strike*	Strike*	Strike*	Strike*
ALB.	Strike	Arb.	Arb.	Arb.	Strike	Arb.
SASK.	Strike	Strike	Arb.	Strike	Arb. by	Strike either party's request
MAN.	Strike	Strike	Arb.	Strike	Arb.	Arb.
ONT.	Strike	Arb.	Arb.	Arb.	Strike	Strike*
QUE.	Strike* Strike*,‡	Arb. Strike*	Arb.	Limited	Limited	Strike*
N.B.	Strike	Arb.	Arb.	Limited Strike*	Strike	Limited Strike*
N.S.	Strike	Strike	Strike§	Strike#	Limited Strike**	Arb.
P.E.I.	Strike	Arb.	Arb.	Arb.	Arb.	Arb.
NFLD.	Strike	Strike	Strike‡‡	Limited Strike§§	Strike	Limited Strike

Note Most provinces permit government enterprise employees to strike. Arbitration is required in PEI and, for the most part, Alberta. Some provinces subject government enterprise employees to essential service designations.
* Essential services provisions stipulate that certain employees will be or may be required to continue working during a strike.
Except for the city of Winnipeg, where the method is arbitration at the request of either party.
‡ In Quebec, health care and education workers are not permitted to strike over local and regional issues.
§ It should be noted that, at least according to Jackson (1995:317), there have been no recorded strikes by firefighters in Canada. Strikes by police have occurred, but only extremely rarely.
# According to Thompson and Swimmer (1995:11), two large hospitals use arbitration instead.
** Nova Scotia schoolteachers are not permitted to strike over local and regional issues.
Arbitration is used for members of the provincial police force, the Royal Newfoundland Constabulary.
‡‡ Arbitration in St. John's, strike elsewhere.
§§ The union can demand arbitration if more than 50 percent of a bargaining unit is designated as essential and thus prohibited from striking. The same is true in the Nfld. civil service.

Source: Adapted from Thompson and Swimmer (1995:7–8) and updated by the author.

Moreover, most European countries that bar some public sector groups but not others from striking have at least attempted to provide some kind of policy rationale for the exclusion, by basing it on the essential nature of the work performed by these groups. Where essentiality as such is not at issue, as in the case of career civil servants in Germany and Japan, the workers in question enjoy some sort of quid pro quo in the form of relatively high pay, considerable job security, and (at least in the case of the German *Beamte)* a good deal of political clout (Reynolds, 1995; Jacobi et al., 1995). In contrast, Canadian public sector strike bans are often unconnected to the essentiality of the work being performed, and those groups barred from striking are not necessarily rewarded in other ways (as by receiving high salaries).

At the end of the day, one can only speculate on the reasons for the evolution of what Drache and Glassbeek (1992:344) have described as Canada's "patchwork" system of public sector collective bargaining. Given the otherwise irrational, even contradictory nature of many of the provisions we have been discussing, it seems likely that local political considerations have played an extremely important if not pivotal role in that evolution.

Bargaining Unit Determination

Another key difference between public and private sector collective bargaining has to do with the way in which bargaining units are determined. In the private sector, as we pointed out in the previous chapter, this determination is normally made by the labour relations board, generally with considerable input from the parties involved (see Ponak and Thompson, 1989:387). Indeed, where the parties agree, the labour board will not normally interfere. Where they do not agree, the board will base its decision largely on what seems likely to make for the most harmonious union-management relationship.

In contrast, public sector bargaining units are most often spelled out in public sector legislation (Fryer, 1995:345). Under *PSSRA*, federal public servants were initially divided into some 76 different occupational groups (Swimmer, 1995:370), leaving the PSSRB little if any authority to determine bargaining units (Ponak and Thompson, 1989:387).[24] New Brunswick followed the federal government's lead, authorizing a number of occupationally based province-wide bargaining units (Fryer, 1995:345). In contrast, B.C.'s public service act spells out three bargaining units, and a single province-wide unit is named in the legislation of Alberta, Manitoba, Nova Scotia, Ontario, and P.E.I. (Fryer, 1995). Some statutes go even farther, spelling out the only union that can legally represent government employees. While some analysts (i.e., Fryer, 1995:345) suggest that legislative determination of the bargaining agent appears to go against the Charter's "freedom of association" provision, various Supreme Court cases have made it clear that "freedom of association" does not include the right to choose one's own bargaining agent (Thompson and Ponak, 1995:432; Cavalluzzo, 1988).[25]

BRITISH COLUMBIA FEDERATION OF LABOUR
www.bcfed.com

Scope of Bargainable Issues

Yet another important difference is the scope of issues that may be negotiated in the private and public sectors. In the private sector, the parties are free to negotiate pretty well any provision they want pertaining to the terms and conditions of employment, so long as it is not illegal. In most public sector acts, the scope of bargainable issues is severely limited. A modified form of the old sovereignty doctrine would appear to apply in some cases. For example, the *PSSRA*, a rather liberal act in certain other respects, does not allow bargaining over any issue that would require parliamentary legislation, except for the appropriation of funds (Swimmer, 1995:371). What this means in practical terms is that many issues that are central to private sector bargaining become management rights in the public sector more or less by default (Swimmer, 1995). Under *PSSRA*, for example, there is no bargaining over criteria for appointments, promotions, layoffs, job classification, and technological or organizational change (Swimmer, 1995:371–372). While some of these restrictions may be understandable, given the federal government's need to apply the merit principle to prevent favouritism in appointments and promotions, the merit principle does not explain the government's refusal to allow its public servants to bargain over technological change. Even less does it explain the government's refusal to allow its employees to bargain over pensions (Swimmer, 1995:371), a position also taken by every province except Saskatchewan (Fryer, 1995:345)[26]. Given that all permanent federal government workers are required to pay a sizeable percentage of their salaries into the pension plan, the government's refusal to allow bargaining over this issue seems decidedly inequitable, to put it mildly.

Most provincial public sector acts are only slightly more liberal than *PSSRA* with respect to the scope of bargainable issues. Many do allow bargaining over technological and organizational change (Swimmer, 1995:372), but most prohibit bargaining over employee training programs, appointments, and promotions (Fryer, 1995:345). Somewhat more justifiably, perhaps, given the paramilitary nature of fire and police departments, both, in particular the latter, often forbid their employees to bargain over disciplinary issues and superior-subordinate relations (Jackson, 1995:319; Ponak and Thompson, 1995).[27]

As Ponak and Thompson note (1995:431), such severe restrictions on the scope of bargaining may well hurt the bargaining process by creating frustration on the part of unions, thereby preventing trust from emerging. Indeed, the restrictions can themselves be a source of increased conflict, in that the parties may wind up wasting a good deal of time and energy bickering about what can and cannot legally be bargained over, rather than engaging in productive negotiations (Ponak and Thompson, 1995). Almost certainly, restricting the scope of bargainable issues does not eliminate conflict over these and other issues. For example, during a period in the 1980s when wage controls applied to the federal public service, effectively eliminating public servants' ability to bargain over money, the number of grievances under *PSSRA* increased sharply (*Current Scene,* 1991), a finding very much in line with the theory of public sector conflict advanced by Hebdon (1992).

Dispute Resolution Procedures

To most Canadians, the single most important difference between public and private sector collective bargaining lies in the different procedures for resolving disputes in the two sectors. As noted earlier, the conciliation-strike routine is all but universal in the private sector. Only very rarely are other procedures, such as back-to-work legislation or the imposition of binding arbitration, invoked, and then only in large federal-jurisdiction strikes with a substantial public interest component, such as railway or airline disputes.

In contrast, the essential (or allegedly essential) nature of much public sector work has led policy-makers to devise a broad array of special dispute settlement procedures for that sector. As these procedures are dealt with in more detail in Chapter 12, they will be discussed only briefly here. The alternative public sector procedures discussed here include conventional interest arbitration, final offer arbitration, choice of procedures, and the controlled strike. Other procedures, such as med-arb and back-to-work legislation, have been left to Chapter 12.

Conventional Interest Arbitration

Conventional interest arbitration is the method normally used for resolving disputes involving police, firefighters, and other public sector workers whose services are considered so essential to the public health, safety, or welfare that they cannot be allowed to withdraw them. In addition, as noted earlier, it is also used for many civil servants, teachers, and other public sector workers whose work may or may not be truly essential, but whom the government has nonetheless, for whatever reason, forbidden from striking.

Under conventional interest arbitration, arbitrators are normally free, within certain broad limitations, to fashion an award comprising the union's position, the management's position, or their own (Ponak and Thompson, 1989). Some jurisdictions, notably Alberta (Ponak and Thompson, 1995:427), require arbitrators to take the government's ability to pay into account in arriving at public sector awards; however, it is not clear what effect, if any, such statutory provisions have had on arbitration awards. The major advantage of conventional, as opposed to final offer arbitration (discussed below) is that, because arbitrators can "split the difference" in fashioning their awards, those awards are likely to be more acceptable to both sides (Ponak and Thompson, 1989:394). A major disadvantage is that, particularly in cases where parties use arbitration frequently, they can lose their ability to bargain, preferring to leave hard decisions to the arbitrator rather than making them themselves. Most evidence suggests that conventional arbitration systems lead to lower rates of negotiated settlement than systems that allow strikes and lockouts (Ponak and Thompson, 1989, 1995). While final-offer arbitration (FOA) appears to offer a way around this difficulty, it has not, for reasons to be discussed shortly, been very widely adopted in Canada.

Final-Offer Arbitration (FOA)

Under FOA, arbitrators have little discretion in fashioning their awards. They must choose either the union's or employer's position for the entire package, if that is how the award is being made, or for each issue. The idea behind FOA is that because the risk of "losing" is so great, particularly when the award is being made as a package rather than issue by issue, most parties would rather settle on their own (see Godard, 1994:353–354). FOA has been fairly widely adopted in American public sector legislation, and the evidence suggests that it generally achieves a significantly higher rate of negotiated settlements than does conventional arbitration (Ponak and Thompson, 1995:438). Nonetheless, it has seldom been adopted in Canada, and some (i.e., Thompson and Ponak) suggest that it will not likely be more widely adopted in the near future. One major criticism of this approach is that it can lead to bad collective agreements, at least in cases where both sides submit unreasonable proposals (Ponak and Thompson, 1995). Another is that it can foster a damaging win-lose mentality that will hurt the parties' efforts to build a more constructive relationship.

Choice of Procedures (COP)

Under choice of procedures, one party or the other (in Canada, normally the union) is given the right to choose between the traditional conciliation-strike route and binding arbitration. Initially devised for *PSSRA,* COP soon spread to a number of provinces and U.S. states (Ponak and Thompson, 1989:396–397). In Canada, the federal government's intention was to come up with a system that would give public service unions the right to strike, yet lead to arbitration in most cases. For *PSSRA's* first decade or so, COP generally fulfilled this expectation. However, after 1976, the public service unions' growing militancy and anger at the government's wage-price controls led them to choose strikes rather than arbitration most of the time. In addition, experience with arbitration boards and conciliation boards suggested that the latter were willing to address a broader range of issues, including some technically beyond the permissible scope of bargaining (Swimmer, 1995:375–376). For these reasons, the Public Service Alliance no longer allows its bargaining units to choose arbitration (Swimmer, 1995:377), and even the less militant Professional Institute of the Public Service of Canada has long had a policy of encouraging its bargaining units to opt for the conciliation-strike route (Swimmer, 1995). Given its growing lack of acceptability to the public service unions, COP seems unlikely to be more widely adopted; indeed, many of the provinces and states that tried it have since abandoned it (Ponak and Thompson, 1995:439).

Controlled Strikes

The controlled strike, based on the designation of certain employees who must remain on the job to provide essential services, has become the most common option in jurisdictions that permit public sector workers to strike. Indeed, every jurisdiction except Saskatchewan that permits public sector strikes now has some kind of designation procedure in place. Under *PSSRA*, Treasury Board decides who should be considered essential and the PSSRB rules in the event of any dispute between Treasury Board and the union (Swimmer, 1995). Elsewhere, the usual procedure is for the union and public sector employer to negotiate acceptable levels of designation, with the final decision left to a labour board or some other impartial tribunal in the event of a dispute (Thompson and Ponak, 1995:439). Often the negotiations over designation are long and difficult, sometimes as difficult as the actual collective agreement negotiations themselves (Thompson and Ponak, 1995:439–440).

In principle, the controlled strike should often be the most attractive option for governments, because it ensures the continuation of essential public services without removing unions' right to strike. In practice, administering such strikes has often been fraught with difficulties.[28] The most serious problem, particularly in hospital settings where the approach has most often been used (see Haiven, 1995), is knowing how many employees to designate as essential. If the figure is set too low, public health and safety could be at risk. If it is set too high, the union may not be able to carry on an effective strike (Thompson and Ponak, 1995). Often, labour tribunals ruling on designation levels have erred on the side of caution, in some cases ludicrously so. During a 1989 hospital strike in B.C., one hospital saw 110 percent of its usual nursing complement designated as essential (Haiven, 1995:256)! An option already in place in Newfoundland (see Table 9.3) that might prevent public sector employers from designating excessive numbers of employees as essential, is to allow the union to take the dispute through to binding arbitration in cases where designation exceeded a certain level, such as 50 percent. The reason such an option could work is that, in recent years, governments have been increasingly reluctant to submit public sector disputes to arbitration, disliking the loss of control and possible expense entailed in arbitrated settlements.[29]

IS A TRANSFORMATION POSSIBLE?

Our review of the differences between public and private sector collective bargaining has identified a number of important employer, employee and union, and legislative and policy differences between the two sectors. Based on this review, we conclude that bargaining is generally more difficult in the public sector, and that that sector will find it significantly harder than the private sector[30] to move away from a strongly adversarial form of industrial relations towards one based more on trust and the formation of strategic alliances between unions and management (see Chaykowski and Verma, 1992).

As has long been recognized in the literature, fragmented public sector management authority generally makes bargaining both longer and more difficult than it is in the private sector. Such negative effects are likely to be even more serious when, as is now often the case, the actual public sector employers are changing rapidly, owing to major restructuring in education and health care in several provinces, and regionalization of government in Ontario (Marshall, 1998). In government departments, the division of authority between an administrative head (the deputy minister) and a political head (the minister) tends to aggravate employer fragmentation still farther.

For the most part, unionized public sector employees do not appear to have significantly different bargaining objectives from their private sector counterparts. However, because these workers, many of whom are professionals, are generally better-educated and more accustomed to having some say in determining working conditions than most unionized private sector workers, they may well have higher expectations of the bargaining process and of worklife in general. At a time when public sector workers' employer, the government, appears generally unwilling to meet either their extrinsic needs for job security and at least stable income, or their intrinsic needs for job satisfaction and a feeling of recognition and respect for a job well done, their frustrations have mounted to dangerous levels. It is no small irony that this group of workers, which initially tended to eschew adversarial union actions such as strikes and the filing of grievances, has, over the past three years, become the most militant part of the Canadian labour movement, accounting for about half the person-days lost to strikes over the past two years (see Chapter 12 for more details).

Unlike private sector workers, those in the public sector generally have little say in the determination of their bargaining units. In some cases, the relevant public sector legislation may even specify the union to which they must belong. The range of issues that they can negotiate is generally far narrower than the range of permissible private sector issues, and they are also severely restricted with regard to industrial action. Many, including some whose duties most would classify as far from essential, are barred from striking altogether. Even those public sector workers permitted to strike must generally go through lengthy designation processes and sometimes multiple-stage conciliation. And even when a public sector strike is legal, government is likely to legislate workers back to their jobs in the name of the public interest. All of these, particularly the restrictions on bargainable issues and on the right to strike, are also major sources of frustration for public sector workers.

Even more important, the lack of economic bottom-line indicators in much public sector bargaining arguably makes it more difficult for the parties to find a basis for agreement than it is in the private sector. To the extent that private sector industries have managed to transform their industrial relations systems (see Chaykowski and Verma, 1992), the need to maintain profitability and market share under conditions of increased global competitiveness has driven such transformation. The evidence suggests that unions may be willing to relax hard-won work rules if they sense that the increased efficiency that results from doing so will ultimately lead to greater revenues in which their members will share. But an industrial relations transformation cannot be manufactured out of nothing. Where there is little likelihood that increased effort or concessions at the bargaining table will lead to increased revenues in which union members will share, as is the case in most of the public sector, what incentive do workers have to work harder or unions have to make concessions? While some recent observers (i.e., Warrian, 1996) argue that the public sector is now undergoing a fundamental transformation that will require that sectors' unions to rethink their traditional adversarial approach, it isn't at all clear what approach they should use instead. We would argue that until public sector unions have something to gain from relaxing their traditional adversarial stance towards government, they will almost certainly continue to maintain it. To date, only in British Columbia, and possibly in Saskatchewan, have governments given the public sector unions any reason to believe they might have something to gain from a different approach.

Overall, it appears that the potential for conflict is greater in the public than in the private sector, while the possibilities for defusing it through collective bargaining are less, even at times when the bargaining process is working more or less as it is supposed to. At present, with anything approaching free public sector collective bargaining more the exception than the rule across Canada, the potential for public sector conflict is that much greater. In the past, better job security and higher levels of pay and benefits may have served as a kind of quid pro quo in return for the greater restrictions on public sector employees' actions. Now, with downsizing as much a fact of life in government departments as in large private corporations, and with government no longer playing a leadership role in such matters as pay equity, such a quid pro quo no longer seems to exist.

In short, in the current economic and political climate, it would be wishful thinking to expect any transformation away from adversarial public sector industrial relations any time soon. With governments returning increasingly to unilateral regulation of public sector workplaces (see Thompson and Swimmer, 1995:434), only ever-increasing levels of conflict can be expected, as those governments clash with large, well-organized public sector unions made up of people who have become more and more irate over their loss of job security and basic bargaining rights, and who seem more and more prepared to take bold, militant action in support of those rights. While the general public certainly has a strong stake in seeing lower levels of public sector conflict, particularly in health care and education, it has not thus far mobilized itself in such a way as to convince government of the need to put maintenance of these vital services on a par with deficit and tax reduction. For whatever reasons, governments at all levels have paid far more attention to citizens in their role as taxpayers than in their role as consumers of public services. Only intense public pressure on governments to reorder their priorities seems likely to achieve any significant reduction in public sector conflict, even in the short term.

But as we have tried to show throughout this chapter, the problems with Canadian public sector bargaining go beyond governments' heavy-handed approach to the current economic crisis. In this connection, it is perhaps useful to bear in mind that for the roughly 30 years during which most Canadian public sector workers have enjoyed bargaining rights, free public sector bargaining has taken place in at most half of those years in most jurisdictions. With all the evidence pointing towards governments' more or less permanent abandonment of free public sector bargaining (Swimmer, 1995:405), it may now be time not to tinker with the existing system, but to overhaul it to ensure both continued high quality of public services for Canadians, and basic bargaining rights for the men and women providing those services.

QUESTIONS
FOR DISCUSSION

1) How does work in the public sector differ from work in the private sector (if at all)?

2) Why is the public sector important to any study of IR?

3) Discuss the main stages of the evolution of public sector collective bargaining.

4) What was the significance of the *Public Service Staff Relations Act*?

5) What are the main *employer* differences between the public and private sectors?

6) What are the main *employee and union* differences between the two sectors?

7) What are their major *legislative and policy* differences?

8) Why are special dispute resolution methods needed for the public sector? Discuss some of these methods, indicating which appear to you to be most promising, and which most problematic.

9) What's the significance of the federal government's apparent abandonment of its traditional leadership role in employment and pay equity?

10) How (if at all) do you think governments can meet their commitments to deficit and debt reduction while maintaining free collective bargaining in the public sector?

11) Based on what you have learned so far, would you like to work in the public sector? Would you recommend that a friend or relative apply to work in that sector? Why, or why not?

SUGGESTIONS
FOR FURTHER READING

Swimmer, Gene, and Mark Thompson (Eds.). (1995). *Public sector collective bargaining in Canada*. Kingston: Queen's IRC Press. An indispensable book for anyone with an interest in the public sector. It should be required reading for all staff and management at Treasury Board. Contains articles on subjects ranging from collective bargaining to compensation and pay equity. Of particular note are the papers on health care, by Larry Haiven; on public sector union growth, by Joe Rose; on provincial public service issues, by former NUPGE president John Fryer; and on comparative public sector issues, by P.B. Beaumont.

Warrian, Peter. (1996). *Hard bargain: Transforming public sector labour-management relations*. Toronto: McGilligan. This author argues that the public sector is in a state of fundamental transformation, driven by equally fundamental economic constraints, and that traditional, highly adversarial public sector labour-management relations pose a major impediment to needed change and must be radically restructured.

Zussman, David, and Jak Jabes. (1989). *The vertical solitude: Managing in the public sector.* **Halifax: Institute for Research on Public Policy.** This study on public sector management deserves to be better-known than it is. It provides significant research evidence in support of its thesis that managing in the public sector is a different, and in many ways more difficult, job than managing in the private sector.

ENDNOTES

[1] As noted by Fryer (1995:355), in 1994 the Prince Edward Island government unilaterally rolled back public sector pay by 8.5 percent. Such a reduction amounts to roughly one month's pay per year, in a province where pay levels already lag behind those in most of the rest of Canada.

[2] The Alberta government has also imposed draconian cuts on its public servants (Fryer, 1995:360).

[3] Through the 1980s and early 1990s, as noted by Beaumont (1995:424–425), there was an unusually high rate of public sector strike action in such countries as Belgium, France, Greece, and Portugal. More recently, 1996 saw a series of major public sector strikes in Germany and a general strike sparked by public sector unions in France.

[4] An exception was 1991, the year of the federal public service strike, when the public sector accounted for 57 percent of all person-days lost.

[5] Determining the share of union members in the public and private sectors is not an exact science, as Rose (1995:23) notes, since official statistics do not classify union members by public or private sector status. Our estimate was obtained by summing the number of members of public sector unions enumerated in the 1997 *Workplace Information Directory* and dividing that number by the total number of union members listed in that directory for 1996.

[6] See Peirce (1989) for a more detailed discussion.

[7] Rose (1995:21) notes that as of 1945, there were about 40 000 public sector union members, or roughly 5 percent of the country's total union membership. Almost certainly most would have been outside municipal workers, who faced less daunting legal obstacles to unionization partly because municipal workers have always been covered by general labour acts rather than by special, and generally more restrictive, public sector legislation. For a more detailed discussion of the eventual of municipal collective bargaining, see Graham (1995:181–183).

[8] This structure has since been simplified considerably. The largest public service union, the Public Service Alliance of Canada (PSAC) now negotiates with the government at seven bargaining tables. Each table negotiates issues in both a master agreement and individual agreements covering specific groups (Swimmer, 1995:392).

[9] In 1994, Ontario passed a new public service employment act granting its public servants the right to strike (Fryer, 1995:346).

[10] Between 1965 and 1974 (Ponak and Thompson, 1995:440), back-to-work legislation was invoked 12 times, or just slightly more than once a year. Six of the 12 back-to-work laws were in Quebec.

11 For a useful discussion of this change of attitude, see Godard (1994:262–263).

12 These preferences were clearly reinforced by the public service unions' actions. During the mid 1970s, the relatively moderate Professional Institute of the Public Service of Canada (PIPSC) began an internal PR campaign to encourage its members to abandon arbitration in favour of striking. In 1985, PSAC went further, passing a motion at its national convention requiring all bargaining units to choose the conciliation- strike route (Swimmer, 1995:377).

13 In addition to the famous "Common Front" strike of 1972 (discussed in the labour history chapter), major public sector disputes during the 1970s and early 1980s included 21 complete or partial work stoppages on the Montreal Transit system (19 of them illegal), a nine-month shutdown of the Quebec City public transit system in 1979, and a six-week strike of Montreal's blue-collar workers in 1980 (Boivin and Déom, 1995:471).

14 For as long as Bill 19 remained in effect. When an NDP government replaced Vander Zalm's Socreds in 1991, one of its first acts was to repeal this bill and the Compensation Stabilization program that had frozen public sector wages since 1982 (Craig and Solomon, 1996:365). The new government also did away with Bill 19's sweeping definition of essential services and replaced it with more limited essential services legislation roughly comparable to the Quebec legislation described earlier in the chapter (Craig and Solomon, 1996:235).

15 In other words, if public servants received a 1 percent wage increase, 1 percent of all public servants would have to be laid off.

16 Throughout the Mulroney years, cabinet members, Commons committee heads, and Conservative MPs frequently attacked public servants and other public employees in the press. In a particularly notable attack, Commons Finance Committee chair Don Blenkarn said that after Ottawa voters turned out several Conservative MPs in favour of Liberals in the 1988 federal election, public servants should be prepared to take what was coming to them.

17 Initially, the Klein government sought to eliminate taxing authority for all boards. It backed down following a threatened constitutional challenge by the Catholic boards (Thomason, 1995:280).

18 CBC Radio News Report, Thursday, September 10.

19 As the final version of this chapter was being prepared (January 1999), the province's health care support employees were embroiled in a dispute with the hospital associations. After staging a one-day strike during the first week of January, CUPE (the union representing the health care workers) agreed to return to the bargaining table and not to stage any more strikes (CBC Radio News, January 10, 1999).

20 As we note elsewhere in the chapter, this has begun to change in recent years, as more provinces, including Ontario and Alberta, have moved towards direct, centralized control over the school system.

21 For a useful discussion of the issues contained in this paragraph, see Ponak (1982).

22 In 1992, the author had nearly 200 hours of teaching assistance in an introductory IR course. In 1998, he had just 50 hours for a similar course with only 20 percent lower enrollment.

23 The one important exception here is construction, where many provinces have introduced private-wide bargaining to combat the historical imbalance of power between strong building trade unions and weak construction employers and employer associations (Rose, 1992:189–190).

[24] In subsequent changes to *PSSRA*, this number was reduced to 26 (Swimmer, 1995:390–391).

[25] Whatever the merits of any Charter-based challenges to statutory designation of public sector bargaining agents, such designation appears to violate a key principle of Canadian labour legislation, namely that the employer should have no hand in the formation or operation of a union. Since government is ultimately the employer of all public sector workers, especially public servants, statutory designation of the bargaining amounts to the employer's choosing which union will represent its workers. Somewhat similar provisions do exist in a few private sector labour acts; for example, Quebec's construction act (discussed in the previous chapter) specifies that construction workers must belong to one of five duly recognized associations.

[26] The restriction on bargaining over pensions applies not just to federal and provincial public servants, but also to many municipal employees, teachers, and health care workers (Thompson and Ponak, 1995:431).

[27] Jackson (1995:319) notes that police departments conduct discipline under a military-style code free from the "diluting influence of civilian arbitrators and just-cause provisions."

[28] For a fascinating if sometimes horrifying first-hand account of a controlled hospital strike in Vancouver, see Weiler (1980).

[29] As Craig and Solomon (1996:315–316) note, the government of Quebec has long refused to submit most disputes in the public and parapublic sectors to arbitration for just this reason.

[30] That is, than most private sector industries.

CHAPTER 10

BARGAINING STRUCTURE
AND THE NEGOTIATION PROCESS

"And that's our final offer!" Negotiators often try to make it look as if their settlement was achieved only at the last minute, after a frenetic all-night session. This way, their constituents will be convinced that the negotiator "gave it her best shot."

The negotiating process is critical in the IR system since in unionized workplaces, most outcomes are established through collective bargaining. Indeed, negotiations play an important role even in non-unionized establishments. We start this chapter with a consideration of bargaining structure, which may have a good deal to do with determining the relative balance of power between the parties, and may also be a factor in the ease or difficulty of negotiations. Next, we look at the negotiating process itself. An important part of this examination will be a discussion of the concept of a settlement zone, and the issues to which the settlement zone concept does and does not apply.

COLLECTIVE BARGAINING: A BRIEF OVERVIEW

Collective bargaining may be defined as "the determination of terms and conditions of employment through negotiations between employers and representatives of employees" (Rogow, 1989b:44). In Canada, as in most industrialized countries, such bargaining is conducted within a well-defined legal framework. In the two previous chapters, we discussed that framework as it applies to the private and public sectors, respectively. Here and in the next chapter, our concern is with the negotiation process itself, as well as with the structure of collective bargaining and the collective agreements that are its direct results. In the two subsequent chapters (strikes and grievances), our concern will be with the two types of conflict most commonly arising out of the collective bargaining process.

Bargaining Structure

Bargaining structure is of considerable importance to any discussion of collective bargaining because particular types of structure have been related to higher strike levels, higher levels of inflation, and even conflict within unions (Anderson, 1989b). In addition, structure has been associated with bargaining power, the types of issues that are negotiated, and the internal politics on both sides of the bargaining table (Anderson, 1989b; Chaykowski, 1995:230–231).

At its simplest level, "collective bargaining structure" answers the question "Who bargains with whom?" (Rogow, 1989a:132). This is important information to know, since it is difficult to evaluate any bargaining process without knowing to which parties any agreement eventually negotiated will apply (Chaykowski, 1995:231). As we'll see later in the section, different bargaining structures are commonly distinguished from one another through the number of unions, employers, work establishments, and/or employees involved (Rogow, 1989a:132).

A more detailed definition is offered by Thomas Kochan (1980:84), who defines bargaining structure as "the scope of employees and employers covered or affected by the bargaining agreement." Kochan goes on distinguish between the **formal** structure, which is the negotiation unit (i.e., those employees and employers legally bound by the terms of the agreement), and the **informal** structure (i.e., other employees or employers affected by the results of a negotiated settlement through pattern bargaining or some other process that is not legally binding). In this section, our main concern is with formal structures, though informal structures will be briefly discussed in connection with pattern bargaining.

It is also important to distinguish between the **certification unit,** or the group of employees designated by a labour board as appropriate for collective bargaining, and the **negotiation unit,** or the grouping of employees that actually takes part in such bargaining (Anderson, 1989b; Rogow, 1989a). The actual negotiation unit may comprise several different certification units, assuming the parties agree (Anderson, 1989b:212).[1] Though not unknown in the private sector, joint or coordinated bargaining by several different unions has been more frequent in the public sector, as in the case of Quebec's 1972 Common Front, which as we noted earlier was formed by the CSN, QFL, and the CEQ (provincial teachers' federation) to bargain with the provincial government on behalf of the province's teachers, hospital workers, and civil servants (Boivin, 1989:416). In some cases, the combination may also be made at the instigation of the employer, who may wish to negotiate with a unit composed of similar groups of employees in several plants or even to combine with other employers in the same industry (Anderson, 1989b:212). It should, however, be noted that multi-employer bargaining is comparatively rare outside the public sector (see Chapter 9) and the construction industry (Rose, 1986, 1992), where it has often been legislatively mandated to help promote greater labour-management stability.

Types of Bargaining Structure

The most basic distinction is between **centralized** structures (involving relatively few sets of negotiations per jurisdiction or industry with each covering relatively large numbers of workers), and **decentralized** structures (those involving large numbers of negotiations per jurisdiction or industry with each covering relatively few workers). By international standards, Canadian bargaining structure is quite decentralized (Chaykowski, 1995; Anderson, 1989b; Rogow, 1989a), with negotiations most often occurring between a single employer and a single union (Chaykowski, 1995), unlike the situation prevailing in many European countries, such as Germany and Sweden (Adams, 1995a). At least in the private sector, Canadian bargaining structures have also been becoming increasingly decentralized in recent years, owing mainly to the breakdown of traditional multi-employer or pattern bargaining arrangements in several major industrial sectors (see Rose, 1986; Forrest, 1989). The reasons for Canada's generally decentralized bargaining structure and for the recent tendency towards even greater decentralization will be discussed in some detail later in this section.

Six basic types of bargaining structure have been identified in the literature (Chaykowski, 1995:231–232; Anderson, 1989b. Also see Rogow, 1989a). These structures are differentiated from each other according to (a) the number of employers involved (one or many); (b) for single employers, the number of establishments or specific places of businesses involved (one or many); and (c) the number of unions involved (one or many). Each of the six types is discussed below.

SINGLE-PLANT, SINGLE-UNION, SINGLE-EMPLOYER This is one of the most common bargaining structures and involves negotiations at a single workplace. It often occurs because the employer operates at one location only, has only one unionized establishment, or has different unions at different locations (Chaykowski, 1995:231); however, in some cases it may also occur because of the wishes of the employer or union. This type of structure is very common in bargaining between universities and their faculty associations and has also been found to be quite common in such industries as forestry, mining, and manufacturing (Anderson, 1989b). One reason for the frequency of this type of structure in Canada has been labour boards' tendency to use workers' "community of interest" as a major criterion in certification unit determination. This criterion generally pushes labour boards in the direction of smaller and more homogeneous units (Rogow, 1989a:139; Anderson, 1989b:221).

SINGLE-EMPLOYER, MULTI-ESTABLISHMENT, SINGLE-UNION This structure, which is also quite common, involves the negotiation of a single collective agreement across several different workplaces by the same employer and union. It offers useful economies of scale for both employers and unions in situations where the employer runs an integrated operation across a number of generally similar establishments (Chaykowski, 1995:232), and is most common in public administration, transportation, and communications (Anderson, 1989b). In public administration, for instance, the Public Service Alliance (as we noted in Chapter 9) negotiates nationwide agreements with the federal government (Chaykowski, 1995:232). In telecommunications, province-wide agreements are the norm, with separate units for operators, craft workers, and sales and clerical employees (Verma and Weiler, 1992:419). Though this is not common, in some cases a labour board will require that certification be on a multi-plant basis, as in the case of Nova Scotia's "Michelin Bill" (Anderson, 1989b:221), passed to make union certification more difficult and thus to prevent the Michelin Tire plant from leaving the province.

SINGLE-EMPLOYER, SINGLE-ESTABLISHMENT, MULTI-UNION This type of bargaining structure involves a negotiating partnership between two or more unions within the same workplace, as when production workers represented by an industrial union negotiate together with maintenance workers represented by a craft union (Chaykowski, 1995:232). It is quite rare in Canada (Chaykowski, 1995; Anderson, 1989b:214), probably because in most situations where workers from different occupations within the same establishment feel they have enough in common to bargain together, they will already have joined the same union.

SINGLE-EMPLOYER, MULTI-ESTABLISHMENT, MULTI-UNION This is another relatively rare type of structure, found mostly notably in the railway industry where operating union coalitions bargain as a group with each of the major railways

(Chaykowski, 1995:232). Where it does occur, it is most likely to be found in industries made up of a few very large employers and a larger number of small craft unions (Chaykowski, 1995).

MULTI-EMPLOYER, MULTI-ESTABLISHMENT, SINGLE-UNION   This type of structure is most apt to be found in industries characterized by large numbers of relatively small employers and a single dominant industrial or craft union (Chaykowski, 1995). Among the industries in which it is most often found are trucking, fishing, and forestry (Anderson, 1989b:214). This type of structure is also found in health care, especially in bargaining with registered nurses, who typically are represented by a single, province-wide union (Chaykowski, 1995:232; Haiven, 1995).

MULTI-EMPLOYER, MULTI-ESTABLISHMENT, MULTI-UNION This most centralized type of bargaining structure is rarely one that parties choose for themselves. It is found most often in the construction industry, where it has generally been imposed by governments in a bid to bring labour peace following major disputes (Chaykowski, 1995:232; Rose, 1992:190; Boivin and Déom, 1995; see also the discussion of Quebec construction legislation in Chapter 8). Under this type of structure, bargaining is normally conducted through a certified employers' association rather than by individual employers (see Rose, 1992:190). In some cases, as in British Columbia's construction industry, supplementary legislation may also provide for bargaining through a province-wide council of trade unions—the union equivalent to an employers' association (Rose, 1992; Anderson, 1989b:215).

Reasons for Canada's Decentralized Structure

A key reason for Canada's generally decentralized bargaining structure is the fact of provincial jurisdiction over most labour relations matters. This tends to make national-level bargaining quite difficult (Chaykowski, 1995:231), except in interprovincial industries under federal jurisdiction, given that such things as certification procedures and bargaining unit determination criteria tend to differ significantly from province to province.

 "LABOUR NEGOTIATIONS AT ONTARIO PROCESSING PLANTS"
www.ontariopork.on.ca/News_PR/porknews9709.html

Given provincial jurisdiction, a second important reason is labour boards' tendency to determine bargaining units according to criteria that generally favour the creation of relatively small, homogeneous bargaining units rather than larger, more heterogeneous, more broadly based ones (Rogow, 1989a). As noted earlier, boards often place very considerable emphasis on the creation of an IR "community of interest" in determining appropriate bargaining units. In practice, this often means, for example, emphasizing the differences between office and production workers in the same establishment, rather than emphasizing their common interests. This is evidenced by the tendency of both Ontario and federal boards to create separate units for these groups (Rogow, 1989a:141).[2] Another criterion often used by boards, that of facilitating unionization whenever a majority of employees wish it, has also tended to lead to the creation of small and relatively homogeneous bargaining units, since smaller units are generally more cohesive and easier to organize (Rogow, 1989a:139).

In some cases, to be sure, labour boards have also been guided by the desire to facilitate harmonious bargaining relations between the parties. Where this criterion is primary, boards are more apt to rule in favour of larger, more inclusive bargaining units, since more inclusive units can often reduce (or even eliminate, assuming they are all-inclusive) the possibility of conflict between units, and can also facilitate broader and longer-term bargaining objectives, and more generally reduce labour-management conflict (Rogow, 1989a:139–140). However, such a situation is more the exception than the rule. Except in the construction industry and in British Columbia, where broader-based bargaining has long been promoted as a matter of public policy, the creation of "communities of interest" has generally been given greater weight than the reduction of conflict or creation of viable longer-term bargaining relationships (Rogow, 1989a:140–141).

A third reason has to do with the attitude of North American employers, many of whom seem, on principle, to oppose broader-based bargaining, particularly any sort of multi-employer bargaining that would require them to surrender some of their control over bargaining to an employers' association (see Adams, 1995a). While such a position is understandable in hard times, when, for example, an employers' association may sign an agreement containing wage provisions that a marginal firm will find difficult or even impossible to meet, many employers' opposition to this type of bargaining appears to be rooted in something deeper than economic calculation (see Rogow, 1989a).[3] Some simply take visceral exception to any bargaining arrangements requiring them to subordinate their own interests to those of the employer group represented by the association, or to relinquish any measure of control over how their enterprises are run. For others, the opposition to multi-employer bargaining may be more firmly rooted in an individualistic philosophy that sees the creation of broad-based employer groups as an implicit recognition of the existence of fundamental class distinctions in society—something they are not prepared to accept (Adams, 1995a:503). At least modest evidence in support of employers' general opposition to multi-employer bargaining is offered by Sauvé, whose 1971 study found unions reasonably interested—and employers significantly less interested—in exploring sectoral-level bargaining. Given that Sauvé's research was conducted at a time of fairly high inflation, when more centralized bargaining arrangements could well have seemed attractive from a purely economic perspective (see below for a more detailed discussion), one might reasonably suppose the employers' opposition to have been based primarily on broad philosophical or ideological considerations of the type we have just been discussing.

REASONS FOR INCREASED DECENTRALIZATION While many Canadian employers dislike centralized bargaining structures for reasons other than economic ones, the economy has been the major reason for the increase in decentralized Canadian bargaining structures and the breakdown of many previously centralized ones in recent years. The Canadian IR system has by no means been alone in this trend towards greater decentralization. All across the industrialized western world, "decentralization" and "flexibility" have become "industrial relations catchwords" over the past two decades (Scheuer, 1992:168). In the United States, a change in the product market and increased competition from non-unionized firms helped lead to the break-up of **pattern bargaining** arrangements that had prevailed in the rubber tire industry since shortly after the Second World War (Kochan, McKersie, and Cappelli, 1984), whereby the agreement negotiated between the United Rubber Workers and its chosen target among the four largest tire companies became the agreement for all four, and thus most of the industry.[4] In Sweden, employers seeking more flexibility pushed bargaining from the national to the industry level, and even in some cases to the company level (Adams, 1995a; Hammarstrom, 1993; Kjellberg, 1992). Similar moves have taken place, generally at the behest of employers, in such countries as Denmark (Scheuer, 1992; Ferner and Hyman, 1992b) and Italy (Ferner and Hyman, 1992a). Even the German system, long considered among Europe's most stable, has made certain moves, albeit smaller ones, in the same direction (Jacobi, Keller, and Muller-Jentsch, 1992).[5]

"NEW COMPETITION LAW FOR SOUTH AFRICA"
www.ahi.co.za

In Canada, increased competition, driven sometimes by trade liberalization and sometimes by other factors, has arguably been the major cause of decentralization of bargaining structures over the past two decades. Sometimes, one of the weaker firms in a centralized or pattern bargaining arrangement finds it can no longer meet the industry standard and remain competitive, with the result that it withdraws from the centralized arrangement. Soon other firms are likely to find themselves in a similar position and likewise withdraw. Once that starts happening, the centralized arrangement's demise is virtually inevitable. In other cases (as in the case of General Motors' unsuccessful attempt to do away with pattern bargaining in its 1996 negotiations with the Canadian Auto Workers), an industry leader sets out with the avowed intention of ending the arrangement.

Growing competitive pressures, created in part by the increased deregulation of previously heavily regulated industries, led to the dissolution of employer associations in the railway, pulp and paper, and trucking industries (Rose, 1986a:3). In meat-packing (Forrest, 1989), the source of the increased competitive pressures was somewhat different. Here, the industry was faced with over-capacity and aging, inefficient plants at a time when red meat consumption was shrinking owing to a pronounced change in consumer tastes (Forrest, 1989:402). However, the end result was pretty much the same, as first one firm and then another withdrew from the old pattern bargaining arrangement and the union was forced to agree to such major concessions as a two-year wage freeze and a **two-tier wage scheme,** whereby newly hired workers were paid about half what existing workers were getting, at the Gainer's plant in Edmonton (Forrest, 1989). Here, as in other cases, the end of the pattern bargaining arrangement led to a sharp erosion of the union's bargaining power (Forrest, 1989:403), as it lost its ability to take wages out of competition.

One major industry that has so far been able to resist the shift to decentralized bargaining structures has been the auto industry (Kumar and Meltz, 1992). One of the main reasons why the industry has been able to retain its long-standing pattern bargaining arrangement, even in the face of growing foreign competition, has been a bilateral Canada-U.S. Auto Pact, which created an integrated continental market in auto products and parts manufacturing while maintaining previous levels of Canadian production and employment (Kumar and Meltz, 1992). However, as foreign competition, particularly from Japan,[6] became more severe during the 1990s, even this most venerable of pattern bargaining arrangements was put to the test. Only a determined struggle by the Canadian Auto Workers in its 1996 strike against General Motors (discussed in detail in Chapter 12) allowed pattern bargaining to survive. It is by no means clear that pattern bargaining will survive the next round of auto negotiations, although the union will almost certainly do its best to preserve it.

The discussion to this point has been almost entirely concerned with the private sector. In the public sector, a more difficult economic climate tends to lead in the opposite direction, as provincial governments increasingly concerned with holding down public sector compensation costs come to play a more and more direct role in public sector bargaining (Muir, 1971). For example, in elementary and secondary education, bargaining has, over the past three decades, moved from the local to the provincial level in Quebec, New Brunswick, Nova Scotia, and Saskatchewan (see Gallagher and Wetzel, 1980). More recently, centralized teacher bargaining has been adopted in British Columbia, in a move strenuously opposed by the provincial teachers' federation (Thomason, 1995:286–287). As this chapter is being written, the province of Ontario is moving from local to province-wide bargaining in education. The provincial government's assumption of control over the education system was a key issue in the 1997 and 1998 teachers' strikes. Teachers' federations' almost universal opposition to centralized bargaining is sometimes based on the belief their members can get a better deal at the local level, and almost always on the belief that they and their members will have more control over their jobs and more say in educational policy decisions affecting them and their students. In Saskatchewan, one province where centralized teacher bargaining appears to have been brought off without a great deal of opposition from the teachers' federation, input on local issues is assured through a two-tier bargaining system, whereby items of general applicability such as wages and retirement benefits are negotiated provincially and issues of purely local significance are left for local-level negotiators to hammer out (Anderson, 1989b; Gallagher and Wetzel, 1980). A similar two-tier public sector bargaining structure has been devised in Quebec (Boivin and Déom, 1995:429).

Effects of Different Bargaining Structures

EFFECTS ON EMPLOYERS AND UNIONS The first thing to be said about different types of bargaining structure is that their effects on different parties tend to be different depending on whether the economy is weak or strong. In good times (i.e., high parts of the business cycle marked by low unemployment and usually relatively high inflation), private sector unions generally favour decentralized bargaining structures. Under such structures, at times when the demand for labour is high and employers are very much interested in maintaining labour peace, they can often **whipsaw** employers, that is, use one settlement with one employer as the basis for obtaining similar or (generally) better terms with others (Gallagher and Wetzel, 1980). At such times, many employers are willing to give up some degree of control and enter into multi-employer bargaining agreements, because these will combat whipsawing by establishing a common wage scale throughout the industry (Gallagher and Wetzel, 1980). Indeed, some well-known centralized bargaining arrangements, including most notably the national-level bargaining that prevailed in Sweden from the 1950s through the 1980s (Kjellberg, 1992:96), have actually been started at the employers' behest, with an eye to moderating wage settlements. Other benefits employers may seek from multi-employer bargaining include a reduction in work stoppages and scale economies in negotiations and contract administration, as well as reduced uncertainty about labour costs and, therefore, about product pricing (Rogow, 1989a:146). Even though they may not like some of the results of centralized multi-employer negotiations, in particular the loss of their ability to whipsaw, unions also share in some of these gains, such as scale economies in negotiations, and may also achieve other benefits, such as the ability to bring better negotiators to the table or to deal with more senior members of management (Rogow, 1989a). For these reasons, they can sometimes be convinced to go along with the centralized bargaining arrangements.

In bad times, (again confining ourselves to the private sector), it is unions who usually favour centralized bargaining arrangements, while employers often seek to escape from them. Now, whipsawing is often done by employers, who may obtain concessions from the union in one negotiation and use this initial set of concessions as the basis for even greater ones in another negotiation. So long as the bargaining structure remains centralized, it is harder for an employer to force concessions on a union, and the costs of a strike are apt to be considerably greater. As well, employers' attempts to rid themselves of unions, which have become increasingly frequent since the early 1980s (see Kochan et al., 1984; Fisher and Kushner, 1986; Rose, 1992), are a good deal harder to pull off under centralized than under decentralized bargaining. Ending centralized arrangements also means that employers are free to bargain based on their own particular circumstances, rather than having to take into account the circumstances of other firms that may not be as efficient or as well-run and that may thus serve to "drag them down" under centralized bargaining. At a time of ever-increasing competitiveness, this kind of flexibility means a good deal to most employers.

Other Effects

WAGES In general, decentralized structures lead to bargaining outcomes determined mainly by market forces (Anderson, 1989b:229). With regard to wages, this means greater dispersion between higher and lower-paid workers and greater union–non-union wage differentials (Anderson, 1989b). For example, in Sweden, the devolution of bargaining from the national to the industry level during the late 1980s and early 1990s was accompanied by increased wage dispersion (Kjellberg, 1992). In good times, decentralized structures generally lead to higher wage settlements, since unions can whipsaw employers into accepting their terms (Anderson, 1989b; Gallagher and Wetzel, 1980; Rogow, 1989a). In bad times, such structures typically lead to lower compensation levels, as employer whipsawing (Rogow, 1989a:151) and increased competition from non-union firms allow employers to force unions to agree to productivity improvements, wage freezes, or even more radical measures such as outright pay cuts or two-tier wage systems (Anderson, 1989b:229; Forrest, 1989; Rose, 1986a).[7]

CANADA SAFEWAY LTD. ON LABOUR ISSUES AND NEGOTIATIONS
www.safeway/mblabour.com

In contrast, centralized structures are marked by a significantly greater degree of government involvement both in the bargaining process and in any subsequent dispute settlement processes (Rogow, 1989a:154). This increased involvement is understandable, given that much more is usually at stake in centralized negotiations—both because they directly cover more workers and because they are often "trend-setters" for other agreements, including pattern bargaining arrangements or government-decreed extension across entire industries (Rogow, 1989a). With respect to outcomes, these structures generally lead to greater similarity of wages, benefits, and other terms of employment across industries or jurisdictions (Rogow, 1989a:152).

INFLATION   At the macro-economic level, centralized systems have been associated with lower levels of inflation than decentralized ones (Tarantelli, 1986), at least in good economic times.[8, 9] Again, more moderate settlements are likely to result at least in part from unions' loss of the ability to whipsaw. In addition, there is often a different political dynamic at work in centralized systems, many of which have traditionally been found in countries with strong labour or social democratic parties with a good chance of forming the government, such as Sweden, Denmark, and Austria (see Tarantelli, 1986). When such a party forms the government, the labour movement will often be able to achieve much of its agenda politically and may well be induced to agree to lower wage settlements in return for pension and tax reform, price controls, a full employment guarantee, or other government policies favouring workers and unions (Adams, 1989). The promise of favourable government policies can also induce unions to call fewer strikes than they otherwise would (Adams, 1989; Tarantelli, 1986).

STRIKES   An argument often advanced in favour of more centralized bargaining structures is that they lead to fewer strikes and less time lost due to those strikes (Anderson, 1982 and 1989b; see also Rogow, 1989a). That centralized structures should lead to fewer strikes seems almost axiomatic, given that such structures involve many fewer sets of negotiations at any given time than decentralized ones. In addition, larger negotiations with more at stake are likely to be conducted by more skillful and experienced negotiators (Rogow, 1989a:149). Managers with real decision-making authority are more likely to be at the table or at least in close contact with the management negotiating team (Rogow, 1989a:146, 151). And because of the relatively greater importance of centralized negotiations, governments, as noted above, are more apt to intervene both to prevent strikes and to end them quickly should they occur (Rogow, 1989a:154).

Internationally (see Adams, 1989, 1995a), the evidence strongly suggests that centralized systems result not just in fewer strikes, but in the loss of less working-time. A similar conclusion was reached by Perry and Angle (1981) in their study of strike activity in U.S. transit systems. However, for Canada, a study by Gunderson, Kervin, and Reid (1986) finds a higher probability of strikes in bargaining units of greater than 1000 employees. A study by Rose (1986a) of construction industry disputes finds that, although strike frequency decreased in larger bargaining units, the number of workers involved and average strike duration both increased. Another study cited by Anderson (1989b:230) finds a lower probability of strikes in single-plant units than in multi-plant, single-employer structures. Such results have led various commentators to warn that more centralized Canadian bargaining structures are not a panacea for reducing industrial conflict (Anderson, 1989b; Rogow, 1989a:150). There is also reason to believe that centralization may lead to increased wildcat strikes, due to increased internal union conflict and membership dissatisfaction with the union (Rogow, 1989a; Stern and Anderson, 1978).

Why has centralization led to a reduction in working time lost to strikes internationally, but not in Canada? The likeliest explanation is that here, centralized structures have not been accompanied by a widespread shift of conflict from the bargaining table to the political arena, as they generally have in European countries such as Sweden and Germany. That is primarily because labour or social democratic parties such as the NDP or PQ, with which unions might make such political bargains, have never formed the government federally, and have only occasionally done so at the provincial level. Lacking the political option that many European unions possess, Canadian unions have used the increased strike power that centralized structures undeniably provide (see Rogow, 1989a:146) to help them achieve their ends through the collective bargaining process. Thus it is not centralization itself, but the shift in the locus of conflict that often accompanies it that seems to be the main reason for reduced industrial conflict levels in European countries with centralized structures. This serves as an excellent illustration of the point made by Mishel (1986), that bargaining structures cannot meaningfully be studied in isolation from other, broader aspects of the economic and political environment.

The Bargaining Process

The effects of greater centralization of the bargaining process are somewhat mixed. On the one hand, centralization seems to make negotiations go more smoothly because of the superior negotiators generally conducting them and the presence or availability of senior management with real authority. On the other hand, because in centralized bargaining each side represents a greater number of union or management factions, internal or intraorganizational bargaining becomes more complex, with the result that negotiations as a whole tend to go more slowly (Mishel, 1986:151). There is also evidence that centralized negotiations may increase local union negotiators' and rank-and-file members' feelings of alienation from the negotiations and from the centralized negotiators, who are less likely to be closely attuned to specific local conditions and issues (Mishel, 1986:153). Such feelings of alienation may well be a factor in the higher incidence of wildcat strikes found in centralized structures (Mishel, 1986; Anderson, 1989b:231).

Representational Issues

Perhaps the greatest single criticism of centralized structures is that they tend by their very nature to encompass issues of general importance, leaving out issues of more local concern and thus causing local union members and lower-level managers to feel left out. One consequence of this is that local union officials and lower-level management may become reluctant to administer collective agreements adequately, because they resent having to enforce agreements they feel they had little or no hand in fashioning (Anderson, 1989b:231). Other consequences include an increased incidence of wildcat strikes (discussed above) and higher rates of contract rejections (Anderson, 1989b). In addition, centralized negotiations tend to cover a narrower range of issues (Rogow, 1989a:153), which can also be a source of resentment when local parties feel their concerns haven't been adequately addressed at the bargaining table.

One way around this problem is to use two-tier or multi-tier bargaining systems (discussed earlier in the section). Such systems have long been used in a number of European countries (Adams, 1989); in Canada, they are generally confined to the public sector (Gallagher and Wetzel, 1980; Hébert, 1995). While two-tier and multi-tier bargaining systems are no panacea to the representational problems raised by centralized bargaining, and may even generate certain tensions of their own (Rogow, 1989a:153), the evidence suggests they can help reduce a number of the problems associated with centralization, particularly when the union is careful to solicit local input throughout the bargaining process, as appears to have been the case in Saskatchewan (Gallagher and Wetzel, 1980).

Summary

Bargaining structure is a significant aspect of collective bargaining because it can help determine such things as the parties' relative bargaining power, the types of issues that are raised at the table, the speed and ease with which negotiations are concluded, and even the degree of conflict within union and management teams. A key distinction is that between decentralized and centralized structures. In general, unions prefer decentralized structures in good times because they can then whipsaw employers into granting them higher wage increases than they might otherwise be able to obtain. Conversely, in bad times, it is employers who prefer decentralized structures, both because such structures allow greater flexibility and control at the individual workplace level, and because they facilitate employer whipsawing of unions. Internationally, centralized structures have generally been associated with lower rates of inflation, unemployment, and industrial conflict; however, this does not generally appear to have been the case in Canada. While the reasons for Canada's divergence from the international pattern are not entirely clear, one explanation may be that in Canada, unlike most European countries, centralized bargaining has not been accompanied by a shift in the locus of most industrial conflict from the workplace level to the political arena. To the extent that this is true, the main reason for the lower rates of industrial conflict found in many European countries may not be centralization as such, but rather the shift from economic to political bargaining. Another, related reason may be that in countries with decentralized bargaining structures, like Canada, collective agreements (discussed in the next chapter) are generally longer, more detailed, and cover a broader range of issues than they do in countries with more centralized bargaining structures. The greater range of issues typically negotiated here could well be a cause both of longer negotiations and of more frequent bargaining breakdowns.

THE NEGOTIATION PROCESS

A study of the negotiation process is an important part of any IR course because collective bargaining, through which collective agreements are concluded, involves detailed, often highly complex negotiations between unions and management organizations. While these negotiations have certain things in common with more conventional commercial negotiations, they also differ from commercial negotiations in a number of important respects. In this section, we take a brief look at the significance of negotiation in general before looking at some special features of union-management negotiations. The discussion then turns to the stages of negotiations and the concept of a settlement zone (including situations in which the settlement zone may not apply). We then take a closer look at the role played by bargaining power and at specific negotiating strategies. The chapter concludes with a brief discussion of ways to improve the bargaining process.

Negotiation in Everyday Life

The collective bargaining simulations that many instructors include in introductory IR courses are designed to give students a taste of the negotiating process. Not all introductory IR students will earn their living as union or management negotiators. But almost everyone, other than those pledged to live their lives as hermits or ascetics, will need negotiating skills. Such skills are important in obtaining a job, getting a promotion or transfer, raising children, making a marriage work, and arriving at a reasonable divorce settlement if it doesn't work, not to mention buying a house or a car. For example, a recent study showed that job seekers who negotiate over salary and benefits before signing up earn an average 3 to 4 percent more in compensation than those who do not—a difference that can add up to many thousands of dollars over a working lifetime (Kunde, 1998). Nor is the need for good negotiating skills confined to the workplace. In modern, two-career marriages, with both husband and wife often heavily overcommitted both at home and at work, frequent negotiation is needed to ensure domestic duties are apportioned fairly, children are adequately looked after, and the husband and wife get enough "quality time" both together and alone. And in divorce cases, good negotiating skills can mean the difference between a reasonably amicable separation agreement, essentially crafted by the parties themselves, that costs a relatively modest amount to draw up and the sort of nightmarish scenario involving lengthy court proceedings where the parties spend upwards of $10 000 each and have nothing to show for it other than a relationship that is even more embittered than it was prior to the divorce.

All in all, it is not going too far to suggest that negotiating ability is one of the most critical life skills a person can possess. Those who possess it are far likelier to succeed professionally, make and keep friends, and have happy and successful marriages and family lives than those who do not.

The Qualities of a Good Negotiator

Like a number of other aspects of the IR system, negotiation is often misrepresented in the media, giving members of the general public a false impression of what goes on at the bargaining table. Some, when asked what qualities a negotiator should bring to the table, would undoubtedly reply: "The ability to lie, cheat, and deceive and manipulate others for one's personal benefit." Others would probably include: "A willingness to engage in crass, boorish, aggressive behaviour aimed at intimidating one's opponents."

People taking this view fail to recognize that, particularly in labour negotiations, there is usually a long-term relationship to consider. Possibly a negotiator **could** succeed in taking unfair advantage once. But in the long run, such behaviour doesn't pay in labour negotiations. The other side will remember, and will be far less likely to trust you or your team in future negotiations. By and large, loud-mouthed, aggressive behaviour, outbursts of temper, personal attacks on members of the opposing side, and attempts to deceive the other side are the mark of the amateur;[10] more experienced negotiators are less likely to resort to threats (Kervin, 1989:205). Professionals know they will likely to have to face the same negotiator sitting across from them at some point in the future, and govern their conduct accordingly. As Lewicki, Saunders, and Minton (1997:232) note, negotiators will readily justify resorting to an ethically dubious "hardball" strategy when they are facing people whose behaviour they have previously experienced as exploitative, arguing that anticipatory self-defence legitimizes their actions. In the long run, the most successful negotiators are generally those who behave like the negotiator they would like to face on the other side of the table.

While negotiators do best when they adopt a bargaining style compatible with their own personalities (Fisher and Williams, 1989:203), and even experts sometimes disagree as to the precise qualities a good negotiator needs, most would list the following as important:

- a liking for people
- a liking for negotiation
- a knowledge of what they want
- excellent speaking and, above all, listening skills
- a clear knowledge of their objectives
- creativity in attempting to achieve those objectives
- empathy—the ability to put themselves in the other team's shoes
- persuasive ability
- persistence
- courage
- a good sense of humour
- the willingness to take risks
- honesty and integrity (Fisher and Williams, 1989:187–189, 202–3).

"INDUSTRIAL RELATIONS AND COOPERATIVES"
www.ilo.org/public/english/65entrep/papers/dulfer.htm

We have emphasized listening skills because it is by careful listening that the negotiators picks up cues from the other side. Often what is not said may be even more important than what is said, as issues that had previously seemed important to the other side simply fade from the table (Fisher and Williams, 1989:203). A sense of humour is also important because humour can be an excellent way to defuse the tension bound to arise during long and difficult bargaining sessions (Fisher and Williams, 1989).

Special Features of Union-Management Negotiations

People observing a union-management negotiation for the first time are often bewildered by its length and complexity. As Fisher and Williams note (1989:190–191), many commercial negotiations are concluded in half an hour or less. In many labour-management negotiations, the parties often haven't even started addressing the issues after half an hour. It may be weeks or even months before they so much as raise monetary issues, much less settle them. For much of this time, they may be arguing over comparatively minor issues. Why spend so much time bickering over a whole slew of peripheral issues when any fool could predict the whole thing will come down to wages and job security in the end (as probably happens at least 90 percent of the time)? Moreover, the process often involves lengthy set speeches, threats that neither party has any intention of carrying out, and numerous other rituals and posturings (Sass, 1989) that would be more appropriate in a theatrical performance than in what is, after all, a business transaction. Why can't the parties simply "talk turkey" from the outset and get the job done quickly, the way most commercial negotiators do (Fisher and Williams, 1989:191)?

There are at least four reasons for the generally far greater length and complexity of union-management negotiations. First, such negotiations typically address a far broader range of issues than do most commercial negotiations. Also, many of these issues are more complex than issues raised in the typical commercial deal. Second, union-management negotiations are quite strictly regulated by statute (Fisher and Williams, 1989). A union's need to ensure, for example, that it is complying with its statutory duty to represent all its members fairly may lead it to introduce a broader range of issues than it otherwise would, and to spend a fair amount of time on seemingly peripheral issues that it knows are unlikely to form part of the eventual settlement. Third (and not unrelated to the previous point) union-management negotiations are **representative negotiations,** at the end of which negotiators must emerge with a settlement acceptable not just to them but to their principals (senior executives on the management side, the membership on the union side), who have the ultimate say as to whether the tentative agreement is accepted or rejected (Fisher and Williams, 1989). Fourth, union-management relationships are generally long-term in nature (Fisher and Williams, 1989). Most have a history; most will also have a future. In arriving at a settlement, union and management negotiators must try to come up with solutions that will not merely meet the parties' immediate needs today, but will help them build or maintain an effective working relationship over the medium to long term. Since such a process involves making projections and educated guesses about the future and gets into the parties' feelings and perceptions as well as objective economic issues, it will almost inevitably be more complex than a commercial negotiation that addresses only economic issues and that is often set at a single point in time, or at most involves projection over, a time span of a year or two.

Broader and More Complex Range of Issues

In negotiating an agreement for, let us say, the purchase of 1000 desks for a government department, the negotiator for the department and the supplier normally need only be concerned with three things: the quality of the desks, their delivery date, and their price. Since the desks' quality can usually be ascertained on the spot by means of a direct inspection, this leaves two items to be negotiated: price and delivery date. Granted, there may be room for minor trade-offs here (i.e., "We'll give you $10 more per desk if you agree to a firm delivery date of September 1"); however, with only two variables, the room for creative packaging is rather limited.

"CUPE BARGAINING REPORT" ON TEACHING ASSISTANTS
www.zoo.utoronto.ca/BOARD1/messages/45.html

In contrast, union-management negotiations typically cover a broad range of issues including wages, many different benefits, job security, hours of work, vacation leave, work rules, procedures for layoff, transfer, and promotion, and various health and safety issues, in addition to the rights and responsibilities of the union and management organization (see Chapter 11 on the collective agreement for more detail). Even a cursory look at the above list will reveal a large number of possible trade-offs: wages for job security, benefits for wages, work rules for wages, or wages for reduced hours, to mention just a few. Because the typical work organization has many different occupational classes and groups of workers, changes in any of the above items may not be uniform across the entire work force, but could well affect members of different groups quite differently. All of this means that costing of tentative proposals and packages can be lengthy and complex, which in turn is likely to add considerably to the length and complexity of the overall negotiation process.

As well, not only are there more issues to consider in the typical union-management negotiation, but the issues themselves are often more complex. In a commercial negotiation such as the one described above, the process by which the desks are made is normally of little importance to either negotiator, so long as its costs are known and the desks can be delivered at the agreed time. In contrast, in a labour negotiation, the production process may well be critical, since it will affect not just the cost of the goods and services in question, but the way work is organized in the manufacturing facility, the ease with which that work is done, and in some cases even the health and safety of the people doing the work. Jointly negotiated rules regulating a work process are typically far more conceptually difficult and practically complex than provisions governing how money will be apportioned. In particular, the costing of such issues may be extremely difficult. Moreover, some issues, such as those involving protection against workplace discrimination and harassment or the establishment of a joint union-management committee to address certain issues, may by their very nature be more or less intangible or at least not readily quantifiable, and hence difficult to evaluate within the overall context of a set of negotiation results.

Because of the breadth and complexity of issues involved in most labour-management negotiations, more is often at stake here than in commercial negotiations, and emotions can run high on both sides, particularly as the strike deadline approaches. This too can complicate bargaining, not just between the parties, but within each of the negotiating teams.

Statutory Regulation of Collective Bargaining

Unlike many other kinds of negotiations, union-management ones are heavily regulated by government. To begin with, collective negotiations cannot even take place until a union receives certification from a labour board as the exclusive bargaining agent of those whom it represents (Fisher and Williams, 1989). As well, the union will remain those workers' bargaining agent until a majority of them to vote to terminate the process by decertifying the union. Since, as we pointed out in the labour law chapter, decertification can take place only at certain times, this fact alone inevitably makes most union-management relationships at least medium-term in length (see below for more details).

While Canadian labour relations law generally says little about the *content* of collective agreements, certain items, such as grievance procedures and minimum contract durations, are considered compulsory (Fisher and Williams, 1989). Perhaps more important, collective agreements cannot contain any provision that would be illegal under employment standards, human rights, or health and safety legislation. For example, no agreement can contain a provision paying less than the minimum wage or allowing workers to work more hours than the maximum allowable under employment standards legislation (Fisher and Williams, 1989:191–192). Similarly, agreements establishing separate locker-room facilities for workers of different races or paying women less than men for the same job would also be illegal (Fisher and Williams, 1989:192).

Labour relations legislation imposes much stricter restrictions with regard to the bargaining process. This is most obvious in the case of strikes and lockouts. Even in the private sector, no union can strike or employer lock out until the agreement has expired and, in most cases, until some kind of conciliation process has been attempted and certain time limits have passed. In the public sector, additional restrictions are often imposed, such as further time limits or extra steps to the dispute resolution process (see the discussion on Quebec in the public sector chapter for an example). In some cases, strikes are barred altogether, forcing the parties to take their disputes to binding arbitration. Habitual resort to arbitration can hinder the bargaining process through the **narcotic effect,** whereby the parties become dependent on arbitration and lose the ability to fashion their own agreements, or the **chilling effect,** whereby the parties refuse to make concessions in the expectation, or at least hope, that the arbitrator will arrive at a middle position, thereby relieving them of the need to make hard decisions on their own (Godard, 1994:353). Even when strikes and lockouts are permitted, a compulsory conciliation process may simply have the effect of delaying serious bargaining until after the conciliator has issued his or her findings. Indeed, some analysts suggest that the effect of the conciliation process, and its associated time delays may simply be to harden the parties in their positions by giving them more time to prepare for a strike, thus making a strike that much more likely (Godard, 1994:350).

At the table, both sides are required to bargain in good faith and with an eye to concluding an agreement (Fisher and Williams, 1989:192). In addition, the union has in most jurisdictions a duty to represent its members fairly, which in some cases (see Chapter 8 for details) applies to the negotiation process as well to the handling of grievances. While Canadian labour boards do not take a consistent approach to bad-faith bargaining (Fisher and Williams, 1989), in general the duty to bargain in good faith would probably expedite the bargaining process somewhat, as delaying tactics such as reneging on previous concessions or adding new proposals would likely be ruled breaches of good-faith bargaining (Fisher and Williams, 1989).

The effects of duty of fair representation (DFR) provisions in labour legislation are somewhat harder to gauge, since labour boards very rarely find unions in breach of this duty on the basis of their conduct at the bargaining table. Where such a breach is found, it is normally on the basis of provisions favouring certain select groups (such as union officials), or a severely flawed or misleading consultation process (Fisher and Williams, 1989:193). It is not clear that statutory DFR provisions cause most unions to conduct negotiations any differently than they otherwise would. To the extent that such provisions *did* have an effect, it would probably be to slow down the process some-what, as for example by causing the union to raise issues addressing the needs of each of its major factions, regardless of the relative importance of those issues to the mem-bership as a whole, and thus to bring more issues to the table than it otherwise might.

The Nature of Representative Negotiations

Both union and management negotiators generally represent diverse constituencies, and both must obtain approval (from constituents and principals, respectively) before the collective agreement can take effect. Often members of the various management or union factions will be part of the bargaining team, leading chief negotiators to "put on a good show" with an eye to convincing those team members that they have genuinely expended their best efforts on their behalf (Fisher and Williams, 1989). In the eyes of observers like Bob Sass (1989:170–172), it is the need to meet con-stituents' psychological as well as economic needs that explains much of the other-wise irrelevant or even ludicrous ritual and ceremony often connected to the negotiation process. As well, such ritual and ceremony can serve broader strategic purposes, since they can help conceal one's own bottom line while one is busily probing for that of the other side (Sass, 1989:172).

On management teams, production managers often seek provisions granting them greater flexibility, such as permitting supervisors to do work normally done by bargaining unit members (Fisher and Williams, 1989:194). Those from finance and accounting are generally most concerned with cost containment (Fisher and Williams, 1989), while those from IR and HR are often most concerned with maintaining harmonious union-management relations, and, therefore, may be more inclined to accommodate the union.[11] The management negotiators may be hard-pressed to come up with a settlement that adequately meets all these conflicting objectives. Similarly, on the union side, younger workers with mouths to feed and mortgages to pay are likely to put greatest emphasis on up-front wages. Older workers in high tax brackets are likely to favour deferred payments such as pensions; women will generally push for maternity benefits and flexible hours provisions allowing them to take time for family matters when they need to (Fisher and Williams, 1989).

Knowing each of these constituencies' different preferences, the wise negotiator will include provisions addressing each of those preferences in the initial bargaining package, and will keep at least one of each group's major priority items on the table for as long as is reasonably possible. In this way, the negotiator can at least let constituents or principals know that she or he gave the issues in question his or her "best shot" (Fisher and Williams, 1989:199). Even then, the **intraorganizational bargaining** within each team (Walton and McKersie, 1963) will be fierce during team caucuses; in some cases it may actually be more difficult than the union-management negotiations themselves (Fisher and Williams, 1989:194). Not only does intraorganizational conflict complicate and lengthen the bargaining process; it is also associated with higher levels of bargaining impasses and strikes (Gunderson, Hyatt, and Ponak, 1995:393). Internal political battles may pose particular difficulties for unions, because they are democratic organizations and because their activities, unlike those of many management organizations, are generally highly visible and their leaders' freedom of action often quite severely circumscribed. A company president or CEO can, in most cases, ultimately impose a negotiation package on a bickering management team.[12] Union leaders rarely have that power, because in most cases settlements must be ratified by a formal vote of the members.[13] To the extent that team members' differing positions on key issues represent legitimate divisions within the rank-and-file, such an imposed settlement would almost certainly be rejected, even if the team members could be made to agree with it. In fact, a tentative agreement that is sufficiently unpopular with the membership can wind up costing both the union negotiator and the union president their jobs. One reason why many strikes end up being over wages, even when money didn't seem to be the most important issue before or during negotiations, is that this is one issue around which union officials can normally rally members from all different factions of the organization—something that's important if a strike is to be sustained for any length of time (Gunderson et al., 1995).

The Long-Term Nature of Union-Management Relationships

Fisher and Williams (1989:194) compare union-management relationships to marriages. In many cases, the relationship has lasted for several decades; in most, the expectation is that it will last for several more decades. For better or for worse, the parties seem to be "stuck with each other." Even a management organization that doesn't particularly like the union that represents the company's workers will often stick with that union because it is familiar with it and understands its leaders and strategy; better the devil one knows than the devil one doesn't know.

The long-term nature of union-management relationships offers both advantages and disadvantages for the bargaining process. By definition, most long-term relationships have a significant past, aspects of which are likely to resurface at each succeeding round of negotiations. Where the parties have had a cooperative relationship, they are more likely to work together to produce "win-win" outcomes on as many issues as possible (Kervin, 1989:185). Where the past relationship has been very bad, a large accumulation of unsettled grievances may complicate negotiations, and the parties may view everything in "win-lose" terms, even to the extent of being more interested in punishing the other side than in making positive gains for themselves (Kervin, 1989). As Lewicki et al. (1997) notes, negotiators who have previously experienced exploitative behaviour from the other side are much more likely to engage in it themselves. Difficult negotiations (often the result of a bad long-term relationship) may also be marked by a greater emphasis on intangibles, such as face-saving or the appearance of toughness (Kervin, 1989), or by arguments over fundamental issues of principle such as the union's right to exist, which are far more difficult to settle than issues such as wages and benefits.

However, the long-term nature of the union-management relationship may help improve the bargaining process. In general, union-management negotiators are less likely to engage in exploitative or manipulative behaviour than people engaged in "one-shot" transactions precisely because they realize that such behaviour is likely to have serious long-term effects on the relationship.

Where the relationship is likely to continue for some time, it may make sense to make specific efforts to improve the relationship, as for example, by establishing joint problem-solving committees or other mechanisms (Fisher and Williams, 1989:195).

In addition to being a good long-term investment in a better relationship, establishing such mechanisms can be a good way to start a negotiation, since it shows the parties they can work together to solve problems and may thus facilitate later discussions over more contentious issues such as the economic package. Kervin (1989:195) points out that, for the most part, cooperation is more apt to emerge when the parties' bargaining power is roughly equal, although this is not the case when their previous relationship has been highly competitive.

To establish joint problem-solving mechanisms requires a fair degree of trust on both sides. Where such trust is lacking, and particularly in cases where it may have been destroyed because of previous hard-nosed or unethical tactics (Fisher and Williams, 1989:195), it will first be necessary to restore that trust, perhaps through the application of an organization development technique such as one of those discussed in Downie (1989), or a preventive mediation program such as one of those offered by a number of provincial governments. Once trust has been established or restored, both sides must work hard at maintaining it, as trust is far more easily destroyed than restored (Fisher and Williams, 1989:195).

The Role of Bargaining Power

Ideally in negotiations, one would like to move in the direction of as much union-management cooperation as possible. However, even the most cooperative relationship will almost certainly feature a significant degree of competition over money (Kervin, 1989). In less cooperative relationships, competition is likely to permeate most, if not all, aspects of the bargaining process. Where competition is present, what chiefly determines bargaining outcomes is the extent to which each side is able to exert **bargaining power** over the other.

The literature offers a number of definitions of the term "bargaining power." Perhaps the most widely quoted definition is that of Leap and Grigsby (1986): the ability to resist another's proposal in favour of a proposal more favourable to one's own side. Godard's definition (1994:339) is not dissimilar, but has a slightly different emphasis. In his view, each side has bargaining power, and therefore is likely to win concessions from the other side, to the extent that a work stoppage imposes direct and indirect costs on the other side.[14]

As Godard sees it, the direct sources of union bargaining power result from the union's ability to impose losses on management during a strike. In the private sector, these losses will take the form of lost profit and market share. In the public sector, they take the form of increased public sympathy for the strikers (and their cause) and a corresponding loss of confidence in the government (Godard, 1994). This explains why public sector unions, as we noted in Chapters 6 and 9, generally devote so much of their time and effort to publicity campaigns. The greater the union's ability to impose such strike costs on management, the likelier management is to make concessions and to bring the strike to an end (Godard, 1994).

The indirect sources of union bargaining power "entail the costs to management of increased exit and recalcitrance due to worker discontent and adversariness after a strike" (Godard, 1994). In the first instance, and at the most obvious level, this refers to the costs management incurs when any significant number of workers quit, particularly highly skilled ones who may be difficult to replace, and in situations involving highly complex and capital-intensive technologies (Godard, 1994). But such costs can also include increased grievances, increased absenteeism and sick leave, and in more extreme cases even an increase in spoiled goods, vandalism, and sabotage, as workers seek to get back at an employer they feel has treated them unfairly in any way they can. Finally, the indirect costs to the company may include a loss of public faith that can lead to reduced profit and market share. Such a loss of public faith is most apt to occur in situations where the conflict has been a bitter and lengthy one, and the union has used negative publicity campaigns or a boycott. Because such a direct attack on a company can lead to job losses or even the failure of the entire enterprise, the boycott is a tactic requiring great caution.

The direct sources of management bargaining power relate to the economic cost, to workers, of a strike or lockout (Godard, 1994). Such direct bargaining power is reduced to the extent that lost income can be replaced by temporary or part-time work, or by strike pay (Godard, 1994). However, in most cases strike pay replaces only a small proportion of workers' regular wages or salaries, and temporary jobs rarely pay nearly as much as regular full-time ones. Therefore, this source of management power is likely to remain a potent one except in very good economic times, when striking workers may find it relatively easy to locate a new full-time job, and when a firm may need to make up for production losses after a strike with large amounts of overtime (see Godard, 1994). It's also usually easier for workers to find another job in large, diversified labour markets than in small ones or in rural areas, which may be one reason why employers sometimes like to build new plants in small towns or rural areas rather than in big cities. In any event, the greater management's ability to impose costs on workers through a strike or lockout, the likelier management will be to extract concessions, such as wage and benefit reductions or the easing of rigid work rules, at the bargaining table (Godard, 1994)

The indirect sources of management bargaining power relate to the possibility of job losses resulting from lost business following a strike, and the possible imposition of harsher working conditions, such as heavier workloads or stricter discipline (Godard, 1994:339–340). Again, this latter source of power can be reduced, to the extent that the union is successful in fighting heavier workloads or stricter discipline through its grievance process.

As the history of the Canadian labour movement illustrates, bargaining power can shift quite quickly. Often, such shifts in bargaining power are the result of large-scale economic and political trends. During the Great Depression, for example, with production severely curtailed and jobs at a premium, bargaining power swung very markedly towards employers. Once war was declared and most able-bodied young male workers were sent to the front, power shifted quite markedly in the opposite direction, although the government did what it could to mitigate the effects of this shift by imposing wage controls, freezing workers in essential employment, and limiting employees' right to quit or shift jobs (Morton, 1995:142–143). Through the 1970s, workers and their unions generally continued to enjoy a fair degree of bargaining power; however, things shifted quite quickly as a result of the recessions that came in the wake of the two major energy shocks of the 1970s, particularly the major recession of 1981–1983. The shift in bargaining power was perhaps felt most acutely in the construction industry, which is always especially sensitive to economic downturns. In Canada, it was felt most acutely of all in Alberta, where the economy had been booming prior to the recession due to high oil revenues, and where unionized construction workers had won a 28 percent wage increase in 1982 (Rose, 1992:206). By 1984, with the bottom having fallen out of the oil industry, and the construction market extremely depressed, the province's unionized contractors were facing severe competition from cheaper, non-unionized ones.[15] Having previously failed to reopen the 1982–1984 agreement to defer scheduled wage increases, the Alberta Construction Labour Relations Association came to the table in 1984 demanding wage rollbacks of $5 to $6 per hour. When the unions refused, the employers' association staged a series of legal 24-hour lockouts, then terminated all collective agreements and imposed much lower wages and harsher terms and conditions of employment unilaterally (Rose, 1992). To all intents and purposes, this spelled the end of collective bargaining in Alberta construction for the next four years (Rose, 1992).

ALBERTA LABOUR MEDIATION SERVICES
www.gov.ab.ca/lab/what/mediat.html

The Stages of Negotiation

One can think of negotiations as passing through four major stages: settling in, consolidation, finalization, and mopping-up (Fisher and Williams, 1989:189). It's generally best, when negotiating, to take one's time and try to go through all the stages. Attempts to push the other side too fast can result in unnecessary resistance; overly rapid concessions can lead to trouble on one's own side, and perhaps even to rejection of the tentative agreement if constituents don't believe you have fought hard enough on their behalf.

Settling in, the first stage, is a time for opponents to feel each other out and get to know each other (Fisher and Williams, 1989), particularly if the chief negotiators haven't been to the table together before. Normally it's best to begin with some non-committal pleasantry about the weather or something else other than the bargaining agenda. It's also usually best to negotiate items in reverse order of their importance, because less important items are generally easier to settle. A particularly good idea may be to start with an item that can be seen as a "win-win" for both sides, like a joint committee to control the cost of grievances. Once a few minor items have been settled, teams are more likely to have developed the momentum needed to tackle the more major items, like wages and job security.

The second stage, consolidation, is normally by far the longest. It is here that each side puts forward its positions and arguments and learns about the other side's priorities (typically through the simple dropping of certain less important demands). The consolidation stage often requires several caucuses (team meetings) to allow each side to assess the other side's demands and priorities and come up with an appropriate response to them; it is generally considered good strategy not to agree to anything important without calling a caucus (Fisher and Williams, 1989:203). The overall aim of this stage is to hone one's own bottom line—the least your team is prepared to agree to—as well as to develop an understanding of the other side's bottom line. While bottom lines may change in response to information exchanged at the table or (in real life negotiations), in response to changes in the economic or political environment within which negotiations are being conducted (Fisher and Williams, 1989:189), changes in a team's bottom line should not be made lightly. Particularly in the later stages of negotiations, it's important for the chief negotiator to remind his or her team members periodically of the bottom line to which they have committed themselves (Fisher and Williams, 1989:199).

Where two teams' bottom lines (in terms of wages or the overall cost of the agreement) intersect, then a **settlement zone** (see Figures 10.1a and 10.1b) can be said to exist (Fisher and Williams, 1989:189). Where they do not intersect, then there is no settlement zone. If management prefers to hold the total compensation increase to 1 percent, but can live with an increase up to 3 percent, while the union would prefer an increase of 4 percent but can live with an increase as low as 2 percent, then the settlement zone is between 2 and 3 percent. Assuming the teams have good negotiators and allow the process to work as it should, they'll very likely come in with a settlement somewhere in that range. If, on the other hand, management's bottom-line range is from -1 to +1 percent but the union's is still between 2 and 4 percent, then no settlement zone exists, and the parties will reach a bargaining impasse unless one or both gives in on the monetary package, or on some non-monetary issue (such as work rules or job security) that is considered important enough to allow some relaxation of the other side's monetary bottom line.

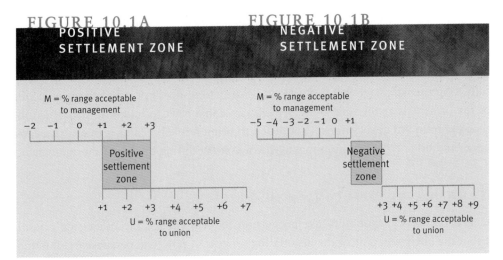

FIGURE 10.1A
POSITIVE SETTLEMENT ZONE

FIGURE 10.1B
NEGATIVE SETTLEMENT ZONE

Source: Prepared from sketch by author.

More important, perhaps, are those cases where a settlement zone does not exist, not because the parties have not moved far enough, but because the issue over which they disagree is one of fundamental principle, not quantifiable, and thus not amenable to the sort of trade-off inherent in the very notion of a settlement zone (Kervin, 1984). For this reason, disputes over such issues tend to be longer, more bitter, and far harder to settle than disputes over monetary issues; often such disputes are only resolved after some kind of direct government intervention (Kervin, 1984). A union's right to exist is such an issue; one can't realistically agree that the plant will operate with a union from January through June, then be union-free for the rest of the year. Health and safety and human rights issues also involve matters of fundamental principle, which explains why, as we pointed out in some detail in Chapter 7, they are regulated primarily through legislation, rather than being left solely to the vagaries of collective bargaining.

Where a settlement zone does exist, it is discovered during finalization, or the actual reaching of a settlement (Fisher and Williams, 1989:189). Unlike consolidation, which usually lasts for a long time, finalization is normally quite quick. The experience of reaching a settlement is difficult to describe in words, though most people who have ever negotiated will know intuitively what that experience feels like.[16] Sometimes agreement is reached only after the parties have all but given up hope. It is apparently common for negotiators to report feeling quite depressed just prior to this stage (Downie, 1984). Often the final settlement is triggered by a corridor or washroom meeting of the two principal negotiators, followed by a last-minute concession or repackaging that makes a previously unpalatable package at least marginally acceptable to the other side. In this regard, a prudent negotiator is like a wise parent; he or she will always hold a goodie or two in reserve for use in truly desperate situations (Williams, 1982, Lewicki et al., 1997).

Mopping up generally means drafting specific language for provisions to which the chief negotiators have agreed in principle. It may also entail attending to letters of intent or troubleshooting issues subsequently raised by one's constituency or principals (Fisher and Williams, 1989:189). It is important to attend to this stage carefully. Contract language that is not carefully drafted or does not reflect the true intent of the principals at the time of agreement can come back to haunt all concerned in the next round of negotiations, in addition to being fertile breeding ground for grievances and other types of union-management conflict during the life of the agreement.

Negotiating Strategy and Tactics

In general, good negotiators use persuasion to help change the other side's mind about the likely outcome of the negotiating process. A powerful persuasive technique (Fisher and Williams, 1989:187–189) involves planting a seed of doubt in the other negotiator's mind, as by depicting a credible scenario regarding a given issue that differs significantly from what the other side seems to expect. If the seed of doubt has been well planted, the other side should come to modify its position on related issues (Fisher and Williams, 1989:189).

"NEGOTIATION SUPPORT SYSTEMS AND NEGOTIATING AGENTS"
interneg.carleton.ca/interneg/research/misc/nss_na

Effective persuasion does not happen by accident. In addition to superior communication and listening skills on the part of the negotiator, it requires thorough preparation on the part of the entire team, the careful development of a firm yet sufficiently flexible bottom line, and the judicious use of a number of specific negotiating tactics.

Preparation for Bargaining

Often success in negotiations can be attributed to a team's superior preparation. A good starting point is to canvass one's constituency or principals to determine what issues they would like to resolve from bargaining, the relative importance of those issues, and how long a lawful work stoppage they are prepared to stage or take (Fisher and Williams, 1989:199).

With the team's general objectives established, detailed preparations can begin. On the management side, this may well include monitoring workers' attitudes and concerns, getting a read on the overall economic and political environment within which negotiations will be conducted,[17] monitoring the union's developments, monitoring local or industry wage developments to get a sense of a reasonable "ballpark"

Researcher pores over past settlements in her industry. In negotiations, good preparation is often half the battle.

figure for the final settlement,[18] and conducting background research aimed at developing proposals for non-wage issues (Godard and Kochan, 1982:128–130). Such background research may in turn entail conducting interviews or soliciting written submissions from line managers (Godard and Kochan, 1982:129–130), reviewing company policies and the administration of the current agreement, and examining any outstanding grievances or arbitration decisions resulting from the previous agreement, in addition to examining data drawn from suggestion boxes or employee exit interviews (Williams, 1982:213). With this broad range of information in hand, the management team can start developing and costing specific wage and benefit proposals (Godard and Kochan, 1982:129; Fisher and Williams, 1989:200).

For the union team, the overall objective of preparation is pretty much the same as it is for management: to obtain as thorough a knowledge of the general and specific economic and political environments as possible to arrive at bargaining proposals that are realistic and stand a reasonable chance of acceptance, in addition to meeting as many of the needs of the union's members as possible. But because of the union's statutory obligation to represent members fairly, and because unions generally operate in a far more public and open fashion than do management organizations, the *process* of preparation may be somewhat different. Like the management team, the union will solicit members' written input on contract proposals, and will conduct background research into comparable settlements in the area and industry. Then,

both to receive further input and to help ensure members buy into any tentative settlement eventually negotiated, the union will typically hold one or more general membership meetings at which both general and specific bargaining objectives are
discussed. It has been this author's experience that, unlike most typical union meetings (see Chapter 5), this type of meeting is generally very well attended.[19] At these
meetings, the union leadership and negotiating team will normally take pains to
ensure that proposals are put forward to address the needs of all major constituencies within the union. After these meetings, still further written input may be solicited, and the union may also inform members of ongoing developments through
a series of "Negotiation Newsletters."

Developing the Bottom Line

For both union and management teams, the bottom line is normally developed at
prenegotiation meetings. It is important that, by the end of these meetings, all issues
be divided into three categories: bottom-line issues, over which the union or management team is prepared to strike or take a strike; trading issues, which are important but that can be bought by the other side in return for an equivalent concession;
and "throwaway items," or items of less importance that will be given up after a good
fight, for show (Fisher and Williams, 1989:200). Within these categories, individual
issues should be rank-ordered. Also, to the extent possible, the opponent's anticipated demands should be classified in similar fashion (Fisher and Williams, 1989).

"PERSPECTIVES ON REPRESENTATION AND ANALYSIS OF NEGOTIATION"

interneg.carleton.ca/interneg/research/misc/boston_gdn

In addition to helping teams develop their bottom line, such meetings may serve
as "dress rehearsals," where the other side's expected positions are examined in
preparation for the actual negotiations (Fisher and Williams, 1989:202). Another
purpose of the prenegotiation meeting is to build teamwork and esprit des corps with
an eye to ensuring all team members remain committed to the team's agreed issue
positions. At such meetings, team members are assigned roles such as the taking of
notes, collection of data, costing, or observing the other side's reactions (Fisher and
Williams, 1989). Part of these meetings may also be devoted to tactical decisions such
as how to begin negotiations, or whether the chief negotiator will be the team's sole
spokesperson and, if not, under what conditions others should speak. Most teams
usually find it best to allow the chief negotiator to do all the talking, except in the
case of specific technical issues, such as costing, where the team member assigned to
the role may be better informed and thus better able to help the team's cause

(see Fisher and Williams, 1989:203).[20] In such cases, the chief negotiator should specifically ask the individual in question to speak to a given point or points, and the team member should be sure to confine himself or herself to those points.

Specific Negotiating Tactics

Researchers such as Kervin (1989:186) have identified five different types of bargaining move: concessions, trade-offs, promises, threats, and procedural moves. The ability to use all five judiciously is critical to almost any negotiator's success. In addition, good negotiators generally have the ability to find a critical focal point for a settlement, and to package items in a way that both constituents and opposing negotiators find acceptable. As well, they know how to make opening moves that are far enough away from their intended bottom line to allow a fair amount of room to maneuver, but not so far away, or so unreasonable, as to lead the other side to believe that they aren't really interested in striking a deal. Perhaps a simple example from outside the world of industrial relations may help here. If one is offered $30 000 for a quarter-interest in a property known to have been appraised at $200 000, one may not be prepared to accept the offer, but one will likely also get the sense that the person making the offer is at least interested in the property. If, on the other hand, one is offered $2000 or even $10 000 to $15 000, one will almost certainly see the offer as a clear sign of lack of interest and start contacting other prospective buyers.

OPENING MOVES   "What's a reasonable opening position?" is a question that instructors who use collective bargaining simulations in their introductory IR courses are probably asked more than any other. The question is never an easy one to answer. Usually, all one can say is, "It depends."

What, exactly, might an initial position depend on? Among the relevant factors would surely be inflation levels, one's own level of experience and that of one's opponents, and (in classroom simulations), the amount of time available for the exercise. As a general rule, a union team could do worse than set an initial target of twice what it expects to receive for the monetary package. For management teams, the process of establishing an initial position may be a bit more difficult in these times of very low inflation. A position of, say, half what they expect to give eventually leaves very little room to maneuver in situations where the final settlement seems likely to be in the 2 to 3 percent range. What the management team must do in this case is assume a likely final settlement of, say, 2.5 percent, and then subtract from that figure as much as the union team seems likely to add in its initial position. In this case, this means that the management team's initial position will be to call for a freeze in the total compensation package.

In addition, both sides should initially put forward far more issues than they expect to be on the table at the end of negotiations. The main reason for this strategy, often termed the "blue sky" or "large demand" approach (Craig and Solomon, 1996:272), is to allow ample room for trade-offs along the way.

One of the few things all the negotiation experts agree on is that the initial position should *not* be the same as the bottom line. Again, many bargaining novices tend to wonder why so much time is wasted on the seemingly meaningless if not irrational ritual of arriving at a final settlement when to a great extent the terms are known before negotiating even starts (Craig and Solomon, 1996:203). Why doesn't management simply make a "firm, fair, and final offer" on a take-it-or-leave-it basis, and end all the palaver right there? Unfortunately, space limitations do not permit a detailed discussion of this question here. However, one reason surely lies in the fact that the process of collective bargaining, as distinguished from its economic outcomes, is considered by most citizens of democratic societies to be of value in and of itself. The use of Boulwarism[21] (to give the aforementioned take-it-or-leave-it approach its official name) essentially prevents collective bargaining from occurring, which is why such approaches have been ruled illegal in both Canada and the United States (Craig and Solomon, 1996:204; Godard, 1994:288). A related reason is that serious negotiations seem, for whatever reason, to help people both appear and feel more competent. By eliminating the negotiating process as such, Boulwarism eliminates a potentially important source of satisfaction (Godard, 1994, Lewicki et al., 1997:47). Beyond that, various studies have found that those who make more extreme initial offers get better settlements than those who make more modest ones (Lewicki et al., 1997:45)

Initial offers should also not be overly precise. Far better for a union to demand 3 percent than 2.89 or 3.11 percent. Indeed, it is not uncommon for a union, in making its initial demands, to call simply for a "substantial increase" or an increase "sufficient to allow our members to catch up with five years of inflation." Phrasing a demand in this way can be an effective technique, since it forces management to start thinking about just what would constitute a "substantial" increase, and may thus lead to a quicker meeting of minds than a more rigid numerical demand would.

CONCESSIONS AND TRADE-OFFS A concession is a move that entails taking a position closer to, or even identical with, the other side's latest position. One might at first think rapid concessions the key to success in negotiation; however, the literature indicates otherwise. A pattern of a tough opening position followed by gradual concessions appears to be much more successful most of the time (Godard, 1994:204).[22] For one thing, such a pattern convinces one's own constituents that one has done one's best in their behalf, and thus reduces the likelihood of rejection of the tentative deal. For another, it allows the opposing negotiator to feel he or she has had some influence on the process (Kervin, 1989). From a psychological perspective, it is

Would you want this man as your chief spokesperson? Most collective bargaining specialists say frequent use of threats is typically the mark of the amateur.

also better to start tough and gradually ease up than to start soft and be forced to toughen up after criticism from team members. In the latter instance, opponents are apt to get their backs up, and a strike may well be the ultimate result. Where concessions are made, they are generally more effective if done conditionally, in the form of a "tit-for-tat" or possible trade-offs (i.e., making a concession on one item in return for the opponent's roughly equal concession on other) than if done unconditionally (Kervin, 1989), perhaps because they suggest the concession maker is dealing from a position of strength rather than from one of weakness.

THREATS AND PROMISES   A threat suggests some action that will hurt the opponent (i.e., leaving the bargaining table) if or unless the opponent makes a certain move. A promise, though sometimes unconditional, typically offers the opponent some benefit in return for a move on its part (Kervin, 1989:186). While threats are not uncommon (Kervin, 1989:205), experienced negotiators tend to use them sparingly, since they are likely to evoke hostility and lead to counterthreats and reduced joint outcomes (Kervin, 1989). Given that most labour-management negotiations are conducted under strict deadline pressure and that normally a work stoppage can occur should negotiations reach an impasse, it is usually best to let this fact speak for itself, rather than getting an opponent's back up unnecessarily.

The impact of promises is less clear, since various studies have shown their effect on opponents' compliance to range from significant to none (Kervin, 1989). However, negotiators who make promises are perceived by opponents to be more trustworthy and cooperative, which suggests that the use of promises could lead to a quicker settlement so long as the negotiator is perceived to have the authority to fulfill them (Kervin, 1989).

PROCEDURAL MOVES   Procedural moves include actions such as suggesting or making a change in the bargaining process (Kervin, 1989:186). Such a change could take the form of a request for a caucus, a request for a change in the time or place of the next negotiating session, or a request for mediation (Kervin, 1989).

On the surface, such moves appear to be neutral, like a baseball hitter's request for time from the umpire. As in the case of the baseball example, however, such requests can throw an opponent's timing off and generate considerable uncertainty, and they can also seriously impede the flow of negotiations. For this reason, when such changes are initiated unilaterally, especially if they are at all frequent or occur during the late stages of negotiations when timing is everything, they are often interpreted as hostile acts. Significantly, the use of such procedural moves has been associated with an increased rate of bargaining impasses and strikes (Kervin, 1989:202). But where a procedural move, such as a request for mediation, is initiated jointly, it may signal increased willingness to work together and thus help lead to a quicker settlement.

FOCAL POINTS   Experienced negotiators have the knack of proposing settlement terms that "seem to make sense" to opponents because of their symmetry, simplicity, or obviousness, or because they are in line with previous, well-known settlements (Kervin, 1989:204). In the words of Thomas Schelling (1957:435): "The 'obvious' place to compromise frequently seems to win by some kind of default, as though there is simply no rationale for settling anywhere else." From this perspective, much of the negotiator's skill may lie in finding just what that obvious place is and pointing it out to constituents and the other side. Settlements that can be expressed in round numbers or that split the difference between the two sides' most recent offers seem to possess "focal quality," to use Schelling's terminology. So, too, do settlements that rely on common, generally accepted indicators. Far better, in devising a cost-of-living formula, to rely on the Consumer Price Index than on some other possibly more accurate, but definitely more obscure inflation index. In this case, any possible benefits (in terms of increased fairness) to be derived from using the alternative index would likely be far outweighed by the greater difficulty of using that index.

PACKAGING   Packaging is the art of combining several different positions into a comprehensive final offer. Often it entails the use of several different types of move at once (concessions, trade-offs, promises, threats).

Research has found that the packaging of issues leads to a higher rate of settlement than dealing with issues one at a time (Kervin, 1989:206). There are a number of possible reasons for this. For one thing, a package is generally offered at the end of negotiations. At this stage, it offers the opportunity to end the proceedings once and for all—an opportunity that the other side may well be glad to avail itself of, if it can do so without loss of face. For another, it presents a clearer and more immediate picture of the bargaining scenario as a whole than do deals pieced together issue by issue. This can be helpful in convincing constituents or principals that their issues have been addressed in some way, even if not entirely to their satisfaction. Finally, and quite simply, a skillfully prepared package has the ring of authority about it. Far more than further movement on individual issues, a package suggests that the negotiator offering it is serious about settling. This note of finality also carries with it an implicit threat—that of withdrawing from negotiations if the package is not accepted—that can likewise encourage the other side to settle.

Desire to Settle

The previous discussion has focussed on a number of generally accepted techniques for reaching settlement. Implicit in this discussion has been the assumption that both sides want to settle and possess the ability to do so (Godard, 1994:342). While it seems obvious that both sides should want to settle, this isn't necessarily the case. Moreover, even when both sides do want to settle, one or both may be prevented from doing so by factors at least partly beyond their control. For example, a management group might genuinely want to offer workers more money, but be unable to do so because of strict cost-control measures coming out of the head office. Similarly, a union local might be willing to accept management's demand for a relaxation of certain work rules, but be prevented from doing so by national union policy.

When a settlement is not reached and any mandatory third-party intervention proves unavailing, a strike or lockout is the usual result. To the pure economist, most strikes are irrational, particularly in times of low inflation. But as we point out in more detail in Chapter 12, strikes serve more than simply economic functions; a strike that is economically irrational may be quite rational from a political perspective. Management may want to push the union into a strike it knows it can't win, as a means of asserting more control over the workplace and possibly even getting rid of the union at a later date.[23] A union may feel the need to call a strike to build its members' internal solidarity, or even to serve as a reality check on some members' extravagant expectations (Gunderson, Hyatt, and Ponak, 1995:382–383). Either or both sides may view such a strike as an investment in longer-term bargaining power vis-à-vis the other side—a case of "short-term pain for long-term gain" (Fisher and

Williams, 1989:197). Alternatively, they may simply be so caught up in the strike's political objectives and ramifications that they don't even concern themselves with its immediate costs.

To sum up, and at the risk of belabouring the obvious, if both sides don't want to settle, then most likely they *won't* settle. No amount of persuasion, repackaging of offers, or jawboning by a conciliator or mediator is likely to be of much use so long as either or both parties are operating on the basis of a different agenda.[24]

Ways of Improving the Bargaining Process

In a situation where a union and management group may have a history of acrimonious negotiations, but be sincerely interested in turning things around, there are a number of options open to them for improving the bargaining process.

One approach that has been tried and often found to be effective is that of **early negotiations,** or **prebargaining** (Downie, 1989:265–266). Normally, most negotiations are conducted under extreme time pressure due to the imminent threat of a strike or lockout. While the threat of a work stoppage can lead to a settlement, it can also generate tension and hard feelings. Starting negotiations well ahead of time can remove most of that tension and lead to a more productive, problem-solving atmosphere. Early-bird negotiations seem to work best when there is a target date and a well-thought-out time frame for negotiations (Downie, 1989:266).

Another well-known approach is **single-team** bargaining (a variation of integrative bargaining, discussed in the union impacts chapter), which has union and management representatives seated next to each other at a round table rather than across from each other at a rectangular one in a bid to promote joint problem-solving. When the approach was tried out at Labatt Breweries, a pioneer in single-team bargaining during Tom Crossman's time as personnel director, it not only involved the use of a round table (or sometimes no table at all), but also the elimination of single spokespersons for the two sides, a strategy normally recommended (including here) as being the most efficient and effective way to proceed (Downie, 1989:267).

 "SUPPORT FOR GROUP DECISIONS AND NEGOTIATIONS
    interneg.carleton.ca/interneg/research/misc/intro_gdn.html

Even where the parties prefer not to sit at a round table, they can still move away from traditional confrontational bargaining marked by distrust, high levels of conflict, and an emphasis on "win-lose" outcomes, towards what Fisher and Ury (1983) have described as **principled bargaining.** This approach focusses on the parties' underlying interests rather than on the positions they may take at the bargaining table (Chaykowski, 1995:247). It works by separating team members' personalities from the problems under discussion, developing objective criteria for negotiating outcomes that involve fairness in both standards and procedures, and devising options that give rise to "win-win" or mutual gains situations rather than to "win-lose" or zero-sum ones (Chaykowski, 1995). While it is not clear how widely principled bargaining has been adopted in Canada, Chaykowski (1995:247–248) notes that it has been adopted by a number of major corporations and unions; two of the unions that appear to have adopted it most widely are the Steelworkers and Communications, Energy and Paperworkers (CEP).

Yet another possibility may be to substitute voluntary arbitration for the threat of a strike or lockout. While mandatory interest arbitration, as we note elsewhere in the book, generally hurts the bargaining process, a substitute dispute resolution process voluntarily selected by both parties can sometimes help it (Downie, 1989:264–265). Such an approach has been taken in such varied industries as the U.S. steel industry and the clothing industry in Ontario. In the latter, the number of disputes actually referred to arbitration was extremely low, suggesting that the voluntarily chosen mechanism may indeed have improved the bargaining process (Downie, 1989:265).

Again, we must emphasize that the use of mechanisms like those just described presupposes a certain degree of trust, as well as a joint willingness to settle. Where the trust isn't there, the parties may wish to work specifically on improving their relationship, using either an organizational development technique, such as one of those described by Downie (1989:268–270), or one of the preventive mediation programs now run by most provincial governments.

STILL A MYSTERY?

Despite researchers' best efforts to learn more about the negotiation process, it remains in many ways as much an art as a science (Kervin, 1989; Sass, 1989). Rituals that may appear irrelevant or even ridiculous to those unfamiliar with the process will be seen, on closer examination, to be key elements to achieving success in many cases. Study of effective negotiating technique and of successful negotiations from the past can help provide some understanding of the process; however, in the last analysis, there is no substitute for hands-on experience.

"THE ART OF WAR"
www.mit.edu/people/dcctdw/AOW/toc.htm

Negotiating processes and outcomes are affected by broad environmental factors, such as the state of the economy or type of bargaining structure in place, and by the parties' previous bargaining history (whether cooperative or conflictual), the negotiators' skill and experience, the specific tactics they use, and the degree of intraorganizational conflict within each team. The most successful strategy appears to be one in which the negotiator initially stakes out positions far better than those she or he eventually expects or even hopes to achieve, then moves in the opponent's direction slowly, by means of gradual trade-offs and concessions. As well, cooperation and successful joint outcomes are likelier when the two sides' bargaining power is roughly equal.

Negotiations also proceed more smoothly when there is at least a reasonable degree of trust between the two sides. Where this trust is lacking, it may be necessary to take specific measures to build (or rebuild) the relationship, ideally before entering into negotiations. Assuming some measure of trust already exists, the bargaining process can also be improved through such mechanisms as prebargaining well in advance of the strike deadline, single-team or principled bargaining, or, in appropriate circumstances, voluntary arbitration.

Perhaps most important of all—and far too often overlooked in the IR literature—is the parties' willingness and ability to settle. Where either or both are lacking, no settlement is likely to be reached, no matter how skilled the negotiators or how effective their techniques may have proven in other instances.

QUESTIONS FOR DISCUSSION

1) Have you ever been part of a union-management negotiation? If so, what was the experience like? Do you think it's something you would enjoy doing again?

2) If you haven't been part of a union-management negotiation, have you had any other sort of negotiating experience, either individually or as a member of a group? What was that experience like?

3) Explain why bargaining structure is important in collective bargaining.

4) Distinguish between centralized and decentralized bargaining structures, and explain why private sector unions generally prefer decentralized structures in good times, but centralized ones in bad times.

5) Why have Canadian private sector bargaining structures become more decentralized in recent years? Why have public sector bargaining structures generally become more centralized?

6) From a comparative perspective, what are the main effects of different types of bargaining structure?

7) Would simply centralizing Canadian bargaining structures likely lead to a reduction in industrial conflict? Why, or why not?

8) How do union-management negotiations differ from other types of negotiation?

9) Discuss the role of bargaining power in negotiations.

10) List the four stages of negotiation, and explain why it's important to go through all of them.

11) Discuss the concept of a settlement zone, and identify some issues to which this concept would, and would not, apply.

12) Why do seasoned negotiators seldom make threats? What are some tactics they would be more likely to use?

13) What are some ways of improving the bargaining process? Which of these seem most promising to you?

SUGGESTIONS FOR FURTHER READING

Fisher, E.G., and Brian Williams. (1989). Negotiating the union-management agreement. In J. Anderson, M. Gunderson, and A. Ponak (Eds.). *Union-management relations in Canada* (2nd ed.). Don Mills, ON: Addison-Wesley. Somewhat uneven, but contains a wealth of practical advice on how to negotiate.

Forrest, Anne. (1989). "The rise and fall of national bargaining in the Canadian meat-packing industry." *Relations Industrielles*, 44(2). A well-written account of the effects of changes in bargaining structure on union and management bargaining power in a major Canadian industry.

Lewicki, Roy, David Saunders, and John Minton. (1997). *Essentials of negotiation*. Chicago and Toronto: Irwin. A thorough and very readable study of negotiation that moves beyond traditional negotiation contexts into such emerging areas as multilateral, cross-cultural, and international negotiations.

Sauvé, Robert. (1971). "La négociation collective sectorielle." *Relations Industrielles*, 26(1). Those who read French will find that this study offers some perceptive insights into why Canadian bargaining structures have evolved as they have. Deserves to be better-known in the English IR community.

Schelling, Thomas. (1957). "Bargaining, communication, and limited war." *Journal of Conflict Resolution*, 1(1). This classic (and beautifully written) study, which is not limited to union-management negotiations, explains the crucial concept of the focal point. A must for anyone with a broader interest in negotiating theory.

Sethi, Amarjit (Ed.). (1989). *Collective bargaining in Canada*. Scarborough, ON: Nelson. A very good collective bargaining text. Contains articles on a very broad range of subjects, from negotiating technique to quality of working life and technological change. Not all are equally strong, but the pieces by Kervin (the science of bargaining), Sass (the art of bargaining), Lemelin (quality of working life and collective bargaining), Rogow (bargaining structure), Swimmer (public sector bargaining), and Sass and Stobbe (health and safety issues) are first rate. Another book that deserves to be far better known than it is.

Tarantelli, Ezio. (1986). "The regulation of inflation and unemployment." *Industrial Relations*, 25(1). A masterful study in comparative political economy that links bargaining structures to inflation and unemployment.

Walton, Richard, and Robert McKersie. (1991). *A behavioral theory of labor negotiations: An analysis of a social interaction system* (2nd ed.). Ithaca: ILR Press. Revised edition of the classic work on union-management negotiations.

ENDNOTES

[1] As Anderson (1989:212) notes, both must agree to the combination of certification units into a negotiation unit for a binding collective agreement to be signed.

[2] For a perceptive and thoughtful critique of the Ontario board's prevailing practice through the mid 1980s, see Forrest (1986), especially pages 846–847.

[3] Similarly, as Rogow notes, union leaders may favour centralized bargaining arrangements even at times when such arrangements are not in the union's economic interest, because of their philosophical belief that such arrangements can better promote worker solidarity than more "individualistic" decentralized ones.

[4] Through most of the postwar period, the "Big Four" tire manufacturers accounted for 85 percent of industry sales (Kochan, McKersie, and Cappelli, 1984:31).

[5] For a very useful overview of these developments, see Ferner and Hyman (1992b), especially pages xx–xxii.

[6] As late as 1966, according to Kumar and Meltz (1992:56), less than 1 percent of the cars sold in Canada were manufactured in Japan. By 1990, that figure had grown to more than 25 percent.

[7] See Mishel (1986) for a useful discussion on the interaction between bargaining structure and economic conditions.

[8] It is not likely that centralized systems would have such an effect in bad times. In connection with this point, it should be noted that most of Tarantelli's data were compiled prior to the major recession of 1981–1983. At the same time, it should also be noted that inflation is generally of far less concern in bad times than in good.

[9] Centralized systems have also been associated with lower levels of unemployment (Tarantelli, 1986). For one thing, the social democratic governments under which such systems are adopted have tended to follow full-employment policies as a matter of principle. For another, the political bargaining in which these governments often engage with labour movements often leads to trade-offs, like the Swedish active labour market policy (Hammarstrom, 1993:200), which in turn have led to full employment guarantees in return for the unions' pledge to restrain wage demands and in some cases strike activity.

[10] A notable exception here was the Canada Post dispute in 1997, when, as we note in Chapter 12, management negotiator Jean Lafleur shoved union negotiator Phillipe Arbour to the floor as the latter attempted to enter a management hotel suite in Hull. The incident did little to improve the flow of negotiations or win public support for the corporation. It also led to Lafleur's immediate replacement as chief management negotiator.

[11] As we pointed out in the management chapter (Chapter 3), the growing ascendancy, within management teams, of people from finance and accounting has been associated with the

generally tougher stance taken by most management organizations at the bargaining table over the past two decades. So, too, has the relative decline in influence of people from IR and HR, the two management constituencies most strongly committed to collective bargaining and maintaining labour peace.

12 An excellent example appears in the "Bridgetown Manufacturing Company" case in Craig and Solomon (1996:501–505).

13 For an interesting exception, see the brief discussion of the end of the Eaton's strike in Ontario in 1985, found in Fisher and Williams at page 193. In this case, union officials, who had sole ratification power, signed a memorandum of agreement to end the strike so that striking employees could get their jobs back and union members crossing picket lines could not vote against the agreement.

14 Godard's original wording is "strike" rather than work stoppage. However, management could presumably impose such costs through a lockout as well as a strike—hence the use of the broader term here.

15 As Rose notes (1992:206), by 1993 the union–non-union wage differential had increased to about $6.60 per hour!

16 The closest analogy the author can come up with (with apologies to readers who are not cooks) is that of preparing a cream or béchamel sauce. Such sauces seem to take an eternity to thicken, but then do so almost instantaneously. Also (another key element of the analogy), if it is not diligently attended to at the precise moment it is ready, the sauce will be ruined.

17 If one's business is export-oriented, this may entail monitoring ongoing political developments and trade policies in the countries to whom one is primarily interested in exporting.

18 Human Resources Development Canada puts out a number of publications listing various wage settlements, as do a number of provincial labour departments.

19 On at least two occasions, attendance was in excess of 50 percent of the organization's total membership, a particularly remarkable achievement given that on both those occasions, the meetings were held during the summer when a fair number of members were out of town.

20 Teams may wish to modify this rule in classroom simulations where peer evaluation is in effect, as it most often is, to prevent the chief negotiator from being at an unfair advantage when peer grades are being handed out. One way to do this is for the chief negotiator to assign all team members to speak on given issues or at certain times. Another is simply to ensure that all are given roles that give them plenty of useful work to do, and to ensure as well that each team member's contribution is duly noted in the introduction to any reports that are handed in to the instructor before or after the simulation.

21 Named for one Lemuel Boulware, vice-president of General Electric during the 1950s, who regularly took this approach to collective bargaining.

22 In connection with this general point, it may be relevant to note that Kervin (1989:203) suggests that negotiators are generally more tolerant of early hostile moves, which they view as "just part of the ritual" of negotiations, than of later threats, which are more likely to be regarded as exploitation or betrayals of trust.

23 Again, the Bridgetown case in Craig and Solomon (1996) offers an excellent illustration of this kind of behaviour.

24 Herein (in the author's view) lies the fallacy of compulsory conciliation.

CHAPTER 11

THE COLLECTIVE AGREEMENT

In longshoring, prior to modernization, unions tried to use work rule provisions to protect their members' jobs and prevent injures from lifting loads that were too heavy.

Collective agreements are closely related to the negotiating process discussed in the previous chapter, because they serve as a written record of negotiation results. In this chapter, we begin by discussing some of the functions served by collective agreements and the evolution of Canadian agreements through the twentieth century. From there, we go on to look at the

most common types of agreement provisions. We conclude the chapter with a brief discussion of what collective agreement provisions may say about a union-management relationship, and of the overall strengths and weaknesses of collective bargaining as a means of regulating workplace conflict.

THE SIGNIFICANCE OF COLLECTIVE AGREEMENTS

Collective agreements—the tangible result of the negotiation process—are central to the Canadian IR system (Giles and Jain, 1989; Giles and Starkman, 1995). These documents are of such importance because, in unionized establishments, they regulate many aspects of the day-to-day relationships between workers, unions, and employers (Giles and Starkman, 1995), including such important matters as workers' rates of pay and hours of work, their working conditions, and (at least in the private sector),[1] the processes for layoffs, promotions, and transfers. They also spell out specific management and union rights and provide a mechanism (normally some kind of grievance procedure) for handling any disputes that may arise during their lifetime.

"AVERAGE ANNUAL RATE INCREASES FOR NEW COLLECTIVE AGREEMENTS"

www.statcan.ca:80/cgi-bin/Cansim/cansim.cgi?matrix=4041&cq=&order_id=

By European standards (see Adams, 1995a:503), most Canadian and American agreements are quite long and detailed. There are, as we'll soon see, a number of reasons for this. Perhaps the most important is that, due in large measure to the relative political weakness of these two countries' labour movements (Giles and Starkman, 1995:341), they have concentrated most of their attention on collective bargaining and detailed regulation of work at the individual workplace level. In addition, alternative mechanisms such as works councils, through which many workplace-level matters are regulated in European countries such as Germany and the Netherlands (Adams, 1995a:506), are virtually unknown here. As a result, the collective bargaining process takes on more importance and is forced to address a considerably broader range of issues than is generally the case in most other industrialized countries.

SOME FUNCTIONS OF COLLECTIVE AGREEMENTS

The primary function of the collective agreement, at least from a legal point of view, is to set out the terms and conditions of employment to be followed by the union and management organization for a given period of time (Giles and Jain, 1989). In this respect, a collective agreement isn't all that different from other kinds of contracts

(Giles and Jain, 1989). IR scholars and practitioners, however, would argue that there are significant differences between a collective agreement and, for example, a contract to supply 10 000 shovels to the Department of National Defence. This is because, unlike ordinary commercial contracts, collective agreements regulate ongoing social relationships between groups and organizations (Giles and Jain, 1989). Increasingly, governments have come to recognize the unique nature of these agreements. Most important, as we noted in the labour law chapter, the labour relations legislation that undergirds those agreements is primarily regulated by labour boards, which are specialized tribunals staffed by experts in the fields, rather than by the courts. In arriving at their decisions, these boards frequently place greater importance on maintaining the ongoing labour-management relationship than on legal niceties (see Carter, 1995). Moreover, a special procedure—grievance arbitration—has arisen to handle disputes arising out of the interpretation of collective agreements.

PERSPECTIVES ON COLLECTIVE AGREEMENTS

Collective agreements mean different things to different people, depending upon their perspective and their role in the IR system. To the dedicated unionist, it is a bible to which he or she will almost invariably refer in time of need or doubt. Many unionists carry a copy of their agreement with them at all times, so as never to be caught unprepared in the event of a dispute with management (see Giles and Starkman, 1995:343). To most IR and HR managers, on the other hand, it is probably something between a nuisance and a necessary evil. On the one hand, collective agreements complicate managers' work to some extent, since they represent a second set of regulations (along with the company's personnel policy) to which these managers must conform. But they can also simplify managerial work, as by eliminating the need for individual wage negotiations or judgment calls on which workers to lay off first in times of economic downturn. From a slightly different perspective, managers who favour such participative management practices as total quality management and self-directed work teams may see detailed collective agreements as barriers to the achievement of the trust needed if such participative practices are to succeed.

As for IR academics, institutionalists generally look on collective agreements very favourably, as being, in effect, mini-constitutions that bring some measure of self-government and industrial democracy to the workplace (Giles and Jain, 1989:320).[2]

"NUMBER OF AGREEMENTS FOR NEW SETTLEMENTS BY INDUSTRY"

www.statcan.ca:80/cgi-bin/Cansim/cansim.cgi?matrix=4051&cq=&order_id=

On the other hand, neoclassicists and managerialists often view collective agreements, particularly their work rule provisions, as both inefficient and wasteful and an infringement on management's right to run enterprises as it sees fit (Godard, 1994:315). At the other end of the spectrum, those taking a radical/political economy perspective (i.e., Panitch and Swartz, 1988) see collective agreements as doing little to rectify the fundamental power imbalance between workers and management. From this perspective, collective bargaining and collective agreements may even be viewed as means to help management solidify its control over the workplace, making mid-term strikes illegal and turning union officials into "managers of discontent" by ensuring that they compel their members to comply with the contract (Giles and Jain, 1989:320).

EVOLUTION OF CANADIAN COLLECTIVE AGREEMENTS

In 1901, as Giles and Jain (1989:318) note, Local 713 of the Carpenters' Union signed an agreement with Niagara Falls contractors that contained only eight brief clauses governing such basic issues as wage rates, hours of work per day, holiday and overtime pay rates, and security of employment for union members. Today, many collective agreements are far longer, often reaching 100 pages or more and not infrequently containing a variety of appendices, letters of understanding, and wage schedules in addition to the main text (Giles and Jain, 1989:321). Also, unlike the Carpenters' agreement, written in plain English, many of today's agreements are written in complex, even convoluted legal jargon that makes them barely understandable to the workers and supervisors who must live by them on a daily basis (Giles and Jain, 1989). Why have Canadian agreements become so long and involved? And why must they be written in such complex language that the people who work with them most closely have difficulty understanding them?

One reason, particularly for the greater length of today's agreements, lies in the growth of larger and more bureaucratic workplaces and the industrial unionism that arose in response to that development. The Carpenters' Union of 100 years ago represented a quite homogeneous group of people performing similar work under roughly similar conditions. In addition, as skilled craftsmen, they would have enjoyed considerable freedom in how they did their jobs and would likely have been unwilling to sign any agreement providing for detailed regulation of their work methods.

With the growth of large factories employing sizeable numbers of unskilled and semi-skilled workers, employers (as we noted in Chapter 3) became very interested in regulating the work process to extract the maximum possible amount of labour from their workers. Detailed regulation was also necessary to provide some degree of uniformity in production standards and personnel policies. In situations where close personal supervision of each worker was no longer possible, management organizations needed formal rules and procedures to ensure that the goods their plants produced were of uniform quality and to prevent the sort of nightmarish morale problems that would have arisen had supervisors been free to interpret company personnel policy in their own way (Radforth, 1991). With no customary craft practices or traditions governing the way unskilled or semi-skilled factory work was to be done (Curtis, 1966), management now held virtually unlimited sway over the work process. In large, bureaucratic organizations like auto plants and steel mills, the degree of regulation could be quite extreme. The industrial unions that these factory workers joined (once the legislation had been passed enabling them to do so) could not do away with bureaucratic regulation of the work process. Even their own officials would have been forced to admit that no one can operate an efficient auto plant or steel mill without detailed, written rules. What the unions could do was ensure some degree of protection for workers' interests (such as rules specifying how work was to be assigned, how layoffs and transfers were to be handled, or how many people would be required to perform certain jobs).

The growth of larger workplaces meant that a single establishment might be employing workers performing many different jobs. Once these workers joined industrial unions, their agreements had to make provision for all those different types of workers. This meant, typically, separate wage schedules for each occupational grouping in the plant. It also meant a far broader range of work rules, since the same rules governing work methods could not realistically be expected to apply to an assembly line worker, a shipping clerk, and a member of the maintenance staff. All these wage schedules and sets of work rules have added considerably to the length of the typical Canadian agreement.

In recent years, Canadian workplaces haven't generally grown larger, but they have made increasing use of a broad range of new technologies and chemical substances of various kinds. The increasingly rapid pace of technological change has led unions to negotiate provisions seeking to protect workers against the adverse effects of such change, such as loss of employment or income (see Economic Council of Canada, 1987; Peirce, 1987). As well, unions have sometimes achieved provisions forbidding or restricting the use of surveillance cameras or electronic monitoring devices (Peirce, 1987:31–32). The widespread adoption of computer-based office technology that started in the 1980s led some unions to negotiate provisions allowing pregnant women operating computer terminals to change jobs with other workers, giving full-time computer operators regular rest breaks, and providing those operators with free eye examinations (Peirce, 1987:32–33). Meanwhile, the introduction of many new, potentially hazardous substances into Canadian workplaces has led unions to negotiate a variety of health and safety provisions governing procedures for using such substances, protective equipment, and the like. Again, these provisions, sometimes addressing quite complicated technical issues, have helped add to Canadian agreements' length and complexity.

ASSOCIATION OF LABOUR RELATIONS AGENCIES
www.state.vt.us/vlrb/alra.htm

Over the past decade, increased foreign competition, liberalized trade, and poor economic conditions have put considerable additional stress on the IR system, as we pointed out in Chapter 2. Growing numbers of layoffs have led most unions to make job security a priority. On the one hand, this has driven unions to negotiate employment and income security provisions when they can, and when they can't, to negotiate severance pay provisions or other ways of at least partially cushioning the impact of layoffs. On the other hand, it has sometimes led unions to demand greater control over pension plans (Giles and Starkman, 1995:349), and to negotiate increased involvement in the new forms of work organization that employers have often introduced in an attempt to make their firms more competitive (Giles and Starkman, 1995:343).

Another important source of collective agreement length and complexity has been the Canadian work force's growing diversity. During the early postwar period, newly unionized unskilled and semi-skilled workers pushed their unions to negotiate a broad range of fringe benefits, such as pension plans, life and medical insurance, dental plans, layoff allowances, and paid vacation and sick leave time, that would have been of little concern to the turn-of-the-century craft unionist (Curtis, 1966). Later, as large numbers of women entered the work force and signed union cards, unions began negotiating maternity leave and family leave provisions, anti-discrimination and anti-harassment clauses, and in some cases provisions establishing on-site workplace child care centres.[3] Similarly, the entry of large numbers of ethnic and religious minorities into unionized workplaces required unions to place additional emphasis on negotiating anti-discrimination and anti-harassment provisions, as well as provisions requiring employers to accommodate those of different religious backgrounds by providing time off for major religious observances, or creating a different work schedule when necessary. The hiring of increased numbers of people with disabilities, spurred by human rights legislation, led unions to negotiate special provisions governing building accessibility, or in some cases even redesigning jobs to allow them to be performed by those with disabilities (see Carter, 1997).

Still another source of complexity is rooted in employers' resistance to unions. Though they were eventually unable to stop unions from entering their establishments, they continued to seek to restrict their activities as much as possible, reducing the issues subject to union influence by means of detailed management rights clauses (discussed in more detail below) and adhering to collective agreements in a narrowly legalistic way (Giles and Jain, 1989:319). Moreover, under the prevailing Canadian doctrine of residual management rights, it is generally accepted by most arbitrators that any right not specifically granted to the union in the collective agreement is reserved to management (Giles and Starkman, 1995:345–347). In addition, with mid-term strikes banned and a minimum contract duration of one year, Canadian unions are "locked in" to the terms of the agreement for its full duration. Except in very rare cases, Canadian agreements don't contain "reopener" provisions allowing for the renegotiation of issues during the life of the contract (Giles and Jain, 1989:319). Therefore, to protect their members' interests, unions have been forced to negotiate extremely detailed and comprehensive collective agreement provisions limiting the rights of management in the areas of greatest concern to those members. As well, because grievance arbitration (discussed in Chapter 13) has become highly legalistic, contract language must be drafted with great care—undoubtedly further adding to the documents' complexity in many cases (Giles and Jain, 1989).

For the past two decades in particular (see Carter, 1997), collective agreements have been required to conform to a variety of laws beyond labour relations statutes. These include, most notably, work standards laws, health and safety legislation, and human rights laws (all discussed in Chapter 7 on employment legislation). Typically, unions and management have incorporated such legal requirements explicitly into their collective agreements (Giles and Starkman, 1995:342). While there are frequently good reasons for this, one being to allow issues such as sexual harassment to become subject to the agreement's grievance procedure as well as to a human rights tribunal or the courts, the incorporation of external legislative requirements has become a further source of collective agreement complexity.

MAIN TYPES OF COLLECTIVE AGREEMENT PROVISION

An Overview of Collective Agreements

One's first reaction, on looking into the bewildering array of highly legalistic clauses and sub-clauses, schedules, and letters of intent that makes up the typical Canadian agreement, is likely to be to throw up one's hands in despair and then head for the nearest telephone to engage the services of a labour lawyer or IR specialist to make some kind of sense of the otherwise mysterious document. After the shock wears off, though, and after one has examined a number of collective agreements, one comes to see that, in many ways, most agreements resemble each other quite closely. Most begin with a brief statement outlining the agreement's general purpose and, if the document is at all complex, with a list of relevant definitions (Giles and Jain, 1989:321).

Next comes a group of clauses outlining the rights and obligations of the parties (management rights and union recognition clauses), defining the bargaining unit, and, typically, providing for grievance procedures or (in some cases) other means of resolving conflict such as joint committees (Giles and Jain, 1989; Godard, 1994:305).

INDUSTRIAL RELATIONS RESEARCH ASSOCIATION
www.ilr.cornell.edu/iira/

The second major group of clauses typically covers wages and hours of work. Included here are wage and hours schedules governing different groups of workers, provisions governing overtime pay, shift premiums for work at night, vacation allotments, and provisions for both paid and unpaid leave (Giles and Jain, 1989:321).

A third group of provisions (not always grouped together in the agreement) governs work rules, broadly defined. Here, in addition to rules governing how work is assigned and performed, one finds provisions governing technological change and the methods used for layoffs, transfers, and promotions (Giles and Jain, 1989). The fourth and last major group of provisions concerns the work environment, again broadly defined (Giles and Jain, 1989). Such provisions may include disciplinary procedures, health and safety clauses, and anti-discrimination and anti-harassment clauses of various kinds.

If wage schedules are at all detailed and complicated, they are generally placed in an appendix, along with other issues considered too lengthy to be included in the main text (Giles and Jain, 1989). The agreement's back pages may also contain letters of intent or memoranda of understanding typically intended to spotlight issues to be addressed more fully in subsequent rounds of negotiations. A good example of such a letter of intent is the one contained in the 1984 agreement between Carleton University and CUPE, the union representing the university's support staff. This letter called for a joint eight-person union-management committee to make recommendations on all matters of concern related to the installation and use of computer terminals, including the testing of such terminals, the method of transferring workers away from such terminals for health-related reasons, and the plan for dealing with computer-related health hazards (Peirce, 1987:33–34).

Union and Management Rights and Conflict Control Provisions

These "ground rule" provisions, found in virtually all Canadian agreements, delineate the respective workplace rights of management and the union and provide for the handling of disagreements over interpretation, normally through a grievance procedure, but also sometimes through joint committees or other more proactive means. In addition, provisions in this group often specify the bargaining unit and members to whom the agreement applies, either directly or by listing members of excluded groups, such as management or in some cases professional staff.

Of greatest importance here are management rights and union rights and security provisions. Management rights provisions refer to clauses affirming management's right to run the enterprise as it wishes, subject to the limitations of the collective agreement. Such clauses may be either general or specific. In the latter case, they may spell out specific rights management reserves to itself, such as the right to hire, promote, transfer, or lay off workers, as well as to dismiss or suspend them. A good example of such a provision is Article 8.01 of the agreement between Bell Canada and the Communications Workers of Canada, which states that "[t]he Company has the exclusive right and power to manage its operations in all respects…(in particular) it has the exclusive right and power to hire, promote, transfer, demote, or lay-off employees, and to suspend, dismiss, otherwise discipline employees." Article 8.02 qualifies these rights by stating that their exercise "shall not contravene" the agreement's provisions.

Union rights and security provisions officially recognize the union's place in the enterprise. In addition, they grant specific rights for union officials, such as stewards, and address the rather controversial issue of how dues are to be collected.

The vast majority of Canadian agreements contain a provision stating that the employer recognizes the union as the workers' official bargaining agent. Many such provisions also state which employees are to be considered members of the bargaining unit. Management and confidential labour relations personnel are virtually always left out, though in a sense this exclusion is redundant since such employees are excluded from unionization in every Canadian jurisdiction in any case. In some cases, as in Article 9.01 of the Bell-CWC agreement, members of other groups such as part-timers and casuals may also be excluded; the Bell agreement specifically excludes "occasional" workers, whom it defines as people working no more than three weeks per year.

Beyond contract language generally recognizing their right to exist, unions need more specific provisions to ensure their presence is felt in the workplace on an ongoing basis. This means that their officials, in particular their stewards, need to be free to represent members' interests without management harassment. With this in mind, unions will frequently seek to negotiate provisions allowing them access to company facilities, such as offices or bulletin boards, to enable them to carry out their duties. Along similar lines, stewards' rights provisions, such as Article 5.01(b) of the Bell-CWC agreement, have become fairly standard features of Canadian agreements. This article states that union stewards, chief stewards, or local officers may handle grievances or attend meetings with the company during their regularly scheduled working hours, without deduction of the time spent at these activities or loss of wages, provided that each union official arranges things in advance with his or her immediate supervisor, and subject to service requirements. In some cases (Giles and Starkman, 1995:349), the company will reserve the right to limit the amount of time stewards can devote to union duties if it deems the time taken for such duties excessive.

Union security provisions address the issue of whether employees are required to be union members and if so, within what time frame. A number of types of union security clause are found in Canadian agreements. The strictest are the so-called "closed shop" provisions stating that the employer will hire only individuals who are already union members. Closed shops are most typically associated with the existence of hiring halls, organized and run by unions to provide employers with the number of workers they may need at any given time. Such arrangements are commonest in industries like construction and longshoring, where the work is temporary in nature and the workers' real attachment is to their trade and union rather than to the firm. "Union shop" provisions do not require union membership as a condition of employment, but do require all employees to join within a specified time period after being hired. A "modified" union shop provision requires all those hired after a given date to join the union. The weakest type of union security provision, the so-called "maintenance of membership" provision, does not compel anyone to join the union or pay dues, but does require anyone who has already joined or joins in the future to remain in the organization (Giles and Jain, 1989:326). "Rand formula" clauses (discussed in Chapters 4 and 8) do not require anyone to join a union, but do require all bargaining unit members to pay union dues, on the basis that non-members benefit just as much from the union's efforts in their behalf as do members. A good example of such a provision is Article 3.01 of the Bell-CWC agreement, which states that all current bargaining unit members shall pay union dues and all hired or transferred into the unit shall pay dues within 30 days after being hired or transferred. Where no union security provision is in place, the situation is referred to as an open shop.

As of 1994 (Giles and Starkman, 1995:349), about 55 percent of all Canadian agreements imposed some type of union membership requirement. The commonest types were the union and modified union shop, each with just over 20 percent. Closed shop provisions were found in less than 10 percent of all agreements, and maintenance of membership provisions, in just 3 percent. Rand formula arrangements were the commonest of all, found in more than 39 percent of all agreements. Open shops, increasingly common in the United States because of the "right-to-work" provisions of the *Taft-Hartley* amendments to that country's labour relations act, are a comparative rarity here; in 1994 they were found in just 6.5 percent of all agreements.

Conflict-control provisions address the issue of how disputes arising during the life of the agreement will be handled; in some instances they also establish preventive mechanisms, such as joint committees, designed to reduce or redirect labour-management conflict. Such provisions include "no-strike" clauses whereby the union agrees it will not strike during the life of the agreement and management agrees it will not lock out and provision for grievance arbitration of some kind as the mechanism for resolving mid-term contract disputes. Both types of provision are found in the vast majority of Canadian agreements. In many cases, grievance procedures are much more specific. Many agreements specify a list of acceptable arbitrators. Others provide for a single arbitrator instead of a three-person panel; still others name a standing umpire or establish various types of expedited arbitration procedure (Gandz and Whitehead, 1989:250–252), one of the more imaginative of these being the Port of Vancouver's dockside arbitration approach (J. Weiler, 1984).

Grievances, as we will point out in more detail in Chapter 13, are costly and time-consuming for both unions and management organizations. Recognizing this, thoughtful unions and management organizations often make provision for joint committees, with an eye to addressing ongoing problems on a proactive basis, thereby preventing them from becoming formal grievances. As of 1994, such committees were found in about 53 percent of all agreements, covering more than 60 percent of all employees (Giles and Starkman, 1995:352). Most were general committees designed to address a broad range of issues; however, some were specifically devoted to particular issues such as technological change. The effectiveness of these committees, like that of the health and safety committees now mandatory in almost all jurisdictions (discussed in Chapter 7) appears to vary widely, depending on the nature of the relationship between the parties and management's willingness to grant the committees significant decision-making authority.

In a few cases, unions and management organizations have gone beyond committees to negotiate broad, framework-style agreements, variously known as joint governance arrangements or social contracts (Verma, 1995; Giles and Starkman, 1995), normally involving a trade-off whereby the union agrees not to strike for a fairly lengthy period (typically in the vicinity of five years) and to moderate its wage demands in return for job security and increased involvement in organizational decision-making. These agreements, which were discussed in some detail in Chapter 6 (union actions and impacts), mean that the union becomes, in effect, a full partner in managing the organization (Verma, 1995), and thus entail a fundamental transformation away from its traditional role as workers' advocate.

Wage and Hours Provisions

Since most people work primarily for the pay they receive, wages and hours are, as Giles and Jain (1989) note, at the heart of the collective agreement. Compensation issues are normally among the more difficult items to negotiate and are typically left to the end of the process, after less contentious issues have been settled (see Fisher and Williams, 1989).

Wages

Most agreements contain various wage schedules detailing hourly, weekly, bi-weekly, monthly, or sometimes even annual pay rates for workers in different groups. Production and other blue-collar workers are normally paid an hourly basis, while office, white-collar, and professional workers are typically paid on a weekly or monthly basis (Giles and Starkman, 1995:357). Premium wages (most often 50 percent above the usual rate) are normally paid for overtime work (typically anything beyond 40 hours in a week or 8 in a day); sometimes an extra premium (normally at least twice the usual rate) will be paid for work on Sundays or holidays. Premium wages may also be paid for shift work, for work performed at night, or for unusually onerous or unpleasant work, such as unloading animal carcasses from ships' holds. In some cases, special clauses will provide "standby pay" for those who must remain on call when off-duty, or "reporting pay" for those called into work for short periods (Giles and Starkman, 1995:353).

In addition to accounting for different jobs, wage schedules often take workers' length of service into account. Such "step increments" become particularly important in situations where there is little opportunity for promotion (as in the case of much public sector work in recent years). Schedules often contain four to six steps within each job category,[4] with workers normally receiving a one-step raise each year providing their performance remains satisfactory (Giles and Starkman, 1995:356).

"WAGE INCREASES IN NEW COLLECTIVE AGREEMENTS"
www.statcan.ca/english/Pgdb/People/Labour/labour14.htm

When inflation was high, as it was in the late 1970s and early 1980s, many unions sought to protect their members' real wages by negotiating cost of living allowance (COLA) clauses. The basic idea behind such provisions is to adjust wages to the inflation rate so workers' purchasing power is maintained through the life of the contract. COLA clauses typically provide some, though not complete, protection against inflation. Often they are triggered only at a certain rate of inflation (i.e., 3 percent). Also, some COLA clauses don't cover the full contract period and some provide for less than full adjustment to the inflation rate. With the sharp decline in inflation since the early 1980s, COLA clauses have become far less common in Canadian agreements, accounting for only about 13 percent of all Canadian agreements in 1993 compared with 30 percent in 1981 (Giles and Starkman, 1995:358). Another consequence of the drop in inflation has been that few of the remaining COLA clauses have been triggered (Giles and Starkman, 1995).

While most unionized workers are paid a regular wage or salary, some are under incentive systems whereby they are paid wholly or partially on the basis on the amount of work performed. Unions generally dislike incentive systems, particularly individual systems that they typically criticize as "pitting worker against worker." As well, piecework systems are often difficult and costly to administer and can lead to considerable workplace conflict (Giles and Starkman, 1995:357). For these reasons, they have generally been uncommon in Canadian agreements, except in the clothing industry, where half the labour force work under such arrangements Grant, 1992:233), and in logging and other parts of the forest sector (Radforth, 1982; Giles and Starkman, 1995:357).[5] As Figure 11.1 illustrates, significantly fewer of the collective agreements monitored by the Workplace Information Directorate of Human Resources Development Canada contain piecework systems than 10 years ago (Fawcett, 1998). However, "team-oriented" incentive plans such as gain-sharing, group incentive plans, and, in particular, profit-sharing plans, increased during the same period (Fawcett, 1998).

Still another form of compensation system is the "pay-for-knowledge" system whereby workers are paid a different hourly, weekly, or monthly rate depending on the

FIGURE 11.1

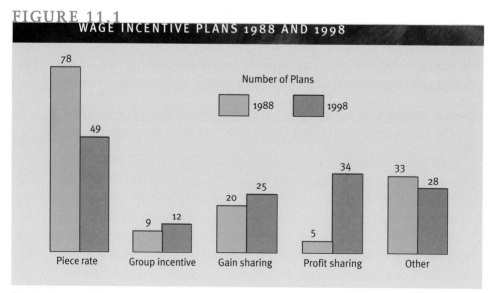

Source: Fawcett, 1998.

number of skills they have mastered (see Halpern, 1984). Normally, mastery must be demonstrated by passing specific tests covering the skill or skills in question. Such systems are most common in socio-technical systems environments and other workplaces using self-directed work teams, where it is necessary for workers to have a broad range of skills to function effectively as team members. An example of a pay-for-knowledge pay schedule drawn from the Shell Sarnia socio-technical systems case (Halpern, 1984) may be found in Table 11.1.

Benefits

In addition to wages, compensation packages in collective agreements generally include a variety of fringe benefits. Nationwide, fringes comprise more than 30 percent of total compensation costs (Halpern, 1984:358). In unionized establishments, the figure is almost certainly higher, since (as we noted in earlier chapters), many unionized workers prefer to take as much as possible of their compensation in the form of non-taxable benefits rather than taxable wages, and employers also like to use such benefits (particularly pension plans) as a means of reducing costly turnover. The benefits most commonly found in collective agreements include pension plans, disability and medical insurance, sick leave, extended health care, life and accident insurance, and dental insurance. Some agreements also contain provisions entitling workers to a given number of days off a year for religious or unspecified personal reasons.

Table 11.1
BASIC MONTHLY SALARIES

Team Members (Shift)	Basic Monthly Salaries	Hourly Rate Equivalents
Phase 12	$1 698	$10.47
Phase 11	$1 643	$10.13
Phase 10	$1 588	$9.79
Phase 9	$1 536	$9.47
Phase 8	$1 483	$9.14
Phase 7	$1 429	$8.81
Phase 6	$1 376	$8.48
Phase 5	$1 322	$8.15
Phase 4	$1 269	$7.82
Phase 3	$1 215	$7.49
Phase 2	$1 162	$7.16
Phase 1	$1 124	$6.93
Team Members (Craft) Journeymen	$1 551	$9.56

Source: Halpern, 1994, Basic Monthly Salaries, Pay-for-Knowledge Progression, Shell Sarnia Plant.

Agreement provisions normally spell out the details of the various plans, the eligibility rules (often linked to seniority, especially in the case of pension plans), and the respective contributions to be made by the employer and employees towards the cost of the various plans.

In recent years, there have generally been few new benefits, as cost-conscious employers have sought to reduce benefits or shift more of their costs to employees (Giles and Starkman, 1995:359). However, one new benefit that has been introduced with some regularity is prepaid legal services (Giles and Starkman, 1995). Another, perhaps in recognition of the growing stresses faced by workers in today's difficult economy, is the employee assistance program, which enables workers to receive counselling on a broad range of issues, from alcohol- and drug-related problems to marital and financial ones.

Work Hours

Hours of work have been of enormous importance to the Canadian labour movement since the nineteenth century, when, as we noted in the labour history chapter, demands for a shorter work day were a rallying cry around which the entire movement could unite.[6] Hours provisions have taken on renewed importance in recent years, with the growing recognition that shorter hours may be the best solution to persistent demand-deficient unemployment (see Chapter 2; Reid and Meltz, 1995; Gunderson and Reid, 1998; Peirce, 1998a, 1998b).

Most agreements stipulate normal working hours per week for those working on different jobs. The most common arrangements are still weeks of 35 to 40 hours during regular daytime hours; however, various alternative arrangements such as shift work and shorter or longer hours having been growing more frequent in recent years (see Chapter 2; see also Giles and Starkman, 1995:353). In the case of shift work, agreements may provide for the rotation of shifts among employees or the scheduling of shifts by seniority (Giles and Starkman, 1995), which typically means that more senior employees can pick preferred daytime shifts. Other provisions stipulate the length of time allowed for lunch breaks, coffee breaks, and washroom breaks (Giles and Starkman, 1995). Vacation and holiday pay provisions state how much vacation workers at given seniority levels will be entitled to, which days will be considered paid holidays, and how much of a premium will be paid to those required to work on those holidays. Finally, the growing presence of women in the work force has led to clauses providing maternity leave beyond the minimum provided through unemployment insurance, the right to accumulate seniority while on maternity leave, and to take time off to care for sick family members or attend parent-teacher interviews at school (Giles and Starkman, 1995:354).

As we pointed out in some detail in Chapter 2, the growing presence of women in the workplace has also led to demands for more flexible working hours to allow working mothers (and sometimes fathers) to attend to family responsibilities. A good example of this tendency towards more flexible hours is found in Article 18.02 of the Bell Canada-CWC agreement, which states that the basic workweek will be 38 hours for a five-day week, but that the hours may be averaged over a two-week period on the basis of ten days totalling 76 hours of work. Other agreements, especially in the public sector, may go even farther and provide for a compressed work week, whereby the employee works the regular number of hours over a two-week period, but may work only eight or nine days during those two weeks. Such arrangements are often extremely popular with employees (see CLMPC, 1997 for examples), since they allow a long weekend every week or two weeks and provide needed time during business hours to attend to family matters. However, these arrangements sometimes meet with management resistance, either because they complicate scheduling and create difficulties in maintaining service (CLMPC, 1997) or simply because the managers in question don't feel comfortable with anything other than orthodox "nine-to-five" scheduling, particularly in situations where employees may be working without supervision.

In a bid both to reduce unemployment and to allow workers to better attend to family responsibilities, European labour movements have been pushing shorter hours increasingly hard in recent years. During the spring of 1998, the Danish labour movement, spearheaded by the country's large female labourers' union, staged a general strike in support of a sixth annual week of paid vacation (*Better Times*, 6/98). While the Danish workers were not completely successful in achieving this result, they did win two additional paid days off per year as well as various other concessions. Determined efforts by other countries' labour movements have resulted in legislation providing for a 35-hour week by the year 2000 in France and Italy (Peirce, 1999), and the general achievement, through collective bargaining, of a 36-hour week in the Netherlands (Peirce, 1999).[7]

The Canadian labour movement has been far from monolithic on the issue of shorter work hours (A. Jackson, 1997), in part because many lower-paid workers feel they need overtime pay to help make ends meet. However, a number of unions have taken the lead in negotiating agreements providing for reductions in either regular work hours or overtime hours or both in return for job creation. Among those unions is the Canadian Auto Workers (CAW), which in 1993 negotiated a deal with Chrysler providing for a reduction in the work day from 8 to 7.5 hours and a substantial reduction in overtime. As a result of this agreement, over 800 jobs were saved (Donner, 1994; Canadian Labour Market and Productivity Centre, 1997; Peirce, 1999). A similar deal in 1995 between the United Steelworkers of America (USWA) and Alcan Aluminium Company in Jonquière, Quebec, whereby workers put in standard 40-hour weeks, but were paid for only 38 hours, allowed for the rehiring of 125 previously laid-off workers at the plant (CLMPC, 1997; Peirce, 1999).

The Canadian union that appears to have gone the farthest to promote shorter working hours is the Communications, Energy and Paperworkers' Union (CEP). For a number of years, the CEP has promoted a broad-brush approach to reduced hours including longer leaves, reduced and flexible hours for workers with family responsibilities, and a shorter work week or shorter work year featuring longer vacations and increased family and educational leaves (Peirce, 1999). The union has also called for "time banking," which would allow workers to defer part of their regular or overtime salary and take it as paid leave time at a later date. A number of CEP locals have negotiated reduced overtime or shorter work weeks in return for agreements to create or save jobs. For example, the CEP local at a Shawinigan, Quebec, pulp mill reduced overtime and worked some overtime at straight time pay to provide 55 additional jobs (White, 1997a:170). Similarly, CEP members at a Polysar rubber plant in Sarnia, Ontario, proposed a reduction in the standard week to 36 hours, at some loss in pay, to help prevent layoffs (White, 1997a).

"CAW MEMBERS AT AIR CANADA RATIFY COLLECTIVE AGREEMENT"

www.caw.ca/communications/contact/26.41.html

Nonetheless, the most recent evidence suggests that Canadian unions overall are generally putting a fairly low priority on shorter work hours, in contrast to many European unions. A survey conducted by Kumar, Murray, and Schetagne (1998) found that reducing work hours was an extremely important priority for only 20 percent of the responding unions, whose combined membership accounts for about 60 percent of all Canadian union members (1998:Table 9). Only about 11 percent of those unions reported that restrictions on overtime had been a top bargaining priority in the most recent round of negotiations, and only 8 percent indicated that they had been highly successful in achieving such restrictions in that round (Kumar et al., 1998:Tables 10 and 11).

Work Rules and Job Control Provisions

Without unions, management would have complete control over how work was organized and performed. At the bargaining table, unions seek to wrest some degree of control over work rules stating how work is to be done, as well as over the criteria for layoffs, transfers, promotions, technological change, and larger-scale work force reductions. Since workers' belief that they are entitled to basic job rights almost inevitably conflicts with management's desire to maximize flexibility and control, job control and work rules provisions can be among the most bitterly contested in the entire agreement (Giles and Starkman, 1995:360). Managerialists and neoclassicists argue that such provisions lead to inefficiency, in addition to interfering with management's right to run the enterprise as it sees fit. To buttress their arguments, such people may cite "horror stories," such as provisions stipulating that only licensed electricians be allowed to change light bulbs (Godard, 1994:315) or, in the theatre, that a minimum of four duly certified stagehands will be required to move a sawhorse on a set. But unionists, along with IR academics adopting more liberal perspectives, argue that such provisions are needed to protect employment levels, maintain some degree of quality of working life, and in some cases protect workers' health and safety (Godard, 1994:364). These people would argue that while "horror stories" of the type just cited do exist, they are comparatively rare, and that most work rules do not seriously harm workplace efficiency.

Hiring Process and Job Assignment

The strongest protection a union can achieve for its members is a "closed shop" provision (discussed earlier in the chapter) allowing only its members to be hired. Such provisions have never been common in Canada; they are found mainly in industries such as construction and longshoring, where the union also often maintains a hiring hall. Another, related form of control over job assignment may be obtained through the joint union-management dispatch systems that have often been used in longshoring (see Giles and Starkman, 1995:361). Unions may also obtain a measure of control over hiring and, in some cases, over the number of people admitted to the trade through provisions establishing union-management apprenticeship programs, requiring vacancies to be filled from within the organization when possible, and preventing supervisors and other non-bargaining unit employees from performing jobs normally done by their members (Giles and Starkman, 1995:360). Management's strongest weapon here is the probationary period, found in about 70 percent of all major Canadian agreements (Giles and Starkman, 1995). Workers on probation, which normally lasts three to six months but may last a good deal longer, can be let go should management deem their work to be unsatisfactory. Unlike permanent employees, they cannot avail themselves of the collective agreement's grievance procedure; thus a probationary period allows management considerable control over the hiring process, even in cases where the union may have negotiated other sorts of restrictions (Giles and Starkman, 1995).

Work Rules

Work rules provisions get at the very heart of the production process. They regulate such things as the speed of assembly lines and production processes, the number of people who must be assigned to a given job, the maximum allowable workload, and the question of who is to be allowed to do certain jobs. In longshoring in the Port of

Montreal (Shipping Federation, 1972; Picard, 1967), collective agreement provisions traditionally sought to protect employment by placing a maximum on the size of sling loads, requiring a given number of certain classes of worker for each gang in addition a given minimum overall gang size, and requiring certain numbers of relief men under certain circumstances (Picard, 1967, Rules 11 and 12). The maximum sling load restriction was given up in 1967 in return for the granting of job security to a certain number of "permanent" longshoremen. However, the gang minimums and restrictions on which members could be asked to perform particular jobs remained in place, causing the Shipping Federation to complain of serious inefficiencies and to propose, in a 1972 brief to Judge Alan Gold, the port's standing arbitrator, that management be allowed to determine how many men would be required to perform any given job and that all employees be required to perform any work for which they were qualified (Shipping Federation, 1972:19).

Workload restrictions are also an important part of bargaining in education. Teachers and university professors say that in order for them to provide quality education, there need to be restrictions both on the numbers of students they are asked to teach and on the numbers of classes or courses to which they are assigned. Such restrictions are needed, they argue, so that they will not be swamped with marking and preparation work. Additionally, public school teachers say they need time to "recharge themselves" during the school day. Workload was a major issue in both the 1997 and 1998 Ontario teachers' strikes (discussed in more detail in the strike chapter). It has also been an important issue in Quebec teachers' ongoing battle with the provincial government (CBC Radio News, October 6, 1998).[8]

Job Control

Job control provisions govern the criteria to be used for changes in the firm's internal labour market, especially promotions, transfers, and layoffs. Like workload and work rule provisions, they are often the source of considerable conflict between workers and management, since management generally prefers to retain its control over such decisions, while workers normally prefer that such decisions be made on the basis of seniority (Giles and Starkman, 1995:362). The rationale behind seniority is that long-serving workers, who have invested much of their working lives in the organization, should be entitled to preferential consideration for promotion and transfers and greater security against layoffs (Giles and Starkman, 1995). Another argument in favour of seniority is that by providing an objective, impersonal standard for personnel decisions, it eliminates the possibility of arbitrary or unfair management actions (Giles and Starkman, 1995), which in turn can increase workers' morale and productivity (see Freeman and Medoff, 1979).

Seniority provisions are used in two different ways: to determine a worker's status with respect to accrued benefits such as vacation time, severance pay, and pensions; and to determine his or her status relative to other workers in situations involving promotions, transfers, layoffs, choice of shifts, and the like (Godard, 1994:315–316). The first type of provision, known as benefit status provisions, are generally uncontroversial; the second type, known as competitive status provisions, are often far more so, for reasons that will be discussed presently.

Within the "competitive status" group, provisions applying to layoffs and recalls are the most common. Such provisions, typically stating that layoffs will be made in reverse order of seniority and that recalls will be in direct order of seniority, were found in about three-quarters of all major Canadian agreements in 1994 (Giles and Starkman, 1995:362). Such provisions are favoured by almost all workers and may well be preferred even by some managers, since they spare managers the necessity of making painful individual decisions as to who will be let go during economic downturns.

The use of seniority as a criterion for promotions is a good deal more controversial. Nonetheless, provisions of this kind remain quite common in Canadian agreements. In 1994, such provisions were found in nearly 60 percent of all major Canadian agreements—only a slight reduction since 1986 (Giles and Starkman, 1995). Seniority-based promotion provisions run the gamut from those that use seniority alone to clauses stating that it will be used only in situations where the workers' skills and abilities are more or less equal. In between, there is a broad range of provisions stipulating that some mix of ability and seniority will be used. Not untypical is the Coca-Cola Company provision described in Godard (1994:316) that the employee in question must possess the ability to do the job. Managers often dislike seniority-based promotion provisions because they mean that the individual promoted is often not the best person for the job, which over time may lead to reduced efficiency. In addition, many workers also dislike these provisions, because they sense that an individual's ability, motivation, and effort do not matter as much as his or length of service. For this reason, seniority-based promotion provisions have often been criticized as demotivating.

Many collective agreements also contain bumping rights that allow senior workers who have been laid off to take the jobs of more junior workers, who in turn may take the job of even more junior workers and so on down the line (Giles and Starkman, 1995:363). Such bumping provisions were found in about half of all major collective agreements in 1994 (Giles and Starkman, 1995). Managers generally dislike bumping provisions, particularly those that set up lengthy organization-wide bumping chains, since they can lead to considerable uncertainty as to who will be doing which jobs within the organization.[9] As a result, most bumping provisions restrict bumping rights in some way or other, either by limiting them to certain locations or departments or by requiring that "bumping" employees possess the ability to do the job within a minimal period of time (Giles and Starkman, 1995:363; Godard, 1994:318–319).

Seniority provisions have come under increasing attack in recent years. For one thing, the negative efficiency implications of such provisions, especially when applied to promotions, may be more severe now than in the past when, in many large industrial plants, workers and jobs might be more or less interchangeable. Increasingly, this is no longer the case; a worker's ability to do one job may be no guarantee of his or her ability to do a different job. Another concern is, on the one hand, that seniority-based layoff provisions may inadvertently discriminate against women, minority group members, and people with disabilities, who, as the "last hired," would of necessity be the first laid off and the last recalled under most existing layoff arrangements (Giles and Starkman, 1995:363). On the other hand, it could also be argued that seniority-based layoff provisions, in particular, take on particular importance at a time when many firms are cutting labour costs and going in for large-scale layoffs. Without such provisions, one could fairly argue, many organizations might simply lay off their most experienced workers, on the basis that these workers commanded the highest wages and laying them off would achieve the greatest labour cost savings. In addition to being very bad for morale, such a move could be very bad for the organization in anything beyond the exceedingly short term, since it would rob it both of its most experienced workers and of much of its institutional memory. Alternatively, a firm could simply lay off anyone management didn't like, a course of action that could prove equally bad for morale.

In Chapter 2 on the economy, we noted that large-scale layoffs continue to be a way of life across Canada, in both the private and public sectors. So long as these layoffs continue, unions are likely to put a very high premium on maintaining seniority-based layoff provisions, if only to prevent the kinds of arbitrary management action just described.

Technological Change

Workers and employers have battled over technological change from time immemorial (Peirce, 1987). On the whole, the Canadian collective bargaining system has not handled issues related to technological change very well. This really isn't too surprising, given that the purpose of collective bargaining is to fix terms and conditions of employment for a given period of time, whereas technological change is by its very nature destabilizing and often serves to change the balance of workplace power both between management and workers and among different groups of workers (Peirce, 1987; Cardin, 1967). Among the major consequences of such change can be layoffs, loss of income, and deskilling of jobs. In extreme cases, it can even lead to plant closures.

A study from the mid 1980s (Peirce, 1987) found that slightly over half of all Canadian agreements covering 500 or more workers contained some kind of technological change provision. However, in most cases the protection afforded was rather minimal. On average, these "large agreements" contained less than two of the six technological-change-related provisions most commonly coded by Labour Canada. Provisions calling for advance notice or consultation before bringing in technological change were found in slightly less than 40 percent of the "large agreements." Training and retraining provisions related to technological change were found in about 30 percent of those agreements, and employment security provisions, in just over 20 percent. Far less common were clauses providing for technological-change-related labour-management committees, relocation allowances, and notice of layoff related to technological change (Peirce, 1987, Table 1).

INFORMATION HIGHWAY AND WORKPLACE ISSUES
www.reflection.gc.ca/menu2_e.cfm

The large agreement pool appeared to overstate the frequency of technological change provisions within Canadian agreements as a whole. A supplementary study (Peirce, 1987, Table 7) based on examination of agreements covering fewer than 500 workers finds technological change provisions occurring only slightly more than half as often as they did in the "large agreement" pool. The study also finds technological change provisions to be no more frequent in jurisdictions that had relevant legislation in force than in those that did not (Peirce, 1987:4). Beyond that, labour boards appeared to be reluctant to enforce the legislation (Peirce, 1987:95), while arbitrators seemed similarly reluctant to enforce collective agreement provisions related to technological change (Peirce, 1987). In addition, many key areas of concern to Canadian workers, such as the health and safety aspects of new technology and the possible deskilling effects of that technology, were virtually never dealt with through collective bargaining (Peirce, 1987:5, Table 7).

A more recent review (Giles and Starkman, 1995:364–5) suggests that not much has changed since the mid 1980s with respect to the handling of technological change through collective bargaining. There appears to have been a moderate increase in provisions calling for advance notice or consultation with the union; however, other tech-change-related provisions have remained virtually constant. More than 40 percent of all agreements still contain no technological change provisions at all—only a slight decline since 1985. The lack of any real increase in protection against the adverse effects of technological change, despite the past decade's numerous plant closings and layoffs that should have made the issue a priority for unions, lends some credence to Giles and Starkman's contention that Canadian employers have remained "steadfast in their determination to preserve their control over the process of technological change" (Giles and Starkman, 1995:365).

However, there is reason to believe Canadian unions may not have done enough to raise the issue at the bargaining table, at least in the past. The Economic Council's "Working with Technology" survey (Betcherman and McMullen, 1986; Peirce, 1987:59–60) finds that, while technological change had occurred in 80 percent of the unionized establishments surveyed in the five years prior to the survey, negotiations over such change had occurred in only 46 percent of the unionized establishments. When unions did raise technological change issues, they were successful about half the time, a finding that suggests that if unions were to raise these issues more often, collective agreement provisions addressing workers' interests would probably become more frequent (Peirce, 1987).[10] More recently, the survey of major Canadian unions by Kumar and his associates (1998:Table 10) found that technological change was a high bargaining priority with 33 percent of all responding unions, and a moderate priority with another 32 percent. These figures suggest that unions may be more fully appreciating the importance of technological change than they did in the past. What hasn't changed is the limited account of success unions have had in negotiating technological-change provisions. Only about 14 percent of all responding unions reported a high degree of success in this area in their last bargaining round, while another 42 percent reported moderate success (Kumar et al., 1998:Table 11).

Some (i.e., Cardin, 1967; Anderson, 1989b) have suggested that issues like technological change may be handled better under centralized bargaining systems that allow for political bargaining.[11] Others (Task Force on Microelectronics, 1982; Ontario NDP, 1984; Adams, 1985; ECC, 1987; Peirce, 1987) have suggested that collective bargaining over this issue should be replaced (or at least supplemented) with joint committees that would apply in all workplaces, unionized and non-unionized alike, and that would have the power to take issues through to arbitration if the committee were unable to arrive at a consensus. But despite the frequency with which this recommendation has been made, there has thus far been little sign that any Canadian government is prepared to act on it.

Work Force Reductions

With the large-scale restructuring, downsizing, and layoffs that have been taking place in many industries in recent years, job security has become a top priority for unions. An issue of particular concern for many unions is contracting out, or the hiring of an outside firm to do a given job, rather than using existing employees or hiring new ones (Giles and Starkman, 1995:361). In many (perhaps most) cases, the firm to which the work is being contracted will be non-union, which may pose a threat to union membership levels as well as to members' jobs and incomes. In almost all cases, these firms pay their workers substantially lower wages than do the organizations that have contracted out the work to them. Contracting out has been a particularly hot issue in the public sector, as government departments, hospitals, and universities (to give just a few examples) have contracted out food operations, snow and garbage removal, and cleaning services with increasing frequency (Rose, 1995:36).

To help protect their members against the effects of contracting out, unions have negotiated a variety of prohibitions against the practice. Complete prohibitions are rare (Giles and Starkman, 1995; Peirce, 1987, Table 7). Much commoner are prohibitions against moves that may lead to job loss, or prohibitions against contracting out of work to non-union firms. Other agreements contain provisions barring the contracting out of work so long as there are enough regular employees available to do that work.[12]

In recent years, unions have been moderately successful in negotiating contracting-out prohibitions, which were found in about 44 percent of all major collective agreements in 1994 (Giles and Starkman, 1995:362), a substantial increase from their 31 percent frequency in 1985 (Peirce, 1987, Table 7). Interestingly, such prohibitions appear to be far more common in the private than in the public sector. In 1991 (Rose, 1995:36), they were found in 59 percent of all private sector agreements, but only 38 percent of all public sector ones, and a mere 22 percent of all agreements in public administration. More recently, Kumar et al. (1998) found restricting contracting out to have been the responding unions' fourth most important priority overall in their most recent round of bargaining. About 48 percent of all responding unions placed a high priority on this issue, while another 27 percent gave it moderate priority (1998:Table 10). Despite the high importance unions gave this issue, their success in achieving increasing protection against contracting out appears to have been quite modest. Only 15 percent reported a high degree of success with this issue, while another 49 percent indicated they had had moderate success (Kumar et al., 1998:Table 11).

Where unions are not successful in preventing job loss (as through the negotiation of contracting-out prohibitions), they will, at a minimum, seek to cushion the impact of job loss through provisions requiring the employer to give employees notice of impending layoffs or to give severance pay packages to those being laid off. As of 1994, notice of layoff provisions were found in slightly over half of all Canadian agreements, the vast majority providing less than 45 days' notice (Giles and Starkman, 1995:361). The incidence of such provisions doesn't appear to have changed much in recent years; in 1985 (Peirce, 1987, Table 8) they were found in 58 percent of all major agreements. However, it should be noted that notice of layoff provisions may now be less important than in the past, since almost all provinces and the federal jurisdiction have mass termination legislation in place (Giles and Starkman, 1995:361).[13] In many cases, such legislation requires a far longer notice period than most collective agreement provisions do, and in the federal jurisdiction, it also includes a severance pay requirement.

Severance pay packages are a way of giving laid-off employees time to find a new job or adjust to retirement. They take on particular importance when a large number of employees are laid off simultaneously in a community, making new jobs hard to find. In some cases, the severance package may be a lump sum; more often, however, it is based on the number of years of service (Peirce, 1987:9), a typical formula being one week's pay for each year of service to a maximum of 26 weeks. In some cases, those being laid off may also receive career counselling, time off for job searches, or permission to use the employer's facilities in searching for a new job. In addition to severance pay packages, unions may seek to negotiate supplementary unemployment benefits, rights to new job openings in other establishments run by the employer, or the continuation of employer-paid benefits after layoffs have occurred (Giles and Starkman, 1995:361).

Work Behaviour and Work Environment Provisions

Work behaviour and work environment provisions address issues relating to the social and physical environment in which work is performed (Giles and Jain, 1989:340). General rules governing work behaviour and disciplinary methods and more specific prohibitions on certain types of harassment relate to the social environment. Health and safety provisions are concerned with the physical environment.

Most collective agreements permit management to discharge or suspend employees provided there is "just cause" (Giles and Starkman, 1995:366). Whether the employer has in fact shown just cause is something that the union will usually dispute, particularly in discharge cases. Some agreements stipulate special, expedited hearings for discharge cases; others state that an employee's disciplinary record may be "cleared" after a specified period of time (Giles and Starkman, 1995:366–367). While unions normally prefer not to incorporate specific disciplinary procedures into the collective agreement (Giles and Starkman, 1995:366), in some cases there will be specific rules or penalties for offences such as absenteeism (i.e., verbal warning for a first offence, written warning for a second offence, suspension for a third offence, layoff and possible dismissal for a fourth offence).

The handling of discharge and discipline cases by arbitrators represents the one significant modification to the doctrine of residual management rights that otherwise governs the interpretation of Canadian collective agreements. Though most agreements contain a provision that states that arbitrators do not have the power to alter an agreement term or substitute a new provision for an existing provision (Giles and Starkman, 1995:367), in discipline and discharge cases, arbitrators have broad discretion to substitute their own penalties for those imposed by the employer. In such cases, especially discharge cases, the onus of proof rests with the employer, and the standard required by arbitrators is generally high (Giles and Starkman, 1995). Except in cases where an employee has been discharged for a single, extremely serious offence such as theft or assault, arbitrators normally expect employers to have imposed progressive discipline (discipline in steps, as indicated in the previous paragraph) to give the employee a chance to mend his or her ways. Where progressive discipline has not been applied, the discharge will normally be overturned at arbitration. Of those workers filing discharge grievances, slightly more than half are reinstated, many with some back pay (McPhillips and England, 1995:81). Collective agreements' grievance procedures thus offer workers quite substantial protection against arbitrary disciplinary action by employers.

REPORT OF THE ADVISORY COMMITTEE ON THE CHANGING WORKPLACE

www.reflection.gc.ca/menu_e.cfm

A recent trend, resulting from the growing number of women in the workplace and their increasing prominence within many unions, has been the inclusion of sexual harassment provisions in collective agreements. While human rights legislation (discussed in Chapter 7) provides protection against such behaviour, incorporating harassment provisions into the agreement allows women who believe they have been sexually harassed to avail themselves of the agreement's grievance procedure as an alternative to the often cumbersome and time-consuming procedures established by the legislation. Similarly, the growing number of workers from ethnic and religious minorities has spurred demands for other kinds of anti-discrimination provisions, likewise enforceable through the grievance procedure.

As for health and safety, unions have long been leaders in pushing for safer workplaces. Their contributions in this area are among the most important ones they have made. Even though health and safety issues are the subject of legislation in every Canadian jurisdiction, unions continue to have an important role to play here, as we noted in Chapter 7, both through their role in enforcing legislation that governments might otherwise lack the resources or political will to enforce at all adequately, and through their ability to enhance legislative standards at the bargaining table.

In many cases, unions will insist on the inclusion of provisions allowing workers to be informed about, or to refuse, unsafe work (Giles and Starkman, 1995:367). While such provisions would seem to be redundant since these rights are provided in provincial and federal health and safety legislation, they again allow unions to avail themselves of their agreements' grievance procedures, which in practice may afford a speedier and more appropriate remedy than legislatively established procedures. Beyond that, unions can negotiate any number of industry- or firm-specific clauses, such as provisions requiring employers to cover all or part of the cost of safety equipment (see the Bell-CWC agreement discussed below for a good example) or establishing safety programs or training procedures governing the use of potentially hazardous equipment (Giles and Starkman, 1995).

RECENT TRENDS IN COLLECTIVE AGREEMENT PROVISIONS

Evidence from the 1998 survey by Kumar and his associates suggests a renewed concern by unions with traditional bread-and-butter issues of wage protection, job security, and pensions. The survey also shows just how difficult unions are finding it to achieve major success on *any* bargaining issue, but especially on "non-traditional" issues not related to wages, benefits, or job security.

The six items of high priority to the greatest number of unions in the most recent bargaining round were, in descending order: protection of current wages and benefits, protection against layoffs, increasing the union's role in workplace decision making, restriction on contracting out and outsourcing, provision of advance notice of organizational change, and improvements in pensions and retirement benefits (Kumar et al., 1998:Table 10).[14] Out of these six items, protection of wages and benefits was the one on which the greatest proportion of unions (49 percent) had achieved a high degree of success (see Table 11.2). On only two of the remaining five issues(layoff protection and improved pensions(did more than 20 percent of the responding unions report a high degree of success. The unions' most notable "failure" was in achieving an increased role in workplace decision making. While 49 percent of the unions had indicated that this was a high priority in the last bargaining round, only 6 percent said that they had achieved a high degree of success on this issue.

As Table 11.2 further indicates, unions were also notably unsuccessful in guaranteeing minimum levels of employment, controlling or regulating workloads, achieving workplace adjustment provisions, and regulating the pace and nature of workplace change. What is not clear from the Kumar et al. study is whether unions were less successful in achieving workplace control provision than traditional "bread-and-butter" provisions because management resisted such provisions more strongly at the table, or because, in the final analysis, members placed a lower priority on workplace control than they did on the bread-and-butter items.

A finding potentially great significance to unions, particularly public sector unions and other representing large numbers of women, is that in several areas of special interest to women, such as flextime, family-related leaves, and child-care facilities, the number of unions reporting a high degree of success was *greater* than the number that had put a high priority on the issue prior to the last round of negotiations. For example, fewer than 6 percent of the unions had placed a high initial priority on flextime,

Table 11.2

DEGREES OF SUCCESS IN THE MOST RECENT BARGAINING ROUND*

		High %	Modest %	Low %
Protect current wages and benefits	(n=87)	49.4	41.4	9.2
Lay-off protections	(n=80)	25.0	38.8	36.3
Increase union role in workplace decision-making	(n=86)	5.8	50.0	44.2
Restrict contracting-out/out-sourcing	(n=80)	15.0	48.8	36.3
Advance notice of organizational change	(n=77)	16.9	42.9	40.3
Improved pensions and early retirement provisions	(n=81)	23.5	44.4	32.1
Increase wage and benefits	(n=86)	14.0	47.7	38.4
Consultation and mechanism on change	(n=77)	11.7	41.6	46.8
Improved training and retraining opportunities	(n=80)	13.8	50.0	36.3
Merger/amalgamation protections and protocols	(n=77)	18.2	27.3	54.5
Cost-of-living adjustments	(n=81)	11.1	29.6	59.3
Guarantees of minimum levels of employment	(n=77)	5.2	37.7	57.1
Control or regulate workloads	(n=79)	7.6	53.2	39.2
Technological change protections	(n=78)	14.1	42.3	43.6
Labour adjustments provisions	(n=74)	6.8	47.3	45.9
Better severance pay provisions	(n=79)	12.7	35.4	51.9
Regulate working hours/shift schedules	(n=81)	14.8	48.1	37.0
Access to financial information	(n=79)	13.9	35.4	50.6
Regulate the pace and the nature of workplace change	(n=78)	6.4	43.6	50.0
Health and safety improvements	(n=80)	12.5	46.3	41.3
Increase worker control and responsibility	(n=79)	7.6	35.4	57.0
Policy on harassment	(n=79)	16.5	36.7	46.8
Employment equity policies	(n=77)	14.3	31.2	54.5
Family-related leaves	(n=77)	14.3	39.0	46.8
Restriction on overtime	(n=76)	7.9	23.7	68.4
Flex time	(n=77)	11.7	33.8	54.5
Child care facilities	(n=75)	5.3	10.7	84.0

*Note: items are arranged in order of the degree of importance placed on them by unions (Kumar, Murray, and Schetagne 1998, Table 10)

n=number of respondents

Source: Kumar, Murray, and Schetagne, 1998.

but 12 percent reported achieving a high degree of success on this issue. This finding suggests that greater emphasis on issues of particular interest to women might well bear fruit at the bargaining table, which in turn could help make unions a more attractive proposition to women over the longer term.[15]

Collective Agreements and the Union— Management Relationship

A collective agreement provision can tell a knowledgeable reader a good deal about the nature of the relationship between the union and management that have negotiated that provision. For example, provisions laying out harsh disciplinary procedures or rigid limitations on who can perform certain jobs or the number of people required to perform them are often found in highly adversarial union-management relationships, where there has been a long history of mistrust between the parties. Such provisions also appear to be characteristic of declining industries, such as longshoring and coal mining, where management's need to curb labour costs comes into direct conflict with the union's need to preserve its members' jobs and income.[16] Conversely, provisions that allow the parties a greater degree of latitude, or suggest some significant sharing of workplace power or responsibility, are generally characteristic of more positive union-management relationships. Such provisions are more likely to be found in industries that are growing, or at least stable, such as telecommunications. The point here is that where collective agreement provisions impose increased costs on management (as many such provisions do), they are less apt to lead to serious union-management conflict in situations where at least part of the increased costs may be compensated for by a growth in revenues and profits.

Adapting and elaborating on some terminology devised by Godard (1994) to classify management attitudes towards unions, we would describe provisions in which the delineation of the union's and management's respective territory and rights is extremely detailed or minute as characteristic of an exploitive relationship between the parties. Here, the focus is quite simply on how much each side can extract from the other; there is generally little concern about the impact agreement provisions will have on the overall union-management relationship or even on the enterprise's long-term viability. Quite a number of these kinds of provisions can be found in collective agreements between the Shipping Federation of Canada, representing shipping company owners in the Port of Montreal, and Local #375 of the International Longshoremen's Association, representing the port's longshoring workers. For instance, Rule 44 of the Picard Commission Report, which for a time served as the agreement between the parties, actually stipulated that toilets and washrooms be provided in sheds, and close to the docks where there were no sheds (Picard, 1967)! This author has never seen a comparable provision in any other collective agreement he has examined. The evident need to spell out management's obligation to provide workers with such basic amenities as sanitary facilities near their work sites or food service facilities (also specified in the Picard Report) points to an appalling level of mistrust between the longshoremen and the shipowners, ample evidence of which may be obtained from examining the history of that relationship (see Picard, 1967). By the same token, examples like the light bulb and sawhorse ones quoted previously point towards the union's desire not just to maintain employment levels (though this is part of the rationale for such provisions), but also to punish management for perceived past wrongs by making it far more difficult for management to deploy workers.

Agreement provisions that, without in any way suggesting a fundamental change in the nature of the employment relationship, are phrased in more general terms and allow some latitude in interpretation may be thought of as characteristic of accommodative union-management relationships. In such relationships, while the parties' interests may still diverge sharply in many cases, particularly when it comes to monetary issues, both are also concerned with the viability of the enterprise and with maintaining a good long-term relationship. In general, the parties to such relationships would tend to agree that extremely detailed and minute delineation of union and management "territory" in agreement provisions is often not the best way to achieve such a relationship.

A number of examples of such accommodative provisions may be found in the agreement between Bell Canada and the Communications Workers of Canada. For example, Article 12.01, on health and safety, states: "Both parties...recognize the need to ensure the safety and protect the health of all employees." Article 12.02 states that it is the company's responsibility to introduce "reasonable procedures and techniques" to provide for workers' health and safety, while for its part the union may make suggestions for improvements in this area. Article 12.05 stipulates that the company will pay for all required safety equipment except safety footwear, for which the company will contribute a substantial share of the cost, depending on the type of shoe or boot required. A related provision (Article 18.36) dealing with video display terminals (computer terminals) stipulates that operators will not normally be scheduled more than two hours on duty without a relief or meal period. When such a relief or meal period cannot be scheduled, the employee will be entitled to take a five-minute rest break after two hours' continuous work on the terminal. While leaving no uncertainty as to who is in charge of running the enterprise (as Article 12.02 in particular indicates), the provisions just cited point to a willingness on the part of Bell to accommodate workers' reasonable needs in the area of safety equipment and rest breaks for computer operators. Even more important, Article 12.01 suggests a willingness to share responsibility for health and safety issues and provides at least implicit recognition that here may be a "win-win" area for both parties. Normally the degree of trust needed to arrive at this kind of recognition must be built up over a number of years. Provisions of this kind are, therefore, generally characteristic of mature and stable bargaining relationships.

Occasionally (though rarely in Canada), one finds agreements that go beyond the accommodative approach just described to adopt an egalitarian approach. In place of detailed "control" provisions, such agreements tend to feature broad, rather general statements of principle. The best-known and most-studied Canadian agreement of this kind, that between the Shell Chemical Plant in Sarnia, Ontario, and Local 9-148 of the Oil, Chemical and Atomic Workers Union, does not contain a management rights provision or a formal grievance procedure (Halpern, 1984). The agreement also contains no specific work rules or job control provisions, beyond a stipulation that layoffs will be made in order of reverse seniority, providing that the remaining employees are capable of meeting all job requirements (Halpern, 1984:73). A foreword making up about one-fifth of the agreement's very modest length states that its purpose is "to establish an enabling framework within which an organizational system can be developed and sustained that will ensure an efficient and competitive world-scale Chemical Plant operation and provide meaningful work and job satisfaction for employees" (Halpern, 1984:70). The agreement also reflects the management's and union's mutual commitment to a number of key principles, such as a belief that employees are responsible and trustworthy and are capable of making proper decisions related to their work arrangements "if given the necessary authorities, information and training" (Halpern, 1984). Such an agreement was adopted because both sides recognized that a collective agreement "composed of tight rules and regulations" would be inconsistent with the plant's workplace design, based on "minimal specification," encouragement of exploration, and a high degree of mutual trust (Halpern, 1984:51).

Beyond explicit contract provisions, the way in which parties interpret an agreement can offer important insights into their relationship. In mature, accommodative relationships, management and the union will tend to interpret the agreement judiciously and will not always seek to turn every apparent "violation" of the agreement into a formal grievance. Indeed, such relationships often feature proactive, problem-solving mechanisms like joint committees whose aim is to prevent most workplace problems from developing into grievances. In exploitive relationships, in contrast, each apparent "violation" of the contract is seen as a way to score political points against the other side. In extreme cases (like the highly conflictual relationship between Canada Post and the Canadian Union of Postal Workers), grievances may be used as a political weapon by both sides (Gandz and Whitehead, 1989; Stewart-Patterson, 1987; Godard, 1994:360). For example, a union may file large numbers of grievances just before or during negotiations as a means of putting pressure on management. For its part, management may "stonewall" on settling grievances, refusing to settle as a means of proving its toughness and resolve to the union. Such politicization of the grievance process, of which an excessively formal and legalistic interpretation of the collective agreement is often part and parcel, has frequently been associated with poor overall organizational performance (see Gandz and Whitehead, 1989:244).

SOME PROBLEMS WITH COLLECTIVE AGREEMENTS

The excessively legalistic interpretation of collective agreements that appears to be characteristic of exploitive union-management relationships is just one of the problems associated with such agreements. Another is that even the most detailed agreement cannot possibly cover all possible workplace situations. In particular, as we noted already, technological change, plant closures, and other large-scale changes over which the union may have very limited control may alter the ground rules quite considerably. While some Canadian jurisdictions have provided workers and their unions with limited legislative protection against the adverse effects of technological change, for the most part such legislation has been weak, and its enforcement haphazard at best (ECC, 1987; Peirce, 1987). It has also been observed that many unions appear to have been reluctant to raise technological change issues at the bargaining table (Betcherman and McMullen, 1986). Taken together, these facts suggest that the issue may be one better handled through other forums than collective bargaining. At a more fundamental level, the case of technological change raises the even broader issue of how well collective bargaining, which is designed to stabilize terms and conditions of employment for a given period (see Cardin, 1967), can realistically be expected to operate in an increasingly global economy marked by almost instantaneous transmission of information, rapid movement of goods, services, and capital across international borders, and constant fluctuations in exchange rates (Giles and Starkman, 1995:342–343).[17]

INTERNATIONAL CONFEDERATION OF FREE TRADE UNIONS
www.icftu.org

Even leaving aside such large-scale global issues, the interpretation of collective agreements is often an extremely complex business. This becomes most apparent when a case is taken to arbitration. Then the complexity can be measured in terms of dollars spent and the number of person-hours utilized in processing the case. But this is not the only way in which collective agreements' complexity is manifested. Some provisions, as was noted earlier, can be so difficult to interpret that neither supervisors nor union stewards really understand them. In part because many provisions are so difficult to interpret, and in part just to make life easier all around, collective agreements tend to be unevenly enforced in the workplace. Union officials and managers alike may decide simply to ignore certain provisions, and may also, for whatever reason, not avail themselves of all the rights allowed them by the agreement. Should, at a later date, either side decide to start sticking more closely to the "letter of the law," such earlier laxness could come back to haunt them (see Godard, 1994:363).

Another more fundamental criticism of collective bargaining is that it assumes at least rough equality between the parties. In practice, this doesn't always exist, particularly not in bad economic times, when (as at present) the balance of power tends to shift strongly in the direction of employers. Where such a balance of power does not exist, it becomes harder for unions to negotiate effectively, and the collective bargaining process does less well at defusing workplace conflict than it otherwise would. Should the power imbalance continue for any length of time, the conflict may well resurface in the form of increased grievance rates, higher levels of official or unofficial strike action (as in the case of Ontario's teachers), or increased absenteeism and sick leave (see Shellenbarger, 1998), all of which may have severely negative consequences for both the organization and its employees.

A BLESSING OR A CURSE?

Though collective bargaining has been widespread in Canada since the end of the Second World War, the process, and the agreements that are its fruits, have remained controversial. A particular concern has been the evolution of collective agreements into long, detailed, often highly legalistic documents. Has this evolution been healthy for the Canadian IR system? Though there are different schools of thought within union and management camps, by and large unionists and academics supportive of unions would say that this evolution has been healthy. While they admit that interpreting agreements is often difficult and costly, most would argue that workers and their unions have few alternatives to detailed rules spelling out workers' and unions' rights, given Canadian unions' political weakness and their need to negotiate detailed provisions to get around management rights clauses and the doctrine of reserved management rights. In contrast, managers and the IR academics who support them tend to view the evolution as unhealthy, citing among other things the increased cost of negotiating and administering detailed and complex agreements and such agreements' tendency to reduce trust. A growing concern here is that detailed work rules and complex job classification systems may reduce firms' ability to respond quickly to rapid changes in the global economic and political environment.

The literature offers a number of examples, like the Shell Sarnia case discussed previously, Quebec's "social contracts" (discussed in earlier chapters), and British Columbia's "social contract" with its health care workers (discussed in the public sector chapter), which seem to point towards a different, less legalistic sort of collective agreement. But such arrangements are still quite uncommon in Canada. Moreover, most—other than the Shell Sarnia agreement—have come about only after substantial government intervention. Due in large measure to that intervention, the various "social contracts" have provided workers with a significant degree of job and income security. Where employers are unable or unwilling to provide such security, and as long as the doctrine of residual management rights prevails, it is probably not realistic to expect unions to give up the detailed work rules and job control provisions that may represent workers' only protection against loss of employment or income, whatever such provisions' effects on the firm's efficiency may be (Godard, 1994:315). The point here would seem to be that if employers want their workers to be concerned about the firm's longer-term survival, they will need to give those workers reason to believe they have some kind of longer-term future with the firm.

Another concern is whether collective agreements provide workers with adequate protection and serve as a means of achieving economic and industrial democracy, as proponents such as Paul Weiler (1980) maintain. Here, the evidence is mixed. On the one hand, collective agreement provisions do provide workers with far more say over their terms and conditions of employment than they would enjoy in non-unionized establishments. In matters involving discharge and discipline, in particular, grievance procedures serve as a significant check on what would otherwise be management's unfettered ability to discipline and terminate workers at will. In other areas (technological change being a prime example), the continued application of the residual management rights doctrine has meant that agreement provisions have often afforded little protection in practice, and may even have discouraged serious bargaining over the issue. Indeed, some (i.e., Giles and Starkman, 1995:368) argue that collective agreement administration's emphasis on residual management rights may even bolster management's control over workplaces. While this may be an overstatement, most would likely agree with these authors' contention that, in general, collective agreement clauses fall far short of providing for any real sharing of workplace power.

CANADIAN INDUSTRIAL RELATIONS ASSOCIATION
www.business.mcmaster.ca/cira

Many of the current problems with Canadian collective bargaining and collective agreements may ultimately be structural in nature. The basis of most Canadian agreements is detailed regulation of individual workplaces. In an ever more global economy where individual employers and management organizations are forced to operate under conditions of increasing uncertainty and often have very little control over their economic environment, workplace-level bargaining seems unlikely to be able to address many of Canadian workers' and unions' most pressing concerns, such as those relating to job and income security. The fact that in recent years, many of the most successful collective bargaining arrangements have been brought about only after substantial government intervention suggests that more centralized bargaining structures accompanied by some kind of political bargaining could be of considerable help. However, with employers pushing for greater flexibility and even further decentralization, as was noted in the previous chapter, any significant increase in centralization seems unlikely. Unless and until it occurs, collective bargaining seems likely to remain adversarial and conflict-ridden, and the collective agreements resulting from it will likely continue to be, for the most part, long, complex, and highly legalistic documents reflecting, in some sense, the often bitter power struggles that have accompanied their drafting.

QUESTIONS FOR DISCUSSION

1) Get a collective agreement. Read through as much of it as you can. Are you able to make sense of it? If not, why are you having difficulty?

2) Try to determine, from some key clauses of the agreement, what kind of union-management relationship the parties have.

3) Why are Canadian agreements generally quite long and detailed, by international standards?

4) Discuss the evolution of Canadian agreements. What has contributed to their growing length and complexity? In your view, has this evolution been healthy?

5) List the four main types of agreement provisions and, using the agreement you read for questions 1 and 2, try to identify one or more provisions of each type in that agreement.

6) How does seniority play a role in Canadian agreements? Overall, is that role healthy or not, in your view?

7) Discuss some problems with collective agreements. Might there be ways to get around some of those problems?

SUGGESTIONS FOR FURTHER READING

Giles, Anthony, and Akivah Starkman. (1995). The collective agreement. In M. Gunderson and A. Ponak (Eds.), *Union-management relations in Canada* (3rd ed.). Don Mills, ON: Addison-Wesley. Both this chapter and the Giles-Jain chapter in the earlier (1989) edition of the same book offer an excellent introduction to the collective agreement. In addition to providing a thorough overview of agreement clauses, both chapters take a look at some of the larger issues around collective agreements and collective bargaining in general.

Halpern, Norman. (1984). *Sociotechnical systems design: The Shell Sarnia experience.* (Full bibliographical information appears in the reference to this work after Chapter 3). Contains the now-classic Shell Sarnia socio-technical systems collective agreement with no formal grievance provision and no management rights clause.

Kumar, Pradeep, Gregor Murray, and Sylvain Schetagne. (1998). "Adapting to change: Union priorities in the 1990s." *Workplace Gazette,* fall. Possibly the single most important study yet done on Canadian union behaviour and priorities. It contains detailed survey evidence showing that, by and large, Canadian unions have been adapting to change by taking a defensive stance at the bargaining table, while at the same time seeking to organize new industries and groups of workers. A must read for any serious IR student.

Peirce, Jon. (1987). *Collective bargaining over technological change in Canada: A quantitative and historical analysis.* Ottawa: Economic Council of Canada Discussion Paper #338. A detailed analysis of technological change provisions in Canadian agreements, as well as legislative provisions and arbitration decisions around technological change.

ENDNOTES

[1] As we noted in Chapter 9, these issues are typically treated as management rights rather than bargainable issues under most Canadian public sector bargaining legislation.

[2] See P. Weiler (1980) for an extremely thoughtful and articulate exposition of this perspective from a Canadian point of view.

[3] Violence and other forms of abuse, at home and on the job, are of growing concern to many unions, as well as government policy-makers. To help address these problems, recent agreements signed by the Canadian Auto Workers have included provisions making workplace advocates available to support women facing harassment on the job or abuse at home (Giles and Starkman, 1995:359).

[4] This was the case with pay scales for the Economists', Sociologists', and Statisticians' group of the federal government during the author's time with the Economic Council of Canada.

[5] It may be worth noting that in logging and in the garment industries, the two industries that make the greatest use of piecework systems, most of the labour force is uneducated and many of the workers have few other options for gainful employment (Radforth, 1982; Grant, 1992:232–234). In the clothing industry in particular, extensive use has been made of immigrant women for whom the work is the "port of entry" into the Canadian labour market. These facts suggest that, at least outside of commission sales, where few workers tend to be unionized, piecework systems would probably not be embraced voluntarily by the majority of workers.

[6] For a more detailed discussion of the evolution of shorter work hours, see Hunnicutt (1988) and Peirce (1997, 1999).

[7] Labour movements in several other European countries are now seeking to negotiate shorter working hours or get shorter hours legislation passed. An issue of *Better Times* (October, 1998) outlining many of these developments in detailed reached the author too late to be included in the main body of the chapter.

[8] In the CBC Radio News report, aired at 9 a.m. on October 6, a spokesman for the Quebec teachers' union said that the government believed teachers should be paid less than other

professionals because they do not work as many hours. The union responded by asking its members to keep detailed logs of all the activities they did in a typical week, including preparation, marking, meetings with students and parents, and extracurricular activities such as coaching. The survey found teachers putting in an average of about 39.5 hours per week—a figure that the union spokesman said exceeded the average number of hours put in by other professionals who are being paid more than the teachers. The report did not specify whether the average work week applied just to the school year or was the result of averaging the total number of hours put in during the school year over a 52-week period.

[9] Anecdotal evidence from my students suggests that many workers dislike bumping provisions for essentially the same reason, because they mean that workers will not know for some time whether they have a job or what job they will be doing.

[10] More research is needed to determine why unions have not in fact raised technological change issues more frequently than they have.

[11] A good example would be the Swedish "active labour market system" whereby unions accepted management's right to hire and fire and to deploy new technology in return for income security and retraining rights. The system facilitated both occupational and geographic mobility (Kjellberg, 1992:96–97). For unfortunately brief discussions, see Kjellberg (1992) and Hammarstrom (1993).

[12] Such provisions typically apply primarily in the case of work that would be assigned to regular staff as overtime.

[13] This legislation was discussed in Chapter 7 (employment law).

[14] Interestingly, increased wages and benefits ranked just seventh on the high-priority list, a finding that should, at least to a degree, help dispel the notion of "greedy" unions held by many.

[15] For a somewhat different interpretation, see Kumar, Murray, and Schetagne (1998:95).

[16] In practice, as the reader may already have guessed, there is often considerable overlap between these two factors. The ultimate source of the long-standing mistrust between management and the union may well be the declining long-term economic position of the firm or industry in question.

[17] For an extremely useful and much more detailed discussion of the points raised here, see Giles (1996).

CHAPTER 12

STRIKES

Scenes like this (above) are far more common than scenes like this (below). In most years, well over 90 per cent of Canadian agreements are negotiated without a work stoppage.

In this chapter we discuss the significance of strikes in the Canadian industrial relations system, as well as considering the causes of strikes and some of the policy measures used to control them. We start by defining the term "strike" as it is used in various labour relations acts. Next, we consider different types of strikes and discuss some of the problems involved in measuring strike incidence. From there, we go on to consider the causes of strikes, including both economic and non-economic causes. This analysis includes a discussion of some recent Canadian strikes that have attracted widespread public attention. We conclude with a discussion of some of the dispute resolution methods used to help prevent strikes or reduce their impact, and with an explanation of the recent resurgence in strike activity in Canada.

THE SIGNIFICANCE OF STRIKES

Partly for the wrong reasons, strikes tend to be the aspect of the industrial relations system with which the average person is most familiar. Media coverage of industrial relations developments undeniably centres mainly on strikes, particularly the bitter, emotional type featuring violent picket-line confrontations. Quite simply, stories about conflict sell more newspapers and attract more viewers to TV screens than do stories about negotiation and compromise (Hannigan, 1986). As well, many journalists lack the training, the time, or the support from their superiors needed to provide in-depth coverage of industrial relations developments other than strikes (Hannigan, 1986).

While perhaps inevitable, such media emphasis on violent confrontation can obscure the fact that in most years, well over 90 percent of Canadian agreements are negotiated without a work stoppage. Moreover, even when there is a work stoppage, most employers do not attempt to bring in replacement workers, and the majority of strikes are conducted peaceably. Sensationalist media coverage also tends to obscure the innovative preventive mechanisms being developed all across Canada, of which the various provincial preventive mediation programs are an excellent example.

 LABORNET-IGC "INTERNATIONAL STRIKE PAGE"
www.igc.apc.org/strike

The media's emphasis on strikes gives uninformed readers and viewers the mistaken impression that strikes are the only significant form of industrial conflict. As will be emphasized throughout this chapter, strikes are but one of a number of forms of industrial conflict—one of many methods used by workers to send management the message that they are not happy with what is going on in the workplace. Other forms of conflict range from active ones such as grievances (to be discussed in Chapter 13), vandalism, and sabotage, to more passive ones such as heavy use of sick leave or disability leave, unexcused absenteeism, alcohol or drug abuse, slacking on the job, or quitting. All result in reduced productivity; some (such as alcohol abuse or absenteeism) may arguably lead to far greater productivity losses than do strikes, which have never cost the country as much as one percent of total working time, even in tumultuous years like 1919 (marked by the Winnipeg General Strike) and 1976 (marked by a nation-wide Day of Protest against federal wage controls).

Strikes, then, should not be considered as an isolated phenomenon. Rather, they should be viewed in the larger context of industrial conflict as a whole, of which they are just one manifestation, though certainly a dramatic one. This said, there *are* reasons why strikes are central to industrial relations. As was noted in the labour history chapter, Canadian labour relations law has developed largely in response to bitter, bloody strikes, with an eye to preventing the recurrence of such disputes, or at least making them less bloody. The *Industrial Disputes Investigation Act* of 1907, which made conciliation compulsory for the first time, was a direct response to a lengthy Alberta coal-miners' strike the previous winter (Morton, 1989). Similarly, *PC 1003*, the bill that, in 1944, granted basic collective bargaining rights to Canadian workers, can be linked to bitter wartime strikes in the gold mining and steel industries (MacDowell, 1978, 1982). A sizeable portion of all Canadian labour relations acts is devoted to strikes: what constitutes a strike, when it can take place, which groups (if any) cannot strike, what types of picketing are and are not legal, whether employers can replace striking workers, what procedures the government may use to help the two sides arrive at a settlement, and what special restrictions may be placed on strikes in certain sectors. Indeed, it is probably not going too far to say that a central purpose of labour relations legislation is to regulate strikes with an eye to protecting the public interest and maintaining public peace and order.

This emphasis is not misplaced. While relatively infrequent within the context of the Canadian industrial relations system as a whole and generally less violent than the pitched battles of the early twentieth century (Heron, 1989), strikes can still have extremely severe consequences–including injury or loss of life. Property damage can be extensive. Third parties can be seriously inconvenienced or in some cases injured, especially in public sector disputes. Striking workers may lose their homes or be forced into bankruptcy. And in the aftermath of a strike, particularly a lengthy one, firms may lose customers and market share,[1] or in extreme instances be forced to shut down part or even all of their operations. Strikes may also lead to lasting bitterness between unions and management, or sometimes even within unions. (The latter may well have been the case following the Ontario teachers' strike, discussed below.) Given such a broad array of potentially serious consequences, strikes pose some difficult challenges for policy-makers. Particularly in the case of public sector disputes (P. Weiler, 1980), they may be faced with balancing workers' right to strike in support of their demands with the public's need to continue receiving such essential services as health care.

Conversely, strikes may also have positive effects. Not only may they, in some cases, serve the "cathartic" function discussed by Gunderson, Hyatt, and Ponak

(1995), allowing workers to release pent-up frustration; they can also serve as a kind of "wake-up call" to both union and management. Both in Canada and in other countries, a number of creative joint problem-solving mechanisms have been introduced in the wake of strikes that convinced both sides they would need to restructure their relationship to prevent further strikes from occurring in the future.[2] Without the spur of the strike to prod them into action, the parties might never have developed those mechanisms.

Obviously, strikes are not all there is to industrial relations, as some tabloid newspapers might seem to suggest. But by the same token, they are and have probably always been central to it, albeit in a more subtle way than many would recognize. Given an apparent recent resurgence in strike activity, both in Canada and in many European countries, the topic clearly merits careful consideration.

WHAT IS A STRIKE?

No one can hope to understand the causes of strikes or the best ways of preventing them without understanding what a strike is. Moreover, from a practical perspective, such knowledge is extremely important both for unionists and for IR and HR managers.

In general, a strike must be a "concerted" (i.e., planned) activity, involving a collective refusal to work. Thus an individual worker's refusal to work would *not* be considered a strike, whether or not that refusal was legal.[3] On the other hand, the stoppage need not be a complete one to be considered a strike. In general, Canadian labour relations acts state that a slowdown or other "concerted activity" designed to limit output is a strike. Specifically, the *Canada Labour Code* (section 3[1]) defines a strike as "a cessation of work or a refusal to work or to continue to work by employees, in combination, in concert, or in accordance with a common understanding, and a slowdown of work or other concerted activity on the part of employees in relation to their work that is designed to restrict or limit output." A virtually identical definition may be found in Ontario's *Labour Relations Act* (section 1[1]).[4] Under federal and provincial labour acts, such varied work actions as union-imposed overtime bans (Snyder, 1995:29), rotating Canada Post strikes (Snyder, 1995:29—30), work-to-rule campaigns by railway employees, and a postal union's threat to order its members to stop verifying whether letters bore sufficient postage (Snyder, 1995:30) have all been deemed strikes. So, too, have unions' refusal to cross picket lines, even in cases where the refusal was based on a "fear of picket line violence" (Randazzo, 1995:11), and a union's refusal to handle work that was the subject of a legal lockout between a different employer and a sister local (Randazzo, 1995). All of this suggests that unions should be exceedingly cautious in calling actions such as work-to-rule campaigns, slowdowns, and other partial withdrawals of service.

When May a Legal Strike Occur?

In Canada, legal strike activity is tightly constrained by a variety of what Godard (1994:294) has referred to as "timeliness restrictions." First, the collective agreement must have expired. Second, both sides must have made a "good faith" effort to obtain a settlement. Third, in all Canadian jurisdictions except Saskatchewan, a legal strike cannot be conducted until the government has appointed a third party (usually called a conciliator, but sometimes called a mediator) in an attempt to settle the dispute. In most jurisdictions, a strike will be legal only after the conciliator or mediator has reported his or her lack of success to the government and a certain length of time (normally seven to fourteen days) has elapsed.[5] In some cases, though less often now than in the past, the parties must also have passed through a second stage of conciliation, involving the creation of a tripartite board and the issuance of a public report. In addition, a number of jurisdictions, including British Columbia, require a supervised strike vote to be held, while five jurisdictions, including Quebec, Alberta, and B.C., require a brief (48- or 72-hour) notice period before any strike or lockout can become legal.

Strike Restrictions in the Public Sector

The previous discussion has been concerned only with strikes in the private sector. It's important to bear in mind that in Canada, as in many other industrialized countries (D. Reynolds, 1995; Beaumont, 1995), public sector strikes are generally much more severely restricted than private sector ones.

As we pointed out in the public sector chapter, several jurisdictions, including Alberta, do not allow public servants to strike, instead requiring binding arbitration. Some also bar strikes among other public sector groups such as health-care workers and teachers. Of those provinces that do permit public sector workers to strike, all but one (Saskatchewan) have established a designation process whereby some employees are designated essential and must, therefore, remain on the job in the event of a strike.

Another significant feature of Canadian public sector strikes is the frequency with which legislation is used to end them. Between 1965 and 1993 (Ponak and Thompson, 1995), federal and provincial governments resorted to such legislation 62 times–23 times in Quebec alone. Such legislation is not unheard-of in Canada's private sector, but is rarely used there, and then normally only in the case of disputes involving large, heavily regulated industries in the federal jurisdiction, such as the ports and the railways (Craig and Solomon, 1996), where there is reason to believe that a lengthy dispute could cause innocent third parties serious harm.

The numerous restrictions on public sector strike action have not prevented public sector unions from engaging in strike action–sometimes with great frequency. Indeed, some of the most serious recent Canadian strikes have been public sector ones. Later sections of this chapter consider why this has been the case.

MEASURING STRIKE ACTIVITY AND INTENSITY

It is generally agreed (Adams, 1995a; Ponak and Gunderson, 1995) that Canada's strike record compares poorly to that of most other Western industrialized countries. But what, exactly, is meant by this assertion? On what basis can we compare relative strike intensity in different countries, or, for that matter, in different jurisdictions or industries within Canada?

The most basic measure of strike activity is *frequency*, or the number of strikes occurring in any given jurisdiction during any given period of time (normally a year). While it is useful to know how many strikes have occurred in a jurisdiction, by itself this statistic is of relatively little significance. Of particular importance are the *size*, or number of workers involved in any given dispute, and the *duration*, or the length of time workers remain off the job. The more workers involved and the longer the dispute lasts, the greater its impact will be.

"THE COSTS OF STRIKES AND LOCKOUTS"
yoda.sscl.uwo.ca/~palmer2/Eco020/Syllabus/ex4.html

Both size and duration have varied greatly over the years since the First World War (see Table 12.1). One reason for the variation is that both measures have sometimes been greatly affected by single, large disputes. For instance, the average size of strikes in 1976 was more than three times what it had been the year before, in large measure because of the Day of Protest in October. That one-day political strike also resulted in a duration figure (7.3 days) only about one-third of the previous year's (21.6 days). Similarly, lengthy Canada Post strikes in 1975 and 1981 were key factors in unusually long average strike durations for those years.

Multiplying the number of strikes, or frequency, by size, or number of workers, times duration, gives us the total number of person-days lost in any given jurisdiction or industry. As Table 12.1 shows, this figure has fluctuated greatly over time. In 1975 and 1976, more than 10 million person-days were lost due to strikes and lockouts–more than 100 times as many as were lost in 1930, during the Great Depression. Part of the difference results simply from an increase in the size of the Canadian work force. Part of the difference can also be attributed to rising union membership rates, since only unionized workers are counted in strike data. In 1976, Canada's union density stood at 37 percent, or nearly three times the rate (13 percent) it had been in 1930. It is also necessary to take into account inflation, the 1976 "Day of Protest," labour's generally stronger political position in 1975—1976, and the addition of large numbers of public-sector workers to the ranks of workers eligible to strike.

One more piece of information is needed before we can meaningfully compare relative strike intensity in different jurisdictions or industries. Other things being equal, larger industries and jurisdictions lose more person-days due to strikes simply because

Table 12.1

MEASURES OF STRIKE ACTIVITY, CANADA, 1919–1997

Year	Frequency*	Avg. Size	Duration‡	Person-Days Lost**	As Percentage of Working Time
1919	336	443	22.8	3 400 942	0.60
1920	322	187	13.3	799 524	0.14
1921	168	168	37.1	1 048 914	0.22
1922	104	421	34.9	1 528 661	0.32
1923	86	398	19.6	671 750	0.13
1924	70	490	37.7	1 295 054	0.26
1925	87	333	41.2	1 193 281	0.23
1926	77	310	11.2	266 601	0.05
1927	74	301	6.8	152 570	0.03
1928	98	179	12.8	224 212	0.04
1929	90	144	11.7	152 080	0.02
1930	67	205	6.7	91 797	0.01
1931	88	122	19.0	204 238	0.04
1932	116	202	10.9	255 000	0.05
1933	125	212	12.0	317 547	0.07
1934	191	240	12.5	574 519	0.11
1935	120	277	8.7	288 703	0.05
1936	156	223	8.0	276 997	0.05
1937	278	259	12.3	886 393	0.15
1938	147	139	7.3	148 678	0.02
1939	122	336	5.5	224 588	0.04
1940	168	361	4.4	266 318	0.04
1941	231	377	5.0	433 914	0.06
1942	354	322	4.0	450 202	0.05
1943	402	543	4.8	1 041 198	0.12
1944	199	378	6.5	490 139	0.06
1945	197	488	15.2	1 457 420	0.19
1946	226	614	32.4	4 515 030	0.54
1947	234	442	22.9	2 366 340	0.27
1948	154	278	20.7	885 790	0.10
1949	135	347	22.1	1 036 820	0.11
1950	160	1 200	7.2	1 387 500	0.15
1951	258	392	8.9	901 620	0.09
1952	219	513	24.6	2 765 510	0.29
1953	173	315	24.1	1 312 720	0.14
1954	173	327	25.3	1 430 300	0.15
1955	159	378	31.2	1 875 400	0.19
1956	229	387	14.1	1 246 000	0.11
1957	245	329	18.3	1 477 100	0.13
1958	259	425	24.4	2 816 850	0.25
1959	216	440	23.4	2 226 890	0.19
1960	274	180	15.0	738 700	0.06
1961	287	341	13.6	1 335 080	0.11

Table 12.1 (continued)

Year	Frequency*	Avg. Size	Duration‡	Person-Days Lost**	As Percentage of Working Time
1962	311	239	19.1	1 417 900	0.11
1963	332	251	11.0	917 140	0.07
1964	343	293	15.7	1 580 550	0.11
1965	501	342	13.4	2 349 870	0.17
1966	617	667	12.6	5 178 170	0.34
1967	522	483	15.8	3 974 760	0.25
1968	582	385	22.7	5 082 732	0.32
1969	595	514	25.2	7 751 880	0.46
1970	542	481	25.0	6 539 560	0.39
1971	569	421	11.9	2 866 590	0.16
1972	598	1 180	10.9	7 753 530	0.43
1973	724	484	16.4	5 776 080	0.30
1974	1 218	487	15.6	9 221 890	0.46
1975	1 171	431	21.6	10 908,810	0.53
1976	1 040	1 525	7.3	11 544 170	0.53
1977	806	270	15.3	3 320 050	0.15
1978	1 057	379	18.4	7 357 180	0.32
1979	1 049	441	16.9	7 819 350	0.33
1980	1 028	427	20.8	9 129 960	0.37
1981	1 049	325	25.9	8 850 040	0.35
1982	679	684	12.3	5 702 370	0.23
1983	645	511	13.5	4 440 900	0.18
1984	717	261	20.8	3 883 000	0.15
1985	825	196	19.3	3 125 560	0.12
1986	748	647	14.8	7 151 470	0.27
1987	668	871	6.5	3 810 170	0.14
1988	548	377	23.7	4 901 260	0.17
1989	627	709	8.3	3 701 360	0.13
1990	579	467	18.8	5 079 190	0.17
1991	463	547	9.9	2 516 090	0.09
1992	404	371	14.1	2 110 180	0.07
1993	382	267	14.9	1 516 640	0.05
1994	374	216	19.9	1 605 580	0.06
1995	328	455	10.6	1 582 320	0.05
1996	328	865	11.8	3 339 560	0.11
1997	279	909	14.1	3 573 374	0.12

* Number of strikes in existence during the year in question, whether they began that year or earlier.
"Avg. Size" is obtained by dividing the total number of workers on strike during the year by the frequency figure described in the previous note.
‡ Average days lost per worker on strike is found by dividing total person-days lost by the number of strikers involved.
** Product of frequency (number of strikes) times size and duration.

Sources: 1919—1975, Labour Canada, *Strikes and Lockouts in Canada,* various issues; 1976—1997 data provided by Work Stoppage Bureau, Workplace Information Directorate, Human Resources Development Canada.

there are more collective agreements expiring than in smaller industries and jurisdictions, and because these agreements cover a greater number of workers. Yet the number of person-days lost compared to the number worked may be minuscule in a large jurisdiction. It is, therefore, usual to divide the number of person-days lost by the number of person-days worked, so that the former can be expressed as a percentage of time worked.

With this figure in hand, we can compare relative strike intensity in different industries and jurisdictions. Granted, different countries' data are seldom totally comparable. To begin with, there is the issue of whether "strike" data includes only strikes, or also includes lockouts, as in the case of Canada. For the period 1977 to 1985 (Labour Canada, 1982, 1986), about 10 percent of the workers involved in disputes were involved in a lockout rather than a strike; during this same period, lockouts accounted for about 16 percent of the total person-days lost.[6]

Even more important is the size threshold that must be crossed before a country will say that a dispute constitutes an official strike. In Canada, all disputes in which one or more person-days of work are lost are counted as strikes. In the United States, only disputes involving 1000 or more workers are counted. The immediate result of these two countries' different size thresholds is that the United States's record *looks* far better than it would were the Canadian definition of an official strike applied. It is also possible (Gunderson, Hyatt, and Ponak, 1995) that the large work stoppages, which are the only ones officially reported in the United States, have different causes than the smaller ones that make up the lion's share of Canadian disputes. But despite these and other measurement problems,[7] one can generally make reasonably accurate international or inter-industry strike comparisons using a measure such as percentage of working-time lost.[8]

Recent Trends in Canadian Strike Activity

As Table 12.1 illustrates, 1996 and 1997 were years that marked a dramatic reversal of a number of long-term trends in Canadian strike activity. In general, Canadian strike intensity had been declining steadily since the mid 1970s. But in 1996, the proportion of working-time lost due to strikes was more than that double that of the previous year, as was the number of sector workers legally barred from striking (Swimmer and Thompson, 1995). As well, in many cases where public sector strikes are officially legal, back-to-work legislation, which has frequently been invoked in the case of Canadian public sector disputes, makes those strikes far shorter than they would otherwise have been. And even when public sector strikers are not ordered back to work, the mere *threat* of back-to-work legislation may well make the strike shorter than it would otherwise have been, as in the case of the 1991 Toronto Transit Commission strike (Craig and Solomon, 1996, 412–413).

Given all these factors, the 1996 and 1997 data are significant. As Table 12.2 indicates, 42 percent of all person-days lost to strikes in Canada in 1996 were in the public sector, a major increase over the proportion lost in any of the previous four years and a figure almost certainly greater than the proportion of union members from the public sector eligible to strike. The greater number of public sector person-days lost was due almost entirely to the longer duration of strikes in that sector (18.3 days as compared to 9.4 in the private sector). This was the only time since 1976 when public sector strikes lasted longer on average than private sector ones. Nineteen-ninety-seven saw the public sector accounting for an even larger proportion (55 percent) of person-days lost due to strikes. This time, the greater number of lost workdays was due almost entirely to the greater *size* of public sector disputes, which involved an average of 3297 workers, as compared to 310 workers for private sector disputes.

MANAGEMENT SUPPORT SERVICES INCORPORATED: "COUNTER UNION CORPORATE CAMPAIGN STRATEGIES"
www.mgmtsupportservs.com/index.htm

When the 1996 data are broken down by industry (not shown in tables), we find that public administration accounted for 33.6 percent of the person-days lost–just over one-third of the total, and considerably higher than the proportion of the Canadian work force employed in that sector. Remarkably, it is also higher than the 31 percent figure for 1991, a year when there was a nation-wide federal public service strike. Other sectors accounting for a sizeable proportion of person-days lost in 1996 were manufacturing, trade, and the service industries.

Another significant finding is that by far the greatest number of workers involved—just under 46 percent of the total—were in the "Various Industries" category. These appear to have been workers from both private and public sector organizations (mainly the latter) who staged a series of one-day general strikes in various Ontario cities to protest provincial government policies. Thus, nearly half the workers involved in strikes in 1996 were involved in political disputes.

In 1997, (see Figure 12.1) service industries accounted for the largest share (42.5 percent) of person-days lost due to strikes. This undoubtedly reflects the impact of that year's massive Canada Post and Ontario Teachers' Federation strikes. Other sectors accounting for a sizeable proportion of person-days lost included manufacturing (21 percent), transportation and utilities (17 percent) and trade (13 percent). Though the strikes in trade and manufacturing did not involve a great many workers, they tended to be very long (an average of 41.9 days in the former sector, and 34.5 days in the latter), a finding that lends some support to the observation that, in bad times, private sector strikes tend to be less frequent, but longer than in good times.[9]

Table 12.2

STRIKES AND LOCKOUTS, CANADA, BY PUBLIC VERSUS PRIVATE SECTOR STATUS, 1976–1997.

Public Sector

Year	Frequency (% of total)	Size	Duration (Days)	PDL	% Time Lost (% of total)
1976	226 (22)	393 427	5.6	2 219 400	0.10 (19)
1977	191 (24)	61 409	13.0	800 800	0.04 (24)
1978	212 (20)	148 697	8.0	1 188 810	0.05 (16)
1979	208 (20)	234 022	10.2	2 385 420	0.10 (30)
1980	244 (24)	227 616	14.0	3 193 820	0.13 (35)
1981	271 (26)	110 121	20.1	2 210 430	0.09 (25)
1982	121 (18)	273 020	3.3	895 230	0.04 (16)
1983	95 (15)	215 841	9.9	2 129 160	0.09 (48)
1984	108 (15)	31 334	18.3	571 970	0.02 (15)
1985	158 (19)	51 466	12.2	628 470	0.02 (20)
1986	128 (17)	214 209	3.7	795 650	0.03 (11)
1987	105 (16)	397 558	2.2	884 750	0.03 (23)
1988	76 (14)	93 592	23.2	2 166 800	0.08 (44)
1989	139 (22)	340 718	4.9	1 657 820	0.06 (45)
1990	119 (21)	60 820	12.9	785 760	0.03 (15)
1991	115 (25)	215 576	6.6	1 429 050	0.05 (57)
1992	80 (20)	73 930	6.7	496 390	0.02 (24)
1993	85 (22)	56 155	6.3	355 210	0.01 (23)
1994	55 (15)	26 169	15.8	413 830	0.01 (26)
1995	55 (17)	44 125	4.1	182 882	0.01 (12)
1996	76 (23)	76 088	18.3	1 389 198	0.05 (42)
1997	56 (20)	184 626	10.6	1 948 070	0.07 (55)

Private Sector

Year	Frequency (% of total)	Size	Duration (Days)	PDL	% Time Lost (% of total)
1976	814 (78)	1 192 794	7.8	9 324 770	0.43 (81)
1977	615 (76)	156 238	16.1	2 519 250	0.11 (76)
1978	845 (80)	251 925	24.5	6 168 370	0.27 (84)
1979	841 (80)	228 364	23.8	5 433 930	0.23 (70)
1980	784 (76)	211 387	28.1	5 936 140	0.24 (65)
1981	778 (74)	231 211	28.7	6 639 610	0.26 (75)
1982	558 (82)	191 108	25.2	4 807 140	0.20 (84)
1983	550 (85)	113 631	20.3	2 311 740	0.09 (52)
1984	608 (85)	155 582	21.3	3 311 430	0.13 (85)
1985	671 (81)	110 867	22.5	2 497 090	0.10 (80)
1986	620 (83)	270 046	23.5	6 355 820	0.24 (89)
1987	563 (84)	184 324	15.9	2 925 420	0.11 (77)
1988	472 (78)	113 204	24.2	2 734 460	0.10 (56)
1989	488 (78)	104 029	19.6	2 043 540	0.07 (55)

Table 12.2 (continued)

Year	Frequency (% of total)	Size	Duration (Days)	PDL	% Time Lost (% of total)
1990	460 (79)	209 651	20.5	4 293 430	0.15 (85)
1991	348 (75)	37 758	28.8	1 087 040	0.04 (43)
1992	324 (80)	76 010	21.2	1 613 790	0.06 (76)
1993	296 (78)	45 629	25.5	1 161 430	0.04 (77)
1994	319 (85)	54 687	21.8	1 192 750	0.04 (74)
1995	273 (83)	105 034	13.3	1 399 439	0.05 (88)
1996	252 (77)	207 656	9.4	1 950 362	0.07 (58)
1997	223 (80)	69 066	23.5	1 625 304	0.05 (45)

PDL = person-days lost

Percentage of time lost due to strikes was calculated against time worked by total non-agricultural paid workers.

Source: Work Stoppage Bureau, Workplace Information Directorate, HRDC.

FIGURE 12.1 STRIKES AND LOCKOUTS BY INDUSTRY, (PERSON-DAYS LOST), CANADA, 1997

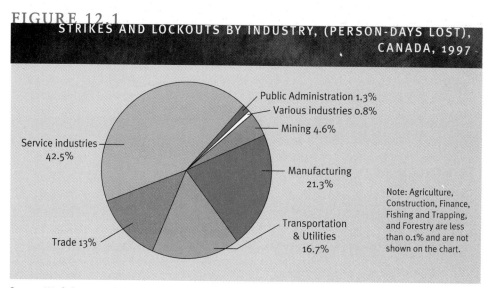

Note: Agriculture, Construction, Finance, Fishing and Trapping, and Forestry are less than 0.1% and are not shown on the chart.

Source: Work Stoppage Bureau, Workplace Information Directorate, HRDC.

An equally interesting finding is that Ontario far outstripped other provinces in terms of strike activity in 1996 and 1997 (see Table 12.3). In 1996, Ontario account-ed for 77 percent of the workers involved in strikes and 59 percent of total person-days lost, though only 40 percent of all Canadian strikes occurred there. Similarly, in 1997, Ontario accounted for 69 percent of the workers involved in strikes and 53 percent of all person-days lost, but only 39 percent of all strikes. Indeed, these figures likely understate Ontario's contribution to the national strike total, since many striking fed-eral jurisdiction workers, such as Canada Post employees, were employed in Ontario.

Table 12.3

Jurisdiction	Number (% of total)	Workers Involved (% of total)	Person-Days Lost (% of total)
STRIKES AND LOCKOUTS IN CANADA, BY JURISDICTION, 1997			
Newfoundland	5 (2)	1 185*	10 990*
P.E.I.	NONE	0	0
Nova Scotia	3 (1)	401*	15 730*
New Brunswick	2 (1)	63*	12 230*
Quebec	105 (38)	7 599 (3)	209 610 (6)
Ontario	109 (39)	175 869 (69)	1 891 680 (53)
Manitoba	8 (3)	772*	13 860*
Saskatchewan	4 (1)	587*	19 420 (1)
Alberta	10 (4)	11 756 (5)	474 690 (14)
B.C.	14 (5)	7 489 (3)	366 920 (11)
Federal	19 (7)	47 971 (19)	558 244 (16)
TOTAL	**279 (100)**	**253 692(100)**	**3 339 560(100)**

* Less than 1%

Percentages may not add to 100, due to rounding.

Source: Work Stoppage Bureau, Workplace Information Directorate, HRDC.

Historically, Quebec, British Columbia, and Newfoundland have generally seen the highest levels of strike intensity. Through the 1980s, these three provinces generally had at least double the rate, in terms of person-days lost per paid worker, of any other (Labour Canada, various years). As recently as 1986, Quebec and B.C. alone accounted for about three-quarters of the workers involved in all Canadian strikes, and 70 percent of the person-days not worked (Workplace Information Directorate, 1998). Ontario's levels were typically far lower, in part because civil servants and many other public employees were not allowed to strike, as they were in the other three provinces just mentioned. While strike activity in these provinces has been declining in recent years and increasing in Ontario, which in 1993 granted its civil servants the right to strike, in no recent year has any single province as completely dominated the strike scene as Ontario did in 1996 and 1997

Part of the reason for Ontario's high 1996 strike intensity was undoubtedly the General Motors strike (discussed below in more detail), which took place during the fall of 1996. But an equally if not more important factor was a wave of public sector strikes, political in nature and intended as a protest against the provincial government's budget-cutting policies, during the early months of the year. The teachers' strike (also discussed in more detail below) was a key factor in the province's high strike intensity in 1997. Of the remaining jurisdictions, only Alberta, British Columbia, and the federal jurisdiction accounted for any significant number of person-days lost.

Looking more generally at the pattern of Canadian strike activity since the end of the First World War, it is by and large true, as economically oriented analysts have suggested, that strike activity tends to rise and fall with the business cycle, rising in inflationary periods and declining in times of recession or depression. This would appear to have been particularly the case with respect to strike **frequency**, perhaps somewhat less so with respect to size and duration. Certainly a desire to keep pace with rising inflation was an important factor in the wave of strike activity that followed the two world wars and also occurred in the middle and late 1970s and very early 1980s. Along similar lines, it is worth noting that strike frequency fell off very sharply starting in 1982, a recessionary year that marked the end of the last significant wave of inflation seen in this country—and the beginning of a second round of wage controls for most public sector workers.

At the same time, it is important not to overlook the various pieces of labour legislation, especially *PC 1003* (1944) and the *Public Service Staff Relations Act* (1967), which granted collective bargaining rights to large numbers of new workers. The increase in strike intensity immediately following the passage of these two pieces of legislation should not be considered simply a response to inflation. In part it was a reflection of the fact that more workers were now legally entitled to go on strike. In part, as well, it may have reflected pent-up frustration over non-economic as well as economic issues, to which the newly unionized workers could now, for the first time, legally respond by striking.

 ## IWA-CANADA STRIKES AND LOCKOUTS LINKS PAGE
www.cowichan.com/union/iwa/strklink.htm

At the industry level, it is difficult to uncover trends over time, because a few large disputes can account for the lion's share of person-days and work-time lost in any given year, thus "skewing" the longer-term data considerably. However, an examination of that data over the past decade (years other than 1996 not shown) does suggest that the relative number of strikes and proportion of person-days lost appear to be declining somewhat in manufacturing, and increasing in public administration and service industries (including health care and education). In part, these findings may simply reflect changes in the country's industrial structure and in labour relations legislation. As was noted in Chapters 2 and 4, relatively fewer Canadian workers than in the past are employed in manufacturing, and that sector's union density rates have also declined, meaning that a smaller proportion of those Canadian workers legally entitled to strike are in manufacturing. In addition, various legislative changes, including most notably the granting of strike rights to Ontario's public servants in 1993, have meant that a greater proportion of those Canadians legally entitled to strike are in public administration.

But it would probably be a mistake to attribute growing public-sector strike intensity solely to structural factors. As a number of observers (Ponak and Thompson, 1995) point out, and as we pointed out in the public sector chapter (Chapter 8), the decade of the 1990s was a period marked by large-scale privatization, contracting-out of government work, service cuts, and layoffs of public sector workers. Such developments were obviously the source of extreme frustration and stress for many public sector workers. One should also not overlook provincial and federal governments' all but nationwide imposition of public sector wage controls, which had the effect of removing many public sector workers' ability to bargain over money. In the short run, the wage controls may have reduced public sector strike intensity, as appears to have been the case for the early "90s. Over the longer term, though, particularly when added to the other frustrations and stresses of public sector worklife in the 1990s, the wage controls could well prove a spur to renewed militancy, as public sector workers seek to make up some of the ground lost through years of wage controls, freezes, or in some cases even actual rollbacks.

In the private sector, innovative new bargaining arrangements may be helping to reduce strike intensity in some traditionally strike-prone manufacturing industries. Such arrangements appear to be particularly common in the province of Quebec (Boivin and Déom, 1995; Chaykowski and Verma, 1992). Here, the provincial government has played an active role in brokering "social contracts," especially in the steel and pulp and paper industries, in which unions have signed long-term collective agreements containing no-strike clauses in return for job security and a guarantee of government investment in plant modernization. Most typically, the social contracts provide for wage arbitration after three years (Boivin and Déom, 1995). The social contracts, which in Quebec at least, appear to be part of a broader trend towards cooperative rather than adversarial union-management relations (Boivin and Déom, 1995), have not really taken hold in the public sector, either in Quebec or elsewhere in Canada, except to a limited degree in British Columbia's health care sector (Craig and Solomon, 1996). While this writer is not aware of the extent to which social contracts are being used in the private sector outside of Quebec, their growing prominence in Quebec would logically point towards lower strike intensity in that province, and, to a lesser extent, towards relatively lower private (as opposed to public sector) strike intensity, both in Quebec and in Canada as a whole. It may not, therefore, be a coincidence that strike intensity has in fact dropped in Quebec, which in 1996 accounted for only 13 percent of Canadian person-days lost, and, in 1997, just 6 percent, despite the large share of the country's workforce and union membership that it accounts for.[10]

By Type of Strike

It is useful to know whether a given strike has occurred during the negotiation of a first agreement, during renegotiation, or during the life of the contract. Typically, these three different types of strike have a different dynamic.[11] First-agreement strikes often centre on the fundamental issue of the employer's willingness to bargain with the union. Renegotiation disputes are more often about money, while wildcat strikes, or strikes occurring during the life of the agreement, often revolve around a very specific issue, such as the actions of a particular supervisor or anger over a co-worker's suspension. Wildcat strikes may also be a sign of rank-and-file discontent with the union's leadership.

As Table 12.4 indicates, renegotiation strikes have almost always resulted in the greatest number of person-days lost. During the 1970s, wildcat strikes sometimes involved a greater number of workers than renegotiation disputes; however, because they are illegal in almost all Canadian jurisdictions and frequently not sanctioned by union leaders, these disputes are generally extremely very short relative to other strikes. Both their relative frequency and their proportion of person-days lost appears to have diminished, although in this connection it's important to bear in mind that Workplace Information Bureau data by type of strike cover only disputes involving 500 or more workers, and hence we lack information on smaller disputes, which might reveal different trends. There are a number of possible explanations for the decline in wildcats.

First, health and safety legislation in all Canadian jurisdictions (McPhillips and England, 1995) allows workers to refuse to continue working in conditions they consider unsafe. Such legislation has essentially eliminated what was formerly a major cause of wildcats. Second, a number of organizations have come up with innovative and speedy forums for resolving grievances, such as the dockside arbitration used in the Port of Vancouver (J. Weiler, 1984). While such innovative dispute resolution methods may not have eliminated wildcats altogether, they do appear to have reduced their incidence (J. Weiler, 1984). Finally, in today's tougher economic climate, employers and managers may well be taking a harder line on wildcats. Knowing that they will likely be held legally accountable should they walk out during the life of the agreement, workers and unions may be more reluctant to do so than they were at times when management might have been more willing to look the other way.

SOME RECENT DISPUTES

In this section, we stop to take a closer look at four Canadian strikes that have occurred since 1996. While this section does not pretend to offer a representative treatment of all recent Canadian strikes, the four disputes we have chosen should provide some sense of the kinds of issues of greatest concern to Canadian workers and their unions.

Table 12.4
STRIKES AND LOCKOUTS IN CANADA INVOLVING 500 OR MORE WORKERS, BY CONTRACT STATUS, VARIOUS YEARS

1976

Status	Number (% of total)	Size (% of total)	PDL (% of total)
First Agreement	2 (1)	1 543*	79 100 (1)
Renegotiation	134 (76)	608 111 (41)	7 995 000 (88)
Wildcat	40 (23)	879 755 (59)	1 013 980 (11)
Other	1 (1)	750*	750*
TOTAL	**177 (100)**	**1 490 159 (100)**	**9 088 830 (100)**

1981

Status	Number (% of total)	Size (% of total)	PDL (% of total)
First Agreement	1 (1)	1242 (1)	890*
Renegotiation	66 (67)	189 585 (79)	6 061 120 (98)
Wildcat	32 (32)	49 625 (21)	107 140 (2)
Other	——	N/A	N/A
TOTAL	**99 (100)**	**240 452 (100)**	**6 169 150 (100)**

1986

Status	Number (% of total)	Size (% of total)	PDL (% of total)
First Agreement	——	N/A	N/A
Renegotiation	71 (80)	412 770 (96)	5 635 450 (99)
Wildcat	17 (19)	16 016 (4)	27 460*
Other	1 (1)	1 300*	10 400*
TOTAL	**89 (100)**	**430 086 (100)**	**5 673 310 (100)**

1991

Status	Number (% of total)	Size (% of total)	PDL (% of total)
First Agreement	——	N/A	N/A
Renegotiation	32 (88)	215 577 (99)	1 447 890 (100)
Wildcat	4 (13)	2 800 (1)	4 510*
Other	——	N/A	N/A
TOTAL	**36 (100)**	**218 377 (100)**	**1 452 400 (100)**

1996

Status	Number (% of total)	Size (% of total)	PDL (% of total)
First Agreement	2 (6)	2 800 (1)	70 500 (3)
Renegotiation	26 (76)	125 159 (49)	2 286 090 (88)
Wildcat	4 (12)	46 934 (18)	144 496 (6)
Other	2 (6)	83 000 (32)	83 000 (3)
TOTAL	**34 (100)**	**257 893 (100)**	**2 584 086 (100)**

* = less than 1%
PDL = person-days lost
N/A = not applicable
Percentages may not add up to 100, due to rounding.

Source: Work Stoppage Bureau, Workplace Information Directorate, HRDC.

GM Canada and CAW (1996)

The National Automobile, Aerospace, Transportation and General Workers Union of Canada (CAW) won historic concessions from General Motors Canada following a three-week October, 1996 strike involving roughly 26 000 production, maintenance, and warehouse employees. The strike, which had some major spin-off effects, including the layoff of auto parts workers in Ontario and several U.S. states (Bertin et al., 1996), was primarily over the issue of outsourcing, or contracting-out of work. Prior to the dispute, GM was doing significantly less outsourcing than Ford or Chrysler (Bourette, 1996a; Alexandroff, 1996). It had sought to change that situation, initially refusing to go along with the three-year moratorium on outsourcing that the CAW had already negotiated with Chrysler (Alexandroff, 1996; Bourette and Grange, 1996). Also at issue was a provision in the old contract that allowed supervisors to demand that workers stay after their shift had ended and put in mandatory overtime (Grange, 1996). Interestingly enough, the issue of mandatory overtime nearly proved a deal-breaker, holding up a tentative settlement for several days after the seemingly more contentious issue of outsourcing had been settled (Grange, 1996; Bourette, 1996b).

"GM CANADA AND CAW PREPARED FOR LONG STRIKE"
www.theautochannel.com:8080/news/archive/general/19961010.html

Under the terms of the new agreement, overwhelmingly ratified on October 23, the main elements of the "pattern" established with Chrysler were maintained. While the union allowed GM to sell two plants, affecting about 3500 workers, the affected workers would have their wages and benefits protected under new ownership for at least three years, and their pension benefits protected for at least nine years (Grange, 1996). In return, the company agreed to a three-year moratorium on plant closures and on outsourcing of any major operations. Even more important, GM agreed (as had Chrysler) to replace any jobs for which it contracted out the work (Grange, 1996; CBR, 11/96).

Like their Chrysler counterparts, GM workers received a 2 percent annual wage increase plus a COLA clause, which at 2 percent inflation would mean an additional 1.5 percent annual pay increase. Employment standards laws, such as the right to refuse unsafe work, enacted by the previous NDP provincial government were entrenched in the agreement to protect workers against any weakening of those laws by the new Conservative government (CBR, 11/96). On hours of work, the union gained on two fronts: through the elimination of the contentious mandatory overtime provision, and through an additional 10 scheduled paid days off over the life of the agreement. Both of these provisions, the latter in particular, were expected to create additional employment (CBR, 11/96).

While CAW president Buzz Hargrove was at pains not to call the GM settlement a victory, given the uncertain future awaiting workers at the two affected plants, most observers viewed the deal as a win for the union. Perhaps the most significant long-term impact will turn out to have been the survival, at least for the time being, of pattern bargaining in the Canadian auto industry. Had GM been able to impose poorer terms on the CAW than Chrysler had, it is almost certain that auto industry pattern bargaining would have come to an end. Also significant are the work hours provisions, which have been cited in a major study on workplace innovations as a prominent example of a union's choosing to reduce hours in order to save jobs (CLMPC, 1997).

Ontario Teachers' Federations (1997)

Ontario's teachers, not historically noted for their militancy, staged Canada's largest strike of 1997. The dispute, officially illegal since it took place during the life of the contract, saw 126 000 elementary and secondary school teachers leave their classrooms for two weeks in protest over the provincial government's Bill 160, designed to do away with the province's 129 local school boards and centralize power over public education in Toronto. Wages and working conditions as such were not the primary issues, though teachers were extremely upset over a proposal to reduce their preparation time significantly.

THE EDUCATION QUALITY IMPROVEMENT ACT (ONTARIO'S BILL 160)
ncboard.edu.on.ca/bill160.htm

From a short-term perspective, the teachers could be said to have lost the strike, since their action did not in any way change the government's mind. Bill 160 was enacted into law December 1, just three weeks after the teachers returned to the classroom (Mackie, 1997a). Indeed, from this perspective, one would have to agree with Jeffrey Simpson's view that the strike was one in which everybody lost–students and parents as well as teachers (Simpson, 1997). But if one assumes that the strike was essentially a political action aimed at turning Ontarians against the provincial government, then the teachers may well have been successful. The government was embarrassed when, on November 3, Mr. Justice James MacPherson ruled against its request for a back-to-work injunction (Downey, 1997), saying that "no irreparable harm" had as yet occurred and hence the injunction would not be justified. Two days later, the *Globe & Mail* commented that despite the disruption the strike was causing, most Ontarians appeared to prefer the teachers' version of events to the government's.

To be sure, some of the good will teachers had won initially was dissipated because of the strike's bizarre ending. Despite the failure of the government's injunction bid and the existence of significant public support, the unions themselves decided to end their strike after two weeks. This action revealed significant intra-organizational conflict within the teachers' federations. Late in the strike's second week, the three federations representing elementary teachers opted to return to work (Mackie and Lewington, 1997), apparently leaving the more militant secondary federations little choice but to follow suit. Both rank-and-file teachers and members of the general public were puzzled by the unions' seemingly inexplicable change of heart. Many were bitter, such as the Toronto Grade 12 student who said (Fine and Rusk, 1997), "The government got what it wants. Now that the teachers are back in school, it's like they're backing down. We lost two weeks of school for nothing." At this writing, it remains unclear why the teachers returned to their classrooms when they did.

Though the strike's abrupt ending certainly did little to help the teachers' cause, they may still have been the overall winners in the public opinion battle. The Ontario labour movement's response to the government's handling of the teachers' strike was to announce plans for a province-wide general strike (Hess, 1997). And polls taken about a month after the strike ended showed two-thirds of all Ontarians believed the government was changing things too fast (Mackie, 1997b). Nor did the end of the strike mean the end of the teachers' battle with the government. Late in November, the province's principals and vice-principals, angry at having been expelled from the teachers' federations and designated as management, announced they were considering resigning their posts and returning to the classrooms (Galt, 1997). While this did not happen after the exclusion of principals and vice-principals from the federations took effect, the new policy left a legacy of lasting bitterness.

During the fall of 1998, as we pointed out in Chapter 9, further teachers' strikes took place across much of the province (Galt, 1998; Green 1998). This time, the major issue was the teachers' loss of preparation time. Even in cases where the teachers did not leave their classrooms, they often refused to participate in extracurricular activities such as coaching or the supervision of dramatics. Since 1997, the teachers have widened the scope of their anti-government activities, engaging in a wide variety of publicity campaigns, including the boycotting of wineries and other firms found to have donated money exclusively to the governing Conservative party (Lakey, 1998). Education funding appears likely to be a major issue in the provincial election expected sometime during 1999.

Canada Post and CUPW (1997)

Over the years, Canada Post and the Canadian Union of Postal Workers (CUPW) have maintained what has arguably been the country's single most acrimonious labour-management relationship. Between 1965 and 1991, postal workers went out on strike eight times, some of the disputes lasting more than five weeks, some involving the use of strike-breakers (Ponak and Thompson, 1989), and most ending only after passage of back-to-work legislation.

SUMMARY OF THE CANADA POST STRIKE

canadaonline.miningco.com/library/bl/blpost.htm

In the past, the federal government provided Canada Post with sizeable subsidies. Over the years, it had earned notoriety as "a textbook case of a flabby, hidebound operation" as well as a strike-prone, money-losing government agency (McCarthy, 1997). In recent years, especially since it became a Crown corporation rather than operating as a government department, Canada Post has been expected to turn a profit. At the same time, the corporation has been losing a significant share of its business to courier services, e-mail, and other forms of communication.

Canadian Union of Postal Workers member speaks for many postal workers in expressing frustration at the slow pace of postal negotiations.

With a drop in letter volume estimated at 50 percent (*Le Droit*, 1997), Canada Post's position was that it had no choice but to cut jobs and to ask remaining employees to work harder. While the corporation claimed it was seeking nothing more than a full day's work for a full day's pay, the union claimed that it wanted letter carriers to walk faster than rates established as international standards 30 years ago, and that its real aim was to get them to "walk faster, take shorter lunches, and incur a greater risk of injury" (Fine, 1997b).

Though CUPW was seeking a wage increase, job security and work intensification were the two major issues, as Round 9 of the long-running battle began November 19, following a long period of uncertainty.

Tensions between the corporation's management and the union were showcased in an episode just before the beginning of the strike in which management negotiator Jean Lafleur shoved union negotiator Phillipe Arbour to the floor as Arbour attempted to enter a management hotel suite in Hull, Quebec (*Le Droit*, 1997). The incident proved a public relations disaster for Canada Post's management, already under heavy fire for its arbitrary and inefficient practices and for failing to do more to enlist workers' loyalty (Corcoran, 1997; Grange, 1997).

Previous postal strikes have often provoked waves of public outrage. This one did not—partly because new communications technologies have somewhat reduced Canadians' dependence on the postal service. (To be sure, some businesses heavily dependent on mail orders, such as Columbia Record Company, saw orders drop to nearly nil and were as a result forced to lay off their workers [Leitch and MacDonald, 1997].) A more important reason, however, seems to have been that, as in the case of the Ontario teachers' strike, people appeared more inclined to believe the union's than the management's version of events. Where previous postal union heads had sometimes struck a defiant note, CUPW president Darrell Tingley's tone was one of regret, as he announced that proposed job cuts and workload increases had left the union with no choice but to strike (*Le Droit*, 1997). This contention was never seriously disputed. Moreover, the key issues of job security and work intensification were undoubtedly issues to which ordinary Canadians could relate.

The strike ended December 4 with the passage of the *Postal Services Continuation Act*. This legislation extended the term of the existing agreement to include the period beginning August 1, 1997, and ending on the day on which a new collective agreement would come into effect (excluding the strike period). The new agreement will run until July 21, 2000. The legislation provides for wage increases of 1.5 percent on February 1, 1998, 1.75 percent on February 1, 1999, and 1.9 percent on February. 1, 2000 (*CBR*, 12/97).

The legislation stated that the Minister of Labour would appoint a mediator-arbitrator to consider all matters remaining in dispute between the corporation and the union at the time of his or her appointment. The mediator-arbitrator would have 90 days to mediate. Any matters not settled within that time period would be addressed through arbitration (*CBR*, 12/97). At this writing, the med-arb process is continuing. While the outcome remains uncertain, observers of many different political stripes agree that the corporation and the union will need to achieve fundamental change in their still highly fractious relationship if the corporation is to survive into the next century.

CFB Goose Bay (1998)

In a dispute perhaps more similar to strikes of the late nineteenth century than to those of the late twentieth (see Chapter 4 for details), the residents of the small Labrador community of Goose Bay united in a rare show of solidarity, bringing the town to a virtual standstill for one day in a protest over proposed job losses at Canadian Forces Base Goose Bay–one of the community's major employers. Unlike the other three strikes discussed in this section, the Goose Bay action was not limited to union members, but took in businesspeople, public officials, and the general public as well.

At issue was the federal government's awarding of a major contract for support services at CFB Goose Bay to a private, British-based company, Serco. The contract, expected to cover "everything from plowing roadways and janitorial work at the base to firefighting, air traffic control and security" (*Western Star*, 1998), was also expected to reduce the base's work force from over 600 to about 415. In addition, there were to be significant reductions in wages, benefits, and job security (Hebbard, 1998b).

Angered by the threat of job losses, which in the view of some residents could be so severe as to threaten the community's survival,[12] the Happy Valley-Goose Bay town council declared February 3, 1998 a day of mourning. The town manager then urged all local residents and businesses to take part (Hebbard, 1998a). Members of the Goose Bay Local of the Union of National Defence Employees, joined by other residents, put up a picket line around the base, preventing all but those with essential business from entering. In addition, between 500 and 700 people marched through the town to protest against the privatization (Hebbard, 1998b), while another 100 marched through the base's gates to the contractor's offices (*Globe & Mail*, 1998). Following a declaration of support from the Labrador North Chamber of Commerce (Hebbard, 1998a), virtually all area businesses, including restaurants, gas stations, and fast food outlets, remained closed for the day.

Summing up the reasons for the one-day general strike, local union president Terry Quinn said, "[the threat of job losses] is putting the whole community in a state of stress....A couple of people said 'enough of this' and said we're going over to shut 'er down now and they went over an' shut 'er down." (Hebbard, 1998a). The day after the strike, a delegation of leading Labrador public officials met with the federal Defence Minister (Hebbard, 1998b).

Despite that meeting, the protest did not change the government's decision to award the contract, nor did it put a halt to the job losses resulting from the contract. But at least one local observer (Pomeroy, 1999) has suggested that it did result in improved severance packages for affected employees and higher wages for those employed by the contractor, since the government is now providing such employees with a guarantee of at least 75 percent of their previous wages for one year (Pomeroy, 1999). At a minimum, the protest appears to have cushioned the blow from the contracting-out, though this same observer admits that it isn't clear what will happen in 1999. "If there hadn't been a protest, people would've been a lot worse off," is his conclusion. [13]

Some Common Themes

While the four strikes just discussed had different origins and ended in different ways, it's possible to discover a few, more or less, common themes. The first of these is job security. For various reasons, workers in all four cases were at risk of losing their jobs. In the case of the Ontario teachers, there was the fear that provincial education restructuring would lead to major job loss. In the other disputes, the fear was that jobs would be lost to outside contractors.

Work intensification and hours of work were major issues in three of the four disputes. At Canada Post, letter carriers resented the prospect of having to work longer days carrying heavier mail sacks over longer routes. At GM, enforced overtime likewise caused resentment. For the Ontario teachers, loss of preparation time meant scrambling to make up that time in their already crowded schedules.

Wages, often the most important issue in a strike, were a concern in both the GM and Canada Post strikes. They were, however, of considerably less importance than job security or work intensification and work hours. On the other hand, unpopular government policies were factors in three of the four disputes (all except GM). Such policies were crucial in the case of the CFB Goose Bay and Ontario teachers' strikes, which were called as direct protests against those policies.

WHAT CAUSES STRIKES?

Having looked in some detail at four recent Canadian strikes, and the causes for those strikes, we can now step back a bit and consider the issue of strike causes more generally. In few cases, other than certain wildcat strikes, is the cause likely to be single or simple. Leaving aside for the moment strongly inflationary periods, where strike action is often necessary to prevent rapid erosion of workers' real wages, experience suggests that most Canadian strikes appear to require: (1) serious medium- or long-term worker frustration, typically the result either of poor labour-management relations or an extremely difficult economic environment, or both, and (2) a triggering incident or incidents that can serve to channel that frustration, and around which union leaders can mobilize broad support for strike action. In the case of a now-famous Canada Post strike staged by CUPW in 1981, frustration had arisen from the long-standing poor relationship between management and the union and, in the eyes of some observers (Morton, 1989), the corporation's mismanagement. The triggering incident for the lengthy dispute appears to have been Canada Post's refusal to meet the union's demand for a maternity leave provision. In some unions, such an issue might not have proved of sufficiently broad appeal to have led to strike action. Here, it undoubtedly helped that about 40 percent of CUPW's members were women (Craig and Solomon, 1996, 53). More often, wages are likely to be the triggering issue. In many cases, wage issues by themselves might be insufficient to provoke a strike, particularly in deflationary periods. But given that almost everyone could use more money, an employer's refusal to meet a union's wage demand will often prove to be the "last straw" when antagonistic relationships marked by large accumulations of grievances or employer attempts to diminish the union's influence have already sown the seeds of conflict.

Beyond this, there is now a large body of literature relating strikes to various economic causes such as unemployment, inflation, nominal and real wage levels, and profits. A smaller, but still significant, literature exists on such socio-political and cultural determinants as community cohesion, union leaders' values and ideologies, decision-making authority, and intraorganizational conflict within unions and management organizations. Some attempts have also been made to link strikes to bargaining unit size and to the bargaining history of particular organizations.

While much of this literature is interesting and important, space precludes a detailed consideration of most of it here.[14] It should also be noted that a good deal of the literature, especially the more economically oriented portion of it, presumes a background in econometrics and statistics and, in general, gets into research issues that are too complex for most beginning students.

Strike causation is undeniably a complex issue. Realistically, an introductory text can do little more than scratch the surface. Here, we propose three fairly generic approaches that provide some tools for understanding strike causes without getting into heavy-duty statistics or complex research methodology issues. In applying these approaches, readers should be aware that, in the last analysis, each bargaining relationship and set of strike issues is unique. To fully understand the causes of any given strike, one must know the players and the history of their interactions with each other, in addition to understanding the economic, political, and cultural environment within which those interactions are and have been conducted. This said, the generic or "framework" approaches discussed below *can* make readers aware of some of the more common patterns of strike causation.

Within any given negotiation, an unavoidable strike may result from fundamental disagreement over an issue of principle (maternity leave in the 1981 Canada Post strike, the union's continued right to exist in other cases). A settlement zone doesn't exist in the case of such issues because they are really not quantifiable, and hence any numerical compromise is impossible. One cannot have a union shop on Tuesdays and Thursdays, but a non-union shop the rest of the week. As well, when strikes do arise over such issues of fundamental principle, they are apt to be longer and more bitter than those over less fundamental issues such as money (Kervin, 1984). Other unavoidable strikes may result from either party's desire to change the bargaining framework or structure (as in the case of the GM strike discussed above), or from *intraorganizational* conflict within the union or management group. In the latter case, the strike, though perhaps irrational from an economic perspective, may be seen as necessary to help maintain internal cohesion within the union or management group. Speaking of the need some unions have to call occasional strikes for this purpose, Reynolds notes (p. 428) that "[u]nused weapons become rusty." Strikes are also extremely difficult to avoid in situations where, typically because of a history of bad relations, one party feels driven to use a strike to punish the other.

Mistakes or Collective Voice?

John Godard's (1994) distinction (similar but not identical to Reynolds's) is between strikes that result from mistakes, generally in the negotiation or ratification process, and those more appropriately regarded as unions' expressions of their members' collective voice. In the former group (Godard, 1994:343—346) he includes disputes resulting from immature or flawed bargaining relationships, as well as those caused by negotiators' lack of skill, inexperience with each other, or inability to get along. Another cause, often related to union intraorganizational conflict, can be individual workers' miscalculations, which may lead them to reject tentative agreements that their leaders know are probably the best they can realistically hope for. The complexity of the situation itself can also be the source of mistakes that lead to strikes. Here again, intraorganizational conflict may lead to negotiating errors. More fundamentally, such errors are more apt to occur in situations where difficult issues are at stake, where bargaining structures are complex, or where many different occupations and classes of worker are being represented.

The "strikes as mistakes" perspective also covers disputes resulting from an asymmetry of information. Typically, this takes the form of the management's possessing more complete and up-to-date financial information than the union. The union may then be caught in the position of not knowing whether or not management is telling the truth when it claims it cannot afford to meet the union's demands, and thus being forced to call a strike in order to call the management's bluff.[15]

Godard (1994:343—346) argues that while the "strikes as mistake" approach has its uses, it's wrong to view strikes only as mistakes, given the conflict he sees as inherent in employment relationships generally. In his view, it is generally more useful to view strikes as expressions of unions' collective voice. With this approach, what primarily determines whether or not a particular situation will lead to a strike are the extent and intensity of worker discontent, union leaders' ability to mobilize that discontent, the union's strike power, and management's willingness and ability to "buy off" discontent through generous wage settlements or progressive human resource policies. Also relevant are the availability of other means of expressing discontent (especially quitting) and the presence or absence of cohesive community support, which may prove necessary, particularly in the case of a lengthy or bitter strike.

"PEOPLE'S STRIKE AGAINST PRIVATISATION DEEMED SUCCESSFUL"

www.skyinet.net/users/courage/intl/puertorico2.htm

Both Godard's and Reynolds's approaches help explain why, despite the existence of a formidable array of dispute resolution mechanisms (discussed below), Canada has continued to have relatively high strike intensity by international standards. As the reader will observe, a number of Canadian dispute resolution mechanisms, such as back-to-work legislation, are reactive. Most of those that are proactive, such as conciliation and mediation, are approaches designed to prevent mistakes from occurring in the negotiation process. The assumption here is that if the parties can communicate reasonably effectively, behave decently towards each other, and convey accurate information at the table, a strike should not be necessary. Often, such interventions are useful in preventing strikes or at least in reducing their length and severity. But they are of little value where a settlement zone simply does not exist (in many cases involving intraorganizational conflict), or in situations (as in the "industrial conflict" perspective described by Kervin [1984]) where the conflict extends beyond the workplace and permeates virtually all aspects of the worker's lives, as in strikes occurring in single-industry mining towns. It would be naive to view such strikes as "mistakes." Here, a strike is almost always an overt expression of serious long-term discontent–discontent of the same variety, normally, which led the striking workers to unionize in the first place.

The one key question left largely unanswered, even in Godard's more comprehensive discussion, is why worker discontent takes the form of strikes under some circumstances but not others. Why, in particular, do some countries (and provinces within Canada) appear to have consistently lower strike intensity than others?

Strikes and Workplace Conflict: The Big Picture

In attempting to answer the questions just posed, it's important to bear in mind, once again, that strikes are just one of many possible forms of workplace conflict. Such conflict may find either individual or group expression. Moreover–and this is key to the discussion that follows–some IR systems' arrangements for handling "alternative" types of conflict, such as worker grievances, seem far likelier than others to reduce the sort of worker frustration that's likely to lead to strike action later on.

STATISTICS CANADA "TIME LOST IN WORK STOPPAGES"
www.statcan.ca:80/cgi-bin/Cansim/cansim.cgi?matrix=28&cq=&order_id=

Let's suppose our job is to find out why Canada has normally had higher strike intensity than Germany. Even if we confine our investigation to strikes that are the result of mistakes, there are some good reasons, as the literature (Adams, 1995a; Bamber and Lansbury, 1993) has already established, why the Canadian system should lead to more such mistakes than the German one. Most important, within the highly centralized German system, bargaining is normally conducted at the national industry level between an employers' association and an industrial union. This means there are many fewer sets of negotiations going on whose failure could lead to a strike. It also means that negotiators on both sides are apt to be highly experienced, and therefore less apt to make mistakes than the inexperienced negotiators who often hammer out deals in Canada. As well, German collective agreements themselves are simpler and cover a smaller range of issues than Canadian ones, since in Germany a good many issues are left to be resolved at the enterprise level. This also reduces the likelihood of negotiating error.

A final point concerns information asymmetry. In Canada, as noted above, unions may well be forced to call strikes to find out the true state of affairs from employers who may or may not be telling the truth. In Germany, this would seldom if ever be necessary. Most corporations have worker directors, and works councils, whose officers are generally active unionists, and who are legally entitled to full and accurate information about the firm's performance (Adams, 1995a). Union negotiators thus go to the table with pretty much the same information about the firm as their management counterparts.

Less often discussed in the literature is the question of how grievance arrangements may increase or decrease the likelihood of strike action, assuming now that we are dealing with strikes as collective expressions of union members' frustration and discontent. An aggrieved German worker (Adams, 1995a) has a broad range of avenues for possible redress, including his works councillor, his local union officer, his immediate supervisor, or the union's local office. If these approaches fail, the worker may take his case to a Labour Court. The Labour Court has jurisdiction over a far broader range of issues than does a Canadian arbitration panel (Adams, 1995a), and hence the likelihood of a complaint's being heard by the court is that much greater. All in all, the German approach to grievances suggests a desire to see individuals' workplace complaints resolved as quickly as possible. By allowing the individual worker to retain "ownership" of his grievance, the German system also seeks to "uncouple" individual workers' frustrations from the sort of collective frustrations that can lead to strikes. The works councils, which can legally take disputes through to arbitration, can also help to defuse at least some of the collective frustrations arising at the shop-floor level.

"THE PRESSURES OF PATCO: STRIKES AND STRESS IN THE 1980S"

www.lib.virginia.edu/journals/EH/EH37/Pels.html

With its broad range of options, then, the German approach to grievances probably serves to defuse a large portion of individual workers' frustrations and discontents. Here it is in sharp contrast to the Canadian approach, which relies almost exclusively on a single mechanism: the formal grievance process. Under this procedure, the grievance is filed by the union, not by the individual worker. Ultimately it is the union that will decide whether or not the grievance gets carried forward. While there have been many improvements in recent years (see Chapter 13 for details), the process is still generally costly, legalistic, and extremely slow. A minuscule proportion of all grievances are carried through to arbitration (Gandz, 1979); most are either settled by the parties or withdrawn. It is not generally considered a breach of the union's statutory duty of fair representation for it to use individuals' grievances for political purposes, trading off the possibility of individual redress for the organization's larger collective aims. As well, many grievances are filed for avowedly tactical or political purposes. In unhealthy organizations, it is common for unions to file large numbers of grievances during or just before negotiations. At the extreme, as in the case of Canada Post, the existence of huge numbers of unsettled grievances may itself be a possible cause of strike action. Even in less extreme cases, unsettled grievances add to everyone's frustrations and tend to make negotiations that much more difficult.

Overall, Canadian approaches to grievances seem likely to increase both individual and collective frustration. The major sources of frustration for individuals are the slowness of the process and their loss of control over it. For unions, serving as their members' collective voices, the major sources of frustration are probably the slowness and costliness of the process and its likelihood of leading to intraorganizational conflict. For example, aggrieved individuals whose cases haven't been heard may, at negotiation time, put severe pressure on union executives and negotiating teams—possibly pressing them to go in directions they would rather not take and that the organization as a whole would benefit from not taking.

The German approach to grievances appears to be based on two important assumptions: (a) the individual's right to have his case heard, and (b) the desirability of defusing workplace conflict at an early stage. In contrast, the Canadian approach seems to be founded on a pluralistic desire to balance unions' power with that of management. The idea here appears to be that if unions are given the greatest possible latitude with respect to worker grievances, subject of course to the limitations of duty of fair representation provisions, this will be another "weapon" that can help them get to a level playing field with management. Both systems' aims are worthy. The question is whether Canadian society as a whole, or even the Canadian labour movement, is best served by grievance arrangements that offer individual workers little guarantee of a hearing, while increasing union-management conflict by allowing individuals' frustrations to feed into and exacerbate that conflict, personalizing it, as it were. Arguably, Canadian grievance arrangements have helped make strikes longer and more bitter, a conclusion that receives at least modest support from the long average duration (by international standards) of Canadian strikes in most years.

The preceding discussion does not pretend to be a complete analysis of comparative Canadian and German strike intensity. Hopefully it *has* given readers some insight into the complexity of strike causation, and into some of the many different ways in which strikes are related to other kinds of industrial conflict. Clearly, here is an area where further research is badly needed.

DISPUTE RESOLUTION METHODS

Canadian jurisdictions have developed a variety of dispute resolution methods for use in helping to prevent strikes, or, in some cases, as alternatives to strikes. Virtually all involve the use of a neutral third party. These methods work in various ways. In mediation and, increasingly, in conciliation as well, the neutral assumes a more interventionist role, working actively with the parties in an attempt to reach a settlement. In arbitration, normally used after one or more other methods have failed, the neutral actually establishes the terms and conditions of the new agreement. In establishing an arsenal of dispute resolution methods and in deciding which ones to use on any given occasion, Canadian governments seek to strike a balance between allowing the parties as much freedom as possible to settle their own disputes and protecting the public interest. For example, compulsory arbitration is virtually unheard-of in the private sector. Its main use is with groups such as police and firefighters whose services are deemed so essential to public welfare and safety that they can't be allowed to go on strike. Similarly, conciliation boards are now all but unknown in private sector disputes, though they are still used from time to time in high-profile public sector ones (Craig and Solomon, 1996; Godard, 1994).

In one important respect, Canadian government intervention in the IR system appears to go beyond "striking a balance." The compulsory conciliation provision found in most Canadian labour acts seems both highly interventionist by international standards, and inconsistent with the general principle of voluntarism underlying the Canadian IR system, which was discussed in some detail in the labour law chapter (Chapter 8). While there may be some rationale for retaining the procedure in disputes with a substantial public interest component, it is not at all clear why a conciliator should be used to help resolve disputes in, say, shoe factories. It's also not clear, as Godard (1994:352) points out, whether the process actually winds up doing more good than harm. Undoubtedly some strikes have been averted as a result of compulsory conciliation. On the other hand, it's entirely possible that without it, unions and management organizations would have become more creative in thinking up their own ways to resolve disputes, and thus averted other strikes in that way.[16]

Compulsory Conciliation

Compulsory conciliation was first introduced into Canadian labour legislation in 1907, when it was written into the *Industrial Disputes Investigation Act (IDI Act)*. Some version of compulsory conciliation continues to be part of every Canadian labour act except that of Saskatchewan.

Under compulsory conciliation, a government official, normally someone from the labour ministry, meets with the parties to determine the possibilities of settlement. Increasingly, conciliators have come to play active roles in attempting to resolve disputes, functioning more and more as mediators in fact if not name. Indeed, in two jurisdictions, British Columbia and Alberta, mediators are used instead of first-stage conciliators. As noted earlier in the chapter, a conciliator must report his or her lack of success to the labour minister and, in addition, a certain length of time must generally have elapsed before a strike or lockout can become legal.

The second stage of the conciliation procedure, still "on the books" in most Canadian jurisdictions, is the conciliation board. Under this procedure, a tripartite board comprising a neutral, a management representative, and a union representative meets. Where used, the board operates more formally than a single conciliation officer, eliciting presentations from the parties and making recommendations as to the appropriate terms of settlement (Godard, 1994). However, as noted above, conciliation boards are increasingly rarely used. While a number of criticisms have been levelled against the boards, the most significant appear to be the delays they cause and their tendency to interfere with the parties' willingness to negotiate a settlement on their own (the so-called "chilling effect"). A number of jurisdictions have substituted mediation for the second stage of the conciliation process; the *Canada Labour Code* allows for a mediator or conciliation commissioner in addition to the traditional officer and board (Craig and Solomon, 1996). Quebec and British Columbia have done away entirely with second-stage conciliation.

Mediation

In theory, mediation involves more active intervention on the part of the third-party neutral than does conciliation, though the boundaries between them are becoming increasingly blurred in practice. Unlike conciliation, mediation is usually voluntary, although as noted above, it has been incorporated as the first stage of the conciliation process in two Canadian jurisdictions and as the second stage in several others.

Depending on the nature of the negotiations and the experience of the negotiators, the mediator may be called on to do such things as meeting with the parties to determine what their key issues are, discovering where the "settlement zone" lies, acting as a go-between, actively pressuring the parties to compromise so that an agreement may be reached, and dealing with the media both during negotiations and after a tentative agreement has been reached (Craig and Solomon, 1995; Downie, 1989; Godard, 1994). Experience suggests that there is no one "best way" to mediate; people with varying backgrounds and personal styles have proven successful. It is, however, generally agreed that effective mediators must be honest and impartial, have good listening skills, know how to keep a secret, and have a good sense of timing (Craig and Solomon, 1996). As with negotiators (Fisher and Williams, 1989), courage is also required; frequently the mediator will find himself or herself "out on a limb," directly confronting the very real possibility of devastating failure.[17]

Mediation of various types is being used more and more frequently, both within the IR system and for other purposes, such as resolving child custody disputes in divorce cases. A survey of the Ottawa-Hull "Yellow Pages" for 1998 found 62 active mediation practices in the English section and another 20 in the French section. The ad for one of those practices put the matter most succinctly: "Mediate, Don't Litigate." While there are many reasons for mediation's growing popularity, the two most important are probably its significantly lower cost compared to formal litigation, and its less adversarial nature. Those using mediation seem to find the process less traumatic than going to court would be. The trend towards using mediation to resolve a wide range of disputes is a far-reaching one that will bear careful observation in the coming years.

Arbitration

Interest arbitration, in which a neutral acceptable to both sides or a tripartite panel chaired by such a neutral establishes the terms and conditions of the new collective agreement, is often used in Canada's public sector, normally after the failure of one or more of the methods described above. Note that interest arbitration should not be confused with rights or grievance arbitration, which has to do with interpreting the existing contract. (This type of arbitration will be discussed in Chapter 13, on grievances). Note as well that compulsory interest arbitration is virtually never used in the private sector. In general, both management and unions prefer to negotiate their own contracts rather than turning the decision over to a third party. On occasion, however, voluntary arbitration is used. Not uncommon in the United States, where it has been tried in industries as varied as steel and major league baseball, it is rarer in Canada. However, it has been used in the Ontario clothing industry (Downie, 1989) and in some university settings such as the University of Ottawa (Craig and Solomon, 1996).

Binding interest arbitration is the normal method of resolving contract disputes involving essential employees such as police and firefighters, whose services are generally considered so crucial that they cannot be allowed to strike.[18] Without the ability to present their case before a neutral third party, these groups would be at a severe disadvantage in bargaining. Aside from such clearly essential workers as police and firefighters, arbitration is substituted for the usual conciliation-strike route in varying ways across Canada. The approaches taken here range from that of Quebec, which specifically rejects arbitration except in the case of police and firefighters (Hébert, 1995), to those of Alberta, Manitoba, and P.E.I., where public servants continue to be denied the right to strike and must, therefore, submit to binding interest arbitration. In certain jurisdictions, other groups, such as teachers and nurses, must likewise go to arbitration. In the federal public service under *PSSRA* and in certain provinces under similar acts, public servants may choose either binding interest arbitration or the traditional conciliation-strike route.

An examination of the various pieces of Canadian public sector bargaining legislation reveals little overall consistency as to which groups are and are not permitted to strike. In general, however, the tendency has been for provincial governments to move away from arbitration of non-essential public sector workers. Notably, the province of Ontario granted its public servants the right to strike in 1993 (see above). One reason why, in these tough economic times, provincial governments are tending to look with less favour on arbitration is their fear that arbitrators will impose awards whose costs they are unable, or at least unwilling, to meet. To get around this problem, some jurisdictions (i.e., Alberta) have explicitly laid out public sector arbitration criteria, including the province's ability to pay (Ponak and Thompson, 1989).

However, the imposition of such criteria does raise the question of whether affected employees are really getting a fair and impartial hearing, given that the arbitrator's hands have in effect been tied with regard to monetary issues.

There are two major types of interest arbitration: *conventional* and *final-offer* (FOA). Under conventional arbitration, the arbitrator is given considerable latitude in fashioning an award. He or she may, and often does, pick and choose among the positions submitted by the parties. With FOA, there is no such latitude. The arbitrator must choose either the management's position or the union's. FOA may be used either on a total-package basis, or issue-by-issue. An intriguing variation (see Craig and Solomon, 1996:319) is tri-offer FOA, where, in addition to the positions advanced by management and the union, the arbitrator may pick the recommendations of a fact-finder.

Conventional arbitration has been criticized on a number of counts. Some have been concerned at its cost, others at the slowness with which settlements are achieved through it compared to settlements achieved in other ways. The two most common criticisms are (a) that groups that use it regularly may become so dependent upon arbitrators that they lose their ability to fashion their own settlements (the so-called "narcotic effect") and (b) that it inhibits genuine bargaining by removing the incentive for the parties to make hard choices, since they know the arbitrator is there to make the choices for them at the end of the day. This latter effect is commonly as the "chilling effect." While there is no consensus in the literature on the extent to which such effects exist in Canada, there is at least some reason to believe they may be significant problems.

The use of FOA, especially in its total-package form, would seem to provide a good way around any possible chilling or narcotic effects. In principle, the possibility of having an arbitrator reject one's entire package and select that of the other side should be a very severe disincentive to unreasonable behaviour, and an equally strong incentive for the parties to settle on their own. Some evidence cited by Ponak and Thompson (1989:394–396) suggests that, under FOA, the rate of freely negotiated settlements is a good deal higher than under conventional arbitration. Nonetheless, FOA has found little favour in Canada, though it has become relatively common in U.S. public sector bargaining.[19]

Mediation-Arbitration (Med-Arb)

Med-arb, as it is commonly known, is a hybrid form of dispute resolution that has not often been used in Canada, but that lately has become more prominent because of its use in certain high-profile public-sector disputes. Most notably, it was used to help resolve a national railway strike in 1995 (Craig and Solomon, 1996) and more recently has been used to help resolve issues still outstanding after the 1997 postal strike. As the name suggests, this approach involves the neutral's functioning first as a mediator, then, if the parties are unable to settle on their own within a given period of time, as an arbitrator. Judge Alan Gold, who for some years was standing arbitrator for the Port of Montreal and who often used med-arb (Gold, 1993), suggests that med-arb may work best where there is a standing arbitrator or umpire who knows the industry and the players extremely well.

Among the criticisms of med-arb, perhaps the most serious is that having acted as a mediator could prejudice a person's decision as an arbitrator (Craig and Solomon, 1996). Judge Gold, however, indicates (1993) that this had not been a problem, at least in his experience. Given the relatively small amount of experience Canada has had with med-arb, it would probably be premature to pass judgement as to its effectiveness.

Back-to-Work Legislation

Back-to-work legislation is used to end public sector strikes that have reached a point where government officials believe that, if they continued, they would pose significant risk to the public health, safety, order, or welfare. Such legislation has often been used to end strikes at Canada Post and in the Quebec public sector. Sometimes (as in the most recent Canada Post strike), it is followed by a referral to med-arb or straight arbitration.

While occasional use of back-to-work legislation is perhaps inevitable in any country that allows public sector workers to strike, the frequency with which this legislation has been used in Canada (see above) suggests there is something seriously wrong with existing public sector bargaining arrangements.

SUMMARY

Overall, there appears to have been a gradual but significant trend away from formal investigative mechanisms such as second-stage conciliation, and in the direction of more informal facilitative mechanisms such as mediation. The conciliation process itself has evolved into something very much like mediation in most jurisdictions. Within the public sector, arbitration, initially envisaged as the normal option under *PSSRA's* "choice of procedures" approach, has recently found less favour with both management and unions. A number of jurisdictions (notably Ontario) that formerly used arbitration to resolve disputes with their public servants have moved to the conciliation-strike route. Meanwhile, med-arb, though still relatively uncommon, is becoming more prominent because of its occasional use in high-profile public sector situations. Also in the public sector, federal and provincial governments continue to make frequent use of back-to-work legislation.

A NEW WAVE OF STRIKE ACTIVITY?

Earlier this decade, some observers (i.e., Gunderson, Hyatt, and Ponak 1995) were predicting an end to what they saw as a 35-year wave of Canadian strike activity. That prediction appears to have been premature. The past two years have seen a marked resurgence of strike activity, to its highest levels since 1990. Particularly note-worthy are the high concentration of strike activity in the public sector and in Ontario, and the avowedly political nature of many of the disputes. In this respect, Canada (and especially Ontario) has been in line with larger international trends. The past two years have seen a wave of general and public sector strikes, many political in nature, in such diverse countries as Brazil, Germany, France, and Greece. The caus-es of these disputes have been equally diverse; they have ranged from a desire to stop the murder of Brazilian street children to protests against French government cut-backs and the desire to achieve a shorter workweek in Greece (*Better Times,* 11/97).

One reason for Canada's low strike intensity earlier in the decade may have been the prevalence of public sector wage controls, which almost certainly led to a reduced incidence of public sector strikes during those years. To the extent that earlier strike public sector strike levels were held artificially low, the recent rise in strike activity could be considered, at least in part, a statistical artefact. But it would be a mistake to write off the recent strike resurgence as *solely* a statistical artefact. In Ontario, where strike activity over the past two years has included a number of one-day com-munity-wide "general strikes," the phenomenon almost certainly reflects broad and continuing anger at provincial government policies, especially at cutbacks in health care and education. As the recent teachers' strikes demonstrated, this anger does not appear to be confined to public sector workers; it is broadly shared by the general public as well. In other provinces, public sector strikes reflect anger over years of pay freezes, increased workloads due to downsizing and restructuring, and job insecurity.

From an economic perspective, the recent resurgence of public sector strike activ-ity is entirely logical. Members of many public sector groups have seen a substantial erosion in real purchasing power over the past decade. The resurgence is also consis-tent with the theory of conflict developed by Hebdon (1992) and with the view of conflict that has been advanced here. Due to the restrictions that have been placed on it recently, the collective bargaining process has been far less able to defuse conflict than was the case in the past. The result seems to have been that frustrations have risen to the point where they are likelier to result in strike action.

The situation of Canada's public sector workers raises a critical public policy issue. How can governments pursue fiscally responsible policies while maintaining adequate public services, without allowing public sector workers' frustrations to become so great that they trigger unacceptably high levels of strike activity, comparable say to those of the 1970s? The last chapter offers some tentative answers to this question.

One hopeful development might be B.C.'s 1993 "social accord" with its health care workers, which provided for strong contract language on job security, modest wage increases, and reduced work hours during a time of major health care restructuring (Craig and Solomon, 1996: 365). It is, of course, possible that any kind of public sector social contract will remain in bad odour with the labour movement, owing to Ontario's unfortunate experience with its social contract legislation. Still, it may be possible for other governments to learn from the Ontario experience, and make sure unions are fully involved from the outset any time such legislation is proposed.

In the private sector, Quebec's social contracts in the steel and pulp and paper industry seem quite promising. It isn't entirely clear to what extent such contracts have penetrated other sectors of the economy; however, the presence of many elements of the social contracts in agreements under the Quebec Federation of Labour's Solidarity Fund (Boivin and Déom, 1995) suggests that the approach has probably been more generally applied. Further research is needed on the extent to which the social contracts and similar arrangements have lowered strike intensity in Quebec. Still, given that Quebec has, within a decade, gone from being one of the country's most to one of its least strike-prone provinces, the social contracts and other elements of the province's approach to reducing labour-management conflict will bear closer observation elsewhere in Canada.

Within the IR profession, a great deal of research and practical activity have focussed on the development of dispute resolution methods designed to prevent strikes or at least minimize their impact on "innocent" third parties. Many of these methods have proven useful. However, Canada's continued relatively high strike intensity suggests that, by themselves, dispute resolution methods are not enough. This chapter has suggested that, in addition, attention must be paid to broader institutional factors, such as Canada's generally decentralized bargaining structure and the ways in which the grievance procedure feeds into and aggravates existing sources of union-management conflict. In the public sector, the recent resurgence of strike activity coupled with governments' frequent use of back-to-work legislation suggests the need for a fundamental rethinking and retooling of that sector's collective bargaining arrangements.

QUESTIONS FOR DISCUSSION

1) Have you ever been on strike? What was the experience like? If you haven't been on strike, try to find a friend or relative who has been, and ask that person what the experience was like.

2) What's special about the way unions operate during and immediately before a strike?

3) Legally speaking, what is a strike?

4) What is the most accurate way of comparing strike intensity across different jurisdictions, industries, or countries?

5) At which points in history was Canadian strike activity highest and lowest? Why?

6) Why does strike activity now appear to be on the increase again, after a number of years of very low strike incidence?

7) What were the major causes of the four recent strikes discussed in the mini-cases?

8) Describe the various theories of strike causation discussed in the chapter. Why does the "strikes as mistakes" theory not explain much strike activity?

9) What are some methods of dispute resolution used to prevent strikes or lessen their impact once they've started? Which ones are used mainly in the public sector? Which seem most effective? Are there serious problems with any?

10) Assume you have been appointed provincial labour minister. What steps would you take to reduce strike intensity in your province? Would these steps involve any curtailment of basic union rights? If so, how would you justify that?

SUGGESTIONS FOR FURTHER READING

Adams, Roy. (1995a). "Canadian industrial relations in comparative perspective." In M. Gunderson and A. Ponak (Eds.), *Union-management relations in Canada*. Don Mills, ON: Addison-Wesley. Contains a useful discussion of industrial conflict that suggests conflict may depend more on structures than on processes (such as dispute resolution systems).

Hebdon, Robert. (1992). "Ontario's no-strike laws: A test of the safety valve hypothesis." In *Proceedings* of the 28th Conference of the Canadian Industrial Relations Association, held in Kingston, Ontario, in 1991. Quebec City: CIRA. Fascinating discussion of conflict that strongly suggests that suppressing conflict in one way (as by making strikes illegal) merely causes it to resurface in other ways. An article that should be much better-known than it is.

Kervin, John. (1984). "Strikes: Toward a new typology of causes." In *Proceedings* of the 21st Annual Meeting of the Canadian Industrial Relations Association, held in Guelph, Ontario. Offers an extremely helpful classification scheme for different types of strikes, including a discussion of policy approaches suitable for each. A useful corrective to the Panglossian optimism of those who think that all we need to do to prevent strikes is to be of good will and learn how to communicate better.

ENDNOTES

1 Recent news reports suggest that this has been the case in the aftermath of both the Canada Post strike and the earlier strike against United Parcel Service in the United States.

2 The point that a strike or other crisis can serve as a catalyst for introducing such mechanisms is well made by Verma (1995). For a discussion of this point within the American setting, see Woodworth and Meek (1995).

3 Such a refusal would be legal if the employee in question believed working conditions to be dangerous. See the employment law chapter for more detail on this point.

4 The Ontario act contains one or two extremely minor differences in wording from the *Canada Code* definition.

5 In the case of Ontario, seven days must have elapsed since the release of a conciliation board report or fourteen days since the Labour Minister's decision not to appoint such a board (the so-called 'No-Board' report). Under the *Canada Labour Code*, seven days must have passed in either case.

6 More recent data do not distinguish between strikes and lockouts, and, therefore, a comparable breakdown is not available for the more recent period.

7 For a brief discussion (probably quite adequate for the needs of most beginning students), see Gunderson, Hyatt, and Ponak (1995:374–375).

8 An alternative, though basically similar, measure is the number of days lost per paid worker per year.

9 As we note elsewhere in the chapter, this does not generally hold true for public sector strikes, which are often artificially "shortened" through governments' use of back-to-work legislation or the threat of such legislation.

10 For a very useful discussion, see Kervin (1984).

11 In a remarkable indication of how far public opinion appeared to have shifted towards the postal workers and away from Canada Post management, *Globe & Mail* columnist Terrence Corcoran, arguably that paper's most outspoken right-wing and pro-business voice, produced a November 21 commentary on the dispute that excoriated the corporation's management—and did not have a single negative thing to say about the union.

12 CBC Radio News Report, 7 a.m., Wednesday, February 4, 1998.

13 Pomeroy also suggests that the Goose Bay protest may have helped make the government more careful about the way in which it has handled other military base privatizations.

14 For a fairly detailed overview, see Gunderson, Hyatt, and Ponak (1995:383–395).

15 The author does not agree with the rather dismissive attitude towards this perspective taken by Gunderson, Hyatt, and Ponak (1995:384). These writers state that while the asymmetric information perspective is appealing, it is not clear that the firm's private information "is so important in today's world of sophisticated information-processing. In addition, it is not clear why the parties do not agree to contractual arrangements whereby compensation depends on the true state of the firm, since that information is revealed over time." Such a statement seems naive in the extreme. Sophisticated computers or not, it is still possible to conceal information. As to why the parties do not agree to contractual arrangements of the

sort just described, the reason should be self-evident. They do not agree to them because at least one of the parties (more likely management) believes it can get a better deal by concealing the true state of affairs than by being open. Nor is it necessarily self-evident that such information will be revealed over time (or at least in time to be of any benefit to the union). Had it not been in a fair number of employers' interest to conceal relevant information, unions would not have started calling strikes to obtain this information, and the asymmetric information perspective as such would never have been devised.

[16] Throughout most of this paragraph, I am heavily indebted to the thoughtful discussion provided by Godard at pages 349 to 352.

[17] For a useful and interesting discussion of the mediation process and the characteristics of good mediators, see Craig and Solomon (1996:300–306).

[18] A few jurisdictions, mainly in the Atlantic region, do permit police to strike.

[19] For an interesting discussion, see Ponak and Thompson (1989:395–396).

CHAPTER 13

GRIEVANCES:
RESOLUTION AND PREVENTION

Grievance media-
tion can bring
smiles to the faces
of both sides—as
well as lower bills.

The grievance process is important in that it provides a
way other than the traditional mid-term strike to resolve problems
arising out of the interpretation of collective agreements. It is also important in
that it provides workers with a certain measure of workplace voice and a forum
through which they can express discontent about workplace conditions without
fear of employer reprisal. In this chapter, we begin by examining the overall sig-
nificance and functions of the grievance process. After a look at a specific case,
we go on to examine grievance procedures and outcomes. We then consider some
criticisms of the conventional arbitration process and some innovative new dis-
pute settlement mechanisms that have arisen in response to those criticisms.

GRIEVANCES AND THEIR SIGNIFICANCE

As we've pointed out throughout this book, worker-management conflict is a fact of life in most workplaces. Strikes, which are perhaps the most dramatic manifestation of such conflict, were discussed in the previous chapter. Here, we are concerned with grievances, a less dramatic, but often equally profound, manifestation of worker-management conflict.

COMMISSION ON THE FUTURE OF
WORKER-MANAGEMENT RELATIONS
www.irl.cornell.edu/library/e_archive/Dunlop/dunlop.contents.html

WHAT IS A GRIEVANCE?

Strictly speaking, a grievance (Gandz, 1982:289) is an allegation that one or more provisions of a collective agreement has been violated, and a claim for redress for any damages resulting from that violation. While one could apply the term to most types of employee complaint, such as those resulting from arbitrary or excessively harsh supervisory practices or the behaviour of co-workers (Gandz, 1982), using the term in its more general sense could result in ambiguity. It is, therefore, probably wiser, for purposes of this course, to apply the term "grievance" only to allegations of collective agreement violation.

The Function and Significance of Grievances

The grievance process is of great significance in the Canadian IR system because it provides a forum for the resolution of disputes arising out of the collective agreement. Under Canadian legislation, mid-term strikes are banned,[1] although individual workers are, as we noted in Chapter 7, allowed to refuse work they believe unsafe. Otherwise, the rule is "Work now; grieve later" (Godard, 1994:363). As we noted in the labour law chapter, collective agreements in every Canadian jurisdiction must contain procedures, culminating in binding arbitration, for the resolution of disputes over the interpretation and application of the agreement. For example, section 48(1) of the *Ontario Labour Relations Act* states that every collective agreement shall provide for the final and binding settlement by arbitration, without a work stoppage, of all differences between the parties arising from the interpretation, application, administration, or alleged violation of the agreement, including any question as to whether the matter is arbitrable. Where such procedures are not explicitly written into an agreement, the labour board will normally deem them to have been included (see *OLRA*, sec. 48(2), for a rather lengthy example of such a "deemed" provision).

Because of the "Work now, grieve later" rule, it's vital that aggrieved employees have a quick and relatively inexpensive mechanism for obtaining redress. It has been well established (see Rose, 1986b) that failure to address grievances quickly can lead to more serious labour relations difficulties(including wildcat strikes and other forms of industrial conflict(later on. Initially, in both Canada and the United States (Thornicroft and Eden, 1995; Nolan and Abrams, 1997), grievance arbitration appears to have resolved most problems fairly expeditiously. However, since the early postwar period, it has tended to become lengthier, more formal, more highly legalistic, and a good deal costlier (Nolan and Abrams, 1997; Arthurs, 1988). The reasons for these developments are discussed later in the chapter, along with a number of remedies that have been worked out in recent years.

 AMERICAN ARBITRATION ASSOCIATION
www.adr.org

In addition to maintaining the integrity of the agreement by providing a mechanism for ensuring that its terms are adhered to (Godard, 1994:359), the grievance process serves a number of other functions. First, and perhaps most important, it provides a system of industrial jurisprudence under which individuals can seek redress without fear of reprisal from superiors (Godard, 1994:360–361). By thus protecting workers from arbitrary treatment from superiors, the grievance process serves as an important mechanism of individual and group voice (Godard, 1994:360; Freeman and Medoff, 1984). Next to the higher wages that unions normally provide workers, the grievance process may well be the most compelling reason for people to join unions. Beyond that, the process can provide a forum for supplementary negotiations over items left vague in the agreement (Godard, 1994:359–360). It can also serve as a political mechanism for resolving intraorganizational conflict within both management and union sides. As Godard notes (p. 360), a union official may pursue a grievance more to satisfy a certain faction within the organization than because she or he believes the case has merit as such. Likewise (Godard, 1994), lower-level managers may encourage the union to pursue a certain grievance in the hopes it will persuade senior management to change a policy they dislike or find unworkable. Management may also "hang tough" on a particular grievance or set of grievances to prove a point to the union or to their superiors.

Finally, the grievance process can be used as a pressuring device in an attempt to induce management to address issues not covered by the collective agreement. As Godard notes (1994), an agreement may contain no provision on contracting out—an issue that could cost union members jobs or income. Though they cannot grieve over this issue where there is no relevant agreement provision in place, what they can do is file a large number of grievances over other provisions contained in the agreement, thereby causing management considerable inconvenience, if not disruption, and possibly getting them to rethink their position on contracting out.[2] While this is a perfectly legitimate use of the grievance process, it is also a controversial one, since (particularly around negotiation time) it can lead to large accumulations of grievances not arising out of the complaint of any individual union member. Habitual use of the grievance process for this purpose, as is the case in organizations such as Canada Post (Stewart-Patterson, 1987), is generally a sign of very poor labour-management relations overall. Indeed, high grievance rates can seriously affect a firm's bottom line. A number of studies, such as those by Ichniowski (1986), have found that establishments with high grievance rates perform more poorly in terms of both labour efficiency and product quality than those with lower grievance rates.

FEDERAL MEDIATION AND CONCILIATION SERVICE
labour-travail.hrdc-drhc.gc.ca/eng/fmcs.cfm

Types of Grievances

It is useful to distinguish between **individual, group,** and **policy** grievances. As the name implies, an individual grievance involves the application of the agreement to one member. An example would be a grievance by Mary Jones alleging that her three-day suspension for chewing gum in the company cafeteria violated the collective agreement in that the suspension was not imposed for just cause. A group grievance results from a combination of similar individual grievances seeking a common redress (University of Ottawa, 1994). For example, a group of workers might file a grievance alleging that the company had failed to pay overtime pay for work after regular working hours. A policy grievance involves a question of the agreement's general application or interpretation (University of Ottawa, 1994). Such a grievance might be initiated over large-scale technological or organizational change or a change in the pension plan. While such grievances are relatively infrequent, they are generally quite serious because they may involve millions of dollars or hundreds of jobs. For this reason, policy grievances are often initiated at a late stage of the grievance procedure, where they can be dealt with by senior management and union officials (Gandz and Whitehead, 1989:241).[3]

Before we go any further, it might be helpful to look at an actual grievance case. We suggest that you read the following case now, then again when you have finished the chapter. See how your view of the case changes as a result of what you've learned. The case is followed by a number of questions; you may wish to answer them now, and again once you've read the rest of the chapter.

DRUGS IN THE WORKPLACE
THE WESTGATE WIDGET CO. CASE[4]

The Westgate Widget Company is a medium-sized manufacturing firm located in Kanata, just outside Ottawa. It employs about 400 people and produces a variety of finished and semi-finished metal products. Since 1986, all its production and office employees, except management and the plant manager's and personnel director's secretaries, have been represented by Local 123 of the Canadian Auto Workers.

In 1994, a new plant manager and personnel director were hired. Prior to their appointment, the company's discipline policies could best be described as casual. So long as the job got down, management generally didn't care too much *how* it got done. By the early 1990s though, the problem was that, all too often, the job simply wasn't getting done. Between 1990 and 1993, there were significant increases in late orders, spoiled goods, absenteeism, and drug and alcohol use on the job.

New plant manager Winston Q.E.D. Wardhaffel and personnel director Jim Carson examined the production and absenteeism data and concluded there was probably a connection among the increased rate of absenteeism, on-the-job alcohol and drug use, and the increased rates of late orders and spoiled goods. They were particularly concerned that the company had begun losing market share. If they didn't do something quickly, they reasoned, Westgate Widget could be down the tubes in another two to three years.

In an effort to come up with effective new absenteeism and discipline policies, Wardhaffel did what many another manager in his position has done before: he brought in a consultant from a major New York firm for $2500 per day plus expenses. After shaking his head repeatedly at the company's lax ways and touring the entire plant for several days, the consultant took his laptop into his hotel suite and emerged, two days later, with something he described as a "Flexible Zero-Tolerance Policy" on both absenteeism and alcohol and drug use. Item 1 of that new discipline policy, which was immediately put into effect, reads as follows:

Any employee committing any of the following acts shall be disciplined by reprimand, suspension, or dismissal depending upon the seriousness of the offence and his or her past record...

1) Reporting for work or being present on company property under the influence of unprescribed drugs, or bringing alcoholic beverages or unprescribed drugs onto the premises.

On June 15, 1996, just two years after the consultant's visit, assembly line worker Sally Renwick filed the following grievance:

I was given a medical leave of absence on June 7, 1996, when I went to the Ottawa General Hospital because I was feeling dizzy and light-headed. On Friday, June 11, 1996, I received an e-mail from the Westgate Widget Company stating that I was discharged. I received written confirmation of my discharge on June 14. The company does not have just cause to discharge me, and I am therefore demanding reinstatement with full pay.

The discharge notice issued by the company on June 11 reads as follows:

On Monday, June 7, 1996, you reported for work under the influence of unprescribed drugs. This is a direct violation of Item #1 of the plant rules and regulations, clearly posted on the main bulletin board in the plant lobby and at several other strategic locations. You are hereby informed that your employment with this company has been terminated for (a) being under the influence of unprescribed drugs, and (b) medical unfitness. This termination is effective Friday, June 11, 1996.

Renwick's discharge arose out of incidents at the Kanata plant on June 7, 1996. At 8:00 that morning, Harry Olson, supervisor in the main assembly works, became concerned about the behaviour of Renwick, one of the workers he supervised. He described her as behaving "as if someone were pinching her nose with clothespins. She was twitching and shaking her head around and chewing something violently." He added that he had seen Renwick in a similar state before, but the symptoms had been nowhere near as extreme.

Fearing for her safety, Olson soon assigned Renwick, along with two other women, to the lighter and simpler job of sorting finished parts in the stockroom. At 8:30, when he entered the stockroom to see how things were getting on, he noticed that Renwick's co-workers had stopped work and were staring at her. He said: "Frankly, it was a terrifying sight. Sally was wandering around in a total daze, bumping into things and occasionally colliding with the other women. Her eyes were bugged out as if they were about to come out of their sockets. She was still chewing violently and twitching and rolling her head. As for doing the job, forget it. She dropped eight pieces on the floor just while I was there, and the others said she had put more pieces in the wrong bins than in the right ones. I confirmed this by looking at the bins."

Olson didn't know what to do next. He tried calling the plant doctor, but unfortunately she was away at an all-day seminar and wouldn't be back until the next day. His next move was to call on personnel director Jim Carson. Carson instructed Olson to accompany Renwick to the first-aid office, which was normally under a nurse's supervision. Olson did so, and then left her there and went back to the assembly line. Unfortunately, the nurse was out giving vaccinations in another room, so Renwick was left alone in her office for about half an hour.

At 9:00, Carson came to the first-aid office. He found Renwick lying on the bed but with both legs on the floor. She had obviously been perspiring heavily and appeared to be having some trouble breathing. When Carson asked her what was wrong, she spoke very rapidly, making it almost impossible for him to figure out what she was saying. "She went on and on for the better part of half an hour," he would later testify, "talking about her emotional problems and problems at home; she said her nerves were bad. She was talking about someone who had been hurt on a forklift some time before and was now unemployed. She said she'd taken some nerve pills, but she had not had any drug at that time. Speed was one of the drugs she mentioned, but not at that time."

Just then the nurse, Edna Malone, returned from giving vaccinations and spoke kindly to Renwick, suggesting she rest for a while. She said she would look in on her occasionally and would immediately phone the local hospital for an ambulance if necessary.

Carson left to attend a meeting. When he returned to the first-aid station at noon, he found Renwick asleep. He woke her and accompanied her to Malone's private office, adjoining the first-aid room, where he used the telephone to call her husband. Carson said her body movements were still very exaggerated and her eyes were "flashing around like those of a madwoman."

Carson's secretary, Elaine Dow, stayed with Renwick for much of the morning. Her description of Renwick's actions was similar to Carson's, though she noted that Renwick had fallen asleep just after 11:00. She said Renwick appeared to be chewing something quite violently and that she also had great difficulty sitting still and was constantly crossing and uncrossing her legs. According to Dow, Renwick frequently looked at her fingers, at times digging under one nail with another. She reported seeing a skin rash on Renwick's hands. She said that Renwick wouldn't look at her, and that for the most part she simply hummed and talked to herself. When she did answer a question, which was seldom, she never did so completely, but used disjointed words and phrases. Like Carson, Dow described Renwick as sweating profusely.

Early in the afternoon, Carson arranged for Renwick to see her personal physician at the Ottawa Civic Hospital. This physician was Dr. Thomas Brown, associate professor of internal medicine at the University of Ottawa, who had a small private practice on the side. Dr. Brown said he'd seen Renwick on May 30, when she had come to him complaining of a skin problem. She'd told him then that she believed the skin problem was due to crystals of methedrine coming out of her skin and that there were "insects and other beasties" crawling under her skin, especially at night. After a brief examination he prescribed Valium, describing the phenomenon reported to him by Renwick as "hallucinations."

Brown said that when Renwick arrived at the hospital at 2 P.M. on June 7, she was totally distraught and was obviously hallucinating severely. He described the skin condition on her hands and said that the area under her fingernails appeared to have been dug at, either by her fingers or by a sharp instrument. Her hallucinations by then were taking the form of insects crawling under her skin and snakes crawling on her face. Brown said these symptoms strongly suggested that Renwick had been taking drugs, most likely methedrine (speed). He stated that to reach the point of hallucination from methedrine required prolonged, heavy use—a single dose would almost certainly not cause such symptoms. He further stated that it was unlikely the excessive perspiration was caused by methedrine—that he had, in fact, never seen this symptom in his 15 years of practice—but that with street purchases of the drug one could never be sure what other substances might have been included in the mixture.

After examining Renwick and performing some tests on her, Brown determined that she was under the influence of methedrine and decided to admit her to the hospital. He said that at that time, "Sally was not medically fit for anything." When she came to at 6 P.M. she agreed to undergo treatment, but discharged herself from the hospital at 5 P.M. on June 12. The doctor believed she should have remained in the hospital for at least a week, and that she should then have entered a local drug rehabilitation centre. He could not say why Renwick had discharged herself from the hospital.

At the first, oral stage of her grievance procedure, Renwick said she had been taking drugs on and off for about six weeks prior to June 7. She attributed her condition to serious home problems. Her husband had been unemployed for more than a year and had begun to drink heavily. While he was "the nicest guy in the world" sober, occasionally he would beat her when in his cups. Renwick said she wanted to leave him, but was afraid what he might do to himself, her, and their three children if she did. She admitted having taken methedrine on the morning of June 6 (a Sunday), but said she had felt no ill effects from the drug the next day. She added that she had obtained the drug from a friend, who earlier had obtained it by prescription from her doctor. She claimed to have several witnesses who could be called on to testify that she had not acted abnormally on June 7.

Fred Flint, president of the plant's CAW local, said the company had been far too arbitrary and severe in its discipline. No one had previously been disciplined for drug abuse. However, the company had discharged four workers for alleged drunkenness. Three of the four had been reinstated after arbitration; the fourth had been offered reinstatement, but had refused it in lieu of a year's wages, declaring: "I'd like to enjoy the rest of my life."

Flint cited Renwick's previously flawless 12-year work record as further evidence of injustice on the part of the company. He said: "The company suggests that Ms. Renwick wantonly disregarded its rules and regulations. This is ludicrous, given her desperate personal situation. She could not afford to lose her job. If, as the company suggests, she was under the influence of some drug, then I submit that the influence was involuntary. Involuntary ingestion of a drug cannot be differentiated from the contraction of measles. It is only when the person who is ill refuses treatment that we can condemn that person. Ms. Renwick did submit to treatment, not once but twice. Management has acted in an irresponsible and arbitrary fashion. No arbitrator will let this pass."

CASE QUESTIONS

1) What would you do next if you were Carson? Would you take the case to arbitration? Why or why not?

2) Assuming the case *did* go to arbitration, what do you think the result would be? Why?

3) Comment on the discipline policy under which Renwick was discharged. Does it seem fair and consistent?

4) How do the company's actions fit with the notion of progressive discipline? (You may only be able to answer this question after reading the whole chapter.)

5) On June 12, as noted earlier, Sally Renwick signed herself out of the hospital. Should this have any bearing on the case?

6) If you think the company's actions were helpful and constructive, defend those actions. If you do not agree with the company's actions, describe a course of action that you think would have been more constructive.

7) Suppose that instead of this being Renwick's first drug-related offence, it was her third, and that on the first occasion she had received counselling from the personnel director, and on the second occasion she had been referred to a company-supported employee assistance program (EAP). Suppose further that, after three or four visits to the drug rehabilitation program to which the EAP had referred her, she had stopped going. How should Carson respond in that case? If the case went to arbitration, how would the arbitrator likely rule?

8) What are some ways in which the company might achieve its objectives of reduced absenteeism and substance abuse without resorting to a "zero toler- ance" plan (flexible or not)?

9) Evaluate the company's overall handling of the case (not just the discharge aspect of it). Are there certain things about the way the case was handled that cause you particular concern?

10) Fred Flint, president of the CAW local representing Renwick in her fight against the company, is an old-fashioned unionist who believes that no worker should be subjected to arbitrary dismissal. He has publicly vowed to fight "every single one of these damned cases all the way through arbitration, no matter how much it costs." At the same time, Flint is also a realist. He knows that the union's resources for arbitration cases are limited, and (privately at least) he'll admit that he shuddered when he received the bill for the union's share of the costs for the four previous alcohol-related cases. "Don't quote me on this," the treasurer said later, "but we could probably have put another per- son on staff for what it cost us to take those cases all the way up the ladder." Is there any way to reconcile Flint's insistence on providing top-quality union representation for all discharged workers with his recognition of the reality of limited, if not shrinking, funds to handle grievances?

GRIEVANCE PROCEDURES

Collective agreements generally spell out grievance procedures in fairly considerable detail. A 1978 study by Jeffrey Gandz (quoted in Gandz and Whitehead, 1989) found that Ontario grievance procedures had anywhere from two to seven steps, with three being the most common number. A verbal stage involving a discussion between the grievor (often accompanied by a union steward) and the supervisor appeared in about two-thirds of the procedures, either as the official first stage or as a step preceding the official first stage (ibid.). If the problem could not be resolved verbally, the grievance would then be reduced to writing and submitted to the next level of management above the supervisor. Most grievance procedures contained strict time limits for each stage; however, almost all procedures also contained provisions allowing the parties to opt out of those time limits by mutual consent. A common feature was a semi-offi- cial "extra step" in which senior management and union officials would meet on a regular basis to review cases pending arbitration (ibid.). In some instances, this "extra step" was incorporated as an official stage of the procedure.

Since 1978, despite growing delays in the time it takes cases to be sent to arbitra- tion and some evidence that suggests that at least some of the stages in the typical grievance process achieve few settlements and are thus of little practical use (Brett and Goldberg, 1983), the typical grievance process doesn't appear to have changed much. Most grievance processes that the author has examined contain either three or four official stages; many contain an additional unofficial stage either at the beginning or end of the process. The procedure in the University of Ottawa agreement discussed earlier is slightly more expeditious than some others the author has examined in that it contains only one step between denial of the initial written grievance and referral to arbitration: a meeting between the grievor (accompanied by a union representative) and the Dean to explore the possibilities of settlement. However, by allowing the parties to opt out of the grievance procedure's time limits at any stage, the procedure has failed to address one of the major causes of delay noted in the literature. Another potential source of delay arises from the possibility of using a three-person panel rather than a single arbitrator (see Button, 1990; Ponak and Olson, 1992; Rose, 1986a), although the latter would seem to be the norm.

The procedure outlined in Table 13.1, based on one described by Trotta (1976), would not be untypical, even today.

Table 13.1
A SAMPLE GRIEVANCE PROCEDURE

STEP 1 **(oral discussion, filing of grievance).** Meeting between supervisor and aggrieved employee, accompanied by shop steward. If problem not satisfactorily resolved in three working days, then grievance to be reduced to writing and Step 2 taken.

STEP 2 **(discussion between shop steward and department head).** Shop steward to discuss grievance with department head. If grievance not satisfactorily adjusted within three working days, then Step 3 shall be taken.

STEP 3 **(discussion between senior management and union officials).** Grievance committee consisting of four members appointed by the union to meet with plant manager or his or her appointed representative. The aggrieved employee and a representative from the international union may also be present.

STEP 4 **(referral to arbitration).** If grievance not settled, dispute may be taken to arbitration providing either party has given written notice requesting arbitration within 15 working days after the end of the Step 3 meeting. The parties designate a mutually satisfactory arbitrator. If they cannot agree on one within three days after the arbitration request, then the appropriate government agency shall, at the request of either party, provide both parties with a list.

ISSUES MOST COMMONLY GRIEVED

Discharge and discipline are the issues most commonly grieved by unions. A study by Gandz and Whitehead (1989) of grievances in a basic steelworks found that about half of all grievances were of a disciplinary nature. Seniority accounted for another 15 to 20 percent of the grievances, the remainder being related to such issues as job postings, overtime, health and safety, and the performance of bargaining unit work by supervisors. For Ontario as a whole, a more comprehensive study quoted by Adams (1978:40) found that discharge and discipline cases constituted 37 percent of all grievances sent to arbitration.[5] While management grievances against the union are rare, they do exist. Most typically (as in the case of the steelworks described by Gandz and Whitehead), such grievances would result from an illegal work stoppage.

As for the causes of dismissal, both Adams (1978) and Barnacle (1991) found dishonesty, poor work performance, insubordination, poor attendance, alcohol, failure to get along, and union activity[6] to be the seven types of behaviour most commonly leading to dismissal. There was some difference in the relative frequency of various causes in the two studies. Adams found insubordination and poor attendance to be the most common causes, while in Barnacle's case, the most common causes were dishonesty and poor work performance. Despite these differences, there was not a great deal of difference in the percentage of cases related to each cause, and in both studies, dishonesty, work performance, poor attendance, and insubordination were the four commonest causes of discharge.

THE ARBITRATION PROCESS

Panels Versus Single Arbitrators

Arbitration decisions are made either by single arbitrators or three-person panels. If a three-person panel is used, the union and management each select one member, and the agreed-upon third party neutral serves as chairperson of the board. This effectively makes the chair the decision-maker, since the panel need only reach a majority decision, not a unanimous one (Thornicroft and Eden, 1995:260). Indeed, even if neither nominee agrees with the neutral's decision, the chair's decision will generally be deemed to be the final award (Thornicroft and Eden, 1995; Craig and Solomon, 1996:340).

Numerous studies have found that single arbitrators reach their decisions more quickly than three-person panels, and that the single-person process generally costs a good deal less (Goldblatt, 1974; Rose, 1987; Button, 1990; Thornicroft and Eden, 1995). Other studies (i.e., Barnacle, 1991) have found little difference in grievance outcomes whether a panel and a single arbitrator was used. No doubt as a result, in recent years a decreasing percentage of cases have been heard by three-person panels. For example, in Ontario between 1980 and 1984, about 58 percent of conventional arbitration cases were heard by panels (Rose, 1986a). By 1985–1986, panels were being used in only about a third of those cases (Rose, 1991). Still, a surprising number of organizations continue to rely on the panels. As late as 1985–1988, panels were being used in three-quarters of all Alberta arbitration cases (Ponak and Olson, 1992). Moreover, as we noted earlier, even grievance procedures (like the University of Ottawa's) that allow for a single arbitrator may offer the option of a three-person panel.

It is not at all clear why panels have remained so popular, particularly at a time when organizations are finding it necessary to cut costs in almost every area of their operations. Granted, in certain instances panelists who know the industry could be of help to an arbitrator who does not (see Craig and Solomon, 1996:339).[7] In addition, in complicated policy grievances that are likely to take a long time to be resolved, there might be a certain merit to having union and management representatives available to draw out implications concerning the possible effects of, say, the proposed change in the company pension plan. But such cases are few and far between. In the vast majority of individual and group grievance cases, the use of union and management representatives does little other than waste time,[8] which further increases the grievor's hard feelings and contributes to still further deterioration of labour-management relations within the organization.

The Arbitration Hearing

Arbitration hearings are normally held in neutral settings(most often hotel meeting rooms (Gandz and Whitehead, 1989:249). While there is no requirement that parties be represented by legal counsel, unions and, especially, management organizations have been using legal counsel increasingly in recent years (Arthurs, 1988; Barnacle, 1991). When the union does not use legal counsel, the case is most often presented by a business agent or a national or international representative (Gandz and Whitehead, 1989:249).

Often there will be preliminary objections to a grievance. These include allegations that the agreement's time limits have been breached, that the arbitrator lacks jurisdiction because the provision breached is not in the collective agreement but rather in a subsidiary document such as a letter of intent, or that the grievance has already been withdrawn, abandoned, or settled (Sack, 1994:75–76; Gandz and Whitehead, 1989:249–250). While the respondent may argue that the arbitrator should adjourn the hearing until the preliminary objection has been decided, the normal practice is for the arbitrator to reserve judgment on the preliminary objection and proceed to hear the grievance proper, including his or her ruling on the preliminary objection in the final award. In this way, delay and expense can be avoided (Sack, 1994:69–70,75–76).

Once any preliminary objections have been dealt with, the hearing normally proceeds as follows.

1. Each party makes an opening statement in which the nature of the grievance and issues in dispute are raised (Gandz and Whitehead, 1989:249). Since the union is normally the party filing the grievance, the union will normally speak first. However, in discharge and discipline cases, where the onus of proof is on the employer, the company will normally present first (Sack, 1994:70-71; Peach and Kuechle, 1975:248). The party making the first opening statement has the opportunity to reply to new points raised by the other party (Sack, 1994:77). The grievor's opening statement should include the remedy sought (i.e., reinstatement in the case of dismissal) and the amount of income she or he has lost since the discharge, to guide the arbitrator in making a back pay award (Sack, 1994:79).[9]

2. The party on whom the onus of proof rests (normally the union, except in discharge and discipline cases) calls witnesses, who give evidence, generally under oath (Gandz and Whitehead, 1989:250). Each witness is cross-examined by the other party and then re-examined by the first party. Witnesses may also be questioned by the arbitrator, and by the panelists if there is a three-person panel (Gandz and Whitehead, 1989). It's important to bear in mind that the rules about what kind of evidence an arbitrator can accept are much less strict than those applied to formal court cases. In general, labour relations legislation empowers arbitrators to accept any evidence they consider proper, whether or not such evidence would be admissible in a court of law (Sack, 1994:81–82). It's also important that no witness be "badgered" in cross-examination to the extent that that witness feels unfairly harassed (Sanderson, 1976:66). Should this happen, the other side's representative or the arbitrator may intervene, and the arbitrator's ultimate decision may be negatively influenced (Sanderson, 1976).

   In evaluating the evidence before them, arbitrators will generally hold the parties to different levels of proof, depending on the nature of the grievance (Thornicroft and Eden, 1995:258). In most cases, the standard of civil trials, proof on "a balance of probabilities," is required (Thornicroft and Eden, 1995; Sack, 1994:81). This simply means that the side bearing the burden of proof must establish that its version of the facts is likelier to be true (Sack, 1994:81). However, in discharge cases, particularly those involving allegations of serious misconduct such as theft or dishonesty, a higher standard of proof is usually required. Here, arbitrators will often apply the standard normally used in criminal cases: proof beyond a reasonable doubt (Thornicroft and Eden, 1995:258).

3. The responding party also calls witnesses, who then give evidence and are cross-examined and re-examined as in the case of the first party's witnesses.

4. Each side then presents its closing argument, normally in the same order as the initial presentation (Gandz and Whitehead, 1989:250; Peach and Kuechle, 1975:247). Such closing arguments will frequently cite arbitration decisions made in similar cases (Gandz and Whitehead, 1989:250).

5. The arbitrator then adjourns the hearing. If sitting as the chair of a three-person panel, he or she confers with the nominees. If acting as a sole arbitrator, he or she then prepares the award. If there is a panel, he or she prepares a draft award and seeks input from the panelists. In a number of jurisdictions, there are time limits that the arbitrator or panel must observe. In Ontario, a single arbitrator must issue an award within 30 days after the end of the arbitration hearing, while a panel must do so within 60 days (*OLRA*, section 48[7–8]). However, these deadlines may be extended with the consent of the parties or at the arbitrator's discretion, so long as reasons are given in the award for the extension of the deadline (*OLRA*, section 48[9]). The final written award is then sent to the parties (*OLRA*, section 48[9]). The arbitrator's or panel's decision is binding on the parties and on the employees covered by the agreement affected by the decision (see *OLRA*, section 48[18]).

Enforcement

Most labour acts lay out a procedure for enforcing arbitration awards where either party refuses to comply (Sack, 1994:141). In Ontario, the award may be filed in the General Division of the Ontario Court (*OLRA*, section 48[19]) and enforced in the same way as any other court judgment, through contempt proceedings for continued non-compliance (Sack, 1994:141). Thus, if a party continues to ignore the arbitrator's award after it has been filed with the court, he or she risks a fine or even imprisonment (Thornicroft and Eden, 1995:262).

Judicial Review of Awards

In general, Canadian jurisdictions are reluctant to use the courts to overturn arbitrators' decisions. A number of provinces attempt to limit judicial review of arbitration awards through a privative clause (Thornicroft and Eden, 1995). An example is section 101 of B.C.'s labour act, which provides that except as noted in the act, any arbitration award or decision is final and not open to question or review in a court on any grounds whatever. Another section of the same act does grant the labour relations board limited power to review an arbitration award where a party has been denied a fair hearing or where the award is inconsistent with the principles of the labour act (Thornicroft and Eden, 1995; Sack, 1994:141–142). To date, most other provinces have not granted their labour boards this power (Sack, 1994:142).

Even in jurisdictions whose labour acts do not contain a privative clause, courts will rarely overturn an arbitrator's decision simply because they disagree with it (Sack, 1994). In particular, they are reluctant to question an arbitrator's interpretation of a collective agreement unless that interpretation is patently unreasonable (Sack, 1994:141). Appeals are more likely to be granted in cases where the arbitrator has shown bias, denied a party a fair hearing, or made an incorrect interpretation of a common law principle or a statutory provision lying outside his or her "core area of expertise" (Sack, 1994). Appeals will also be granted in cases where the arbitrator has made a jurisdictional error (i.e., an error relating to a legislative provision limiting his or her remedial powers).[10]

 "CBC V. CANADA (LABOUR RELATIONS BOARD)" CBC APPEAL
www.droit.umontreal.ca/doc/csc-scc/en/pub/1995/vol1/html/
1995scr1_0157.html

ARBITRATION OUTCOMES

To date, there has been no single, comprehensive study on all aspects of arbitration outcomes. There have, however, been a great many studies of a more limited nature seeking to relate arbitration outcomes to such factors as arbitrator characteristics, grievor characteristics, the type of issue grieved, and the use of legal counsel by the two parties.[11] Overall, the evidence appears to be fairly inconclusive as to whether arbitrator and grievor characteristics such as age, gender, education, and experience significantly affect the outcomes of arbitration cases (see Thornicroft and Eden, 1995:268–270). A much more significant issue may be the extent to which women, non-lawyers, and younger people find it possible to enter the profession at all. A 1988 survey by Brian Bemmels (see Thornicroft and Eden, 1995:264) revealed that only 7 percent were women, 63 percent held a law degree, and the average age was nearly 56. Similar results were obtained in several other studies reviewed by Thornicroft and Eden (1995). In principle, it would seem desirable to have a cadre of arbitrators whose demographic characteristics more closely approximated the diversity of the work force. To the extent that the various provincial arbitrator development programs allow more women, non-lawyers, and younger people to enter the field, they will be performing a very useful service indeed.[12]

Discharge Cases

Because the impact of discharge cases both on individual workers and on organizational morale can be so dramatic, these cases are of special importance in industrial relations. For the most part, except in cases involving a single extremely serious offence such as theft, assault, or sabotage, arbitrators expect employers to have applied progressive discipline, whereby the penalties have increased for each succeeding offence and the employee has been made aware of the possibility of further penalties up to and including discharge for any further offences (Adams, 1978; Thornicroft and Eden, 1995).[13] The purpose here is twofold. First, it *informs* employees that their conduct is unacceptable and states what the consequences will be should such conduct continue. Second, it allows them to *correct* the offending behaviour, where this is possible. The development of progressive discipline as the accepted norm for most dismissals arguably represents the single most important modification of the otherwise dominant doctrine of residual management rights. Slightly over half of all discharged employees who grieve their dismissals are reinstated, many with back pay (McPhillips and England, 1995:81).

Progressive discipline has always had a rehabilitative aspect to it (see Adams, 1978:29–30). In recent years, this aspect of progressive discipline has come increasingly to the fore, particularly in cases involving unexplained absenteeism and drug and alcohol use. A growing trend in such cases is for arbitrators to expect employers to have offered employees the chance to rehabilitate themselves, as by referring them to counselling or an employee assistance program. No employee is required to accept counselling or employee assistance. On the other hand, should an employee not be willing to do so, the employer is then entitled to conclude that the employee in question is either unable or unwilling to be helped, and to proceed with appropriate disciplinary measures up to and including discharge.

CORPORATE POLICY AND EMPLOYEE DRUG TESTING
www.ccsa.ca/wisearl3.htm

Somewhat surprisingly, one's likelihood of reinstatement does not seem to depend very heavily on the type of offence one has allegedly committed. In George Adams' 1978 study, 53.5 percent of grievors were reinstated. The proportion of employees reinstated for different categories of misconduct ranged from 38 percent for attendance and 39 percent for poor work performance and dishonesty to 58 percent for union activity and 55 percent for alcohol-related offences. A later (1991) study by Peter Barnacle found that 54 percent of all grievors were reinstated. Slightly over half (51 percent) of all dismissals for dishonesty were sustained, as compared to 25 percent of those for union activity and 35 percent of those for alcohol-related offences. Only 12 percent of all those discharged were exonerated (i.e., awarded full compensation). Interestingly, exactly the same percentage of those discharged for dishonesty were exonerated, a finding which would seem to refute the notion that the reason such a relatively large percentage of those dismissed for dishonesty were reinstated was that arbitrators were not convinced the grievors hadn't committed the acts of which they were accused. Had the arbitrators not been satisfied that the grievors had actually committed the offences in question, they would presumably have had no choice other than to exonerate them completely.

Of far more significance than the type of offence allegedly committed was the grievor's previous disciplinary record. Adams found that a full 94 percent of those with no previous disciplinary record were reinstated, as compared to just under 60 percent for those with a good record or a prior disciplinary warning, and only 39 percent for those with a previous suspension. Similarly, Barnacle found that dismissals were sustained for 68 percent of those with a prior record related to the dismissal offence, and 47 percent of those with some kind of prior record, but for only 23 percent of those with no prior disciplinary record. These findings point strongly towards arbitral use of progressive discipline as a criterion in determining the appropriate penalty for a given offence (see Thornicroft and Eden, 1995:269).

An all-too-familiar criticism of the IR system concerns the length of time it takes to bring most cases before an arbitrator. Adams's study in particular lends some support to this criticism. He found that the longer it took arbitrators to hear cases, the less likely a grievor was to be reinstated or to receive any back pay. In cases heard within three months of discharge, only 29 percent of the dismissals were sustained and 29 percent of the grievors were exonerated. However, in cases heard more than six months after the discharge, 62 percent of the dismissals were sustained and only 10 percent of the grievors exonerated (1978:50–51). Such findings lend support to the hypothesis, discussed in the labour law chapter, that expedited arbitration systems can be of considerable benefit to workers and unions.

Use of Legal Counsel

The use of legal counsel by management and unions has frequently been cited as the cause of delays in arbitration cases (Rose, 1987; Elliott and Goss, 1994; Thornicroft and Eden, 1995). Since lawyers are also expensive, the question naturally arises, why do parties continue to use them? The answer, as revealed by a number of studies (i.e., Goldblatt, 1974; Barnacle, 1991), is quite simple. If you have a lawyer and your opponent doesn't, you are more likely to win the case. If, on the other hand, your opponent has a lawyer and you don't, you're more likely to lose. Therefore, if there is any chance at all that your opponent will be using legal counsel, you would be well advised, from a purely practical perspective, to follow suit.

Barnacle (1991:163) found that, in cases where dismissals were sustained, employers used lawyers 85 percent of the time, but unions used them only 45 percent of the time. On the other hand, where full or partial compensation was awarded, the difference was much narrower, with employers using lawyers 78 percent of the time and unions, 69 percent.

An interesting observation is that lawyers appear to make little difference to arbitration outcomes when neither party uses them or when both parties do (Thornicroft and Eden, 1995:265). This in turn suggests that both sides could achieve substantial time and money savings simply by agreeing not to use legal counsel at all.

Lawyers as Arbitrators

As we noted earlier, both in Canada and the United States, the vast majority of arbitrators come from the legal profession (Barnacle, 1991; Thornicroft and Eden, 1995). This raises the question of whether lawyer-arbitrators arrive at different outcomes than do arbitrators from other professions, such as economics or industrial relations. While space does not permit a detailed discussion of this issue, Barnacle's findings[14] suggest that the differences between lawyers and arbitrators from other backgrounds are generally rather slight. The major difference was that lawyers gave somewhat longer suspensions in cases where employees were reinstated but not fully exonerated (1991:144). Non-lawyers were marginally less apt to sustain a dismissal than lawyers, except in cases involving dishonesty, where the reverse was true (Barnacle, 1991:144–145). Similarly, Thornicroft and Eden's review of eight studies (1995:268) found little difference in outcomes between cases decided by lawyers and those decided by people from different backgrounds.

Other Outcomes

Dastmalchian and Ng (1990) found that grievances were more likely to be granted in organizations with a positive industrial relations climate than in those with a negative one. In another study, this one of the Canadian federal public sector (Ng and Dastmalchian, 1989), the same two authors found that grievances were more often settled at early stages of the internal grievance procedure, and that higher-status employees were more apt to have their grievances granted than lower-status employees.

A number of studies, including most notably one by Brett and Goldberg (1983), have found that grievances are rarely settled at the middle stages of internal grievance procedures. In effect, what seemed to be happening was that middle-level managers and union officials were simply rubber-stamping their subordinates' decisions and passing the matter up to someone with real power to decide the case. This finding, as we will point in more detail shortly, has important implications for the development of grievance mediation systems and other alternatives to conventional arbitration.

CRITICISMS OF CONVENTIONAL ARBITRATION

There is by now a substantial literature on the failings of the conventional arbitration process. Most of this literature (i.e., Nolan and Abrams, 1997; Button, 1990) laments the transformation of grievance arbitration from an informal, speedy, and relatively inexpensive process to a slow, costly, and highly legalistic one. Another major criticism is that, because arbitration has become so slow and so costly, only a very small percentage of all grievances filed—less than 2 percent, according to one study (Gandz and Whitehead, 1989:240) are actually heard by an arbitrator. Still another criticism is that because the union "owns" the grievance process and individual workers cannot, for the most part, file their own grievances, the individual worker has little redress if the union decides not to file his or her grievance (Godard, 1994:360).

In this section, we examine the time delays, costs, legalism, and inaccessibility of conventional arbitration, leaving the broader and more systemic question of union ownership of the process to a concluding section.

Time Delays

If good labour-management relations are to be maintained, it's essential that grievances be resolved as quickly as possible. As the case of Canada Post (see Stewart-Patterson, 1987) attests far too clearly, large backlogs of unsettled grievances often represent industrial relations "time bombs" waiting to explode.[15]

Though most managers and union officials would agree about the importance of settling grievances quickly, the time required to settle grievances under conventional arbitration seems to be increasing. Various studies reviewed by Thornicroft and Eden (1995:267) found the total length of time from the action that inspired the grievance to the issuing of the arbitration award to be anywhere from six to fourteen months, with delays of eight to twelve months most common. At Canada Post, delays of more than a year have often been the norm, with delays of more than two years not uncommon (Stewart-Patterson, 1987). For obvious reasons, lengthy delays are of particular concern in discharge cases; an employee who has lost his or her job and cannot find another will almost certainly undergo considerable hardship. In addition, as was noted above, the longer the arbitration process takes, the less likely employees are to be reinstated. While it is workers who most obviously suffer as a result of slow grievance processes, delays can also come back to haunt employers, as other employees file their own grievances to "protest" inaction on earlier cases, or in some instances even engage in illegal work stoppages (Rose, 1986b).

Costs

Though arbitration may indeed be relatively inexpensive compared to litigation in the courts, it is still far from cheap. Arbitrators' fees (split between the parties, along with other expenses such as the rental of hotel suites and photocopying) typically range from $500 to $2000 per day (Thornicroft and Eden, 1995:261). Their total fees for a case where the hearing itself is finished in one day typically range from $2500 to $5000 (Thornicroft and Eden, 1995); when the hearing is longer, the fees will obviously be proportionally higher. Where there is a three-person panel, panelists must also be paid, lodged, and fed. And when parties use legal counsel, they must pay lawyers' fees that can range from $100 to upwards of $300 per hour (Thornicroft and Eden, 1995). To get the complete picture regarding costs, one must also include the value of the many hours of union and management personnel's time devoted to preparing and presenting arbitration cases. By the late 1980s, one well-known arbitrator was "conservatively" estimating the costs of a single case to be $4400(not including the value of the time spent on the case (see Button, 1990:6). Since then, costs have increased further, so that for a one-day case involving legal counsel and using a three-person panel, the total bill could be as high as $15 000 per side when the value of people's time was taken into account (Elliott and Goss, 1994:9).

Legalism

As Elliott and Goss(1994:12) have noted, arbitration hearings are all too likely to become bogged down in technical legal arguments, rather than concerning themselves with the merits of the grievance at issue. In their view, the problem has been exacerbated by the growing use of legal counsel in recent years and by the excessive number of cases that arbitrators and arbitration panels are forced to read, digest, and incorporate into their awards. Because of this excessive reliance on precedents, arbitrators take significantly longer to write their awards than they otherwise would, and the costs to the parties are greater. Moreover, when at long last awards *are* issued, they are often so weighted down with legal citations as to be very difficult for anyone but a lawyer to understand.

Accessibility

Given the time delays, costs, and legalism of conventional arbitration, it isn't really surprising that so few cases are taken through to arbitration. With most arbitration cases running to four figures if not five, few management organizations and fewer unions could ever hope to take more than a tiny fraction of all grievances to arbitration. While some grievances may be resolved informally, many grievors, including some with very legitimate complaints, simply do not obtain a hearing for their cases. Such workers are likely to feel considerable frustration, and they can pose serious problems both for management and for their own union officials.

ALTERNATIVES TO CONVENTIONAL ARBITRATION

Growing awareness of the problems of conventional arbitration has led to the development of a number of innovative alternatives. The three most important for our purposes are expedited arbitration, which speeds up the arbitration process and reduces its cost, grievance mediation, where a third-party neutral helps the parties negotiate a solution to the grievance to prevent it from going to arbitration, and preventive mediation, where the parties seek to improve communications and develop proactive problem-solving mechanisms that will prevent most problems from becoming formal grievances.

ALTERNATIVE DISPUTE RESOLUTION, ARBITRATION, AND MEDIATION
law.house.gov/314.htm

Expedited Arbitration

Most of the delay in arbitration cases results from cumbersome internal grievance processes, the use of three-person panels, dickering over the choice of an arbitrator or chairperson, the use of legal counsel at hearings, and long waits between the hearing and the issuing of an award. To counter these difficulties, a number of expedited (speeded-up) arbitration systems have been developed both by governments and by unions and management working on their own. Though there are certain differences between the various systems, most observe the principles in Table 13.2.

"ALTERNATIVE DISPUTE RESOLUTION"
www.chapmantripp.co.nz:80/publish/adr.htm

The Canadian Railway Office of Arbitration (CROA) is a good example of a private sector arbitration system that has earned its spurs. This system, which has been in effect since 1965 (Button, 1990:30), uses a standing umpire who normally hears cases starting on the second Tuesday of each month (Button, 1990:36). The umpire will sit for up to three days if necessary (Button, 1990:39), hearing on average 13 cases at a sitting (Button, 1990:36). The grouping of cases means that where there is a delay in one case (as when the parties decide to try to settle the matter themselves)

Table 13.2
THE WAY TO QUICKER ARBITRATION DECISIONS[16]

1) Always use a single arbitrator rather than a three-person panel.

2) Where possible, have a standing umpire who will hear cases at the same time each week or month (i.e., the third Thursday). This allows him or her to hear a number of cases on the same day. It also ensures that the arbitrator "knows the business" and eliminates dickering over fees, since the umpire will be on monthly or annual retainer.

3) If a standing umpire isn't possible, then draw from a list you have agreed on in advance in an order you have agreed on in advance (i.e., alphabetical order), so as to eliminate dickering over the choice of an arbitrator.

4) Agree not to use legal counsel, or at least to restrict its use to complicated policy grievances.

5) Eliminate steps of the internal grievance procedure that don't seem to be producing any significant number of settlements, and consider replacing them with grievance mediation (discussed below).

6) Adhere strictly to time limits in any remaining steps.

7) Simplify procedural requirements as much as possible, by allowing oral decisions in straightforward cases, reducing the use of precedents, and requiring short written decisions very soon after the hearing.[17]

the umpire can simply move on to the next and return to the first when the parties are ready to proceed. Cases are presented in the form of written briefs, which reduces (though it hasn't completely eliminated) the use of legal counsel at hearings (Button, 1990:37).[18] A CROA umpire, M.G. Picher, has suggested that the use of written briefs saves time by helping the arbitrator to focus on the material at hand and reducing the need for rambling, long-winded oral argumentation (Button, 1990). In 1987–1988, the CROA simplified its procedures further by deciding to limit the use of counsel to discharge cases, unless the parties agreed otherwise (Button, 1990). The system has resulted in significant cost savings. For 1987–1988, the average cost per case was $1295 (Button, 1990:41), or 29 percent that of cases heard under conventional arbitration in the province (Rose, 1987). Best of all, the system has succeeded in doing what arbitration was originally intended to do: provide a quick, relatively inexpensive mechanism for resolving disputes over the interpretation of the collective agreement (Rose, 1987:43).

Though the CROA system of expedited arbitration is perhaps the country's best-known private sector system, it is not the only one. An essentially similar grievance commissioner system was adopted in 1972 by Inco and two United Steelworkers locals (Thornicroft and Eden, 1995:273). And in Vancouver, the once strike-plagued longshoring industry has long relied on a "dockside arbitrator" who is on call

24 hours a day and, travelling by motor launch or helicopter if necessary, can be on the site anywhere in the port within an hour or two to render an instant on-the-spot decision orally (J. Weiler, 1984).[19] At various times, other expedited systems have been used in the garment, motor transport, and auto industry in Canada, as well as in numerous American industries (Gandz and Whitehead, 1989:251–252).

As we noted in the labour law chapter, public expedited arbitration systems are in place in four provinces (B.C., Manitoba, Ontario, and Saskatchewan). In all four, expedited arbitration can be combined with prior grievance mediation,[20] further reducing costs and increasing the number of cases resolved. Section 49 of the Ontario act sets out that province's expedited arbitration procedure. Under the *OLRA,* either party may apply to the Labour Minister for appointment of a single arbitrator. The arbitrator, drawn from a list maintained by the ministry, must schedule a hearing within 21 days of the request (section 49[7]) and issue an award within 21 days of the hearing. If both parties agree, the arbitrator may deliver an oral decision immediately after the hearing (section 49[8]). The Ontario legislation also makes provision for prior grievance mediation through a med-arb procedure (section 50).

Over the years, expedited arbitration has become increasingly popular in Ontario. By 1992–1993, some 45 percent of all arbitration awards in the province were of the expedited variety, as compared to 19 percent in 1981–1982 (Thornicroft and Eden, 1995:272). The system has been shown to save both time and money. According to Rose (1991), between 1980–1981 and 1985–1986, expedited arbitration alone saved $2.2 million; prior grievance mediation saved a further $6.4 million. Time savings were even greater, as the average elapsed time between the incident giving rise to the grievance and an expedited award was only four months, compared to eleven months under conventional arbitration (Thornicroft and Eden, 1995:272).

Grievance Mediation

One criticism of all arbitration systems, even the best-designed expedited ones, is that they serve to foster an adversarial mentality by establishing a "winner" and a "loser," thus damaging ongoing relationships (Elliott and Goss, 1994). Grievance mediation, used either on its own or in conjunction with a system of expedited arbitration, can get around this difficulty by helping the parties to resolve their own differences. Instead of damaging the ongoing relationship, it can actually strengthen it by developing problem-solving skills that can later be applied to other areas of the relationship. In addition, its costs are quite low compared to those of arbitration.[21] Arbitration is still available should the parties fail to resolve their dispute on their own. The process is confidential in that, unless both parties consent, nothing said or done there can be used as evidence in subsequent legal proceedings (Thornicroft and Eden, 1995:273). Normally no formal record of the proceedings is kept, except to record any agreement reached (Elliott and Goss, 1994:32). As well, settlements are without prejudice to either party, which means that no precedent created by the settlement can be used in any future cases (Thornicroft and Eden, 1995:273).

 ### "APPROPRIATE DISPUTE RESOLUTION: WHAT IS MEDIATION?"
www.mbnet.ca/~psim/adr3.html

Mediation focusses on effective communication and negotiation skills (Elliott and Goss, 1994:27). The mediator's role is not to "settle" the dispute, but to help the parties communicate and negotiate more effectively, thus increasing the likelihood they will reach agreement on their own (Elliott and Goss, 1994). A typical mediation session might consist of the following four stages (Elliott and Goss, 1994:27–29):

1) Introduction. Here, the mediator explains the process and his or her role and seeks to create an atmosphere in which the parties feel free to speak openly. It is at this time that the ground rules for mediation are laid out.

2) Creating an agenda. Where the parties have not agreed on an agenda beforehand, one is established, normally through brief presentations by the parties outlining the issues they would like to see resolved. After the presentations, which would normally be followed by clarifying questions from the other side and the mediator, key points are identified to form the agenda.

3) Discussing interests. Here, each party has the opportunity to present their side of the story. The mediator will seek clarification of anything that appears unclear and will also seek to ensure that each party hears and understand the other's perspective, whether or not they agree with it. At this stage, common ground and agreed-upon facts are identified, in addition to any facts that may be in dispute. It is at this stage that the mediator seeks to reduce the dispute to its basic elements and to focus on the parties' underlying needs and interests.

4) Problem solving. Here, the mediator takes the information obtained in the previous stages and uses it to help the parties find a mutually agreeable solution, initiating suggestions for a possible solution where appropriate (Thornicroft and Eden, 1995:273). This may be done on either an issue-by-issue or "total package" basis.

The decision as to the best time to use mediation is often a judgment call. Ideally, it should be used at the earliest possible point in the dispute; where a relationship is very poor, it may even be used before the usual Stage 1 grievance meeting (Elliott and Goss, 1994:29). Often, the best stage can be determined empirically, from an examination of settlement rates at different points of the agreement's internal griev-ance process. If there is any step where settlement rates are particularly low, that would be a good place to insert grievance mediation (see Elliott and Goss, 1994:29–30).

Grievance mediation has been used in four provinces, most often as a first stage in an expedited arbitration process. In Ontario, Rose (1991) found that voluntary grievance mediation had saved some $6.4 million between 1980–1981 and 1985–1986. As of the early 1990s (Craig and Solomon, 1996:351), about 80 percent of all expedited arbitration cases were being resolved through mediation. Unfortunately, the Ontario government has since discontinued this most useful and innovative program. However, it remains in effect in Alberta, Manitoba, and B.C., where similar results have been obtained (Elliott and Goss, 1994:41–52), and in the private sector in the United States.[22] For example, in the American bituminous coal industry (Brett and Goldberg, 1983), an industry long notorious for its poor labour-management relations, 153 grievances were mediated between 1980 and 1982. Of these, 89 percent were resolved without arbitration. Likewise, of 2220 grievances mediated by the Chicago-based Mediation Research and Education Project between 1980 and 1982, about 85 percent were resolved without arbitration (Elliott and Goss, 1994:52).[23]

Preventive Mediation

While it is good to reduce the costs and time delays of arbitration through an expe-dited arbitration process, and better to use grievance mediation to prevent grievances from even being taken through to arbitration, it's best of all, where possible, to improve the labour-management relationship so that problems are handled proac-tively, as they arise, before they become formal grievances. This is where preventive mediation comes in. Designed to overcome the problems resulting from mutual mis-trust and poor communications, preventive mediation programs in the federal juris-diction and most provinces seek to help management and unions build and maintain constructive and cooperative working relationships (HRDC, 1994). To this end, a number of the programs, including those of Ontario (Bergman, 1988) and the feder-al jurisdiction (HRDC, 1994) use Relations by Objectives (RBO) workshops to help the parties hone their communications and joint problem-solving skills. A key princi-ple of all preventive mediation programs is that they are purely voluntary (HRDC, 1994; Joyce, 1996).

The federal program includes six components: establishing a labour-management committee, negotiation skills training, committee effectiveness training, relationship by objectives, grievance mediation, and facilitation. The various provincial programs appear to have a fairly similar emphasis, although there are certain differences; for example, the Newfoundland program includes joint supervisor-steward training in collective agreement administration (Joyce, 1996).

Unfortunately, there has thus far been little in the way of evaluation of the various preventive mediation programs. However, some anecdotal evidence (i.e., Joyce, 1996) suggests that the programs have been effective and have found favour with both management and unions. On the RBO workshops that are an important component of many preventive mediation programs, a study by Bergman (1988) found that union-management relationships had improved after the workshops and that participants attributed at least some of the improvement to the RBO experience (Bergman, 1988; Downie, 1989:270).[24]

GRIEVANCES AND INDUSTRIAL CONFLICT MORE GENERALLY

The grievance procedure is a crucial element of the Canadian IR system since it provides workers with some measure of workplace voice and a certain degree of protection against arbitrary dismissal or disciplinary action. While the grievance system appears generally to have worked reasonably well during the early postwar period, since then it has often been criticized for its slowness, costliness, and growing legalism, which taken together have meant that only a very small proportion of all grievances are ever taken through to arbitration.

INTERNATIONAL AGREEMENTS ON LABOUR COOPERATION
206.191.130/doc/nafta/eng/e

In response to these serious criticisms of the conventional arbitration process, governments, unions, and management have developed a broad range of innovative new dispute settlement mechanisms, of which the most important are expedited arbitration, grievance mediation, and preventive mediation. The evidence suggests that grievance mediation has helped resolve a large proportion of grievances without the need for arbitration, and that expedited arbitration has helped to provide a speedier, less legalistic, and less expensive forum for the disposition of unavoidable grievances. While we lack hard evidence on the success of preventive mediation programs, anecdotal evidence to date indicates that these programs have generally had at least some success in improving union-management relations.

Though these and other innovative new dispute settlement mechanisms[25] have contributed significantly to reducing workplace conflict in Canada, major sources of conflict remain unaddressed. One important source of conflict is unions' "ownership" of the grievance process. As noted earlier, an individual cannot normally file a grievance independently; only a union can do so. Inevitably, unions' ownership of the process means that a certain number of grievances will be used for political purposes—perhaps to be traded off for other grievances or even for certain collective agreement provisions. Particularly where labour-management relations are already poor, it also means that large numbers of grievances may be filed not because people feel their collective agreement rights have been violated, but simply as a pressure tactic, perhaps to protest the slow pace of negotiations or an arbitrary management action on some other front.[26] For its part, management may respond by stonewalling, that is refusing to deal with outstanding grievances for a more or less indefinite period of time. While perfectly legal, this kind of use of the grievance process increases labour-management conflict in a number of different ways. First, it overloads the grievance process so that legitimate (perhaps even serious) problems may not be addressed for far too long. Second, particularly when management stonewalls, it becomes extremely difficult to distinguish individual problems from broader political issues. Third, to the extent that individuals' grievances are not addressed in timely fashion, it decreases individuals' satisfaction with both the employer and the union, leading both to increased worker-management conflict and increased intraorganizational conflict within the union.

One could also argue that in the Canadian IR system, the grievance process is simply asked to do far too much. Not only does it serve as a vehicle for individual workplace voice; it must also serve as a vehicle for group and in some cases collective voice. In addition, as we noted earlier, it often serves as a forum for informal union-management negotiations and as a mechanism for helping to resolve intraorganizational conflict within both unions and management groups. Perhaps all this is really more than should be asked of any single process.

The impact of these sources of conflict is likely to be most severe in the public sector, where the grievance procedure has, in addition, extra stress put on it due to the restriction in the scope of bargainable issues in that sector and governments' growing tendency to curtail collective bargaining as such. While these sources of conflict exist in both the public and private sectors, in the latter the parties have clear economic incentives to reduce their effects as much as possible. Money spent on conflict resolution is money not available for profits, wages, or jobs. Recognition of this basic fact has led a growing number of private sector firms and unions to seek to reduce the time and money costs of workplace conflict as much as possible. To this end, they have created joint committees and, in some cases, other informal forums for addressing at least certain types of workplace problems outside of the grievance process. In the public sector, where a bottom line as such does not exist, at least not to the same extent, the costs of conflict are less readily apparent, and thus there is less immediate incentive to reduce those costs. Yet the extent of workplace conflict in the public sector may now be even greater than in the private sector, owing to the general restriction of collective bargaining and its consequent inability to serve as a mechanism for reducing conflict. Thus the real need for mechanisms that can help prevent conflict or reduce its effects may be even greater there.[27]

One way to reduce some of the strain on the seriously overloaded grievance process might be to allow any worker to file a dismissal grievance independent of his or her union, on condition he or she was willing to bear half the costs. Beyond that, unions, management, and governments alike will need to continue to search for flexible, creative, and low-cost mechanisms for defusing workplace conflict.

QUESTIONS FOR DISCUSSION

1) If you are in a union, read your collective agreement's grievance procedure. How many steps does it contain? Can time limits be waived? If a grievance is sent to arbitration, will there be a single arbitrator or a three-person panel? If you aren't a union member, find and read a collective agreement and answer the same questions.

2) What are some benefits of the grievance process to workers, unions, and organizations? In your view, do the benefits outweigh the drawbacks?

3) Why has grievance arbitration become a lengthy, costly, and legalistic process?

4) List the steps in a "typical" grievance procedure.

5) Describe a typical arbitration hearing.

6) What seem to be the key factors in determining whether someone filing a dismissal grievance is reinstated or not?

7) Discuss some ways in which Canadian unions, management organizations, and governments have tried to speed up the arbitration process and reduce the number of grievances being sent to arbitration.

8) What are some inherent sources of grievance activity, particularly in the public sector? If you were an IR director in the public sector, how might you try to go about reducing grievances in your organization?

9) How has your view of the grievance process changed as a result of your having read this chapter?

10) Would you be more or less likely to reinstate Sally Renwick than you would have been after you first read the Westgate Widget case? If your position has changed, explain why.

11) What lessons does the Westgate Widget case have to teach about the relationship between grievances and organizations' overall management practice?

496 CANADIAN INDUSTRIAL RELATIONS

SUGGESTIONS FOR FURTHER READING

Barnacle, Peter. (1991). *Arbitration of discharge grievances in Ontario: Outcomes and reinstatement experiences.* Kingston: Queen's IRC Research and Current Issues Series No. 62. Not hammock reading by any means, but an astoundingly thorough and systematic analysis of discharge outcomes and reinstatement experiences in more than 800 Ontario discharge cases. Similar studies are badly needed for other jurisdictions.

Brett, Jeanne, and Stephen Goldberg. (1983). "Grievance mediation in the coal industry: A field experiment." *Industrial and Labor Relations Review, 37.* A groundbreaking early study of grievance mediation in one of the United States's most conflict-ridden industries.

Elliott, David, and Joanne Goss. (1994). *Grievance mediation: How and why it works.* Aurora, ON: Canada Law Book Co. A bit evangelical at times, but contains a wealth of information about how to conduct grievance mediation and the results of grievance mediation in both Canada and the United States.

Rose, Joseph. (1986b). "Statutory expedited grievance arbitration: The case of Ontario." *Arbitration Journal, 41:4.* Important early study of the results of Ontario's expedited arbitration system.

Weiler, Joseph. (1984). "Grievance arbitration: The new wave." In J. Weiler and P. Gall (Eds.), *The labour code of British Columbia in the 1980s.* Calgary and Vancouver: Carswell. Interesting and well-written discussion of a number of alternatives to conventional arbitration, including the Port of Vancouver's "dockside arbitration" system, by a man who served for many years as the port's arbitrator.

ENDNOTES

[1] At least one recent Canadian writer (Haiven, 1990) is critical of the ban on mid-term strikes.

[2] The grievance process is often used for this purpose in the public service or other branches of the public sector, where (as noted in Chapter 9), the scope of bargainable issues is generally considerably restricted.

[3] At the University of Ottawa (University of Ottawa, 1994), such grievances are initiated at step three of the grievance procedure. As well, the potentially greater seriousness of group grievances is reflected by the fact that they are initiated at step two of the procedure.

[4] This case has been adapted from one used by Peach and Kuechle (1975). The author has condensed and adapted this case with the permission of the copyright holder, Ivey Management Services. Reproduction of this material is prohibited. Further, this material is not covered under authorization from CanCopy or any other reproduction rights organization.

[5] This figure would almost certainly overrepresent the proportion of discharge and discipline-related grievances, given that unions send most discharge grievances through to arbitration.

[6] The majority of discharges under this category relate to illegal work stoppages. Others relate to refusals to cross picket lines, to union organizing, or to the conduct of union business.

[7] Of course, a useful way around this particular problem would to be appoint a standing umpire who knew the industry.

[8] Goldblatt (1974) found that cases involving a single arbitrator were settled, on average, about 50 days sooner than those involving a three-person panel. Rose (1987) found that in Ontario during the early 1980s, the difference was 131 days.

[9] Sack also advises grievors to list their attempts to seek employment and the responses they have made, so they can prove to employers that they have made an honest attempt to mitigate (lessen) the damages resulting from the dismissal.

[10] See Sack (1994:141–142) for an interesting and somewhat more detailed discussion of the issues covered in this section.

[11] For a useful if brief review of these studies, see Thornicroft and Eden (1995:262–265 and 268–270).

[12] Such programs have now been established in four provinces: Newfoundland, Ontario, Alberta, and British Columbia. For a brief description, see Thornicroft and Eden (1995:264–265).

[13] For an original and thought-provoking critique of progressive discipline and the assumptions behind it, see Eden (1992).

[14] Admittedly, Barnacle's sample of non-lawyer arbitrators was very small, since more than 80 percent of his arbitrators were lawyers.

[15] In fairness, Canada Post has, since 1992, been using an expedited arbitration system for many of its grievances. This system, which features an agreement with the union not to use lawyers, minimal use of witnesses, and the exchange of essential documents a week before arbitration hearings, has resulted in quicker handling of arbitration cases (Casselman, 1998). It should also be noted that discharge grievances are not handled through this system, except with the agreement of both parties, and decisions are not precedent-setting (Casselman, 1998). Despite the expedited system, the backlog of unsettled grievances remains large(almost 100 000 cases—although this represents a smaller number than was often the case in the past (Casselman, 1998).

[16] This list is an adaptation and expansion of one developed by Rose (1987).

[17] Some organizations set a maximum length for decisions under their expedited arbitration programs; others do not allow reasons with decisions.

[18] Counsel can, of course, be used to prepare the briefs, but this doesn't affect the course of the hearing, though it does affect the cost of the process.

[19] As Craig and Solomon (1996:352) note, the oral decision takes effect immediately, but must be confirmed by a brief written decision as soon as possible (normally within 48 hours).

[20] Sometimes called something else, but the process is generally pretty much the same.

[21] Elliott and Goss (1994:18) estimate that grievance mediation costs are less than 15 percent those of arbitration.

[22] As Thornicroft and Eden (1995) note, there is little evidence available on private sector grievance mediation results in Canada.

[23] For more detailed results of grievance mediation in the American private sector, see Feuille (1992). Feuille's study also includes cost and time data.

24 See Downie (1989) for a more detailed discussion of RBO and other related organizational development techniques.

25 See Elliott and Goss (1994) for a detailed discussion of a broad range of these mechanisms.

26 Again, this has often been the case with Canada Post. Stewart-Patterson (1987) indicates that during the 1980s, a sizeable proportion of all grievances filed against the corporation had nothing to do with the collective agreement as such.

27 All this isn't to suggest that such mechanisms don't exist there (for an example, consider the Ontario Crown Employees' Settlement Board discussed by Thornicroft and Eden at p. 274). It is to suggest that there may be certain obstacles to the creation of such mechanisms in the public sector.

CHAPTER 14

KEY THEMES AND ISSUES

Homework: a blessing or a curse?

In this chapter, we step back from the examination of specific issues and topics that has dominated the previous chapters, with an eye to seeing where the Canadian IR system as a whole has been going, and where it may be headed in the years to come. The chapter centres on seven key themes that, in our view, raise critical issues of public labour policy. It features a look at these seven key themes and at some important findings related to each, as well a discussion of policy suggestions arising out of each theme. The chapter closes with a brief discussion of areas where further IR research appears to be most urgently needed.

This book has tried to provide an introductory survey of industrial relations that is both comprehensive and comprehensible. Along the way, we have examined such diverse topics as the Canadian economy's impact on management practice and the types of actions unions engage in, the growth of a broad range of employment legislation, and such forms of industrial conflict as strikes and grievances.

In this chapter, the aim is to try to put the pieces together, and to take a broader look at the Canadian IR system and some of the directions in which it seems to be headed. We will do this through an examination of seven key themes that, to some extent at least, seem to cut across the specific treatment of various topics in the previous thirteen chapters and raise important issues for IR policy-makers. In what follows, we start by looking at the themes themselves.

LABOUR NET (CANADA)
www.labournet.ca

KEY THEMES

The first of the seven key themes (see Figure 14.1) is the increasingly precarious nature of work in today's globalized and highly competitive economy—a fact that has important implications for all the actors in the IR system. Our examination of today's economy in Chapter 2 suggests that the past decade's changes have gone far beyond those normally associated with fluctuations of the business cycle. Quite simply, the world of work is a fundamentally different and far less secure place than it was 50 or even 15 years ago. Due largely to such developments as globalization, trade liberalization, deindustrialization, and governments' growing preoccupation with deficits and the debt, unemployment has remained stubbornly high throughout the past decade, and even most of those who have jobs enjoy little real job security, and are often working far longer hours than workers of their parents' generation did. As Chapter 3 shows, Canadian management has responded to the tougher economic environment in various ways. On the one hand, many firms have sought to motivate workers and involve them more directly in their work through such innovative practices as self-directed work teams, job rotation, and total quality management. On the other hand, in many firms there appears to have been at least a partial reversion to the coercive drive approach that prevailed prior to the First World War. The growing lack of job security is a key element of that approach, as are the low pay, minimal benefits, irregular hours, and enforced overtime found throughout much of the economy, but especially in the private service sector, which in recent years has been the major source of new jobs.

Related to the precarious nature of work is the continued, even growing, lack of meaningful representation for many workers. Only about one-third of all Canadian non-farm workers are union members, and only a slightly higher proportion than that are covered by a collective agreement. Despite the Charter, many still don't even enjoy the legal right to join a union. In the private service sector, determined employer opposition will make it extremely difficult for unions to make appreciable headway, as is evidenced by the McDonald's chain's willingness to close a legally certified branch at Saint-Hubert, Quebec, rather than operate it as a unionized establishment (King, 1998). Elsewhere, the growth of self-employment, homeworking, and short-term and contractual work arrangements seems likely to pose equally severe challenges for unions. In the public sector, membership rates have remained high, but the actual number of members has already begun to fall in some sub-sectors, owing to reductions in employment levels. This trend seems likely to continue, if not accelerate, in the future. An equally disturbing trend is the continuing lack of meaningful bargaining rights for public sector union members. This issue is of sufficient importance that we will treat it as a separate theme later in the section.

LABORNET (USA)
www.igc.org/labornet

The third major theme, and one related to both the two previous ones, is the restructuring and reordering of the labour movement to enable it to meet the serious representational challenges posed by today's economy. As we noted in Chapter 5, the Canadian labour movement has historically been quite fragmented by international standards. Smaller unions generally find it more difficult to carry out such activities as organizing, research, publicity, and legislative lobbying, all of which are critical for unions operating in the current environment. In recent years, there have been a number of important union mergers, such as that of the Communications, Energy, and Paperworkers' unions. Big industrial unions like the Auto Workers and Steelworkers have also expanded their traditional boundaries and have begun organizing workers in the private service sector (Murray, 1995; Murdock, 1997). There has also been a growing recognition that the Canadian labour movement will need to form effective sectoral alliances with unions in other countries, particularly the United States and Mexico, if it hopes to deal with the giant multinational corporations on anything approaching even terms (Lipsig-Mumme, 1995).

"THE REORGANIZATION OF THE WORKPLACE IN SERVICE INDUSTRIES"
socrates.berkeley.edu/~iir/ncw/wpapers/bailey_b/index

Related to the labour movement's restructuring is its expansion of its traditional range of activities. In addition to collective bargaining, grievance-handling, and political activities, Canadian unions have become involved in a broad range of business ventures. While such involvement has not been without controversy, inside the labour movement or outside it, a growing number of unions and labour federations have come to see it as an essential tool for preserving members' jobs. The same can be said of unions' involvement in joint governance ventures with management, something that has become an especially prominent feature of the Quebec IR scene in recent years. And many unions, particularly in the public sector, have also begun to go in for a broad range of publicity campaigns. As for organizing, a number of unions have changed their approach to better reach the women, ethnic minority group members, and part-time workers they will need to attract if they are to maintain their membership levels. Among other things, this revamped organizing approach has meant that women are now organizing women, and immigrants, their fellow immigrants (Galt, 1994). In place of the economic cost-benefit calculus used by most traditional male organizers, many of the new organizers are focussing more on empowerment in their bid to sign up new members (Bronfenbrenner, 1992; Crain, 1994).

The four remaining themes all relate more or less directly to government's role in the IR system, both as the regulator of that system and as the provider of public services and employer of public sector workers. As will soon become readily apparent, that role, and in particular government's attitude towards workers and unions, has changed significantly over the past two decades (see Godard, 1994:262–274).

FIGURE 14.1

SEVEN KEY THEMES

1) Increasingly precarious nature of work.

2) Continuing lack of meaningful worker representation.

3) Restructuring of the Canadian labour movement.

4) Individualization of labour law.

5) Restriction of public sector bargaining.

6) Development of innovative new conflict resolution methods.

7) Shift in government's role in the IR system.

The first of these four themes has to do with what, for want of a better term, might be described as a tendency towards the "individualization" of labour- and employment-related law. In recent years, the vast majority of new legislative initiatives in these areas have addressed individual, as opposed to collective, rights (see Adell, 1988b). In particular, there has been a dramatic expansion of human rights legislation. However, there have been remarkably few new initiatives aimed at enhancing workers' collective right to form unions, to strike, or to carry out other union activities. Though labour relations legislation as such has not changed significantly over the past two decades, workers' collective unionization rights may now be less well-protected than they were, owing both to incremental legislative changes such as a shift from a card count to a vote as evidence of certification in several jurisdictions, and a growing tendency to interpret collective agreements in the light of anti-discrimination provisions contained in human rights acts (Carter, 1997). While this new "duty to accommodate" the needs of minority group members and people with disabilities has been held to apply even to the extent of rewriting collective agreement provisions or agreeing to waive their application (Carter, 1997:197–198), the Charter's freedom of association clause has not been found to provide any protection for such basic union rights as the right to join a union, to strike, or to picket (England, 1988). Taken together, such developments signal a definite if gradual shift in legislative emphasis away from collective rights and in the direction of individual rights (see Adell, 1988b).

A far more dramatic public policy shift has been the virtual abolition of free collective bargaining in much of the public sector. Across the country, open public sector bargaining has become more the exception than the rule, as governments have used legislation to extract concessions from their own employees, rather than attempting to do so at the bargaining table (Swimmer and Thompson, 1995:1). Moreover, even where collective bargaining has been conducted, the public sector unions have had a hard time advancing their members' interests at the table, due to the generally severe restrictions governments place on the scope of issues they are prepared to negotiate (Fryer, 1995). The increasing restrictions placed on this country's public sector workers have had important implications for the IR system as a whole, as we will see in later sections of this chapter.

CANADIAN POLICY RESEARCH NETWORKS
www.cprn.com

A third public policy theme relates to the many new, often quite innovative, ways that governments have devised for reducing union-management conflict. These have ranged from a transformation of the conciliation process into something more closely resembling mediation (Carter, 1995) to the establishment of expedited arbitration, grievance mediation, and preventive mediation programs in many jurisdictions. Such developments, together with several provincial governments' assumption of responsibility for the training of arbitrators (Thornicroft and Eden, 1995:264–265), indicate a pattern of increased government intervention in the conflict resolution process. Given the high costs and lengthy delays of the conventional arbitration process, in particular (Thornicroft and Eden, 1995:261, 266–267), government-sponsored alternatives have generally been welcomed by both managers and union officials. However, the new conflict-resolution techniques appear to have been only partially successful in reducing union-management conflict, for reasons we will be discussing shortly.

Our fourth and final public policy theme concerns a different kind of shift in governments' conception of their role in the IR system, and of the significance of labour relations legislation to society. In the past, governments viewed their regulatory role primarily as that of keeping the peace. Collective bargaining, as the preamble to the 1984 version of Ontario's *Labour Relations Act* indicated, was to be fostered as a positive public policy leading both to improved union-management relations and greater democracy in society as a whole. Today, governments are more apt to view their role in the IR system as that of facilitating, if not directly promoting, economic growth. This change in emphasis has been reflected in the officially stated purposes of the current (1995) version of the *OLRA*.[1] While facilitating collective bargaining and promoting the expeditious resolution of workplace disputes are two of those purposes, several of the other purposes have a more purely economic emphasis. These include recognition of the importance of workplace parties' adapting to change, the promotion of flexibility, productivity, and employee involvement in the workplace, and, most important of all, recognition of "the importance of economic growth as the foundation for mutually beneficial relations amongst employers, employees and trade unions" (*OLRA*, section 2[5]). To the extent that this kind of shift in emphasis is indeed reflected in Canadian labour legislation, the implications for the IR system could be profound.[2]

KEY FINDINGS

Precarious Employment

Chapter 2 offered detailed evidence of the growing precariousness of employment in Canada. To begin with, even official unemployment rates have remained stubbornly high, particularly in the Atlantic region and among youth. When discouraged workers, involuntary students, and involuntary part-time workers are factored in (O'Hara, 1993; Peirce, 1998a), it becomes clear that the official rates, as bad as they are, have for some time significantly understated the extent of the country's unemployment problem (see Figure 14.2). An especially disturbing development has been a sharp increase in the average duration of unemployment, which nearly doubled between 1980 and 1991 (Gunderson and Riddell, 1993).

We also noted in Chapter 2 that the wave of mergers, restructuring, and downsizing that has occurred throughout the past fifteen years has left few unscathed (Donner, 1994). Public sector workers, once reasonably well protected from layoffs, have been as hard hit as their private sector counterparts, as have large numbers of managers (Payne, 1998) and people with graduate and professional degrees, including many in computer-related industries (Bryan, 1998).

Even those still employed have been forced to adjust to profound changes in the way in which work is organized and scheduled, changes that have made many jobs far more difficult and stressful and that have reduced employment security for large numbers of Canadians. As Chapter 2 pointed out, there have been large increases in the rate of part-time, temporary, and contractual work, home-based work, and self-employment. In all, such "atypical" arrangements have very nearly become the norm, with only 54 percent of all employed workers putting in standard hours as of 1995 (Sheridan, Sunter, and Diverty, 1996). While the conditions under which home-based and contractual employees work vary enormously, relatively few of these employees enjoy fringe benefits, and many don't have the right to join a union.

CENTRE FOR THE STUDY OF LIVING STANDARDS
www.csls.ca

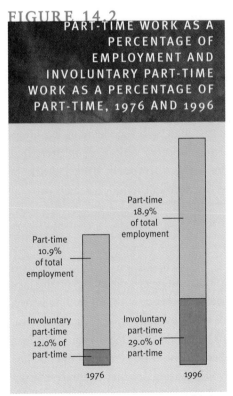

FIGURE 14.2

PART-TIME WORK AS A PERCENTAGE OF EMPLOYMENT AND INVOLUNTARY PART-TIME WORK AS A PERCENTAGE OF PART-TIME, 1976 AND 1996

Part-time
18.9%
of total
employment

Part-time
10.9%
of total
employment

Involuntary
part-time
12.0% of
part-time

Involuntary
part-time
29.0% of
part-time

1976   1996

Source: Part-time employment: CLMPC, Table A1 (1976); Statistics Canada, Cat. No. 71-201-XPB (1996). Involuntary part-time: CLMPC, Table A2 (1976 and 1996); Statistics Canada Cat. No. 71-001-XPB, Table 19 (1996).

Not the least disturbing aspect of the unemployment situation is that high rates of unemployment and underemployment continue to exist alongside a rapidly growing rate of overtime(much of it unpaid. In all, nearly one-fifth of all Canadian workers put in paid or unpaid overtime in 1997, the average amount worked over the first four months of that year being nine hours (*Better Times*, 9/97).

Both unemployment and overwork can be very bad for people's physical and mental health. The links between high unemployment and increased incidence of such "social pathologies" as liver cirrhosis, mental hospital admissions, and crime have been known for some time (see Carrothers, 1979). More recently, it has been observed that overworked, stressed-out workers are more likely to be absent from work (Shellenbarger, 1998) and to face more or less serious conflicts between their work and their family responsibilities (Coates, 1991; Duxbury, Higgins, Lee, and Mills, 1991). The combined stress resulting from economic insecurity and overwork seems to have been particularly hard on women, who (for the most part) continue to bear the major portion of family responsibilities (Coates, 1991; CLC, 1997). While some unions, including most notably the Communications, Energy and Paperworkers, have sought to achieve shorter hours through collective bargaining, the labour movement itself is not unanimous on this issue (Jackson, 1997), and in any case efforts to achieve shorter hours often meet with determined resistance from employers, who would rather work existing workers harder than bring in additional ones.

Recently, there has been growing awareness that the ongoing wave of layoffs and restructuring not only isn't good for workers, but may be bad for business as well. A recent study by Conference Board of Canada researcher Carolyn Farquhar (Bryan, 1998) suggests that most major restructurings have failed to achieve the objective of improving long-term profitability and that companies that downsized showed no performance gains compared with other companies after two or three years. Indeed, virtually all the cuts were eventually reversed through new hiring because companies found they simply couldn't do without the skills of the large numbers of middle managers who had been laid off (Bryan, 1998).

There is also good reason to believe that today's growing lack of employment security may be a cause of workplace conflict, as it frequently was around the turn of the century (see Chapter 3 for a detailed discussion of this issue). At Starbucks coffee shops in B.C., for example, workers' desire for adequate and regular working hours has been a major impetus behind a Canadian Auto Workers' unionization drive that has succeeded in organizing a number of the shops (Murdock, 1997). Lack of employment security also appears to have been an issue in the unionization drive at McDonald's (see King, 1998).

Lack of Representation

Chapters 5 and 8 offer evidence as to the continuing and, very possibly, growing lack of meaningful representation for Canadian workers. To begin with, more than fifteen years after the freedom of association provisions of the Charter took effect, the members of many occupational groups continue to be denied the legal right to join a union. While the exclusion of management and confidential IR personnel may be justifiable, given public policymakers' desire to avoid creating conflict-of-interest situations, the same cannot be said of the exclusion of professionals, agricultural workers, and domestics, all of whom are denied unionization rights in a number of jurisdictions (Peirce, 1989). There is good reason to believe that these continuing exclusions may be associated with lower overall union membership rates. In general, the provinces with restrictive exclusion policies have significantly lower membership rates than those with more liberal policies in this area. To make matters worse, a number of the groups excluded from unionization are also excluded from protection under various areas of employment legislation, as we pointed out in Chapter 7. As a result, a number of the country's least fortunate workers not only enjoy no meaningful workplace representation, but little or no protection with regard to such matters as hours of work and overtime.

As of 1997, fewer than 35 percent of the country's paid non-agricultural workers were union members, and well below half were covered by a collective agreement. In much of the private sector, union membership rates have already begun to drop due both to structural shifts in employment and a decline in density rates within individual sectors. As a result, there are many fewer union members in such traditional union strongholds as manufacturing and construction than there were two decades ago. The pressures on union membership are likely to be even more severe in the years ahead (Murray, 1995), given the far greater rate of employment growth in the private service sector than in either the private goods-producing sector or the public sector. While membership rates have increased in the private service sector, thanks in part to determined organizing drives by a number of unions, they remain very low there compared to rates in most of the rest of the economy. For example, in 1997, only about 10 percent of those employed in trade and finance/insurance/real estate were union members (Akyeampong, 1997). Given the difficulty and expense of organizing unions in this sector, and continuing determined employer resistance to unionization, it seems unlikely that membership rates in this area will ever approach rates in the good-producing or public sectors, or that increases there will make up for the losses attributable to deindustrialization and public sector cutbacks.

Other trends that seem likely to lead to a decline in union membership include the growth of small and medium-sized businesses, at the expense of larger ones, and the growth in part-time and other forms of insecure employment. As we noted in Chapter 5, membership rates are a good deal lower in small and medium-sized businesses than they are in larger ones, and for part-time as opposed to full-time workers. As for the effect of other trends, people working at home are extremely difficult to organize, and those on short-term contracts are often ineligible for membership (as in the federal public service). For the growing numbers of self-employed individuals, union membership is generally a moot point (see Figure 14.3).

The increase in layoffs and growing lack of job security could affect union membership in another way, as well. In today's economy, far fewer workers than in the past seem likely to stay with firms for a long time. Given that membership rates are far higher among workers with long job tenure, the trend towards declining job security seems likely to lead to a long-term decline in membership rates.

FIGURE 14.3

SOME KEY FINDINGS

- Increased overtime exists alongside continuing high unemployment.
- A growing number of workers are employed on a part-time, temporary, or contractual basis and have few, if any, benefits.
- Many groups continue to be denied the right to join unions.
- Traditional industrial unions are becoming larger and are representing more workers from many different industrial sectors.
- More jurisdictions have enacted employer freedom to communicate provisions.
- Denial of basic bargaining rights and governments' hard line on pay equity have led to increased conflict in the public sector.
- Expedited arbitration and grievance mediation programs have resulted in substantial savings in time and money.
- Governments increasingly view their role in the IR system as that of promoting economic development.

Finally, continuing government deregulation and privatization are likely to reduce union membership rates in a number of different sectors. In health care, the move towards community-based care is leading towards an increase in the contracting-out of services formerly provided by publicly funded bodies (Haiven, 1995), most of whose staff were traditionally unionized. This trend will almost certainly lead to a reduction in union membership rates, given that the subcontractors are far less likely to be unionized. Similarly, the deregulation of the residential construction industry in Quebec, which was described in Chapter 8, seems almost certain to lead to lower construction membership rates in that province, if it has not in fact already done so.

Changes in Union Structure and Actions

While the Canadian labour movement remains, in general, highly fragmented, with a large number of workers still represented by small unions, there are signs that this situation is beginning to change. The past decade has seen a growing number of union mergers. Since 1990, for example, the Canadian Auto Workers have merged with half a dozen smaller craft and industrial unions (Murray, 1995:178). In addition, the Canadian Paperworkers Union, the Communications and Electrical Workers, and the Energy, Chemical and Atomic Workers Union merged in 1992 to form a single union, the Communications, Energy and Paperworkers of Canada (Murray, 1995:177), which is now among the most influential private sector unions in the country. Since the initial merger, the CEP has also merged with the Southern Ontario Newspaper Guild and with the National Association of Broadcast Employees and Technicians (Craig and Solomon, 1996:191). As well, traditional industrial unions like the Steelworkers and Auto Workers have significantly expanded their jurisdictions. The former have organized security guards and hotel and restaurant workers as well as zoo guards and Montessori school teachers (Murray,

1995:178). Since their 1993 merger with the Canadian branch of the Retail, Wholesale and Department Store union (Murray, 1995:178), they have also begun extensive organizing efforts in the retail sector. The Auto Workers have also begun organizing in the service sector, as evidenced by the Starbucks example discussed earlier. Indeed, by 1994, the CAW had diversified its membership to such an extent that only about 40 percent of its members were working in its "core" auto and auto parts industries (Craig and Solomon, 1996:191).

Taken together, such developments point towards a broad evolution of industrial unions into something approaching general unions, willing to represent workers across industrial sectors (Murray, 1995:178). By 1997 (see Table 5.6), five such industrial-general unions, as we might call them, represented about 850 000 workers, or roughly half of the country's private sector union members. A sixth large union, the Teamsters, which has long claimed to be a general union, represented another 95 000 workers. The increasing dominance of these six unions (the CEP, CAW, Steelworkers, United Food and Commercial Workers, and Service Employees International, as well as the Teamsters) may go some way towards overcoming the country's traditionally fragmented union structure.

Thanks in part to the entry of large, well-financed industrial unions into the service sector, organizing efforts in that sector have increased, with unions starting to take on some of the larger retail chains, such as McDonald's and Wal-Mart. There are signs, as well, that the character of union organizing has begun to change, as unions like the Service Employees discover that empowerment and a desire for skills recognition may be more powerful organizing tools than a desire for money (Crain, 1994; Lipsig-Mumme, 1995) and that organizing is often more effective when organizers reflect the diversity of the groups the union is seeking to organize (Crain, 1994; Galt, 1994).

In the political sphere, the link between the labour movement and the NDP and PQ remains tenuous, due mainly to the recent tendency of NDP and PQ governments to turn on their erstwhile labour allies once in office. In Ontario, where the NDP link has been most severely questioned, the labour movement's extreme dislike of the current Conservative government could help restore that link (see Gollom, 1998).[3] However, with the NDP still very low in the polls in the province (Brennan, 1998) and a close race shaping up between the Conservatives and the Liberals, it is also possible that unionists, along with other Ontarians, will wind up voting Liberal in an attempt to get rid of the Conservatives.[4] Whatever the eventual fate of the labour-NDP link, it seems likely that the recent trend towards more targeted and issue-oriented union political action represented by the establishment of various humanity and social justice funds will continue.

In Chapter 6, we noted that unions' participation in business ventures ranging from the creation of venture-capital funds to the buyout of failing firms has increased dramatically over the past two decades. Perhaps most noteworthy here has been the Quebec Federation of Labour's Solidarity Fund, which has not only created or saved thousands of jobs, but significantly advanced the cause of industrial democracy in the province's workplaces (Boivin and Déom, 1995:460). The Fund has also helped promote greater labour-management cooperation in the province, at least in part through the "social contracts" it has helped put in place (Boivin and Déom, 1995:460–461). The success of the Solidarity Fund and of other labour-supported business ventures, such as Vancouver's Greystone Properties and the Manitoba Federation of Labour's Crocus Investment Fund, suggests that such ventures will be an increasingly important aspect of union action in the future.

Individualization of Labour Legislation

While the trend towards individualization of labour legislation is a subtler and more gradual one than some of the others described in this chapter, it has nonetheless had some significant effects on the way such legislation is interpreted and other (albeit lesser) effects on the content of that legislation. Both sets of effects seem, if anything, likely to increase in the years ahead.

The most important finding here, as noted in Chapters 7 and 8, has been the increasingly broad application of the duty to accommodate to collective agreements. This duty has been construed to extend far beyond the protection of women, minority group members, and people with disabilities from workplace discrimination and harassment. Among other things, employers have been expected to draw up different work schedules for people whose religious beliefs forbid work on particular days of the week, and to redesign jobs to allow people with disabilities to perform them more easily (Carter, 1997). In other cases, they have been expected to waive certain collective agreement provisions that inadvertently discriminated against members of certain groups. As Carter has noted, such requirements would seem to fly in the face of core collective bargaining principles such as equal application of all collective agreement provisions and the barring of special treatment for individual workers without the union's express consent (Carter, 1997:186). While it remains unclear exactly to what extent arbitrators will be prepared to allow the individual human rights contained in human rights legislation to prevail over the collective rights embodied in collective agreements, the evidence to date suggests that over the long term, the application of the duty to accommodate could significantly alter, if not dilute, the "collective" character of collective agreements.

As for actual legislative provisions, the most significant development is the growth in employer freedom to communicate provisions. In 1998, such provisions were part of seven jurisdictions' labour acts (all except the federal jurisdiction, Saskatchewan,

Quebec, and Newfoundland), a sharp increase from the three jurisdictions that had the provisions in place in 1984 (LLCG, 1984).[5] There are, as was noted earlier, significant differences in the scope and wording of the seven provinces' freedom to communicate provisions. However, all are based on the same principle: that of condoning, if not actively encouraging, direct communication by employers to individual employees on a broad range of issues, including those related to collective bargaining.[6] Normally, under collective bargaining, communication by the employer on issues related to terms and conditions of employment would be made through the union, and would thus be of a collective nature. At a minimum, the freedom to communicate provisions appear to contemplate the establishment of a second, parallel communications link, between employers and individual employees, or employees in small groups. Particularly when such communication is related to unionization, or to issues contained in the collective agreement, it has the potential to undercut the union's workplace role quite significantly.

In a less direct way, the shift, in several jurisdictions, from a card count to a vote as evidence of union membership may also be having an "individualizing" effect. Here, our greatest concern is that the switch from a card count to a vote opens up the possibility of direct employer communication with individual employees regarding the desirability of unionization, a possibility that, as we noted earlier, may reduce the union's likelihood of success in its certification bid (Weiler, 1983; Mills, 1989). The likelihood that direct employer communication with employees could have such an effect may well be greater in those jurisdictions (Alberta, Nova Scotia, and Ontario) with both a vote procedure and employer free speech provisions in force.[7]

The one positive development in this area from the unions' perspective has been a 1991 Supreme Court of Canada ruling that overturned a federal prohibition on political activity among its public servants (Swinton, 1995:68). In the case of Osborne v. Canada (Treasury Board),[8] the Supreme Court ruled that this prohibition, contained in section 33 of the federal *Public Service Employment Act,* violated the Charter's freedom of expression guarantee.[9] While the rationale for this ruling may have been a desire to protect individual rights, its effect has been to enhance public servants' collective ability to engage in partisan political activity and politically oriented publicity campaigns, an ability that has become increasingly important at a time when few public servants enjoy free collective bargaining rights.

Lack of Public Sector Bargaining

For the public sector, as Chapter 9 showed, the past decade has been one of great, even traumatic change—much of it unilaterally imposed by government, as in the case of Alberta's health care restructuring (Haiven, 1995) and Ontario's ongoing restructuring of both its health care and education systems. Going beyond the wage freezes and rollbacks of the 1980s, these restructuring efforts have led and are continuing to lead to job losses in health care and education. They have also been marked by a centralization of provincial control, as evidenced by the Alberta government's elimination of public school boards' taxing authority (Thomason, 1995) and Ontario's "Bill 160," which will severely restrict and eventually eliminate local school boards.

Even where governments have taken less draconian measures than in Ontario and Alberta, free public sector bargaining remains the exception rather than the rule, as governments have continued to prefer achieving results through legislation rather than through negotiations with their employees. The scope of public sector bargaining has remained quite limited, compared to that of private sector bargaining, and governments have continued to make frequent use of back-to-work legislation, as in the case of the renewed wave of Ontario teachers' strikes in September, 1998 and a lockout of Saskatchewan power employees (CBC Radio News report, October 19, 1998).

Because of the complicated reorganizations going on, many public sector workers (such as Ontario hospital staff affected by the wave of hospital mergers) don't know how long they will continue to have a job, or, even if they do continue to have one, what they will be doing. Those who have managed to survive the cuts are often badly overworked, and their morale, and in some cases their health, have been severely affected. Making matters worse, particularly for the public sector's large contingent of female workers, is the federal government's apparent abandonment of its traditional leadership role in the area of pay equity, as evidenced by its August 1998 decision to appeal the Human Rights Tribunal's earlier award of back equity payments to thousands of current and past public servants.

Frustrated by their inability to achieve change through negotiations, public sector workers have increasingly taken their fight to the media and the political arena. As we noted in both Chapters 6 and 9, the public sector unions have become increasingly adept at using the media to get their message across to the public. While continuing to make heavy use of the traditional print media, these unions have also used such varied tactics as bus ads, billboards, radio and TV spots, and electronic publicity campaigns. Politically, they have mounted a series of increasingly intense and bitter campaigns against the governments responsible for cutting public services—and their members' jobs. In Ottawa, officials from CUPE and the provincial Teachers' Federation were among the speakers at an October 1998 demonstration aimed at toppling the Conservative regime of Mike Harris (Gollom, 1998). In Quebec, public servants angry at the federal government's appeal of the pay equity award were widely credited with making the difference in a narrow Bloc Quebecois by-election win over the favoured Liberal candidate (Aubry and Bryden, 1998).

The combination of a threat to their jobs and loss of workplace autonomy resulting from centralization has angered public sector workers in many parts of Canada, but nowhere more than in Ontario. Through 1996 and early 1997, they spearheaded a series of one-day general strikes across the province (CBR, various issues). During the fall of 1997, the province's teachers staged an illegal province-wide strike (described in detail in Chapter 12), which was followed by a series of strikes during the fall of 1998. Despite numerous restrictions on the right to strike in the public sector, that sector accounted for more than 40 percent of the person-days lost to strikes in 1996, and more than half the days lost in 1997. Ontario, which experienced the lion's share of the public sector disputes in both years, accounted for more than half of the person-days lost to strikes in both years. The increase in public sector disputes was primarily responsible for the sharp increase in the national percentage of working time lost to strikes in 1996, and a further increase in 1997.

Innovative Dispute Resolution Mechanisms

The past two decades have seen the introduction of a broad range of innovative new dispute resolution mechanisms. These have ranged from first-contract arbitration, in cases where the employer appears to be unwilling to conclude a collective agreement with the union, to expedited arbitration, grievance meditation (often used in conjunction with expedited arbitration), and various types of preventive mediation programs. In addition, traditional conciliation has evolved into something more closely resembling mediation, and various hybrid forms, such as med-arb, have been tried out in certain situations. Various studies have indicated that a number of these mechanisms have been quite effective in reducing conflict, resolving grievances more quickly, and improving union-management relations. For example, a study of first-contract arbitration in Canada showed that the imposition of an initial agreement was helpful in establishing a longer-term bargaining relationship, especially in smaller bargaining units in Quebec (Sexton, 1987). In Ontario, the use of expedited arbitration in conjunction with grievance mediation has resulted in substantial savings in both time and money while grievance mediation remained in effect (Rose, 1986b; 1991). Similar results have been achieved through the use of grievance mediation on its own. In Canada, as in the United States, the process has generally resulted in negotiated settlements in 70 to 90 percent of the cases (Brett and Goldberg, 1979; Goldberg, 1989; Thornicroft and Eden, 1995). In addition to saving substantial amounts of time and money, the adoption of a collaborative, problem-solving approach to grievances can improve the parties' overall relationship (Goldberg, 1989; Thornicroft and Eden, 1995). While there is less hard evidence available to date about the effects of the various provincial preventive mediation programs, anecdotal evidence (Joyce, 1996) suggests that these programs have also helped improve union-management relationships.

But despite all the attention devoted to developing innovative new dispute resolution mechanisms and the undoubted usefulness of many of those mechanisms, workplace conflict remains a severe problem in many organizations. As we noted earlier, public sector strike activity has increased sharply since 1995. In addition, a number of organizations, such as Canada Post, continue to stagger under the weight of a huge pile of unsettled grievances.[10] Evidence such as this suggests that while the innovative new settlement mechanisms have been useful, they have done little to address some of the more deep-seated causes of labour-management conflict, especially in the public sector. Here, the low level of strike activity in Quebec, where unions have been heavily involved in joint governance ventures with management, may offer some useful lessons for the rest of the country.

Shift in Governments' Regulatory Role

Comparative evidence suggests that where governments view their main role in the IR system to be that of promoting economic development, workers' freedoms tend to be quite severely restricted. For example, between 1953 and 1987, South Korean union activity was considerably restricted to fit the requirements of the government's growth-oriented economic policy (Young-ki, 1993). Despite the existence of laws officially protecting workers' right to organize, these laws were generally ignored. Dispute settlement was most often through direct government intervention, often carried out with total disregard for workers' civil rights or even their personal safety (Ravenhorst, 1990). In many other developing countries, especially in Asia and Africa, it has been commonly maintained by governments that unfettered trade union action such as the right to strike is a "luxury" that most developing nations simply cannot afford (see Peirce, 1996).[11] To prevent such a threat to their economic growth, governments have taken a variety of measures ranging from the substitution of arbitration for the right to strike in Ghana (Kassalow, 1963) to the deregistration of unions and virtual curtailment of collective bargaining in Singapore (Leggett, 1993). For these reasons, any signs of a shift in the government's IR role towards that of promoting economic development should be of serious concern.

To date, the strongest evidence of governments' shift in IR emphasis has been the Newfoundland government's unsuccessful attempt to create a separate labour relations regime structured more or less along Third World lines in its 1995 enterprise zone legislation (Peirce, 1996). In addition to providing firms relocating to Newfoundland with a lengthy tax holiday, the legislation would have forbidden employees of these firms from striking—a ban almost unprecedented in the private sector during peacetime. Instead, contract disputes would have been submitted to three-person arbitration panels, with the chair to be chosen by the province's labour minister. As well, the maximum permissible pay raise would have been the provincial inflation rate. The legislation's labour relations provisions were eventually withdrawn in the face of harsh criticism by various business groups (Peirce, 1996). Some felt that the separate labour relations regime amounted to unfair competition for existing businesses. Others pointed out that the legislation could give the province a bad image by suggesting it was strike-prone, when, in fact, it was not. While the exact reasons for the Newfoundland government's deletion of the labour provisions from the legislation remain unclear, what can be said is that had they remained in place, they would have established a precedent that other provinces, especially poorer ones, might well have been quick to follow.

The negative response to Newfoundland's legislation on the part of both business and labour groups (Peirce, 1996) suggests that such a drastic shift in government's IR policy role may not be politically acceptable to large numbers of Canadians. Other moves in this direction have been of a more gradual and incremental nature. They include the insertion of economically oriented provisions into various labour acts' prefaces and purpose statements,[12] and an increase in employer free speech provisions in those labour acts. Somewhat more significant has been Ontario's removal of its labour board's previous power to certify a union with less than majority support as a remedy for grossly unfair employer labour practice. This policy change, which occurred in June 1998 (Adams, 1998), could have the effect of sending employers the signal that the province will do nothing to stand in the way of business growth, even if it means that workers' right to join a union without employer interference is trampled on in the process. It will be interesting to see if other provinces follow Ontario's lead in removing this power from their labour boards.

"EXPLORING OPTIONS: A DISCUSSION PAPER FOR LABOR RELATIONS ISSUES"
www.netfx.iom.net/ace/summary.htm

POLICY SUGGESTIONS AND PROPOSALS FOR ACTION

The following policy suggestions and proposals for action rise directly from the findings just discussed (see Figure 14.4). While some of the proposals go against the grain of the current trend towards smaller government, it is important to note that recent economic and political developments have worked severe hardship on many Canadians in addition to leading to increased workplace conflict. It's also important to bear in mind that several of these proposals have already been put forward elsewhere (as in the case of the recommendation on work hours, some of which is drawn from the 1994 Donner Commission report), and that most are of a fairly incremental nature.

FIGURE 14.4
SOME KEY POLICY SUGGESTIONS AND ACTION PROPOSALS

- Introduce experience rating of EI premiums.
- Reduce both overtime and regularly scheduled work hours.
- End exclusions from unionization rights of all groups other than management and confidential IR personnel.
- Create stronger international linkages between unions.
- Remove employer free speech provisions from labour relations acts.
- Establish a Royal Commission on public sector IR.
- Increase the scope of public sector bargaining.

With respect to the economy, there may not be much governments to do to ensure workers a greater degree of job security; however, one measure the federal government might consider is fairly steep experience rating of EI premiums, which would mean that firms laying off large numbers of workers would be forced to pay significantly higher premiums than other firms.

On the issue of work hours, a situation where many workers are working far more hours than they would like to be while others work far fewer, or even none at all, is bad for workers and their families, bad for the country and the economy as a whole, and not even very good for business in anything beyond the extremely short term. Here, there *are* things governments can do. One would be to amend employment standards legislation to increase the premium that must be paid for overtime work. Another would be to reduce the number of hours that must be worked before overtime must be paid, which is currently as high as 48 in some jurisdictions. In addition, all provinces should provide workers with the right to refuse overtime after putting in a standard week, a right currently available in only three provinces. With such a provision in place, workers asked to put in long overtime hours on short notice would not be forced to choose between their jobs and their families, as many now are (see Shellenbarger, 1997). Finally, all provinces, instead of just half of them as is now the case, should set strict limits on the number of hours anyone can be required to work without a labour ministry permit. Such permits should not be easy to obtain, and those seeking to make frequent use of them should be viewed with suspicion. The point behind all these policy proposals is to try to provide employers with every possible incentive to hire additional workers to meet extra demand, rather than simply working existing staff longer and harder.

 EUROPEAN INDUSTRIAL RELATIONS OBSERVATORY ONLINE
www.eiro.eurofound.ie

There are also things governments can do to help bring about shorter regular hours of work, even short of legislating them, as a number of European countries have in recent years (Hayden, 1998).[13] For example, firms could be given financial assistance to create jobs by reducing hours, as is already being done in the province of Quebec (Donner, 1994). Another option is the proposal advanced by Frank Reid (1997; also Gunderson and Reid, 1998) to amend employment standards law to allow anyone wishing to work shorter hours to do so, at an equivalent reduction in pay. Leave policies could also be made more flexible to allow workers wishing to leave their jobs for a time for family or other personal reasons to do so without penalty, thus opening up a job for an unemployed worker. In the meantime, part-time work could be made somewhat more attractive for those forced to work on this basis through the mandatory pro-rating of such benefits as sick leave, pension plans, and paid health and dental plans (see CLMPC, 1997), where these are enjoyed by full-time workers in the same establishment.

In an economy such as the present one, marked by frequent job changes and a growing incidence of part-time and temporary work, it will never be easy for unions to represent all those wishing such representation. Still, there may be ways to facilitate greater representation somewhat. First, the outright exclusion of groups other than management or confidential IR personnel from unionization rights seems simply unconscionable, as well as being a clear violation of the Charter's freedom of association provision, and should be ended at once, as should the exclusion of those groups from coverage under employment standards legislation. Second, to facilitate the unionization of homeworkers and other hard-to-organize workers, unions should be provided with their e-mail addresses and other necessary information to allow them to conduct organizing campaigns among such workers.[14] Third, in all provinces (including Ontario), the labour board should continue to have the power to certify a union with less than majority support where an unfair employer labour practice has clearly prevented employees' true wishes regarding unionization from becoming known. In our view, there was more than adequate protection for employers' interests from the old section 11(2) of the *OLRA*, which provided that a union would not be certified (even with majority support) when a union had engaged in an unfair labour practice that had prevented employees' true wishes from becoming known.

AUSTRALIAN CENTRE FOR INDUSTRIAL RELATIONS RESEARCH AND TRAINING
sue.econ.su.oz.au/acirrt/intro.htm

Finally, given workers' growing lack of attachment to a particular job and workplace, community unionism of the sort described by Carla Lipsig-Mumme (1995) would seem to make a good deal of sense. A key focus of such unionization would need to be the development of new representative structures in which the union and community would share (Lipsig-Mumme, 1995:216). With such structures in place, a worker who lost his or her job could continue to draw on the union for support rather than being left totally isolated, as is now all too often the case.

On the subject of union structure and actions, the recent trend towards larger and more diverse unions seems a healthy one, one likely to provide members with a broader range of services than they would otherwise be able to obtain. Although even the country's most powerful unions still face an uphill battle in their bid to organize the private service sector, by and large they seem likelier to succeed in this venture than smaller unions—even those specializing in representing private service sector employees. Given today's economic realities, the trend towards increased union participation in business ventures and joint governance schemes with management also seems a healthy one, provided there are adequate safeguards in the latter case, to ensure that the venture is not simply an indirect way of weakening or even destroying the union.[15] As for the question of stronger international linkages between unions, an issue also raised by Lipsig-Mumme (1995), these seem essential if unions are to provide adequate representation to workers in a globalized economy marked by growing dominance of multinational corporations. While full-blown international bargaining is probably some years away, there's still a good deal that unions from different countries could do short of that, such as provide each other with bargaining information or logistical or financial support.

"FINANCIAL WARFARE" AND "THE GLOBAL FINANCIAL CRISIS"
www.interlog.com/~cjazz/chossd.htm

Because the individualization of labour law is quite a subtle trend, it is difficult to know what policy measures to suggest to help ensure that this trend does not have seriously adverse effects on collective worker representation by unions. One fairly widespread trend that we have noted with some concern is the increase in employer free speech provisions in labour relations acts. In our view, such provisions directly conflict with fundamental union rights set forth in labour relations acts, and should, therefore, be deleted from those acts as soon as possible. In the meantime, such provisions should be closely monitored to ensure they are not having a harmful effect on workers' right to join and participate in the unions of their choice. The extent to which the duty to accommodate requires modification of collective agreements will also bear monitoring. Given the ambivalence that Carter (1997) has described many arbitrators as feeling towards reading this duty into collective agreements, this may be the time for a broader public debate on the appropriateness of arbitration as a forum for human rights issues beyond those explicitly contained in collective agreements.

To even begin to untangle the knotty issue of public sector bargaining would require a book-length study all to itself. For now, suffice it to say that the growing level of conflict in this sector, coupled with governments resorting more frequently to back-to-work legislation and the use of statutory wage freezes and rollbacks, suggests that current public sector IR arrangements are not working—indeed, have not worked for some time—and need to be fundamentally rethought. Given the virtual certainty of even greater conflict as the restructuring of Ontario's health care and education systems is carried out, a Royal Commission on public sector labour relations and collective bargaining comparable in scope to the Woods Commission of the 1960s seems most urgently needed. Such a commission would doubtless offer many detailed recommendations for ways to improve labour-management relations and the collective bargaining process. The suggestions offered here are made in the spirit of seeking to reduce unnecessary conflict at a time when a good deal of conflict seems more or less unavoidable.

The severe restrictions on the scope of public sector bargaining in most jurisdictions are, in our view, one such source of unnecessary conflict. While government departments may not be able to allow their employees to bargain over issues covered by merit plans, such as the criteria for appointments and promotions (Swimmer, 1995:371), merit plans do not explain the exclusion of such issues as technological change, employee training programs, or (most shocking of all) pension plans from the list of bargainable issues (Swimmer, 1995; Fryer, 1995). We would, therefore, urge all jurisdictions to grant their public sector workers the ability to negotiate all issues not specifically barred because of civil service merit plans. The greater the range of bargainable issues, the better public sector bargaining will be able to defuse or at least reduce labour-management conflict.

The issue of public sector workers' right to strike has been so often and so hotly debated that we hesitate to say anything at all on this point. However, our examination of current public sector legislation in Chapter 9 suggests that the pattern of Canadian jurisdictions' restrictions on this right is, by and large, neither consistent nor at all firmly grounded in any sort of public policy rationale. Ideally, these restrictions should apply consistently across different jurisdictions. At a minimum, all such restrictions should be based on *some* type of policy rationale. One would be hard-pressed indeed to find any policy justification for Nova Scotia's granting of the right to strike to teachers, hospital workers, and even police, but not to civil servants—or for Manitoba's granting of that right to hospital workers, but not teachers or civil servants.

A third, at least potential, source of tension concerns the way in which public sector bargaining units are generally determined. In the private sector, such a determination is made by a labour relations board comprising labour relations professionals. In determining the appropriate bargaining unit, a labour relations board will, as we noted in Chapter 8, generally strive to take both employees' and the employer's wishes into account to the extent possible. In the public sector, many bargaining units are determined legislatively—often for reasons that may have little or nothing to do with industrial relations. Allowing employees and public sector managers some say in determining the appropriate bargaining unit might be a good way to begin building harmonious relations between the parties. So, too, might turning final bargaining unit determination over to a public sector labour board made up of professionals rather than leaving it to legislators whose knowledge and understanding of labour relations issues may be all but non-existent.

Canada's public sector unions will also need to form broad-based coalitions with the general public. The basis for such coalitions seems natural. As the users of public services like health care and education, Canadians share with the unions an interest in maintaining adequate levels of government funding for those services. Through their publicity campaigns, unions such as CUPE and PSAC have begun to earn greater public support for their cause. But much more needs to be done if governments are to be moved away from their single-minded concern with debts and deficits and convinced of the importance of maintaining adequate levels of public services. Given the broad support that pay equity enjoys, within the public at large as well as within the labour movement, the pay equity issue could prove a useful one for the labour movement to use in building broad-based coalitions, and there have lately been signs that PSAC, in particular, has begun to use the issue in just this way.

Canada's record in implementing innovative dispute resolution systems is an admirable one. We applaud these innovations and would urge the various jurisdictions to continue developing new ones. At the same time, it is important to recognize that much (perhaps even most) labour-management conflict may arise from reasons other than poor communication or faulty information, and hence not be amenable to resolution by even the most innovative of mechanisms. Here, we would agree with Roy Adams (1995a:515) that to a large extent, conflict appears to be more strongly related to structure than to process.

At various points in the book, we have spoken of certain more fundamental sources of conflict. In the public sector, the denial of bargaining rights is one such source. Elsewhere, the decentralized structure of Canadian bargaining and the fact that so much conflict tends to be worked out in the workplace rather than in the political arena may be two more. In this connection, the apparent success of Quebec "social contracts" in bringing peace to that province's once tumultuous labour scene at least brief mention. What seems most noteworthy about these social contracts is not simply the long-term peace agreement that the parties sign, but the transformation of the union into almost a co-manager of the enterprise through joint administration of the agreement and the provision of detailed information to it and employees on the firm's financial situation (Boivin and Déom, 1995:461). Here, in short, we have something approaching European-style political bargaining (see Adams, 1989; 1995), with unions regarded by both management and government as a full and legitimate partner, and job security their reward for the acceptance of a long-term no-strike pledge. To bring about such social contracts entails a good deal more than simply changing the mechanisms through which labour-management disputes are to be resolved.

The shift of the government's role in the IR system is another trend that is sufficiently general that it is hard to propose specific policy measures in response to it, beyond urging the government of Ontario to repeal its recent withdrawal of the labour board's power to certify with less than majority support as a remedy for grossly unfair employer labour practices. Here, we would only suggest that as Noah Meltz (1989) has so aptly said, industrial relations involves considerations of equity as well as of economic efficiency. To the extent that public policy makers (including makers of IR policy) ignore considerations of equity in formulating or changing that policy, conflict seems likely to increase both in the workplace, and in society at large.

WHERE FURTHER RESEARCH IS NEEDED

Both in this chapter and throughout the book as a whole, we have indicated various issues that seem to us in need of further research. The list below, while by no means definitive, has tried to include those items where such research seems most urgent from a public policy perspective (see Figure 14.5).

FIGURE 14.5

SOME KEY RESEARCH ISSUES

1) Which approaches to reducing work hours would work best in the Canadian context?

2) How well have other countries maintained public sector workers' bargaining rights while proceeding with deficit and debt reduction?

3) How successful have the new "general" unions been in organizing private-sector service workers?

4) To what extent has the "duty to accommodate" affected collective bargaining?

5) What are the major barriers to effective enforcement of employment legislation, and how can those barriers be overcome?

Canada is far from alone in facing stubbornly high unemployment rates. The current employment crisis is pretty much a global affair. In France and Italy, unemployment has been in double digits for much of the past decade.[16] Even Sweden, which prior to the 1990s rarely experienced rates of more than 3 percent, is now in double digits, while Germany, arguably Europe's most prosperous country, has seen its rates creep up to almost 8 percent.

What is different about the unemployment crisis in different countries is the way in which governments, business, and labour have responded to it. In Canada, with the partial exception of Quebec,[17] governments have done little either to stimulate the economy or to spread existing jobs around more evenly by reducing work hours. Their major response to the crisis to date has been to cut social programs such as employment insurance, thus making life even harder for those who become unemployed. Businesses have all too often cut jobs and then worked remaining staff longer and harder. Unions have sometimes negotiated shorter hours or overtime reductions, but the labour movement as a whole, in the words of one of its own chief spokespeople (A. Jackson, 1997) has not taken a united stance on the issue. As we suggested earlier in the chapter, the economic and social costs of this laissez-faire approach to the problem are becoming increasingly evident.

"EXPERIENCED WORKERS AND NEW WAYS OF ORGANIZING WORK"
socrates.berkeley.edu/~iir/ncw/wpapers/shaiken.index.html

In most European countries, the response has been quite different. In Europe, with the notable exception of the United Kingdom, national labour movements have solidly united around demands for a significantly shorter work week (generally 35 hours). Their efforts have resulted in a legislated 35-hour week in such countries as France and Italy (see Hayden, 1998; see also Figure 14.6) and may well do so in Germany, where a Social Democratic government has just taken over from the longstanding conservative government of Chancellor Helmut Kohl. In the Netherlands, a shorter (36-hour) week has been achieved through a tripartite business-government-labour agreement (Peirce, 1999). Even the business community has been supportive of shorter hours in some cases. In France, while opposed to the current Socialist government's legislation, many business leaders had no difficulty in signing on to the voluntary approach of the previous, conservative government, which featured tax reductions for firms creating jobs through the use of shorter work weeks (Peirce, 1999).

The initiatives just described represent just a few of the approaches tried by various European countries. More research is needed to discover other such initiatives, to determine which might be best suited for use in a Canadian context, and to find out how effective these initiatives have been at reducing unemployment and the social and economic costs associated with it.[18]

Canada is also not alone in facing a crisis in its public sector. As Beaumont (1995:414) notes, the 1980s was a tough decade for the public sector in most advanced industrialized countries. To date, the evidence suggests that the 1990s have been even tougher, with widespread privatization, contracting out, wage freezes, and reductions in government expenditures on public services generally the order of the day (see Beaumont (1995:426–427). More research is needed to determine whether other industrialized countries have been able to maintain public sector workers' basic bargaining rights better than Canada has over the past decade, and, if so, by what means they have managed to ensure continuation of those rights.

FIGURE 14.6

The shorter work week is a hot issue across Europe, as the cover from "32 Hours" coordinator Anders Hayden's recent report on the subject amply attests.

Source: Hayden, 1998.

Both in this chapter and in the chapter on union structure, we noted that many traditional industrial unions are in the process of evolving into something like general unions, due both to mergers and to their increasing willingness to organize workers from far beyond their traditional jurisdictions. Further research is needed to see how this new style of Canadian union operates, what these unions' organizing approaches are, and how successful they have been at attracting new members, particularly from the service sector. Comparative research would also be helpful to determine the extent to which traditional industrial unions in other countries, such as the United States, are undergoing a similar evolution.

At several different points in this book, we have pointed out the challenges posed to collective agreement interpretation by the duty to accommodate. Here, Donald Carter's 1997 study has broken important new ground by illustrating some of the ways in which collective agreement interpretation has already been modified because of arbitrators' application of this duty. Further research is needed to determine to what extent the duty to accommodate affects the collective bargaining process, and where arbitrators decide that undue hardship has resulted from application of that duty.

The last item on our proposed research agenda has to do with enforcement of employment legislation. In Chapter 7, we noted that enforcement of both work standards and health and safety legislation has been a significant problem in a number of Canadian jurisdictions over the years. Given ongoing government budget cuts in labour- and employment-related areas, there is every reason to believe that this situation will get worse before it gets better. More studies similar to Roy Adams' 1987 study of employment standards enforcement in Ontario are needed to determine to what extent work standards, health and safety, and human rights legislation are actually being enforced in Canadian workplaces, what the main barriers to effective enforcement appear to be, and how (if at all) Canadian jurisdictions have managed to get around those barriers.

As we said earlier, the above list should be considered suggestive rather than definitive. No doubt many readers will by now have their own ideas as to where further research is most urgently needed. Perhaps the one thing that can be said with certainty about the rapidly changing field of IR is that it offers almost limitless research opportunities for people of intelligence and imagination with an interest in public policy issues.

QUESTIONS FOR DISCUSSION

1) Do you agree with the author's choice of seven key themes summarizing the main directions of Canadian IR today? If you do, which seem to you most important? If you don't, which themes would you say are of most relevance?

2) Do you think Canadian union membership is likely to increase, decline, or stay about the same in the near future? What factors are most likely to lead it to increase or decrease, in your view?

3) Why is enforcement of existing legislation such an important issue? What do you think governments, employers, and unions can do to ensure that existing legislation is adequately enforced?

4) Do you agree with the choice of issues for further research? If you don't, which issues seem to you most in need of research?

5) Are there topics you feel should have been covered in this book, but were not? What are these topics? How might they be covered in some other way? What type of coverage should they receive in subsequent editions?

6) Overall, what would you say are some of the most important things you've learned from this book? If you plan to take further courses in this area, what would you like to learn from those courses?

SUGGESTIONS FOR FURTHER READING

Chaison, Gary. (1996.) *Union mergers in hard times.* (Full bibliographical information in reference at end of Chapter 6). This very interesting comparative study suggests that Canadian and American unions, in particular, will have to become a good deal larger and much more diversified to compete. Contains a useful section on the formation of the Communications, Energy and Paperworkers.

Donner, Arthur (chair). (1994.) *Report of the advisory group on overtime and hours of work.* Ottawa: Supply and Services. Contains a useful background discussion on the issues and some sensible but quite modest policy recommendations. Canadian governments' almost universal failure to adopt these modest recommendations illustrates the serious, nationwide lack of political will around these issues. At a time when most European countries are seriously debating a 35-hour or even 32-hour week, it's nothing short of pathetic that we can't even guarantee people a 40-hour week.

Galt, Virginia. (1994.) "Reinventing the labour movement." *Globe & Mail,* June 6. Useful account, by a veteran labour reporter, of how the labour movement is having to adapt to organize women, immigrants, and young people in the private service sector. (Note: This article is reprinted in the 1996 edition of Craig & Solomon's textbook, cited in the general reference list.)

ENDNOTES

1 The purposes, found at the beginning of the act after the list of definitions, may be said to fulfill roughly the same objective as the old preamble did.

2 Another of the new purposes, that of encouraging communication between employers and employees in the workplace (section 2[4]), might be regarded as not altogether consistent with that of fostering collective bargaining, at least to the extent that direct communication between the employer and individual employees is what is being referred to here.

3 On October 17, 1998, about 8000 unionists, unaffiliated working people, and members of various left-oriented political parties marched to Ottawa's Congress Centre to protest the Conservative provincial government's policies.

4 An Angus Reid poll released October 17, 1998, found the Conservatives with the support of 42 percent of Ontario voters, and the Liberals with 40 percent support. The NDP trailed far behind at 12 percent (Brennan, 1998). Canadian Auto Workers' president Buzz Hargrove's announcement, in late November 1998, that he would be voting Liberal in the next provincial election is likely to do little to reverse the NDP's lowly poll standing.

5 It may or may not be a coincidence that two of the three provinces that do not have freedom to communicate provisions in place, Newfoundland and Quebec, have the country's highest union membership rates.

6 Taken in conjunction with section 2(4) of the *OLRA*, which officially includes the improvement of employer-employee communications as an express purpose of the act, the Ontario provision could be said to have the effect of encouraging such communication. So could the P.E.I. provision, which as noted in Chapter 8 specifically refers to communications around collective bargaining and terms and conditions of employment.

7 Again, it may or may not be coincidental that of the three provinces in this group, Alberta has by far the country's lowest union membership rates, while the other two both rank among the five lowest and well below the national average.

8 (1991), 82 D.L.R. (4th) 321 (S.C.C.)

9 As Swinton (1995:68) notes, similar prohibitions against public servants' political activity were in place in a number of provinces. Presumably the court's decision in the Osborne case would have had the effect of invalidating those provincial prohibitions, as well as the federal one.

10 This despite Canada Post's creative expedited arbitration program, described in some detail in Chapter 13.

11 For a more detailed discussion of the rationale behind some of these trade union restrictions, see Low (1963).

12 These remarks were quoted in various newspapers including the *Ottawa Citizen* and *Globe & Mail* on October 20, 1998.

13 A legislated four-day week, as suggested by O'Hara (1993) would be the author's personal choice. However, it is clear from statements made by unionists such as Andrew Jackson (1997) that the labour movement would not be united behind such legislation. Given the absence of solid labour movement support, and with the virtual certainty of strong business opposition, such legislation is probably not politically feasible in the current Canadian climate; united labour support is generally essential if such legislation is to win passage and be effective.

14 In addition to Ontario, provinces that have inserted such statements into their labour acts include Alberta.

15 Proposed changes to Part I of the *Canada Labour Code* that have been passed by Parliament, but not officially put into effect, would do just that.

16 See Lemelin (1989) and Downie (1989) for useful discussions of this issue.

17 The source for the unemployment data contained in this paragraph is the U.S. Department of Labor's Bureau of Labor Statistics, as quoted in the 1998 *World Almanac*, p. 144.

18 There, as we noted earlier, the government has provided financial assistance to firms creating jobs by reducing work hours. In addition, the government has also negotiated shorter hours in some of its contracts with its own employees, thereby setting a "best practice" example in this area.

19 Major developments from European countries are tracked regularly in *Better Times*, the newsletter of the Toronto-based "32 Hours" organization devoted to achieving shorter working hours.

CBC ✺

CBC Video Cases

ABSENT AND ACCOUNTED FOR

In the past, many companies tended to be rather casual about attendance. If someone was sick, there were usually lots more people available to do the job. At Toronto Hydro, for example, about 100 of the organization's 1400 employees were typically absent on any given day.

Today, this casual attitude towards attendance has gone the way of the automatic 10 percent annual pay raise and the open-bar office Christmas party. In the wake of large-scale downsizing, rightsizing, and restructuring, companies feel the need to ensure that the people they're paying to work are actually there to do the job.

No one can deny that absenteeism is a serious problem. Statistics Canada says that it costs the Canadian economy about $10 billion a year. In a recent survey, 75 percent of all Canadian companies said they recognize absenteeism as a problem.

To help combat absenteeism, Canadian companies have adopted a variety of approaches ranging from "attendance awareness" programs and stricter monitoring to actually phoning up workers who have called in sick to ask them if they'll be able to come in later that day, or if not, when they will be able to return to work. Software companies have developed a broad range of software designed to keep track of who is absent and for how long. Some of this software even tracks disciplinary action for absenteeism.

This new, "get-tough" approach to absenteeism has been far from uncontroversial. Proponents, like Toronto Hydro human resource manager Jeff Rosenthal, argue that such an approach is necessary to reduce absenteeism and the high costs associated with it. But critics, like Bruno Silano, president of Toronto Hydro's CUPE Local #1, contend that all the absenteeism management programs do is increase the stress on already overworked employees who often work under hazardous conditions and, he says, need to feel free to take the sick days provided for in the collective agreement without being made to feel guilty about doing so.

Others, like human resource management consultant Marti Snye, the author of *Corporate Abuse*, suggest that attendance management programs fail to address the real reasons for absenteeism, which in her view are overwork, stress, burnout, and work/family conflicts. At the same time, at least one major Canadian company, the Canadian Imperial Bank of Commerce, has done what it can to reduce absenteeism resulting from work/family conflicts by providing its employees, a majority of whom are women and parents, with flexible hours, compressed work hours, and other ways of meeting their family responsibilities more easily.

Video Resource: "Attendance Police" from *Venture* #646, June 15, 1997.

Will today's tougher corporate stance towards absenteeism achieve significant reductions in absenteeism and cost savings in the long term? Only time will tell. One thing is clear. For most Canadian workers, the days of phoning in sick every time they feel marginal are over.

QUESTIONS

1) What strategies are Canadian companies using to try to reduce absenteeism?

2) Why do some union leaders and others criticize the new attendance management programs?

3) Do you think attendance management programs are justified? Why, or why not? If you don't think the type of programs you saw in the video are justified, what approach would you take, as a human resource manager, to try to reduce absenteeism in your organization?

CBC ✸

CASE
V.2
CBC Video Cases
SOME WORK AND SOME PLAY

High unemployment has become a virtual epidemic throughout the industrialized world. Even countries as prosperous as France and Germany have not been immune. Both have recently been suffering from double-digit unemployment which in turn has led to massive labour unrest.

One country which has proved an exception to the global pattern is the Netherlands. Lately it has become the envy of the rest of Europe with its 6.5 percent unemployment rate— about half that of most other European countries. Somehow, the Dutch seem to have managed to discover just about the right balance between work and play, while maintaining global competitiveness. As journalist Paul Workman suggests, the Netherlands is now "the closest thing Europe has to a tiger economy."

What makes the Dutch experience particularly remarkable is that fifteen years ago, the country's economy was in such bad shape that people used to refer to the "Dutch disease." Wages and unemployment were both high, and far too many people were on welfare.

How did the Netherlands turn things around? To start with, former Prime Minister Ruud Lubbers managed to induce the country's unions to accept a wage freeze and sign on to an agreement with business and government. In return for this, Dutch workers were given the

---

Video Resource: "A Place That Works." From *The National*, March 26, 1997.

shortest working hours in Europe. Initially, the experiment led to widespread public protest. Business leaders were skeptical as well. In time, however, most Dutch people, including business leaders, came to realize that shorter hours didn't have to mean reduced productivity. Quite the reverse.

Today, seeing that their wages and jobs are protected and that the country's economy is growing, unionized workers have become "amazingly cooperative" in accepting employers' demands for flexibility. The head of the country's metalworkers' union went so far as to encourage the country's only steel mill to modernize, even though the modernization would mean the loss of about 10 000 jobs. When asked how he could justify such a course of action to his members, the union leader pointed out that the mill was still running, unlike steel mills in neighbouring countries which had not gone in for modernization. Moreover, the remaining workers enjoy a 33-hour week and five weeks' annual vacation. Union-management cooperation has become such a way of life in the Netherlands that in 1996, the country didn't experience a single strike or lockout.

One key to the "Dutch miracle" is job-sharing. Another is extensive part-time work. For example, the metalworkers' union leader's wife, a social worker, works only part-time to allow herself more time with her children and more time to engage in her own pursuits, such as reading and study. She is one of a great many Dutch part-timers. In all, 33 percent of all Dutch workers are part-timers, compared with 19 percent of Canadian workers. But there's a big difference. In the Netherlands, unlike Canada, part-timers enjoy the same perks and benefits as their full-time counterparts, including pension rights.

Far from interfering with the country's economic competitiveness, its family-friendly approach seems to have made the Netherlands even more competitive. As Paul Workman notes, it has become the seventh largest exporter in the world. Fully 45 percent of all companies starting a new business in Europe choose to locate in the Netherlands.

While there are concerns that even the robust Dutch economy may not be generating enough entry-level jobs for low-skilled workers, the country's political leaders appear confident the Netherlands can meet this challenge as it has met so many others in the recent past.

QUESTIONS

1) How did Prime Minister Lubbers set about curing the "Dutch disease"?

2) What role did the unions and unionized workers play in turning the "Dutch disease" into the "Dutch miracle"?

3) What advantages do you see to the Dutch approach to unemployment? What disadvantages?

4) Do you think the Dutch approach would work in Canada? Why or why not?

SOLIDARITY BENEATH THE GOLDEN ARCHES OR WHAT'S THE MCBEEF?

What would make workers at McDonald's restaurants want to unionize, despite the many risks involved?

Though the burger chain's wages are low, unionization isn't mainly about money, insists one-time Employee of the Month Martin LePage who changed his career to become a full-time union organizer earlier this winter. Rather, it's about working conditions.

"The managers often yell at kids who are a bit slow with the pickles and make them feel like nothing," LePage says.

"They keep telling you, 'Oh, you're so great. You're so wonderful.' Then they make you clean the toilet bowl. Or you've got to go up and shovel the snow off the roof with your bare hands, without gloves, without protective equipment of any kind. For that they'll give you an apple pie."

LePage's career plans underwent an abrupt shift during the winter of 1998, after he organized the McDonald's outlet in St-Hubert, Québec. It was the first time any North American McDonald's outlet had been unionized.

To say the company was unhappy with this development is an understatement. Rather than operate the St-Hubert outlet unionized, they simply closed it down, leaving LePage and his co-workers without a job — and determined to fight the company tooth and nail.

Now he vows he won't be satisfied until every McDonald's outlet in the province of Québec has a union. Since he can't legally organize in the restaurants, he spends a good deal of his time going around to schools and telling the students there, many of whom will soon be working in places like McDonald's if they aren't already, what a union can do for them.

Though not all the students are receptive to his message, many are. As evidence of what a union can do for workers in the fast-food business, a friend of LePage's who recently organized a Harvey's restaurant points to seniority rights, a wage scale, improved job security, and regular coffee breaks as just a few of the benefits.

This doesn't mean that unionization will be an easy sell, now or for the near future. The company and other fast-food restaurants have always resisted fiercely in the past, and all the evidence suggests they're likely to go on resisting. The question is whether the Martin LePages of the world, aided by some powerful allies from the mainstream labour movement, can do what it takes to succeed in the face of that resistance.

QUESTIONS

1) Why might many McDonald's workers want a union? Why might many others not be so enthusiastic at the prospect?

Video Resource: "McUnions," from *The National*, May 26, 1998.

2) Why are McDonald's and other fast-food chains so fierce in resisting unionization?

3) Do you think Martin LePage is taking the right approach in stressing working conditions over wages?

4) Do you think LePage and others like him will succeed in organizing large numbers of McDonald's and other fast-food establishments? Why, or why not?

APPENDIX II   Cases

Health and Safety Case

C.L.R.B. DECISION NO 757, BOARD FILE 950-99, SEPTEMBER 28, 1989

A skilled machinist returns from vacation to find his shop in a state of total chaos. Because of the slippery condition of the floor around his wheel reprofiling machine, he slips and falls, injuring his finger. The next day he refuses to work until the situation is remedied. Should he be penalized for this action?

Parties: Spielberg / Canadian National (CN)
Forum: Canada Labour Relations Board
Jurisdiction: Canada

The worker was a machinist who had been employed by CN for about 10 years. He had an unblemished employment history with CN and his expertise had been recognized. His specialized job involved essentially the reconditioning of locomotive wheels that had worn out and had deteriorated over time. He was expected to be able to reprofile three or four pairs of wheels during a normal shift if the machine used for the purpose was in good working order.

The worker was also an active member of the workplace health and safety committee, responsible for questions on health and safety in the shop. He had submitted written reports on several occasions disclosing shortcomings in the shop facilities, particularly in the wheel reprofiling section where he worked. Before he went on vacation, he had reported the fact that the platform around the wheel reprofiling machine was slippery and had no guardrail, which posed a danger to health and safety. On his return from vacation, he found the shop in a state of total disorder. The reprofiling machine required repairs and the dangers and deficiencies he had reported in writing had not been remedied. The worker refused to work because of the slippery condition around the machine, which had caused him to slip and fall the day before, resulting in injury to his finger. He requested that a Labour Canada officer be called to investigate the matter. The shop foreman refused and instead assigned the worker to perform other duties.

Source: Adapted from Canadian Labour Relations Board Decision No. 757 Board File 950-99, 9/28/89, record #8994. © 1989, CCH Canadian Ltd. Reprinted from *Canadian Employment Safety & Health Guide* with permission. Some deletions have been made by the author for the purposes of this book and names have been changed.

He later received a summons to a disciplinary hearing for alleged lack of productivity. The hearing led to the worker's being assessed 10 demerit points under the company's personnel management procedure known as the "Brown System" in disciplinary matters. Once an employee had accumulated a certain number of demerit points, he could be subject to dismissal.

The worker filed a complaint with Labour Canada alleging that his employer, in imposing the 10 demerit points against him, had contravened section 147(a) of the Canadian Labour Code prohibiting any disciplinary or reprisal action against an employee who has exercised his rights under the Code or has sought the enforcement of any of the provisions of Part II of the Code. In this case, the complainant alleged that the disciplinary action taken by CN against him was the result of his insistence that safety standards should be complied with and of the fact that he had exercised his right to refuse unsafe work under Part II of the Code. The employer, in reply, essentially argued that the penalty imposed had no connection with the complainant's availing himself of the provisions of Part II of the Code.

QUESTIONS

1) Will the Board allow the machinist's penalty of ten demerit points to stand? Why, or why not?

2) If you were the machinist's superior, how would you have handled this situation?

3) If you were senior management, in what light would you view the foreman's behaviour? How might you respond to the incident?

4) What might the machinist do, another time, to help ensure safe conditions without putting his own neck on the line to the same extent?

CASE
HS.2   Health and Safety Case
CANADA LABOUR RELATIONS BOARD,
DECISION NO 743. MAY 18, 1989

Two flight attendants file complaints against their employer for alleged contravention of section 147 of the Canada Labour Code, which prohibits the employer from taking disciplinary action against those who refuse to work in conditions they consider

Source: Adapted from CLRB Decision No. 743, 5/18/89, record #8989. © 1989, CCH Canadian Ltd. Reprinted from *Canadian Employment Safety & Health Guide* with permission. Some deletions have been made by the author for the purposes of this book and names have been changed.

unsafe. The flight captain inspects all the equipment that the crew reports to be unsafe and clears it for flight. When the attendants walk off the job, they are given the choice of resigning or being terminated. Should this action stand?

Record Number: 8989
Parties: Arthur / Jones / Bradley Air Service
Forum: Canada Labour Relations Board
Jurisdiction: Canada

Two flight attendants had filed complaints against their employer for alleged contravention of section 147 of the Labour Code. This provision of the Code prohibits the employer from taking reprisal or disciplinary action against an employee for refusing to work because of concern for safety and health. Having arisen from the same incident, the complaints were heard together.

The complainants were part of a plane crew scheduled to work on a charter flight from Mirabel to San Andras, Columbia. The flight departure was delayed, which considerably upset the crew. The crew had expressed their dissatisfaction to the flight supervisor and had suggested getting another crew to double for them so their extended duty day would be shortened. During the pre-flight safety check, the complainants had also reported certain non-functioning equipment on board the aircraft. The flight captain, however, cleared all the items specified as not being safety hazards to the flight. The complainants had decided to walk off the job and had no further contact with their employer until they were advised that they had no flight schedule and that they had the choice to resign or be terminated. After much discussion, the complainants were served their letters of termination. Complaints were filed with the Canada Labour Relations Board in accordance with section 133 of the Code.

··· ··· ···

As to the length of the duty day that the complainants had claimed to be harmful to their health, the Board found abundantly clear from the evidence that the entire crew was upset from the start of the delays. The respondent had understood the complainants' concerns about their extended duty day for that charter flight, but it was impossible to locate another crew on such short notice and the employer was critically short of flight attendants at the time. Scheduled departure times for charters were often delayed and delays, such as occurred in this case, were an unavoidable feature of a flight crew's conditions of employment. The complainants had also refused the respondent's offer for them to be switched to an alternative flight, which would have resulted in a duty day of similar duration as their original schedule.

QUESTIONS

1) What would your ruling have been had you been the adjudicator in this case?

2) Do you think the flight attendants' behaviour was constructive? What might you have done differently had you been in their position?

3) What might the employer have done differently (if anything)?

4) Recently there has been a significant increase in crashes and near-crashes caused by defective equipment, such as faulty insulation or wiring. Does this cast the attendants' behaviour in a different light?

CASE
C.1

Certification Case

Should a union be certified when it appears an employer has had a hand in generating support for it?

United Electrical, Radio, and Machine Workers of America (UE), Applicant, v. **Square D Canada Electrical Equipment Inc.**, Respondent, v. Square D Employees' Association, Intervener.

Before: D. E. Franks, Vice-Chairman, and Board Members J. D. Bell and H. Simon. September 15, 1980.

···   ···   ···

In order to establish its status as a trade union for the purpose of section 1(1)(n) of the Act, the intervener adduced evidence concerning the formation of the Square D Employees' Association at a meeting at the Holiday Inn in Kitchener on May 22, 1980. The minutes of the meetings were filed with the Board as was a copy of the constitution adopted at that meeting. On the basis of the evidence before the Board concerning that meeting, the Board finds that the intervener has established its status within the meaning of section 1(1)(n) of the Act.

The applicant alleges, however, that because of the employers' conduct in this matter, section 12 of the Act prohibits the Board from certifying the intervener as a bargaining agent. That section provides as follows:

"The Board shall not certify a trade union if any employer or any employers' organization has participated in its formation or administration or has contributed financial or other support to it or if it discriminates against any person because of his race, creed, colour, nationality, ancestry, age, sex or place of origin."

On the afternoon of May 13, 1980, Mr. Joel Johnson, the plant manager of the respondent, assembled the employees of the respondent at a meeting and read to them from a prepared text which was filed with the Board at the hearing. The text of his remarks reads as follows:

"A number of employees have indicated to me that they have been approached by union representatives. Some of these employees have questioned the reason for the company remaining silent on this issue.

I would like to say that prior to relocating into Waterloo, Company representatives came into this area to take a survey of wages and benefits. What has been established here is the result of this survey.

Lowest hourly rate is 5.19/hour
Highest hourly rate is 7.54/hour

Source: Adapted from 0363-80-R; 0412-80-R, in Ontario Labour Board Reports, 1980, pp. 1324–1329. Some deletions have been made by the author for the purposes of this book and names have been changed.

How many companys [sic] in Waterloo can match these rates?

Square D pay 100% of OHIP

      100% of Group Insurance Plan

Have 12 stat. Holidays + an excellent vacation plan

Bereavement allowance

Jury Duty allowance

If employees feel that they have other problems or complaints they are certainly entitled to have these mutually resolved.

This could be achieved by (1) individuals meeting with their supervisor or manager, (2) Employees forming an Employee Committee, and (3) if neither of these were to satisfy the employees then a Union could be the answer. If employees feel that a union is the only answer to their problems then that is your right, but please make sure that the union selected is one that will act 100% on *your* behalf." (emphasis indicated in notes)

The evidence is that after finishing these remarks, Mr. Johnson added that he would answer no questions in relation to his statement. There is a substantial conflict between the evidence given by witnesses for the applicant and Mr. Johnson. A number of witnesses for the applicant say that Mr. Johnson added that if anyone wanted to talk to him about this matter, they could come and see him afterwards. Mr. Johnson, however, denies having made such an invitation.

Two days later, on May 15, the evidence is that a petition was circulated around the respondent's premises to the effect that a shop association should be set up by the employees. The Board heard evidence concerning the conduct of two employees involved with this petition.

The evidence of Donna Switzers is that on the afternoon of May 15, just before the afternoon break an employee, Sam Brown, approached the employees in her department at their work stations. He asked them to sign the petition in favour of a shop association. At the time when Brown was in the area, the foreman, Engels, was at his desk, which is in the area. Switzers' evidence is that Brown was with the group of employees for a sufficient length of time that Engels, the foreman, would have been aware of his presence. Engels, however, said nothing concerning this disruption of work in his area. The witness regarded this as unusual since, as a foreman, he does not allow talking in his area.

The other incident in relation to this petition involves Don McNeil. There is some dispute about McNeil's status as an employee. The position of the respondent is that McNeil is a lead hand. The applicant disputes this and claims that he is a foreman or is sufficiently close to being a foreman as to be perceived by employees as part of management. Mr. Johnson, in his evidence, denied that McNeil is a foreman. This is supported by other evidence that confirms that McNeil does not wear the distinctive jacket of a foreman and that he punches a time card.

Of singular interest is an event that occurred while Mr. McNeil was circulating the petition to form a shop association. The evidence of Tom Dover is that on May 15, just after lunch, McNeil came to his area and called a group of employees together. In the course of discussions concerning the formation of a shop association, Bill Olson, who later became the president of the intervener, asked McNeil what would happen if they did not sign the petition. Would management know that they were with the UE? McNeil replied, yes they would know. Not surprisingly, all the employees in the area signed the petition to form a shop union. This evidence was not denied and in fact Mr. McNeil was not called as a witness in this case.

On Friday, May 16, McNeil and others called a meeting of the employees in the plant at noon hour. The meeting was held in the parking lot adjacent to the respondent's plant. The meeting was chaired by McNeil and there was a substantial discussion concerning the formation of a shop association, as a result of which a committee was struck. They in turn contacted a solicitor and the events of May 22 resulted in the formation of the intervener association.

The Board also heard evidence of two subsequent events concerning the conduct of Tim O'Connor and Fred Walker after the formation of the intervener on May 22. The evidence of Sam Duryea is that on May 23, in the afternoon, Walker spent a good ten to fifteen minutes talking to two employees in the presence of one of the foremen, Mr. Delaney. Apparently, Delaney did not interfere with the discussions notwithstanding the recent instructions concerning such activity. In his evidence, however, Mr. Walker denied that he engaged in any organizing activity for the intervener during working hours.

The applicant argues that the events must be taken as a whole and dealt with as a matter of timing and atmosphere.

Although Mr. Johnson's speech is a very carefully worded and guarded statement, there is no doubt that the employer's preference was made quite clear given the context of that speech. The opening remarks can only be interpreted as a reference of the organizing campaign of the applicant trade union. Thus, the concluding remark that the union selected should be one that would "act 100% on *your* behalf" can only reasonably be interpreted as a preference against the applicant UE and in favour of an employee committee.

QUESTIONS

1) In what ways (if at all) did the employer demonstrate a preference for the Square D Employees' Association over the United Electrical, Radio, and Machine Workers?

2) Why do most labour relations acts bar certification in cases where employers have participated in a union's formation or administration or have otherwise supported a union?

3) If you were a labour board member, would you certify the Square D Employees' Association? Why, or why not?

4) Do you feel that the employers' behaviour can be justified on the basis of "employer freedom to communicate" provisions such as those discussed in the text? Why or why not?

When a union is seeking to represent a bargaining unit containing large numbers of seasonal, part-time, and casual employees, who should be considered a bargaining-unit member for the purpose of determining whether the union has sufficient support to entitle it to a representation vote?

Canadian Union of Public Employees, Local 79 and The Corporation of the City of Toronto
Ontario Labour Relations Board, R. O. MacDowell, Chair; J. A. Rundle, Member; and H. Peacock, Member. July 3, 1996.

J. James Nyman, for union.
E. T. McDermott, for employer.
No. 2603–95–R.

R.O. MACDOWELL, CHAIR
(H. PEACOCK, MEMBER, CONCURRING)

This is an application for certification in which CUPE Local 79 seeks to represent a large group of City employees who are currently unrepresented. A significant number of those employees have sought membership in the union and have indicated in a secret ballot vote that they want the union to represent them. The question in this case is whether the union is entitled to certification as their bargaining agent — that is, whether the Board can give legal effect to the wishes of employees recorded in the representation vote.

The union and the City are no strangers to the collective-bargaining process. CUPE Local 79 already represents some 2800 "white-collar" employees in the so-called "inside workers' bargaining unit." CUPE Local 43 (a sister local) represents a bargaining unit of 1800 "blue-collar" workers in the "outside workers' bargaining unit." Employees represented by the two CUPE locals work in proximity to the unrepresented workers affected by this application.

The two CUPE locals have been involved in collective bargaining with the City for decades. The issue in this case is whether another group of City employees is entitled to participate in that process.

The present application relates to a body of employees variously described as "part-time," "seasonal," or "casual," who work in the City's parks, community centres, and recreation programs. Their hours of work and work locations vary considerably, as does the actual work that they do. The number of casuals actively employed at any particular time also varies with the season and with the program mix offered by the City.

Source: Adapted from OLRB, No. 2603-95-R, in 32 CLRBR (2nd), 1996, pp. 1–49. Some deletions have been made by the author for the purposes of this book and names have been changed.

The parties are *agreed* that for the purposes of this certification application the unit of employees appropriate for collective bargaining should be described as follows:

> all casual employees employed by the corporation of the city of Toronto in the Recreation Division of the Department of Parks and Recreation, save and except supervisors, persons above the rank of supervisor, and persons for whom the applicant or any other trade union held bargaining rights as of October 10, 1995.

However, the parties are *not* agreed on the number of employees in this unit for the purposes of the application. In other words, the parties agree on the *description* of the bargaining unit, but they do not agree on its *composition*.

The term "casual employee" (or "recreation casual") is used by the City for payroll purposes to describe these casual workers in a general way, and distinguish them from the "regular" inside or outside workers who are already represented by CUPE. For convenience, we will use the same terminology in this decision. However, it is important to note that the term "casual employee" (as used by the City and applied to a particular individual) does not necessarily connote a continuing employment relationship with the City, either in a common-law contractual sense, or for the purpose of certification under the *Labour Relations Act, 1995*. That is one of the issues that divides the parties. Since these "recreation casuals" work intermittently, there is a dispute about just how many of them actually were "employees" at the time the certification application was filed.

Counsel for the City advised that, over the course of the year, the City hires as many as 2400–2500 of these "casual workers" who work for various lengths of time in the parks, playgrounds, and recreation centres scattered throughout the City. The peak program period is during the summer months when, we were told, the City needs roughly 1500 additional employees to work as lifeguards, supervise wading pools, organize sports activities, administer camp programs, and so on. Many of these individuals are students employed during their school vacation period, so when the summer is over, their jobs end and they go back to school. They may or may not return the following summer.

In the fall, the complement of casuals drops considerably. Counsel for the City advised that, for the autumn programs, between 700 and 900 individuals are engaged for activities as diverse as square dancing, piano lessons, or Red Cross certification. In the winter, *yet another group* of workers is engaged in respect of indoor programs or outdoor winter sports activities at the City's parks, ice rinks, and arenas.

We were told that only a small group of "recreation casuals" are working continuously — primarily because they have a skill (for example, piano training) that is in constant demand for particular programs or at a particular recreation centre. However, that core group comprises only 200 to 400 workers (the parties disagree about the numbers). The rest of the recreation casuals come and go in accordance with the City's needs. There is no necessary carry-over between, say, those casuals who act as lifeguards or supervise the wading pools in the summer, and the casuals who clean the ice rinks in the winter. The composition of the casual group is continuously changing.

The City says that up to 75 percent of the summer casuals are hired again in the following summer (the union disputes the percentage). But there is no legal commitment to do so. Nor is there any obligation on the casual to return if asked. In this sense, the casual workers' situation is quite different from someone with enforceable "recall rights" under a collective agreement.

...   .

By any measure, there is a substantial turnover of casual employees, since the number and composition of the casual group depends upon the seasons, the program mix that the City chooses to offer, and, of course, their own availability to return to a program that has been offered before. Indeed, it is interesting to note that even the City had difficulty identifying the precise number of casuals who had been employed over the past year. We were told that compiling a list of casuals was difficult because the work locations were geographically diverse and many of the payroll records were kept manually.

This application for certification was filed on October 10, 1995 — that is precisely a month before Bill 7 came into effect. The material filed with the application therefore reflects the scheme of the Act that was in effect prior to November 10, 1995. However, because Bill 7 had certain retroactive features, it is agreed that the Board is obliged to apply the new Act to this application, even though it was filed "under the old system."

In support of this application for certification, the union has submitted 738 "membership" cards, and has estimated that, at the time the application was filed, the size of the bargaining unit was 840 persons. We were told that the union had been organizing for a number of months prior to the application, so its estimate is presumably based upon its contact with the various workplaces and its understanding of the ebb and flow of program activity. The union's estimate is generally consistent with the City's own estimate of the number of casuals *actively* working in the fall programs (see above).

In each case, the union card is signed by the individual worker concerned, is witnessed by another person, and indicates that the signer is applying for membership in the union. There is no real challenge to the form of this membership evidence either from the City or from any of the individuals who signed the cards. There is no reason to believe that the cards do not mean what they say: that the person signing the card wants to be represented by the trade union in a collective-bargaining relationship with the City.

The City has filed material in response to this application (which, as noted, was launched prior to the passage of Bill 7). The City's filing identified some 369 persons who were actively at work on Tuesday, October 10, 1995, the day on which the certification application was made.

The City has also filed a schedule of some 2455 other persons labelled "recreation casuals" who were not at work on the application date, but who had worked for the City at some point in the previous year. For the overwhelming majority of these individuals, the City has indicated that they were not scheduled to work on the application day, and that their expected date of return or recall was "unknown." The City's position is that all of these individuals (369 + 2045 = 2414) should be considered to be "employees in the bargaining unit" for the purposes of this certification application, *and further that if less than 40 percent of them have signed union membership cards, there can be no representation vote.*

It remains to be determined whether Bill 7 actually requires the kind of *pre-vote* arithmetic calculation proposed by the City, and, if it does, whether such calculation should be based upon the City's proposed list, material from the union, or some revised version of the City's list that emerges from inquiry or litigation. *The City asserts that an examination of this kind is required before any representation vote can be ordered.* The union's proposed interpretation of Bill 7 avoids this *pre-vote* exercise altogether — or, more accurately, shifts the focus to one of determining voter eligibility *after* the vote is ordered, rather than whether a vote should be taken at all. We shall have more to say about that later. At this point, it may be helpful to "do the arithmetic" in order to illustrate the dimensions of the problem.

For the 369 persons actively at work on October 10, 1995 (*i.e.*, literally "in" the proposed bargaining unit on the application date), the union has submitted 201 membership cards, which represents about 54 percent of the persons listed by the City as being at work on October 10. For the other 2045 persons not at work on October 10 (and for the most part not scheduled to return to work at any known date), the union has gathered a further 344 cards. Since the union's card-signing campaign took place in the weeks prior to the filing of the application for certification, it appears that by the time the application was filed, quite a number of the casuals who were working during the summer and had signed cards at that time, were no longer actively employed.

The union clearly has the support of the majority of the employees actively at work on October 10, 1995, and, therefore, unequivocally in the bargaining unit on the date the union applied for certification. Since the City says that there are around 900 individuals working in its fall programs, it is also clear that a significant proportion of them want to be represented by the union. However, if the bargaining unit actually contains 2400 to 2500 "employees" as the City claims, then the union's level of "card support" in that much larger group is only around 25 percent of this much larger number. And if the size of the bargaining unit is somewhere between 369 and 3000, it is currently impossible to determine the union's level of card support in percentage terms, without examining the actual situation of each person named on the employer's list to see whether such individual should be treated as an "employee" in the bargaining unit for the purposes of the certification process.

It is impossible to predict how long such analysis would take, particularly if the "facts" or their characterization are disputed, so that the Board would have to make specific determinations with respect to individual workers. But the union's estimate of "many months" is not at all unreasonable — especially if the test for inclusion in the bargaining unit for certification purposes ultimately turns on each individual's personal situation, his or her intention to return to work, or the likelihood that she or he will return to the program, position or location in which she or he had worked before. This could be a mammoth task, involving hundreds of individual inquiries, and by the time it was completed, the bargaining unit under review would likely have undergone significant change.

The nature of the inquiry urged upon us by the employer warrants some further elaboration, because it highlights what might be described as a "systemic concern" in the interpretation of Bill 7. The "process problem" raised by the City in this case is not at all unique. If the employer's interpretation of Bill 7 is right, quite a number of cases may require such pre-vote litigation to sort out the employee list. And that, in turn, may significantly impact on the way in which the Board handles certification applications under Bill 7. In other words, while the characteristics of this work group are a little unusual, the legal issue raised by the employer is extremely important for the way in which the certification process works generally — and ultimately whether the new system can actually deliver the five-day votes that are contemplated by the statute.

We should note that in this particular case, the union could not reasonably have known the precise number of "employees" in the bargaining unit, for, as we have already indicated, even the employer had some difficulty compiling a complete list. The union would have had some general information about the bargaining-unit size from its members in the field, from the casuals themselves and from an earlier application that was filed in the spring and later withdrawn. But the union would not know the precise number or identity of the employees in the bargaining unit in October, even where, as here, the bargaining-unit description was agreed upon.

An agreement on the bargaining-unit *description* does not mean that there will be agreement on bargaining unit *composition.*

...   .

If uncertainty about the "employee list" is a basis for litigation, then there may be quite a lot of it. And if a "list dispute" of this kind can delay the "quick vote" contemplated by Bill 7, then there may be quite a few votes that are delayed — despite the terms of the statute.

...   .

On November 21, 1995, the Board (differently constituted) established a "voting constituency" for this application, based upon the agreed-upon bargaining-unit description. The Board also directed that a representation vote be taken, so that the "employees" affected by this application (whatever their number) could indicate, by secret ballot, whether or not they wanted to be represented by the union. In so doing, the Board took into account the material before it, its reading of what Bill 7 required, and the parties' agreement with respect to the bargaining-unit description. The Board was satisfied that the union's material demonstrated the requisite "appearance" of support required by section 8 of the Act, so that the union's right to certification depended on a test of employee wishes.

The City disagreed. The City took the position that no vote of employees *could* be taken, that no vote of employees should be taken, and further that if a vote were taken, the vote should not be counted and the wishes of employees should not be revealed.

The parties did not agree on the composition of the proposed bargaining unit, so they did not agree on the list of eligible voters in the voting constituency. The City maintained that there were 2500 to 3000 persons who were "employees" in the bargaining unit entitled to participate in the vote, and apparently sent letters to those individuals (or many of them) advising them of the vote and urging them to exercise their franchise. The union's view was that the votes consisted of the 800 or so employees actually at work in the City's fall programs when the application was filed.

To avoid delay, the union agreed that a vote could be taken using the City's expanded voters' list. But the union's agreement was made without prejudice to its position that the City's list grossly overstated the number of employees in the bargaining unit and thus the number of eligible voters.

The union's position was that the City's list contained the names of a large number of persons who were no longer "employees" on the City's payroll. In the union's view, the City had "loaded the list" with a huge number of names in order to precipitate "front end" litigation over the list, and derail the quick-vote procedure contemplated by Bill 7. The union points out that delaying the vote was in the employer's interest because in a bargaining unit like this one employee turnover would erode the union's base of support. And on a more general plane, if a union had to meet a test of correctness with respect to bargaining-unit size, it would significantly impede any union's ability to organize employees.

...   .

The representation vote in the instant case was taken on December 8, 1995. There were four separate polls in various parts of the city, with voting hours extending to 8 p.m. so that any individuals interested in the process would have an opportunity to exercise their franchise. Voters were invited to signify by secret ballot whether or not they wished to be represented by the trade union in a collective bargaining relationship with the City.

The turnout was quite low — only 342 persons. The union says that this low turnout reflects the casual workers' lack of actual attachment to the workplace, whatever their notional "employment status" might be, and points out that, in any case, everyone had an opportunity to vote, whether or not they chose to do so.

···   ···   ···

In the result, a significant majority of the ballots cast in the representation vote were cast in favour of the union. In other words, all of the arguably eligible voters were given an opportunity to cast ballots, the ballots were counted, and the union "won" the vote.

The union is content with that result. The City is not.

···   ···   ···

None of the employees (or potential employees) in the bargaining unit affected by this certification application has raised any challenge to the Board's decision to direct that a representation vote be taken to test their wishes. No employee has raised any question about the manner in which the vote was conducted. Nor does any employee or potential employee oppose the union's request that a certificate should issue based upon that representation vote. This case is a contest between the "institutional parties."

···   ···   ···

THE SCHEME OF THE ACT UNDER BILL 7

Bill 7 was introduced into the Legislature in October 1995 and became law about a month later on November 10, 1995. Much of the Bill was directed to repealing features of "Bill 40." But in addition, Bill 7 made a number of other changes, including a revised certification process.

The new scheme no longer permits certification based on membership cards alone. A representation vote has now become the exclusive method of testing employee wishes and is a requirement in every case.

However, in opting for "a vote in every case," the Legislature has not simply reverted to the former process for obtaining and conducting a representation vote. Instead, the Legislature has created an entirely new and quite different mechanism, relying on very quick five-day votes, to measure the employee wishes, while at the same time limiting the employer's opportunity to improperly interfere with the employees' freedom of choice.

The secret ballot replaces the signed membership card as the means of testing the employees' appetite for collective bargaining. But like the previous card-based model, the new system is designed to avoid a protracted "campaign" where the union and employer compete for the loyalties of employees. Because of the tight time-frames, there is less opportunity for behaviour that could attract unfair labour practice charges (quite a number of these are filed each year). The new system makes it very clear that time is of the essence: it is not just "a vote in every case;" the statute contemplates a *"quick* vote in every case."

The five-day time-frame mentioned in the statute is the most critical characteristic of the new certification scheme. It not only defines the nature of the process, it also requires the Board to develop new administrative structures in order to meet the five-day target. Indeed, it is a target that we think the Board is required to meet if it can; moreover, it is a target that the Legislature must have intended that the Board *could meet* in most cases, applying the words of the new statutory scheme. The new certification process reflects a legislative trade-off: the elimination of the (relatively) *quick* card-counting model for certification, and the substitution of the *quick* vote model instead.

QUESTIONS

1) Why is the *City of Toronto* case potentially of great importance?

2) Whose arguments do you find more convincing: those of the employer or those of the union? Why?

3) What's the significance of "Bill 7," which has since been incorporated into the *Ontario Labour Relations Act*?

4) If you were the chair of the Ontario Labour Relations Board, would you allow the representation vote to stand? Why, or why not?

5) If you would not allow the representation vote to stand, how would you then proceed in this case?

6) There is considerable debate in the IR literature as to whether certification votes should be decided by a majority of bargaining unit members or a majority of those voting? Which do you think is the fairer standard, and why?

CASE UL.1   Unfair Labour Practice Case

When a union organizing drive is being carried out at the same time as a company is losing major contracts, and some employees find their hours reduced but not others, under what circumstances does this constitute an unfair labour practice?

James Gordon et al. and 113239 Canada Ltd. c.o.b. as Hill's Limousine Service and International Brotherhood of Electrical Workers, Local 228

Canadian Labour Relations Board, J. Philippe Morneault, Vice-Chair; Véronique L. Marleau, Member; and Sarah E. FitzGerald, Member. October 4, 1996.

Board File No. 745–5229.
Decision No. 1184.

Source: Adapted from CLRB File No. 745–5229, Decision No. 1184, in 32 CLRBR (2nd), 1996, pp. 122–136. Some deletions have been made by the author for the purposes of this book and names have been changed.

DECISION OF THE BOARD

I.

On November 28, 1995, five employees filed an unfair labour practice complaint against their employer, Hill's Limousine Service ("Hill's" or the "employer"), alleging that the employer has been discriminating against them by reducing their hours of work and consequently their incomes. They say that Hill's is doing so because of their membership in or participation in the administration of a trade union, in this case the International Brotherhood of Electrical Workers, Local 2229 (IBEW).

Section 94(3)(a)(i) of the Canada Labour Code states:

94.(3) No employer or person acting on behalf of an employer shall

    (a) refuse to employ or to continue to employ or suspend, transfer, lay off or otherwise discriminate against any person with respect to employment, pay or any other term or condition of employment or intimidate, threaten or otherwise discipline any person, because the person,

        (i) is or proposes to become, or seeks to induce any other person to become, a member, officer or representative of a trade union or participates in the promotion, formation or administration of a trade union.

IBEW filed an application for certification in May 1994. In July 1994 the Board certified the trade union to represent a bargaining unit of Hill's chauffeurs, chauffeur/dispatchers and chauffeur/driver trainers. The complainants say that prior to the May 1994 application, and as the more experienced drivers employed at Hill's, they received more work hours. They allege that Hill's has reduced their hours of work since May 1994 by assigning work to less experienced drivers hired,

- after IBEW's May 6, 1994, application for certification,
- after IBEW's September 1994, notice to bargain,
- after Hill's created the position of assistant manager in October 1994, and
- in November 1995.

The employer denies harbouring anti-union feelings and maintains that the hours of all drivers were reduced when it lost a major contract representing 70 percent of the company's business. Hill's says that it distributed the remaining work hours among its drivers as equitably as possible, subject to their availability. The employer says it did so to maintain the interest of all drivers in working for Hill's. Hill's describes all of its drivers as "essentially casual."

In the employer's view, an award of lost income to the complainants will, in effect, establish a system of driver seniority that has never existed at Hill's and that IBEW has not, to date, succeeded in obtaining through bargaining.

II.

Certain matters raised by the parties during the hearing may be briefly stated.

1. *Exclusive representation by certified bargaining agent*

The employer challenged the fact that IBEW did not file this complaint on behalf of the named employees, nor did it appear as an interested party at the hearing. James Gordon, one of the complainants, represented the five employees before the Board.

Although this type of complaint is usually filed on an employee's behalf by a trade union, the Code does not prevent employees from filing their own complaints. Section 97(1) of the Code [am. S.C. 1991, c. 39, s. 2] allows "any person or organization" to make such a complaint. The right is not restricted to trade unions.

···   ···   ···

A section 94(3) complaint attracts the reverse onus of proof set out in section 98(4):

98. (4) Where a complaint is made in writing pursuant to section 97 in respect of an alleged failure by an employer or any person acting on behalf of an employer to comply with subsection 94(3), the *written complaint is itself evidence that such failure actually occurred and, if any party to the complaint proceedings alleges that such failure did not occur, the burden of proof thereof is on that party.* [Emphasis added]

As discussed in *Air Atlantic Ltd. and C.A.W.* (1986), 68 di 30, 87 CLLC ¶16,002 (CLRB No. 600), the employer is usually the only person who really knows the reason for its actions and this is why Parliament gave section 94(3) meaning by shifting the burden of proof. The freedom to join a trade union and to participate in its lawful activities is an important right afforded by the Code. In consequence, section 94(3) requires that an employer satisfy the Board that the actions complained of were not motivated in any way by anti-union animus.

···   ···   ···

If Hill's evidence does not satisfy the Board that the employer's actions were devoid of anti-union animus, the presumption in section 98(4) remains operative, and the employer will be found to have violated section 94(3).

IV.

In presenting its case, Hill's initially called as witnesses Jane Dunn, the general manager, and Phil Olson, former operations manager. Ms. Dunn, a former manager, became general manager in early 1994 and reports to the president, Mr. Zed. She hires drivers and oversees daily operations. The positions of operations manager (when it was staffed) and assistant manager (once created) report to her.

Ms. Dunn gave the following testimony. She hires people-oriented drivers who have flexible schedules. Drivers know they are hired on a part-time, "as needed" basis. There are no guaranteed hours and no maximum number of hours. There has never been "full-time" work. Hill's maintains on average a pool of about 30 drivers to meet its needs. There is a high turnover in drivers because of the nature of the work and part-time hours.

Ms. Dunn explained the significance a single contract can have for Hill's. In 1993, Hill's obtained a contract with Lufthansa for the Ottawa-Mirabel Airport run. This required three to nine trips per day. "At one point" (upon which Ms. Dunn did not elaborate), this contract accounted for 60 percent of the company's hours. In late October/early November 1995 (about one month prior to the filing of this complaint), Hill's received three months' notice from Lufthansa that the contract would terminate in January 1996. Ms. Dunn says the loss of that work has never been replaced.

Ms. Dunn also noted that in June 1994 (one month after the application for certification), Lufthansa ceased paying for stand-by driver hours, and that this affected in particular the work of Thomas Goudet (a complainant). June 1994 was, however, a particularly busy month, and Ms. Dunn stated that Hill's almost doubled its complement of drivers in order to service the transportation needs of a visiting Argentinean delegation for one week.

Ms. Dunn agreed that the employer's records show that only 7 of 35 drivers employed at the time of the May 1994 application for certification were still employed in November 1995 when the complaint was filed.

With respect to the creation of the assistant manager's position, Ms. Dunn explained that in October 1994, Hill's hired Ms. Samantha Cohen. The employer had decided that, for security reasons, it required more of a management presence at its operations. IBEW did not dispute the creation, duties, or staffing of the assistant manager's position. Ms. Cohen was one of the drivers hired by Hill's about six months earlier, following the application for certification. The position was offered first to James Gordon (a complainant). Ms. Dunn knew that he declined because of an ongoing commitment to trade-union matters. Mr. Gordon and Mr. Hancox (another of the complainants) were known members of the team negotiating a first collective agreement.

Ms. Dunn further testified that before Ms. Cohen's hiring as assistant manager, Phil Olson, the operations manager, did the dispatching. He was assisted by a number of drivers acting as relief dispatchers. After Ms. Cohen's hiring and until Mr. Olson was laid off in January 1996 (about two months after the filing of this complaint), they shared the dispatch function. With one exception, drivers were no longer asked to work as relief dispatchers.

Ms. Dunn is still called upon on occasion to do dispatch work. In her opinion, the system at Hill's does not ensure that work is equally distributed among the drivers. The main or senior drivers are given a certain number of hours; that is, those drivers who have worked for Hill's for about a year and who know the cars and the business receive the first offers and are called for all sorts of work. However, she believes that all drivers are offered enough work to keep them busy.

One or two days in advance, Hill's dispatcher schedules drivers to satisfy the bookings. Ms. Dunn says the key is to "cover the work with qualified, suitable drivers." The dispatcher assesses driver availability from monthly posted sheets on which drivers indicate available dates. Drivers also verbally advise dispatchers of circumstances affecting availability. Over time, the dispatcher "gets a feeling" for each driver's availability and preferred work.

Phil Olson, former operations manager, gave the following testimony concerning his dispatching practices while employed at Hill's. The length of a driver's employment was not a factor. He dispatched based on availability, something he "got a feel for over time." He telephoned drivers in alphabetical order. Whoever called back first was given the assignment. Sometimes he would schedule a specific driver if the booking came from a steady client with whom the driver had developed a rapport.

Mr. Olson explained that he tried to give all drivers a minimum of 30 hours per week. He recalls that Mr. Zed, president, had on a few occasions, over the years, discussed a restriction of driver hours. Sometime in 1993, Hill's drivers complained about uneven work distribution. However, it was not until Hill's began hiring more drivers "in the 1994 to 1995 period" that Mr. Zed told him to restrict all drivers to 30 hours per week.

V.

Bob Lewis, a former Hill's chauffeur, testified on behalf of the complainants. Mr. Lewis started driving for Hill's in September 1994 and quickly developed a friendship with Ms. Cohen, the new assistant manager. They lived in the same neighbourhood and drove to and from work together in Ms. Cohen's car. On occasion they enjoyed a social drink together.

Mr. Lewis testified that Ms. Cohen told him that in doing her dispatch work, she was restricting driver hours because the union campaign was hurting both the employer and the newer drivers. Hill's wanted to get rid of drivers who supported the union. She named various individuals in this regard. Mr. Lewis also says that on at least two occasions, Ms. Cohen told him that she preferred to give work to him or "Xavier" rather than to "those union guys," and that she described him as one of the "nice" guys.

Believing the union was not in his best interests, and in the Board's view, seeking to benefit from the situation, Mr. Lewis offered to help get rid of the union. He was told to keep his eyes open and report back to the office. Mr. Lewis testified that, in January 1995, Mr. Zed told him that he would take care of him if he wrote an incident report that helped Mr. Zed to suspend James Gordon. Mr. Lewis understood this to mean that he would be dispatched to the better bookings, and perhaps receive limousine work. Mr. Lewis agreed to write the letter and says that Ms. Cohen told him what to write and Phil Olson typed it. Mr. Gordon was suspended. Mr. Lewis admitted before the Board that he knew that the letter he signed contained false statements.

Mr. Lewis testified that a few months after this January incident he complained about a decrease in hours and the distribution of work. He says that Ms. Cohen told him the following: Business was slow and it was the fault of the union guys that he was not getting more hours, because Hill's could not fire them. Mr. Lewis was already receiving preferential treatment, but the union guys had to get some hours, although they were being given the less desirable bookings. He recalled her giving him an example of dispatching Mr. Gordon on a Toronto run that did not pay for all hours he had to wait with the limousine.

Mr. Lewis testified that he experienced a change of heart in "late spring" of 1995. At this time and again "in the summer" of 1995, he exchanged information about his past earnings at Hill's with drivers who support the trade union. From the information he gathered, it was clear to him that he had been receiving preferential treatment.

For reasons not material to this case, Mr. Lewis left Hill's employ in the fall of 1995.

VI.

In rebuttal testimony Ms. Cohen, the assistant manager, denied the anti-union comments attributed to her by Mr. Lewis. In her view, Mr. Lewis was initially friendly to her because he wanted to ride to and from work with her. When he finally purchased his own car, he pressured her as a friend for more hours because of car payments. After a few months, she tired of his repeated complaints about insufficient hours. Their friendship soured.

Ms. Cohen testified that she was told, upon being hired, to distribute the hours equally among drivers, about 30 hours each. She says however that the 30-hour rule is not cast in stone and it is not a problem to exceed that number. Ms. Cohen mentioned a book in which she maintains a running total of each driver's hours. She says that she telephones those drivers with the fewest hours first, if they show as being available.

Ms. Cohen confirmed that, ultimately, the matter of which driver is assigned to a particular booking lies completely within her discretion.

VII. DETERMINATIONS

Merits of the Complaint

The testimony and documentary evidence satisfies the Board that following the May 1994 application for certification and a busy period in June 1994, the employer introduced changes in its dispatching practises that were not communicated to the drivers.

The employer says that there were fewer work hours to distribute because of the loss of a major contract, but the evidence did not show what contract the employer was referring to. The Lufthansa contract work did not finish until January 1996, after the filing of the complaint. Testimony concerning the loss of stand-by driver hours gave no indication of the number of lost hours or drivers affected, nor whether any new business subsequently made up for this loss. With respect to the testimony about the hiring of many new drivers in June 1994 to provide services to a visiting Argentinean delegation, the pay records do show that June 1994 was a busy month for Hill's drivers. But neither Ms. Dunn nor Mr. Olson provided a satisfactory explanation for the employer's decisions to retain, after June, all of the newly hired drivers and to modify the dispatching practice in order to distribute work more evenly over the enlarged driver group. The employer claimed a loss of overall business and therefore fewer work hours to distribute, but the pay records show little variance in the gross amount paid to the driver group as a whole in the months prior to the May 1994 certification application, and in the months after the busy June 1994, for example, July to November 1994. What did change was the manner in which the work hours were distributed among the drivers. In short, the Board finds that the employer's explanation on this point is insufficient. Furthermore, it does not stand up to scrutiny.

The pay records requested by the complainants reveal that over time certain drivers who had enjoyed a consistent level of earnings prior to the May 1994 application for certification (including the majority of the complainants as top earners), saw their earnings begin to fluctuate and/or decline. As the months passed, many of the drivers employed at the date of the certification application left Hills' employ, and were replaced through new hirings. The employer's evidence does not satisfy the Board that the departure of so many employees in the May 1994 to November 1995 time period was usual for its operations. Given the nature of the complaint and the burden of proof, a single statement by Ms. Dunn that there is a high turnover in the industry is insufficient.

· · ·   · · ·   · · ·

The only pay records available to the Board that show driver earnings in the time period prior to the application for certification (the "PAC" period), were pay records for the immediately preceding four months: January to April 1994. These PAC period records show that four of the five complainants were consistently among a group of about six drivers earning the greatest earnings. In comparison, in a four-month period leading up to the filing of the complaint — July to October 1995 (the "reference period") — only one complainant consistently remained in the group of top earners. The reference period is discussed further below.

The change in four of the five complainants' earnings "rankings" (if we may use that term) between the PAC period and the reference period is shown below:

Range of PAC Monthly Rankings	Range of Reference Period Monthly Rankings
Driver "A": 2nd - 3rd	1st - 4th
Driver "B": 3rd - 4th	8th - 10th
Driver "C": 2nd - 5th	6th - 9th
Driver "D": 4th to 6th	6th - 11th

More specifically the Board noted from the pay records that:

- The amount of each complainant's gross earnings in the January to April 1994 PAC period, and the amount of gross earnings for the bargaining-unit driver group as a whole in those months, were reasonably steady. Consequently, the earnings rankings enjoyed by the complainants as between each other and in comparison with the driver group as a whole were also steady. The consistency permits the Board to draw conclusions about the usual earnings of the complainants in the PAC period.

- The Board compared earnings in the four-month PAC period with earnings in a four-month reference period that does not include November 1995, even though this was the month in which the complaint was filed. Driver earnings decreased markedly in November 1995 at which time the parties had reached the stage of legal strike or lockout in their bargaining. Having regard to the employer's explanation for its work distribution that month, the Board decided against including November 1995 in the reference period for the purpose of assessing similarities to or difference from earnings from the PAC period.

In the reference period, gross earnings for the bargaining-unit driver group as a whole were also reasonably steady, but the proportion of each complainant's earnings had decreased when compared to proportions in the PAC period. Two other drivers working at Hill's in the PAC period had, over time, moved into the top earners group. In the reference period, these two drivers showed gross monthly earnings around or well above their PAC earning levels, despite the employer's assertion that it was distributing work more equally over the entire driver group. Further, three drivers hired after the certification application were, by the time of the reference period, consistently among the top earners.

●●●   ●●●   ●●●

It was no secret to Hill's that the longer-term employees were seeking seniority recognition in a first collective agreement.

QUESTIONS

1) Do you find the employer's denial of anti-union motivation credible?
2) Do you accept the employer's statement that hours reductions for certain drivers were imposed merely for business reasons?
3) Had you been the chair of the labour board, what would your ruling have been in this case? Why?
4) How might the employer avoid having further unfair labour practice complaints brought to the board in the future?

Arbitration Case

IVACO ROLLING MILLS LTD. AND UNITED STEELWORKERS OF AMERICA, LOCAL 7940

In filling a vacant position, an employer must decide between two very good candidates, one of whom has more seniority with the organization, but the other of whom has experience specifically related to the position in question. Which candidate should he or she choose?

Heard: September 16 and November 17, 1997; Ontario; B. Adell
Decision rendered: December 24, 1997
D. Lipton and others, for the Union.
G. Rontiris, J. Van Massenhoven and others, for the employer.

AWARD

The grievor claims that she ought to have been given the posted position of permanent mill recorder for which she applied in January 1997 and that was awarded to Mr. Dave Thomas. The company argues that although the grievor was senior to Mr. Thomas and of similar skill and ability, awarding him the job was justified by the fact that she would have needed a significant amount of training in order to be able to do it, while he needed none. The grievor also claims that she was in fact given the position, and that it was wrongly taken away from her. On this aspect of the grievance, the company's response is that the member of management who led her to believe that she was being given the job simply made an error.

Collective Agreement Provisions

The applicable collective agreement was signed on February 20, 1997, but was effective from December 1, 1996. The following provisions of article 8 (Seniority) and article 9 (Job Posting) are pertinent:

8.03 (a)

The parties recognize that job opportunities shall increase in proportion to seniority. It is therefore agreed that:

(i) In all cases of promotion and transfer the following factors will be considered:
  1) seniority
  2) the skill, ability, and related experience of the applicants.

Source: Adapted from 1–69 L.A.C. (4th), pp. 1–11. Some deletions have been made by the author for the purposes of this book and names have been changed.

N.B. Instructors may find this case helpful in connection with Chapter 11, on the collective agreement.

When the factors mentioned in (2) are relatively equal amongst the applicants, the applicant with the most seniority will be awarded the job, recognizing that job opportunities shall increase in proportion to seniority. If none of those applying has the required skill, ability, and related experience to perform the work then the Company may fill the job from any source available.

···   ···   ···

(iii) In all cases of a job award, the promoted employee will be entitled to a familiarization period of one (1) Week, followed by a trial period not exceeding thirty (30) Working days.

···   ···   ···

9.01(a)

A permanent job becomes vacant in the event the incumbent leaves the service of the Company, or is promoted, demoted, permanently transferred, or when a new job is created.

9.01(b)

A temporary job becomes vacant when the incumbent is ill, injured, on an approved leave of absence, or being trained for a period exceeding thirty (30) working days. A temporary job will also become vacant in the case where the job is for a special task of a definite term that is to be for less than six (6) months. In such case, the terms and task shall be indicated on the job posting. The Company shall not use this provision to by-pass the usual job-posting mechanism set out in article 9.01(a).

···   ···   ···

9.06

The Company may fill any vacant job on a temporary basis while the posting procedures are being invoked. The experience acquired by the employee placed on the job during this temporary period will not be considered if he is one of the applicants.

9.07

A job shall not be considered vacant for posting where the job will not last beyond thirty (30) working days.

At the time of the posting of the job in issue in this case, the collective agreement provided that a job did not have to be posted if it was not expected to last more than six months. The February 1997 agreement shortened that period to 30 days.

Facts

The union called as witnesses Mr. James Donleavy, rod mill superintendent, and the grievor. The company called Mr. Mike Stone, personnel and industrial relations manager. There was little disagreement on the facts.

Duties of the Mill Recorder's Job

The May 1996 job description for mill recorder described the purpose of the job as being "[t]o provide an accurate record of details pertaining to the Rod Mill rolling operations." From that job description and the other evidence before me, perhaps the most central function of the mill recorder is to keep a detailed descriptive record of every interruption of production during the shift, so that such interruptions can be kept to a minimum in the future. An example of the rod mill delay report prepared by a mill recorder for one shift in August 1997 listed about 20 delays in production and set out more than a dozen items of information about each one, including a fairly detailed statement of the cause. Much of this data is entered into the computer system by the mill recorder. Other important aspects of the duties of the job include recording production data and recording the extent of usage of roller guides, so that they can be changed before they wear out. To gather the information needed for these reports, the mill recorder has to have the interpersonal and communication skills to be able to go out onto the mill floor and gather detailed information by talking to members of the crew. He or she also needs extensive familiarity with the layout and operation of the rod mill, and the writing and computer skills to record and input the information clearly and accurately.

Both Mr. Donleavy and Mr. Stone testified that anyone with no previous experience as a mill recorder would need at least three weeks' training in that job, and that during that time the trainee would have to be accompanied more or less constantly by an experienced mill recorder. This evidence was not challenged. Nor was it in dispute that there is normally only one mill recorder on duty at a time, and that providing training for the grievor would have required the assignment of another mill recorder to work with her for the three-week period.

Qualifications of the Grievor and Mr. Thomas

The grievor was hired by the company in March 1990. She was a high-school graduate with experience in several industrial, health care, and clerical jobs. At Ivaco, she did a wide variety of office and clerical jobs, and did them well. She also took continuing education courses in accounting and computers, and got high marks in them. Since April 1994 she had worked as a maintenance clerk in the machine shop — the foundry side of the plant, where many of the billets used in the rod mill are cast. In that position, she was responsible for preparing certain reports on operations and maintenance in the melt shop. She spent most of her time in the office and the melt shop maintenance area, though she would often go onto the melt shop floor, and she learned quite a lot about the duties of the various trades. One of the reports for which she was responsible — the furnace delay report — had some similarities to the rod mill delay report mentioned above. The furnace delay report periodically lists delays in the operation of the melt shop furnace, with data on their length and cause. However, it is much less detailed than the rod mill delay report, and it relates to the other side of the plant.

The grievor's experience had given her a good familiarity with the melt shop, but less familiarity with the rod mill. Her knowledge of the rod mill came largely from the fact that she had worked there for two weeks during the 1995 summer shutdown, when she did a report on maintenance that was to be carried out. Also, in her capacity as a health and safety officer for the office, technical and clerical unit, she would walk through the rod mill from time to time, checking for potential safety hazards. According to the most recent analysis pursuant to the SES job evaluation system, the position of maintenance clerk did not score very far below that of mill recorder (249.9 points as compared to 254.8), and the two jobs had the same score (25 points) on the component factor of "on-the-job experience and training."

Mr. Thomas was hired by the company as a student (a secondary-school graduate who would be going on to college) for the period from February 1995 until the fall of that year. During that period, he worked for two months as a scrap yard clerk and general clerk, and for the rest of the time as a temporary mill recorder. On April 11, 1996, he was hired as a part-time general clerk in the production department, supervised by Mr. Brad Parker as foreman. On April 18, 1996, he was assigned to be a temporary mill recorder. Because the vacancy he filled was expected to be (and in fact was) of short duration, the collective agreement exempted it from the posting requirement. On May 21, 1996, Mr. Thomas was assigned to a week's work as maintenance clerk. On May 27, June 3, and July 7, 1996, he again received temporary assignments as a mill recorder — assignments that were again exempt from the posting requirement because they were expected to be of short duration.

In August 1996, a permanent mill recorder, Mr. Harold Holt, took a temporary position outside the bargaining unit. According to the undisputed evidence, the company expected that Mr. Holt's absence would be temporary, but that it would be for more than six months, so his mill recorder's position was posted under article 9.01 (b). Mr. Thomas was the only applicant. There is no dispute that he was properly awarded the position.

In the course of the grievor's testimony, she was asked whether she had seen the August 1996 posting. She was uncertain, first answering that she had, then indicating that she probably had not. In any event, there was no challenge to the propriety of that posting, and the grievor did not apply for the job at that time. If she had applied for it, and if there had been a competition between her and Mr. Thomas, it was clear from the collective agreement (and accepted by both sides) that Mr. Thomas experience as a mill recorder prior to that point could not have been used in his favour, as it had been acquired in unposted assignments. The grievor's seniority, her basic skill and ability, and her experience in various jobs in the plant would have given her a strong claim to the job.

The January 1997 Competition for the Permanent Mill Recorder's Job

In January 1997, Mr. Holt decided not to return to his position as a mill recorder. That created a vacancy for a permanent mill recorder, which the company posted pursuant to the collective agreement on January 14. Two employees applied for the position — the grievor, and Mr. Thomas.

The grievor was interviewed by Mr. Donleavy and Mr. Bolton on January 28. Mr. Donleavy was favourably impressed by her and, as he put it in his testimony, he thought she was clearly capable of learning the mill recorder's job. However, he was acting under a misapprehension at the time of the interview. According to his evidence, which was unchallenged and was straightforward and credible, he was accustomed to applying the rod mill collective agreement rather than the office, clerical, and technical agreement. The promotion and transfer provision in the rod mill agreement was not a "relatively equal" provision. Instead, it stated that on promotion or transfer, seniority was to govern as long as the senior candidate "has the skill and ability to perform the work to be done." Mr. Donleavy wrongly believed that this sort of "threshold" provision applied to the competition for the mill recorder's job. Because he formed the opinion that the grievor had the skill and ability to learn the job and do it well, he thought she was entitled to it, and he told her so at the end of the interview. There was some difference between his recollection and the grievor's as to what he actually said, but nothing turns on that difference. It is clear that he thought she would get the job and that he told her as much. This is confirmed by the fact that Mr. Donleavy gave her an authorization for the issue of a pair of suitable boots, and that she immediately picked up those boots from the storeroom.

Right after the interview, Mr. Donleavy asked Mr. Bolton to go to see Mr. Stone and tell him of the result. It was not in dispute that Mr. Bolton, as manager of personnel and industrial relations, was the member of management who had the authority to decide whom to choose for the job in question, within the limits set by the collective agreement. Mr. Stone realized that Mr. Donleavy had been under a misapprehension about what the applicable collective agreement provisions said. He immediately conferred with Mr. Donleavy and Mr. Bolton, and pointed out that fact. After a brief discussion, he told Mr. Donleavy and Mr. Bolton that Mr. Thomas would be given the job rather than the grievor, because she would need training and he would not. Later, that day or at the beginning of her shift the next, Mr. Bolton or Mr. Donleavy told the grievor what had happened. Mr. Donleavy apologized to her for his error, and assured her that he still thought she had been a good candidate for the job. She then brought this grievance.

Analysis

Article 8.03(a)(i) is a "relatively equal" clause, which gives seniority a lower priority than "skill, ability and related experience." Seniority only prevails when two or more applicants are "relatively, equal" (that is, approximately equal) on the criteria of skill, ability, and related experience.

…   …   …

The extensive body of arbitral jurisprudence on the application of "relatively equal" clauses has taken the form outlined in the following terms by J. Sack and E. Poskanzer, *Contract Clauses: Collective Agreement Language in Canada*, 3rd ed.:

> Under a clause which states that "seniority shall govern provided ability is relatively equal" arbitrators are loath to interfere with management's assessment of the relative abilities of different employees. This is so even though it has been held that, if the margin of ability is less than substantial, then qualifications are relatively equal.

Union counsel forcefully argued that the presence in article 8.03(a)(i) of the words, "recognizing that job opportunities shall increase in proportion to seniority," should be interpreted to limit the thrust of the "relatively equal" clause and put a good deal more weight on seniority. However, in the context of the article as a whole, those words do not appear to be intended to detract substantially from the priority given to skill, ability, and related experience.

…   …   …

The undisputed evidence shows that the grievor is an able, conscientious, and versatile employee, and I formed a very favourable impression of her during her testimony. She has done a wide variety of jobs in response to company's needs, and she has done them well. The evidence on Mr. Thomas, though much briefer, was to the same effect. There is no question that the grievor's basic level of skill and ability is substantially equal to Mr. Thomas's and that she is capable of learning the mill recorder's job. But it was admitted that she would need no less than three weeks' training to be able to do that particular job on her own, while Mr. Thomas needed no training.

Whatever the wording of the collective agreement, the appointment of Mr. Thomas to the permanent mill recorder's job could obviously not stand if the company had acted with an improper purpose at some point in the chain of events leading to that appointment — for example, if the company had known all along that the August 1996 vacancy would probably be permanent, but had posted it as a less attractive temporary vacancy in order to dissuade others from applying and thereby give Mr. Thomas privileged access to the specific experience needed to override any claim of more senior employees to the permanent job. The union did not allege any such impropriety in connection with the August 1996 posting, and the evidence would not support an allegation of that sort. Union counsel did bring out the fact that Mr. Thomas is the son of a senior foreman in the rod mill, though not a foreman to whom the mill recorders report. Counsel did not claim that there was anything wrong with hiring the son of a member of management, but did suggest that the familial relationship should lead to especially close scrutiny of the company's reasons for choosing Mr. Thomas for the permanent mill recorder's job. I agree. However, even after such scrutiny, I can find no evidence that Mr. Thomas's appointment was the result of any improper factors.

QUESTIONS

1) What's the significance of collective agreement provisions providing that promotion be based wholly or partly on seniority?

2) What type of seniority provision was in effect in this case? How much weight would it give to seniority in promotion decisions?

3) The grievor had the opportunity to apply for the vacant temporary position that gave Mr. Thomas experience related to the mill recorder position, but did not apply to that position. Should this be a relevant factor in the arbitrator's decision?

4) After the grievor's interview for the position, one member of senior management was so confident she had the job that he had her issued a pair of boots. How much weight should this action be given in the arbitrator's decision?

5) Had you been the arbitrator, what would your decision have been, and why?

Arbitration Case
FORDING COAL LTD. AND UNITED STEELWORKERS OF AMERICA, LOCAL 7884

Does an employer's prohibition of cellular phones in the workplace constitute an unreasonable infringement on employee's personal privacy?

Heard: November 5, 1997;
Decision rendered: January 21, 1998; British Columbia; D. L. Larson
Lynn Jenning, for the Union.
R. E. Lester, for the employer.

AWARD

The issue in this case is whether a rule established by the Company on September 11, 1996, that prohibits all employees from bringing personal cellular telephones into the workplace is valid.

The evidence relating to how the rule came about is not in dispute. Michael Wilson, superintendent, employee relations, testified that the matter did not arise out of any particular incident, but that it was generally based upon concerns relating to safety, productivity and efficiency. He testified that until the fall of 1996, cell phones were not a problem because they had not been a reliable means of communication in Elk Valley. However, when B.C. Tel established a new cell site and began to sell the service in the local mall, he concluded that it could become a problem and issued the policy.

When asked what was behind his safety concern, he replied that he became alive to the dangers of cell phones from news reports, combined with the fact that mining is inherently hazardous and that one must do everything possible to reduce the risk. He said that this mine encompasses a large geographic area with constant traffic on the haulage roads. It is an open pit mine with huge equipment, including 170 and 240 ton Wabco trucks, on roads that can have a pitch of up to eight degrees and that must share the roads with a lot of other smaller vehicles.

As for productivity and efficiency, Mr. Wilson said that the mine is operating on very small margins, which requires maximum efficiency in order to remain profitable. He said that he could not even endorse the use of cell phones during breaks because that would be difficult to monitor and human nature being what it is, if employees were to have phones, they would use them during working time, particularly to take calls.

Source: Adapted from 2–70 L.A.C. (4th), pp. 33–43. Some deletions have been made by the author for the purposes of this book and names have been changed.

N.B. Instructors may find this case useful in connection with Chapter 7 on employment law.

The Union conceded that there was good reason to be concerned with safety. Bill James, national representative, testified that they concurred that employees should not be permitted to use cell phones while operating heavy equipment or working in the plant because there are already a significant number of accidents. But he said that the Union considered that it would be appropriate that shop stewards and safety representatives be permitted to carry them. He said that would involve only 20 to 25 employees, equal to about 3 percent to 4 percent of the total workforce, depending upon the number of active stewards. Further, he said they would be distributed into all areas of the property over three shifts.

Currently employees have access to the Company hard-wire phone system by permission. If a foreman is not immediately accessible, the procedure is that the employee may request a truck driver to call the foreman on his two-way radio. The foreman will normally then come around some time later and if he thinks that it is important, will either take the employee to a telephone or arrange for someone else to do it.

It is not without significance that the employees of outside contractors who work on the property are permitted to use cell phones. Mr. Wilson explained that the Company tries not to interfere with the way they run their businesses. They usually have other customers who need to have access to them. On the other hand, he said that the allegations that Dan Wilcox, a management employee who works in the Purchasing Department, has been given permission to use a cell phone is incorrect and that what he has is a cordless phone that only works within a limited range from the base unit. Mr. Wilcox was not called as a witness and, since it involved a singular instance, even if true, I do not consider it to be sufficient to affect the integrity of the policy.

Sally Neal, who is classified as Pit Utility in the Mine Production Department, was a shop steward from 1994 to 1995. She is currently a safety representative for the Union. She testified that her job is located at the "spoils," which is where the large Wabco trucks dump overburden. The spoils tend to be a fair distance from the actual mine, but a "dump shack" has been set up by the Company to provide shelter. It has also been equipped with a two-way radio although Ms. Neal testified that the majority of the time it does not work. That was not disputed by the Company, which explained that the problem stems from the fact that the shack is on skids and is moved frequently.

She gave two examples of occasions when she was refused the use of Company phones in her capacity as a safety representative. She said that on December 18, 1996, she expressed concern to her foreman, Sam Golzo, that the shack had been placed on the opposite side of the road from the spoil. The problem was that it put her in a position of having to cross the road in the face of traffic. Her supervisor responded by giving her an alternate assignment of driving the buses that take employees to and from the mine. She said that she arrived at the mine at 1:30 p.m. during the lunch break. When Mr. Golzo came by she asked him if she could use the phone, to which he replied that he would have to ask Dave Downing, a control foreman. Over the radio, Mr. Downing asked if the call was for personal or union business. She said that when she told him that it was union related, he replied, "no," but he told her to take her lunch and wait for him. When he arrived at the dry, she said that she asked him why he did not permit her to use the phone during her lunch break. He explained that if she wanted to use the phone for union business she would have to book off work. But when she requested a union book off he refused it because there were too many off that day. She was then told to wait for Mr. Golzo to take her down to the buses. The result was that she ended up waiting a total of about 80 minutes including her lunch break, not being able to use the phone even though it was no more than 20 feet away.

The other example that she gave happened on July 6, 1997. On that day a rock went through the windshield of a front-end loader driven by Fred Arnold. When it was reported to her, she asked for permission to go and see it. When she got there she felt that it was a dangerous occurrence that required investigation. In the course of the investigation she asked for permission to use the phone to call Brad White at home in order to determine whether a screen guard might be the solution. Mr. Downing denied the request, stating that the investigation should be completed first, and that if she still felt that she would like to talk to Mr. White arrangements would be made. Based on that evidence, the Union took the position that a Company rule prohibiting all employees from possessing cellular phones on Company property is not reasonable in its application within the rule set out in *Re Lumber & Sawmill Workers' Union. Loc. 2537, and KVP Co.* (1965), 16 L.A.C. 73 (Robinson). While it conceded that there was a legitimate safety concern, specifically relating to employees using cell phones while working and operating machinery, it argued that the current rule is too broad and could not be supported by reference to any of the standard tests in the cases. Accordingly, it proposed that Union officials, including shop stewards and health and safety representatives should be permitted to possess cellular telephones on Company property. Under the proposal, those officials would be entitled to use the phones in the following circumstances:

(a) as of right, on their own time, without prior authorization;

(b) as may be necessary on Company time, with authorization, which authorization would not be unreasonably withheld; and

(c) as of right, during authorized leave for the purpose of conducting union business.

• • •   • • •   • • •

The Company takes quite a different position. On the authority of *Re British Columbia Railway Co. and C.U.T.E.,* Loc. 6 (1982), 8 L.A.C. (3d) 250 (Hope), Mr. Lester argues that the better view is now that an arbitration board does not have an inherent jurisdiction to determine whether a rule published by an employer is reasonable: *Bank of British Columbia v. Union of Bank Employees. Loc. 210* (1982), 133 D.L.R. (3d) 228 (S.C.), but can only monitor the application of the rule under its right to determine whether an employee has been disciplined for just and proper cause: *Re Religious Hospitallers of Hotel-Dieu of St. Joseph of the Diocese of London and Service Employees' Union. Loc. 210* (1983), 11 L.A .C. (3d) 1.51 (Saltman). As for the argument that the policy interferes with the administration of the Union, Mr. Lester says that, in point of fact, there is nothing in the policy that restricts the Union. He said that while the Union might like to be able to operate in a certain way, it has never had the right to use cell phones on Company property and that what it really wishes to do is enhance, facilitate, and improve the way that it carries out its functions. Since it is not a current right, he contends that the only way that it can be acquired by the Union is in the normal way, through collective bargaining.

• • •   • • •   • • •

Is the use of cell phones in the nature of a personal right similar to the right to privacy? Ms. Jenning took up that point by arguing firstly, that for the Company to suggest that the use of cell phones by employees would be an enhancement of their existing rights should not be accepted. Secondly, she said that prior to the policy, employees had a right to bring cell phones to work just as they have a right to bring a lunch and that, instead of the Union seeking to obtain enhanced rights, it is the Company that seeks to limit individual employee rights.

There would appear to be some support in the collective agreement that safety representatives are distinguishable from shop stewards and that they could be enabled to use cellular telephones, based upon the fact that their investigative responsibilities are not constrained in the same manner as shop stewards. Without deciding the matter, under Article 7.02 a steward must obtain permission from his supervisor in order to take time off from work "to attempt to resolve a grievance," although that provision equally provides that the supervisor will not arbitrarily or unreasonably withhold permission. By contrast, no similar requirement is imposed on safety representatives under Article 8. Article 8.02 requires that the foreman and safety representative will determine whether an investigation of an accident is required and if they cannot agree, the matter may be referred under subsection (c) to a referee process. In the event of a complaint that a condition is unsafe or an unusual hazard exists, a safety representative may investigate under Article 8.07 on the condition that a complaint must first be made and the employee is not satisfied with the decision of his or her supervisor.

In those circumstances, one could conclude that the use of cellular telephones by safety representatives could be more easily accommodated because they are less regulated. A safety representative is entitled to initiate an investigation depending upon certain objective conditions, while a shop steward may be refused permission to take time off work by the subjective decision of a supervisor that there are overriding operational requirements.

However, while safety representatives and shop stewards have been given different degrees of independence, nowhere does the collective agreement purport to give either of them a right to use cell phones. Further, there is nothing in the investigative procedures contained in Articles 7 and 8 that would permit me to imply such a right. Accordingly, I have no jurisdiction to determine whether the current policy that prohibits all employees from bringing cellular phones to the workplace is reasonable. Even more, I have no jurisdiction to decide whether the proposal put by the Union is better; nor can I mandate an alternative.

The fact is that the rule is not arbitrary in the sense that it is based upon considerations of safety, a matter which is conceded by the Union. Indeed, it is difficult to see how cell phones could be made completely safe by virtue only of the employee being a shop steward or a safety representative. The concern expressed by Mr. Wilson was not that regulations could not be prescribed for when they could be used, as was proposed by the Union, but that these same employees will also be driving heavy equipment or operating plant machinery and that if they have them they will use them.

QUESTIONS

1) Why did management impose the ban on cellular phones in the first place? Do you think the ban was justified?

2) Is it reasonable for the union to argue that a ban on the use of cellular phones by union stewards and health and safety representatives constitutes interference with the union's workplace activities?

3) What would your decision have been had you been the arbitrator? Why?

4) Would the fact that outside contractors are allowed to use cellular phones, at least under certain conditions, affect your decision in this case?

5) The union has served notice that if this grievance is denied, it will challenge the ban as an unfair labour practice. Do you agree with this approach? If not, what alternative course might the union take?

CASE A.3

Arbitration Case

SUDBURY GENERAL HOSPITAL AND ONTARIO NURSES' ASSOCIATION, LOCAL 13

Does the exclusion of management personnel from unionization rights under the labour relations act prevent individuals from simultaneously occupying a part-time management position and a position in a part-time bargaining unit?

Heard: November 25, 1997; Ontario; I. G. Thorne, S. Ursel, and Y. Campeau
Decision rendered: January 27, 1998
J. Janczur and others, for the union.
P. C. Hennessy and others, for the employer.

AWARD

The Association has grieved that an individual holds positions at the Hospital as a part-time registered nurse and as a part-time employee in a position excluded from the bargaining unit, i.e., a management position. The Association contends that an individual cannot at the same time be a member of the bargaining unit and a member of management, and that the Hospital is in breach of the collective agreement in permitting this situation to come into being.

The parties proceeded on the basis of an agreed statement of facts, as follows:

1. Mary Carter is the trauma coordinator at Sudbury General Hospital. The position of trauma coordinator is a management position and is excluded from the bargaining unit.

2. Mary Carter commenced employment as trauma coordinator in 1991. When she commenced employment as trauma coordinator in 1991, the trauma coordinator position was a full-time position.

Source: Adapted from 70 L.A.C. (4th), pp. 9–21. Some deletions have been made by the author for the purposes of this book and names have been changed.

3. On July 2, 1996, Mary Carter was awarded a temporary part-time position in the Intensive Care Unit, which is a bargaining unit position.
4. On September 9, 1996. Mary Carter was awarded a regular part-time position in the Intensive Care Unit, a position which she continues to hold.
5. Since commencing employment in the Intensive Care Unit, Mary Carter has continued as trauma coordinator on a part-time basis, a position that continues to be a management position.

Also in evidence were the postings for the temporary part-time position and for the regular part-time position mentioned in the above statement, together with a list of the applicants interviewed in connection with each posting, and a letter dated December 6, 1996, from the Association to the Hospital regarding this grievance.

We were advised that Ms. Carter had been notified of this hearing, but had chosen not to attend.

On September 10, 1996, the Association filed a grievance claiming a "violation of the collective agreement in the Employer's decision regarding the Trauma Director position" and asserting that the position should be within the bargaining unit. The remedy that the Association sought at the hearing was that Ms. Carter should removed from the bargaining unit position in the Intensive Care Unit and that the position should then be posted in accordance with the collective agreement. In view of this change in the remedy requested, the Employer asked that the original grievance be withdrawn by the Association or dismissed by this board. The letter of December 6, 1996, referred to the change in the Association's stance. The letter referred to a grievance regarding the alleged impropriety of an incumbent holding a position in the ICU in the bargaining unit and the position of trauma director, a management position. The letter also purported to put the Hospital on notice "... that our position at arbitration will be that she should not have been awarded the bargaining unit ICU position."

...   .

The Hospital was of the view that nothing in the collective agreement prohibited one person from holding positions within and outside the bargaining unit and asked that the grievance be dismissed in any case.

Counsel for the Association elaborated on the Association's position that no one person could simultaneously hold a position in the bargaining unit and a management position. Such a situation was contrary to the scheme of the *Labour Relations Act, 1995*, S.O. 1995, c. 1, Sch. A, counsel argued, and assigning a bargaining unit position to a member of management was inconsistent with the collective agreement taken as a whole, since it existed to protect the rights and positions of members of the bargaining unit. What had occurred was also a specific violation of Article B-2 of the local agreement and of Article 10.11(a) of the central collective agreement. The former article restricted management from acting in a manner inconsistent with the collective agreement, while the latter prohibited nurses in supervisory positions excluded from the bargaining unit from performing duties normally performed by nurses in the bargaining unit, and its breach deprived other nurses of the right to claim positions available within the unit.

In counsel's submission this was more than a question of whether a member of management was doing bargaining unit work and was more fundamental: a member of management could not at the same time be in the bargaining unit. Membership in the bargaining unit of such a person would entitle her to attend meetings of the Association, to vote on Association matters, and to seek election to an office within the Association. Underlying the Association's position, counsel maintained, was the principle that it was persons who were excluded from the bargaining unit under the legislation, not positions. He illustrated this argument by reference to ss. 1(3), 15, 53, 70, and 114 of the *Labour Relations Act, 1995,* all of which were said to demonstrate the arm's-length nature of the relationship between employer and unions conceived by the legislation.

···   ···   ···

In the Hospital's submission, the Association was not able to show any violation of the collective agreement. Article B-1 restricted management from acting in a manner inconsistent with the provisions of the agreement, but the Association had not been able to show such an inconsistency, counsel maintained. The Association could show no breach of Article 10.11 since no evidence had been brought forward to show the impact of Ms. Carter having been awarded a bargaining-unit position and thus the tests set out in that article had not been met. In fact, counsel pointed out, Ms. Carter was the sole applicant for the temporary position so that no opportunity was lost to members of the bargaining unit; thereafter, in the Hospital's view, Ms. Carter was herself a member of the unit and entitled to the same consideration as any other member when she applied for the regular part-time position. Further, contrary to the Association's assertion, Article 19.04(b) of the central agreement appeared to contemplate what the Association said was prohibited: a member of the bargaining unit could be temporarily assigned to a higher classification not included in the bargaining unit.

···   ···   ···

Certain provisions of the collective agreement are relevant to the parties' submissions:
In the local agreement:

Article A — Recognition

A-1 The Hospital recognizes the Association as the bargaining agent of all lay, part-time Registered and Graduate Nurses, employed by the Sudbury General Hospital of the Immaculate Heart of Mary at Sudbury, engaged in a nursing capacity, save and except Head Nurses, persons above the rank of Head Nurse, full-time employees, and persons specifically excluded by the decisions of the Ontario Labour Relations Board dated the 15th day of December 1970.

Article B — Management Rights

B-2 It is agreed that the Hospital may exercise any of the rights, powers and functions or authorities which the Hospital had prior to the signing of this Agreement, except those rights, powers, functions or authority which are abridged or modified by this Agreement, and these rights shall not be exercised in a manner inconsistent with the provisions of this Agreement.

In the Central agreement:

Article 10 — Seniority

10.11(a) Nurses who are in supervisory positions excluded from the bargaining unit shall not perform duties normally performed by nurses in the bargaining unit which shall directly cause or result in the layoff, loss of seniority or service or reduction in benefits to nurses in the bargaining unit.

Article 19 — Compensation

19.04(b) Where the Hospital temporarily assigns a Registered Staff Nurse to carry out the assigned responsibilities of a higher classification (whether or not such classification is included in the bargaining unit) for a period of one (1) full tour or more, at times when the incumbent in any such classification would otherwise be working, the nurse shall be paid a premium of one dollar and twenty cents ($1.20) per hour for such duty in addition to her or his regular salary. The Hospital agrees that it will not make work assignments which will violate the purpose and intent of this provision.

The contents of the sections of the *Labour Relations Act, 1995* referred to in argument can be summarized. Section 1(3)(b) provides that "... no person shall be deemed to be an employee ... who, in the opinion of the Board, exercises managerial functions or is employed in a confidential capacity in matters relating to labour relations." Section 15 requires the Labour Relations Board not to certify a union "... if an employer ... has participated in its formation or administration or has contributed financial or other support to it ...." Similarly, section 53 deems an agreement between an employer and such an employer-influenced union not to be a collective agreement for the purposes of the Act. Section 70 prohibits an employer from participating in or interfering with the formation, selection or administration of a union. Section 114(2) assigns to the Labour Relations Board the determination of any question whether a person is an employee within the meaning of the Act.

The issue raised by the grievance appears to be a novel one, at least in the sense that there seem to be no reported awards dealing directly with it. While we heard no direct evidence on the point, it is reasonable to suppose that the sort of situation that might give rise to this issue is more likely to occur at the present time than might have been the case in the past. Budgetary pressures on hospitals have forced staff reductions and realignments of responsibilities. Layoffs, bumping, or other circumstances may oblige employees to apply for positions involving a new mix of responsibilities. That seems to have been Ms. Carter's situation: her position outside the bargaining unit was reduced from a full-time to a part-time one and she applied for a vacancy in the part-time bargaining unit. Fortunately for her, she was able to obtain a temporary part-time position for which she was the only applicant. This may well have seemed a satisfactory situation for all concerned. In any event, no issue was made of Ms. Carter's status until after her later successful application for the regular part-time position. One way of looking at the present dispute is to consider, as the Hospital does, that at the time of her application for the latter position, Ms. Carter was a member of the bargaining unit with seniority. Another way of looking at it, as the Association does, is to take the view that by virtue of her holding a part-time management position, Ms. Carter was precluded from becoming a member of the bargaining unit and thus was not entitled to apply for the vacant position.

There is some support in the collective agreement for the view that individuals and not simply positions are excluded from the bargaining unit. Article A-1 in the local agreement does speak in terms of the exclusion of "... persons above the rank of Head Nurse ... and persons specifically excluded by the decisions of the Ontario Labour Relations Board ...." Beyond that, the Association cannot point to any specific provision that would preclude an individual from holding a part-time management position and a part-time bargaining unit position. Article 10.1 1(a) indicates a priority for nurses within the bargaining unit so far as the performance of duties normally performed by nurses is concerned, but it must be said that the article is directly applicable only in circumstances that have not been shown to be present here. On the other hand, the Hospital can point to Article 19.04(b) as an indication that the parties have not excluded the possibility that one individual may both be a member of the bargaining unit and a person assigned to act in a management position; again it must be said that the application of the article is restricted and could be viewed as an agreed exception to the principle of mutual exclusivity of management and bargaining-unit work — if such a principle exists.

This brings us to the Association's central contention: that the whole scheme and structure of the legislated labour relations regime supports its view that one person cannot be both in management and in the bargaining unit, and that this explains the lack of a clear reference to the point in the collective agreement.

•••   •••   •••

12. The identification of management is fundamental to the scheme of collective bargaining, as set out in the Labour Relations Act. What is contemplated is an arm's-length relationship between the employees represented by a bargaining agent, on the one side, and the employer acting through management on the other side. The Act attempts to create a balance of power between these two sides by insulating one from the other. Employees, therefore, are protected from management interference and domination by the prohibitions against employer interference with trade union and employee rights.

Management, by the same token, is protected by excluding from collective bargaining either persons exercising managerial functions, or persons employed in a confidential capacity in matters relating to labour relations. Collective bargaining rights, therefore, are not universal, but must be qualified by the need to preserve a countervailing force on the employer side.

It should be borne in mind that in this passage the Board was explaining why it was important to determine who was identified with management in ruling on an application for certification, a matter fundamental to the process of collective bargaining. The passage makes clear the Board's view of the need to create a balance of power and to protect each side from the sort of interference it describes. These concerns seem somewhat remote from the situation described to us in this case. It was suggested on behalf of the Association that if Ms. Carter were permitted to hold a position within the bargaining unit, she would be entitled to seek union office and otherwise participate in the affairs of the Association. We are uncertain whether that might be seen as management interference in the affairs of the Association or alternatively as a breach of duty by a member of management, but in any event there is no evidence that Ms. Carter has actually participated in union affairs in support of one interest or the other.

•••   •••   •••

While none of the judicial and arbitral decisions before us directly considers the issue raised in this case, *Re Miller (supra)* does touch on one aspect of the problem. The decision of the Divisional Court examined an arbitration award that had determined that a newly created position of assistant manager was not within a bargaining unit stipulated to consist of "... all ... employees save and except the Manager." In a judgment quashing the award the Court observed:

There is nothing in the Labour Relations Act which provides that a voluntary collective agreement which covers persons other than employees as defined in the Labour Relations Act is invalid ...

In this respect it is fair to say that the Court seemed to accept that it was open to the parties to extend the benefits of a collective agreement to individuals who might otherwise be deemed not to be members of the bargaining unit. That is consistent with our understanding of the capacity of the parties in this case to determine in their collective agreement whether one individual may simultaneously hold a part-time management position and a part-time bargaining unit position, or not.

We must say that any intention the parties may have had in this regard is unclear. It may be that their intent would become clear if there was evidence demonstrating some adverse affect on the interests of one party or the other. However, it is difficult to say that such an adverse effect has been demonstrated on the particular facts of this case. Ms. Carter, employed part-time in a management position, applied for a temporary part-time position within the bargaining unit. She was the only candidate and was appointed. It cannot be said that her appointment caused any loss to any member of the bargaining unit at that time. If other qualified applicants had come forward, the issue of Ms. Carter's right to apply for the position might properly have been raised. As matters stood, however, it does not appear that either party saw any impediment to her appointment. Rather than diminishing the bargaining unit, therefore, Ms. Carter's appointment made her a member of it. The situation was a little different when she applied for the regular part-time position since there were other applicants for that position from within the bargaining unit. However, by that time, it appears, Ms. Carter had been treated as a member of the bargaining unit for some time without objection.

•••   •••   •••

The parties may wish to consider whether the issue raised by this grievance is one that should divide them. The drawing of a rigid line could work to the disadvantage of nurses both inside and outside the part-time bargaining unit who wished to pursue a job opportunity on the other side of the line. The parties may prefer to negotiate more precisely the extent to which a part-time employee may occupy a bargaining-unit position and one in a higher classification.

QUESTIONS

1) Given today's economic climate, what is the significance of this case?

2) Does the case provide you with what you consider adequate information concerning the nature of Ms. Carter's duties as trauma coordinator? If not, what additional information might be helpful?

3) Whose arguments do you find more convincing: the Hospital's or the Nurses' Association's?

4) If you were the arbitrator, what would your decision have been, and why?

5) What might the parties do to help prevent such cases from being taken to arbitration in the future?

ALCOHOL AND DRUG ABUSE— THE BELL CANADA CASE

At what point can an employer dismiss an employee for absenteeism on the basis that the employee is simply unable to meet job requirements?

In the Matter of an Arbitration Between Bell Canada ("the Company") And Communications Workers of Canada ("the Union") And in the Matter of a Grievance of Helen Barry; A hearing in this matter was held in Toronto on January 25, 1984.

AWARD

This is a grievance against discharge. The grievor, Ms. Helen Barry, also grieves a letter of warning dated August 3, 1982. Both the warning and the discharge relate to the grievor's rate of innocent absenteeism. It is on that basis that the grievor was discharged pursuant to the following letter dated January 31, 1983:

> Helen Barry
>
> Your health problems continue to prevent you from fulfilling your obligation to be at work on a regular and consistent basis. This situation was reviewed in our letter dated 1982 08 03.
>
> We regret, that in view of the circumstances, your employment with Bell Canada will terminate effective Monday, 1983 01 31.
>
> "Velma Haire"
> Manager Operator Services
> Intercept

The foregoing letter of termination followed the earlier warning letter dated August 3, 1982, which is as follows:

> Miss Helen Barry
>
> This letter confirms our discussion of 1982 08 03 concerning your complete absence record. As you are aware, we do consider it to be excessive. Your absence record demonstrates that you are unable to report for work on a regular and consistent basis. If this performance continues, we will be obligated to terminate your employment with Bell Canada.

Source: Adapted from Craig and Solomon (1993), pp. 429–433. Some deletions have been made by the author for the purposes of this book and names have been changed.

"Velma Haire"
Manager Operators Services Intercept/SOST
6 Fl. 15 Asquith Avenue,
Toronto, Ontario

The grievor maintains that both the warning letter and her termination were without just cause, contrary to the provisions of the collective agreement. She seeks reinstatement without loss of seniority and with full compensation for wages and benefits lost.

The facts are not disputed. The evidence establishes that the grievor is afflicted both by alcoholism and the abuse of prescription drugs. These difficulties caused the grievor chronic absenteeism throughout the entire period of her employment with the Company. The grievor was first employed as an operator for the period of one year in 1969. She voluntarily left the Company at that time to return to school. She was subsequently rehired as an operator in the centralized intercept office of the Company on Asquith Street in Toronto on September 14, 1981. The evidence of Ms. Velma Haire, manager of Operator Services at the time of the grievor's employment, establishes beyond any doubt that Ms. Barry recorded an excessive and unacceptable rate of absenteeism. While the grievor's record was adduced in evidence in some detail, it suffices to say that the Board is satisfied, on the unchallenged evidence before it, that the grievor's rate of absence between the time of her re-employment and the letter of warning of August 3, 1982, was approximately 45 to 50 percent of her scheduled work time. We are satisfied that that rate of absence was far in excess of the average of other employees in the same division of the Company's operations and that the grievor's recurring and intermittent absences caused substantial inconvenience and disruption to the normal operations of her department.

The evidence also establishes that on a number of occasions the grievor received verbal counselling from Ms. Haire with respect to the rate and causes of her attendance problems. The evidence establishes that Ms. Haire met with the grievor in January, February, and May of 1982 with a view both to impressing upon her the seriousness of her ongoing absenteeism and to offering any assistance, including medical assistance, that might help to correct her problem. While Ms. Haire had grounds to suspect that alcohol might be at the root of Ms. Barry's attendance problems, she had no firm evidence to confirm that suspicion. The grievor generally justified her absences in terms of short-term illnesses and family problems, offering explanations that her supervisor was not in a position to challenge. On November 4, 1982, Ms. Haire met with the grievor following another period of absence. Without confronting her or suggesting the nature of her problem, her supervisor did emphasize that, as an employee, she could take advantage of the Company's benefit plan, which included some measure of wage protection during an extended leave of absence for illness, including mental illness, alcoholism, and drug addiction. The grievor did not pursue that suggestion, and made no further inquiries either of the Company or her Union with respect to the possibility of treatment with the support of the Company's benefits plan.

The grievor's medical absences were monitored by the Company's medical health physician, Dr. Roberta Hall. In the normal course, documentation provided by the grievor in relation to her absences was forwarded to Dr. Hall. The documents were in the nature of confidential memoranda from her own physician that established that she was medically unfit for work and under a doctor's care. Although the Company's physician had as many as six interviews with the grievor relating to her medical absences and her ongoing ability to work, she did not treat Ms. Barry or give her any medical examination. In the course of her encounters with the grievor, Dr. Hall developed a concern that she might be abusing herself chemically. On several occasions she wrote reports to the grievor's supervisors, based on the medical records before her, indicating that in her view there was little or no basis to expect improvement in Ms. Barry's rate of attendance in the future. On four occasions Ms. Haire requested that Dr. Hall do an employee health assessment with respect to the grievor's future employability. Each time the report returned to Ms. Haire expressed a pessimistic prognosis for her future attendance. However, the evidence of Dr. Hall, and a memorandum that she wrote to Ms. Haire, establish that she did not view the grievor's situation as hopeless. In a memorandum dated December 16, 1982, Dr. Hall noted that in light of the grievor's age (30 years) and good physical condition it would be within her ability to end the problems giving rise to her absences, and that she could correct her attendance pattern in a period of three to six months. Unfortunately, Ms. Barry's attendance pattern was not corrected. The grievor continued to believe that she could solve her own problem without medical assistance or outside help. In the result, her attendance problems continued, and indeed worsened, until the point of her termination.

Evidence was adduced respecting the grievor's change of attitude and her efforts at medical rehabilitation after her discharge. By her own account, following her termination, the grievor's abuse of alcohol increased and was further complicated by her continuing intake of prescription drugs, including a compound of codeine and barbiturates, a sedative, and valium. Her own concern increased when she began to have progressively longer memory black-outs; in the earlier stages these were as short as five minutes and eventually lasted as long as a half-day in which she would have no recollection of what she had done. According to the grievor's evidence she first acknowledged that she was an alcoholic and drug-dependent in the spring of 1983. In June of that year she approached her family physician, Dr. Joseph Tillman, and asked for medical help for her alcohol and drug dependency. Dr. Tillman referred her to the Donwood Institute where she was admitted for seven weeks of treatment on July 15, 1983.

A letter from Dr. J. Cohen, co-ordinator of medical services at the Donwood Institute, was adduced in evidence by agreement. It establishes that the grievor was diagnosed as having no substantial medical or psychiatric problems other than her alcohol and drug dependency. During her treatment she participated in an educational program of lectures and discussion groups and in group therapy. According to Dr. Cohen's letter, Ms. Barry took good advantage of her seven weeks' treatment and made appropriate gains during that time. She appeared positively motivated at the time of her discharge. She was then given a prescription for 50 mg Tempacil to be taken twice a day and was scheduled to participate in the Institute's two-year "continuing health services program" for continuing support during her recovery.

Her record of progress and attendance in that program has been less than perfect. She suffered relapses in September, October, and November of 1983, although she did re-attend at the Institute on two occasions in December of 1983 and January of 1984 respectively, at which times she is described as appearing "well and chemically clear." Dr. Cohen's letter indicates that maintaining regular contact at the Donwood Institute would provide the grievor with the support necessary to work towards a complete recovery from her illness. Dr. Tillman also indicates, in a letter filed by the agreement of the parties, that the grievor has responded well and is now taking Antabuse, and that he sees "a good progress."

Substantial argument was addressed to the issue of the admissibility and weight to be given to evidence respecting the facts of the grievor's condition as they evolved after her discharge. Counsel for the Company argued that the correct arbitral authority in this regard looks to the date of termination as the appropriate time to determine whether the prognosis for the grievor's attendance was such as to justify her termination. In his submission subsequent events cannot be admitted to alter the merits of the grievor's case or to establish that the Company did not have just cause for her termination.

Counsel for the Union argued that a board of arbitration is entitled to take into account circumstances arising after the discharge of an employee for innocent absenteeism, particularly as they may have a bearing on the discretion of the arbitrator to fashion a remedy with regard to the future employment of the grievor. Counsel for the Union referred the Board to *Re Canada Post Corporation and Canadian Union of Postal Workers* (1982), 6 L.A.C. (3d) 385 (Burkett) and another case involving the parties to the instant matter, *Re Bell Canada and Communications Workers of Canada* (1983), 10 L.A.C. (3d) 285 (Shime). The decision of the board chaired by Mr. Shime, which was apparently unanimous, plainly rejects the approach taken by arbitrators Rousseau and Frumkin in the cases noted above. In that case, as in the instant case, the grievor was an alcoholic who did not recognize or admit his problem until his dismissal. Between the time of his discharge and the arbitration of his grievance, the employee received treatment, joined Alcoholics Anonymous, and became a complete abstainer. Taking into account the grievor's work record, his seniority, and his rehabilitative steps, the board then reinstated the grievor, without compensation, subject to a number of conditions relating to continued rehabilitative treatment and his record of employment in the next two years.

It is generally accepted that an employer may terminate with justification when it is shown that an employee has a blameless shortcoming that undermines his or her employment relationship and where it is reasonably probable that the conditions giving rise to that shortcoming are not likely to improve. Blameless absenteeism, including absenteeism for alcoholism, can therefore entitle an employer to end the employment relationship if it is established that the employee has been and will continue to be incapable of regular attendance at work.

The evidence in the instant case establishes that the Company has an enlightened policy with respect to the treatment of employees suffering from alcohol and drug dependencies. Among the materials filed in evidence is a notice distributed by the Company's personnel headquarters establishing a generous and sophisticated plan "for identifying and treating those employees with a health problem caused by alcohol and drug abuse." Without relating the details of that plan, it specifically acknowledges that alcohol and drug abuse are to be treated as an involuntary illness. The plan reflects an offer of assistance to the afflicted employee involving five components: identification, confrontation, referral, treatment, and rehabilitation. Unfortunately, in the instant case, the best efforts of Ms. Haire and Dr. Hall did not succeed in bringing the grievor to the critical acknowledgement of her own drug dependence. If the grievor had recognized her own problem, and bearing in mind that the refusal to recognize alcoholism is itself part of the illness, Ms. Barry would in all likelihood have had the advantage of a leave of absence with medical benefits to help her overcome her problem, as well as the ongoing support of her employer in full awareness of the similar comment by the unanimous board chaired by Mr. Shime, noted above. In that instance the board reinstated the grievor.

QUESTIONS

1) What is "innocent" absenteeism? How is the idea relevant to this case?

2) What should be the critical test that an arbitrator applies in deciding cases of this type?

3) If you had been the arbitrator, what would have been your award, and why?

4) Do you think there is anything else the company could have done to help Ms. Barry with her problems?

FIGHTING AND THE USE OF A
KNIFE — THE MCKAY CASE

What circumstances, if any, would justify an arbitrator's reinstating a man discharged for attacking a fellow employee with a knife?

In the Matter of an Arbitration between Canadian National Railway Company and Division No. 4, Railway Employees Department A.F. of L. — C.I.O. And in the Matter of the Grievance of A. McKay [The case was heard by a single arbitrator]; A hearing in this matter was held at Montreal on June 13, 1979.

AWARD

JOINT STATEMENT OF ISSUE

On October 6, 1978 Electrician A. McKay was working the 1600 to 2400 hours shift in the passenger car paint shop at Transcona Main Shops. At approximately 2115 hours an altercation occurred involving Mr. McKay and carman apprentice J. Jacot.

During the altercation Mr. McKay drew a utility knife from his tool pouch and Mr. Jacot was cut on the little finger of his left hand.

An investigation was conducted and the electrician was discharged for his part in the altercation.

The International Brotherhood of Electrical Workers appealed the company's decision requesting that Mr. Ward be reinstated in his former position and that the discipline assessed be similar to that assessed the other persons involved in the incident.

The company declined the appeal.

From the statement of all the employees concerned, it is clear that there was a fight between the grievor and another employee, and that as a result the other employee was injured (his hand was cut) by the grievor's utility knife. What is not clear is the degree of responsibility of the various persons involved.

The grievor did participate in a fight and for that (except in clear cases of self-defence) some discipline would be warranted. He did, as well, draw from his pocket (and from the pouch protecting the blade) his utility knife. The use of any weapon, or the use of a tool as a weapon (even if the blade was very short) is obviously wrong, and for that too the grievor would be subject to discipline. I do not consider that the grievor was deliberately attacked by

---

Source: Adapted from Craig and Solomon (1996), pp. 588–589. Some deletions have been made by the author for the purposes of this book and names have been changed.

another employee or employees, so that he was in reasonable fear of serious injury. I do not consider, then, that there was that degree of justification that would excuse resort to such a weapon in the circumstances. Thus, for his participation in the fight, and especially for his use of a knife, I consider that the grievor would be liable to severe discipline.

It is necessary, however, in assessing the penalty imposed on the grievor to consider all the circumstances of this incident, as well as the grievor's disciplinary record. In this case the grievor, an electrician, had relatively short seniority, but had a clear disciplinary record and was regarded as a good employee. He was considered by his supervisor to be cooperative and of a good disposition. It appears that he immigrated to Canada from the Philippines a few years ago, and is of relatively slight build.

On the evening in question the grievor had been speaking to his wife on the telephone, mounted on a pillar just outside a foreman's office, with respect to their sick child. Several other employees, carmen and carman apprentices, were nearby, and one of them was anxious to use the telephone. The group considered that the grievor had been too long on the telephone and began to make noise, sing songs and, it seems, beat on a garbage can. While the evidence is conflicting on the point, it seems most likely that one of the employees, Mr. Jacot, actually threw a garbage can against the pillar on which the telephone was mounted. The grievor thought, perhaps not entirely without reason, that it was aimed at him, although I doubt that it really was.

Finally, the grievor hung up the telephone and some conversation took place between him and Mr. Jacot. Mr. Jacot, a carman apprentice, is a younger man than the grievor and is taller and heavier. The accounts of the matter differ, but it appears to me that the most probable account of what occurred is that Mr. Jacot taunted the grievor and invited him to fight. I have no doubt, from the material before me, that whatever the particular incidents may have been, Mr. Jacot was the overall aggressor, and that the grievor's conduct was provoked by the actions of the younger man and by the taunts of his companions. That the grievor was in fact frightened is, I think, the case, although obviously his reaction to the situation was an improper one.

As to the severity of the penalty imposed on the grievor, it is to be noted that there were six persons involved, to some extent, in the incident: the grievor on one hand and five other employees. Of those five, two would appear not to have been substantially implicated, and were not disciplined. Two others were assessed 10 and 20 demerits, respectively, for unnecessary harassment of a fellow employee. These penalties would appear to reflect the involvement of the employees concerned. The fifth member of the group that was harassing the grievor was Mr. Jacot, who was assessed 30 demerits and was suspended for 10 days. That is a substantial penalty and was, it would appear, merited. None of the penalties just described were appealed and they are not before me for determination.

QUESTIONS

1) What circumstances would justify the use of a knife in a fight?

2) If you were the arbitrator, what factors would you take into account in deciding what penalty to impose on Mr. McKay?

3) What would be your ruling in this case, and why?

DISCIPLINE FOR POOR PERSONAL APPEARANCE — THE EMPRESS HOTEL CASE

Under what circumstances can an employee's personal appearance justify disciplinary action by an employer based on the employee's alleged violation of company personnel policy?

Empress Hotel and Canadian Brotherhood of Railway Trainmen, Local 726

I. THE GRIEVANCE

The union grieves that employer had no "just and reasonable" cause when it suspended Jason White, a former employee of the hotel, for refusing to cut his hair when asked to by the chief steward, Brian Johnson. Because (1) there was no policy prohibiting male employees from wearing pony-tails, and (2) even were there such a policy, it would be unreasonable and, therefore, unforceable, no proper grounds existed for disciplining White.

The employer relies, in defending the discipline, on its written "Grooming Policy," which, in addition to requiring that its employees be "impeccably groomed," contains the following relevant passage:

> Employees must ensure that their hair is clean and well groomed at all times. Employees with long hair should ensure that it is neatly tied back and away from their face.

According to the employer, a case-by-case application of that policy over the years has resulted in a management practice of not permitting male employees working in certain "front-line" positions (such as White's position in the Garden Café, namely, that of busperson) to wear their hair below their collar, and/or in a pony-tail. White was apparently the first male employee working in one of those specified "front-line" areas who, when asked, refused to cut his hair. According to the employer, the practice of not permitting pony-tails is a reasonable one in that — were it to permit men working in those positions to wear pony-tails — it would harm one of the very things that give it a competitive edge over its growing number of competitors, namely, its image of gentility and class. Hence, the discipline of White was justified.

The union's response is as follows. The only employer policy regarding hair (length or otherwise) is that cited above, a policy in respect of which White was always in strict compliance. As for the employer's unwritten policy of prohibiting those of its male employees working in

---

Source: Adapted from Craig and Solomon (1996), pp. 541–543. Some deletions have been made by the author for the purposes of this book and names have been changed.

N.B. This case may be useful in connection with Chapter 7 on employment law or Chapter 2 on the economy.

certain jobs from wearing pony-tails, the union says that that policy is unenforceable: not only because it is inconsistent with the terms of the written policy dealing with precisely the same subject, but also because such a policy would constitute, even were it to stand alone, a patently unreasonable invasion of an employee's privacy.

Because White resigned from his employment before the commencement of this hearing, the parties agreed that the matter proceed as a kind of "policy" grievance. The remedy sought by the union is simply a declaration that the employer had no just and reasonable cause for imposing any form of discipline on White.

II. THE EVIDENCE

Because there is so little factual dispute between the parties, I can be very brief in my summary of the evidence that was led. Before White was hired as a busperson on September 22, 1990, he was told that, as a condition of employment, he must have his long hair cut. He agreed, cut his hair, was hired, and worked in that position in the Garden Café until his lay-off in the spring of 1992.

When he was recalled to work on May 2, he showed up with hair that was in fact longer than it had been at the time of his hire. When advised by Johnson that he must get his hair cut before his next shift, White agreed and proceeded to work that shift. At the request of Johnson, he removed his elastic band and worked with his hair hanging loose. On his next scheduled workday, White showed up for work — with his hair uncut. He was suspended at that time.

No one disputed that White was always meticulous in his appearance, and that his hair was always clean, neat, tidy and combed. Scott Hunt and Judy Nelson, two fellow employees, testified that, although White had not wanted to get his hair cut at the time he was hired, he did so in order to get the job. Both they and Johnson testified that White was an exemplary employee in terms of service: "very efficient, good to customers;" "good rapport with customers;" "very well-mannered;" "affable," and "held himself well."

With reference to one of the hotel's "10 Commitments to Customers," namely, that employees be "impeccably groomed," Hunt stated that White was. According to Hunt, White's hair style and length at the time of his recall conformed in every respect to the employer policy in respect to same. Both Hunt, who was the local chairperson from 1989 to 1992, and Nelson, the shop steward for the Garden Café, testified that they had never heard of a customer complaint or employer concern regarding White.

Both Hunt and Nelson gave undisputed evidence that several of the women working in the Garden Café not only had hair that was longer than White's (at the time of his recall), but that they did not always wear their hair pulled back off their face. As for the male employees, they testified that at least one or two of them had hair that touched on or was below their collars: one of them had to push his hair back to keep it off his face. As well, at least one male employee in the banquet department wore his hair in gelled spikes from time to time.

In cross-examination, Hunt agreed that — if all of the male employees working in the Garden Café had pony-tails — the atmosphere would be more "relaxed" than is presently the case. He added that White never gave him the impression of being "laid back and easygoing."

In redirect, Hunt referred to a grievance that arose some two years ago regarding a male employee wearing an earring in his ear. The employer ultimately withdrew the discipline and "it is now quite common" for the male employees to wear earrings.

Both union and employer witnesses testified to the pride they take in the fact that the Empress Hotel is a "class" operation. No one disagreed with Johnson's evidence that it has the "highest standards and quality of any hotel in Victoria." As well, no one disputed the fact that the hotel industry in Victoria is becoming increasingly competitive, and that the Empress' success, to date, has been due in no small part to the fact that it has managed to maintain, and in fact foster, a unique image of gentility, elegance, and "heritage character." Not a single union witness disputed the fact that they want the employer to continue to project a "clean, crisp, and efficient" image. What they did dispute, however, was the employer's assertion that White did not fit that image; according to both Hunt and Nelson, White was at all times "clean, crisp, and efficient." According to Johnson, White had fit that image, but only until the day he showed up for work with a pony-tail.

Johnson testified that — when White was recalled — his hair fell just below his shoulders. When Johnson told him that he would have to get it cut, White replied that he did not believe that employer policy required him to do so. He nevertheless agreed to do so.

When asked why he told White to take it out of a pony-tail for that day's shift, Johnson replied: "because it (the pony-tail) was not acceptable to either the employer's or my standards." In terms of the clientele serviced by the Garden Café, Johnson stated that 75 percent of them are hotel guests, comprised — for at least five months of the year — by "high profile business clientele." According to Johnson, those "business-oriented clientele" would simply "not be used to male employees wearing pony-tails in the context of this kind of hotel." In his opinion, allowing males to wear pony-tails would lower the image of the hotel, and "could cost the hotel business;" this is a "definite concern."

Johnson stated that the kinds of establishments that would allow pony-tails would be "younger, noisier, not as conservative," such would be "consistent with the attire" worn in such places: "more lackadaisical, not as neat." Johnson stated that, based on his observations of other "upper-end" hotels in Victoria, no male employees wear pony-tails in such places.

In addition, Johnson testified that various staff members had commented, when White showed up for work with a pony-tail, that such was not acceptable in the Garden Café.

When White returned to work on May 5 with his hair still uncut, Johnson felt that he had no option but to suspend him until he got it cut. According to Johnson, this was the first time that any employee had refused to abide with his instructions as to how they should wear their hair. Johnson testified regarding a number of male employees to whom he had spoken in the past in this regard. In every case, the employee ultimately conformed to his expectations: "only White failed to improve his grooming."

In cross-examination, Johnson agreed that it was not until after White's return to work on May 2 that he first became aware of the employer's written grooming policy (cited above). He stated that his primary concern that day was the fact that White's hair was not "well groomed." When asked why he did not, after reading the policy, permit White to keep his pony-tail, Johnson replied "because it was not appropriate; not well-groomed." Johnson did not agree that a male employee could both have a pony-tail and be well-groomed at the same time.

Johnson agreed that White's pony-tail was "neat," and further agreed that "it was messy when not in a pony-tail."

As for whether more and more of the Garden Café's clientele have long hair, Johnson said that their standards have not changed over the years: only 0.5 percent of the male customers have long hair. When asked whether he had any statistics to back up his statement that "pony-tails are not acceptable in the public eye," he replied that he had never done a survey in this regard. It was simply his "opinion" and that of management's.

In answer to a question from me, Johnson testified that the policy he was enforcing on both May 2 and 5 was an "unwritten policy," "just an understanding," namely, that "the length of a man's hair should be collar length and neatly trimmed." Johnson was unable to say why this policy was not in writing.

Asked to comment on the May 7 "suspension letter" written to White from the human resources department, Johnson stated that both the written and unwritten policy regarding hair length were being referred to in the following passage:

> Jason, we as your employer, have every right to ask you to comply with Hotel standards which indicate very clearly in the Employee Handbook, which you signed on commencing work, that one's hair must be neat and well-groomed. It is painfully apparent that yours is neither. It states very clearly in the Collective Agreement that "the management and operation of the Hotel and the direction and promotion of its working force is the exclusive responsibility of the Hotel ..."

He added that, while he thought White's hair was "neat," he did not think it was "well-groomed." Why not? Because it was "over the ears."

David Jackson, the general manager of the hotel, testified that the $52 million renovation recently concluded was aimed at reinforcing the hotel's unique, first-class character in an increasingly competitive market-place. As for the employer's written "grooming" policy, Jackson testified that the employer is careful to apply that policy in ways that are appropriate to the particular circumstances at hand. Thus, for example, certain male employees working in "front-end" jobs are permitted to wear pony-tails: *e.g.*, the security guard. In terms of the Garden Café, the employer has always consistently applied the policy in a way that prohibits male employees from wearing their hair below their collars.

According to Jackson, hotel guests would be "disappointed" if they saw males wearing pony-tails working in the Garden Café: it would not be what they would expect to see in a heritage property; "it would be the only jarring element to their trip."

In cross-examination, Jackson testified that — while he assumes that "opening the floodgates" to men wearing pony-tails would damage the hotel's image — no survey had been conducted in this regard, "it is a judgment call based on many years of business." When asked whether the employer's oral policy is in contravention of the written policy, Jackson replied, "no — it is the interpretation of well-groomed. A better choice of words would perhaps have been 'appropriately well-groomed'."

In answer to a question from me, Jackson testified that he was more concerned about the negative impact on business of pony-tails than was the case with males wearing earrings: "Pony-tails are more evident, higher profile."

III. MY REASONING AND CONCLUSION

What is in issue in these proceedings is the enforceability or otherwise of a unilaterally promulgated employer policy. In order for *any* such policy to be enforceable, it must meet the following criteria:

1. it must be consistent with the collective agreement

2. it must not be unreasonable

3. it must be clear and unequivocal

4. it must be brought to the attention of the employee affected before the company can act upon it

5. the employee concerned must have been notified that a breach of such a rule could result in his discharge if the rule is used as a foundation for discharge

6. such a rule should have been consistently enforced by the company from the time it was introduced

QUESTIONS

1) What's the special significance of the Empress Hotel case in today's multicultural workplace?

2) Do you think the company's personnel policy as presently laid out is enforceable?

3) What would the company have had to do to make its policy enforceable?

4) What are the key issues governing cases involving an employee's personal appearance?

5) What would the employer have to prove to justify disciplinary action against White?

6) Had you been the arbitrator, what would your decision have been?

7) Would this case have been a good one to take to med-arb or prior grievance mediation? Had you been a grievance mediator, what might your advice have been?

REFERENCES

ABELLA, Irving. (1975). "Oshawa, 1937." In *On strike: Six key labour struggles in Canada 1919–1949*. Toronto: Lorimer. Reprinted in L.S. MacDowell and I. Radforth (Eds.). (1991). *Canadian working class history*. Toronto: Canadian Scholars' Press.

ADAMS, George. (1998). *Canadian labour law*. Aurora, ON: Canada Law Book.

_____. (1978). *Grievance arbitration of discharge cases*. Kingston: Queen's Univ. Industrial Relations Centre.

ADAMS, Roy. (1995a). "Canadian industrial relations in comparative perspective." In M. Gunderson and A. Ponak (Eds.), *Union-management relations in Canada* (3rd ed.). Don Mills, ON: Addison-Wesley. Some use has also been made of Adams' comparative chapter in the 2nd edition (1989) of the same book.

_____. (1995b). *Industrial relations under liberal democracy: North America in comparative perspective*. Columbia, SC: Univ. of South Carolina Press.

_____. (1993). "'All aspects of people at work': Unity and division in the study of labour and management." In R. Adams and N. Meltz (Eds.), *Industrial relations: Its nature, scope, and pedagogy*. Metuchen, NJ: Scarecrow Press.

_____. (1987). "Employment standards in Ontario: An industrial relations systems analysis." *Relations Industrielles*, 42. Reprinted in LLCG. (1991). *Labour law: Cases, materials and commentary* (5th ed.). Kingston: Queen's IRC Press.

_____. (1985). "Should works councils be used as industrial relations policy?" *Monthly Labor Review*, 108:7 (July).

ADELL, Bernard. (1988a). "Law and industrial relations: The state of the art in common law Canada." In G. Hébert, H. Jain, and N. Meltz (Eds.), *The state of the art in industrial relations*. Kingston and Toronto: Queen's Univ. Industrial Relations Centre and the Univ. of Toronto Centre for Industrial Relations.

_____. (1988b). "Introduction." In *Labour law under the Charter: Proceedings of a conference sponsored by Industrial Relations Centre/School of Industrial Relations and Faculty of Law, Queen's University*. Kingston: Queen's Law Journal and Industrial Relations Centre.

AKYEAMPONG, Ernest. (1997). "A statistical portrait of the trade union movement." *Perspectives on Labour and Income*, Cat. No. 75-001-XPE, winter. Ottawa: Statistics Canada.

ALEXANDROFF, Alan. (1996, October 17). "Outsourcing's future on the line." *The Globe & Mail*, p. B-2.

ANDERSON, John. (1989a). "The strategic management of industrial relations." In *Union-management relations in Canada* (3rd ed.).

_____. (1989b). "The structure of collective bargaining." In *Union-management relations in Canada* (3rd ed.). Use has also been made of Anderson's bargaining structure chapter in the 1st edition (1982) of the same book.

_____. (1979). "Local union democracy: In search of criteria." *Relations Industrielles*, 34.

ANDERSON, John, and Morley Gunderson. (1982). "The Canadian industrial relations system." In *Union-management relations in Canada* (1st ed.).

ANDERSON, John, Morley Gunderson, and Allen Ponak. (1989). "Frameworks for the study of industrial relations." In *Union-management relations in Canada* (2nd ed.).

ARNOPOULOS, Sheila. (1974). Various *Montreal Star* articles, reprinted as "Immigrants and women: Sweatshops of the 1970s." In I. Abella and D. Millar (Eds.), (1978). *The Canadian worker in the twentieth century*. Toronto: Oxford Univ. Press.

ARTHURS, Harry. (1988). "The right to golf." In *Labour law under the Charter*.

ARTHURS, Harry, Donald Carter, Judy Fudge, Harry Glassbeek, and Gilles Trudeau. (1988). *Labour law and industrial relations in Canada*. Toronto: Butterworths. Some use has also been made of the 1993 edition of this same book.

ASH, Philip. (1967). "Measurement of industrial relations activities." *Journal of Applied Psychology*, 51:5. Reprinted in A. Nash and J. Miner (Eds.). (1973). *Personnel and labour relations: An evolutionary approach*. New York: MacMillan.

ASHENFELTER, Orley, and John Pencavel. (1969). "American trade union growth." *Quarterly Journal of Economics*, 83.

AUBRY, Jack. (1998, July 30). "Windfall 'a long time coming' for underpaid workers." *Ottawa Citizen*, p. A-1.

AUBRY, Jack, and Joan Bryden. (1998, September 16). "Candidate blames PS for by-election loss." *Ottawa Citizen*, p. A-1.

BAIN, George, and Farouk Elsheikh. (1976). "Trade union growth in Canada: A comment." *Relations Industrielles*, 31.

BAKER, William. (1983). "The miners and the mediator: The 1906 Lethbridge strike and Mackenzie King." *Labour/Le travailleur*, 11 (spring). Reprinted in *Canadian working class history*.

BALDERSTON, C.C. (1933). "Recent trends in personnel management." *Management Review*, 22:9. Reprinted in *Personnel and labour relations*.

BAMBER, Greg, and Russell Lansbury. (1993). *International and comparative industrial relations* (2nd ed.). London and New York: Routledge.

BAMBER, Greg, and Gillian Whitehouse. (1993). "Appendix: Employment, economics, and industrial relations: comparative statistics." In *International and comparative industrial relations* (2nd ed.).

BARBASH, Jack. (1988). "The new industrial relations in the U.S.: Phase 2." *Relations Industrielles, 43.*

_____. (1984). *The elements of industrial relations.* Madison: Univ. of Wisconsin Press.

BARNACLE, Peter. (1991). *Arbitration of discharge grievances in Ontario: Outcomes and reinstatement experiences.* Kingston: Queen's IRC Research and Current Issues Series #62.

BEAN, Ron. (1994). *Comparative industrial relations: An introduction to cross-national perspectives* (2nd ed.). London: Routledge.

BEATTY, David. (1987). *Putting the 'Charter' to work: Designing a constitutional labour code.* Montreal: McGill-Queen's.

_____. (1983). "Ideology, politics, and unionism." In K. Swan and K. Swinton (Eds.), *Studies in labour law.* Toronto: Butterworths.

BEATTY, David, and Steve Kennett. (1988). "Striking back: Fighting words, social protest and political participation in free and democratic societies." In *Labour law under the Charter.*

BEAUCHESNE, Eric. (1998, April 30). "Force jobless to move." *Ottawa Citizen,* p. A-1.

BEAUMONT, P.B. (1995). "Canadian public sector industrial relations in a wider setting." In G. Swimmer and M. Thompson (Eds.), *Public sector collective bargaining in Canada.* Kingston: Queen's IRC Press.

BEMMELS, Brian. (1998). "Gender effects in discharge arbitration." *Industrial and Labour Relations Review, 42:1.*

"BENEFITS given to same-sex spouses." (1998, February 7). *Toronto Sun,* p. 20.

BERCUSON, David, and David Bright (Eds.). (1994). *Canadian labour history: Selected readings.* Toronto: Copp Clark Longman.

BERGMAN, Paul. (1988). *Relations by objectives: The Ontario experience.* Kingston: Queen's IRC Research and Current Issues Series #55.

BERRIDGE, John. (1995). "The United Kingdom." In Ingrid Brunstein (Ed.), *Human resource management in Western Europe.* Berlin and New York: de Gruyter.

BERTIN, Oliver et al. (1996, October 4). "Layoffs mount in wake of GM strike." *The Globe & Mail,* p. B-1.

BETCHERMAN, Gordon, and Kathryn McMullen. (1986). *Working with technology: A survey of automation in Canada.* Ottawa: Economic Council of Canada.

BETCHERMAN, Gordon, Kathryn McMullen. Christina Caron, and Norm Leckie. (1994). *The Canadian workplace in transition.* Kingston: Queen's IRC Press.

BETTER Times. (1997) and (1998). Various issues.

_____. (1997, November). Unsigned article in issue on European labour action in support of shorter working hours.

BLAND, Susan. (1983). "Henrietta the homemaker, and Rosie the riveter." *Women's Study Journal, Atlantis.* Reprinted in *Canadian working class history.*

BLEASDALE, Ruth. (1981). "Class conflict on the canals of Upper Canada in the 1840s." *Labour/Le travailleur, 7* (spring). Reprinted in *Canadian working class history.*

BLOCK, Richard. (1993). *Unionization, collective bargaining and legal institutions in the United States and Canada.* Kingston: Queen's Univ. IRC Press.

BOIVIN, Jean, and Esther Déom. (1995). "Labour-management relations in Quebec." In *Union-management relations in Canada* (3rd ed.). Use has also been made of Boivin's Quebec chapter in the 1st (1982) and 2nd (1989) editions of the same book.

BOURETTE, Susan. (1996a, July 15). "Outsourcing tops CAW agenda." *The Globe & Mail,* p. B-1.

_____. (1996b, October 22). "GM deal believed within reach." *The Globe & Mail,* p. A-3.

BOURETTE, Susan, and Michael Grange. (1996, October 10). "CAW walkout closes all GM Canada's plants." *The Globe & Mail,* p. A-1.

BRAVERMAN, Harry. (1974). *Labor and monopoly capital.* New York: Monthly Review Press.

BRENNAN, Richard. (1998, October 18). "Tories, unions at war." *Ottawa Citizen,* p. A-1.

BRENNER, Harvey. (1973). *Mental illness and the economy.* Cambridge: Harvard Univ. Press.

BRETT, Jeanne, and Stephen Goldberg. (1983). "Grievance mediation in the coal industry: A field experiment." *Industrial and Labor Relations Review, 37.*

_____. (1979). "Wildcat strikes in bituminous coal mining." *Industrial and Labor Relations Review, 32.*

BRONFENBRENNER, Kate. (1992). "Seeds of resurgence: Successful union organizing strategies." Paper presented at 1992 Annual Meeting of the American Sociological Association.

BROWN, H.F. (1934–1935). "Industrial relations activities survive a critical test." *Personnel Journal, 13.* Reprinted in *Personnel and labour relations.* New York: MacMillan.

BROWN, Lorne. (1970). "Unemployment relief camps in Saskatchewan, 1922–1936." In *Saskatchewan history.* Saskatoon: Saskatchewan Archives Board. Reprinted in *Union-management relations in Canada* (3rd ed.).

BRUCE, Peter. (1990). "The processing of unfair labour practice cases in the U.S. and Ontario." *Relations Industrielles, 45.*

_____. (1989). "Political parties and labor legislation in Canada and the U.S." *Industrial Relations, 28* (spring).

BRUNSTEIN, Ingrid. (Ed.). (1995). *Human resource management in Western Europe.* Berlin and New York: de Gruyter.

BRYAN, Jay. (1998, October 7). "Stampede of downsizing did not increase profits." *Ottawa Citizen,* p. F-2.

BRYCE, George, and Pran Manga. (1985). "The effectiveness of health and safety committees." *Relations Industrielles, 40:2.*

BULLEN, John. (1986). "Hidden workers: Child labour and the family economy in late nineteenth-century urban Ontario." *Labour/Le Travail, 18* (fall). Reprinted in *Canadian working class history.*

BUREAU of Labor Statistics, U.S. Dept. of Labor (BLS). (1997). Data on U.S. minimum wages, 1950–1997. In *World Almanac,* 1998 edition.

BUTTON, Tony. (1990). *The Canadian railway office of arbitration alternative.* Kingston: Queen's IRC School of Industrial Relations Research Essay #29.

CANADA Labour Views. (1997). Article from January 24 on Ontario Labour Relations Board certification of a union at a Wal-Mart department store. Article from November 17 on changes to workers' compensation legislation in Ontario.

CANADIAN Auto Workers (CAW). (nd). "CAW statement on the reorganization of work."

CANADIAN Labour Congress (CLC). (1997). *Women's work: A report.* Ottawa: Author.

CANADIAN Labour Market and Productivity Centre (CLMPC). (1997). *Changing times, new ways of working: Alternative working arrangements and changes in working time.* Ottawa: Author.

CANADIAN Paperworkers' Union (CPU). (1990). "The team concept and the restructuring of the workplace." *CPU Journal, 10:2.*

CANADIAN Union of Public Employees (CUPE). (nd). List of courses prepared by and available from the union's education department.

CANSIM. (1998). Statistics Canada, CANSIM, Matrix 3472 (employment by industry). Ottawa: Statistics Canada.

CARDIN, Jean-Real. (1967). *Canadian labour relations in an era of technological change.* Economic Council of Canada Special Study #6. Ottawa: Supply and Services.

CARPENTER, C.U. (1903, April). "The working of a labor department in industrial establishments." *Engineering Magazine, 25:1.* Reprinted in *Personnel and labour relations.*

CARROTHERS, Arthur W.J. (Chair). (1979). *Report of the commission of inquiry into redundancies and lay-offs.* Ottawa: Supply and Services (Labour Canada). This report contains a discussion of Harvey Brenner's "social pathology" statistics relating unemployment to physical and mental illness and crime.

CARTER, Donald. (1997). "The duty to accommodate: Its growing impact on the grievance arbitration process." *Relations Industrielles, 52.*

_____. (1995). "Collective bargaining legislation." In *Union-management relations in Canada* (3rd ed.). Use has also been made of Carter's labour law chapters in the 1st (1982) and 2nd (1989) editions of the same book.

CASSELMAN, Karen. (1998, December 21). Labour relations officer, grievances and arbitration section, Canada Post. Telephone interview.

CAVALLUZZO, Paul. (1988). "Freedom of association—Its effect upon collective bargaining and trade unions." In *Labour law under the Charter.*

CCH. (1998a, May). Information on employment standards legislation. In *Employment standards.* Don Mills, ON: Author.

_____. (1998b, May). "Human rights legislation." In *Employment standards.* Don Mills, ON: Author.

_____. (1998c, May). "Health and safety legislation" (including workers' compensation). In *Employment standards.*

_____. (1998d, May). "Labour relations legislation." In *Employment standards.*

CHAISON, Gary. (1996). *Union mergers in hard times: The view from five countries.* London and Ithaca: ILR Press.

_____. (1982). "Unions: Growth, structure, and internal dynamics." In *Union-management relations in Canada* (1st ed.). Use has also been made of the union structure chapter by Gary Chaison and Joseph Rose in the 2nd (1989) edition of the same book.

CHAISON, Gary, and Joseph Rose. (1991). "The macrodeterminants of union growth and decline." In G. Strauss, D. Gallagher, and J. Fiorito (Eds.), *The state of the unions.* Madison: IRRA Press.

_____. "Turnover among the presidents of Canadian national unions." *Industrial Relations, 16.*

CHAYKOWSKI, Richard. (1995). "The structure and process of collective bargaining." In *Union-management relations in Canada* (3rd ed.).

CHAYKOWSKI, Richard, and Anil Verma. (1992). "Canadian industrial relations in transition." In R. Chaykowski and A. Verma (Eds.), *Industrial relations in Canadian industry.* Toronto: Dryden.

CHRISTIE, Innis. (1980). *Employment law in Canada*. Toronto: Butterworths.

CLARKE, Oliver. (1993). "Conclusions." In *International and comparative industrial relations* (2nd ed.).

CLEGG, Hugh. (1976). *Trade unionism under collective bargaining: A theory based upon comparisons of six countries*. Oxford: Blackwell.

COATES, Mary Lou. (1992). "Is there a future for the Canadian labour movement?" Kingston: Queen's IRC Current Issues Series.

_____. (1991). "Work and family issues: Beyond 'swapping the mopping and sharing the caring.'" Kingston: Queen's IRC Press Current Issues Series.

COHEN, Marjorie. (1987). *Free trade and the future of women's work*. Toronto: Garamond/CCPA.

COLLECTIVE Bargaining Review (CBR). (1996) and (1997). Various issues. Ottawa: HRDC.

COMMONS, John et al. (1918). *History of labor in the United States*. New York: Macmillan.

_____. (1909, November). "American shoemakers: 1648–1895." *Quarterly Journal of Economics*, 24.

COMMUNICATIONS Workers of Canada (CWC). (1992). Organization chart outlining the union's main activities.

CORCORAN, Terence. (1997, November 21). "First, fire post management." *The Globe & Mail*, p. B-2.

COWDRICK, Edward. (1934–1935). "Collective bargaining in 1934." *Personnel Journal*, 13:5. Reprinted in *Personnel and labour relations*.

CRAIG, Alton. (1967). "A model for the analysis of industrial relations systems." Paper presented to the Annual Meeting of the Canadian Political Science Association held in Ottawa.

CRAIG, Alton, and Norman Solomon. (1996). *The system of industrial relations in Canada* (5th ed.). Scarborough, ON: Prentice-Hall. Some use has also been made of the 1st (1983) edition of the same book.

CRAIN, Marion. (1994). "Gender and union organizing." *Industrial and Labor Relations Review*, 47:2.

CRISPO, John. (1982). "The future of Canadian industrial relations." In *Union-management relations in Canada* (1st ed.).

CUNNINGHAM, J.B., and T.H. White (Eds.). (1984). *Quality of working life: contemporary cases*. Ottawa: Supply and Services (Labour Canada publication).

CURRENT Scene: The current industrial relations scene in Canada. (1991). Kingston: Queen's University Industrial Relations Centre.

CURTIS, C.H. (1966). *The development and enforcement of the collective agreement*. Kingston: Queen's Industrial Relations Centre.

DASTMALCHIAN, Ali, and Ignace Ng. (1990). "Industrial relations climate and grievance outcomes." *Relations Industrielles*, 45.

DAVIS, Edward, and Russell Lansbury. (1993). "Industrial relations in Australia." In *International and comparative industrial relations* (2nd ed.).

DEERY, Stephen, and Richard Mitchell (Eds.). (1993). *Labour law and industrial relations in Asia*. Melbourne: Longman.

DEUTSCH, Arnold. (1979). *The human resources revolution: Communicate or litigate*. New York: McGraw-Hill.

DIGBY, C., and W. Craig Riddell. (1986). "Occupational health and safety in Canada." In W. Criag Riddell (Ed.), *Canadian labour relations*. Toronto: Univ. of Toronto Press.

DITCHBURN, Jennifer. (1998, June 23). "Ottawa dropping court fight over same-sex benefits." *London Free Press*, p. A-10.

DONNER, Arthur (Chair). (1994). *Report of the advisory group on overtime and hours of work*. Ottawa: Supply and Services.

DOWNEY, Donn. (1997, November 4). "No 'irreparable harm,' judge finds." *The Globe & Mail*, p. A-11.

DOWNIE, Bryan. (1992). "Industrial relations in elementary and secondary education: A system transformed?" In *Industrial relations in Canadian industry*.

_____. (1989). "Union-management co-operation in the 1980s and beyond." In *Union-management relations in Canada* (2nd ed.). Some use has also been made of the same author's chapter on the same subject in the 1st (1982) edition of the same book.

_____. (1985). Statements in human resource management class, Master of Industrial Relations program, Queen's University, winter term.

_____. (1984). Remarks on the negotiation process in the negotiation and conflict resolution course in the School of Business, Queen's University, fall term.

DRACHE, Daniel. (1984). "The formation and fragmentation of the Canadian working class: 1820–1920." *Studies in Political Economy*, 15 (fall). Reprinted in *Canadian labour history*.

DRACHE, Daniel, and Harry Glassbeek. (1992). *The changing workplace: Reshaping Canada's industrial relations system*. Toronto: Lorimer.

DUBIN, R. (1959). "Constructive elements of industrial conflict." In A. Kornhauser et al. (Eds.), *Industrial conflict*. New York: McGraw-Hill. Reprinted in *Labour law*, (5th ed.).

DULLES, Foster R., and M. Dubofsy. (1984). *Labour in America: A history* (4th ed.) Arlington Heights, IL: Harlan Davidson.

DUNNETTE, Marvin. (1971). "Research needs of the future in industrial and organizational psychology." Paper presented at 1971 American Psychological Association meetings, Washington, D.C. Reprinted in *Personnel and labour relations*.

DUNNETTE, Marvin, and Bernard Bass. (1963). "Behavioral scientists and personnel management." *Industrial Relations, 2* (May). Reprinted in *Personnel and labour relations*.

DUNLOP, John. (1958). *Industrial relations systems*. Carbondale, IL: Southern Illinois Press.

DUXBURY, L., C. Higgins, C. Lee, and S. Mills. (1991). "Balancing work and family: A study of the federal public sector." Ottawa: no publisher.

EASTMAN, Byron. (1983). "Canadian union growth." *Relations Industrielles, 33*.

EATON, J.K. (1975). "The growth of the Canadian labour movement." *Labour Gazette, 75*.

ECONOMIC Council of Canada (ECC). (1987). *Innovation and jobs in Canada*. Ottawa: Supply and Services.

ECONOMIC Council of Newfoundland and Labrador (ECNL). (1989). "Equity capital and economic development in Newfoundland and Labrador." Ottawa: Economic Council of Canada Local Development Paper #8.

EDEN, Genevieve. (1993). "Industrial discipline in the Canadian federal jurisdiction." *Relations Industrielles*, 48:1.

_____.(1992). "Progressive discipline: An oxymoron." *Relations Industrielles*, 47:3.

EHRENBERG, Ronald, and R. Smith. (1985). *Modern labor economics*. Glenview, IL: Scott-Foresman.

ELLIOTT, David, and Joanne Goss. (1994). *Grievance mediation: How and why it works*. Aurora, ON: Canada Law Book.

ENGLAND, Geoffrey. (1988). "Some thoughts on constitutionalising the right to strike." In *Labour law under the Charter*.

_____. (1987). "Part-time, casual, and other atypical workers: A legal view." Kingston: Queen's Univ. Industrial Relations Centre, Research and Current Issues Series Paper #48.

ENGLISH, Michele (Manager, Nfld. Workers' Compensation Board). (1995) and (1996). Personal conversations and presentations to various industrial relations classes at Memorial University.

EPSTEIN, Abraham. (1932). "Employees' welfare: An autopsy." *American Mercury*, 25:99 (March). Reprinted in *Personnel and labour relations*.

EVENSON, Brad. (1998, July 30). "Equal pay for women is still decades away." *Ottawa Citizen*, p. A-3.

ERSKINE, Lillian, and Trevor Cleveland. (1917). "New men for old." *Everybody's, 36* (April). Reprinted in *Personnel and labour relations*.

FASHOYIN, Tayo. (1991). "Recent trends in industrial relations theory and research in developing countries." In R. Adams (Ed.), *Comparative industrial relations: Contemporary research and theory*. London: Harper Collins Academic.

FAWCETT, Blair. (1998). "Selected provisions in major collective agreements: Wage incentive plans, 1988 to 1998." *Workplace Gazette*, fall.

"FEDERATION to end role as central labour group." (1997, August 22). *The Globe & Mail*, p. A-8.

FERGUSON, G.V. (1935). "An Alberta prophet (1935 model.)" *Canadian Forum*, April. Reprinted in J.L. Granatstein and P. Stevens (Eds.) (1972). *Forum*. Toronto: Univ. of Toronto Press.

FERNER, Anthony, and Richard Hyman. (1992a). "Industrial relations in the new Europe: Seventeen types of ambiguity." Introduction to A. Ferner and R. Hyman (Eds.), *Industrial relations in the new Europe*. Oxford: Blackwell.

_____. (1992b). "Italy: Between political exchange and micro-corporatism." In A. Ferner and R. Hyman (Eds.), *Industrial relations in the new Europe*. Oxford: Blackwell.

FEUILLE, Peter. (1992). "Why does grievance mediation resolve grievances?" *Negotiation Journal*, 8:2 (April).

FINE, Sean. (1997a, November 21). "Post office, CUPW inch toward deal." *The Globe & Mail*, p. A-8.

_____. (1997b, November 22). "Letter carriers balk at Canada Post workload demands." *The Globe & Mail*, p. A-4.

FINE, Sean, and James Rusk. (1997, November 11). "Teachers look to voters to give meaning to strike." *The Globe & Mail*, p. A-4.

FINKEL, Alvin. (1986). "The cold war, Alberta labour and the Social Credit regime." *Labour/Le Travail*, 21 (spring, 1988). Reprinted in *Canadian working class history*.

FISCHER, Frank. (1968). "The personnel function in tomorrow's company." *Personnel*, 45:1 (January-February). Reprinted in *Personnel and labour relations*.

FISHER, E.G., and Brian Williams. (1989). "Negotiating the union-management agreement." In *Union-management relations in Canada* (2nd ed.). Some use has also been made of Williams' negotiation chapter in the 1st (1982) edition of the same book.

FISHER, E.G., and S. Kushner. (1986). "Alberta's construction labour relations during the recent downturn." *Relations Industrielles*, 41:4.

FISHER, Robert, and William Ury.(1983). *Getting to yes: Negotiating agreement without giving in.* New York: Penguin.

FISHER, Sandra, and Jon Peirce.(1995). "Labour education in Newfoundland." *Workers' Education,* 10 (October).

FITCH, John. (1917). "Making the boss efficient." *Survey, 38* (June 2). Reprinted in *Personnel and labour relations.*

FLANDERS, Alan. (1970). "Collective bargaining: A theoretical analysis." In A. Flanders (Ed.), *Management and unions.* London: Faber and Faber. Excerpt reprinted in LLCG. (1991). *Labour law: Cases, materials and commentary* (5th ed.). Kingston: Queen's IRC Press.

FOOT, David. (1997, October 14). "Youth unemployment: A 'bust' priority." *The Globe & Mail,* p. A-23.

FORREST, Anne. (1997). "Securing the male breadwinner." *Relations Industrielles, 52:*1.

_____. (1989). "The rise and fall of national bargaining in the Canadian meat-packing industry." *Relations Industrielles, 44:*2.

_____. (1986). "Bargaining units and bargaining power." *Relations Industrielles, 41:*4.

FORSEY, Eugene. (1985). "Labour and the Constitution in Atlantic Canada." In E. Forsey (Ed.), *Perspectives on the Atlantic Canada labour movement and the working class experience.* Sackville, NB: Mount Allison University Centre for Canadian Studies.

_____. (1982). *Trade unions in Canada, 1812–1902.* Toronto: Univ. of Toronto Press.

FRANK, David. (1983). "The trial of J.B. McLachlan." In *Historical papers* (pp. 208–225). Reprinted in D. Frank and G. Kealey (Eds.). (1995). *Labour and working-class history in Atlantic Canada.* St. John's: Institute of Social and Economic Research.

_____. (1976). "Class conflict in the coal industry: Cape Breton, 1922." In G. Kealey and P. Warrian (Eds.), *Essays in Canadian working-class History.* Toronto: McClelland & Stewart. Reprinted in (1991) *Canadian working class history.*

FREEMAN, Richard. (1989). "On the divergence in unionism among developed countries." Washington: National Bureau of Economic Research Working Paper #2817.

FREEMAN, Richard, and James Medoff. (1984). *What do unions do?* New York: Basic Books.

_____. (1979). "The two faces of unionism." *The Public Interest,* 57.

FRIEDMAN, Milton. (1962). *Capitalism and choice.* Chicago: Chicago Univ. Press. Excerpt reprinted in *Labour law.*

FRYER, John. (1995). "Provincial public sector labour relations." In *Public sector collective bargaining in Canada.*

FUDGE, Judy. (1988). "Labour, the new Constitution, and old style liberalism." In *Labour law under the Charter.*

FUERSTENBERG, Friederich. (1993). "Industrial relations in Germany." In *International and comparative industrial relations* (2nd ed.).

GUNDERSON, Morley, Douglas Hyatt, and Allen Ponak. (1995). "Strikes and dispute resolution." In *Union-management relations in Canada* (3rd ed.). Use has also been made of the strike chapter by John Anderson and Morley Gunderson from this book's 1st (1982) edition.

GUNDERSON, Morley, John Kervin, and Frank Reid. (1989). "The effect of labour relations legislation on strike incidence." *Canadian Journal of Economics,* 22.

_____.(1986). "Logit estimates of strike incidence from Canadian contract data." *Journal of Labour Economics, 4:*2 (April).

GUNDERSON, Morley, L. Myszynski, and J. Keck. (1990). *Women and labour market poverty.* Ottawa: Advisory Council on Status of Women. In *Labour law.*

GALENSON, Walter, and R.S. Smith. (1978). "The United States." In J. Dunlop and W. Galenson (Eds.), *Labor in the twentieth century.* New York: Academic.

GALLAGHER, Daniel, and Kurt Wetzel. (1980). "Centralized multi-employer negotiations in public education: An examination of the Saskatchewan experience in the public sector." *Journal of Collective Negotiations in the Public Sector, 9:*4.

GALT, Virginia. (1998, September 8). "Unions dispute claim work day below average." *The Globe & Mail,* p. A-6.

_____. (1997, November 22). "Mass resignation contemplated by principals." *The Globe & Mail,* p. A-12.

_____. (1994, June 6). "Reinventing the labour movement." *The Globe & Mail.*

GANDZ, Jeffrey. (1979). "Grievance initiation and resolution: A test of the behavioural theory." *Relations Industrielles,* 34.

GANDZ, Jeffrey, and J.D. Whitehead. (1989). "Grievances and their resolution." In *Union-management relations in Canada* (2nd ed.). Some use has also been made of Gandz's grievance chapter in the 1st (1982) edition of the same book.

GANNON, Marvin. (1972). "Entrepreneurship and labor relations at the Ford Motor Company." *Marquette Business Review* (summer). Reprinted in *Personnel and labour relations.*

GEORGE, Claude. (1968). *The history of management thought.* Englewood Cliffs: Prentice-Hall.

GÉRIN-LAJOIE, Jean. (1993). "Quelques contrastes entre les secteurs privé et public au Québec." In *The Industrial Relations System: Proceedings of the 29th Annual Conference of the Canadian Industrial Relations Association.* Charlottetown, P.E.I., Canada.

GILES, Anthony. (1996). "Globalization and industrial relations." In *The globalization of the economy and the worker: Selected papers presented at the 32nd Annual Canadian Industrial Relations Conference.* Montreal, QC, Canada.

GILES, Anthony, and Akivah Starkman. (1995). "The collective agreement." In *Union-management relations in Canada* (3rd ed.). Use has also been made of the collective agreement chapter by Giles and Jain in the 2nd (1989) edition of the same book.

GLASSBEEK, Harry, and S. Rowland. (1979). "Are injuring and killing at work crimes?" *Osgoode Hall Law Journal,* 17, pp. 506–594.

GODARD, John. (1995). "Labour and employee relations in the Canadian private sector: Report to participants in the LERS Survey." University of Manitoba Faculty of Management. Working paper.

_____. (1994). *Industrial relations: The economy and society.* Toronto: McGraw-Hill Reason.

_____. (1991). "The progressive HRM paradigm: A theoretical and empirical re-examination." *Relations Industrielles,* 46.

GODARD, John, and Thomas Kochan. (1982). "Canadian management under collective bargaining." In *Union-management relations in Canada* (1st ed.).

GOETSCHY, Janine, and Annette Jobert. (1993). "Industrial relations in France." In *International and comparative industrial relations* (2nd ed.).

GOLD, Alan. (1993, May). Conversation with the author in Montreal.

GOLDBERG, Stephen. (1989). "Grievance mediation: A successful alternative to labor arbitration." *Negotiation Journal,* 5.

GOLDBLATT, H. (1974). *Justice denied.* Toronto: Labour Council of Metropolitan Toronto.

GOLLOM, Mark. (1998, October 18). "Protesters challenge Harris." *Ottawa Citizen,* p. A-2.

GOSPEL, Howard, and C. Littler. (1982). *Managerial strategies and industrial relations.* London: Heineman.

GOULDEN, Joseph. (1972). *Meany.* New York: Atheneum.

GRAHAM, Katherine. (1995). "Collective bargaining in the municipal sector." In *Public sector collective bargaining in Canada.*

GRANGE, Michael. (1997, November 21). "Canada Post costs the issue." *The Globe & Mail,* p. A-8.

_____. (1996, October 24). "GM contract approved by members of CAW." *The Globe & Mail,* p. A-10.

GRANT, Michael. (1992). "Industrial Relations in the Clothing Industry: Lessons for Survival." In *Industrial relations in Canadian industry.*

GREEN, Sara Jane. (1998, September 9). "Catholic teachers angry at being on the picket line." *The Globe & Mail,* p. A-7a.

"GROUP hopes for Goose Base answers." (1998, February 5). *St. John's Evening Telegram,* p. 5.

GUNDERSON, Morley. (1986). "Alternative methods for dealing with permanent layoffs and plant closings." In W.C. Riddell (Ed.), *Adapting to change: Labour market adjustment in Canada.* Toronto: Univ. of Toronto Press. Reprinted in *Labour law.*

GUNDERSON, Morley, and Allen Ponak. (1995). "Industrial relations." In *Union-management relations in Canada* (3rd ed.).

GUNDERSON, Morley, and Frank Reid. (1998). "Worksharing and working time issues in Canada." Montreal: Institute for Research in Public Policy.

_____. (1995). "Public sector strikes in Canada." In *Public sector collective bargaining in Canada.*

GUNDERSON, Morley, and Douglas Hyatt. (1995). "Union impact on compensation, productivity, and management of the organization." In *Union-management relations in Canada* (3rd ed.). Use has also been made of Gunderson's 1989 chapter on the same topic from the 2nd edition (1989) of the same book.

GUNDERSON, Morley, and W.C. Riddell. (1993). *Labour market economics: Theory, evidence and policy in Canada* (3rd ed.). Toronto: McGraw-Hill Ryerson.

HAIVEN, Larry. (1995). "Industrial relations in health care: Regulation, conflict and transition to the 'wellness model'." In *Public sector collective bargaining in Canada.*

_____. (1990). "Hegemony and the workplace: The role of arbitration." In L. Haiven, S. McBride, and J. Shields (Eds.), *Regulating labour.* Toronto: Garamond.

HAIVEN, Larry, Stephen McBride, and John Shields. (1990). "The state, neo-conservatism, and industrial relations." In *Regulating labour.*

HALPERN, Norman. (1984). "Sociotechnical systems design: The Shell Sarnia experience." In J.B. Cunningham and T.H. White (Eds.), *Quality of working life: contemporary cases.* Ottawa: Supply and Services (Labour Canada publication).

HAMMARSTROM, Olle. (1993). "Industrial relations in Sweden." In *International and comparative industrial relations* (2nd ed.).

HANNIGAN, John. (1986). "Laboured relations: Reporting industrial relations news in Canada." Toronto: Univ. of Toronto Centre for Industrial Relations.

HAYDEN, Anders. (1998a, April). "35-Hour week shakes Europe." In *Ontario New Democrat*, p. 11.

———. (1998b). *Europe's new movement for work time reduction*. Toronto: 32 Hours.

HEBBARD, Gary. (1998a, February 3). "Union, backers block Goose Bay Base." *St. John's Evening Telegram*, p. 4.

———. (1998b, February 4). "Delegates to meet defence minister today to plead case for air base contract." *St. John's Evening Telegram*, p. 3.

HEBDON, Robert. (1992). "Ontario's no-strike laws: A test of the safety valve hypothesis." In *Proceedings* of the 28th Annual Conference of the Canadian Industrial Relations Association.

HÉBERT, Gérard. (1995). "Public sector collective bargaining in Quebec." In *Public sector collective bargaining in Canada*.

HENEMAN, Herbert. (1969). "Toward a general conceptual system of industrial relations: How do we get there?" In Gerald Somers (Ed.), *Essays in industrial relations theory*. Ames, IA: Iowa State Univ. Press.

———. (1960, July). "Manpower management: New wrapping on old merchandise." In Univ. of Minnesota Industrial Relations Center "Special Release" 2. Reprinted in *Personnel and labour relations*.

HERON, Craig. (1996). *The Canadian labour movement: A short history*. Toronto: Lorimer. Considerable use has also been made of the 1989 edition of the same book.

———. (1984). "Labourism and the Canadian Working Class." *Labour/Le Travail*, 13 (spring). Reprinted in *Canadian labour history*.

HESS, Henry. (1997, November 27). "Ontario unions set out plan to unseat Tories: Mass walkout is centrepiece of scheme." *The Globe & Mail*, p. A-6.

HÉTHY, Lajos. (1991). "Industrial relations in Eastern Europe: Recent development and trends." In *Comparative industrial relations*.

HOLMAN, Worthington. (1904). "A 5000 brain-power organization." *System*, 4:2 (August). Reprinted in *Personnel and labour relations*.

HUMAN Resources Development Canada (HRDC). (1998). Selected work stoppage data from the Work Stoppage Bureau, Workplace Information Directorate.

HUMAN Resources Development Canada (HRDC). (1994). Federal preventive mediation program description.

HUNNICUTT, Benjamin. (1988). *Work without end: Abandoning shorter hours for the right to work*. Philadelphia: Temple Univ. Press.

HUNT, Gerald. (1997). "Sexual orientation and the Canadian labour movement." In *Relations Industrielles*, 52:4.

HUTCHINSON, Allan. (1998, April 20). "What the supreme court said, and didn't say, on gay rights." *Toronto Star*.

HYMAN, Richard. (1983). "A critical view of industrial democracy systems." In *Essays in collective bargaining and industrial democracy*. Toronto: CCH Canadian. Excerpt reprinted in *Labour law*.

———. (1975). *Industrial relations: A Marxist introduction*. London: MacMillan.

ICHNIOWSKI, Casey. (1986). "The effects of grievance activity on productivity." *Industrial and Labor Relations Review*, 40.

JACOBI, Otlo, Berndt Keller, and Werner Muller-Jentsch. (1992). "Germany: codetermining the future." In *Industrial relations in the new Europe*.

JACKSON, Andrew (Chief Economist, CLC). (1997). Presentation at "32 Hours" conference, Toronto, November 22.

JACKSON, Edward T. (1998). "Worker ownership and community economic development." Paper presented to CLC conference on Jobs and the Economy, Ottawa, February.

———. (1997). "ETIs: A tool for responsible pension fund investment." *Making Waves*, 8:2.

JACKSON, Edward T., and François Lamontagne. (1995). "Adding value: The economic and social impacts of labour-sponsored venture capital corporations on their investee firms." Ottawa: CLMPC.

JACKSON, Edward T, and Jon Peirce. (1990). "Mobilizing capital for regional development." Ottawa: Economic Council of Canada Local Development Paper #21.

JACKSON, Richard. (1995). "Police and firefighter labour relations in Canada." In *Public sector collective bargaining in Canada*.

JENSON, Jane, and Rianne Mahon. (1993). "North American labour: Divergent trajectories." In J. Jenson and R. Mahon (Eds.), *The challenge of restructuring: North American labour movements respond*. Philadelphia: Temple Univ. Press.

JOHNSTON, T.L. (1962). *Collective bargaining in Sweden*. London: Allen and Unwin.

JOYCE, George (Conciliator, Nfld. Ministry of Labour). (1996). Statements made to various industrial relations classes at Memorial University concerning the Ministry's preventive mediation program.

KASSALOW, Everett. (1963). "Unions in the new and developing countries." In E. Kassalow (Ed.), *National labor movements in the postwar world*. Chicago: Northwestern Univ. Press.

KEALEY, Gregory. (1985). "The Canadian working-class: Past, present and future." *In Perspectives on the Atlantic Canada labour movement and the working class experience.*

_____. (1984). "1919: The Canadian labour revolt." *Labour/Le Travail*, 13 (spring). Reprinted in *Canadian labour history.*

KEALEY, Gregory, and Bryan Palmer. (1982). *Dreaming of what might be: The Knights of Labour in Ontario, 1880–1900.* Cambridge: Cambridge Univ. Press.

_____. (1981). "Bonds of unity: The Knights of Labor in Ontario." *Histoire Sociale/Social History.* Reprinted in *Canadian working class history.*

KERVIN, John. (1989). "The science of bargaining." In A. Sethi (Ed.), *Collective bargaining in Canada.* Scarborough: Nelson.

_____. (1988). "Sociology, psychology and industrial relations." In *The state of the art in industrial relations.*

_____. (1984). "Strikes: Toward a typology of causes." In *Proceedings of 21st Annual Meeting of Canadian Industrial Relations Association.* Guelph, Ontario, Canada.

KING, Carlyle. (1944). "The CCF sweeps Saskatchewan." *Canadian Forum*, July. Reprinted in *Forum.*

KING, Mike. (1998, March 19). "Golden arch enemies: Teamsters declare war on McDonald's." *Ottawa Citizen*, p. C-1.

KILPATRICK, Ken. (1998, March 9) "Maple Leaf vote 'won on fear.'" *Toronto Star*, p. B1.

KJELLBERG, Anders. (1992). "Sweden: Can the model survive?" In *Industrial relations in the new Europe.*

KOCHAN, Thomas. (1980). *Collective bargaining and industrial relations.* Homewood, IL: Irwin.

KOCHAN, Thomas, and Paul Barrocci. (1985). *Human resource management and industrial relations: Text, readings, and cases.* Boston: Little Brown.

KOCHAN, Thomas, and Paul Osterman. (1994). *The mutual gains enterprise: Forging a winning partnership among labor, management, and government.* Boston: Harvard Business School Press.

KOCHAN, Thomas, Robert McKersie, and Peter Cappelli. (1984). "Strategic choice and industrial relations theory." *Industrial Relations*, 23:1.

KUMAR, Pradeep.(1993). *From uniformity to divergence: Industrial relations in Canada and the United States.* Kingston: Queen's IRC Press.

KUMAR, Pradeep, Gregor Murray, and Sylvain Schetagne. (1998). "Adapting to change: Union priorities in the 1990s." *Workplace Gazette*, fall.

KUMAR, Pradeep, and Noah Meltz. (1992). "Industrial relations in the Canadian automobile industry." In *Industrial relations in Canadian industry.*

KUNDE, Diana. (1998, October 10). "Skilful salary negotiation can pay off for job seekers." *Ottawa Citizen*, p. K-5.

KUWAHARA, Yasuo. (1993). "Industrial relations in Japan." In *International and comparative industrial relations* (2nd ed.).

LABOUR Law Casebook Group (LLCG). (1991). *Labour law: Cases, materials and commentary* (5th ed.). Kingston: Queen's IRC Press. Use has also been made of the draft 4th edition (1984) of the same book.

LABOUR law under the Charter: Proceedings of a conference. (1988). Kingston: Queen's Law Journal and Industrial Relations Centre.

LIPSEY, Richard, Douglas Purvis, Gordon Sparks, and Peter Steiner. (1982). *Economics* (4th ed.). New York: Harper and Row.

LABERGE, Roy. (1976). *The labour beat: An introduction to unions.* Ottawa: Media Algonquin.

"LABOUR protest closes town." (1998, February 4). *The Globe & Mail*, p. A-4.

LACEY, Robert. (1986). *Ford: The men and the machine.* Toronto: McClelland & Stewart.

LAFFER, Kingsley. (1974). "Is industrial relations an academic discipline?" *Journal of Industrial Relations*, 16 (March).

LAKEY, Jack. (1998, May 14). "Winery boycotted for backing Tories." *Toronto Star*, p. B-1.

LARSON, Simeon, and Bruce Nissen (Eds.). (1987). *Theories of the labor movement.* Detroit: Wayne State Univ. Press.

LAWSON, Chris (Communications Specialist, CUPW). (1998). Personal interview. September 8.

LAXER, James. (1986). *Leap of faith: Free trade and the future of Canada.* Edmonton: Hurtig.

LEAP, T.L., and D.W. Grigsby. (1986). "A conceptualization of collective bargaining power." *Industrial and Labor Relations Review*, 39.

LEGGETT, Chris. (1993). "Singapore." In *Labour law and industrial relations in Asia.*

LEITCH, Carolyn, and Gayle MacDonald. (1997, November 28). "Postal strike an economic disaster." *The Globe & Mail*, pp. A-1, A-3.

LEMELIN, Maurice. (1989). "Quality of working life and collective bargaining: Can they co-exist?" In A. Sethi (Ed.), *Collective bargaining in Canada.* Scarborough: Nelson.

LEWICKI, Roy, David Saunders, and John Minton. (1997). *Essentials of negotiation.* Chicago and Toronto: Irwin.

LEWIS, Gregg. (1986). *Union relative wage effects: A survey.* Chicago: Univ. of Chicago Press.

LIPSIG-MUMME, Carla. (1995). "Labour strategies in the new social order: A political economy perspective." In *Union-management relations in Canada* (3rd ed.).

_____. (1989). "Canadian and American unions respond to economic crisis." *Journal of Industrial Relations*, 31.

LIPTON, Charles. (c1973 [1967]). *The trade union movement of Canada, 1827–1959.* Toronto: NC Press.

LOGAN, Harold. (1948). *Trade unions in Canada.* Toronto: Macmillan.

LONG, Richard. (1992). Conversation with the author in Toronto, July.

LORWIN, Val. (1954). *The French labor movement.* Cambridge: Harvard Univ. Press.

LOWE, Graham. (1980). *Bank unionization in Canada: A preliminary analysis.* Toronto: Univ. of Toronto Centre for Industrial Relations.

LOW, Stephen. (1963). "The role of trade-unions in the newly independent countries of Africa." In *National labor movements in the postwar world.*

MacDONALD, Robert. (1967). "Collective bargaining in the postwar period." *Industrial and Labor Relations Review*, 20:4 (July). Reprinted in *Personnel and labour relations.*

MacDOWELL, Laurel Sefton. (1982). "The 1943 steel strike against wartime wage controls." *Labour/Le Travailleur*, 10.

_____. (1978). "The formation of the Canadian industrial relations system during World War II." *Labour/Le Travailleur*, 3. Reprinted in *Canadian working class history.*

MACKIE, Richard. (1997a, December 2). "Every last Tory backs education law." *The Globe & Mail*, p. A-3.

_____. (1997b, December 16). "Tories moving too fast for voters." *The Globe & Mail*, p. A-4.

MACKIE, Richard, and Jennifer Lewington. (1997, November 7). "Three unions to teach Monday." *The Globe & Mail*, p. A-1.

MAHONEY, Jill. (1998, September 8). "Job action means longer vacation for some students." *The Globe & Mail*, p. A-6.

MAKI, Dennis. (1982). "Political parties and trade union growth." *Relations Industrielles*, 37.

MALLES, Paul. (1976). *Canadian labour standards in law, agreement, and practice.* Ottawa: Supply and Services.

MANLEY, John. (1986). "Communists and autoworkers: The struggle for industrial unionism in the Canadian automobile industry, 1925–1936." *Labour/Le Travail*, 17 (spring). Reprinted in *Canadian working class history.*

MARSHALL, Stan (Research Officer, CUPE). (1998). Telephone interview, September 9.

MARTINELLO, Felice. (1996). "Correlates of certification application success in British Columbia, Saskatchewan, and Manitoba." *Relations Industrielles*, 51.

MATSUDA, Yasuhiko. (1993). "Japan." In *Labour law and industrial relations in Asia.*

MATHEWSON, Stanley. (1931–1932). "A survey of personnel management in 195 concerns." *Personnel Journal*, 10:4. Reprinted in *Personnel and labour relations.*

MAY, Kathryn. (1998, July 30). "Two hundred thousand share in landmark award." *Ottawa Citizen*, p. A-1.

McCALLUM, Margaret. (1986). "Keeping women in their place: The minimum wage in Canada, 1910–1925." *Labour/le Travail.* Reprinted in *Canadian working class history.*

McCAMBLY, James. (1990, August 21). "Why Canadian labor needs to stay politically neutral." *The Globe & Mail*, p. A-15. Reprinted in A. Craig and N. Solomon. *The system of industrial relations in Canada* (4th ed.). Scarborough, ON: Prentice-Hall.

McCARTHY, Shawn. (1997, November 22). "Can Canada Post deliver?" *The Globe & Mail*, pp. B-1, B-6.

McCORMACK, Ross. (1975). "The industrial workers of the world in Western Canada, 1905–1914." *Historical Papers.* Reprinted in *Canadian working class history.*

McINTOSH, Robert. (1987). "The boys in the Nova Scotia coal mines, 1873–1923." *Acadiensis*, 16:2 (spring). Reprinted in *Labour and working-class history in Atlantic Canada.*

McKAY, Ian. (1991). "None but skilled workmen." From *The craft transformed.* Reprinted in *Canadian working class history.*

_____. (1983). "Strikes in the Maritimes: 1901–1914." *Acadiensis*, 13:1 (fall). Reprinted in *Canadian labour history.*

McKINLEY, Patrick.(1997, August 22). "Labour group to fold." *Winnipeg Free Press*, p. B-1.

McPHILLIPS, David, and Geoffrey England. (1995). "Employment legislation." In *Union-management relations in Canada* (3rd ed.). Some use has also been made of the same authors' employment legislation chapter in the 2nd edition (1989) of the same book.

MELTZ, Noah. (1989a). "Industrial relations: Balancing efficiency and equity." In J. Barbash and K. Barbash (Eds.), *Theories and concepts in comparative industrial relations.* Columbia, SC: Univ. of South Carolina Press.

_____. (1989b). "Interstate versus interprovincial differences in union density." *Industrial Relations*, 28.

_____. (1985). "Labor movements in Canada and the United States." In Thomas Kochan (Ed.), *Challenges and choices facing American labor.* Cambridge: MIT Press.

MILLS, D. Quinn. (1989). *Labor-management relations* (4th ed.). New York: McGraw-Hill.

MINNEHAN, Robert, and W.S. Paine. (1982). "Bottom lines: Assessing the economic and legal consequences of burnout." In W.S. Paine (Ed.), *Job stress and burnout: Research, theory, and intervention perspectives.* Beverly Hills: Sage.

MISHEL, Lawrence. (1986). "The structural determinants of union bargaining power." *Industrial and Labor Relations Review*, 40:1.

MITCHELL, Nancy. (1996). "Coming to a national park in your area: ETOs." *Alliance*, summer.

MOOGK, Peter. (1976). "In the darkness of a basement: Craftsmen's associations in early French Canada." *Canadian Historical Review*, 58. Reprinted in *Canadian working class history.*

MORTON, Desmond.(1995). "The history of the Canadian labour movement." In *Union-management relations in Canada* (3rd ed.). Use has also been made of Morton's labour history chapter in the 1st and 2nd (1982 and 1989) editions of the same book.

_____. (1990). *Working people: An illustrated history of the Canadian labour movement.* Toronto: Summerhill.

MORTON, Desmond, and Terry Copp. (1980). *Working people.* Toronto: Deneau & Greenberg. Some, although less, use has also been made of Morton's 1984 and 1990 editions of the same book.

MOUAT, Jeremy. (1990). "The genesis of Western exceptionalism: British Columbia's hard-rock miners, 1895–1903." *Canadian Historical Review*, 71. Reprinted in *Canadian working class history.*

MUIR, J. Douglas. (1971). "Decentralized bargaining: Its problems and direction in the public education systems of Ontario and the Western provinces." *Relations Industrielles*, 26.

MURDOCK, Rebecca. (1997). "Organizing the service sector: The fight for 40 at Starbucks." *Canadian Dimension*, 31:6 (November).

MURRAY, Gregor. (1995). "Unions: Membership, structure, and actions." In *Union-management relations in Canada* (3rd ed.).

MURRAY, Thomas. (1971, March). "It's hell in personnel." Reprinted in *Personnel and labour relations.*

NELSON, Joyce. (1998). "The art of the deal." *Canadian Forum*, April.

NG, Ignace. (1992). "The probability of union membership in the private sector." *Relations Industrielles*, 47.

NG, Ignace, and Ali Dastmalchian. (1989). "Determinants of grievance outcomes: A case study." *Industrial and Labor Relations Review*, 42:3.

NIVEN, M.M. (1967). *Personnel management, 1913–63: The growth of personnel management and the development of the institute.* London: Institute of Personnel Management.

NOLAN, Dennis, and Roger Abrams. (1997). "Trends in private sector grievance arbitration." In J. Stern and J. Najita (Eds.), *Labor arbitration under fire.* Ithaca and London: Cornell Univ. ILR Press.

NYLAND, Chris. (1989). *Reduced worktime and the management of production.* Cambridge: Cambridge Univ. Press.

O'HARA, Bruce. (1993). *Working harder isn't working.* Vancouver: New Star.

Ontario Federation of Labour (OFL). (1994). *Annual program report.* Toronto: Author.

ONTARIO New Democratic Party (ONDP). (1984). Report on the future of work presented at the party's 1984 policy convention in Hamilton, Ontario, Canada.

OSTERMAN, Paul.(1988). *Employment futures: Reorganization, dislocation, and public policy.* New York: Oxford University Press.

OSTRY, Sylvia, and Mahmood Zaidi. (1979). *Labour economics in Canada* (3rd ed.). Toronto: MacMillan.

OWEN, John. (1989). *Reduced working hours: Cure for unemployment or economic burden?* Baltimore and London: Johns Hopkins Univ. Press.

OWEN, William. (1940–1941). "Decentralize personnel work." *Personnel Journal*, 19. Reprinted in *Personnel and labour relations: An evolutionary approach.*

PACHOLIK, Barb. (1998, April 3). "Ruling confirms gays entitled to same benefits as heterosexuals." *Saskatoon Star-Phoenix*, p. A-3.

PALMER, Bryan. (1986). "Listening to history rather than historians: Reflections on working-class history." *Studies in Political Economy*, 20 (summer). Reprinted in *Canadian labour history.*

PANITCH, Leo, and Donald Swartz. (1988). *The assault on trade union freedoms: From coercion to consent revisited.* Toronto: Garamond.

PATTERSON, John. (1901, January). "Altruism and sympathy as factors in works administration." *Engineering Magazine*, 20. Reprinted in *Personnel and labour relations.*

PAYNE, Melanie. (1998, April 11). "Headhunters thrive in tighter job market." *Ottawa Citizen*, p. J-4.

PEACH, David, and David Kuechle. (1975). *The practice of industrial relations.* Toronto and New York: McGraw-Hill Ryerson.

PEIRCE, Jon. (1999). "The case for a shorter work week." Ottawa: Carleton Centre for the Study of Training, Investment and Economic Restructuring. Publication pending.

_____. (1998a, May 14). "Plenty of militancy left in Canadian unions." *Toronto Star*, p. A-14.

_____. (1998b, March 20). "Jobless rate still far too high." *Toronto Star.*

_____. (1996). "The sad saga of the late and little-lamented Newfoundland 'white paper' provisions on labour relations." In *Proceedings* of the 1995 Canadian Industrial Relations conference. Montreal, QC, Canada.

_____. (1995). "George Meany and the decline of the American labour movement." St. John's: Memorial Univ. School of Business. Working paper.

_____. (1993). "An end to American exceptionalism?" In *The Industrial Relations System: Proceedings of the 29th Conference of the Canadian Industrial Relations Association.* Charlottetown, P.E.I., Canada.

_____. (1989). "Exclusions from collective bargaining legislation in Canada." Unpublished Master of Industrial Relations essay. Kingston: Queen's Univ. Industrial Relations Centre.

_____. (1987). "Collective bargaining over technological change in Canada: A quantitative and historical analysis." Ottawa: Economic Council of Canada Discussion Paper #338.

PELLEGRINI, Claudio. (1993). "Industrial relations in Italy." In *International and comparative industrial relations* (2nd ed.).

PERRY, James, and Harold Angle. (1981). "Bargaining unit structure and organizational outcomes." *Industrial Relations*, 20:1.

PICARD, Laurent (Chair). (1967). *Report of the inquiry commission on the St. Lawrence ports.* Ottawa: Department of Labour.

POMEROY, Bert. (1999). Editor, the *Labradorian.* Telephone interview with the author, January 15.

PONAK, Allen, and Corliss Olson. (1992). "Time delays in grievance arbitration." *Relations Industrielles,* 47.

PONAK, Allen, and Mark Thompson. (1995). "Public sector collective bargaining." In *Union-management relations in Canada* (3rd ed.). Use has also been made of Ponak's public sector chapter from the 1st (1982) edition of the same book, and Thompson's public sector chapter from the 2nd (1989) edition.

PONAK, Allen, and Morley Gunderson. (1995). "Future directions for Canadian industrial relations." In *Union-management relations in Canada* (3rd ed.).

POSNER, R. (1977). *Economic analysis of the law* (2nd ed.). Toronto: Little Brown. Excerpts reprinted in *Labour law.*

PUBLIC Service Alliance of Canada (PSAC). (1998). Various information leaflets and notices to members (mainly, though not entirely, on the issue of pay equity).

RADFORTH, Ian. (1991). Statements made during various labour history classes, Univ. of Toronto, fall semester.

_____. (1982). "Woodworkers and the mechanization of the pulpwood logging industry of Northern Ontario: 1950–1970." *Historical Papers/Communications historiques.* Reprinted in *Canadian labour history.*

RANDAZZO, Daniel. (1995). *The 1995 annotated Ontario labour relations act.* Scarborough, ON: Carswell.

RAVENHORST, A.M. (1990). "Industrial relations in Korea: The backdrop to the current drama." *Comparative Labor Law Journal,* 11:3. Quoted in Park Young-ki. (1993). "South Korea." In *Labour law and industrial relations in Asia.*

REID, Frank. (1997). Presentation at "32 Hours" conference, November 22. Toronto, ON, Canada.

_____. (1982). "Wage-and-price Controls in Canada." In *Union-management relations in Canada* (3rd ed.).

REID, Frank, and Noah Meltz. (1995). "The economic environment." In *Union-management relations in Canada* (3rd ed.). Use has also been made of the same authors' chapter on the economy from the same book's 2nd (1989) edition, cited in the text as Meltz and Reid (1989).

REITSMA, Stephen. (1993). "The Canadian corporate response to globalization." Ottawa: Conference Board of Canada Report #106-93.

REUTHER, Victor. (1976). *The brothers Reuther and the story of the UAW.* Boston: Houghton Mifflin.

REYNOLDS, David. (1995). "The right to strike in the public sector: A comparative analysis of Canada, Germany, Japan, and Sweden." Unpublished paper: St. John's, Nfld.

REYNOLDS, Lloyd. (1982). *Labor economics and labor relations* (8th ed.). Englewood Cliffs: Prentice-Hall.

RICHARD, K. Peter (Commissioner). (1997). *The Westray story: A predictable path to disaster.* Province of Nova Scotia (no place of publication given).

RICHARDSON, J. Albert. (1985). "The role of organized labour in today's Atlantic Canada." In *Perspectives on the Atlantic Canada labour movement and the working class experience.*

ROBB, Roberta. (1987). "Equal pay for work of equal value: Issues and policies." In *Canadian Public Policy,* 13. Reprinted in *Labour law.*

ROBERTS, Wayne, and John Bullen. (1985). "A heritage of hope and struggle: Workers, unions, and politics in Canada, 1930–1982." In M. Cross and G. Kealey (Eds.), *Modern Canada 1930s–1980s.* Toronto: McClelland & Stewart. Reprinted in *Canadian labour history.*

ROBINSON, Archie. (1981). *George Meany and his times: A biography.* New York: Simon and Schuster.

ROBINSON, Ian. (1994). "NAFTA, social unionism, and labour movement power in Canada and the United States." *Relations Industrielles*, 49:4 (fall).

_____. (1990). *Organizing labour: Exploring Canada-U.S. union density divergence in the post-war period.* New Haven: Yale University Ph.D. dissertation.

ROGOW, Robert. (1989a). "The structure of collective bargaining." In *Collective bargaining in Canada*.

_____. (1989b). "Collective bargaining law." In *Collective bargaining in Canada*.

ROSE, Joseph. (1995). "The evolution of public sector unionism." In *Public sector collective bargaining in Canada*.

_____. (1992). "Industrial relations in the construction industry in the 1980s." In *Industrial relations in Canadian industry*.

_____. (1991). "The emergence of expedited arbitration." *Labour Arbitration Yearbook*, I.

_____. (1987). "Innovative grievance arbitration systems." Hamilton: McMaster Univ. Faculty of Business Research.

_____. (1986a). "Legislative support for multi-employer bargaining: The Canadian experience." *Industrial and Labor Relations Review*, 40:1.

_____. (1986b). "Statutory expedited grievance arbitration: The case of Ontario." *Arbitration Journal*, 41.

_____. (1982). "Construction labour relations." In *Union-management relations in Canada* (1st ed.).

ROSE, Joseph, and Gary Chaison. (1990). "New measures of union organizing effectiveness." *Industrial Relations*, 29.

SACK, Jeffrey. (1994). *Winning cases at grievance arbitration.* Toronto: Lancaster House.

SANDERSON, John. (1976). *Labour arbitrations and all that.* Toronto: Richard de Boo.

SASS, Bob. (1993). "The work environment board and the limits of social democracy in Canada." *International Journal of Health Services*, 23.

_____. (1989). "The art of collective bargaining." In *Collective bargaining in Canada*.

SASS, Bob, and Mark Stobbe. (1989). "Collective bargaining and health and safety issues." In *Collective bargaining in Canada*.

SAUVÉ, Robert. (1971). "La négociation collective sectorielle." *Relations Industrielles*, 26:1.

SCHELLING, Thomas. (1957). "Bargaining, communication, and limited war." *Journal of Conflict Resolution*, 1:1.

SCHEUER, Steen. (1992). "Denmark." In A. Ferner and R. Hyman (Eds.), *Industrial relations in the new Europe.* Oxford: Blackwell.

SCOTT, F. R. (1945). "Ode to a politician." Reprinted in M. Wilson (Ed.). (1969). *Poets between the wars.* Toronto: McClelland & Stewart.

_____. (1932). "Communists, senators, and all that." *Canadian Forum*, January. Reprinted in *Forum*.

SEEGER, Pete. (1972). *The Incompleat Folksinger.* Lincoln: Univ. of Nebraska Press.

SETHI, Amarjit (Ed.). (1989). *Collective bargaining in Canada.* Scarborough, ON: Nelson.

SEXTON, Jean. (1987). "First contract administration in Canada." In *Proceedings* of the spring, 1987 meeting of the IRRA. Boston, Massachusetts, America. Reprinted from *Labour Law Journal* (August).

SHELLENBARGER, Sue. (1998, October 7). "Time off is workers' answer to stress." *Ottawa Citizen*, p. G-32. (Reprinted from *Wall Street Journal*).

_____. (1997, December 22). "The worst work-family train wrecks of 1997." *The Globe & Mail*, p. B-11.

SHERIDAN, M., D. Sunter, and B. Diverty. (1996). "The changing workweek: Trends in weekly hours of work." *Canadian Economic Observer.* Ottawa: Statistics Canada Cat. 11-010-XPB (September).

SHIELDS, John. (1990). "Building a new hegemony in British Columbia." In L. Haiven, S. McBride, and J. Shields (Eds.), *Regulating labour.* Toronto: Garamond.

SHIPPING Federation of Canada. (1972). Brief on job security submitted to Judge Alan Gold (arbitrator for the Port of Montreal).

SIMPSON, Jeffrey. (1997, November 11). "In the end, everybody lost when the teachers walked out." *The Globe & Mail*, p. A-20.

SIMS, Andrew (Chair). (c1996 [1995]). *Canada Labour Code, part I, seeking a balance.* Ottawa: Minister of Public Works and Government Services.

SINGH, R. (1976). "Systems theory in the study of industrial relations: Time for reappraisal?" *Industrial Relations Journal*, 7 (fall).

SLICHTER, Sumner. (1929). "The current labor policies of American industry." *Quarterly Journal of Economics*, 43 (May). Reprinted in *Personnel and labour relations*.

SMITH, Anthony. (1993). "Canadian industrial relations in transition." *Relations Industrielles*, 48.

SNYDER, Ronald. (1995). *The annotated Canada labour code.* Scarborough: Carswell.

SOKOLIK, Stanley. (1969). "Reorganize the personnel department?" *California Management Review*, 11:3 (spring). Reprinted in *Personnel and labour relations*.

SOLOMON, N., P. Andiappan, and D. Shand. (1986). "Canadian union presidents: An empirical study." *Relations Industrielles*, 41.

STAT CAN (1998). "Labour force update." Statistics Canada, Cat. No. 71-005-XPB, winter. Ottawa: Author.

_____. (1997). "Labour force update: Youths and the labour market." Statistics Canada, Cat. No. 71-005-XPB, spring. Ottawa: Author.

STEED, Judy. (1994, January 9). "Algoma's man of steel." *Ottawa Citizen.* Reprinted in *The system of industrial relations in Canada* (4th ed.).

STERN, R.N., and J.C. Anderson. (1978). "Canadian strike activity: Union centralization and national diversity." In J. Stern (Ed.), *Proceedings* of the 30th Annual Meeting of the Industrial Relations Research Association. Madison: IRRA.

STEWART-PATTERSON, David. (1987). *Post-mortem: Why Canada's mail won't move.* Toronto: MacMillan.

STOREY, Robert. (1983). "Unionization versus corporate welfare: The Dofasco way." *Labour/Le Travailleur* (fall).

STRAUSS, George. (1991). "Union democracy." In G. Strauss et al. (Eds.), *The state of the unions.* Madison: IRRA Press.

SUMMERS, Clyde. (1991). "Unions without majorities: The potential of the NLRA." In *Proceedings* of the 43rd Annual Meeting of the Industrial Relations Research Association. Madison: IRRA.

SWIMMER, Gene. (1995). "Collective bargaining in the federal public service of Canada: The last twenty years." In *Public sector collective bargaining in Canada.*

SWIMMER, Gene, and Mark Thompson. (1995). "Collective bargaining in the public sector: An Introduction." In *Public sector collective bargaining in Canada.*

SWINTON, Katherine. (1995). "The Charter of Rights and public sector labour relations." In *Public sector collective bargaining in Canada.*

_____. (1983). "Enforcement of occupational health and safety: The role of the internal responsibility system." In *Studies in labour law.* Reprinted in *Labour law.*

SWINTON, Katherine, and Kenneth Swan. (1983). "The Interaction Between Human Rights Legislation and Labour Law." In *Studies in labour law.* Reprinted in *Labour law.*

TARANTELLI, Ezio. (1986). "The regulation of inflation and unemployment." *Industrial Relations,* 25:1.

TASK Force on Microelectronics. (1982). *In the chips: Opportunities, people, partnership.* Ottawa: Supply and Services.

TERKEL, Studs. (c1975 [1972]). *Working.* New York: Avon.

THOMASON, T., H. Zwerling, and P. Chandra. (1992). "Labour relations in the Canadian textile industry." In *Industrial relations in Canadian industry.*

THOMASON, Terry. (1995). "Labour relations in primary and secondary education." In *Public sector collective bargaining in Canada.*

THOMPSON, Mark. (1995a). "The management of industrial relations." In *Union-management relations in Canada* (3rd ed.).

_____. (1995b). "The industrial relations effects of privatization: Evidence from Canada." In *Public sector collective bargaining in Canada.*

_____. (1982). "Collective bargaining by professionals." In *Union-management relations in Canada* (1st ed.).

THOMPSON, Mark, and Allen Ponak. (1992). "Restraint, privatization, and industrial relations in the public sector in the 1980s." In *Industrial relations in Canadian industry.*

THOMPSON, Mark, and Gene Swimmer. (1995). "The future of public sector industrial relations." In *Public sector collective bargaining in Canada.*

THORNICROFT, Kenneth, and Genevieve Eden. (1995). "Grievances and their resolution." In *Union-management relations in Canada* (3rd ed.).

TRACY, J.S. (1987). "An empirical test of an asymmetric information model of strikes." *Journal of Labor Economics,* 5.

TROFIMENKOFF, Susan. (1977). "102 muffled voices: Canada's industrial women in the 1880s." *Women's Study Journal, Atlantis.* Reprinted in *Canadian working class history.*

TROTTA, Maurice. (1976). *Handling grievances: A guide for management and labor.* Washington: Bureau of National Affairs.

TROY, Leo. (1992). "Convergence in international unionism et cetera: The case of Canada and the U.S.A." *British Journal of Industrial Relations,* 30.

UNITED Steelworkers of America (USWA). (1991). *Empowering workers in the global economy, a labour agenda for the 1990s.* Papers prepared for a conference in Toronto, October 1991.

UNDERHILL, Frank. (1932). "The cooperative commonwealth federation." *Canadian Forum,* August. Reprinted in *Forum.*

UNIVERSITY of Ottawa. (1994). Collective agreement between Univ. of Ottawa and Association of Part-Time Professors, Univ. of Ottawa.

VERMA, Anil. (1995). "Employee involvement in the workplace." In *Union-management relations in Canada* (3rd ed.).

_____. (1992). Statement made in Ph.D. seminar in advanced industrial relations topics. University of Toronto Centre for Industrial Relations, winter term.

VERMA, Anil, and Joseph Weiler. (1992). "Industrial relations in the Canadian telephone industry." In *Industrial relations in Canadian industry.*

VERMA, Anil, and Peter Warrian. (1992). "Industrial relations in the Canadian steel industry." In *Industrial relations in Canadian industry.*

VERMA, Anil, T. Kochan, and R. Lansbury (Eds.). (1995). *Employment relations in the growing Asian economies.* London: Routledge.

WORKPLACE Information Directorate (WID), Human Resources Development Canada. (1998). Data on strikes obtained from Work Stoppage Bureau.

_____. (1997). *Directory of labour organizations in Canada.* Ottawa: HRDC. Use was also made of the 1993 and 1996 editions of the same book.

WALTON, Richard, and Robert McKersie. (1991). *A behavioral theory of labor Negotiations: An analysis of a social interaction system* (2nd ed.). Ithaca: ILR Press.

_____. (1963). *A behavioral theory of negotiations.* New York: McGraw-Hill.

WARD, Bob. (1974). *Harvest of concern.* Toronto: Ontario Federation of Labour. Reprinted in *The Canadian worker in the twentieth century.*

WARRIAN, Peter. (1996). *Hard bargain: Transforming public sector labour-management relations.* Toronto: McGilligan.

WEBB, Sidney and Beatrice Webb. (c1920 [1897]). *Industrial democracy.* New York: Longmans.

WEILER, Joseph. (1984). "Grievance arbitration: The new wave." In J. Weiler and P. Gall (Eds.), *The labour code of British Columbia in the 1980s.* Calgary and Vancouver: Carswell.

WEILER, Paul. (1983a) "Promises to keep." *Harvard Law Review,* 96:8 (June).

_____. (1983b). "Protecting the worker from disability: Challenges for the eighties." Report to Ontario Ministry of Labour. Reprinted in *Labour law.*

_____. (1980). *Reconcilable differences: New directions in Canadian labour law.* Toronto: Carswell.

WEINER, Nan. (1995). "Workplace equity." In *Public sector collective bargaining in Canada.*

WELLS, Don. (1993). "Are strong unions compatible with the new model of human resource management?" *Relations Industrielles,* 48.

WHITE, J.F. (1932). "Deportations." *Canadian Forum,* July. Reprinted in *Forum.*

WHITE, Julie. (1997a). *Changing times: Shorter hours of work in the Communications, Energy and Paperworkers' Union.* Ottawa: CEP.

_____. (1997b). Conversation with the author concerning the CEP's educational activities around work hours, December.

WHITE, Robert. (1995). "Workers' education builds strong rights." *Workers' Education,* 10 (October).

WINPISINGER, William. (1989). "A machinist and a left-of-center progressive." In P. Quaglieri (Ed.), *America's labor leaders.* Lexington, MA: Lexington Books.

WOOD, S.J. et al. (1975). "The 'industrial relations system' concept as a basis for theory in industrial relations." *British Journal of Industrial Relations,* 3 (November).

WOODWORTH, Warner, and Christopher Meek. (1995). *Creating labor-management partnerships.* Reading and Don Mills: Addison-Wesley.

WORKPLACE Gazette. (1998). Table of selected employment standards provisions in Canada, in summer. Ottawa: HRDC.

WORTHY, James. (1948). "Changing concepts of the personnel function." *Personnel,* 25:3 (November). Reprinted in *Personnel and labour relations.*

YODER, Dale. (1962). *Personnel management and industrial relations* (5th ed.). Englewood Cliffs: Prentice-Hall.

YOUNG-KI, Park. (1993). "South Korea." In *Labour law and industrial relations in Asia.*

ZUSSMAN, David, and Jak Jabes. (1989). *The vertical solitude: Managing in the public sector.* Halifax: Institute for Research on Public Policy.

ZWERLING, Harris. (1997). "Obesity as a covered disability under employment discrimination law: An analysis of Canadian approaches." *Relations Industrielles,* 52:3.

PHOTO CREDITS

INDEX

private sector labour law, 277
public sector, 335-36
recognition of collective
bargaining, 117, 265
right to strike, 158
"right-to-work" provisions, 87,
157
strikes, 425
union membership rates,
157-59
"union-free" zones, 83, 85, 87
Unjust dismissals, 233
Unsafe work, right to refuse, 248,
254-55, 415

V

Vacation pay, 404
Vancourver City Savings Credit
Union, 201
Vancouver, 111
Vander Zalm, Bill, 314
Venture capital corporations
(VCCs), 200-2
Vietnam War, 135, 172, 183
Violence
pre-industrial, 102-3
workplace, 255
Voluntarism, 271, 273

W

Wages
during Second Industrial
Revolution, 107
in twenties, 112
collective agreement provision,
401-3
collective bargaining structure
and, 358-59
compensating differentials,
45-47
in competitive market, 44

control, 132, 312-15, 316-17,
318-19, 320-21
cuts, 48
in fifties, 124
direct impact of unions, 205-6
dispersion, 208
economic conditions and, 24-25
in sixties, 131
equilibrium, 44
indirect impact of unions, 207-8
"locked in" union, 48
minimum, 48, 209, 223-24,
229-30
part-time work, 34-35
premium, 401
and price controls, 132, 311
protection of, 416
renegotiation, 48
strike issue, 450
two-tier scheme, 356
two-tier schemes, 133
Wagner Act. *See* National Labor
Relations Act
Web of rules, in systems theory,
9-10
Webb, Sidney and Beatrice,
189-200
Welfare capitalist management,
76-78, 92
Westray Mine disaster, 241-42
Whipsawing, 357-58
Wilson, Michael, 316
Winnipeg General Strike, 18,
111-12
Women, 131
collective bargaining issues,
311, 328, 404, 416, 418
during first Industrial
Revolution, 104
non-unionized work force, 121
in public sector fields, 303
unionization of, 151-52
workforce participation, 31-33,
124, 395

Woods, H.D. (Buzz), 16, 128
Woods Task Force Report, 281
Woodsworth, J.S., 118
Work
changing patterns of, 3-5
hours, 230, 404-6, 450, 462
intensification, 450
rules, 211-12
social and economic
significance, 2
unsafe, 248, 254-55, 415
Work actions, 430
Work force
changing charactertics, 3-5,
28-29
demography, 29-31
diversity, 33, 395
non-unionized, 7, 93-94
women, 31-33, 124
Work hours
flexible, 38
polarization of, 36, 47, 62-63
Work standards legislation
effectiveness, 228-31
enforcement, 230-31
hours of work, 224, 230
individual termination, 227
minimum wages, 224
overtime pay, 224, 230
paid holidays, 227
pregnancy and parental leave,
228
scope and provision, 223-24
vacation entitlement, 224, 227
Work teams, 86, 91, 192
Work-to-rule campaigns, 430
Workers' compensation, 249-51
Workers' Unity League (WUL),
114, 115
Working Opportunity Fund, 201
Working Ventures, 200
Workload, 407-8
Written briefs, 489